Windows® XP Professional: The Complete Reference

Guy Hart-Davis

McGraw-Hill/Osborne

New York   Chicago   San Francisco
Lisbon   London   Madrid   Mexico City
Milan   New Delhi   San Juan
Seoul   Singapore   Sydney   Toronto

The McGraw·Hill Companies

McGraw-Hill/Osborne
2600 Tenth Street
Berkeley, California 94710
U.S.A.

To arrange bulk purchase discounts for sales promotions, premiums, or fund-raisers, please contact **McGraw-Hill**/Osborne at the above address. For information on translations or book distributors outside the U.S.A., please see the International Contact Information page immediately following the index of this book.

Windows® XP Professional: The Complete Reference

1234567890 DOC DOC 0198765432

ISBN 0-07-222665-X

Publisher
Brandon A. Nordin

Vice President & Associate Publisher
Scott Rogers

Editorial Director
Roger Stewart

Acquisitions Editor
Megg Morin

Project Editor
Jenn Tust

Acquisitions Coordinator
Tana Allen

Technical Editor
Will Kelly

Copy Editors
Marcia Baker, Lisa Theobald, Pamela Woolf

Proofreader
Marian Selig

Production and Indexing
Apollo Publishing Services

Illustrators
Melinda Lytle, Lyssa Wald

Series Design
Peter F. Hancik

This book was composed with Corel VENTURA™ Publisher.

This book is dedicated
to Rhonda and Teddy.

Acknowledgments

I'd like to thank the following people for their help with this book:

- Roger Stewart for suggesting the book and making it happen
- Megg Morin for developing the book
- Tana Allen for handling the acquisitions end of the book
- Jenn Tust for coordinating the editing and production of the book
- Will Kelly for reviewing the manuscript for technical accuracy and contributing helpful suggestions
- Marcia Baker, Lisa Theobald, and Pamela Woolf for editing the manuscript
- Apollo Publishing Services for laying out the pages and indexing the book
- Marian Selig for proofreading the book

About the Author

Guy Hart-Davis has written more than 20 critically acclaimed computer books, including *The XP Files* from Osborne, and has contributed to more than a dozen books by other authors. He specializes in Windows XP (both Professional and Home Edition), Microsoft Office, Visual Basic for Applications, and MP3.

About the Technical Editor

Will Kelly has spent his evenings and weekends technical reviewing computer books since 1994 working most recently with Osborne McGraw Hill. He lives in Springfield, VA and works as a consultant for Internet, telecommunications, and the internal technology groups of companies in the Northern Virginia/Washington, DC area.

Contents

Part II

Working and Communicating

Part IV

Using Windows XP Professional on a LAN

Introduction

Windows XP Professional is Microsoft's latest desktop operating system for use in the "professional" environment—by corporations, organizations, smaller companies, and individual users who require an operating system for business use rather than home use. Windows XP Professional combines stability and good performance on even modest hardware (by 2003 standards) with ease of use and an attractive and streamlined user interface that most users find easier and faster than earlier Windows interfaces.

Like its consumer-oriented sibling Windows XP Home Edition, Windows XP Professional is built on Microsoft's "New Technology" foundation previously used for Windows NT and Windows 2000. But while Windows XP Home Edition is designed for home use and home-office use, Windows XP Professional includes networking, management, and security features intended to make it the ideal network client in medium-sized and large domain-based networks running Microsoft's server software, Windows 2000 Server and Windows.NET Server. You can also use Windows XP Professional in workgroups or on standalone computers, but you get fewer benefits from doing so.

Who Is This Book For?

Windows XP Professional: The Complete Reference is primarily designed for intermediate and advanced users of Windows XP Professional on Windows-based client-server networks. This book refers to such networks as "corporate" networks, because that's what many of them will be, though others will be the networks of enterprises, non-profit organizations, government organizations, or military forces. If you're on such a network, your computer is likely to be administered centrally by administrators using the administration and management features Windows 2000 Server and Windows.NET Server offer. You're likely to be able to customize your Windows XP Professional configuration only a little and administer it even less (if at all).

This book is also intended for people using Windows XP Professional on standalone computers (for example, working at home or from home) or on small networks, such as small-office networks and home-office networks. If you're using Windows XP Professional in such a situation, you're likely to have much more control over your computer than if you're on a corporate network. Throughout the book, you'll find advice on the actions you may be able to take and the settings you may be able to choose. In Chapter 27, you'll find specific advice for managing Windows XP Professional on standalone or workgroup computers.

This book isn't really designed for network administrators, because anyone who's administering a Windows domain-based network of any size will need a book about Windows 2000 Server or Windows.NET Server as their primary reference. This book assumes that you're getting the user end of the Windows XP Professional network experience rather than doing the administration. However, if you're a power-user who does some low-level administration on the side, or if you want to move into administration, you should find much of this book's content useful.

What Is This Book's Approach?

As the user of a computer running Windows XP Professional, you need to know what features the operating system offers for making your work easier and how to use those features effectively. You also need to know a bit of why certain features might not be available to you (for example, because your network administrator has chosen to disable them) and why certain features can behave in different ways depending on how Windows XP Professional is configured. To that end, this book outlines some of the restrictions that an administrator may impose on computers running Windows XP Professional in a domain-based network, telling you not the precise names of the control features involved but the effects that you'll see if they're applied to your computer.

For some topics, this book discusses administrative restrictions more extensively than for other topics. This is because some applications and features typically can pose more of a threat to the computer's or the network's security than other features, so administrators have tighter control of them. For example, Internet Explorer, the Microsoft web browser included with most installations of Windows XP Professional, includes configuration settings for many features that affect the computer's security, such as using cookies, running scripts, and installing software on demand. So administrators can choose settings to control these features centrally to avoid users coming to (or causing) grief.

This book assumes that you're using Windows XP Professional in a business context. So it doesn't dwell on consumer-oriented features such as Windows Movie Maker (a modest video-editing application) or topics such as tuning into Internet radio or turning your computer into a ferocious gaming platform. If you can make a convincing business case for editing video, using Internet radio, or playing games at work when your job description doesn't include such a task, chances are that you're smart enough to figure out how to use such features by yourself, so this book lets you investigate them on your own.

What's in This Book?

This book is divided into 43 chapters arranged in seven parts. The following subsections discuss their contents.

Part I: Installing, Configuring, and Customizing

Part I shows you how to install, configure, and customize Windows XP Professional. If you're using the operating system (OS) in a domain environment, you may be able to perform only some of the actions described in these chapters. However, be sure to read Chapter 1 to understand the features Windows XP Professional offers.

Chapter 1 discusses Windows XP Professional's features, benefits, and uses. Chapter 2 shows you how to install the OS manually, while Chapter 3 discusses the options that may be available to you for automating installation of the OS. Chapter 4 shows you how to set up dual-boot or multiboot configurations so that you can boot both Windows XP Professional and one or more other operating systems on the same computer.

Chapter 5 covers how you can customize what Windows XP Professional does at startup and shutdown. Chapter 6 shows you how to transfer files and settings to Windows XP Professional from another installation of Windows and how you can use Windows Update to keep the OS up-to-date. Chapter 7 describes how to customize the Windows XP interface for ease of working. Chapter 8 discusses how to customize Windows Explorer to suit your needs.

Chapter 9 explains how to install and uninstall applications on Windows XP Professional. Chapter 10 shows you how to add hardware to your computer and configure it to work with Windows XP Professional. Chapter 11 discusses how to manage events and improve performance. Chapter 12 shows you how to set up, configure, and manage printing.

Part II: Working and Communicating

Part II shows you how to use Windows XP Professional's basic features for working and communicating.

Chapter 13 describes how to use the Windows XP interface effectively—logging on, logging off, navigating the interface, managing files and folders, and more. Chapter 14 shows you how to run applications, print, and send faxes. Chapter 15 runs through the essentials of using Windows XP for audio and video.

Chapter 16 covers how to use Windows XP's two instant-messaging clients, Windows Messenger and NetMeeting, for real-time chat and application sharing. Chapter 17 shows you how to use Messenger and NetMeeting for audioconferencing and videoconferencing. Chapter 18 tells you what you need to know about using Windows XP Professional on a laptop.

Part III: Security, Backup, and Disaster Recovery

Part III covers the security, backup, and disaster-recovery features Windows XP Professional includes.

Chapter 19 explains what Encrypting File System (EFS) is, what it does, and how to use it. Chapter 20 covers Group Policy and local policies, the main tools that administrators use to configure Windows XP Professional remotely. Chapter 21 discusses what digital certificates are and how to get, install, and manage them. Chapter 22 explains what auditing is, what you can audit on Windows XP Professional, and how to use auditing.

Chapter 23 explains how to use Backup Utility to back up and restore data to protect against loss, how to use System Restore to recover from configuration problems, and how to use the Automated System Recovery (ASR) feature. Chapter 24 provides a wider-ranging discussion of recovering from disaster, showing you which recovery tool is appropriate for which kind of problem.

Part IV: Using Windows XP Professional on a LAN

Part IV explains how to use Windows XP Professional on a local area network (LAN).

Chapter 25 shows you how to configure network connections and access network drives. Chapter 26 discusses how to configure and troubleshoot TCP/IP connections, including how to use many of the command-line TCP/IP utilities that Windows XP Professional provides.

Chapter 27 covers managing Windows XP Professional in a standalone or small-office environment. This is a far-reaching chapter that starts by explaining the key differences between workgroup and domain configurations; describes how to use Fast User Switching, how to share folders and printers on the network, and manage users and groups; and finally shows you how to configure Outlook Express for security and effectiveness.

Chapter 28 describes how to configure and use wireless LAN connections in both peer-to-peer networks and networks that use access points. Chapter 29 explains how to install and configure extra networking components provided with Windows XP Professional but not normally included in installations. Chapter 30 discusses how to secure your network traffic with IP Security (IPSec) and TCP/IP filtering.

Part V: Using Remote Network Connections

Part V contains four chapters that cover using remote network connections. Chapter 31 shows you how to configure and use incoming connections (including parallel-port connections and infrared connections) and virtual private network (VPN) connections. Chapter 32 explains how to use Remote Desktop Connections to remotely control a computer running Remote Desktop. Chapter 33 describes how the Remote Assistance help feature works and how to use it. Chapter 34 discusses how to work with Telnet, the text-mode remote-networking tool.

Part VI: Using the Internet Effectively

Part VI shows you how to use Windows XP Professional's Internet features. Chapter 35 discusses the considerations for connecting Windows XP Professional to the Internet. Chapter 36 describes how to configure Internet Explorer for security and effectiveness and how to use Internet Explorer effectively. Chapter 37 covers installing and using Internet Information Services (IIS) for hosting a web site, and Chapter 38 covers how to use the FTP service included in IIS to run a basic FTP site.

Part VII: Managing and Automating Windows XP Professional

Part VII discusses how to manage your disks, Registry, and services under Windows XP Professional, as well as how to schedule tasks to perform operations automatically.

Chapter 39 covers disk management—everything from formatting a disk to creating dynamic disks and volumes. Chapter 40 explains how to work with the Registry to adjust configuration settings that you can't access through the Windows XP interface. Chapter 41 shows you how to schedule tasks using the Scheduled Tasks folder, the schtasks command, and the at command. Chapter 42 describes how to use and customize Microsoft Management Console (MMC) configuration consoles. Chapter 43 explains what services are, what they do, and how to manage them.

Conventions Used in This Book

To make its meaning clear without using far more words than necessary, this book uses a number of conventions, three of which are worth mentioning here:

- Note, Tip, and Caution paragraphs highlight information to draw it to your notice.

- The pipe character or vertical bar denotes choosing an item from a menu. For example, "choose File | Open" means that you should pull down the File menu and select the Open item on it. Use the keyboard, mouse, or a combination of the two as you wish.

- Most check boxes have two states: *selected* (with a check mark in them) and *cleared* (without a check mark in them). This book tells you to *select* a check box or *clear* a check box rather than "click to place a check mark in the box" or "click to remove the check mark from the box." (Often, you'll be verifying the state of the check box, so it may already have the required setting—in which case, of course, you don't need to click at all.) Some check boxes have a third state as well, in which they're selected but dimmed and unavailable. This state is usually used for options that apply to only part of the current situation.

The Complete Reference

Part I

Installing, Configuring, and Customizing

The
Complete
Reference

Windows **XP**

Chapter 1

Windows XP Professional: Features, Benefits, and Uses

This chapter discusses the features that Windows XP Professional provides, points out the benefits that Windows XP Professional offers over previous versions of Windows, and explains the uses for which Windows XP Professional is intended.

Features of Windows XP Professional

This section describes the most compelling features of Windows XP Professional. Some of these features are new in Windows XP Professional. Others are improved versions of features included in Windows 2000 Professional, Windows NT 4 Workstation, or Windows 9x (Windows 95, Windows 98, Windows 98 Second Edition, and Windows Me).

Code Base, Migration, Updating, and Recovery

This section discusses the features related to Windows XP Professional's code base, migrating users to Windows XP Professional, keeping Windows XP Professional updated, and recovering from disaster.

NT Code Base for Stability

Windows XP Professional is built on Microsoft's New Technology (NT) code base to deliver stability. Windows XP Professional uses a protected memory model that prevents one application from overwriting memory used by another operating system (OS).

Files and Settings Transfer Wizard

The *Files and Settings Transfer Wizard* lets you quickly transfer document files and settings from one computer to another. This feature greatly simplifies the process of migrating a user from one computer to another or from one version of Windows to another.

Windows Update

Windows Update is a feature that can automatically connect to Microsoft's Windows Update web site and download updates to Windows XP Professional and the Microsoft applications that are typically included with it (such as Internet Explorer and Windows Messenger). Administrators can then decide whether to install the updates. Administrators can also configure Windows Update not to run. For example, in a corporate setting, administrators may turn off Windows Update, and then install updates and patches automatically by using management features.

Windows Update is a key feature of Windows XP Professional because it provides a mechanism for patching security holes and defective code. At this writing, Windows XP Professional has been shown to have some serious security holes, which makes Windows Update all the more important.

All operating systems (OSs) and all software applications include bugs—they're more or less a fact of programming life when software becomes functional enough to be useful. But because Microsoft's OSs and applications are so widely used, they're a favorite target of malefactors. Worse, Microsoft has included some powerful but poorly secured features in its OSs and applications that malefactors love to exploit. For example, the Visual Basic for Applications programming language included with Microsoft's major applications (Word, Excel, Access, Outlook, and others) can affect not only the host application but other applications and the OS as well. As a result, macro viruses in VBA host can automatically send e-mail messages and attachments, create and delete files, format drives, and more. Scripts in Windows XP Professional and applications such as Outlook Express can automatically execute a wide variety of actions on your computer without your consent.

Consider the following selection of security problems that surfaced in summer 2002:

- A bug in Windows Media Player that would let an attacker execute a script on your computer. This bug was patched in June 2002.

- A problem with the implementation of checking digital certificates (a means of authentication and verifying identity in electronic communications) that could let an attacker dupe Internet Explorer into believing it had established a secure connection with a web site. Because secure connections are typically used by e-commerce sites, this problem meant that millions of supposedly secure transactions might not have been secure. This problem was patched in September 2002.

- A flaw in the Java Virtual Machine (JVM) in Internet Explorer that could give an attacker complete control of your computer. This bug was patched in September 2002.

- A security vulnerability in Windows XP's Help and Support Center that allows an attacker to delete files on your computer by sending you a deliberately malformed URL. This vulnerability was fixed in Windows XP Service Pack 1.

- Two serious bugs in Remote Desktop Protocol (RDP), the protocol used for Remote Desktop sessions. One bug makes it relatively easy for an attacker to analyze a captured communications session to work out a user's keystrokes. The other bug lets an attacker crash a system that's configured to accept Remote Desktop connections. These bugs were discovered by a third-party security developer in April 2002, but weren't announced publicly until they were fixed in Windows XP Service Pack 1 (September 2002).

By using Windows Update and (preferably) by installing Windows XP Service Pack 1, you can protect your computer against these attacks. By using Windows Update, you should also be able to protect your computer against future attacks that exploit newly discovered vulnerabilities. Windows Update also lets Microsoft push out improvements to Windows XP and the applications that come with it (for example, by adding features or by making existing features work better).

So Windows Update is a strong and positive feature for Windows XP Professional. Unfortunately, there's a downside to Windows Update as well. Having Windows Update apply updates to your computer automatically involves involuntary acceptance of the End-User License Agreements (EULAs) that Microsoft applies to those updates. Recent (at this writing) updates have included language such as the following:

■ "Microsoft may provide security related updates to the OS Components that will be automatically downloaded onto your computer. These security related updates may disable your ability to copy and/or play Secure Content and use other software on your computer."

■ "You acknowledge and agree that Microsoft may automatically check the version of the OS Product and/or its components that you are utilizing and may provide upgrades or fixes to the OS Product that will be automatically downloaded to your computer."

Some user advocates have raised concerns that by accepting such EULAs, you agree to Microsoft's automatically installing software on your computer at its discretion. However, if you don't accept these conditions, your computer remains exposed to serious security problems, such as those detailed earlier in this section.

Besides any worries that you may have about EULAs, you should be aware that Microsoft regards patches as "tactical responses" with timeliness the "overriding consideration." Microsoft states: "Service packs, in contrast, can be much more extensively tested, and thus the quality is much higher." Few Windows XP Professional users find such words reassuring when they refer to critical security patches that Windows Update installs by default on their computers. If such patches have quality much lower than the fixes in service packs, how good can they be?

Automated System Recovery

Automated System Recovery (ASR) lets you make a backup of your system that you can restore by booting from the Windows XP Professional CD and supplying ASR with a floppy containing configuration-file information and with the backup file.

Remote Desktop

Remote Desktop is the new name for Terminal Services. Windows XP Professional includes a one-connection version of Terminal Services, which lets you control your computer remotely by using Remote Desktop Connection from any 32-bit version of Windows.

Hardware-Related Features

Windows XP Professional includes several new hardware-related features, from a version of the OS designed for the Intel Itanium processor to the ClearType font-improvement feature.

x86 and Itanium Versions

Windows XP Professional comes in a 32-bit version designed for x86 processors (for example, Pentium II, Pentium III, Pentium IV, Celeron, Athlon, and Duron processors) and a 64-bit version designed for the Intel Itanium processor.

Because computers using Itanium processors are about as rare—and as expensive—as large diamonds at this writing, this book doesn't discuss the 64-bit version of Windows XP Professional.

Hardware Compatibility and Device Driver Rollback

Windows XP Professional is compatible with a wide range of hardware. The Windows XP Professional installation CD contains drivers for many devices, and you can download others via Windows Update.

When you update a driver, Windows XP Professional stores the details of the previous driver you used so that you can easily revert to it if the updated driver isn't satisfactory.

Power-Saving Features for Portable Computers

Windows XP Professional features processor power control for mobile processors that can run at different speeds when plugged in rather than when running on batteries. To further save battery power, Windows XP Professional dims the screen automatically when a portable computer is running on batteries.

ClearType

Windows XP Professional includes *ClearType,* a font-improvement feature that smoothes the rendering of fonts on LCD monitors.

Help Features

Windows XP Professional includes two powerful help features: Remote Assistance and Help and Support Center.

Remote Assistance

Remote Assistance is a new help mechanism that lets you invite a friend, acquaintance, or administrator to help you solve a problem by connecting to your computer, viewing your display remotely, and communicating with you using text-based chat or voice. You can choose whether to let your helper take control of your computer so that he can help you solve the problem. In Windows XP Professional, administrators can also offer unsolicited help to users.

Remote Assistance works the other way as well: you can help someone else solve a problem.

Help and Support Center

Windows XP Professional's *Help and Support Center* integrates Help files stored on your hard drive with a capability to search the Microsoft Knowledge Base and other online sources of help for further information.

Administration, Multiuser Support, and Fast User Switching

Windows XP Professional is designed for use as a secure multiuser OS. When used in a standalone or workgroup configuration, Windows XP Professional's Fast User Switching feature enables multiple users to be logged on to the same computer at the same time.

Administration Features

Windows XP Professional includes features for integrating tightly with Windows 2000 Server and Windows.NET Server to simplify software installation, maintenance, and administration. In its corporate role (discussed in "Corporate Use," later in this chapter), Windows XP Professional is designed to log on to Windows domains and to be managed by the Windows 2000 Server and Windows.NET Server administration tools. For example, a domain administrator can install Windows XP Professional by using Remote Installation Services (RIS), install applications on Windows XP Professional by using IntelliMirror, and use group policy objects to control the configuration and behavior of Windows XP Professional clients. This remote administration saves much time and effort over configuring each computer manually.

Multiuser Support

Like Windows NT Workstation and Windows 2000 Professional, Windows XP Professional is designed to be a secure multiuser client OS. You can set up multiple user accounts on the same computer. Users have their own customized settings (if you allow them to) and their own folder structure that other users can't access.

Fast User Switching (Workgroups Only)

Windows XP Professional supports multiple concurrent user sessions on standalone computers and workgroup computers, but not on computers connected to a domain. At any given time, one user session can be active, while all other user sessions are disconnected. The *active* session appears on screen. Any *disconnected* sessions are hidden in the background. After you finish working, you can either log off (to end your session) or *switch user*, which disconnects your active session so that another user can log on. The applications you left open remain running in the disconnected session, so when you log back on, you can resume work where you left off. This feature is called *Fast User Switching*.

When used in a domain, Windows XP Professional doesn't use Fast User Switching. Only one user can be logged on to the computer at a time. No session can be disconnected.

Software Compatibility, Capabilities, and Applications

This section discusses software compatibility issues, Windows XP Professional's software capabilities, and notable features of the applications and applets typically included in Windows XP Professional installations.

Software Compatibility and Compatibility Mode

Windows XP Professional can run many of the applications that run on Windows 95, Windows 98, Windows Me, Windows NT 4, and Windows 2000 Professional. Many applications run seamlessly, but some applications need you to manually apply Windows XP Professional's Compatibility mode settings, which emulate the earlier versions of Windows on which older applications were designed to run.

Windows XP Professional can also run many DOS applications.

However, some older applications don't run on Windows XP Professional, not even in any compatibility mode. If you need to use an application that won't run on Windows XP Professional, you have three choices:

- Stay with your previous version of Windows so that you can run the application.

- Set up Windows XP Professional as a dual-boot with your old version of Windows so that you can boot into the old version when you need to run the application. Unless you need the application only occasionally, this solution is poor.

- Install PC-emulation software such as Virtual PC (www.connectix.com) or VMWare (www.vmware.com) on Windows XP Professional so that you run an emulated PC with the old version of Windows that can run the application. Because emulation is slow and doesn't provide full access to your computer's peripherals (for example, USB or FireWire devices), this solution works only for productivity applications that require neither blazing performance nor direct access to peripherals.

Support for Multiple Languages Simultaneously

Windows XP Professional lets you use multiple languages simultaneously. (By contrast, Windows XP Home Edition lets you use only one language at a time. You can switch from one language to another.)

Faxing

Windows XP Professional includes basic faxing capabilities.

CD Burning

Windows XP Professional includes basic CD-burning capabilities for creating both data CDs (in the Orange Book format) and audio CDs (in the Red Book format).

Audio and Video Features

Windows XP Professional includes a new version of Windows Media Player, which can play everything from MP3 files to DVDs (with added DVD-player software).

Windows Image Acquisition (WIA) makes it easier to connect scanners, video cameras, or digital cameras to computers running Windows XP Professional.

Improvements to Windows Explorer

The version of Windows Explorer in Windows XP Professional features several improvements, including the following.

WebView and ListView   *WebView* and *ListView* present two, three, or four panes on the left side of a Windows Explorer window containing actions relevant to the selected item or items, navigation links to folders related to the current folder, and details on any selected item or items. "WebView and ListView" in Chapter 8 discusses WebView and ListView.

Folder Templates   Windows Explorer includes customized folder templates for music folders and picture folders that contain links for manipulating the music files or pictures.

The folder templates for picture folders include Filmstrip view, discussed next.

Filmstrip View   Windows Explorer's new *Filmstrip view* provides an easy means of browsing through graphics files. Filmstrip view displays a row of miniature pictures across the bottom of the window with an enlarged version of the selected picture above them. Filmstrip view provides buttons for rotating the selected picture clockwise and counterclockwise.

Filmstrip view is available in the Photo Album folder template and the Pictures folder template.

Compressed Folders   Windows XP Professional's version of Windows Explorer can open Zip (ZIP) folders and Microsoft Cabinet (CAB) folders as if they were regular folders. Windows Explorer can create Zip folders, but not Cabinet folders. Windows XP Professional includes the MAKECAB.EXE command-line utility for creating Cabinet folders.

Customizable AutoPlay   In Windows XP Professional, AutoPlay applies not only to CD and DVD drives but also to removable drives such as Zip drives, USB and FireWire external hard drives, PC Cards, SmartMedia cards, CompactFlash cards, and Memory Stick devices. You can customize the actions AutoPlay takes for different types of content.

Enhanced Applets

Like previous versions of Windows, Windows XP Professional includes a number of applets that provide basic functionality. In most corporate settings, these applets have been used for relatively few tasks—in fact, the applets are specifically designed not to provide enough functionality for any but the lightest tasks, so that corporations won't be tempted to forego buying full-fledged applications. For example, the WordPad applet provides word-processing functionality too limited for anyone who needs to create anything more than the simplest document, so most corporations end up buying a full word-processing application to supplement it.

Windows XP Professional features include new and enhanced applets, including the following:

- *Windows Picture and Fax Viewer* provides basic tools for manipulating graphics and for annotating TIFF files. Windows Picture and Fax Viewer takes the place of Image Preview in earlier versions of Windows.

- *Microsoft Paint* can save pictures in a variety of formats and can capture still pictures from a video feed.

- *Notepad* can open text files of any size. (Earlier versions of Notepad could open only small text files.)

- *Command Prompt* automatically uses command extensions, which give some command-prompt commands greater power and ease of use.

Networking Features

Windows XP Professional includes a strong set of networking tools, including the following:

- The *Network Setup Wizard* helps you set up small networks.

- The *All-User Remote Access Service* (AURAS) lets you share an Internet connection with other users of your computer without telling them the user name and password. (AURAS is primarily useful for standalone and workgroup computers.)

- *Internet Connection Sharing* (ICS) provides easy sharing of an Internet connection with other computers on your network. Windows 98 Second Edition, Windows Me, and Windows 2000 Professional include ICS, but Windows XP Professional's version is improved and features Internet Connection Firewall (discussed next). ICS is primarily useful in standalone and workgroup configurations.

- *Internet Connection Firewall* (ICF) is a software firewall that works together with ICS to protect your Internet connection. You can also use ICF on network connections.

- *Automatic Private IP Addressing* (APIPA) lets Windows XP Professional assign itself an IP address when a Dynamic Host Configuration Protocol (DHCP) server isn't available. APIPA is useful both for computers that sometimes connect to a domain-based network and sometimes don't (for example, a sales rep's notebook), and for ad-hoc home networking.

■ *Network bridging* lets you easily connect two separate networks into a single network. This feature is primarily useful in standalone and workgroup configurations.

Benefits of Windows XP Professional

This section discusses the benefits that Windows XP Professional offers over previous versions of Windows used in corporate settings: Windows 2000 Professional, Windows NT 4 Workstation, and Windows 9*x*.

For many corporations, Windows XP Professional offers significant benefits over previous versions of Windows.

Benefits Over Previous Desktop Versions of Windows

Windows XP Professional offers three main benefits over all previous desktop versions of Windows: its streamlined user interface, the Windows File Protection feature, and its improved Windows Update feature.

Revamped User Interface

Windows XP Professional offers an updated user interface, which it shares with Windows XP Home Edition. The interface is designed to give you quicker access to your applications and files while providing a pleasing look and user experience. For example, the Windows XP Start menu changes its contents to display shortcuts for the applications you use most frequently. Similarly, Windows Explorer's new WebView and ListView features simplify navigation among the folders you supposedly use most frequently, and the actions you need to take with them and the files they contain. Microsoft has also redesigned the taskbar and the System Tray or notification area.

Some people like Windows XP's new interface. Others don't. If you don't like it, you can easily restore Windows XP Professional to using the "classic" Windows interface that Windows 2000 Professional and Windows 98 used.

Windows File Protection

Windows *File Protection* tries to prevent you from deleting system files. If you succeed in deleting some of them (or if malware does so), Window File Protection restores the files automatically from a cache when it notices the files are missing.

Windows Update

Windows XP Professional's improved version of Windows Update provides an effective way of keeping Windows XP Professional up-to-date. However, in domain environments, administrators may choose to disable Windows Update so that they can apply updates and patches consistently to all computers in the domain.

Benefits Over Windows 2000 Professional

Windows XP Professional offers relatively few benefits over Windows 2000 Professional in corporate settings, where features such as improved image acquisition tend to be less important than in the consumer market.

Windows XP Professional's main benefit is its increased compatibility with more applications than Windows 2000 Professional could run. Windows XP Professional also supports a wider range of hardware than Windows 2000 Professional. For those who use a portable computer in a docked configuration, DualView can provide significant benefits.

From Windows 2000 Professional, Windows XP Professional is an incremental upgrade.

Benefits Over Windows NT 4 Workstation

Windows XP Professional offers significant benefits over Windows NT 4 Workstation. In addition to its greatly increased compatibility with applications and support for a much wider range of hardware, Windows XP Professional offers improved communications (for example, Remote Desktop), security (for example, Encrypting File System and IP Security), and management tools.

Benefits Over Windows 9x

Windows XP Professional delivers significant benefits over Windows 9x. These are the most notable benefits:

Stability

Because they included 16-bit code for backwards compatibility with DOS and Windows 3.1 applications, Windows 9x versions were notorious for their instability. Because Windows 9x didn't protect memory effectively, a badly written application could overwrite memory registers used by another application or by Windows itself. This typically crashed both the offending application and the offended application or Windows. By contrast, Windows XP Professional features a protected memory model that runs each application in its own memory space. If an application crashes, Windows XP Professional can close that application without affecting other applications that are running. Windows XP Professional itself seldom crashes when running compatible software on compatible hardware.

Security

Windows XP Professional includes a large number of security features that Windows 9x versions don't have. For example, Windows XP Professional includes the NTFS file system, the Encrypting File System, and IP Security. Put together, Windows XP Professional's security features add up to a complete system that administrators can use to provide effective security on client and server computers. By contrast, Windows 9*x* versions featured a weak security model that could easily be compromised.

Management Features

Windows XP Professional includes a vast array of management features that Windows 9*x* versions don't have. Essentially, Windows XP Professional is designed to be a centrally managed OS, whereas Windows 9*x* is designed as a standalone OS that can have some management features clumsily grafted onto it.

Support for Multiple Users

Windows XP Professional includes effective support for multiple users, whereas Windows 9*x*'s multiuser support was little more than skin deep. Windows XP Professional lets you keep each user's private files secure from any other user, whereas Windows 9*x* essentially let any user access any other user's files.

Remote Desktop

Remote Desktop allows secure remote access to a computer running Windows XP Professional. Windows 9*x*'s nearest equivalent is NetMeeting's Remote Desktop Sharing feature, which is much less powerful and secure.

Offline Files

Windows XP's Offline Files feature lets you work on files stored on network drives even when you're not connected to the network (for example, if you take a laptop home or on a business trip). Windows 9*x*'s nearest equivalent to Offline Files is Briefcase, which is much less capable. (Windows XP Professional includes Briefcase for any users who still need it.)

Intended Uses of Windows XP Professional

Windows XP Professional is intended for four different uses: corporate use, roaming use, SOHO use, and standalone use. The following subsections discuss these uses briefly.

Corporate Use

Windows XP Professional's primary role is as the preferred client OS for Windows-based client-server networks. Servers in these networks typically run Windows 2000 Server or Windows.NET Server. These networks use Windows domains running Active Directory and use group policies to configure their client computers.

Because it offers strong security features, including Encrypting File System (EFS), Windows XP Professional is good for portable computers. For example, sales reps and traveling executives often need to encrypt their files in case their portable computers are stolen. Even *corridor warriors*—users who carry a computer from meeting to meeting—can benefit from having encrypted files if they leave their computers lying around by mistake.

Roaming Use

Windows XP Professional lets users store their user profiles on a network server rather than on a standalone computer. Users can then log on to any computer attached to the network. When a *roaming* user logs on, XP copies their user profile from the server to the computer they're using, making the user's desktop settings and files available to them.

Roaming profiles offer benefits to both users and administrators. Users can log on from any computer available and enjoy their custom settings on it. Administrators can reduce the number of computers used on the network by not needing to provide a separate computer to each user.

SOHO Use

You can use Windows XP Professional in a small office or home office (SOHO) setting. Because typical *SOHO networks* are peer-to-peer networks based on a workgroup, rather than domain-based client-server networks, and because Windows XP Home Edition contains strong features for peer-to-peer networks, Windows XP Home Edition is as effective in many SOHO networks as Windows XP Professional. But if you need features that Windows XP Professional offers that Windows XP Home Edition doesn't offer, Windows XP Professional is the better choice. For example, if you need to encrypt your files, you need Windows XP Professional rather than Windows XP Home Edition on each computer that will need to store or access encrypted files. Similarly, if you need to share a fax-modem among the computers in your workgroup, you'll need Windows XP Professional on the computer that's doing the sharing. (The computers with which the fax-modem is shared can run Windows XP Home Edition.)

In such situations, you may want to use Windows XP Professional on those computers that need its features and Windows XP Home Edition on those computers that can get by with a smaller feature set.

Windows XP Professional behaves differently in a workgroup than in a domain. Chapter 27 discusses the key differences for using Windows XP Professional in a workgroup setting.

Standalone Use

You can use Windows XP Professional on a *standalone workstation*—a workstation that's not connected to a network. But if your computer doesn't connect to a domain, the only reason to use Windows XP Professional on a standalone computer is if you need the security features that Windows XP Professional offers. If you don't need these features, use Windows XP Home Edition instead.

How Windows XP Professional Differs from Windows XP Home Edition

Windows XP Professional is a superset of Windows XP Home Edition. Table 1-1 lists the major features that Windows XP Professional has that Windows XP Home Edition doesn't have. These features break down into four categories: administration features, security features, hardware features, and software components.

Feature	Explanation
Administration Features	
Domain membership	A Windows XP Professional computer can be a member of a Windows 2000 Server or a Windows.NET Server domain and can be administered centrally through the domain.
Roaming user profiles	Roaming user profiles store user profile data on the server so that users can log on from any client computer and receive their desktop settings and applications.
Remote Installation Services (RIS) support	RIS lets administrators install Windows XP Professional on a computer remotely across a domain-based Windows network.
IntelliMirror support	IntelliMirror lets administrators install applications and updates automatically across a domain-based Windows network.
Group policies and local policies	Group policies let domain administrators configure Windows XP Professional remotely, including installing software via RIS and IntelliMirror. Local policies let you both configure a computer that's not part of a domain and apply policy settings that can be overridden by group policy settings.
Security Features	
Encrypting File System (EFS)	EFS lets you encrypting files and folders for security.
Internet Protocol Security (IPSec)	IPSec lets you secure network and internetwork connections.
Complex permissions	Windows XP Professional supports file and folder permissions that you can set manually via an access control list (ACL).

Table 1-1. *Windows XP Professional Features Not Included in Windows XP Home Edition*

Feature	Explanation
Hardware Features	
Symmetric multiprocessing support (SMP)	Windows XP Professional supports two-processor SMP computers. (Windows XP Home Edition can use only one processor on an SMP computer.)
Dynamic disks	Windows XP Professional supports dynamic disks as well as basic disks. *Dynamic disks* are volumes that span two or more physical disks to create large volumes.
64-bit version	Windows XP Professional comes in a 64-bit version for the Intel Itanium processor, as well as a 32-bit version for x86 processors.
Software Components	
Internet Information Services (IIS) 5	IIS 5 lets you set up a web server that supports up to ten concurrent connections.
Remote Desktop	Remote Desktop lets you control your computer remotely by using Remote Desktop Connection from any 32-bit version of Windows.
Fax sharing	Windows XP Professional can share fax devices with other computers on the network, whereas Windows XP Home Edition can't share fax devices.
Offline Files	Offline Files is a feature that creates a local copy of designated network folders so that you can still access them when your computer isn't connected to the network. Offline files don't work when Fast User Switching is switched on.
Automated System Recovery (ASR)	Windows XP Professional supports ASR, whereas Windows XP Home Edition doesn't.
Support for multiple languages	Windows XP Professional lets you load multiple languages at the same time, whereas Windows XP Home Edition lets you load only a single language at any given time.
Capability to install help files for multiple OSs	Windows XP Professional lets you install the help files for other OSs into Help and Support Center. This feature is useful for reference and for people who need to provide technical support.

Table 1-1.   *Windows XP Professional Features Not Included in Windows XP Home Edition* (continued)

This mere handful of different features may not seem to indicate a huge difference between OSs that share thousands of common features. But these are major features that make a great difference in Windows XP Professional's capabilities and greatly influence the role it plays. In particular, Windows XP Professional's features for centralized management mean that the OS behaves in a different way when connected to a domain than it does when on a standalone computer or a computer that's part of a workgroup.

Summary

This chapter discussed what Windows XP Professional is, the features and benefits it offers, and its intended uses.

The next chapter explains how to install Windows XP Professional manually.

The
Complete
Reference

Chapter 2

Installing Windows XP
Professional Manually

This chapter discusses how to install Windows XP Professional manually and apply service packs when necessary. The next chapter discusses how to use the various methods available of automating the installation of Windows XP Professional.

Whether to install Windows XP Professional manually or automatically is usually an easy choice dictated by the number of computers on which you need to install it, the tools available to you, and whether you have the funds available to buy tools you don't have. For example, if you need to install Windows XP Professional on two computers, manual installation will probably be the quickest way. If you need to install Windows XP Professional on two dozen computers, you'll likely want to automate the installation as far as possible.

Choosing the Type of Installation

If you decide to install Windows XP Professional manually, you also need to choose which installation method to use: upgrade installation, new installation, or clean installation. The following subsections explain the differences and discuss which installation type is suitable when.

Upgrade Installation

An *upgrade installation* installs Windows XP Professional over your previous version of Windows. Windows Setup migrates your settings and applications from your previous version of Windows to XP. So if the upgrade runs successfully, you can start working on XP with the same desktop, settings, and applications as you had on your previous version of Windows. The upgrade version of Windows XP Professional is less expensive than the full version.

New Installation

A *new installation* installs Windows XP Professional in a dual-boot configuration with your previous operating system(OS) so that you can boot either Windows XP Professional or the other version of Windows. You'll need to migrate or reinstall all your applications manually. You can migrate your files and settings by using the Files and Settings Transfer Wizard.

Clean Installation

A *clean installation* installs Windows XP Professional as the only Windows OS on your computer. (Windows XP Professional can be the only OS on the computer, or you can create a dual-boot configuration.) Use a clean installation on a new computer that doesn't have an OS or a computer whose OS (or one of whose OSes) you want to overwrite with Windows XP Professional. You'll need to install all your applications manually after performing a clean installation. You can migrate your files and settings from another computer or from the same computer by using the Files and Settings Transfer Wizard.

Preparing for Installation

Before installing Windows XP Professional, you need to take the basic steps detailed in this section to make sure that your computer is fit to run Windows XP and that you won't lose any functionality as a result of installing Windows XP.

Checking Your Computer's Specification

Make sure your computer is powerful enough to run Windows XP Professional adequately. Table 2-1 lists the minimum specifications and suggests reasonable targets to aim at for good performance.

Also required are a keyboard (or equivalent device) and mouse (or other pointing device). The following subsections contain notes on the requirements and recommendations. Not required, but recommended for most users, are a network card, a sound card, and speakers or headphones.

Processor

Windows XP Professional will run on a processor as slow as a Pentium 166 MMX, but performance is too slow to be practical. At the other extreme, you don't need to buy the fastest processor available. (Most computers display the processor speed during their boot sequence.)

Item	Requirement	Recommendation
Processor	Pentium 233	Pentium III 500MHz or faster
RAM	64MB	128MB or more
Hard disk space	2GB (approx.)	3GB or more
Graphics card and display	SVGA (800×600 pixels) at 256 colors	SVGA or XGA (1024×768) at 65,536 colors or better
CD drive	On computer or available across network	N/A

Table 2-1. *Windows XP Professional Hardware Requirements and Recommendations*

RAM

Windows XP Professional will run on 64MB RAM, but only just. Use 128MB as a bare minimum. Because Windows XP greatly benefits from extra RAM, consider 256–512MB for moderate use. Consider 768MB or 1GB if you use large applications or large data files.

 If you're running Windows XP Professional in a standalone or workgroup environment, and you're using Fast User Switching, you'll need enough RAM for the disconnected user sessions as well as for the active user session.

Most computers display the amount of RAM during their boot sequence. Alternatively, if your computer has a version of Windows installed, double-click the System icon in Control Panel and check the readout on the General page of the System Properties dialog box.

Hard Disk Space

The requirement of 2GB of hard disk space breaks down as follows:

- Approximately 950MB to 1GB for the files in the Windows folder, depending on the components you install.

- Approximately 55MB for the Program Files folder with Windows XP's bundled applications (Internet Explorer, Windows Messenger, Outlook Express, Windows Media Player, and others, depending on your OEM package).

- Space for your paging file, which is used to supplement RAM. Windows XP Professional sets the size of the paging file at 1.5 times the amount of RAM your computer has. You can change this setting as necessary.

- Space for your hibernation file, if your computer can hibernate. Your hibernation file takes up as much space as you have RAM, because the hibernation file saves the data held in RAM. If you're short of space, you can disable hibernation.

Because you will likely need to install applications and create data files, it's a good idea to have plenty of hard disk space on your computer. If your main hard disk doesn't have free space, you can install applications or store data files on a second hard disk provided that your computer's configuration supports it. But if you have a portable computer with a single, small hard disk, you're stuck.

If you have a version of Windows installed on your computer, you can check the amount of free space on a drive by examining the readout on the General page of the Properties dialog box for the drive.

Graphics Card and Display

Windows XP's interface requires a graphics card and display capable of SVGA resolution (800×600 pixels) or higher at 256 colors or higher. (Windows XP uses VGA—640×480 pixels—resolution only for Safe mode, a mode used for recovering from configuration problems.) 256 colors provide a crude color gradient. 65,536 colors look acceptable for work with everyday business applications. For graphics work, choose 24-bit color or, preferably, 32-bit color.

CD Drive

To install Windows XP Professional, you need access to a CD drive or DVD drive, either on your computer or accessible across the network. Any speed of CD drive will work.

Checking Hardware and Software Compatibility

Check that the hardware and software on your computer is compatible with Windows XP either by running the Upgrade Advisor program or by checking the Hardware Compatibility List (HCL) manually.

Running the Upgrade Advisor

If your computer is running an older version of Windows, run the Upgrade Advisor to identify any hardware components or applications that aren't compatible with Windows XP.

The Upgrade Advisor is included on the Windows XP Professional CD. If AutoPlay displays the Welcome to Microsoft Windows XP screen, click the Check System Compatibility link and then click the Check My System Automatically link.

If AutoPlay doesn't display the Welcome to Microsoft Windows XP screen, choose Start | Run, enter *cd*:**\i386\winnt32.exe /checkupgradeonly** (replace *cd* with the drive letter of your CD drive), and click the OK button to run the Upgrade Advisor. (If you prefer, browse to winnt32.exe and then type the **/checkupgradeonly** switch.)

If your computer has an Internet connection, the Upgrade Advisor asks your permission to connect to the Windows Update site to download updated components for Dynamic Update. Downloading the updates is a good idea because the updated components may be required for your hardware or software. If you download the updates, Upgrade Advisor updates Setup and then restarts Setup.

Upgrade Advisor then prepares an upgrade Report that lists any hardware or software components likely to cause problems with the upgrade. It divides the list into categories such as Blocking Issues (issues that will prevent you from upgrading to Windows XP, such as lack of disk space or RAM), Hardware that Might Need Additional Files, and Software that Does Not Support Windows XP. You can toggle the report between a summary and full details, print it, or save it under a filename of your choice. By default, Upgrade Advisor saves the report to the file upgrade.txt in your Windows folder.

Checking the Hardware Compatibility List

If you don't have a version of Windows already installed on your computer, you won't be able to run the Upgrade Advisor. If you have access to another computer, check the HCL at www.microsoft.com/hcl/ to make sure that XP supports all your hardware. The HCL shows four icons for compatible hardware:

- **Logo icon** The hardware has passed Windows Logo testing and is considered fully compatible.

- **Beta Logo icon** The hardware has passed Windows Logo testing on a prerelease (beta) version of the operating system.

- **Compatible icon** The hardware works with the operating system but hasn't passed Windows Logo testing.

- **Beta Compatible icon** The hardware worked with a prerelease version of the operating system but didn't pass Windows Logo testing.

If the HCL icon for a device includes a CD, the Windows XP CD contains a driver for the device. If the HCL icon includes a red arrow and drive icon, you can download a driver for the device. If a device has no icon on the HCL, it's not compatible with the operating system.

Download any drivers you'll need that aren't on the Windows XP CD. Replace any unsupported devices that you'll need with Windows XP Professional. XP supports a wide range of hardware, so most devices work. Some of those that don't are those whose manufacturers have either gone out of business or decided not to write Windows XP drivers for older products.

Deciding Which File System to Use

Before starting the installation, decide which file system you will use for the partition on which you install Windows XP. Windows XP supports the FAT16 (file allocation table) file system, the FAT32 file system, and version 5 of the NT File System (NTFS).

Windows XP can convert FAT16 and FAT32 partitions to NTFS, but it can't convert NTFS partitions to FAT16 or FAT32 without reformatting them. Reformatting a partition destroys all the data on it.

Using NTFS for Your Windows XP Partition

Use NTFS for any clean or new installation of Windows XP. NTFS is required for most of Windows XP Professional's security features, encryption, quotas, and compression. NTFS is also more space-efficient than FAT32 on partitions of 8GB or more, and its performance doesn't degrade on larger volumes the way that FAT32's performance does. Windows XP can create NTFS partitions up to 16TB (terabytes) using its default cluster size. If you adjust the cluster size, Windows XP can create NTFS partitions up to 256TB. By contrast, Windows XP can't create FAT32 partitions larger than 32GB, although you can create larger FAT32 partitions by using other operating systems, such as Windows 98 or Windows Me.

Another advantage of NTFS is that NTFS more closely logs disk activities, enabling quicker restoration of data after a power outage or hardware problem.

Windows NT 4 supports FAT16 and version 4 of NTFS but not FAT32. To create a dual-boot arrangement with Windows NT 4 installed on NTFS 4, you need to apply

Service Pack 4 or a later service pack to Windows NT 4. These Service Packs update Windows NT 4 to NTFS version 5. In most cases, you'll do best to use Service Pack 6a.

Using FAT16 or FAT32 to Enable Windows 9x to Access Your Windows XP Partition

If you want to create a dual-boot configuration in which you can not only boot both Windows XP Professional and Windows 9x but also access the Windows XP Professional partition from Windows 9x, you'll need to use FAT16 or FAT32 for your Windows XP partition.

Use FAT16 only if you need to dual-boot Windows XP Professional with Windows 95 (the first edition, not Windows 95 OSR2) and let Windows 95 access your Windows XP Professional partition.

Use FAT32 if you need to dual-boot Windows XP Professional with Windows 95 OSR2, Windows 98, or Windows Me and let that version of Windows access your Windows XP Professional partition.

Backing Up Your Data

If your computer contains data files of any value, it's a good idea to back them up before installing Windows XP Professional. Files to back up include the following:

- **Document files**   Word-processing documents, spreadsheets, databases, financial data, music files (for example, MP3 and WMA files), video files, and so on.

- **Address book**   For example, the Address Book file. (It's the WAB file with your user name in the \Application Data\Microsoft\Address Book folder.)

- **PDA**   Or the organizer's data folder.

- **E-mail folders**   For example, your Outlook local store file (PST files) and offline store (OST file) for your Exchange Server account; your Outlook Express store folder (if you don't know where this is, choose Tools | Options and click the Store Folder button on the Maintenance tab of the Options dialog box); your Eudora folder; or the folder for any other e-mail application you're using.

- **Web browser bookmarks or favorites**   You may need to use an Export command to save them to a file.

- **Password list (PWL) files**   Back these files up if you're upgrading from Windows 98 or Windows Me to Windows XP. You'll need to apply your passwords manually to Windows XP, but back up the PWL files in case you decide to revert to Windows 98 or Windows Me.

If you're planning to use Windows XP's partitioning utility to repartition your hard drive during installation, it's vital to back up the files, because repartitioning destroys any data on the partitions affected. If you don't repartition your hard drive, installing

Windows XP Professional shouldn't affect your data files, but create a backup to be safe in case anything goes wrong with the installation.

The key to backing up your data is ensuring that you'll be able to restore it on Windows XP if necessary. Check that the backup application and backup device that you're using will run on Windows XP. You may need to run the backup application in Windows XP's Compatibility mode. If the application or device won't run on Windows XP, copy your data files to a location or medium that you'll be able to easily access from Windows XP: a network drive, recordable CD or DVD, removable drive, or hard drive that won't be affected by installation. After installation, copy the files to the Windows XP computer if necessary.

Collecting the Files and Settings You Want to Transfer

If you want to copy files and settings from your old computer to a new computer, from an old hard disk to a new hard disk, or from an existing installation of Windows to your new installation of Windows XP, use the Files and Settings Transfer Wizard to collect the files and settings you want to transfer. (Alternatively, you can migrate your files and settings manually, but in most cases the Files and Settings Transfer Wizard does a good job and saves you a great deal of time and effort.)

The Files and Settings Transfer Wizard can collect files and settings from computers running Windows 95, Windows 98 or Windows 98 Second Edition, Windows Me, Windows NT 4, Windows 2000, Windows XP Home, and the 32-bit version of Windows XP Professional. The wizard can transfer files and settings only to Windows XP.

The Files and Settings Transfer Wizard can transfer files and settings from many Microsoft applications and various third-party applications. See Q304903 in the Microsoft Knowledge Base for a full list of applications whose settings the Files and Settings Transfer Wizard can transfer.

Note	*In a domain setting, the domain administrator may use the User State Migration Tool (USMT) to migrate your settings instead of having you use the Files and Settings Transfer Wizard to transfer them. USMT works only for domain user profiles, not user profiles in workgroups. USMT is essentially a server-based version of the Files and Settings Transfer Wizard. The administrator creates information files defining the application files, system files, user documents, and settings to migrate. The administrator then runs the ScanState.exe application to migrate the files and settings to an intermediate store. From there, the administrator runs the LoadState.exe application to load the files and settings onto a clean installation of Windows XP Professional. The USMT files are in the Valueadd\Msft\USMT folder on standard Windows XP Professional distribution CDs. Some OEM packages of Windows XP Professional don't include the Valueadd folder and its contents.*

To run the Files and Settings Transfer Wizard, insert the Windows XP CD in a CD drive or DVD drive and follow these steps:

1. If AutoPlay displays the Welcome to Microsoft Windows XP screen, click the Perform Additional Tasks link, then click the Transfer Files and Settings link to start the Files and Settings Transfer Wizard. If AutoPlay doesn't run, choose Start | Run, enter **migwiz.exe** in the Run dialog box, and click the OK button. You may need to enter *cd***:\i386\migwiz.exe** (where *cd* is the drive letter of the CD drive) if your CD drive isn't in your path.

> **Tip**   *If the old computer doesn't have a CD drive, you can run the Files and Settings Transfer Wizard from a diskette. To create the disk, run the Files and Settings Transfer Wizard on your new computer, choose New Computer | I Want to Create a Wizard Disk in the Following Drive, and follow the prompts. Insert the disk in your old computer, choose Start | Run, enter a:\fastwiz in the Run dialog box, and click the OK button.*

2. On the Which Computer Is This? page, select Old Computer.

3. On the Select a Transfer Method page, specify the means for transferring the files: Direct Cable (serial only), Home or Small Office Network, Floppy Drive or Other Removable Media, or Other. Direct Cable is good for transferring files from one computer to another, as is Home or Small Office Network (if the choice is available). Floppy disks are too small for convenience, but removable disks work well if both computers have them. Use the Other option to store files and settings on another drive in the same computer.

> **Note**   *The Home or Small Office Network option button is available only if both the source computer and the target computer are on the same TCP/IP subnet. If they're not, either change one of their subnets to match the other, or transfer the files to another computer that both the source computer and the target computer can reach.*

> **Tip**   *The Files and Settings Transfer Wizard can't burn files directly to CD or DVD unless you use a packet-writing program such as DirectCD. You can use the Other option to copy to a file, and then burn that file to the CD or DVD using regular burning software.*

4. On the What Do You Want to Transfer? page, select the Settings Only option button, the Files Only option button, or the Both Files and Settings option button (the default), as appropriate. The list box shows the items that will be transferred. To customize it, select the Let Me Select a Custom List of Files and Settings check box.

5. If you selected the check box, the wizard displays the Select Custom Files and Settings page (Figure 2-1). Use the four Add buttons and their resulting dialog boxes to add files, folders, and settings to the list. Use the Remove button to remove a file, folder, or setting from the list.

6. Click the Next button. The wizard collects the files and settings, wraps them up in a file, and then informs you that it has finished.

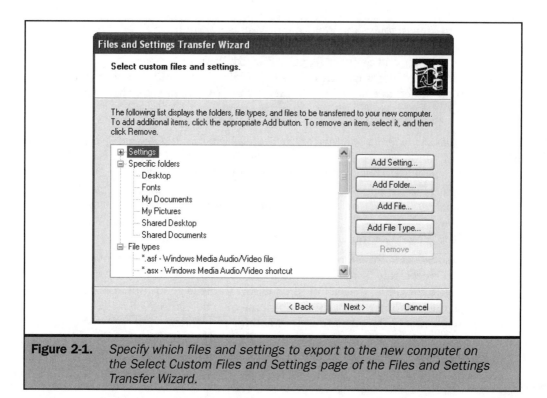

Figure 2-1. *Specify which files and settings to export to the new computer on the Select Custom Files and Settings page of the Files and Settings Transfer Wizard.*

You then apply the files and settings to the new computer as discussed in "Transferring Files and Settings" in Chapter 6.

Collecting Any Necessary Information for the Installation

Collect any information necessary for the installation. For example, collect details of any Internet account you'll need to set up on the computer (account name, password, the ISP's phone number if it's a dial-up connection, and the addresses of your ISP's DNS servers). If you'll be connecting to a domain, make sure you know your user account and password. Also make sure you know any saved passwords on a computer that you're going to upgrade from Windows 98 or Windows Me to Windows XP Professional, because the upgrade will remove the saved passwords so that you'll need to reenter them manually.

Turning Off Antivirus Software and Recovery Utilities

When you're ready to install Windows XP, turn off any antivirus software you're running, because it'll interfere with the upgrade. Also turn off any low-level recovery utilities such as Roxio GoBack, because that will cause trouble too.

Removing Drive Overlay Software

Windows XP doesn't work with drive overlay programs such as Maxtor's MaxBlast, Seagate's Disk Manager, IBM's Disk Manager 2000, or Western Digital's EZ-BIOS. These programs usually display a splash screen on bootup, so it's easy to tell when you're running one of them.

Before installing Windows XP, you'll need to back up your data, remove the drive overlay program, repartition your hard disk, and then restore your data.

Performing an Upgrade Installation

This section discusses how to perform an upgrade installation of Windows XP Professional. An upgrade installation is one in which you install Windows XP Professional on the same partition as your previous version of Windows so that it overwrites that version of Windows and migrates all your existing settings and applications to Windows XP.

When to Choose an Upgrade Installation

Windows XP Professional supports upgrades from Windows XP Home Edition, Windows 2000 Professional, Windows NT Workstation 3.51 or 4, Windows 98 (both first edition and Second Edition), and Windows Me. Windows XP Professional doesn't support upgrades from Windows 95.

If you have one of these versions of Windows installed on your computer and working satisfactorily, together with all the applications you need for your work, an upgrade installation is a good bet.

If the upgrade doesn't work satisfactorily, you can use Windows XP Professional's uninstallation routine to restore your previous version of Windows. If that version of Windows is one of the Windows $9x$ versions (which can't use NTFS), you must not allow the upgrade to convert your hard disk's file system from FAT to NTFS, because that will prevent you from restoring your previous version of Windows if Windows XP Professional proves unsatisfactory.

Preparing for an Upgrade Installation

Before performing the upgrade installation, clean up your hard disk. Follow these steps:

1. Uninstall any applications that you won't use with Windows XP.

2. If your version of Windows includes Disk Cleanup (Start | Programs | Accessories | System Tools | Disk Cleanup), run it to get rid of temporary files, temporary Internet files, downloaded program files, the contents of your Recycle Bin, and other essentially useless files.

3. Defragment your hard disk by running the defragmenter that your version of Windows includes (for example, Start | Programs | Accessories | System Tools | Disk Defragmenter). Windows NT doesn't include a defragmenter, but you can get third-party defragmenters such as Diskeeper (www.diskeeper.com).

Starting the Upgrade Installation

To start the upgrade installation, follow these steps:

1. Boot your current version of Windows.

2. Insert the Windows XP installation CD. If AutoPlay doesn't run, choose Start | Run, enter *cd*:\setup (where *cd* is the drive containing the CD) in the Run dialog box, and click the OK button.

3. Click the Install Windows XP link.

4. Choose the Upgrade item in the Installation Type drop-down list on the Welcome to Windows Setup page.

5. Follow the steps of accepting the license agreement, entering your product key, choosing a type of upgrade report, and letting Dynamic Update download any updated files.

6. Go to "Common Final Steps of Installation," later in this chapter, and finish the installation from there.

Performing a New Installation

This section discusses how to perform a new installation of Windows XP Professional. A new installation is one in which you install Windows XP Professional on a separate partition from your existing version of Windows. This leaves you with a dual-boot multiboot configuration that lets you boot either Windows XP Professional or your previous version of Windows. (If you already had a dual-boot configuration or multiboot configuration, you end up with a multiboot configuration to which Windows XP Professional has been added.)

Preparing for a New Installation

Make sure that you have free space or a partition free on which to install Windows XP. You can create the partition easily during Windows Setup. Alternatively, you may prefer to use a nondestructive partitioning utility such as PartitionMagic or Partition Commander to resize existing partitions and create a suitable new partition from your current version of Windows before beginning the installation.

Before running a new installation from Windows NT 4 Workstation, upgrade Windows NT 4 Workstation to Service Pack 4 or higher. Service Pack 6a is preferable. You can download it from www.microsoft.com/ntserver/nts/downloads/recommended/

SP6/allSP6.asp. (The same service pack is used for both Windows NT 4 Workstation and Windows NT 4 Server.)

 If you're upgrading from Windows NT 4 Workstation, and your computer uses multidisk volumes (such as volume sets, mirror sets, or stripe sets with or without parity), you'll need to either delete them or convert them to dynamic disks before installing Windows XP Professional.

Starting the New Installation

To start the new installation, follow these steps:

1. Boot your current version of Windows.

2. Insert the Windows XP installation CD. If AutoPlay doesn't run, choose Start | Run, enter *cd***:\setup** (where *cd* is the drive containing the CD) in the Run dialog box, and click the OK button.

3. Click the Install Windows XP link.

4. Choose the New Installation item in the Installation Type drop-down list on the Welcome to Windows Setup page.

5. Follow the steps of accepting the license agreement and entering your product key.

6. Choose advanced options, accessibility options, and the primary language and region on the Setup Options page (shown on the left in Figure 2-2). The Advanced Options dialog box (shown on the right in Figure 2-2) lets you specify the following:

   ■ The installation source folder

   ■ The destination folder (for example, to prevent Windows XP from overwriting an existing folder)

   ■ Whether Windows Setup copies all installation files from the CD to the hard disk. Use this option when the CD won't be available after you reboot the computer—for example, if you have a CD-free computer or one that uses a USB or FireWire CD drive. You don't need to choose this option when installing from a network drive, because Windows Setup selects it automatically and prevents you from clearing it.

   ■ Whether to let you choose the installation drive letter and partition during setup. Surprisingly, you don't need to select this option when performing a new installation of Windows XP, even though logically you should need to.

7. Choose whether to let Dynamic Update download the latest files on the Get Updated Setup Files page.

8. After Windows Setup reboots your computer, follow the common installation steps in "Choosing Settings for a New Installation or Clean Installation," later in this chapter.

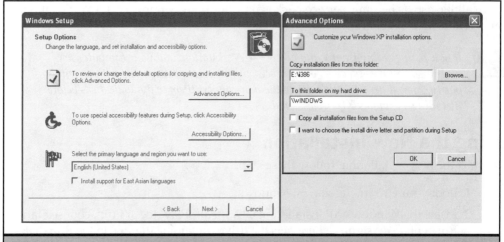

Figure 2-2.   *From the Setup Options page (left), choose advanced options in the Advanced Options dialog box (right), accessibility options, and the primary language and region for the computer.*

Performing a Clean Installation

This section discusses how to perform a clean installation of Windows XP Professional. A clean installation is one in which you install Windows XP Professional from scratch, on a computer that has no operating system installed, a computer whose existing version of Windows or whose other operating system you want to replace, or a computer with a non-Windows operating system that you want to dual-boot with Windows XP.

Preparing for a Clean Installation

If you're installing on a computer that doesn't have an operating system installed, and you have another computer available, check the computer's hardware against the HCL. That's about all the preparation you need to perform.

If the computer contains a non-Windows operating system (for example, Linux or Solaris), use that operating system's tools to remove from the partition on which you intend to install Windows XP any files you want to keep. If necessary, use the operating system's tools or a third-party partitioning utility to rearrange your existing partitions to make space for the Windows XP partition.

You can create the Windows XP partition easily during Windows Setup. Alternatively, you may prefer to use a nondestructive partitioning utility such as PartitionMagic or Partition Commander to resize existing partitions and create a suitable new partition before beginning the installation.

Starting the Clean Installation

To perform a clean installation of Windows XP Professional, follow these steps:

1. Insert the Windows XP Professional CD in your computer's CD drive and boot from the drive. (Change the BIOS's boot settings if necessary.) Setup runs automatically.

Note   *If your CD drive isn't bootable, create boot disks by downloading the compressed boot-disk file from www.microsoft.com/downloads/ and running it to create the set of six boot disks. Insert the first disk and reboot your computer. (You may need to change your computer's BIOS settings to boot from the floppy drive.) After working your way through the boot disks, you'll be able to access your CD drive and continue the installation from there. Alternatively, if you have a Windows 98 startup disk, you can boot from that and then run winnt.exe from the \i386\ folder on the CD.*

2. Press ENTER at the Welcome to Setup screen.

3. If Setup offers to repair an existing installation of Windows XP that your hard disk contains, press ESC.

4. Follow the common installation steps in the next section.

Choosing Settings for a New Installation or Clean Installation

This section discusses the steps common to a new installation and clean installation of Windows XP: partitioning the drive, choosing the installation partition, choosing regional and language options, naming the computer, choosing networking settings, joining a domain or workgroup, and so forth.

Partitioning the Drive and Choosing the Installation Partition

This section discusses how to use Windows Setup's partitioning tool to manipulate partitions and to choose the partition on which to install Windows XP. You need to choose a partition for both a new installation of Windows XP and a clean installation of Windows XP.

After rebooting (for a new installation) or booting from the Windows XP installation CD, Windows Setup displays the partitioning screen (Figure 2-3), which lists the partitions on the disk or disks together with any unpartitioned space.

You can manipulate partitions as follows:

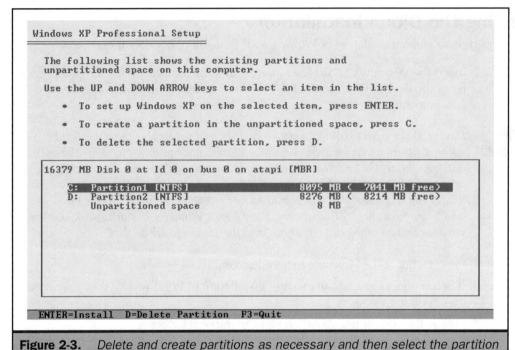

```
Windows XP Professional Setup

    The following list shows the existing partitions and
    unpartitioned space on this computer.

    Use the UP and DOWN ARROW keys to select an item in the list.

        • To set up Windows XP on the selected item, press ENTER.

        • To create a partition in the unpartitioned space, press C.

        • To delete the selected partition, press D.

    16379 MB Disk 0 at Id 0 on bus 0 on atapi [MBR]

        C:  Partition1 [NTFS]                 8095 MB <  7041 MB free>
        D:  Partition2 [NTFS]                 8276 MB <  8214 MB free>
            Unpartitioned space                  8 MB




    ENTER=Install   D=Delete Partition   F3=Quit
```

Figure 2-3.   *Delete and create partitions as necessary and then select the partition on which to install Windows XP.*

- Use the ↓ key and the ↑ key to select the partition or unpartitioned space you want to affect.

- To delete a partition, press D, then press L on the resulting confirmation screen. For a system partition, you have to further confirm the deletion.

- To create a partition on the selected unpartitioned space, press C, type in the size for the partition in megabytes (or accept Windows Setup's suggestion of using the full extent of the unpartitioned space), and press ENTER.

- To install on the selected partition or unpartitioned space, press ENTER. If you chose unpartitioned space, Windows Setup creates a partition using all the space.

If the partition you choose for installation isn't formatted, Windows Setup asks you whether to format it with NTFS or FAT32. If the partition is on clusters that have been formatted before, you can choose between a full format (which scans the disk for bad sectors) and a quick format (which doesn't). It's best to choose the full format. If the partition is on clusters that have never been formatted before, Windows Setup doesn't offer you the choice of a quick format.

Choosing Regional and Language Options

Next, Windows Setup displays the Regional and Language Options page, which summarizes the regional and language settings that Windows Setup will apply to Windows XP by default. (Which settings you get depend on the localization of the version of Windows XP on your installation CD.)

If the defaults don't suit you, change them as follows:

- To change the Standards and Formats settings, click the Customize button and work in the Regional and Language Options dialog box. On the Regional Options tab, you can specify your location (for local information, such as weather and news) and select your preference for standards and formats. You can also click the Customize button on the Regional Options tab to customize the formats (for dates, times, numbers, and currencies) for the location you've chosen. On the Languages tab, you can change your text input languages and install supplemental language features, such as support for complex script and right-to-left languages and support for East Asian Languages. On the Advanced tab, you can choose settings for non-Unicode programs.

- To change your default text input language and method, click the Details button on the Regional and Language Options tab to display the Text Services and Input Languages dialog box. (Alternatively, you can work from the Languages tab of the Regional and Language Options dialog box, as described in the previous paragraph.) To add an input language, click the Add button and use the resulting Add Input Language dialog box to specify the input language and keyboard layout. (For example, you might choose to add a different keyboard configuration, such as one of the Dvorak keyboard layouts, for the same language as you're currently using.) Use the Remove button to remove any installed input language that you don't want to use. Trying to remove the input language that you're currently using results in an error. After adding one or more input languages and clicking the Apply button, you can click the Key Settings button to display the Advanced Key Settings dialog box. This dialog box lets you specify how to turn off the Caps Lock setting (by pressing the CAPS LOCK key or by pressing the SHIFT key) and specify the hot keys to use for switching between your different input languages.

Note *You can also make any of these changes after installation by working through the Regional and Language Options applet in Control Panel, so you don't need to get these settings exactly right during setup.*

Entering Your Name and Your Company's Name

On the Personalize Your Software page, enter your name and your company's name in the format that you want Windows XP to use.

For a clean installation of Windows XP, enter the CD key for your copy of Windows XP. For a new installation, you'll have entered the CD key already.

Specifying the Computer's Name

On the What's Your Computer's Name? page, enter the name you want Windows XP to assign to your computer. In most cases, you'll want to replace the default name that Windows Setup suggests, because it's derived clumsily from the user name you just provided. The constraints for the name are as follows:

- For the name to be readable via network protocols other than TCP/IP, it needs to be 15 characters or fewer.
- If your network uses only TCP/IP, the name can include up to 63 characters, but shorter names tend to be both easier to use and more comprehensible.

Filling In Your Modem Dialing Information

If there's a modem attached to your computer, enter the relevant information on the Modem Dialing Information page: your country or region, the area code, any number needed for using an outside line, and the phone dialing method used (tone or pulse dialing).

Verifying the Date and Time

On the Date and Time Settings page, verify the date, time, and time zone that Windows Setup has chosen for you, and choose whether to adjust the clock for daylight savings time.

Choosing Networking Settings

On the Networking Settings page, choose whether to use Typical Settings or Custom Settings. Which you choose will depend on your network configuration. Typical Settings installs the components shown in the following list:

- **TCP/IP** Transmission Control Protocol/Internet Protocol is Windows XP's preferred protocol and the protocol on which the Internet is based.
- **Client for Microsoft Networks** Client software for connecting to Microsoft networks. Enables Windows XP to access files and printers on the network.
- **QoS Packet Scheduler** Organizes data transmission to maintain quality of service (QoS) for data streams that are sensitive to delays.
- **File and Print Sharing for Microsoft Networks** Enables Windows XP to share files and printers with other computers connected to the same network.

If your computer connects to a server running Novell's NetWare network operating system rather than Windows 2000 Server or Windows.NET Server, you may need to install these components:

- **NWLink IPX/SPX/NetBIOS Compatible Transport Protocol**   Internet Packet Exchange/Sequenced Packet Exchange is the protocol historically used on NetWare networks.
- **Client Service for NetWare**   Client software for connecting to NetWare networks.

For coverage of how to install further networking components, see Chapter 29. For coverage of how to configure TCP/IP manually, see Chapter 26.

Joining a Domain or a Workgroup

On the Workgroup or Computer Domain page, specify whether the computer will be part of a workgroup or join a domain. Enter the workgroup name or the domain name as appropriate.

If you choose to connect to a domain, Windows Setup displays the Join Computer to Domain dialog box. Enter the user name and password for an account authorized to join the computer to the domain. Windows Setup tries to contact the domain. It it's able to do so, Windows Setup proceeds. If not, Windows Setup displays the Network Configuration dialog box, saying that an invalid domain was specified and asking if you want to proceed for now and try joining a domain later. Click the Yes button or the No button as appropriate.

Common Final Steps of Installation

This section discusses the final steps of installation, which are common to all three installation methods: connecting to the Internet, optionally activating and registering Windows XP, and creating user accounts.

Connecting to the Internet

Follow the prompts that Windows Setup provides for connecting your computer to the Internet. If Windows Setup discovers an available Internet connection through a network, it offers you the option of using it. If not, or if you choose not to connect through the network, it lets you specify which type of device to use for the Internet connection (for example, a modem) and the settings to use with it.

Activation and Registration

To reduce software piracy, a retail copy of Windows XP Professional forces you to activate it within 30 days of installation. After 30 days, Windows XP prevents anyone from logging on except to activate the operating system. You can activate Windows XP across the Internet or by making a toll-free phone call.

Windows Setup encourages you to activate Windows XP Professional at the end of setup, but you'll probably want to wait until you've checked that Windows XP agrees with all your hardware. You can activate Windows XP at any time by choosing Start | All Programs | Activate Windows or by clicking the reminder icon in the notification area. Because Windows XP reminds you to activate it each time a Computer Administrator user logs on and "every few days" if you keep a user session running and logged on, your chances of forgetting to activate Windows XP are nil.

Most OEMs who supply computers preloaded with Windows XP activate those copies of the OS, either by performing the process described next or by using a feature called System Locked Preinstallation (SLP). So if you buy a computer with Windows XP on it, you probably won't need to activate it. Similarly, if your company has bought its copies of Windows XP through volume-licensing arrangements from Microsoft, those copies won't need manual activation.

To prevent you from activating the same copy of Windows XP on more than one computer, the activation program generates an eight-digit hardware ID (HWID) by using values it obtains from up to 10 devices on your computer: the video card, amount of RAM, processor type, processor serial number, hard drive, hard drive serial number, primary CD or DVD drive (if any), Media Access Control (MAC) number of the primary network adapter (if any), IDE adapter (if any), and SCSI adapter (if any). During activation, the computer transmits (or you transmit) this HWID number to Microsoft together with a 20-digit product ID (PID) derived from the CD key for your copy of Windows XP. The hardware ID and product ID together comprise the "Installation ID." Microsoft transmits back a 42-digit confirmation ID that activates Windows XP Professional.

Microsoft claims that none of your personal information is transferred during activation. If you doubt this assurance, use the telephone procedure for activation rather than the Internet procedure—but be prepared to type in that 42-digit confirmation ID accurately.

The activation program also monitors your hardware configuration each time you boot up to make sure that Windows XP is still running on the computer on which it was activated. If you change too many of those ten components within a given timeframe, you'll trigger an activation alert and will have to reactivate Windows XP. The threshold is supposedly four of the ten components in a period of 120 days.

If you have to reinstall Windows XP (for example, to recover from a virus), you'll need to reactivate the OS.

If you activate Windows XP, Windows Setup offers you the choice of registering it with Microsoft. If you're already registered with Microsoft, you can merge your Windows XP registration information with your existing information. If not, you'll need to create a new profile. When doing so, be sure to read the small print for options by which you agree to Microsoft and its business partners bombarding you with special offers.

Completing the Network Identification Wizard

If you chose to connect your computer to a domain, Windows Setup launches the Network Identification Wizard, which walks you through adding a domain user to the computer and specifying their access level (Standard User, Restricted User, or a member of one of the groups, such as Administrators). If you choose not to add a user at this time, you can run the Network Identification Wizard at any time by clicking the Network ID button on the Computer Name tab of the System Properties dialog box.

Creating User Accounts

If you chose a standalone or workgroup configuration, Windows Setup displays the Who Will Use This Computer? screen. From here, create a user account for each user that you want to set up now. You can create up to five accounts on this screen. You can create further accounts as necessary after logging on.

These are the constraints for user names:

- Each user name must be unique.

- Each user name can contain from 1 character to 20 characters.

- The following characters are not allowed:

    " [ ] / \ | * + = < > : ; , ?

- Names can't be all spaces, all periods, or a combination of spaces and periods.

By default, Windows Setup makes each account a Computer Administrator account with no password. Because these default settings make a joke of security, you should change them immediately. See Chapter 27 for a discussion of how to do so.

Note *When you upgrade to Windows XP, Windows Setup automatically creates accounts for all users defined on the operating system from which you performed the upgrade. Windows Setup displays the Password Creation dialog box so that you can create a password for all the accounts. (You can then change the password later as necessary.)*

Duplicating an Existing Operating System

The three installation methods described so far cover the needs of most people who will need to install Windows XP Professional themselves. (Many users of Windows XP Professional will have the operating system installed for them, either by their PC's OEM or by their company's network administrators.) But if you're a power user who looks after your own computer, you may want to duplicate your existing operating system before upgrading it so that you can use both that OS and Windows XP Professional with all your applications and settings in place. Doing so will give you a more direct way to compare Windows XP with your existing operating system, because you'll be able to boot either operating system at will and compare how your applications run on the two.

Duplicating an operating system is a complex procedure. The most labor-intensive part of the process is replacing all instances of certain strings of text in the Registry with other strings that refer to the duplicated version of the operating system. Because there may be many hundred or several thousand instances of these strings, replacing them manually is tedious, but still possible. You can make this part of the process painless by getting a third-party Registry-editing application that can perform a global search-and-replace operation, which none of the assorted versions of the Windows Registry Editor can do. Examples of such Registry-editing applications include Registry Search and Replace (which you can find at assorted shareware sites on the Internet), Funduc Software's Registry Toolkit (www.funduc.com), or Norton Registry Editor (www.norton.com).

Note   *See Chapter 40 for a discussion of what the Registry is, what it does, and how you can examine and change it.*

Before duplicating an installation of Windows 2000 or Windows NT 4, back up all files you care about and update your Emergency Repair Disk by using Backup (in Windows 2000) or issuing an **rdisk /s** command. Then follow the procedure outlined in the next section.

Before duplicating an installation of Windows 9*x*, back up all files whose loss would pain you, and make sure that you have a boot floppy for that version of Windows so that you can recover your OS if things go wrong. Then follow the procedure outlined in "Duplicating an Installation of Windows 9*x*," later in this chapter.

Duplicating an Installation of Windows 2000 or Windows NT 4

To duplicate an installation of Windows 2000 or Windows NT 4, follow these steps:

1. Load the Windows XP CD in your CD drive. If your operating system uses AutoPlay, hold down the SHIFT key as you load the CD to override AutoPlay so that the CD doesn't launch Windows XP's setup routine. (Alternatively, cancel out of the setup routine if it runs.)

2. Create a folder to contain the duplicate copy of the OS files. For this example, I'll use the folder C:\WXP.

3. Open a command prompt and issue an **xcopy** command to copy all the files from your current OS's %Windir% folder (for example, WINNT or Windows) to the WXP folder. (%Windir% is a system variable that returns the path to your Windows folder.)

```
xcopy c:\windows c:\wxp /h /i /c /k /e /r
```

| Note | *That handful of switches is worth understanding. /h copies system and hidden files. /e copies empty directories and subdirectories. /i creates destination folders when they don't exist and multiple files are being copied. /r overwrites read-only files. /k copies attributes rather than resetting read-only attributes. And /c forces copying to continue even when errors occur (such as when xcopy tries to copy the SAM and finds it can't do so).* |

4. Configure Windows Explorer to display hidden files and system files.

5. Open boot.ini in a text editor or word processor (for example, Notepad, WordPad, or Word) and add to it a new entry for the duplicated version of the operating system. The easiest way to create this line is by copying the line that refers to the original version of the operating system, pasting it, changing the description, and changing the path to refer to the folder that contains the duplicate version of the operating system. Alternatively, you can type the new line. For example, you might copy and edit the second line shown here to create the third line shown here.

```
[operating systems]
multi(0)disk(0)rdisk(0)partition(2)\WINNT="Windows 2000" /fastdetect
multi(0)disk(0)rdisk(0)partition(2)\WINDOWS="Windows XP" /fastdetect
```

6. Save boot.ini and exit the text editor or word processor.

7. Restart Windows and boot the Recovery Console from the Windows XP Professional CD. (If you had taken it out of the drive, reinsert it first. See "Recovering with Recovery Console" in Chapter 24 for a discussion of the Recovery Console.) When Recovery Console asks you which operating system to start, specify the duplicate installation. Because xcopy won't have copied the security accounts database, Recovery Console won't prompt you for a password.

8. Use the **cd** command to change directory to the %Windir%\System32\config folder for the original installation. Then issue a **copy** command to copy all the contents of this folder to the %Windir%\System32\config folder for the duplicate installation. Doing so copies the Registry files from the original installation to the duplicate installation.

9. Exit Recovery Console and restart Windows. From the boot menu, select the new entry you added to the boot menu—in this example, the Windows XP entry.

10. Log on as an Administrator or as a member of the Administrators group. Use the Registry-editing application to change all instances of the original %Windir% to the new %Windir%.

11. Restart Windows into the duplicate installation again. Log on as an Administrator or as a member of the Administrators group. Upgrade this installation to Windows XP Professional.

Duplicating an Installation of Windows 9*x*

To duplicate an installation of Windows 9*x*, follow these steps:

1. Create a folder to contain the duplicate copy of the OS files. For this example, I'll use the folder D:\Upgrade.

2. Create a Boot folder under the upgrade folder (for example, D:\Upgrade\Boot). Create another Boot folder under your Windows folder (for example, C:\Windows\Boot).

3. Open a command-prompt window and issue an **xcopy32** command to copy all the files from your current OS's %Windir% folder (for example, C:\Windows) to the Upgrade folder:

   ```
   xcopy32 c:\windows D:\upgrade /h /i /c /k /e /r /y
   ```

Note *See the Note in the previous section for an explanation of those switches—they're the same for xcopy32 in Windows 9x as for xcopy in Windows 2000 or Windows NT 4. The exception is the /y switch, which causes xcopy32 to overwrite existing files without prompting.*

4. In Windows Explorer, make Windows show hidden and system files. For example, choose View | Folder Options and select the Show All Files option button in the Hidden Folders section of the View tab.

5. Copy the following files from the root of your boot drive to the \Boot\ folder you created: autoexec.bat, config.sys, io.sys, and msdos.sys.

6. Display the Properties dialog box for the original msdos.sys file (the one in your root folder) and remove the Read-only property. Close the Properties dialog box.

7. Open msdos.sys in a text editor or word processor and change the WinDir, WinBootDir, and (if necessary) WinBootDrv entries to reflect the new Windows directory. Save msdos.sys and exit the text editor or word processor.

8. Restart Windows. Doing so will boot your duplicate copy of Windows in the new folder.

9. Use your Registry editor to replace all instances of the string for the original Windows directory (for example, C:\Windows) with the string for the duplicate Windows directory (for example, D:\Upgrade).

10. Use System Editor, Notepad, or a word processor to change all the instances of the string for the original Windows directory in the System.ini and Win.ini files in the new Windows directory to the string for the duplicate Windows directory. Save these files.

11. Open msdos.sys again in a text editor or word processor and restore the values of WinDir and WinBootDir to their previous value. Save the changes and exit the text editor or word processor.

12. Restart Windows. Doing so will boot your original installation of Windows.

13. Upgrade your original installation of Windows to Windows XP Professional.

14. Move the autoexec.bat file and the config.sys file from your root folder to the Boot folder under your original installation of Windows (for example, C:\Windows\Boot).

15. Move the autoexec.bat file and the config.sys file from the Boot folder under your duplicate installation of Windows to your root folder. Open each file in turn and change any references to the original installation so that they refer to the duplicate installation. Add to the end of autoexec.bat the command **win**. (This command starts Windows 9x.)

16. Edit boot.ini (in the root folder of your boot drive) and add a new entry in the [operating systems] section for Windows 9x:

    ```
    C:\"Windows 9x"
    ```

17. Save and close boot.ini.

18. If you prefer to have Windows XP Professional keep hidden files and protected operating system files hidden from you, open a Windows Explorer window, choose View | Options, and select the appropriate options.

19. Restart Windows and boot Windows 9x from your duplicate installation. You may need to change the path for some of the shortcuts on the Programs menu from the original %Windir% folder to the duplicate installation's %Windir% folder.

Troubleshooting Installation Problems

This section discusses the installation problems and issues that you're most likely to encounter. It covers how to work around CD drive problems; what to do when the installation won't run, when it fails, or when it hangs; how to restore disabled startup programs after an upgrade from Windows 9x; how to revert to your previous OS; and how to remove your previous OS.

Working Around CD Drive Problems

Because Windows XP Professional's only installation medium is a CD, you need a functional CD drive to install it. To install Windows XP on a computer that doesn't have a CD drive, you'll need a computer that does have a CD drive. Connect the two computers using any viable means of connection (infrared, serial cable, parallel cable, network, or crossover cable) and make the CD drive available to the target computer (for example, by sharing the CD drive). Once you've done that, you can either install across the network or create a "flat" and install from that.

Installing Across the Network

The basic way to install Windows XP Professional across the network (in other words, across whatever type of connection you've established between the two computers) is to run the Setup.exe file on the CD from the target computer. As discussed later in Chapter 3, you can also run the winnt.exe program to install from a 16-bit operating system or the winnt32.exe file to install from a 32-bit operating system. By using these programs, you can specify switches that control how Windows Setup runs.

Creating a "Flat"

If for whatever reason you can't install across the network, or if you have only temporary access to the CD-equipped computer but think you may need to install Windows XP multiple times, create a "flat" on the target computer's hard drive.

A *flat* is a copy of the files required for installation. To create a flat, copy the \i386\ folder and the contents of the root directory on the CD to the target computer. (You can copy the entire CD if you like, but you shouldn't need the other folders for the installation, and copying them will cost you about 150MB of space.)

To install from the flat, run the winnt32.exe file or the winnt.exe file as appropriate.

Installing from Boot Disks

To perform a clean installation from a non-bootable CD drive, create Windows XP boot disks as discussed in "Starting the Clean Installation," earlier in this chapter; then boot from the disks.

Installation Won't Run, Fails, or Hangs

If installation won't run, double-check that your hardware is compatible with Windows XP Professional, because an incompatible device is probably causing installation to fail.

If installation fails with the error message "Setup cannot set the required Windows XP configuration information," some hardware on your computer is incompatible with Windows XP. Use Upgrade Advisor or the HCL to pinpoint the offending hardware, remove or replace it, and run setup again.

If an upgrade from Windows 98 or Windows Me fails with the error message "Setup has disabled the upgrade option, could not load the file D:\i386 \Win9xupg \W95upg.dll. Setup cannot continue, because this version can only install as an upgrade," clean-boot into that version of Windows and start the installation again. Failing that, create a flat and install from that.

If installation fails with the error message "Setup has determined that Drive C: is corrupted and cannot be repaired," the error message "No operating system," or "Windows could not start because of the following ARC firmware boot configuration problem. Did not properly generate ARC name for HAL and System path," you're running a drive overlay program that you need to remove. See "Removing Drive Overlay Software," earlier in the chapter, for the bad news.

If your computer appears to hang during installation, give it a few minutes to work out whatever problem it's struggling with. If installation doesn't resume, reboot your computer to restart installation, and let it try again. Windows Setup saves its installation state to disk periodically, so when you reboot it, it should be able to resume installation from the last saved state.

If Windows Setup seems to make progress after restarting installation, let it continue, even if you need to reboot it several times to get all the way through installation. But if installation keeps stopping at the same point, give up on the rebooting, because you've almost certainly got a hardware problem that you need to deal with. If you're upgrading or performing a new installation, reboot one final time and choose the Cancel Windows XP Setup item from the boot menu to cancel the installation and make Windows Setup restore your previous operating system to a working condition. Boot into that operating system and use the Upgrade Advisor or the HCL to identify the hardware device that's causing the trouble. Remove the device or replace it as necessary.

If all your hardware seems compatible, check that you're not running an antivirus program or a boot manager that's interfering with Windows Setup. If not, try the steps outlined in the following subsections, in order and one at a time.

Disabling Advanced Configuration and Power Interface

To disable Advanced Configuration and Power Interface (ACPI), press F7 when Windows Setup displays the banner "Press F6 if you need to load a third-party SCSI or RAID driver" early during installation. Windows Setup doesn't confirm that you've disabled ACPI, but taking this step might enable the installation to run successfully.

Upgrading Your Computer's BIOS

If disabling ACPI does no good, check whether your computer's BIOS needs an upgrade. Visit the manufacturer's web site for a flash upgrade or replace the BIOS.

Changing the Hardware Abstraction Layer

Your last option is to change the *Hardware Abstraction Layer* (HAL) that Windows XP Professional is trying to use. The HAL is a software layer that brokers communication between Windows XP (and Windows NT and Windows 2000) and your computer's hardware. Windows XP comes with a variety of HALs for different types of computers, and using the wrong HAL for your computer may make installation fail.

To specify a different HAL, press F5 when Windows Setup invites you to press F6 to load third-party SCSI or RAID drivers. On the resulting screen, specify the HAL type to use. The choices are

■ Advanced Configuration and Power Interface (ACPI) PC

■ ACPI Multiprocessor PC

- ACPI Uniprocessor PC
- Compaq SystemPro Multiprocessor or 100% Compatible
- MPS Uniprocessor PC
- MPS Multiprocessor PC
- Standard PC, Standard PC with C-Step i486
- Other (use this item only if your computer's OEM has provided you with a device support disk containing HAL information)

Restoring Disabled Startup Programs After Upgrading from Windows 98 or Windows Me

If you installed Windows XP Professional by upgrading from Windows 98 or Windows Me, Windows Setup may have removed some applications from the Startup group. To restore these items, follow these steps:

1. Run the System Configuration Utility. (Choose Start | Run, **msconfig**, OK.)
2. Select the Restore Startup Programs option on the Startup tab and select the check boxes for the applications you want to restore.
3. Restart Windows XP Professional.

Uninstalling Windows XP Professional and Reverting to Your Previous OS

If you upgraded an earlier version of Windows to Windows XP Professional, you can uninstall Windows XP Professional and revert to your previous operating system. If the previous operating system was a Windows 9*x* version, you can uninstall and revert only if you haven't converted the partition involved to NTFS.

When you revert to your previous operating system, you lose any applications you've installed since installing Windows XP Professional. The uninstallation routine warns you of this problem.

 Windows XP stores the files for your previous operating system in the files backup.cab, boot.cab, and backup.$$$ in the undo folder on your boot drive. Don't delete these files manually. When you're sure you no longer need them, use the procedure described in the next section to delete them, so that Windows XP removes the associated entry from the Add or Remove Programs window as well.

To uninstall Windows XP Professional and revert to your previous operating system, follow these steps:

INSTALLING,
CONFIGURING, AND
CUSTOMIZING

1. Choose Start | Control Panel | Add or Remove Programs | Windows XP Uninstall | Change/Remove to display the Uninstall Windows XP dialog box.

2. Select the Uninstall Windows XP option button and click the Continue button.

3. Click the Yes button in the confirmation dialog box. Windows XP Professional uninstalls itself and reboots the computer into the previous version of Windows.

Removing Your Previous Version of Windows

If Windows XP Professional seems to be working well, you can remove your old version of Windows. Follow these steps:

1. Choose Start | Control Panel | Add or Remove Programs | Windows XP Uninstall | Change/Remove to display the Uninstall Windows XP dialog box.

2. Select the Remove the Backup of My Previous Operating System option button and click the Continue button.

3. Click Yes in the confirmation dialog box.

Applying Service Packs

To keep Windows XP Professional up to date, you'll need to use Windows Update (discussed in Chapter 6) to apply updates and patches. You'll also need to apply any service packs that Microsoft releases. As of this writing, Microsoft has released Service Pack 1 for Windows XP Professional. It's likely that the procedure for applying later service packs will be similar to the procedure for Service Pack 1.

 To tell which service pack (if any) is installed, check the System readout on the General tab of the System Properties dialog box (WINDOWS KEY–BREAK). If a service pack is installed, the last line in the System readout gives its number (for example, Service Pack 1).

To apply a service pack, follow these steps:

1. Download the service pack from the Microsoft web site (www.microsoft.com) or obtain it on a CD.

2. Log on to the computer as an Administrator.

3. If the computer uses Fast User Switching, make sure that all other users are logged off so that there are no disconnected sessions.

4. Close all applications.

5. If you have an Automated System Recovery (ASR) set, update it. If not, consider creating one. (See "Automated System Recovery" in Chapter 23 for details.)

6. Make sure that your data files are backed up.

7. Run the service pack's installation routine. How you do this depends on how the service pack is packaged. For example, if you've downloaded a self-extracting file, run it to extract the files and automatically launch the installation routine.

8. Accept the EULA for the service pack.

9. Choose whether to archive your existing operating system files in case you need to remove the service pack later. The disadvantages to archiving these files is that the archive takes disk space—the archive produced when installing Service Pack 1 is around 210MB on a typical system—and makes the process of installing the service pack take a few minutes longer.

10. Restart your computer and make sure that everything is working.

If you chose to archive your existing operating system files, you can remove the service pack by selecting the service pack's entry on the Change or Remove Programs tab of the Add or Remove Programs window (Start | Control Panel | Add or Remove Programs), clicking the Remove button, and confirming the removal.

Summary

This chapter discussed how to install Windows XP Professional. As you've seen, manual installation of Windows XP Professional can be straightforward, involving little more than inserting the Windows XP Professional CD, entering the various pieces of information that Windows Setup needs, and letting Windows Setup handle the rest. On other computers, you may need to troubleshoot installation issues in order to get Windows Setup to complete satisfactorily.

Manual setup is fine when you need to install Windows XP Professional on only a few computers. But if you need to install Windows XP Professional on a large number of computers, you can save a great deal of time by automating the installation process. The next chapter discusses the various possibilities for automating installation.

Chapter 3

Automating Windows XP Professional Installation

A s you saw in the previous chapter, manual installation of Windows XP Professional can be quite straightforward if you prepare adequately for it. But if you need to install Windows XP Professional on many computers, manual installation will take too long and too much effort if your organization runs faster than Tsarist bureaucracy. Instead, you'll want to automate the installation as much as possible.

This chapter assumes that you're not a domain administrator looking to roll out hundreds or thousands of Windows XP Professional workstations in a domain environment but rather a power user who needs to understand the possibilities for installing a more modest number of computers—anything, perhaps, from a few computers to a few dozen. So this chapter concentrates on the tools that Windows XP Professional itself includes for automating installation rather than the tools that Windows 2000 Server and Windows.NET Server provide and the third-party tools available to supplement them. However, this chapter also mentions the Windows 2000 Server, Windows.NET Server, and third-party tools briefly so that you're aware of the possibilities for automating installation.

Automatic Installation Methods

Windows XP Professional supports several methods of automatic installation:

■ Unattended Installation uses an answer file to provide the information usually supplied by a live body during setup. You can create an *answer file* for installing either from a CD or from a network share, which lets you install Windows XP onto a computer that has no CD drive. You can integrate Windows updates and service packs into a *slipstream installation share* so that the copy of Windows XP Professional installed is fully up to date.

■ Disk-imaging solutions let you create a disk image of Windows XP Professional and the applications you want to have on it, then copy this image to the client computers or to disks that you then install in them. Windows XP Professional includes Sysprep, a tool for preparing a disk image from an existing installation of Windows XP. You then copy that disk image to a hard disk that you install in a computer that has the same configuration as the computer on which you prepared the disk image.

■ Remote Installation Services (RIS) is a feature of Windows 2000 Server and Windows.NET Server that automatically installs Windows XP Professional to client computers attached to the network. After using RIS to install Windows XP Professional, you can use IntelliMirror to install applications remotely.

This chapter concentrates on unattended setup, because this is the method you as a Windows XP Professional user can use to install Windows XP Professional automatically on a number of workstations with different hardware configurations. The chapter briefly discusses Sysprep, which can be useful if you buy multiple computers with the same hardware configuration. It also discusses Remote Installation Services and disk-imaging solutions other than Sysprep briefly, on the basis that they're more relevant to domain administrators but that you'd probably like to know a little about them.

Configuring Windows Setup with Switches

The Windows XP Professional installation CD includes two setup programs for installing Windows XP or upgrading to it: winnt32.exe (for 32-bit operating systems) and winnt.exe (for 16-bit operating systems).

These days, you're much more likely to need winnt32.exe than winnt.exe, because you're likely to be upgrading from a 32-bit OS rather than a 16-bit OS. So this section concentrates on using winnt32.exe. However, in some cases, you may still need to use winnt.exe to install Windows XP on a legacy computer (for example, a laptop without a CD-ROM drive), so this section includes brief coverage of winnt.exe but doesn't give examples using it.

winnt32.exe Syntax and Switches

winnt32.exe runs on 32-bit operating systems. It uses the following syntax:

```
winnt32 [/checkupgradeonly] [/cmd:command_line] [/cmdcons] [/copydir:i386\folder_name]
[/copysource:folder_name] [/debug[level]:[filename]] [/dudisable] [/duprepare:pathname]
[/dushare:pathname] [/m:folder_name] [/makelocalsource] [/noreboot] [/s:sourcepath]
[/syspart:drive_letter] [/tempdrive:drive_letter] [/udf:id [,UDB_file]]
[/unattend[num]:[answer_file]]
```

Table 3-1 explains the switches for winnt32.exe.

winnt.exe runs on 16-bit operating systems such as DOS and Windows 3.1*x*. It uses the following syntax.

```
WINNT [/s[:sourcepath]] [/t[:tempdrive]] [/u[:answer file]]
[/udf:id[,UDF_file]] [/r:folder] [/r[x]:folder] [/e:command] [/a]
```

Table 3-2 explains the switches for winnt.exe.

Switch	Explanation
/checkupgradeonly	Runs the Upgrade Advisor and creates an upgrade log. The log is named Upgrade.txt on Windows 9x systems and Winnt32.log on Windows NT or Windows 2000 systems.
/cmd:command_line	Makes Setup execute the specified command during the final phase of Setup.
/cmdcons	Installs the Recovery Console (see "Recovering with Recovery Console" in Chapter 24). You can use this option after Setup, not during Setup.
/copydir:i386\folder_name	Copies the specified folder to the %systemroot% folder during Setup. Useful for copying folders containing items such as additional driver files required for Setup. Use multiple /copydir statements to copy multiple folders.
/copysource:folder_name	Copies the specified folder to a temporary folder in the %systemroot% folder during installation. (%systemroot% is a system variable that returns your system's root folder.) The temporary folder is deleted after Setup completes. Use multiple /copysource statements to copy multiple folders to temporary folders.
/debug[level]:[filename]	Writes debugging information to the specified file or (if no file is specified) to %systemroot%\Winnt32.log. The optional Level argument controls what information is included: 0 (severe errors), 1 (errors), 2 (warnings; the default), 3 (information), or 4 (detailed information). Each level includes all the levels under it—for example, 4 includes 0, 1, 2, and 3.
/dudisable	Turns off Dynamic Update (preventing Setup from downloading additional files) even if the answer file specifies Dynamic Update (DisableDynamicUpdates=No).
/duprepare:pathname	Prepares an installation folder for use with Dynamic Update updates.
/dushare:pathname	Specifies the installation folder prepared with /duprepare so that Setup can include the updates during Setup.

Table 3-1.   *Switches for winnt32.exe*

Switch	Explanation
/m:folder_name	Makes Setup copy replacement files from the specified folder rather than from the default location. If the specified folder doesn't contain the files, Setup reverts to those in the default location.
/makelocalsource	Makes Setup copy all installation source files to the local hard disk.
/noreboot	Stops Setup from rebooting the computer after copying files. Use this option to run another command before completing Setup.
/s:sourcepath	Specifies the location of the source files. You can use multiple /s switches to specify multiple sources. If you do, Setup fails if the first server isn't available.
/syspart:drive_letter	Makes Setup copy the files required for Setup startup to a hard disk and mark the disk as active so that you can install the disk in another computer and run Setup from there. /syspart requires the /tempdrive switch and works only for Windows NT 4, Windows 2000, or Windows XP.
/tempdrive:drive_letter	For use with the /syspart switch. Specifies the temporary drive on which to place the temporary files for installation and (for a new installation) on which to install Windows XP. For an upgrade, /syspart installs Windows XP on the drive from which winnt32.exe was run.
/udf:id[,UDB_file]	Provides the ID that controls how Setup uses the Uniqueness Database file (UDF) to change the answer file provided for unattended setup. UDF entries override entries in the answer file.
/unattend	Upgrades Windows 98, Windows Me, Windows NT, or Windows 2000 Workstation to Windows XP Professional, taking all settings from the previous operating system and accepting the EULA automatically.
/unattend[num]:[answer_file]	Performs an unattended clean installation of Windows XP. num specifies the number of seconds after the end of copying files before restarting the computer. answer_file specifies the answer file containing the installation parameters to use.

Table 3-1.   *Switches for winnt32.exe* (continued)

Switch	Explanation
/s[:*sourcepath*]	Specifies the full path or UNC path to the location of the source files.
/t[:*tempdrive*]	Specifies the drive on which Setup should place temporary files and install Windows XP.
/u[:*answer_file*]	Used with the /s switch. Specifies the answer file to use for Setup.
/udf:*id*[,*UDF_file*]	Provides the ID that controls how Setup uses the Uniqueness Database file (UDF) to change the answer file provided for unattended setup. UDF entries override entries in the answer file. If you don't specify a UDF file, Setup prompts you to insert a disk containing one.
/r[:*folder*]	Creates a folder with the specified name.
/rx[:*folder*]	Creates a temporary folder with the specified name and deletes it after Setup ends.
/e	Makes Setup execute the specified command after the graphical part of Setup ends.
/a	Enables the accessibility options.

Table 3-2. *Switches for winnt.exe*

Examples of Using Setup Switches with winnt32.exe

This section gives you some examples of using setup switches with winnt32.exe. It concentrates on the options you're most likely to find useful.

Running the Upgrade Advisor

To run the Upgrade Advisor, use the /checkupgradeonly switch:

```
winnt32.exe /checkupgradeonly
```

Specifying the Location of Source Files

To specify the location of the Windows XP source files, use the /s switch:

```
winnt32.exe /s:\\AcmeHeavySv01\xpsource
```

To copy files from more than one installation source, using load balancing for a quicker result, use multiple instances of the /s switch:

```
winnt32.exe /s:\\AcmeHeavySv01\xpsource /s:\\AcmeHeavySv02\xpsource
```

Specifying the Location for Temporary Installation Files

To specify the location for temporary installation files, use the /tempdrive switch with the /syspart switch. The following example places the temporary files on, and installs Windows XP on, drive C:.

```
winnt32.exe /s:\\AcmeHeavySv01\xpsource /tempdrive:c /syspart:c
```

Providing Updated Files from Another Installation Source

To provide updated installation files, use the /m switch, as in the following example. This switch makes Setup check the specified folder for each file required. If the folder contains the file, Setup copies that file; if not, Setup copies the file from the default installation source. By putting the latest files in the specified folder, you can create as up-to-date an installation as possible.

```
winnt32.exe /s:\\AcmeHeavySv01\xpsource /m:\\AcmeHeavySv01\wxpdls
```

Creating Permanent Folders During Setup

To create a permanent folder during Setup, use the /copydir switch. The following example copies the my_perm_files folder and its contents to the %systemroot% folder:

```
winnt32.exe /s:\\AcmeHeavySv01\xpsource /copydir:i386\my_perm_files
```

Note *The /copydir switch works a little differently in Windows XP Professional than in Windows 2000. In Windows XP, you need to include "i386\" in the statement (for example, /copydir:i386\myfiles) whereas in Windows 2000 you don't need to (for example, /copydir:myfiles).*

Creating permanent folders enables you to install folders that every computer will need. However, the %systemroot% folder often isn't a satisfactory location for long-term storage of such files. One solution is to use the /cmd switch to move a folder copied using /copydir to a more suitable location at the end of Setup. Another solution is to copy the folders after Setup is complete rather than by using the /copydir switch.

Creating Temporary Folders During Setup

To create a temporary folder that's removed at the end of Setup, use the /copysource switch. Such temporary folders are useful for providing files needed to complete the installation. The following example copies the my_temp_files to the %systemroot% folder:

```
winnt32.exe /s:\\AcmeHeavySv01\xpsource /copysource:my_temp_files
```

Running Commands at the End of Setup

You can run commands at the end of Setup by using the /cmd switch with winnt32.exe (discussed here) or by using a cmdlines.txt file (discussed later in this chapter).

To run a command with the /cmd switch, include the command after the switch. Put double quotation marks around the command if any of the path names or filenames include spaces. (Alternatively, you can reduce filenames and paths to 8.3 format, but doing so is harder than using double quotation marks.) The following example creates a folder named Resources under the Program Files folder:

```
winnt32.exe /cmd"md c:\Program Files\Resources"
```

Preparing a Drive for Use in Another Computer

To prepare a drive for installation in another computer, use the /syspart switch with the /tempdrive switch. /syspart makes Setup copy the startup files for the Setup process to the disk and mark it as active. You then transfer the drive to the target computer and run the rest of Setup. The following example prepares drive E: using a network share:

```
winnt32.exe /s:\\AcmeHeavySv01\xpsource /syspart:e /tempdrive:e /noreboot
```

Because Setup marks the disk specified by /syspart as active, you need to remove the drive before restarting the computer on which you prepare the drive. Otherwise, the computer will try to boot the freshly prepared drive. For this reason, include the /noreboot switch when using /syspart, as in the above example.

Incorporating Dynamic Updates in an Installation Share

Instead of having Setup run Dynamic Update during installation to download the latest files, you can download the files ahead of time and incorporate them in your installation share. You can then run Setup without needing an Internet connection available for downloading the updates.

To incorporate Dynamic Updates in an installation share, use the /duprepare switch:

```
winnt32.exe /duprepare:\\AcmeHeavySv01\xpsource
```

Running winnt32.exe with the /duprepare switch creates a folder named dudrvs in the share and adds update files to it.

Using an Installation Share That Includes Dynamic Updates

To make Setup use an installation share in which you've incorporated Dynamic Updates, use the /dushare switch with the appropriate folder path.

Disabling Dynamic Update During Setup

To disable Dynamic Update during Setup, use the /dudisable switch. Disabling Dynamic Update makes installation run faster, but the installation won't be able to benefit from any update files that are available.

Installing Windows XP Professional via Unattended Setup

To install Windows XP Professional via unattended setup, you create an answer file that supplies the information that you would normally enter manually during the course of an interactive setup.

You can also use a Uniqueness Database File (UDF) to override specified values in an answer file so that you can use the same answer file on different computers. For example, you can use a UDF to provide a different computer name for each computer on which you install Windows XP Professional.

Creating Custom Setup Files

Windows XP Professional includes two tools for creating custom setup files: Setup Manager (discussed in the next section) and Sysprep (discussed later in this chapter). You'll find both of these tools in the Support\Tools\Deploy.cab cabinet folder on the Windows XP Professional CD. To use these tools, extract them to a convenient location on your computer by opening Deploy.cab in a Windows Explorer window and issuing an **Extract** command from the File menu or the shortcut menu for the files. Because you may need the other tools included in Deploy.cab, it's easiest to extract all the contents of the cabinet file to the same location at the same time.

Using Setup Manager to Create Setup Files

Setup Manager can create setup files for use with Windows Unattended Installation, Sysprep installation, or Remote Installation Services. (Setup Manager can't create UDFs. More on this in a minute.) To use Setup Manager, extract it from Deploy.cab as described in the previous section, and double-click the resulting file to run it. Setup Manager runs you through the following steps:

- Specifying whether to create a new answer file or modify an existing answer file that you supply.

- Telling Setup Manager whether the answer file is for Windows Unattended Installation, Sysprep Installation, or Remote Installation Services (RIS).

- Specifying the operating system the answer file installs, in this case, Windows XP Professional.

- Specifying the user interaction level from the following possibilities:

  - **Provide Defaults**   The answer file provides default values that the user reviews and can change.

  - **Fully Automated**   The answer file provides all the information needed to set up Windows XP Professional.

  - **Hide Pages**   Setup displays to the user only the pages for which the answer file doesn't supply all the necessary information.

  - **Read Only**   Setup displays to the user only the pages for which the answer file doesn't supply all the necessary information. When a displayed page contains values provided by the answer file, the user can't change them.

  - **GUI Attended**   The answer file provides information only for the text-based part of Setup. The user completes the graphical part of Setup.

- Choosing whether to create a distribution folder for installing Windows XP Professional or whether you'll install from a CD. If you choose to create a distribution folder, you specify the location of the source files for the folder and the name and location of the distribution folder.

- Accepting the License Agreement (for a Fully Automated installation).

- Working through the 16 pages of settings accessible from the Setup Manager screen shown in Figure 3-1. You can access a page either by clicking its name in the left pane or by clicking the Next button (or the Back button) to move up and down the list of pages. Some pages have fields of required data when you're creating an answer file for a Fully Automated installation, and Setup Manager prevents you from leaving those pages until they are complete. So it's usually easiest to work through the pages in sequence using the Next button. That way, you can be sure that you don't miss a page of information you needed to enter.

Most of these pages are straightforward: the Customize the Software page lets you enter the registered owner name and organization name; the Display Settings page lets you specify color depth, screen resolution, and refresh rate; the Time Zone page lets you specify the time zone for Windows XP Professional; the Telephony page lets you specify a country or region, a city code, any number required to access an outside line, and whether the phone system uses tone or pulse dialing; and so on. The following pages merit comment:

- **Providing the Product Key page**   Lets you specify the product key for Windows XP Professional. Depending on your licensing scheme, you may have to modify the file that Setup Manager creates in order to specify a different product key for each computer.

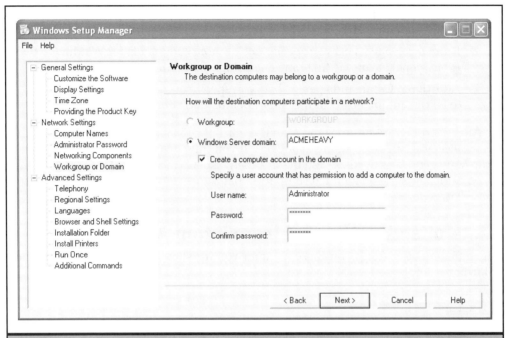

Figure 3-1. *Enter the information required for the setup file on the 16 pages accessible from this screen in Setup Manager.*

- **Computer Names page**   Lets you enter a list of computer names for Setup to assign (one per computer). You can type in a list of names manually, import an existing list of names from a text file that contains one name on each line, or specify that Setup automatically generate computer names based on the organization name supplied. Generally, you'll get more intelligible results by providing the names yourself, even though doing so takes a little more work.

- **Administrator Password page**   Lets you specify the Administrator password for the computer and choose whether to encrypt the password in the answer file, which is often a good idea. You can also choose to make Windows XP Professional automatically log on the Administrator account when the computer starts, either just for the first boot or for multiple boots. Automatically logging on the Administrator account once can be useful for setting up the computer. Beyond that, it's a security risk.

- **Workgroup or Domain page**   Lets you specify the workgroup or domain for the computer to join. If you set the computer to join a domain, you can create a computer account in the domain automatically by supplying the credentials of a user allowed to do so.

- **Browser and Shell Settings page**   Lets you choose between applying default Internet Explorer settings, using an autoconfiguration script created by the

Internet Explorer Administration Kit, or individually specifying proxy settings and default home page settings.

- **Run Once page**   Lets you specify one or more commands for Windows XP Professional to run the first time a user logs on to Windows XP.

- **Additional Commands page**   Lets you specify one or more commands to be run automatically at the end of unattended Setup.

After choosing settings in Setup Manager, click the Finish button. Specify the name for the answer file in the resulting dialog box. If you chose to create an installation source, Setup Manager copies the files from the CD, then displays the Setup Manager Complete screen, which lists the unattended setup files that Setup Manager has created. Choose File | Exit to close Setup Manager.

Contents of an Unattended Installation Answer File

Depending on the settings you chose, your answer file should look something like the following example:

```
;SetupMgrTag
[Data]
    AutoPartition=1
    MsDosInitiated="0"
    UnattendedInstall="Yes"

[Unattended]
    UnattendMode=FullUnattended
    OemSkipEula=Yes
    OemPreinstall=Yes
    TargetPath=\WINDOWS

[GuiUnattended]
    AdminPassword=df9a12636e30a446aadb45603c4027a523c276c80a
    EncryptedAdminPassword=Yes
    OEMSkipRegional=1
    TimeZone=85
    OemSkipWelcome=1

[UserData]
    ProductID=TH1S1-AINTA-VALID-PRODU-CT2ID
    FullName="Peter Acme"
    OrgName="Acme Heavy Industries"
    ComputerName=*
```

```
[Display]
  BitsPerPel=24
  Xresolution=800
  YResolution=600
  Vrefresh=85

[RegionalSettings]
  LanguageGroup=1

[SetupMgr]
  ComputerName0=ACMEHEAVYWK401
  ComputerName1=ACMEHEAVYWK402
  ComputerName2=ACMEHEAVYWK403
  DistFolder=\\ACMEHEAVYSV08\WXPPINST
  DistShare=WXPP_Distribution

[Identification]
  JoinDomain=ACMEHEAVYINDUST
  DomainAdmin=Peter Acme
  DomainAdminPassword=@cm!jo1n42

[Networking]
  InstallDefaultComponents=Yes
```

As you can see, the file starts with a comment line noting that Setup Manager created the file (;SetupMgrTag). The body of the file is broken up into a number of sections, each of which starts with a heading in brackets (for example, [Data] or [Unattended]). Each line represents a setting you specified in Setup Manager. For example, the UnattendMode line reflects the type of unattended installation you chose—"FullUnattended" for the Fully Automated installation option, "DefaultHide" for the Hide Pages installation option, and so on.

You may want to modify the unattend.txt file that Setup Manager produces to produce further customized installations. The change you're perhaps most likely to want to make is customizing the selection of optional components that Setup installs. To do so, include a [Components] section heading in unattend.txt and include a key for the appropriate component. Table 3-3 lists the optional components and the default values in Windows XP Professional.

Item	Name	Default Value
Accessibility Wizard	accessopt	On
Calculator	calc	On
Character Map	charmap	On
Chat	chat	On
COM Internet Services	netcis	Off
Desktop Wallpaper	deskpaper	On
Document Templates	templates	On
Fax Services	fax	Off
Freecell	freecell	On
FTP Service	iis_ftp	Off
Hearts	hearts	On
HyperTerminal	hypertrm	On
Indexing Service	indexsrv_system	Off
Internet Explorer shortcuts	IEAccess	On
Internet Games	zonegames	On
Internet Information Services	iis_common	Off
Message Queuing Active Directory Integration	msmq_ADIntegrated	Off
Message Queuing Core Functionality	msmq_Core	Off
Message Queuing HTTP Support	msmq_HTTPSupport	Off
Message Queuing Local Storage	msmq_LocalStorage	Off
Message Queuing Triggers	msmq_TriggersService	Off
Microsoft Paint	paint	On
Microsoft Script Debugger	iisdbg	Off

Table 3-3.   *Optional Components for Windows XP Professional*

Item	Name	Default Value
Minesweeper	minesweeper	On
MMC Administration Tools for IIS	iis_inetmgr	Off
Mouse pointers	mousepoint	On
MSN Explorer	msnexplr	On
netoc	(Controls whether Setup processes the [NetOptionalComponents] section of the answer file.)	On
Object Packager	objectpkg	On
Personal Web Manager	iis_pwmgr	Off
Phone Dialer	dialer	On
Pinball	pinball	On
Remote Installation Service	reminst	Off
Remote Storage	rstorage	Off
Sample Sound Clips	media_clips	On
Solitaire	solitaire	On
Sound Recorder	required	On
Spider Solitaire	spider	On
Terminal Services ActiveX Client	iis_www_vdir_terminalservices	Off
Terminal Services Client Diss (files for)	TSClients	Off
Terminal Services Web Client	TSWebClient	Off
Utopia Sound Scheme	media_utopia	Off
Volume Control	vol	On
Web Printing Components	iis_www_vdir_printers	Off

Table 3-3. *Optional Components for Windows XP Professional* (continued)

Item	Name	Default Value
Windows Media Player	mplay	On
Windows Messenger	msmsgs	On
WordPad	mswordpad	On
World Wide Web Service	iis_www	Off

Table 3-3.   *Optional Components for Windows XP Professional* (continued)

The [NetOptionalComponents] section of the answer file can contain the items listed in Table 3-4. (This list is for Windows XP Professional. Windows.NET Server and Windows 2000 Server have far more optional components.) This section of the answer file uses the values 1 (install the component) and 0 (don't install the component) rather than the values On and Off.

For example, the following lines prevent Setup from installing WordPad, MSN Explorer, and Pinball:

```
[Components]
mswordpad=off
msnexplr=off
pinball=off
```

Running Setup from CD with an Answer File

To launch Setup from CD using an answer file, create the answer file by using Setup Manager as described earlier in this chapter. Select the Windows Unattended Installation option button on the Product to Install page of Setup Manager and select the No, This Answer File Will Be Used to Install from a CD option button on the Distribution folder page.

Item	Name	Default Value
Print Services for Unix	LPDSVC	0
Simple TCP/IP Services	SimpTcp	0
Simple Network Management Protocol	SNMP	0

Table 3-4.   *[NetOptionalComponents] Components for Windows XP Professional*

When you've finished creating the answer file, rename it from unattend.txt to winnt.sif and copy it to a floppy disk. Load the floppy disk in the floppy drive and boot the computer from the Windows XP Professional CD to run Setup.

Creating UDFs

You can use a Uniqueness Database File (UDF) with winnt32.exe to supplement the answer file, providing answers that take precedence over some of the answers supplied by the answer file. UDFs work only for the graphical part of Setup, not for the text-mode part. Typically, you use a UDF to specify information that varies from computer to computer, such as the computer name, the product code, or the user name. But you can specify just about any value in the UDF if you so choose.

When the UDF contains a key with a value, Setup uses that value. When the UDF doesn't contain a key, Setup uses the value from the key in the answer file. When the UDF contains a key without a value assigned, Setup uses the default value for the key rather than any value specified in the answer file.

A UDF has the same layout as an answer file, being divided up into sections that start with the section name in brackets and that contain statements of the values of keys, one key to each line:

```
[section_name]
firstkey=firstvalue
secondkey=secondvalue
```

If you provide a list of computer names, Setup Manager creates a basic UDF named (by default) unattend.udb. This file contains the [UniqueIds] section heading that lists the unique sections in the UDF and the corresponding sections that contain the data to use in them. In the following example, there's a separate section for each of the two computer names specified, ACMEHEAVYWK401 and ACMEHEAVYWK402:

```
;SetupMgrTag
[UniqueIds]
    ACMEHEAVYWK401=UserData
    ACMEHEAVYWK402=UserData

[ACMEHEAVYWK401:UserData]
    ComputerName=ACMEHEAVYWK401

[ACMEHEAVYWK402:UserData]
    ComputerName=ACMEHEAVYWK402
```

Beyond these basic UDFs, Setup Manager doesn't create UDFs, so you need to create them manually. The easiest way to create a UDF is to build an unattended Setup file using Setup Manager, then use a text editor or word processor to cut and paste it into a UDF.

Using cmdlines.txt to Run Commands

To run multiple commands during installation, use a cmdlines.txt file. Create this text file in a text editor with a [Commands] section heading followed by each command in double quotation marks on a separate line, like this:

```
[Commands]
"command1.exe"
"command2.exe"
```

The commands run after Setup ends but before it reboots the computer. All the commands and any files and folders they affect must be available on the local computer, because network shares aren't available at this point during installation.

Create a folder named OEM in your Windows XP Professional distribution folder. Copy cmdlines.txt to this folder. To let Setup know that cmdlines.txt is there, enter the key OEMPreinstall=Yes in the [Unattended] section of the answer file.

Creating a Slipstream Installation Share

To install a service pack at the same time as Windows XP Professional, instead of needing to apply the service pack to each computer manually, you create a *slipstream installation share* and install from that.

To create a slipstream installation share, follow these steps:

1. Create a folder that will contain the slipstream installation files.

2. Create a folder to contain the extracted service pack files.

3. Copy the Windows XP Professional installation files to the folder you created in step 1 by using an xcopy /e command. For example, the following command copies the files from the CD in drive F: to the Z:\Install\i386 folder:

   ```
   xcopy f:\i386 z:\Install\i386 /e
   ```

4. Extract the service pack files from the self-extracting cabinet by running the file with the /x switch. The following example assumes the service pack is named xpsp1.exe:

   ```
   xpsp1 /x
   ```

5. When the extraction routine prompts you to choose a location for the files, specify the folder you created in step 2.

6. Run the Update.exe command from the Update folder with the –s switch and the location of the first folder:

   ```
   d:\sp1\i386\update\update.exe /s:z:\install
   ```

The Service Pack Setup Wizard then integrates the service pack files into the Windows XP Professional installation folder.

Using Sysprep to Prepare a Disk Image

If you need to install Windows XP Professional and a set of applications on several or many identically configured computers, you can use the Sysprep tool, which is included in Windows XP. As mentioned earlier, you'll find Sysprep in the Support\Tools\ Deploy.cab cabinet folder on the Windows XP Professional CD.

To use Sysprep, follow these steps:

1. Install Windows XP Professional on the C: drive of the source computer. Set the computer up to connect to a workgroup rather than a domain. Assign a blank administrator password.

 Sysprep doesn't always work successfully with an installation drive other than C:. Use C: if possible.

2. Configure Windows XP Professional as necessary.

3. Install on the source computer the applications that you want all the computers to have. Configure the applications.

4. Run Setup Manager as described earlier in this chapter:

   ■ On the Product to Install page, select Sysprep Install to create an answer file for Sysprep. Follow through the rest of Setup Manager to specify the options for the file.

   ■ If necessary, specify an OEM Duplicator String to add to the Registry on the destination computers so that you can easily identify the Sysprep image used for the computer.

   ■ Setup Manager saves the answer file under the name sysprep.inf. Place this file in the %systemroot%\Sysprep folder.

5. Run Sysprep using the following syntax and the appropriate switches. Table 3-5 lists the key switches for Sysprep. (Sysprep has other switches for use with the deployment tool Factory.exe, which is mostly used by OEMs.)

   ```
   sysprep [-quiet] [-nosidgen] [-pnp] [-reboot/-noreboot]
   ```

6. Install the target hard drive in the source computer.

7. Use a third-party cloning application such as Ghost or DriveImage to clone the source disk to the target disk.

Switch	Explanation
-noreboot	Shut down the computer without rebooting.
-nosidgen	Don't create a security identifier (SID) on reboot.
-pnp	Force a refresh of Plug-and-Play information on next reboot.
-quiet	Suppress the confirmation dialog boxes.
-reboot	Reboot the computer after Sysprep finishes.

Table 3-5. *Key Switches for Sysprep.exe*

8. Transfer the target drive to the target computer, boot it, and follow through such parts of the installation process as you chose not to automate using the answer file.

9. After completing the installation process, join the computer to a domain if necessary.

Understanding Remote Installation Services

Windows 2000 Server and Windows.NET Server include Remote Installation Services (the acronym or abbreviation is RIS), a feature for installing an operating system automatically across a network. By using IntelliMirror (of which RIS is a part), an administrator can also install applications remotely. RIS and IntelliMirror together let an administrator deploy a complete computer configuration PC—operating system and applications—to a client PC with minimal interaction. RIS works for deploying not only Windows XP Professional and Windows 2000 Professional but also Windows.NET Server and Windows 2000 Server.

Note *RIS doesn't work for Windows 95, Windows 98, or Windows Me. Administrators who need to install these versions of Windows can use Systems Management Server, a Microsoft product and a member of the Windows 2000 Server family.*

To use RIS, a client computer boots either from a RIS boot disk or from a network card that supports Preboot Execution Environment (PXE). (A PXE-compliant network card contacts a DHCP server for an IP address and the addresses of RIS servers on bootup.) The RIS server uses Active Directory and group policies to determine which OS components to install on the client computer.

Unlike disk-imaging solutions, RIS can accommodate different types of hardware, which makes it an effective solution for deploying operating systems to computers that aren't identical to each other. Remote Installation Services works only in a Windows domain environment and requires Active Directory, group policies, and a fair amount of setup.

Third-Party Deployment Tools

Sysprep is effective for cloning drives for installation in target computers that have the same hardware configuration as the source computer; Remote Installation Services provides powerful and flexible features for deploying Windows XP, Windows.NET Server, and Windows 2000 on domains; and Systems Management Server provides similar features for deploying Windows 9x versions.

For more flexibility, administrators can use third-party disk-imaging tools such as Symantec Ghost Corporate Edition (from Symantec: www.symantec.com) or PowerQuest DriveImage and DeployCenter (from PowerQuest: www.powerquest.com) to deploy Windows XP Professional or other operating systems. These tools have advantages such as the following:

- Neither Ghost nor DeployCenter requires a Windows domain running on Windows.NET Server or Windows 2000 Server. This makes them useful both in workgroup environments and in networks based on non-Windows servers.

- Both Ghost and DeployCenter offer features such as multicast, scripting, and compression.

- DeployCenter can distribute drive images across the Internet, not just across a LAN.

- Ghost can be configured so that users can "pull down" operating system images and applications securely when necessary, thus reducing the amount of administration needed.

Summary

This chapter has discussed the possibilities for installing Windows XP Professional automatically. It has concentrated on the features included in Windows XP Professional for automating installation of the OS, putting emphasis on those features most likely to be useful to you as a Windows XP Professional user rather than as a Windows domain administrator. But it has also mentioned domain-based methods of installing Windows XP Professional automatically and third-party disk-imaging solutions.

The next chapter discusses how to create dual-boot and multiboot configurations so that you can run other operating systems alongside Windows XP Professional.

Chapter 4

Dual-Booting and Multibooting Windows XP Professional

This chapter discusses how to dual-boot and multiboot Windows XP Professional. In a dual-boot configuration, you can boot two operating systems—in this case, Windows XP Professional and another operating system. In a multiboot configuration, you can boot three or more operating systems—in this case, Windows XP Professional and two or more operating systems.

For simplicity, this chapter uses the generic term *multiboot* to refer to boot configurations with two or more operating systems rather than repeating "dual-boot or multiboot" ad nauseam. When only two operating systems are involved, this chapter uses the term *dual-boot*.

Reasons for Multibooting

You may have any of several reasons for wanting to multiboot another operating system with Windows XP Professional:

- You need to run an application that won't run on Windows XP Professional, even with Compatibility mode options applied. (See Chapter 9 for a discussion of Compatibility mode. Briefly, it allows applications designed for earlier versions of Windows to run on Windows XP by mimicking the operating environment they need.) For example, you might need to boot Windows 98 to run ancient accounting software or play a much-loved game that's not compatible with Windows XP.

- You need to use hardware devices for which there are no Windows XP Professional drivers.

- You want to maintain your existing version of Windows while you evaluate Windows XP Professional.

- You develop software or web pages that you need to test on multiple operating systems.

- You need to use another operating system (for example, Linux or Solaris) some of the time and you don't have another computer to run it on, or running it on another computer isn't practical (for example, you need to take your computer with you when you travel).

Alternatives to Multibooting

Before setting up a multiboot configuration, consider the most practical alternative: using emulation to run the other operating systems on top of Windows XP Professional. PC-emulation applications such as Virtual PC from Connectix (www.connectix.com) or VMWare from VMWare, Inc. (www.vmware.com) let you run one or more PC-compatible operating systems on top of Windows XP. (Should you need to run Windows XP under emulation on Mac OS or Linux, you can also get Mac OS versions of Virtual PC and a Linux version of VMWare.)

Each operating system runs in its own *virtual machine*—a hardware PC emulated in software. For example, you could run Windows 98 SE, Windows NT 4 Workstation, Solaris, Linux, and BeOS in virtual machines on top of Windows XP Professional—plus DOS if you liked. Each operating system would have its own virtual machine, and you could network the operating systems with each other if you chose to.

Under emulation, the operating systems run much more slowly than on real hardware, especially when you run more than one virtual machine at once. Emulation requires real RAM and hard-disk space for each virtual machine, and it tends to consume all available processor cycles with a voracity that migrant locusts would envy. Emulation applications typically support a standard set of virtual hardware, so you can't use emulation to test and troubleshoot physical hardware devices.

But where convenience is more important than full-speed performance, emulation is a neat solution. Emulation is widely used by software developers and by help-desk personnel who need to support multiple operating systems from a single computer each without rebooting that computer.

The other alternative to multibooting is to use multiple PCs, one for each operating system you need to run. But for most people this isn't a practical solution.

Disadvantages of Multibooting

Multibooting enables you to run two or more operating systems on the same computer (one at a time), but it also has disadvantages:

■ Each operating system requires a separate partition, so you need more hard disk space. For example, Windows XP Professional requires a minimum of 2GB to run properly, and you'll usually want to give it plenty more space for applications and files. Current distributions of Linux require a similar amount of space. On one of today's monster desktop hard drives, allocating 5–10GB to each operating system you need to multiboot is easy enough. But on a more limited laptop hard drive, it can hurt.

■ You need to install and configure each application on each operating system on which you want to use it. You may even need to buy additional licenses, depending on the licensing terms for the applications.

■ For multibooting with Windows XP: If your non–NT-based operating systems need to be able to access shared drives, you'll need to use FAT or FAT32 on those drives rather than NTFS. FAT and FAT32 are less secure than NTFS.

The first bulleted paragraph above isn't strictly true: In many cases, you can install two or more versions of Windows on the same partition without suffering any ill effects, provided that you use a different %Windir% folder for each of them rather than letting multiple versions install themselves into a Windows folder or a Winnt folder. (Windows 9*x* and Windows XP default to a Windows folder. Windows NT and Windows 2000 default to a Winnt folder.)

However, because all versions of Windows since Windows 95 have used the Program Files folder for their bundled applications, you may run into problems with one version's applications overwriting another version's applications. You may also run into problems when installing the same application on two or more different versions of Windows.

For these and other reasons, Microsoft strongly recommends installing each operating system on a separate partition. In general, this is the safest course to pursue. Another possibility is to use a third-party boot manager (for example, System Commander from V Communications [www.v-com.com] or BootMagic from PowerQuest [www.powerquest.com]) that's capable of automatically rearranging boot files and the active partition for different operating systems.

If your hard drive is configured with a single partition that has an operating system that you want to keep installed on it, use a partitioning utility such as Partition Magic or Partition Commander to shrink that partition and create another partition without destroying your data.

Key Steps to Multibooting Windows

The key steps to multibooting different versions of Windows are to choose the right file systems, to install the operating system in the right order, and to create a boot floppy for Windows XP Professional. The following sections discuss these considerations.

Choose the Right File Systems

To multiboot Windows XP Professional with Windows 9*x*, you need to choose the right file systems for the volumes you use for the operating systems and for your data. These are the main considerations:

- Windows XP Professional supports the NTFS, FAT, and FAT32 file systems.

- Windows 9*x* (Windows 95, Windows 98, or Windows Me) can't read NTFS volumes, so you have to use FAT or (preferably) FAT32 on any volume that Windows 9*x* needs to be able to access. The volume on which you install Windows 9*x* must use FAT or FAT32. So must any volume that contains data files that Windows 9*x* will access.

- Windows XP Professional can use only a limited set of permissions on FAT and FAT32 drives. To secure your files, install Windows XP Professional on its own partition and use NTFS for that partition.

These limitations normally mean that you can't fully secure files stored on a volume that Windows 9*x* needs to access. The best way to get around these limitations is to use a utility such as NTFS for Win98 from Winternals Software LP (www.winternals.com/products/fct/ntfswin98.asp) that enables Windows 9*x* to access NTFS volumes.

Install the Different Versions of Windows in the Right Order

The general rule for installing multiple versions of Windows in the right order falls into two parts:

- Install Windows 9*x* before any NT-based version of Windows.
- Install NT-based versions of Windows in the order in which they were released.

You can install only one version of Windows 9*x* on a computer without using a special boot utility (for example, System Commander). You can install as many NT-based versions of Windows as you have disk space for, including multiple versions of the same operating system if you want. But you need to install them in order because the earlier versions don't know about the boot-sector needs of their successors. For example, if you install Windows NT 4 after Windows XP Professional, Windows NT 4 will boot, but Windows XP won't, because Windows NT 4's boot manager can't handle Windows XP Professional's needs.

Given these constraints, the following is the best order for installing different versions of Windows:

1. Windows 9*x*
2. Windows NT 4 versions (Workstation or Server)
3. Windows 2000 versions (Professional or Server)
4. Windows XP versions (Professional or Home Edition)
5. Windows .NET Server

As discussed in the following sections, you *can* install the operating systems in a different order. But you'll need to do some work to get them all working properly. The following sections assume that Windows XP Professional is your primary operating system and that you want to have it working when you've finished installing operating systems.

Create a Windows XP Professional Boot Floppy

If you aim to end up using Windows XP Professional as your operating system, create a boot floppy after installing Windows XP Professional so that you can recover from problems.

If you currently have Windows XP Professional installed and you need to install an earlier version of Windows, the boot floppy is vital, because installing the earlier version of Windows will prevent Windows XP Professional from booting. The boot floppy that you're about to create is the easiest way to recover from this problem.

To create a boot floppy, follow these steps:

1. Format a floppy disk as usual from Windows Explorer or a command prompt.
2. Copy the files NTLDR, NTDETECT.COM, and boot.ini from the root directory of your boot drive to the floppy. For example, in Windows Explorer, make sure

that Windows Explorer is displaying hidden files and folders and protected operating system files. Then select these three files and issue a Send To | 3 ½ Floppy command from the File menu or the shortcut menu. If your computer uses a SCSI disk, copy the file NTBOOTDD.SYS as well.

| Note | *Those instructions for creating a Windows XP Professional boot floppy assume that Windows XP Professional is running. If you've disabled Windows XP by installing an earlier version of Windows on top of it, use another operating system to copy NTLDR and NTDETECT.COM (and NTBOOTDD.SYS if necessary) from the Windows XP CD to a floppy. Then create a boot.ini file manually and save it on the floppy. See "Editing boot.ini Manually" in Chapter 5 for a detailed examination of the contents of a boot.ini file.* |

Dual-Booting Windows XP Professional with Windows 2000

Dual-booting Windows XP Professional with Windows 2000 (either Windows 2000 Professional or Windows 2000 Server, though the former is more likely) is easy provided that you install Windows 2000 first, and then perform a new installation of Windows XP (as described in Chapter 2). If you install Windows 2000 after Windows XP, the Windows 2000 installation overwrites the Windows XP boot sector, preventing Windows XP from booting anymore.

But if Windows XP Professional is already installed and configured on your computer, you'd probably prefer not to have to install and configure it again. To install Windows 2000 and then repair Windows XP, follow these steps:

1. If you haven't already created a Windows XP boot floppy (as described earlier in this chapter), do so.

2. Boot from the Windows 2000 CD and install it from there into a partition of its own. (Windows XP disables the Windows 2000 installation routine on the assumption that you don't want to install Windows 2000 and thus disable Windows XP.)

3. At this point, Windows 2000 will run as normal. Windows XP startup will either fail with an error message (such as STOP 0x00000074:BAD_SYSTEM_CONFIG_INFO or a message that the \WINDOWS\SYSTEM32\CONFIG\SYSTEM file is missing or corrupt) or won't start at all.

4. Boot from your Windows XP boot floppy into Windows XP.

5. Copy NTLDR and NTDETECT.COM from your Windows XP boot floppy to the root of the boot volume, thus replacing the Windows 2000 versions of these files with the Windows XP versions.

6. Edit boot.ini manually to specify the default operating system and the timeout. (See "Editing boot.ini Manually" in Chapter 5 for a discussion of how to edit boot.ini.)

7. Update your Windows XP boot floppy with the latest version of boot.ini.

The procedure for setting up a dual boot with Windows NT 4 and Windows XP Professional is almost the same as for Windows 2000 and Windows XP Professional. There's one wrinkle worth mentioning. On a computer that has Windows NT 4 installed as a dual-boot with Windows XP, there's a minor problem when you shut down from Windows NT: You'll typically need to hold the power button down for five seconds or more when Windows NT displays the Shutdown Computer notice. This occurs if the computer has Advanced Configuration and Power Interface (ACPI), because Windows NT checks for Advanced Power Management (APM) rather than ACPI.

Note *If one of your operating systems is missing after you try to create a multiboot configuration, use BOOTCFG to rebuild your boot configuration. See "Rebuilding Your Boot Configuration with BOOTCFG" in Chapter 24 for a discussion of BOOTCFG.*

Dual-Booting Windows XP Professional with Windows 9*x*

Like dual-booting Windows XP Professional with Windows 2000, dual-booting Windows XP with Windows 9*x* is easy provided you install Windows 9*x* first, and then perform a new installation of Windows XP Professional (as described in Chapter 2).

If you install Windows 9*x* after Windows XP, the Windows 9*x* Setup routine overwrites the Windows XP boot sector, preventing Windows XP from booting anymore. Once this has happened, you'll need to reinstall or repair Windows XP.

Note *Installing Windows 9x after Windows XP Professional can rapidly get ugly. If you prefer more conventional entertainment than struggling with operating systems, invest in a boot manager such as System Commander from V Communications (www.v-com.com) that manages the intricacies of boot files, partitions, and the master boot record for you.*

If, on a computer that has Windows 9*x* installed as a dual-boot with Windows XP, Windows 9*x* starts without the boot menu appearing at all, chances are that Windows 9*x* has been installed on top of Windows XP. (You'll know if you've done this, but you might not know if someone else has done it for you.) If this is what has happened, Windows 9*x* has overwritten the Windows XP boot files. Again, you'll need to reinstall or repair Windows XP Professional to fix the problem.

Dual-Booting Windows XP Professional with Linux

Because both Windows XP Professional and Linux offer sophisticated setup routines, you can install them in either order—Windows XP Professional first or Linux first—to create a dual-boot configuration with the two operating systems as long as you install them on separate partitions. Choose a custom installation routine for Linux and manually specify which partitions to use, repartitioning the disk if necessary.

If you install Windows XP Professional first, don't install the Lilo boot loader on your MBR when installing Linux, because Lilo will overwrite the Windows XP Professional boot loader and you won't be able to start Windows XP Professional. (If this happens, remove Lilo by opening a terminal window in Linux and issuing the **lilo –U** command for the drive—for example, lilo –U /dev/hda.) When the Linux installation routine offers you the Lilo Configuration screen, select the option to install the Lilo boot record on the first sector of the boot partition. It's also a good idea to create a Linux boot disk either during the installation or afterward.

If you remove Linux from a dual-boot configuration with Windows XP Professional, but you find your computer still tries to boot Linux, boot to DOS from a floppy and restore the MBR by issuing an **fdisk /mbr** command.

Specifying the Default Operating System

If you're using Windows XP Professional's boot manager, you can specify the default operating system to start by choosing it in the Default Operating System drop-down list in the Startup and Recovery dialog box. (To display the Startup and Recovery dialog box, click the Settings button in the Startup and Recovery group box on the Advanced page of the System Properties dialog box.) In this dialog box, you can also configure the length of time to display the boot menu. "Choosing Boot Options in the Startup and Recovery Dialog Box" in Chapter 5 discusses these options in detail.

If you're using another boot manager, use the options it offers to specify the default operating system.

Summary

This chapter has discussed how and why to set up Windows XP Professional in dual-boot and multiboot configurations, and how to deal with the more common problems that result from dual-booting and multibooting.

The next chapter discusses how to customize Windows XP Professional's startup and shutdown.

The
Complete
Reference

Chapter 5

Customizing Windows XP
Startup and Shutdown

This chapter discusses how to customize and control what happens when Windows XP Professional starts up and shuts down. By changing boot options through the Windows XP Professional GUI or by editing the boot.ini file manually, you can control what happens during the boot process: which operating system boots (in a multiboot configuration) and the options it uses. By using the Startup groups, Registry entries, and Services, you can launch applications, open documents, and run scripts on startup. By configuring system failure and debugging options, you can control—to some extent—what happens when Windows XP Professional encounters a serious error. If necessary, you can even set up a user account to log on automatically when Windows XP starts and prevent one or more users from shutting down Windows XP.

Some of the actions in this chapter fall on the watershed between using Windows XP Professional in a domain environment and in a SOHO environment. For a fuller discussion of account management in a SOHO environment, see Chapter 27.

To make the most out of the changes described in this chapter, you'll need to be an administrator. In a domain environment, an administrator may have prevented you from making these changes.

Configuring the Boot Process

Windows XP's boot process is governed by boot.ini, a text file used by NT-based versions of Windows (Windows NT, Windows 2000, and Windows XP) to provide instructions on booting those operating systems and for passing control to other operating systems compatible with the NT boot loader that are installed in a multiboot configuration. boot.ini is a hidden and protected system file located in the root folder of the boot drive, so you need to display hidden files and protected operating system files in Windows Explorer before you can access boot.ini directly from Windows Explorer.

You can affect boot.ini in the following ways:

- By choosing the default operating system, the boot menu delay, and the recovery options delay in the System Startup group box in the Startup and Recovery dialog box, as discussed in the next section.

- By editing boot.ini manually in a text editor (for example, Notepad), as discussed in "Editing boot.ini Manually," later in this chapter.

- By using the BOOTCFG command to automatically adjust or rebuild boot.ini. See "Rebuilding Your Boot Configuration with BOOTCFG" in Chapter 24 for a discussion of BOOTCFG.

boot.ini is crucial to the Windows XP Professional boot process. If you change boot.ini so that it specifies incorrect controller, drive, or partition information, Windows XP Professional won't be able to boot. So make a backup copy of boot.ini before editing it.

INSTALLING, CONFIGURING, AND CUSTOMIZING

Choosing Boot Options in the Startup and Recovery Dialog Box

The easiest—and most limited—way of specifying boot options in Windows XP Professional is to use the options in the System Startup group box in the Startup and Recovery dialog box (Figure 5-1). Display the Startup and Recovery dialog box by clicking the Settings button in the Startup and Recovery group box on the Advanced page of the System Properties dialog box (WINDOWS KEY–BREAK).

The Startup and Recovery dialog box lets you specify the following:

- The default operating system to boot

- The number of seconds Windows XP Professional displays the boot menu of operating systems. The default is 30 seconds, but a shorter time is usually more convenient: long enough to allow you to stop the default selection by pressing ↓ or ↑, but short enough not to unduly delay normal booting into the default operating system.

- The number of seconds to display the Recovery Options menu when Windows XP needs to display it. This default also is 30 seconds, but you may want to set a longer time in case you're not at your keyboard and paying attention when the recovery options menu is displayed.

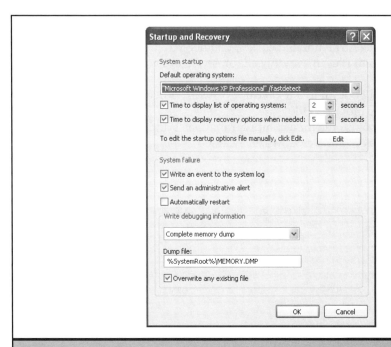

Figure 5-1. *Choose boot options in the System Startup group box in the Startup and Recovery dialog box.*

When you close the Startup and Recovery dialog box, Windows XP Professional automatically writes these changes to the boot.ini file.

Editing boot.ini Manually

If you need to make changes more extensive than the System Startup options in the Startup and Recovery dialog box allow, you can edit boot.ini manually. You shouldn't need to edit boot.ini frequently. These are the most likely circumstances in which you'll need to edit boot.ini manually:

■ You've damaged your Windows XP Professional configuration so that Windows XP won't boot. For example, you or an inconsiderate application may have set the wrong partition active.

■ You need to create a Windows XP boot floppy. The most likely reason for this is that you've installed an earlier version of Windows after Windows XP and that version of Windows has overwritten the Windows XP boot sector, leaving you needing to recover it.

■ You need to add an entry for another operating system to boot.ini manually.

You can open boot.ini by clicking the Edit button in the System Startup group box in the Startup and Recovery dialog box or by more conventional means, such as entering the file's fully qualified name (including the path) in the Run dialog box, double-clicking the file's entry in a Windows Explorer window, or opening the file directly from a text editor or word processor. (As mentioned earlier, you need to display hidden files and protected operating system files in Windows Explorer before you can access boot.ini directly.)

Once you've opened boot.ini in a text editor or word processor, you can edit and save it as you would any other text file.

The following is a boot.ini file for a computer that has Windows XP Professional, Windows XP Home Edition, and Windows 98 installed:

```
[boot loader]
timeout=30
default=multi(0)disk(0)rdisk(0)partition(2)\WINDOWS
[operating systems]

multi(0)disk(0)rdisk(0)partition(2)\WINDOWS="Microsoft Windows XP
Professional" /fastdetect
multi(0)disk(0)rdisk(0)partition(3)\WINDOWS="Microsoft Windows XP
Home Edition" /fastdetect
C:\="Microsoft Windows"
```

Table 5-1 lists the elements that you can use in a boot.ini file.

The final item in the table, /fastdetect, is actually a switch rather than an element. It's included here because it appears in most boot.ini files.

You can apply a dozen or so other switches to boot.ini to affect the boot process. The easiest way to apply these switches is by using System Configuration Utility, a tool

Element	Explanation
[boot loader]	Introduces the first section of the boot.ini file.
timeout=	Controls the length of time for which Windows XP Professional displays the boot menu when the boot menu has more than one entry. (If the boot menu contains only one entry, Windows XP boots it immediately.)
default=	Specifies the disk controller, disk, and partition of the default operating system.
multi()	Specifies the disk controller for an EIDE disk. The first controller is numbered 0. See the sample boot.ini (on the previous page) for examples.
scsi()	Specifies the hard disk controller for a SCSI disk. Used instead of multi(). The first controller is numbered 0, for example, scsi(0)disk(0)rdisk(0)partition(3).
disk()	Specifies the hard disk. This element is used only when the scsi() element is used, but this element is included for EIDE drives as well. The first hard disk is numbered 0.
rdisk()	Specifies the hard disk. The first hard disk is numbered 0.
partition()	Specifies the partition. The first partition is numbered 1.
signature()	Specifies the variable SCSI disk controller. Used in place of multi() or scsi(). The first controller is numbered 0, for example, signature(0)disk(0)rdisk(0)partition(1).
[operating systems]	Introduces the operating systems section of the boot.ini file.
/fastdetect	Prevents the detection of serial mouses on all serial ports. To prevent detection on a particular port, specify it, for example, /fastdetect=COM2.

Table 5-1.   *Elements for a boot.ini File*

primarily used for recovering from disaster, but you can also apply them manually if you prefer. See "Using System Configuration Utility and Clean Boot" in Chapter 24 for a discussion of System Configuration Utility and the meaning of the other boot.ini switches.

Customizing the Startup Groups

Your startup group contains items that run automatically when you log on to Windows XP Professional. By placing shortcuts to applications or documents in the startup group, you can run those applications or open those documents automatically when you log on. You can also run batch files or scripts by placing them in your Startup folder.

Each user has a Startup folder that's located by default in Documents and Settings\ *username*\Start Menu\Programs\Startup. Windows XP also maintains a pan-user Startup folder that's located by default in Documents and Settings\All Users\Start Menu\ Programs\Startup. Items in the latter Startup folder run for each user who logs on.

If your Startup folder isn't in the default location, chances are that an administrator has redirected it to a network location. (See "Understanding Folder Redirection" in Chapter 7 for a discussion of redirection.) For example, an administrator may have redirected your Startup folder to a network location common to all domain users so that each user starts the same set of applications when they log on.

Note   *See Chapter 40 for a discussion of what the Registry is, what it does, and how you can examine and change it.*

If you have the appropriate permissions, you can redirect your Startup folder and the All Users Startup folder by editing the Registry value entries that control them. Your Startup folder's value entry is HKCU\Software\Microsoft\Windows\CurrentVersion\ Explorer\User Shell Folders\Startup. The All Users Startup folder's value entry is HKLM\ SOFTWARE\Microsoft\Windows\CurrentVersion\Explorer\User Shell Folders\Startup. After changing one of these entries, you'll need to log off and back on before the change registers.

Tip   *If you use your startup group to launch a lot of applications, consider launching some of them in minimized windows to keep your Desktop streamlined. To do so, choose Minimized in the Run drop-down list on the Shortcut tab of the Properties dialog box for the shortcut you place in the Startup folder.*

Preventing Your Startup Group from Running at Startup

To temporarily prevent your Startup group from running when you log on to Windows XP Professional, hold down SHIFT when logging on:

- When logging on using the Log On to Windows dialog box, enter your user name and password, hold down SHIFT and press ENTER (or click the OK button).

- When logging on using the Welcome screen, click your user name, enter your password, hold down SHIFT and press ENTER. If you don't have a password, hold down SHIFT and click your user name.

Running Applications Automatically via Registry Entries

If an application is launching automatically when you start Windows XP Professional, but it has a shortcut neither in your Startup folder nor in the All Users Startup folder, chances are that it's being run automatically by a Registry entry. The Registry includes two Run keys and two RunOnce keys—one for your user account and one for the All Users group. An entry in a RunOnce key runs the application the first time the user logs on to Windows XP after the application has been installed. An entry in a Run key runs the application each time the user logs on to Windows XP.

The Run and RunOnce keys for your user account are in the HKCU\Software\Microsoft\Windows\CurrentVersion key. The Run and RunOnce keys for the All Users group are in the HKLM\SOFTWARE\Microsoft\Windows\CurrentVersion key.

You can run applications automatically by creating value entries for them in these keys, but in most cases it's easier, quicker, and more transparent to create shortcuts in the appropriate Startup folder instead. Usually, these Registry entries are created by the installation routines for applications and software components, and you're more likely to want to remove such an entry than create one. To stop the application from running, delete the value entry in the appropriate key.

Note   *In a version of Windows XP Professional upgraded from Windows 9x, applications may also be run by load= or run= lines in the win.ini file, which you'll find in the %Windir% folder. Check which applications win.ini is running and remove any that you'd prefer not to run.*

Running Applications as Services or by Using Scripts

Windows XP Professional also supports two other ways of running applications automatically:

- Applications can be configured to start automatically as services. To prevent an application running that's configured to start automatically as a service, change it to Manual startup. Chapter 43 discusses what services are, what they do, and how you manage them.

- Another way of controlling what happens at startup and shutdown (or at logon or logoff) is to run scripts. See Chapter 46 for a discussion of how to create scripts.

Note *If you're using Windows XP Professional in a domain environment, the administrators will probably assign the scripts through Group Policies.*

Configuring System Failure and Debugging Options

The Startup and Recovery dialog box (discussed earlier in this chapter) also lets you specify what Windows XP Professional should try to do when a system failure occurs and what debugging information Windows XP should write. The previous sentence says "should try to do" rather than "does" because a severe enough crash can bring down Windows XP Professional without giving it a chance to perform the actions specified.

Windows XP Professional offers three System Failure options:

- **Write an Event to the System Log check box** Controls whether Windows XP Professional writes an event to the System log. If this event gets written, you may be able to use it to identify what caused the system failure.

- **Send an Administrative Alert check box** Controls whether Windows XP sends a network broadcast message to administrators warning them that the computer has suffered a system failure. If the alert is sent, a problem on an unattended computer is likely to be noticed and fixed more quickly than if someone has to notice "manually" that a problem has occurred. If you're using the computer, you won't be able to miss the system failure occurring, and you'll no doubt alert an administrator if you can't get the computer running satisfactorily again.

- **Automatically Restart check box** Controls whether Windows XP Professional automatically restarts the computer after a system failure. This option doesn't always work, but it's useful for servers (or workstations providing services to other network users) that are supposed to be available all the time. Clear this check box if you want to see the STOP error that the system failure generates. (A STOP error is often referred to as a Blue Screen of Death, because the STOP error appears on a blue background or occasionally a black background. Blue Screen of Death is sometimes abbreviated to BSOD.)

In the Write Debugging Information group box, specify what debugging information you want Windows XP Professional to write after a system failure and (if applicable) the location for the resulting file. Table 5-2 lists the options.

Option	Explanation
(none)	Write no debugging information.
Small Memory Dump (64KB)	Create a memory dump containing only key memory information. This dump file in named MINI*MMDDYY-NN*.dmp, where *MMDDYY* is the date and *NN* is the number of the dump file created on that day, and is saved in the folder specified in the Small Dump Directory text box.
Kernel Memory Dump	Create a dump that consists of the kernel memory. By default, this file is named memory.dmp and is saved in your %systemroot% folder. You can specify a different filename or location in the Dump File text box. Each dump overwrites any previous dump. Select or clear the Overwrite Any Existing File check box to specify whether to overwrite an existing dump file.
Complete Memory Dump	Create a dump containing all the contents of memory. By default, this file is named memory.dmp and is saved in your %systemroot% folder. You can specify a different filename or location in the Dump File text box. Each dump overwrites any previous dump. Select or clear the Overwrite Any Existing File check box to specify whether to overwrite an existing dump file.

Table 5-2.   *Write Debugging Options*

Setting Up a User Account to Log On Automatically

If you administer the computer, you can set up yourself or another user to log on automatically when Windows XP Professional starts. This feature is most useful in standalone environments, but some administrators choose to use it for environments in which multiple users use the same user account—for example, a computer in a workshop environment or one acting as a public terminal in a coffee shop or at a trade show. In such a case, to minimize the security threat that an automatic logon poses, the administrator will usually use the Guest account or a Limited user account for the automatic login, and lock the account down as comprehensively as possible.

To set up an automatic logon, follow these steps:

1. Launch the User Accounts dialog box by running **control userpasswords2**.

2. Clear the Users Must Enter a User Name and Password to Use This Computer check box.

3. Click the OK button.

4. Enter the user's name and password in the Automatically Log On dialog box.

To bypass automatic logon, hold down SHIFT when the Windows XP Professional splash screen appears while Windows XP loads.

To turn off automatic logon, select the Users Must Enter a User Name and Password to Use This Computer check box once again.

Preventing Users from Shutting Down the Computer

Under normal circumstances, any user who can log on can also shut down Windows XP Professional. But sometimes you may want to prevent certain users from shutting down the computer. For example, if you put a computer on display at a tradeshow or in a kiosk situation, you'll probably want to keep it running.

To do so, deny the appropriate user or users the Shut Down the System right either in Security Settings\Local Policies\User Rights Assignment in Local Security Policy or in Computer Configuration\Windows Settings\Security Settings\Local Policies\User Rights Assignment in Group Policy.

Note *If the computer being shut down by the wrong person would cause significant trouble, protect the hardware as well by preventing access to the power button, the power cord, and the electric supply.*

Summary

This chapter has discussed how to customize Windows XP Professional's startup and shutdown by choosing boot options, customizing the Startup groups, and using other means of running applications automatically. It has also discussed how to set up a user account to log on automatically when Windows XP starts.

The next chapter discusses how to use the Files and Settings Transfer Wizard to transfer files and settings to your copy of Windows XP Professional and how to configure the Windows Update feature to keep Windows XP up to date.

INSTALLING,
CONFIGURING, AND
CUSTOMIZING

Chapter 6

Configuring and Updating Windows XP Professional

T his chapter discusses how to configure and update Windows XP Professional. It starts by covering how to apply previously stored files and settings by using the Files and Settings Transfer Wizard. It moves along to using Windows Update to keep your copy of Windows XP Professional up to date (or preventing Windows Update from running). This chapter finishes by discussing how to install and remove Windows XP components.

If you're using Windows XP Professional in a domain environment, your network administrator may take care of these operations for you: They may use the User State Migration Tool (USMT) to transfer your files and settings, use Software Update Services to apply updates to your computer, and configure your computer so that you can't install or remove components.

Transferring Files and Settings

As you saw in "Collecting the Files and Settings You Want to Transfer" in Chapter 2, you can use the Files and Settings Transfer Wizard to collect files and settings that you want to transfer from an old installation of Windows to a new installation of Windows XP Professional. The new installation of Windows XP can be either on a different computer than the old installation of Windows or on the same computer on which you've performed a new or clean installation of Windows XP Professional. (If you've upgraded your previous version of Windows to Windows XP, Windows Setup should have transferred your files and settings for you.)

Note *As mentioned in Chapter 2, in a domain setting, the domain administrator may use the USMT to migrate your settings instead of having you use the Files and Settings Transfer Wizard to transfer them. To load the files and settings from the intermediate store file onto a clean installation of Windows XP Professional, the administrator runs the LoadState.exe application.*

If you used the Files and Settings Transfer Wizard to store files and settings from your old computer or old version of Windows, load them onto Windows XP Professional by running the Files and Settings Transfer Wizard again.

Note *Before applying your settings to the new computer, install on that computer any applications whose settings you're transferring. Otherwise, the Files and Settings Transfer Wizard won't be able to apply the settings.*

To run the Files and Settings Transfer Wizard, take the following steps:

1. Choose Start | All Programs | Accessories | System Tools | Files and Settings Transfer Wizard.

2. On the Which Computer Is This? page, select the New Computer option button.

3. On the Do You Have a Windows XP Professional CD? page, select the I Don't Need the Wizard Disk. I Have Already Collected My Files and Settings from My Old Computer option button, and follow the prompts to transfer the files.

What the Files and Settings Transfer Wizard and USMT Don't Migrate

The Files and Settings Transfer Wizard and USMT don't migrate the following:

- Display resolution settings. You need to apply these manually.

- Passwords for applications that require them. You'll need to reenter stored passwords. (This is a security measure.) If you upgraded from Windows 98 or Windows Me, you'll need to enter all passwords, from logon passwords and domain passwords through dial-up connection passwords to network share passwords.

- Network printers that aren't available to the target computer.

- Third-party drivers for devices that aren't installed on the target computer.

- Customized screen savers if you've upgraded to Windows XP Professional from Windows 98, Windows 98 SE, or Windows Me. Re-create your customized screen savers manually.

Troubleshooting the Files and Settings Transfer Wizard

If the Files and Settings Transfer Wizard doesn't work, see if its log file contains any indication why not. The log file is named Fastwiz.log. When the source computer is running Windows XP Professional or Windows 2000, the log file is in the Documents and Settings*username*\Local Settings\Application Data folder. When the source computer is running Windows 9*x*, the log file typically lands in the Windows folder. If the log file isn't in one of those locations, or you're feeling lazy, search for it by name.

Make sure there's enough space on the target computer for the Files and Settings Transfer Wizard to unpack the files it's migrating. The Files and Settings Transfer Wizard typically needs about four times as much space as the size of the store that contains the files and settings—for example, 200MB of free space for a 50MB store file. (The Files and Settings Transfer Wizard needs this space because the store file is compressed. The wizard uncompresses the files from the store to a temporary folder, copies them to where they belong, and then deletes the temporary folder.)

Using Windows Update

Windows Update is a tool designed to help you to keep Windows XP Professional current with all the latest updates, patches, and service packs that Microsoft issues.

Because such items are issued as needed rather than on a regular schedule, checking for them is a thankless task. Windows Update's Automatic Updates feature lets you check for them automatically or manually as you prefer.

If your computer connects to a domain, chances are that the domain administrators coordinate Windows updates centrally so as to keep consistent software configurations across the domain's computers. Microsoft has provided two tools to help them do this: the Windows Update Corporate web site and Software Update Services. See "Software Update Services—the Corporate Alternative to Windows Update," a little later in this chapter, for a discussion of these tools.

Using the Automatic Updates Feature

Soon after the first Computer Administrator user (let's assume it's you) logs on to Windows XP, the Automatic Updates Setup Wizard displays a notification-area icon and pop up prompting you to choose settings for Automatic Updates. You can choose from the following three settings on the Notification Settings page of the Automatic Updates Setup Wizard. Alternatively, you can preempt the wizard by pressing WINDOWS KEY–R and choosing from the same settings on the Automatic Updates tab of the System Properties dialog box. The settings are

- **Keep My Computer Up to Date check box**   This check box controls whether the Windows Update controls in the Settings group box are enabled (when this check box is selected) or disabled. If you clear this check box, see "Using Windows Update Manually," later in this chapter, for details on how to check manually for updates. If you choose this setting, it's worth stopping the Automatic Updates service (which runs automatically by default) and setting it for Manual startup so that Windows XP Professional doesn't waste memory or processor cycles on it. See "Starting and Stopping Services" in Chapter 43 for a discussion of how to stop services.

- **Notify Me Before Downloading Any Updates and Notify Me Again Before Installing Them on My Computer option button**   This setting lets you choose whether to download each update and, once you've downloaded it, when to install it. This setting lets you control when Automatic Updates downloads the updates.

- **Download the Updates Automatically and Notify Me when They Are Ready to Be Installed option button**   This setting lets you choose which updates to install and when to install them. The main disadvantage to this setting is that you have little control over when Automatic Updates downloads each update. If you have a slow Internet connection, a large download at a critical time can cause problems.

- **Automatically Download the Updates, and Install Them on the Schedule that I Specify option button**   This setting provides the most automation: Windows XP Professional automatically downloads the updates and installs them on the schedule that you specify by using the two drop-down lists. The first drop-down list offers the settings Every Day and an Every setting for each day of the week—Every Sunday, Every Monday, and so on. The second drop-down list lets you specify the hour at which to install the updates. Choose a time when the installation won't interfere with any of your computing habits—your interactive use, CD burning, all-night downloads, backups, or whatever.

Note *The Automatic Updates settings described in this section reflect changes made in Windows XP Professional Service Pack 1. If your computer has a version of Windows XP Professional without Service Pack 1 (or a subsequent service pack) installed, you won't see the Keep My Computer Up to Date check box or the Automatically Download the Updates, and Install Them on the Schedule that I Specify option button and its scheduling controls. Instead, you'll see a Turn Off Automatic Updating. I Want to Update My Computer Manually option button.*

If you choose to use automatic updating, Automatic Updates checks for updates periodically at times when your Internet connection is available but unused or only lightly used. If you chose the second or third option, Automatic Updates downloads any update files when your Internet connection seems to be quiet. If you or an application starts using the Internet connection, Automatic Updates uses bandwidth-throttling techniques to reduce its download rate so that it doesn't choke the other user.

After downloading the updates, Automatic Updates displays a notification-area icon to let you know the updates are available. Double-click the icon to review the available updates in the Automatic Updates: Ready to Install dialog box. From here, you can click the Install button to install the updates, the Details button to read more about them and decide which to install, or click the Remind Me Later button to tell Automatic Updates to go away for a time period you specify.

The process for the Notify Me before Downloading Any Updates option is similar, except that Automatic Updates displays a notification-area icon to let you know that the updates are ready to download rather than that they're ready to install. Choose which to download and click the Start Download button, or click the Remind Me Later button to gain a reprieve. Once the updates have been downloaded, you get to choose when to install them.

If you chose automatic installation of updates, Automatic Updates proceeds according to the schedule you set.

When Automatic Updates is downloading an update, it displays a notification-area icon from which you can pause downloads and restart them at your convenience.

If you decline an update, you can make Automatic Updates offer it to you again by clicking the Declined Updates button on the Automatic Updates tab of the System Properties dialog box (WINDOWS KEY–R).

Using Windows Update Manually

If you turn off Automatic Updates, or if you want to check right now for the latest updates available, choose Tools | Windows Update from Internet Explorer or choose Start | All Programs | Windows Update. Windows XP Professional opens a browser window to the Windows Update Web site (www.windowsupdate.com).

From the Windows Update Web site, you can run a scan on your computer to determine which new packages are available. The process is easy to understand and doesn't merit description here.

If you have more than one computer, instead of downloading the same update files for each computer, use the Windows Update Catalog to download the update files and save them to a location of your choice. From there, you can apply an update to any computer by running its executable file from that computer.

To use Windows Update Catalog, access the Personalize Windows Update page and select the Display the Link to the Windows Update Catalog under See Also check box. Click the Save Settings button to save your choice. Then access the Windows Update Catalog page by clicking the link in the See Also area of the left column of the Windows Update page. On the Windows Update Catalog page, use the Find Updates for Microsoft Windows Operating Systems link to find the files you want to download.

Removing Windows Update Items

Usually, once you've applied a Windows Update patch, you'll leave it in place so that it can fix whatever problem it's intended to fix. But if you find that a Windows Update patch has removed functionality that you need, or if it seems to have made Windows XP Professional unstable, you may want to remove it.

You can remove some Windows Update patches by using the Windows Components Wizard, as discussed in "Installing and Removing Windows XP Components," later in this chapter. Other patches you can't remove at all. For example, the June 26, 2002 security update for Windows Media Player is not removable. Because this patch fixes severe security problems in Windows XP Professional, many people have chosen to install it.

Software Update Services—the Corporate Alternative to Windows Update

As mentioned earlier, the Windows Update Corporate Web site and Software Update Services are tools for domain administrators who need to keep the clients on their networks up to date.

For the first nine months of Windows XP's release life, the Windows Update Corporate Web site (corporate.windowsupdate.microsoft.com) supplied redistributable versions of the Windows Update packages. Administrators of Windows networks could download these packages and push them out from a central location to client computers.

In summer 2002, Microsoft discontinued posting updates to the Windows Update Corporate Web site and replaced it with Microsoft *Software Update Services* (SUS). Briefly, Software Update Services is a server component that lets an administrator test updates and patches, and then specify via Group Policy (in an Active Directory environment) or via Registry keys which clients and servers will receive them. The Automatic Updates feature on the clients is configured to request updates from the SUS server. If a client is authorized to get the updates, it receives them.

SUS runs on a Windows 2000 Server or Windows.NET Server computer inside the company's firewall. That server can't be the domain controller. (This limitation prevents Small Business Server from using SUS, because SBS runs its own domain controller.) SUS supports critical updates, critical security updates, and security roll-ups (multiple security updates combined into one package), but not service packs. Administrators have to roll out service packs separately.

If your computer is configured to use Software Update Services to update itself, chances are that it will do so outside working hours. It shouldn't need your participation, and you shouldn't need to worry about Windows Update.

Locking Windows Update

If you administer a computer, you can prevent users from installing Windows Update updates by locking Windows Update. You might want to do this if you prefer to examine every Windows Update item yourself before installing it. This locking removes the Windows Update entries from the Windows XP Professional Start menu and from the Tools menu in Internet Explorer.

To lock Windows Update, run the Group Policy snap-in (gpedit.msc) and choose the following settings under Local Computer Policy\User Configuration\ Administrative Templates:

Location	Setting Name	Setting
Control Panel\Add/Remove Programs	Hide the Add Programs from Microsoft option	Enabled
Start Menu and Taskbar	Remove Links and Access to Windows Update	Enabled
Windows Components\ Windows Update	Remove Access to Use All Windows Update Features	Enabled

Users can still access the Windows Update Web site by using their browser, but they won't be able to download any updates from the site.

Installing and Removing Windows XP Professional Components

If you install Windows XP Professional interactively (as discussed in Chapter 2), Windows Setup installs a default set of components, offering you the choice only of customizing the selection of networking components installed. You may want to remove components included in the default set that you don't need at work—for example, Windows Movie Maker, MSN Explorer, Windows Messenger, or Paint. Or you may need to add components that aren't included by default, such as IIS or Fax Services.

Note   *In most cases, your main motivation for removing a component is likely to be to make it unavailable or prevent a user from using it. But if your computer is severely short of disk space, you may want to remove some components to free up as much disk space as possible. This is less likely because most modern hard disks are capacious and the amount of space that you can free up by removing components tends to pale in comparison with the amount that Windows XP Professional takes up anyway. However, if you're pushing an ageing laptop to its limits, you may be grateful for every megabyte you can save. In this case, consider reducing the size of your paging file (see "Configuring the Paging File" in Chapter 39) and turning off hibernation (see "Choosing Power-Management Options" in Chapter 7) to recover more disk space.*

If you install Windows XP Professional automatically (by one of the methods discussed in Chapter 3), you can customize the selection of components that Windows XP Professional includes. This allows you to exclude the components you don't want, so you're less likely to need to remove default components manually. However, you may still need to add extra components after installation when you find you need them.

To install and remove Windows XP components, you use the Windows Components Wizard (Figure 6-1). Launch the Windows Components Wizard by choosing Start | Control Panel | Add or Remove Programs and clicking the Add/Remove Windows Components button in the Add or Remove Programs window. The wizard displays a selected check box for a component that's installed, a cleared check box for a component that isn't installed, and a grayed check box with a check box for a component that has subcomponents some of which are installed and some of which are not installed.

To add a component, select its check box. To remove a component, clear its check box. To add or remove a subcomponent, drill down from its main component by selecting the main component and clicking the Details button. For example, to remove Paint, drill down through the Accessories and Utilities component to the Accessories and

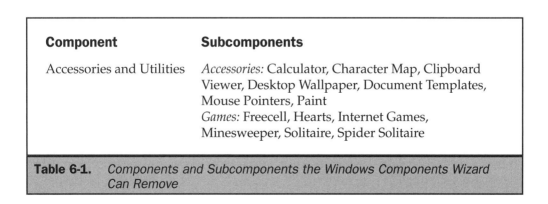

Figure 6-1. *Use the Windows Components Wizard to add or remove Windows XP Professional components.*

Utilities dialog box and from there to the Accessories dialog box. Then clear the Paint check box.

When you've selected and cleared the appropriate check boxes, click the Next button. The Windows Components Wizard checks your selections and adds or removes the components or subcomponents. When installing a component or subcomponent, you'll usually need to supply your Windows XP Professional CD or installation source.

Table 6-1 lists the components and subcomponents you can remove from Windows XP Professional by using the Windows Components Wizard in its default configuration.

Component	Subcomponents
Accessories and Utilities	*Accessories:* Calculator, Character Map, Clipboard Viewer, Desktop Wallpaper, Document Templates, Mouse Pointers, Paint *Games:* Freecell, Hearts, Internet Games, Minesweeper, Solitaire, Spider Solitaire

Table 6-1. *Components and Subcomponents the Windows Components Wizard Can Remove*

Component	Subcomponents
Fax Services	None
Indexing Service	None
Internet Explorer	None
Internet Information Services	Common Files, Documentation, File Transfer Protocol Service, FrontPage 2000 Server Extensions, Internet Information Services Snap-In, SMTP Service, World Wide Web Service (Printers Virtual Directory, Remote Desktop Web Connection, Scripts Virtual Directory, World Wide Web Service)
Management and Monitoring Tools	Simple Network Management Protocol, WMI SNMP Provider
Message Queuing	Active Directory Integration, Common (Core Functionality, Local Storage), MSMQ HTTP Support, Triggers
MSN Explorer	None
Networking Services	RIP Listener, Simple TCP/IP Services, Universal Plug and Play
Other Network File and Print Services	Print Services for Unix
Update Root Certificates	None

Table 6-1.   *Components and Subcomponents the Windows Components Wizard Can Remove* (continued)

The Windows Components Wizard can also remove the components listed in Table 6-2. These components don't appear in the Windows Components Wizard by default. To make them appear, open the file %systemroot%\inf\sysoc.inf in a text editor and delete the word *hide* from the entries for the components. For example, to make WordPad appear in the Windows Components Wizard, change the line "MSWordPad=ocgen.dll,OcEntry, wordpad.inf,HIDE,7" to **MSWordPad=ocgen.dll,OcEntry,wordpad.inf,7**.

Component	Entry in sysoc.inf File
Windows Management Instrumentation	WBEM
Windows Automatic Updates	AutoUpdate
Windows Messenger	msmsgs
Accessibility Wizard	AccessOpt
multimedia	MultiM
Pinball	Pinball
WordPad	MSWordPad

Table 6-2. *Hidden Components That the Windows Components Wizard Can Remove*

Once you've displayed one of these hidden components, you can remove it by running the Windows Components Wizard and clearing the component's check box.

 Note *sysoc.inf also lists as hidden a number of components that the Windows Components Wizard can't remove, such as TerminalServer.*

Summary

This chapter has discussed how to configure and update Windows XP Professional by applying files and settings using the Files and Settings Transfer Wizard or User State Migration Tool, using Windows Update, and installing and removing Windows XP components.

The next chapter discusses how to customize the Windows XP interface so that you can work as smoothly and efficiently as possible.

The Complete Reference

Chapter 7

Customizing the Windows XP Interface for Ease of Working

Microsoft has put a lot of effort into streamlining the Windows XP Professional interface so that it's easy to use. But you can make the interface faster and more efficient by customizing it to suit your style of working. This chapter discusses how to do so if your administrator lets you.

In a domain environment, an administrator may have prevented you from changing some of these settings. For example, an administrator can prevent you from customizing the Start menu or the desktop (perhaps because company policy is to provide the same Start menu and desktop settings to each user). Or an administrator may prevent you from customizing the Recycle Bin so that you can't delete files and folders without confirmation. However, many administrators allow you to configure the interface settings described in this chapter.

Note	*Two of the Windows XP PowerToys, which you can download from the Microsoft Windows XP Downloads site (www.microsoft.com/windowsxp/home/downloads/ powertoys.asp) can make a great difference to the Windows XP Professional interface. The Tweak UI PowerToy is one of the handiest tools for tweaking the Windows XP Professional interface. The Virtual Desktop Manager PowerToy lets you create four separate virtual desktops, which gives you far more space on which to arrange your work.*

Customizing the Start Menu

Windows XP Professional's Start menu (shown on the left in Figure 7-1) is substantially redesigned from the versions of the Start menu in earlier versions of Windows. Microsoft calls the old version of the Start menu the "classic" Start menu. If you don't like the new Start menu, you can restore the classic Start menu as described in the following section.

You can customize the Start menu by adding items to it, removing items from it, and changing the ways in which it displays the items it contains.

Using the Customize Start Menu Dialog Box

Most of the options for customizing the Start menu are located in the Customize Start Menu dialog box. To display this dialog box, right-click the Start button and choose Properties from the shortcut menu; then click the upper Customize button in the Taskbar and Start Menu Properties dialog box. Figure 7-2 shows the two tabs of the Customize Start Menu dialog box.

The General tab lets you

- Select the icon size (Small or Large).
- Specify the number of programs (between 0 and 30) to display in the Most Recently Used Programs area, or clear the list of programs displayed in this area.
- Choose whether to display an Internet item and an E-mail item on the Start menu. If you display these items, you can specify which application they're linked to.

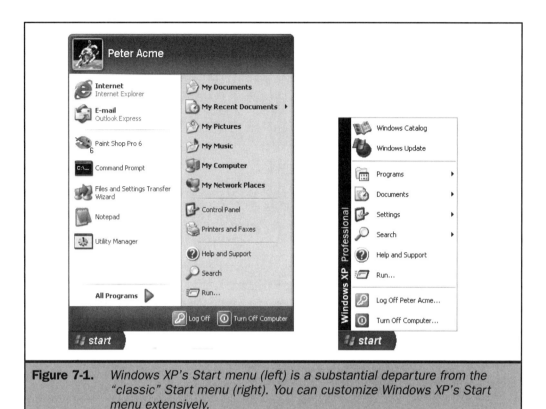

Figure 7-1. Windows XP's Start menu (left) is a substantial departure from the "classic" Start menu (right). You can customize Windows XP's Start menu extensively.

The Advanced tab lets you choose the following:

■ Whether Windows XP Professional should open submenus when you hover the mouse over them. (If you turn this option off, you need to click the submenu item to display the submenu.)

■ Whether Windows XP Professional highlights newly installed applications on the Start menu. Some people like this feature; others don't.

■ Which particular items appear on the Start menu and, for some of them, whether they're displayed as a link or a menu.

■ Whether you can use drag-and-drop on Start menu items. By default, drag-and-drop is on, so you can drag items to the Start menu and drop them there.

■ Whether the Start menu includes a My Recent Documents item. You can clear this list by clicking the Clear List button.

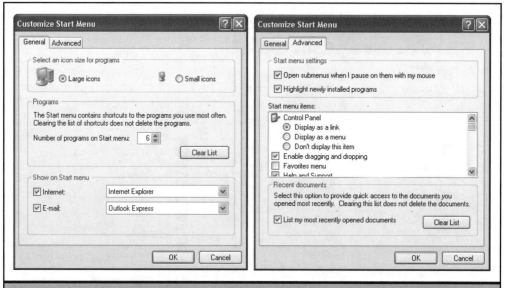

Figure 7-2.   *The Customize Start Menu dialog box*

Adding and Removing Start Menu Items

After choosing options in the Customize Start Menu dialog box, add items to and remove items from the Start menu as follows:

- To place an item on the All Programs menu or one of its submenus, drag it to the Start button, wait for Windows XP Professional to display the Start menu, and then drag it to where you want it to appear, waiting for each menu in turn to be displayed.

- To keep an item permanently on the Start menu, pin it there by right-clicking it on the Start menu, on the desktop, or in a Windows Explorer window and choosing Pin to Start Menu from the shortcut menu. Alternatively, drag the item to the Pinned Items area, or simply drop it on the Start button. To unpin a pinned item, right-click it and choose Unpin from Start Menu. You can rearrange the order of items in the Pinned Items area by dragging them up and down.

- To remove an item from the Start menu, right-click it and choose Remove from This List from the shortcut menu. Removing an item instructs it not to reappear on the Recently Used items area of the Start menu, no matter how frequently you use it.

- To remove an item from the All Programs menu or one of its submenus, right-click it and choose Delete from the shortcut menu.

Restoring the "Classic" Start Menu

If you don't like the Windows XP Professional Start menu, you can restore the "classic" Start menu (shown on the right in Figure 7-1) by right-clicking the Start button, choosing Properties from the context menu to display the Start Menu tab of the Taskbar and Start Menu dialog box, selecting the Classic Start Menu option button, and clicking the OK button.

Customizing the Classic Start Menu

If you like the classic Start menu well enough from using it in previous versions of Windows to prefer it to the Windows XP Professional Start menu, you may well remember how to customize the classic Start menu by working in the Customize Classic Start Menu dialog box (Figure 7-3).

To display the Customize Classic Start Menu dialog box, follow these steps:

1. Right-click the Start button and choose Properties from the shortcut menu to display the Start Menu tab of the Taskbar and Start Menu Properties dialog box.

2. Click the lower Customize button. (If you haven't selected the Classic Start Menu option button, as described in the previous section, do so first.)

The controls in the Start Menu group box let you add a shortcut, remove a shortcut or folder, open a Windows Explorer window to the Start Menu folder (by clicking the Advanced button), sort the Start menu items, and clear your list of recently used documents, applications, and web sites.

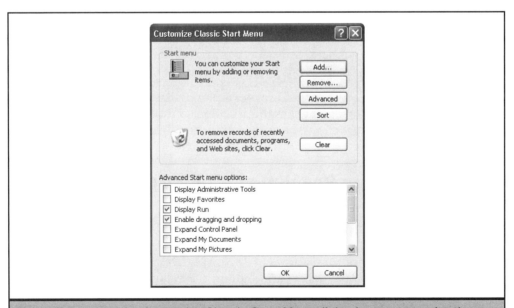

Figure 7-3.   *Use the Customize Classic Start Menu dialog box to customize the classic Start menu.*

The controls in the Advanced Start Menu Options list box let you do the following:

- Specify which items Windows XP Professional displays on the Start menu.
- Choose whether drag-and-drop on the Start menu is enabled.
- Choose whether to "expand" (display a submenu for) folders such as Control Panel and My Documents and My Pictures instead of opening a folder to them.
- Display the Programs menu, when it's too long to fit onto the screen, as a single column with scroll bars top and bottom instead of wrapping it onto a second column.
- Display small icons on the Start menu.
- Use personalized menus, hiding the entries for Start menu items you don't use. To display these items, click the double-arrow button at the bottom of the menu.

Arranging Icons on the Desktop

To provide quick access to your applications and files, you can drag the icons on your desktop into any order you please. Alternatively, you can have Windows XP Professional keep them neatly arranged by using the Arrange Icons By | Auto Arrange command on the desktop's shortcut menu.

To sort the icons, choose Name, Size, Type, or Modified from the Arrange Icons By submenu on the desktop's shortcut menu.

To snap the icons to an invisible grid onscreen, select the Align to Grid command on the Arrange Icons By submenu. This option is most useful for maintaining alignment when you arrange icons manually.

Customizing the Desktop

To customize the desktop, work in the Display Properties dialog box. To display the _ ty Properties dialog box, right-click the desktop and choose Properties from the shortcut menu. Alternatively, choose Start | Control Panel | Appearance and Themes | Display.

Changing the Display Resolution, Color Quality, and Refresh Rate

Most cathode-ray tube (CRT) monitors can display multiple resolutions, whereas most liquid crystal display (LCD) panels can display only one resolution clearly—the same resolution as the number of pixels they have. (Most LCDs can display some other resolutions jaggedly.) Similarly, most CRTs support several different _refresh rates_—the rate at which the display redraws the information its displaying—whereas most LCDs either support only one resolution or only a couple of resolutions. Both CRTs and LCDs support displaying different numbers of colors, or _color qualities_.

When you change one of these settings to a value you haven't used before and click the Apply button or the OK button, Windows XP Professional displays the Monitor Settings dialog box to check that you want to keep the settings. Click the Yes button if you do. But if you have used the setting before, Windows XP Professional applies the change without consulting you.

 On computers that use Fast User Switching, all users have to use the same resolution, refresh rate, and color depth. When one user changes these settings, the settings change for all other users as well.

Changing the Display Resolution

To change the display resolution, drag the Screen Resolution slider on the Settings tab of the Display Properties dialog box (shown on the left in Figure 7-4). Click the Apply button.

Windows XP Professional's GUI is designed for a minimum resolution of 800×600 pixels (SVGA resolution), so this is the minimum resolution you can set on the Settings tab. Windows XP's Safe mode uses 640×480-pixel (VGA) resolution, which requires some simplifications of the GUI.

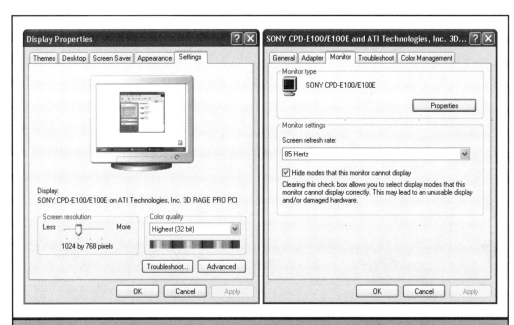

Figure 7-4. *To change the display resolution, drag the Screen Resolution slider on the Settings tab of the Display Properties dialog box (left). To change the refresh rate, use the Screen Refresh Rate drop-down list on the Monitor tab of the Properties dialog box for the monitor and graphics card (right).*

Changing the Number of Colors Displayed

To change the number of colors displayed, change the setting in the Color Quality drop-down list on the Settings tab of the Display Properties dialog box.

The color qualities available, and their descriptions, depend on your graphics card and monitor. Typical settings are 256 colors, Medium (16-bit color), High (24-bit color), and Highest (32-bit color). You may see only some of these settings.

On most graphics cards, Medium color quality gives much faster performance than High color, and High color quality gives faster performance than Highest color quality. Unless you're working with graphics or artwork that requires true color settings, it's a good idea to use Medium color quality to improve your computer's performance.

Changing the Refresh Rate

To change the refresh rate, click the Advanced button on the Settings tab of the Display Properties dialog box to display the Properties dialog box for the monitor and graphics card. Then change the setting in the Screen Refresh Rate drop-down list on the Monitor tab.

For an LCD screen, set the manufacturer's recommended refresh rate. For technical reasons, LCD screens don't flicker unless they're malfunctioning.

For a CRT, set a refresh rate high enough to eliminate flicker, or at least to reduce it as far as possible. Flicker occurs when your eyes notice the screen being redrawn, particularly when you're using a larger monitor, because you see more of a larger monitor in your peripheral vision, where flicker tends to be more noticeable. A refresh rate of 60 Hz (*hertz*—cycles per second) produces significant flicker. At refresh rates between 70 and 75 Hz, most people see little flicker on small monitors. At refresh rates of 85 Hz and above, few people see flicker on even the largest monitors.

By default, Windows XP Professional displays only the refresh rates that your graphics card offers and that your monitor supports, because sending the monitor video signals at rates it doesn't support could damage it. To display all refresh rates, clear the Hide Modes that This Monitor Cannot Display check box. Don't do this unless you've checked the monitor's documentation and are sure that it supports the refresh rate that Windows XP is trying to prevent you from using.

 After changing your display resolution and refresh rate, use your monitor's hardware or software controls to improve the image as far as possible.

 If you can't get satisfactory display results by using Windows XP Professional's built-in controls, consider getting a custom display-tweaking utility such as PowerStrip (www.entechtaiwan.com/ps.htm).

Changing the Look of the Desktop

You can change the look of your desktop either by applying a different theme to it or by configuring its settings manually.

Applying Themes

A *desktop theme* is a suite of settings designed to go together, typically including desktop images, custom mouse pointers, custom sounds, and sometimes a screen saver. Windows XP Professional comes with some basic themes built in. You can buy other themes from Microsoft (for example, in the Windows Plus! pack) and other vendors. Make sure any themes you buy are designed for Windows XP: Because Windows XP Professional has different interface elements than earlier versions of Windows, themes designed for earlier versions don't work properly on Windows XP.

To apply a theme, select it in the Theme drop-down list on the Themes tab of the Display Properties dialog box. To change the settings for a theme, work on the Desktop tab and Appearance tab as described in the next subsection. Once you've customized settings for the current theme, you can save the theme under a new name by clicking the Save As button on the Theme tab. (You don't have to save the theme if you don't want to use it again.) You can delete themes you've saved, but you can't delete Windows XP's built-in themes.

For performance's sake, administrators may prevent you from applying third-party themes to your computer.

Changing the Desktop Background

By default, Windows XP Professional uses a picture as the background to your desktop. You can change it by using the controls on the Desktop tab of the Display Properties dialog box. Select the picture in the Background list box or by browsing to it, and then choose Center, Stretch, or Tile in the Position drop-down list to get the effect you want.

The Background list box lists BMP, JPG, and GIF files in your My Pictures folder, %Windir% folder, your %Windir%\Web folder, and your %Windir%\Web\Wallpaper folder.

To quickly apply a picture as the desktop background, select it in a Windows Explorer window and click the Set As Desktop Background link in the Picture Tasks list. (Alternatively, issue the Set As Desktop Background command from the File menu or the shortcut menu for the file.)

If you prefer not to have a picture on your desktop, select (None) in the Background list box. Use the Color drop-down list to change the background color of your desktop.

Customizing the Items Displayed on Your Desktop

To customize the items displayed on your desktop, click the Customize Desktop button on the Desktop tab of the Display Properties dialog box to display the Desktop Items dialog box. The General tab (shown on the left in Figure 7-5) contains controls for selecting the items displayed on your desktop: the My Documents item, the My Computer item, the My Network Places item, and the Internet Explorer item (for Windows XP Professional installations that include Internet Explorer). You can change the icon displayed for one of these items by selecting the item in the list box and clicking the Change Icon button.

The General tab also contains controls for running the Desktop Cleanup Wizard (which offers to move any unused desktop items to a folder) and turning it off. By default, the wizard runs itself every 60 days. Many people prefer to turn the Wizard off, but if you have a busy Desktop, you may find it useful.

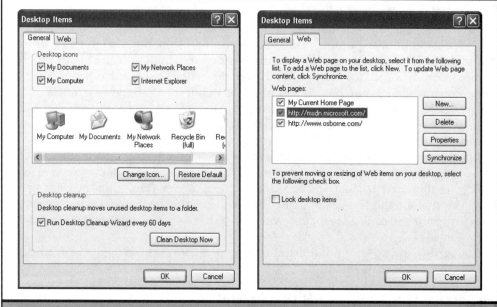

Figure 7-5. *The Desktop Items dialog box contains settings for controlling Desktop items, running the Desktop Cleanup Wizard, and creating and managing Desktop Web pages.*

Adding Web Content to Your Desktop

If you wish, and if your administrator allows you to, you can display web content on your desktop. Web content can greatly enliven the desktop, but like screensavers, it raises questions of what you're doing spending any significant amount of time staring at the desktop rather than working.

To display web content on your desktop, work on the Web tab of the Desktop Items dialog box. To begin with, this contains an item for your current home page, but you can add other pages by clicking the New button and letting the New Desktop Item Wizard walk you through the process of adding either a web page or an item from the Microsoft Desktop Gallery (for example, a stock ticker). For a web page, you can create a schedule using the same process as for offline favorites. (See "Using Offline Favorites" in Chapter 36 for a discussion of offline favorites.)

To configure a desktop web page, select it in the Web Pages list box on the Web tab of the Desktop Items dialog box (shown on the right in Figure 7-5) and click the Properties button. To synchronize a desktop web page immediately, select and click the Synchronize button.

Once you've applied one or more web pages to your desktop, you can adjust a page by moving the mouse pointer over it and using the controls that Windows XP Professional displays. You can display the page either in a window (by issuing the

Reset to Original Size command), full screen (the Cover Desktop command), or take up as much space on your desktop as isn't occupied by icons (the Split Desktop with Icons command).

To lock desktop items in place, either right-click the desktop and choose Arrange Icons By | Lock Web Items on Desktop or select the Lock Desktop Items check box on the Web tab of the Desktop Items dialog box.

To toggle the display of desktop icons, right-click the desktop and choose Arrange Icons By | Show Desktop Icons.

Customizing the Appearance of GUI Elements

As mentioned earlier, a Windows XP Professional theme applies a suite of changes, from the desktop background graphic to the look of individual GUI elements. You can also customize the display of GUI elements manually, as described in this section.

If you've used a previous version of Windows, you may remember that all the features for customizing the appearance of GUI elements were located on the Appearance tab of the Display Properties dialog box. In Windows XP, the Appearance tab of the Display Properties dialog box contains only drop-down lists for specifying the style for windows and buttons, the color scheme, and the font size. Further controls appear in the Advanced Appearance dialog box, which you display by clicking the Advanced button on the Appearance tab.

The Windows and Buttons drop-down list offers two choices: Windows XP Style (the default) and Windows Classic Style. If you select Windows XP Style, your choices of color scheme are limited to Blue (the default), Olive Green, and Silver, and many of the settings in the Advanced Appearance box don't apply.

If you select Windows Classic Style in the Windows and Buttons drop-down list, Windows XP Professional makes available the same wide range of color schemes as previous versions of Windows had, and you can perform extensive customizations in the Advanced Appearance dialog box.

Choosing Desktop Effects

Windows XP Professional also supports *effects* that change the way that Windows XP displays menus, fonts, icons, and windows. To choose effects settings, click the Effects button on the Appearance tab of the Display Properties dialog box and work in the Effects dialog box.

The Effects dialog box offers the following settings:

- For menus and tooltips, you can choose a Fade effect, a Scroll effect, or no effect. You can also choose whether to display shadows under menus for a 3-D effect and whether to hide the underlining of menu-accelerator keys (the keys you press to activate menu items) until you press the ALT key.

- For screen fonts, you can choose Standard smoothing, ClearType smoothing, or no smoothing. ClearType is a font-rendering feature for smoothing fonts on LCD screens.

- For windows, you can choose whether Windows XP displays their contents when you drag them. Displaying just the window frame when moving a window improves performance on an underpowered graphics card.

- For icons, you can choose whether to display large icons rather than regular-sized icons on the desktop and Start menu. Large icons can be easier to navigate, but they can cause complications by making the first pane of your Start menu too large to fit onscreen.

Applying a Screensaver

Windows XP Professional includes a variety of screensavers that you can use to hide the contents of your desktop. The screensaver kicks in after the mouse and keyboard haven't been used for a specified time.

In the days of text-mode operating systems, it was important to use a screensaver to prevent a ghost image being burned into the phosphors of a CRT monitor. Graphical displays and improved monitor technology have largely eliminated this problem, so nowadays you don't need to use a screensaver to save your monitor. But you may still want to use a screensaver to hide your work and lock your computer when you leave it unattended.

For this purpose, the most effective screensaver is Windows XP Professional's built-in Blank screensaver, which simply blanks your monitor, making it look more or less as though it's switched off. However, many people prefer a screensaver that displays something visually striking, something amusing, or something educational.

There's both a conceptual problem and a practical problem with using most striking, amusing, or educational screensavers. On the conceptual front, unless your job description involves staring uselessly at a monitor, you shouldn't be watching your screensaver at all. And on the practical front, if a screensaver is working vigorously to create impressive visuals, it's probably wasting a prodigious amount of processor cycles. If the computer is doing anything useful, such as providing files or other services to other computers on a workgroup, the screensaver will slow down these services instead of letting the PC perform them efficiently without user input.

An honorable exception is Windows XP's My Pictures Slideshow screensaver, which displays each graphic in your \My Pictures\ folder (or another folder you specify) in turn. This screensaver is entertaining without being too demanding, but it's much better suited to the home than the office.

 If your computer is busy rendering video, burning CDs, or burning DVDs when the screensaver starts, the screensaver may ruin the ongoing task. If you perform this kind of task, arrange for the screensaver to start after a delay long enough for any task to complete.

To apply a screensaver, choose it in the Screen Saver list box on the Screen Saver tab of the Display Properties dialog box. If the Settings button is available, click it to display a dialog box in which you can configure the screensaver. Click the Preview button to preview the effect; move your mouse, click, or press a key to cancel the preview. Set the delay in the Wait text box.

In a domain configuration, Windows XP Professional displays the On Resume, Password Protect check box next to the Wait text box. By default this check box is selected, so Windows XP Professional locks the computer when you interrupt the screensaver. Enter your password to unlock the computer.

In a standalone or workgroup configuration using Fast User Switching, Windows XP Professional displays the On Resume, Display Welcome Screen check box next to the Wait text box. By default this check box is selected, so Windows XP Professional displays the Welcome screen when you interrupt the screensaver. Any user can then log on as usual. Clear this check box if you want to resume your user session when you interrupt the screensaver.

You can add third-party screensavers to Windows XP, but because free screensavers are notorious for being infected with Trojan-horse malware and containing dangerously buggy programming, it's best to be wary of them. In any case, your domain administrator may prevent you from adding screensavers for security and performance.

Screensaver files have an SCR extension. Any screensaver files you store in your %Windir%\System32 folder appear in the Screen Saver list box on the Screen Saver tab. But you can also launch a screensaver by double-clicking its SCR file or issuing its name at a command line. Launching a screensaver like this doesn't change your settings on the Screen Saver tab.

Choosing Power-Management Options

This section discusses how to configure power-management options common to desktop and portable computers. "Configuring Power-Management Options for Laptops" in Chapter 18 discusses how to configure power-management options specific to laptops.

To configure power-management options, click the Power button on the Screen Saver tab of the Display Properties dialog box. Windows XP displays the Power Options Properties dialog box.

Most of the options in the Power Options Properties dialog box are easy to understand. These are the main features:

■ On the Power Schemes tab, you can choose from the available power schemes (Home/Office Desk, Portable/Laptop, Presentation, Always On, Minimal Power Management, and Max Battery) to suit the needs of the computer you're using. For example, you might choose Presentation for a computer you're using at a trade show. This setting specifies a timeout of Never for monitor, hard disks, standby, and hibernation, so the computer keeps running even when unattended. Alternatively, you can define a custom power scheme by choosing settings. You can save custom power schemes by clicking the Save As button. If your computer doesn't support standby or hibernation, the Power Options Properties dialog box doesn't offer options for them.

■ The Advanced tab offers assorted power-related options including whether to show a power icon on the taskbar (which is useful for laptops), whether to prompt you for a password when you bring the computer out of standby, and what actions to take when you press the power button or the sleep button on your computer.

■ The Hibernate tab (which appears only if your computer supports hibernation) lets you specify whether to enable hibernation and shows you how much disk space you have free and how much space the hibernation file will require. Usually, hibernation is useful, but you may want to switch it off in order to reclaim disk space on a small disk.

■ The APM tab (which appears only if your computer supports Advanced Power Management) lets you enable or disable Advanced Power Management support.

■ The UPS tab contains controls for configuring an *uninterruptible power supply* (a device that provides backup power if there's an outage). A UPS is a great investment for a standalone or workgroup desktop, as it gives you time to save your work if an outage occurs. A laptop computer typically doesn't need a UPS, as its battery provides enough cushion for most power outages. If your corporation's building has a backup power supply, you probably won't need a UPS.

Customizing the Taskbar and Notification Area

You can customize the taskbar by moving it, resizing it, and changing its behavior. You can also display desktop toolbars either on the taskbar or elsewhere on the desktop.

Locking and Unlocking the Taskbar

By default, the taskbar is unlocked in Windows XP Professional—unless you or someone else has locked it. (The taskbar is locked by default in Windows XP Home Edition.) To toggle the taskbar between locked and unlocked, right-click the notification area and choose Lock the Taskbar from the shortcut menu. A check mark by this menu item indicates that the taskbar is locked.

Once you've positioned and resized the taskbar and any desktop toolbars to your satisfaction, lock the taskbar so that you don't change it unintentionally.

Moving the Taskbar

To move the taskbar, click in any open space in the taskbar and drag the taskbar toward one of the three other edges of the screen. When Windows XP Professional can tell which edge you've chosen, it snaps the taskbar into place.

Resizing the Taskbar

To resize the taskbar, drag its inside edge toward the middle or edge of the screen. When it's positioned horizontally, the taskbar resizes in steps of just over a taskbar button's depth so that it can show one or more full rows of buttons. When it's positioned vertically, the taskbar resizes smoothly because the button width is variable whereas the button depth isn't.

Customizing the Taskbar's Behavior

By customizing the taskbar's behavior to your preferences, you can greatly speed up your work in Windows XP Professional.

Understanding the Taskbar's Basic Behavior

The taskbar is designed to help you navigate between the application windows that you have open. Each application window is represented by a taskbar button. Clicking a taskbar button activates a displayed but inactive application window, restores and activates a minimized application window, and minimizes the active application window. You can work with multiple application windows by selecting the first key, and then holding down CTRL as you select the other keys.

Whether an application receives one taskbar button or one taskbar button for each document it has open depends on whether it uses *multiple document interface* (MDI) or *single document interface* (SDI). MDI displays multiple documents in the same application window, so all the documents are subordinated to the application's taskbar icon. SDI displays each document in a separate application window, and each application window receives its own taskbar icon. (Some applications, such as Microsoft Word and Microsoft Excel, let you switch between MDI and SDI.)

When you have just a few application windows open, the taskbar displays a full-size button for each. When you open enough application windows for space on the taskbar to run short, the taskbar narrows each existing button to accommodate new buttons. When each existing button starts getting unreasonably small, the taskbar groups related buttons onto a single generic button. For example, the taskbar will display generic buttons such as 6 Windows Command Prompt and 23 Internet Explorer. To reach an individual application window, you click the generic button. Windows XP Professional displays a menu of the buttons so that you can click the one you want to affect. You can also work with an entire group of taskbar buttons by right-clicking the group button and choosing the appropriate command (Cascade, Tile Horizontally, Tile Vertically, Minimize Group, or Close Group) from the shortcut menu.

Grouping is effective, but it can be confusing at first, because some categories contain entries for application windows you wouldn't expect them to. For example, a 4 Windows Explorer group button might include two Windows Explorer application window entries, an entry for the Status dialog box for an Internet connection, and an entry for the Sounds, Speech, and Audio Devices group box.

When there's not enough space for reasonably sized taskbar buttons even with grouping, Windows XP Professional displays another row of taskbar buttons below the bottom existing row, together with scrollbars for navigating between the row or rows that are displayed and the row or rows that aren't. Scrolling the taskbar is awkward, but it's better than having indecipherably narrow taskbar buttons.

Configuring the Taskbar's Behavior

To configure the taskbar's behavior, right-click the notification area or open space in the taskbar and choose Properties from the shortcut menu to display the Taskbar tab of the Taskbar and Start Menu Properties dialog box. The Taskbar Appearance group box in this page contains options for the following:

- **Locking the taskbar**   Described earlier in this chapter.

- **Automatically hiding the taskbar**   Making the taskbar automatically hide until you move the pointer to where it's lurking. This option lets you reclaim the desktop space the taskbar takes up.

- **Displaying the taskbar on top of other windows**   This option is on by default. You can turn it and Auto-Hide off so that the taskbar appears onscreen but you can position other windows on top of it.

- **Grouping taskbar buttons**   This option is on by default.

- **Displaying the Quick Launch toolbar**   The Quick Launch toolbar is the most useful of the desktop toolbars. "Using Desktop Toolbars," later in this chapter, discusses the desktop toolbars.

Customizing Taskbar Grouping with Tweak UI

As you saw in the previous subsection, Windows XP Professional offers you only basic control over taskbar grouping: You can choose whether the taskbar groups related buttons.

The Taskbar | Grouping page of the Tweak UI PowerToy lets you configure Windows XP Professional to group taskbar buttons for any application with a given number of windows, to group the applications with the most open windows first, or to group the least-used applications first.

Customizing the Notification Area's Behavior

Windows XP Professional offers the following options for customizing the notification area:

- Select or clear the Show the Clock check box in the Notification Area group box on the Taskbar tab of the Taskbar and Start Menu Properties dialog box to control whether Windows XP displays the clock. (Windows XP Professional displays the clock by default.)

- Select or clear the Hide Inactive Icons check box in the Notification Area group box. If you select this check box (which is selected by default), you can choose custom settings for each of your current notification-area icons by clicking the Customize button and working in the resulting Customize Notifications dialog box. For each notification-area icon, choose the behavior you want: Hide when Inactive (the default), Always Hide, or Always Show.

The Customize Notifications dialog box also offers a Restore Defaults button for restoring default hiding settings to such notification-area icons as have them.

Using Desktop Toolbars

Windows XP Professional includes five built-in desktop toolbars that you can display in any combination you find useful. To toggle the display of a desktop toolbar, right-click the notification area and select its entry on the Toolbars submenu.

Quick Launch Toolbar

The Quick Launch toolbar contains shortcuts to applications. You can add to the Quick Launch toolbar any shortcuts to applications or files you want.

The easiest way to add a shortcut to your Quick Launch toolbar is to drag the icon for the application or file to the Quick Launch toolbar and drop it where you want it to appear. If you display Control Panel in classic view, you can drag Control Panel icons to the Quick Launch toolbar.

To remove a shortcut from the Quick Launch toolbar, right-click its icon, choose Delete from the shortcut menu, and choose the Yes button in the Confirm File Delete dialog box.

You can also customize the Quick Launch toolbar by working in the Quick Launch folder, which you'll find at \Documents and Settings\Username\Application Data\ Microsoft\Internet Explorer\Quick Launch. To open this folder, right-click open space on the toolbar and choose Open Folder. Once the folder is open, you can create or delete shortcuts in it by using the normal techniques.

Language Bar

The Language bar is available and appears by default when you have installed two or more input languages or keyboard layouts on Windows XP Professional. Hover the mouse pointer over the Language bar to display a ScreenTip of the current language and layout. Click the Language bar to display a pop-up menu from which you can change the language or layout, or hide the Language bar. Right-click the Language bar to display a configuration menu for the bar.

Desktop Toolbar

The Desktop toolbar provides an alternative path to the icons on your desktop when you've covered your desktop with application windows. The Desktop toolbar contains an icon for each item on your Desktop together with items for key folders: My Documents, My Computer, and My Network Places. To save space, display the Desktop toolbar at the size of its desktop label, and then click the toolbar to display a menu of its contents.

Address Bar

The Address Bar toolbar is essentially the Internet Explorer Address bar. Enter a URL or folder path to display that site or folder in a browser window.

Links Bar

The Links Bar toolbar is the Internet Explorer Links bar. Display the Links Bar toolbar on the desktop if you need quick access to your links.

To customize the Links Bar toolbar, customize the Links bar in Internet Explorer.

Creating Custom Desktop Toolbars

You can create a custom Desktop toolbar for a folder by right-clicking the notification area, choosing Toolbars | New Toolbar, selecting the folder in the New Toolbar dialog box, and clicking the OK button. This gives you quick access to the contents of the folder.

You can use the same technique to create a custom Desktop Formatting toolbar for a web site, but the result is seldom useful.

Working with Desktop Toolbars

You can reposition and manipulate desktop toolbars as follows:

- To reposition a Desktop toolbar, unlock the taskbar and drag the toolbar's handle to where you want the toolbar to appear. You can dock desktop toolbars on the edge of the screen or float them undocked on the desktop.

- To change a Desktop toolbar's attributes, right-click it and choose View | Large Icons, View | Small Icons, Show Text, Show Title, Always on Top, or Auto-Hide from the shortcut menu.

- If you position a Desktop toolbar at the edge of the screen, you can select its Auto-Hide attribute and its Always on Top attribute to make it hide until you move the mouse pointer to that side of the screen.

- You can close a Desktop toolbar either by right-clicking it and choosing Close Toolbar from the shortcut menu or by right-clicking the notification area and choosing the toolbar's name from the Toolbars submenu. If you display the toolbar as an undocked panel, you can click its Close button to close it.

Customizing Your Keyboard and Mouse Settings

You may also need to customize your keyboard and mouse settings to improve their usability. The following sections discuss the possibilities, which range from changing the speed at which Windows XP Professional reacts to keypresses to applying different mouse pointers and accelerations.

Customizing Your Keyboard Settings

To customize your keyboard settings, choose Start | Control Panel | Printers and Other Hardware | Keyboard to display the Keyboard Properties dialog box.

On the Speed tab, you can change the *repeat delay* (how long Windows XP Professional waits to register a second keystroke when you hold down the key), the *repeat rate* (how quickly Windows XP Professional repeats a character when you hold down the key), and the cursor blink rate.

On the Hardware tab, you can change the type of keyboard and access its Properties dialog box to change its driver.

Customizing Your Mouse Settings

To customize your mouse settings, choose Start | Control Panel | Printers and Other Hardware | Mouse to display the Mouse Properties dialog box. The four tabs of this dialog box offer settings for changing the behavior of the mouse buttons, loading different mouse pointers, configuring the movement and behavior of the mouse pointer, making the mouse pointer more visible, and changing your mouse hardware.

Most of these options are self-explanatory. Here are a few tips:

- Change your double-click speed on the Buttons tab if double-clicking isn't working as you'd like it to.

- Animated mouse pointers can be cute and entertaining, but they slow down your computer's performance.

- You can install third-party mouse pointers by clicking the Browse button on the Pointers tab. Beware of custom mouse-pointer schemes distributed by people or organizations you don't know well enough to trust. Such schemes have been widely used to distribute Trojan-horse malware and attack unsuspecting users' systems.

- The Enhanced Pointer Precision feature (on the Pointer Options tab) controls whether the mouse decelerates quickly when you slow down or stop the movement of the mouse.

- To adjust advanced settings, click the Properties button on the Hardware tab to display the Properties dialog box for the mouse, and then work on the Advanced Settings tab. For a high-sensitivity mouse, you can increase the Sample Rate setting to make Windows XP Professional check the movement of the mouse more frequently. In the Wheel Detection drop-down list, you can change whether Windows XP looks for a mouse wheel (Look for Wheel), assumes the mouse has a wheel (Assume Wheel Is Present), or doesn't try to detect a wheel (Detection Disabled). If your mouse's movement is erratic, you can increase the Input Buffer Length value to store more information about your mouse's movement or turn off Fast Initialization to force Windows XP Professional to detect the mouse properly.

- To adjust even more settings, such as the speed at which Windows XP Professional displays menus when you move the mouse over them, and the mouse's hover time and sensitivity, use the Tweak UI PowerToy.

Customizing System Sounds

Windows XP Professional lets you play sounds to mark a large number of system events, such as your closing a program, an e-mail message arriving, or your doing something Windows XP Professional doesn't like.

As mentioned earlier in this chapter, some themes include custom sounds for various events. You can also manually customize the sounds that Windows XP Professional plays for system events by working on the Sounds tab of the Sounds and Audio Devices Properties dialog box.

To display the Sounds and Audio Devices Properties dialog box, choose Start | Control Panel | Sounds, Speech, and Audio Devices | Change the Sound Scheme. Alternatively, if you have a Volume control icon displayed in the notification area, right-click the icon and choose Adjust Audio Properties from the shortcut menu.

To apply a sound to an event, select the event in the Program Events list box. This list is divided into categories such as Windows, NetMeeting, Phone Dialer, Windows Explorer, and Windows Messenger. Select the sound in the Sounds drop-down list or by browsing to it. The Sounds drop-down list lists the WAV files in the %Windir%\Media folder, so you can make files appear in the list by placing them in that folder.

You can save sound schemes by using the Save As button and apply sound schemes you've saved by using the Sound Scheme drop-down list. You can delete a custom sound scheme by clicking the Delete button.

Note   *Sound schemes you've created are available only to you, not to other users of the computer.*

Using Windows XP Professional's Accessibility Features

Windows XP Professional offers basic accessibility features of users with disabilities. Table 7-1 summarizes these features.

Setting Accessibility Options

You can set up most of the accessibility features by choosing Start | All Programs | Accessories | Accessibility | Accessibility Wizard and working through the wizard's pages.

To change settings manually, choose Start | Control Panel | Accessibility Options | Accessibility Options and work in the Accessibility Options dialog box. The Keyboard tab, Sound tab, Display tab, and Mouse tab contain most of the features detailed in

Table 7-1. The General tab contains controls for specifying when to use the accessibility features, whether to warn the user verbally or with a sound when turning a feature on or off, and whether to turn off the accessibility features after a specified period of idleness.

Feature	Description
Keyboard Accessibility Features	
StickyKeys	Makes the SHIFT, CTRL, ALT, and WINDOWS keys "stick" when you press them so that you don't need to hold these keys down to type key combinations.
FilterKeys	Ignores quick keystrokes (such as those that occur when you accidentally press a key when trying to press another key) and repeated keystrokes caused by holding the key down too long.
ToggleKeys	Beeps to notify you when you press the CAPS LOCK, NUM LOCK, or SCROLL LOCK key.
Show Extra Keyboard Help in Programs	Makes programs that contain extra help about using the keyboard display this help.
On-Screen Keyboard	Displays a keyboard onscreen so that you can type using your mouse.
SerialKeys	Supports alternative input devices.
Sound Accessibility Features	
SoundSentry	Gives visual warnings when the computer is making a sound.
ShowSounds	Shows captions to indicate when the computer is making a sound.
Narrator	Reads text onscreen, including the names of windows, dialog boxes, and controls; menu commands; and the characters you type.

Table 7-1.   *Windows XP Professional Accessibility Features*

Feature	Description
Display Accessibility Features	
High Contrast	Applies your choice of a variety of high-contrast color schemes, some of which offer large controls or extra large controls. This feature can be useful when you need to use a dim laptop screen out of doors.
Cursor Blink Rate	Changes the rate at which the cursor blinks to make it easier to see. Offers a wider range of settings than the setting on the Speed tab of the Keyboard Properties dialog box.
Cursor Width	Lets you widen the cursor to increase its visibility.
Mouse Accessibility Features	
MouseKeys	Lets you control the mouse pointer by using the keys on the numeric keypad.

Table 7-1.   *Windows XP Professional Accessibility Features* (continued)

The following accessibility features are a little harder to find:

- To display Onscreen Keyboard, choose Start | All Programs | Accessories | Accessibility | On-Screen Keyboard.

- To launch Narrator, choose Start | All Programs | Accessories | Accessibility | Narrator.

- The SerialKeys item appears on the General tab of the Accessibility Options dialog box rather than on the Keyboard tab.

Many of the accessibility features are configurable. These options are mostly well laid out and easy to understand, so I won't discuss them here.

Running Magnifier, Narrator, or On-Screen Keyboard Automatically

If you use Magnifier, Narrator, or On-Screen Keyboard consistently, set them to run automatically when you log on. To do so, run Utility Manager (see Figure 7-6) and set the appropriate options for each accessibility feature you want to use.

Figure 7-6.   *Utility Manager lets you specify when to run Magnifier, Narrator, and On-Screen Keyboard.*

Using Shortcuts Effectively

Like earlier versions of Windows, Windows XP Professional lets you create shortcuts that point to files or folders in other locations. Unlike earlier versions, Windows XP Professional tracks the targets to which shortcuts point so that when you move a target file to a new location, Windows XP Professional can repair the shortcuts that point to it.

You can create as many shortcuts as you want to a file or folder to make it easier to access. Deleting a shortcut doesn't affect its target file.

Shortcuts on the desktop, in Windows Explorer windows, and in common dialog boxes (such as the Open dialog box) bear on their lower-left corner a small white box with a black arrow curling upward and clockwise to distinguish them. This box and arrow distinguish a shortcut from the file or folder to which it points. (You can customize or replace the arrow by using the Explorer | Shortcut options of the Tweak UI PowerToy.) Shortcuts on the Start menu and desktop toolbars don't have the box and arrow, because these locations can contain only shortcuts, not files and folders.

Creating Shortcuts

Most installation routines create shortcuts to their program files on the Start menu, on the desktop, in the notification area, or all three. You can create a shortcut to any file manually in any of these ways:

- Run the Create Shortcut Wizard by choosing File | New | Shortcut from an Explorer window or by choosing New | Shortcut from the context menu for the desktop or open space in an Explorer window.

- Right-drag the file to where you want the shortcut, drop it, and choose Create Shortcuts here from the shortcut menu. Windows XP Professional names the shortcut "Shortcut to *filename.*" Rename the shortcut as necessary.

- Drag a file to a destination that accepts only shortcuts, such as the Send To folder or the Quick Launch toolbar.

Customizing Shortcuts

To customize a shortcut, display its Properties dialog box by issuing a Properties command from the shortcut menu. On the Shortcut tab of the Properties dialog box for a shortcut (Figure 7-7), you can change the target file or folder, change the folder in which the associated application should start and the window size it should use, assign a shortcut key or comment to the shortcut, and change the icon for the shortcut. You can also use the Find Target button to open a Windows Explorer window to the folder that contains the target file or folder.

The Properties dialog box for a shortcut to an application includes a Compatibility tab on which you can set Compatibility mode options for the application. These options apply to the application from whichever shortcut you run it, so you can't set different Compatibility mode options for different shortcuts to the same application.

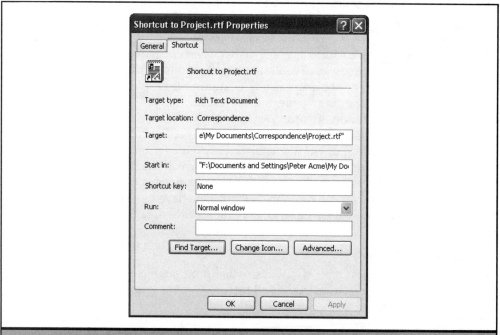

Figure 7-7.   *You can customize a shortcut by working on the Shortcut tab of its Properties dialog box.*

Customizing the Send To Menu

The Send To menu is a convenient mechanism for quickly copying a file or starting an e-mail message with the file as an attachment. The Send To submenu appears on the File menu (File | Send To) and the shortcut menu for files that you can copy or print.

To customize the Send To menu, display the \Documents and Settings*Username*\ Send To folder in an Explorer window. Drag to that folder any program or folder you want to add to the Send To menu, and then choose the Create Shortcut(s) Here item from the shortcut menu.

You can create a cascading menu off the Send To menu by creating a folder within the Send To folder. You can place shortcuts to applications in such a subfolder, but placing a shortcut to a folder in such a subfolder doesn't work.

Configuring the Recycle Bin

The Recycle Bin in Windows XP Professional behaves in the same way as the Recycle Bin in earlier versions of Windows. By default, Windows XP Professional sets aside part of your hard drive to contain the Recycle Bin. When you delete files or folders from your local hard drive, it doesn't actually delete them directly but instead removes them from their current folder and places them in the Recycle Bin. You can recover these files or folders from the Recycle Bin until it becomes so full that Windows XP Professional needs to delete its older contents to make room for new deletions.

To configure the Recycle Bin, right-click its icon on the desktop and choose Properties from the shortcut menu to display the Recycle Bin Properties dialog box (Figure 7-8). This Properties dialog box contains a Global tab with global settings and a tab for each local hard drive installed on your computer.

By default, Windows XP Professional uses a single setting for each local hard drive. To configure separate settings for each drive, select the Configure Drives Independently option button instead of the Use One Setting for All Drives option button on the Global tab. Windows XP Professional then makes available the controls on the drives' tabs of the Properties dialog box.

To make Windows XP Professional delete files and folders immediately rather than placing them in the Recycle Bin, select the Do Not Move Files to the Recycle Bin. Remove Files Immediately when Deleted check box either on the Global tab or the tab for the drive on which you want to make this change.

To change the amount of maximum space the Recycle Bin can consume, drag the Maximum Size of Recycle Bin slider on the Global tab (if you're using one setting for all drives) or on the tab for the appropriate drive.

To suppress confirmation of deletion or of moving objects to the Recycle Bin, clear the Display Delete Confirmation Dialog check box on the Global tab.

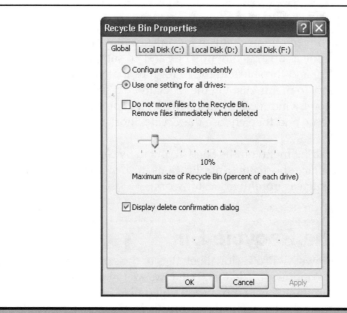

Figure 7-8.   *In the Recycle Bin Properties dialog box, you can configure the Recycle Bin to take up less space, to work differently on different hard disks, not to confirm deletions, and to delete files immediately.*

Customizing the Places Bar in Common Open Dialog Boxes

You can customize the Places bar that appears in common Open dialog boxes such as those displayed by Notepad, WordPad, and Paint. The easiest way to do so is to use the Common Dialogs options in the Tweak UI PowerToy. You can also edit the HKCU\Software\Microsoft\Windows\CurrentVersion\Policies\comdlg32 key in the Registry, but doing so takes much more effort. (See Chapter 40 for a discussion of editing the Registry.) In a domain environment, an administrator may customize the Places bar for you through Group Policy.

Customizing Folders

You can customize any user folder by using the controls on the Customize tab of the Properties dialog box for the folder (Figure 7-9). You can't apply folder templates to system folders, so the Properties dialog box for these folders doesn't include a Customize tab.

The Customize tab offers the following customizations:

■ Applying one of the seven folder templates available in the Use This Folder Type As a Template drop-down list. Documents, Pictures, Photo Album, Music, Music

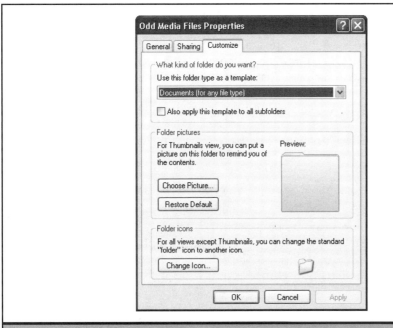

Figure 7-9.   *You can customize user folders by applying any of Windows XP's folder
templates.*

Artist, Music Album, or Videos. The list box lists the roles for which the picture
and music folder types are best suited. Select the Also Apply This Template to
All Subfolders check box if the subfolders will have the same type of content as
their parent folder.

■ Selecting a picture to display on the folder in Thumbnails view. The picture and
music folder types automatically apply pictures by default.

■ Changing the icon used for the folder in all other views than Thumbnails view.
By applying custom icons to folders, you can make them easier to identify at a
glance.

Understanding Folder Redirection

Like other recent versions of Windows, Windows XP Professional encourages you to
save your documents in the My Documents folder structure. The My Documents folder
starts off containing the My Music folder and the My Pictures folder, which Windows
XP Professional's applets, Microsoft applications, and many third-party applications
are built to use by default for document storage. If you start using Windows Movie
Maker, Windows XP automatically creates the My Videos folder for you and uses that
as default storage for videos.

By default, the My Documents folder structure is located on your computer's hard drive unless you're a roaming user. This setting provides good performance and easy access to the files, but unless you are unusually conscientious, it means that your files are unlikely to be backed up. If you *are* a roaming user, the My Documents folder is stored in the roaming profile on the server so that it can be copied to whichever computer you log on to.

In Windows XP Professional, an administrator can redirect the My Documents folder and four other key user folders (the Application Data folder, Desktop folder, My Pictures folder, and Start Menu folder) to network locations. Redirection has three main advantages:

- It centralizes the storage of data files.

- It simplifies data backup. (The administrator can back up the server drive to which all the user folders are redirected.)

- It enables the administrator to replace your computer easily if it breaks or if you win the upgrade lottery. The administrator simply replaces your computer with a default configuration of Windows XP Professional and applications. When you log on, your documents and settings appear to be just where they were on your old computer.

The administrator can specify any of the three different redirection states listed in Table 7-2 to any of the five redirectable folders.

Redirection State	Explanation
No Administrative Policy Defined	The folder stays in its current location.
Basic—Redirect Everyone's Folder to the Same Location	All users' folders are redirected to the same base folder. Typically, each user's folders end up in a folder linked to the user's user name, so each user has a separate set of folders.
Advanced—Specify Locations for Various User Groups	The folder is redirected based on membership of security groups. For example, the folders belonging to all members of the VPs group would be redirected to a different folder than the folders belonging to members of the Mailroom group.

Table 7-2. *Redirection States for the Five Redirectable Folders*

The administrator may give one of your folders a different setting than the other folders. For example, they could redirect your Start Menu folder to the location of a standardized, company-approved Start menu that they inflict on all users rather than let you customize your own Start menu. By customizing the contents of that Start menu, they could push out changes to each computer with minimal effort.

When redirecting a folder, the administrator can choose a number of other settings. The settings most likely to affect you are whether to grant you exclusive rights to the folder and whether to move the current contents of the folder to the new location.

Using Roaming Profiles

If you need to be able to log on from more than one workstation, your domain administrator can set you up with a *roaming profile*. In a roaming profile, your user profile information is stored on the server rather than on your local computer.

When you log on to a computer, Windows XP Professional copies your profile information from the server to the local computer. Depending on the speed of the network and the amount of data in your profile, this can take anything from a few seconds to a few minutes. When the profile information has been copied, your desktop, documents, and configuration information are available on the computer you've logged on to.

Summary

This chapter has discussed how to customize the Windows XP Professional user interface. By customizing items such as the Start menu, desktop, taskbar, notification area, and Send To menu, you can make your work faster and easier. By configuring your keyboard and mouse, and by using accessibility options as necessary, you can make your time at the computer more comfortable. And by using a roaming profile, you can spend time at other computers with all the comforts of home.

The next chapter discusses how to use Windows Explorer and how to customize it to speed up your work.

The Complete Reference

Windows XP

Chapter 8

Using and Customizing Windows Explorer

This chapter discusses how to use Windows Explorer effectively and customize it to make it easier to use. Windows Explorer in Windows XP Professional offers a new look and new functionality, and like its predecessors in earlier versions of Windows, includes a host of configuration options that you can use to customize its behavior.

An administrator can limit the actions you can take in Windows Explorer. In particular, an administrator may remove the Folder Options item from the Tools menu to prevent you from configuring Windows Explorer. An administrator may remove the File menu and the shortcut menu from Windows Explorer, and they can also restrict you in many other ways, from hiding drives so that you can't see them to limiting the changes you can make to the Recycle Bin. This chapter mentions some of the restrictions you may find imposed on you.

Understanding What Windows Explorer Is and Does

At the simplest level, Windows Explorer is the file-management application for Windows XP Professional, as it is for all previous 32-bit versions of Windows. (Windows 3.x used File Manager.) Windows Explorer provides a strong set of graphical tools for creating, deleting, and otherwise manipulating files and folders. For example, you can copy or move a file from one folder to another by dragging it from a Windows Explorer window containing the source folder to a Windows Explorer window containing the destination folder. Or you can set the properties for a folder by selecting and clearing check boxes in a graphical applet launched from Windows Explorer.

If you prefer, you can perform most file-management functions equally well from the command prompt, but doing so involves far more typing. So most users stay with Windows Explorer. Some prefer other graphical file-management tools, such as Ontrack Data International's PowerDesk Pro (www.ontrack.com/powerdesk) or WinAbility Corporation's AB Commander (www.winability.com/abcommander), which offer capabilities beyond those that Windows Explorer provides.

Beyond its file-management role, Windows Explorer is the shell for Windows XP. Windows Explorer runs the Windows desktop and graphical user interface (GUI) in much the same way that Program Manager did in Windows 3.x. If Windows Explorer crashes, your desktop goes with it, which makes it hard for you to interact with your computer. The Start button, taskbar, notification area, and all your desktop icons disappear. (If you want to try this, save all work and close all applications you care about; then use the Processes tab of Task Manager to kill the process called explorer.)

When this happens, Windows Explorer is supposed to restart manually. If it doesn't, you can usually restart it manually by using Task Manager. Display Task Manager by pressing CTRL-ALT-DELETE and (in a domain environment) clicking the Task Manager button in the Windows Security dialog box. Click the New Task button on the Applications tab, enter **explorer** in the Create New Task dialog box, and click OK. Task Manager restarts the Windows Explorer shell, which restores the Start button, taskbar, notification area, your desktop icons, and the functionality they bring.

Beyond providing file-management functions and the Windows XP Professional shell, Windows Explorer is also closely related to Internet Explorer, as its name suggests. If you point Windows Explorer at a URL, Windows Explorer transforms itself into Internet Explorer. Likewise, you can point Internet Explorer at a local folder, and it will take on many of the traits of Windows Explorer, although it won't change the name of its window. (This assumes that your copy of Windows XP Professional includes Internet Explorer as its browser. If you have an OEM package of Windows XP that replaces Internet Explorer with a third-party browser, Windows XP Professional will behave differently.)

This book uses the term "Windows Explorer" to refer to Windows Explorer's file-management functionality and the windows used for this functionality. For other items, such as Control Panel (which is a customized Windows Explorer window), it uses their given names for clarity.

Understanding Windows Explorer's New Looks and Behavior

If you're coming to Windows XP Professional from an earlier version of Windows, you'll notice significant differences in the way that Windows Explorer in Windows XP Professional presents information. You may want to change some of the default settings so that the new version of Windows Explorer isn't so different from previous versions.

Like Windows Explorer in earlier versions of Windows, Windows Explorer in Windows XP Professional offers two different modes: Explore mode and Open mode. Explore mode displays the Folders Explorer bar on the left of the Explorer window, providing quick navigation between the drives, folders, and other locations displayed in the Folders Explorer bar. Open mode doesn't display the Folders Explorer bar, but you can display it manually.

WebView and ListView

Unlike in Windows Explorer in previous versions of Windows, Open mode in Windows XP's Windows Explorer includes two new features, WebView and ListView, which occupy the area taken up in Explore mode by the Folders Explorer bar. WebView and ListView display two, three, or four collapsible panes that provide access to items such as special tasks related to the current folder, File and Folder Tasks, Other Places, See Also recommendations, and Details about the current selection. These panes appear only when the Windows Explorer window is wide enough to accommodate them and the list of the folder's contents comfortably. When you make the window too narrow, Windows Explorer automatically hides the panes.

Figure 8-1 shows the My Documents folder in Open mode. You can see the File and Folder Tasks pane, the Other Places pane, and the Details pane. The File and Folder Tasks pane offers a selection of tasks that you can perform on the currently selected file (in this case) or folder. (This selection varies depending on the file or folder selected.) The Other

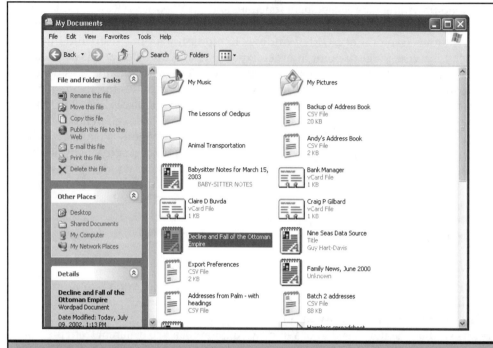

Figure 8-1. *Windows Explorer in Windows XP Professional uses the new WebView and ListView features by default. WebView and ListView display collapsible panes of tasks, links, and details.*

Places pane displays a short list of locations that you may want to access directly from the current folder: in this case, the desktop, the Shared Documents folder, the My Computer folder, and the My Network Places folder. The Details pane displays details on the currently selected file or folder (if any). You can toggle any pane between being displayed and being collapsed by clicking its heading bar.

Note *If on your computer Windows Explorer initially displays the Folders Explorer bar rather than the task panes, click the Folders button on the toolbar to display the task panes.*

By default, the Start menu contains several shortcuts for launching Windows Explorer windows: the My Documents, My Pictures, My Music, My Computer, and My Network Places links. Clicking one of these shortcuts displays the specified folder in Open mode in a Windows Explorer window. To open one of these folders in Explore mode, right-click the shortcut and choose Explore from the shortcut menu.

You can also open a Windows Explorer window in Explore mode by choosing Start | All Programs | Accessories | Windows Explorer or entering **explorer** in the Run dialog box. By default, this window displays the My Documents folder.

WebView and ListView aim to simplify navigation around the folders that Microsoft intends you to use for your documents and settings: the My Documents folder, My Music folder, My Pictures folder, My Videos folder, My Computer folder, My Network Places folder, Control Panel, and so on. But for anyone used to the Folders Explorer bar, navigating via the Other Places pane can be slower than navigating via the folder tree, because you may need to follow two or three links in the Other Places pane to reach a destination.

Similarly, WebView and ListView try to simplify the manipulation of objects such as files and folders in Windows Explorer by displaying in the File and Folder Tasks pane the most widely used commands available for the currently selected object. In previous versions of Windows, these commands were available from the shortcut menu for the object and from the menu bar menus, but usability labs found that four out of five users didn't use the shortcut menu effectively. So Microsoft has added WebView and ListView to Windows Explorer in Windows XP Professional for these four out of five users while still including all the commands on the shortcut menu and the menu bar menus for the fifth user.

If you're that fifth user, you can turn off WebView and ListView permanently. Choose Tools | Folder Options from an Explorer window to display the Folder Options dialog box. (If there's no Folder Options item on the Tools menu, an administrator has restricted the changes you can make.) On the General tab, select the Use Windows Classic Folders option button instead of the Show Common Tasks in Folders option button.

Alternatively, you can click the Folders button on the Standard Buttons toolbar to toggle the display of the Folders Explorer bar in place of the WebView and ListView panes. With the Folders Explorer bar displayed, Windows Explorer has the two-pane view that you're probably familiar with from Windows Explorer in earlier versions of Windows. You can expand a collapsed item in the Folders Explorer bar by double-clicking it or by clicking the + sign to its left. You can collapse an expanded item in the Folders Explorer bar by double-clicking it or by clicking the – sign to its left. And you can move or copy folders by dragging them from one location to another in the Folders Explorer bar.

 If you want Windows Explorer to open each window in Explore mode rather than Open mode by default, edit its file type (as discussed in "Editing a File Type to Change Its Behavior," later in this chapter) and set the Explore action as the default instead of the Open action.

Navigating to Hidden Folders

WebView and ListView also try to discourage you from accessing system files and program files directly via Windows Explorer. By default, when you double-click the icon for the hard disk drive on which Windows XP Professional is installed, Windows Explorer displays a screen telling you "These files are hidden. This folder contains files that keep your system working properly. You should not modify its contents." To see the contents of the drive, click either the Show the Contents of This Drive link in the System Tasks panel or the Show the Contents of This Folder in the main window.

Windows Explorer then shows you the files and folders that aren't protected and hidden. With the protected operating system files hidden, the default structure consists of the Documents and Settings folder, the Program Files folder, and the %Windir% folder (for example, WINDOWS).

If you try to open the Program Files folder or the %Windir% folder, Windows Explorer displays another screen telling you that the files are hidden and that you shouldn't modify them. Again, you need to click the Show the Contents of This Folder link to view the items in the folder. However, you can display the contents of the Documents and Settings folder. You'll find this folder contains an All Users subfolder that contains items common to all users of the computer and a subfolder for each user who has so far logged on to the computer. (Windows XP Professional creates a user's folder structure the first time the user logs on to the computer, not when an administrator creates the user's user account.)

To display hidden files and folders, select the Show Hidden Files and Folders option button instead of the Do Not Show Hidden Files and Folders option button on the View tab of the Folder Options dialog box (Tools | Folder Options). To display protected operating system files, clear the Hide Protected Operating System Files check box on the View tab and then click the Yes button in the Warning dialog box that Windows XP Professional displays.

Once you've displayed hidden files and folders and protected operating system files, the Windows Explorer window for your system drive displays a RECYCLER folder and a System Volume Information folder as well as the Documents and Settings folder, Program Files folder, and %Windir% folder. Depending on the setup of your computer, you'll probably also see the paging file (pagefile.sys), hibernation file (hiberfil.sys), and error log file (ERRORLOG.TXT). "Configuring the Paging File" in Chapter 39 discusses how to configure the paging file for optimum performance.

The %Windir% folder contains your Windows system files. Typically, you'll need to work with the contents of this folder only when things go severely wrong with Windows XP. For example, you might need to access the %Windir% folder directly to repair the Registry.

The Program Files folder is the default location for your application files. Most 32-bit Windows applications are designed to install into the Program Files folder by default. If the drive on which your Program Files folder is located becomes too crowded, you can edit the Registry to temporarily redirect the Program Files folder so as to install applications elsewhere. You normally won't need to work directly in the Program Files folder unless you need to remove an application's files manually.

The Documents and Settings folder holds the folder that contains each user's user profile, which we'll examine in a moment, and the All Users shared profile, as mentioned a moment ago. When you display hidden files and folders and protected operating system files and folders, you also see the Default User folder, the LocalService folder, and the NetworkService folder. The Default User folder contains default settings that are applied when you create a new user profile. The LocalService folder contains files used by local services. The NetworkService folder contains files used by network services. Windows XP Professional keeps these folders locked, because you don't need to access them.

If your computer connects to a domain, your My Documents folder may not actually be located on your computer's hard drive, even if Windows Explorer shows it as being there. The domain administrator may have redirected the Documents and Settings folder to a network location, either for ease of backup and for security or to enable you to use roaming profiles to access your data from any computer on the network rather than just one computer.

You'll easily be able to tell whether your My Documents folder has been redirected. Click the Start button to display the Start menu, right-click the My Documents item, choose Properties from the shortcut menu, and check the location shown in the Target Folder Location text box on the Target tab of the My Documents Properties dialog box. Another indication is that the My Documents folder icon in Windows Explorer windows will include the redirection symbol, a small white square with two blue arrows circling clockwise. This icon appears over the lower-left corner of the folder icon.

If your My Documents folder has been redirected, you won't be able to move it. If your My Documents folder hasn't been redirected, and an administrator hasn't prevented you from moving it, you can move it by clicking the Move button on the Target tab of the Properties dialog box and following the resulting dialog boxes. When you move your My Documents folder, you can choose whether to move the folder's contents as well (including the My Music folder, My Pictures folder, and My Videos folder).

If you have a roaming profile, all your user profile folders are stored on the network so that you can access them from whichever computer you log on.

Folders Contained in a User Profile

A user profile contains the folders listed in Table 8-1.

Folder	Explanation
My Documents or *Username's* Documents	This is the "real" folder that you see as your My Documents folder. It may appear as either My Documents or as *Username's* Documents when viewed in Windows Explorer in the Documents and Settings folder. If a domain administrator has redirected the folder (for example, to a folder on a networked drive), it doesn't appear in the user profile. This folder contains the My Music folder, My Pictures folder, and (after the user starts working with videos) My Videos folder. These folders are also redirected if the My Documents folder is redirected.

Table 8-1. *Folders in a User Profile*

Folder	Explanation
Application Data	This folder contains application-related data such as your Outlook Express identities, your credentials (including your user account's SID), system certificates (including certificate revocation lists or CRLs), your address book, and Internet Explorer settings such as the contents of your Quick Launch toolbar. If a domain administrator has redirected this folder, it doesn't appear in the user profile.
Cookies	This folder contains your *cookie files*—text files used by web sites to store user-specific information so that they can customize the content they present.
Desktop	This folder contains the files, folders, and shortcuts you've placed on their desktop. It doesn't include standard desktop shortcuts such as the Recycle Bin. If a domain administrator has redirected this folder, it doesn't appear in the user profile.
Favorites	This folder contains your favorites (bookmarks) for Explorer and Internet Explorer. The Links subfolder contains the shortcuts that appear on the Links bar in Internet Explorer (and on the desktop's Links toolbar).
Local Settings	This folder contains folders for Application Data (another Application Data folder, one that contains various items including the default CD Burning folder), your browsing history in Internet Explorer, your temporary Internet files (content cached to speed up browsing), and temporary files (files created by applications to store content temporarily while they're working).
My Recent Documents	This folder contains shortcuts to the documents and folders you've accessed recently. This folder feeds the My Recent Documents submenu that appears by default on the Start menu, but it also contains shortcuts to many more recent documents than appear on the Recent Documents submenu.
NetHood	This folder contains the data on the network connections available to the computer. This data appears in the My Network Places folder.
PrintHood	This folder contains your mappings to network printers.

Table 8-1. *Folders in a User Profile* (continued)

Folder	Explanation
SendTo	This folder contains the shortcuts and locations that appear on your Send To menu. Adding a shortcut or folder to this folder adds it to the Send To menu.
Start Menu	This folder contains the shortcuts and folders that appear on your Start menu. If a domain administrator has redirected this folder, it doesn't appear in the user profile.
Templates	This folder contains your user templates. (Some applications may store their templates in other folders.)
WINDOWS	This folder can contain Windows XP Professional settings. In some cases, this folder may be empty.

Table 8-1.   *Folders in a User Profile* (continued)

A user profile also contains the files NTUSER.DAT, NTUSER.DAT.LOG, and NTUSER.INI. Table 8-2 explains these files.

File	Explanation
NTUSER.DAT	This data file contains user-specific information for the Registry. (See Chapter 40 for a discussion of what the Registry is and what it does.)
NTUSER.DAT.LOG	This file contains a log of changes to NTUSER.DAT. Note that if Windows Explorer is configured to hide file extensions for known file types, NTUSER.DAT is listed as NTUSER, and NTUSER.DAT.LOG is listed as NTUSER.DAT, making it easy to confuse these two files.
NTUSER.INI	This file contains initialization information for the user's profile.

Table 8-2.   *Files in a User Profile*

Understanding Files and Folders

If you've worked with a computer at all, you've almost certainly used files and folders. As you know, a *file* is a named object that you use for storing information on a drive. A *folder* is a special type of file that contains files and subfolders.

You can store files and folders on any writable drive that you can access and on which you have permission to create objects. Such a drive can be anything from a *local hard drive* (a physical or logical drive on a hard disk installed on your local computer) to a *networked drive* (a physical or logical drive on a hard disk installed on a network server or web server), a recordable CD or DVD, a removable drive such as a FireWire drive or USB drive, or a floppy disk. Windows XP Professional stores the information contained in a file or folder in one or more clusters on the disk in question, using the file system that the disk uses—for example, FAT12 for a floppy disk, UDF for a recordable CD, or NTFS (for preference) for a hard disk on the local computer or on the server. (A *cluster* is a unit of storage space on a disk.)

Filenames and folder names can be up to 260 characters long, including the directory path to the file or folder. (If you create a folder name that's 260 characters long, you won't be able to create files in it, so it's best to keep folder names considerably shorter.) Filenames and folder names can use all letters and numbers, most punctuation, and most symbols, but can't contain the following characters:

```
*  ?  :  /  \  "  <  >  |
```

Windows XP Professional isn't case sensitive the way Unix and Linux are. To Windows XP, the filenames hello.wav, Hello.wav, and HELLO.WAV all refer to the same file, whereas to Unix and Linux these filenames represent three different files. However, Windows XP Professional preserves the case that you apply to filenames, so it won't change hello.wav to HELLO.WAV.

If you've used Windows 95 extensively, you'll probably remember that it actually stored filenames in the 8.3 format (a filename of up to eight characters, and an extension of up to three letters, with a period separating the two) and overlaid a table of long filenames for the benefit of users and 32-bit applications. Sometimes problems occurred that disrupted the table of long filenames, so files you'd given long filenames suddenly appeared with names in 8.3 format. For example, Tax Workbook 1995.xls would appear only as TAXWOR~1.XLS, which made it difficult to recognize, particularly if there were other files with TAXWOR~ names in the same folder.

Unlike Windows 95, Windows XP Professional actually stores the filenames and folder names in their long format. But so that 16-bit programs can access the files, it maintains a table of short filenames in the 8.3 format. So your file Tax Workbook 2002.xls is stored under that filename, but your 16-bit accounting application can access it under a name such as TAXWOR~9.XLS. When a 16-bit application tries to save an existing file under an 8.3 name, Windows XP Professional saves the file under the existing filename but tells the 16-bit application that it has saved it under the 8.3 name. By contrast, when a 16-bit program creates a new file, it receives the name you specify in the Save As dialog box, which is limited by the capabilities of the 16-bit program. So for these files, the 8.3

filename is the same as the filename under which Windows XP Professional actually saves the file.

Using Views Effectively

To navigate Windows Explorer effectively, make yourself familiar with the views that Windows Explorer offers and what they're best suited for. Table 8-3 lists the views with explanations and comments. To apply a view, choose it from the View menu, the View button's drop-down menu, or the View submenu on the shortcut menu.

Within a view, you can arrange the icons by Name, Size, Type (file type), or Modified (the date on which the file was last modified). Some folders offer other arrangements beyond these basic ones. To arrange the icons, choose the view from the Arrange Icons By submenu on the View menu or shortcut menu.

The Arrange Icons By submenu also offers the Auto Arrange option and the Align to Grid option. The Auto Arrange option causes Windows Explorer to keep the icons

View	Explanation and Comments
Thumbnails	Displays a miniature version of a graphics file and a large icon for any other file type or folder. Good for sorting and manipulating graphics. In Thumbnails view, you can rotate multiple graphics at a time.
Tiles	Displays a mid-sized icon for each file and folder together with brief details about each (for example, file type and size). Good only for folders that contain few items.
Icons	Displays a small icon and the name for each file and folder. Good for navigating folders that contain too many items to navigate in Tiles view but not a huge number of items.
List	Displays a minute icon and the name for each file or folder. Good for navigating busy folders.
Details	Displays a minute icon for each file or folder together with customizable columns of details, such as the file size, file type, and date modified. You can sort by any column by clicking its heading: Click once for an ascending sort, and click again for a descending sort. Good for quickly locating files by name or other details.
Filmstrip	Available only for folders that use the Photo Album folder template or the Pictures folder template. Displays a small preview of each graphic in a filmstrip-like row across the bottom of the window and a larger view of the selected graphic in the main part of the window.

Table 8-3. *Windows Explorer Views and When to Use Them*

arranged automatically in the specified order rather than letting them stray. The Align to Grid option controls whether Windows Explorer arranges the icons according to an invisible grid or allows you to place them wherever you like.

The Arrange Icons By submenu also includes the Show in Groups option, which is a bit more complex and is described in the next section.

The only view that you can customize is Details view. To customize Details view, take either of the following actions:

- Choose View | Choose Details and use the Choose Details dialog box to specify which detail columns to display, the width at which to display them, and the order in which to display them.

- In Details view, right-click a column heading and choose a column from the shortcut menu. (Choosing an already displayed column hides it. Choosing a hidden column displays it.) To change the order in which columns appear, drag a column heading to its new position.

Understanding the Show in Groups Option

Windows Explorer in Windows XP Professional includes a new view arrangement option named Show in Groups, which divides items into categories. You can toggle Show in Groups on and off by issuing a Show in Groups command from the View | Arrange Icons By submenu or the Arrange Items By submenu on the shortcut menu for an Explorer window.

The canonical example of Show in Groups is the My Computer folder, which uses this option by default. Figure 8-2 shows the My Computer folder in its default view, with resources divided into groups by Type.

Table 8-4 explains the groups into which the My Computer folder divides its contents by type.

If you choose to display Control Panel in My Computer, it appears in another category—Other.

You can use the Show in Groups option for any arrangement available from the Arrange Icons By submenu, but only some of the resulting groupings are useful. For example, if you choose Arrange Icons By | Name and Arrange Icons By | Show in Groups for the My Computer folder, you get an alphabetically separated list of drives and objects arranged by the alphabetical order of their names. This is useless. Marginally more usefully, you can arrange the objects by the amount of space they have free.

Another folder that uses the Show in Groups option by default is the Network Connections folder, which by default displays the network connections in groups by type: Dial-up, Incoming, LAN or High-Speed Internet, and Virtual Private Network. You can arrange these icons by Name, Type, Status, Device Name, or Owner.

Other folders for which the Show in Groups option can be useful are the My Network Places folder (which contains links to the network drives available to your computer) and the Printers and Faxes folder (which contains links to all printers and faxes for which

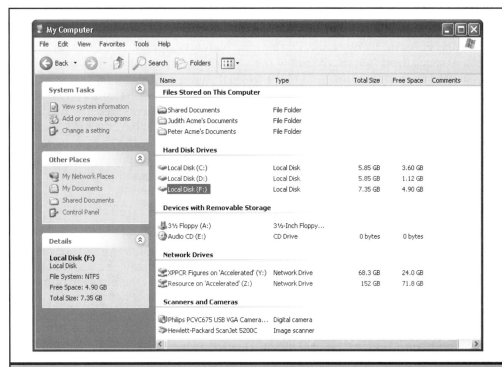

Figure 8-2.   *The My Computer folder uses the Show in Groups arrangement option by default, dividing up the folders, drives, and resources attached to the computer by type.*

Category	Description
Files Stored on This Computer	Each user's My Documents folder and the Shared Documents folder (which is shared among all users of the computer)
Hard Disk Drives	Volumes on hard disks on this computer
Devices with Removable Storage	Removable media such as floppy disks, Zip disks, CD and DVD drives, and memory-card drives (CompactFlash, SmartMedia, MemoryStick)
Network Drives	Network drives to which the user currently has mappings
Scanners and Cameras	Items for any scanners, digital still cameras, or digital video cameras attached to the computer

Table 8-4.   *My Computer Resources by Type*

entries have been defined on your computer). You can arrange the My Network Places folder by Name, Comments, Computer, or Network Location; and you can arrange the Printers and Faxes folder by Name, Documents, Status, Comments, Location, or Model.

In less specialized folders, the Show in Groups option tends to be less useful, but you may find it worth experimenting with to see if some of the groupings suit you. For example, in a documents folder, you can use the Show in Groups option with files arranged by the Modified attribute to get a view of when documents were last modified: Today, Yesterday, Two Months Ago, Earlier This Year, Last Year, Two Years Ago, and (quaintly) A Long Time Ago. These groups can be helpful for locating a document that you know was last modified in a specific timeframe. (Search Companion, discussed in "Searching for Files and Folders," later in this chapter, lets you specify a timeframe for when a file or folder you're searching for was created or modified.)

Making Folders Retain Their View Settings

If you apply different view settings to different folders, you can force Windows Explorer to remember the view used for each folder by selecting the Remember Each Folder's View Settings check box in the Advanced Settings group box on the View tab of the Folder Options dialog box (Tools | Folder Options).

Using the Same View for All Folders

To use the same view for all folders you open in Windows Explorer, choose that view in the current folder. Then choose Tools | Folder Options, click the Apply to All Folders button on the View tab of the Folder Options dialog box, and choose the Yes button in the Folder Views dialog box. Any folders open when you apply this view retain their current view until you close and reopen them.

To reset all folders to their Windows XP Professional default views, click the Reset All Folders button on the View tab of the Folder Options dialog box.

Opening a New Window to the Current Folder's Parent

To open a new window to the parent of the current folder, hold down CTRL and click the Up button.

Compressing Files, Folders, and Drives

Windows XP Professional supports three forms of compression: Cabinet files, Zip files, and compression on NTFS drives. Each form of compression helps you pack more data into less disk space, but the forms of compression are substantially different from one another. You'll benefit from understanding the differences, which the following sections discuss.

Opening and Creating Cabinet (CAB) Folders

Windows XP Professional can open files in the Cabinet (CAB) format. Microsoft packages files for distribution in CAB files. For example, the Windows XP Professional CD includes various CAB files, and Windows XP Professional caches backup copies of driver files in the file %Windir%\Driver Cache\i386\driver.cab.

To open a CAB file, double-click it. Windows XP Professional displays it in an Explorer window as if it were a regular folder.

You're unlikely to need to create CAB files, but Windows XP Professional includes the command-line MAKECAB.EXE utility for doing so. Type **MAKECAB /?** at a command prompt to see the options for the utility.

Creating and Using Zip Folders

Windows XP Professional includes built-in support for opening and creating folders in the widely used Zip format, so that you no longer need a third-party Zip application (such as WinZip or TurboZip).

- Double-click a Zip folder to open it in an Explorer window. To work with a file, you need to extract it from the Zip folder. You can extract it by explicitly issuing an Extract command (choose File | Extract All or click the Extract All Files link in the Folder Tasks pane) or by implicitly issuing an Extract command (for example, drag the file to another folder).

- To compress a selected file to a Zip folder that shares the filename (but not the extension), issue a Send To | Compressed (Zipped) Folder command from the File or shortcut menu.

- To create an empty Zip folder, issue a New | Compressed (Zipped) Folder command from the File or shortcut menu for the folder in which you want to create it. Rename the folder from the default name of New Compressed (Zipped) Folder and then add files and folders to the Zip folder by using drag-and-drop.

 If you don't want to use Windows XP's Zip features, you can unregister them by running the command regsvr32 /u%Windir%\system32\zipfldr.dll from the Run dialog box or from a command prompt. To reregister the Zip features after unregistering them, run the command regsvr32 %Windir%\system32\zipfldr.dll.

Using NTFS Compression

Windows XP Professional can compress files, folders, or entire drives stored on partitions that use NTFS. (Windows XP Professional can't compress FAT32 drives.) In most cases, it makes most sense to compress a whole drive to save as much space as possible.

Compression lets you store more files on your drives, but it slows down access to files because each file needs to be decompressed. If you have a slow hard drive and need to open huge databases or graphical files, or play back large audio or video files, compression may cause a problem. Otherwise, access speed usually isn't a problem.

More of a problem is that you can't use encryption on a compressed file, folder, or drive. If you need to encrypt files or folders, you can't compress them as well. If you need to encrypt only some files or folders, consider keeping them on a separate encrypted drive.

Figure 8-3.   *In the Advanced Attributes dialog box for a file or folder, you can apply (or remove) compression or encryption, but not both at once.*

To compress or decompress a whole drive, display its Properties dialog box, select or clear the Compress Drive to Save Disk Space check box as appropriate, and click the OK button. Windows XP Professional displays the Confirm Attribute Changes dialog box, asking you to decide whether to apply the change to only the drive or to the drive, its subfolders, and their files. Choose the appropriate option button and click the OK button. Windows XP Professional then compresses (or decompresses) the drive. The larger the drive, and the more contents it has, the longer compression or decompression takes.

To compress or decompress a file or folder, display its Properties dialog box and click the Advanced button on the General tab to display the Advanced Attributes dialog box (Figure 8-3). Select or clear the Compress Contents to Save Disk Space check box and click the OK button.

When you click the OK button to close the Properties dialog box for a folder that contains subfolders, Windows XP Professional displays the Confirm Attribute Changes dialog box, asking you to decide whether to apply the change to only this folder or to the folder, its subfolders, and files as well. Choose the appropriate option button and click the OK button. Windows XP Professional then compresses (or decompresses) the file, folder, or folders.

Using the Windows Explorer Toolbars

Windows Explorer has three built-in toolbars: the Standard Buttons toolbar, Address Bar, and Links bar. You can toggle the display of these toolbars by selecting their entries on the View | Toolbars submenu or the shortcut menu displayed by right-clicking any displayed toolbar.

The Standard Buttons toolbar is displayed by default and contains the following buttons:

- **Back button and Forward button**   For navigating along the folder trail. Each button has a drop-down list button to allow you to jump forward or back several steps at once.

- **Up button**   For moving up one level in the folder hierarchy—in other words, to the current folder's parent folder.

- **Search button**   For toggling the display of the Search pane (discussed later in this chapter).

- **Folders button**   For toggling the display of the Folders Explorer bar. If you're using WebView and ListView, the Folders Explorer bar appears in their place.

- **Views button**   For displaying a drop-down menu of views you can apply.

To move back from the keyboard, press ALT+ ← *. To move forward, press* ALT+ → *. To move up one level, press* BACKSPACE. *To activate the Address Bar drop-down list, press* F4. *To refresh the display, press* F5. *You can also navigate by using View | Go To submenu.*

The Address Bar displays the name or address of the current folder. By default, it displays just the folder name, but most people find it more useful to make the Address Bar display the full name. To do so, select the Display the Full Path in the Address Bar check box in the Advanced Settings list box on the View tab of the Folder Options dialog box. Once you've displayed the Address Bar, you can use it to navigate to a folder by using either type-down addressing or the drop-down list of drives and key folders.

The Links bar is Internet Explorer's Links toolbar and provides a customizable set of buttons to URLs or local addresses.

Rearranging the Windows Explorer Toolbars

You can rearrange the Windows Explorer toolbars by unlocking them and then dragging their handles to where you want them to appear. To unlock or lock the toolbars, choose View | Toolbars | Lock the Toolbars or right-click any displayed toolbar and choose Lock the Toolbars from the shortcut menu.

Customizing the Windows Explorer Toolbars

You can customize the Windows Explorer toolbars and the Internet Explorer toolbars by choosing View | Toolbars | Customize or right-clicking any displayed toolbar and choosing Customize from the shortcut menu and working in the resulting Customize Toolbar dialog box (Figure 8-4). This dialog box lets you move buttons from the Available Toolbar Buttons reservoir to the toolbar (and vice versa); rearrange the order of buttons on the toolbar; choose whether to display text labels for all buttons, some, or none; and choose between large and small icons.

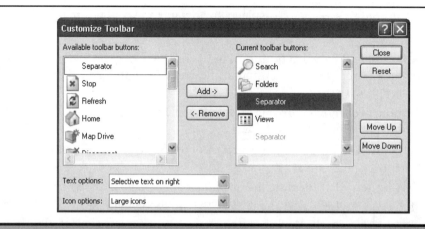

Figure 8-4.   *You can customize the Windows Explorer and Internet Explorer toolbars by using the Customize Toolbar dialog box.*

Customizing Windows Explorer's Behavior

You can customize some aspects of Windows Explorer's behavior by choosing settings in the Folder Options dialog box (Tools | Folder Options). This chapter has described some of the key settings already. This section mentions other settings that you may want to experiment with.

General Tab Options

The General tab of the Folder Options dialog box lets you choose between using WebView and ListView (Show Common Tasks in Folders option button) and using Windows classic folders; between opening each folder in the same window and opening each folder in its own window (as Windows 95 used to do by default), and between single-clicking and double-clicking to open an object.

Click the Restore Defaults button to restore the default settings for the options on this tab.

View Tab Options

The View tab of the Folder Options dialog box lets you apply your current view to all folders and reset Windows XP Professional's default views on all folders. The Advanced Settings list box offers settings for the following:

- Searching automatically for folders and printers on network drives.
- Displaying file-size information when you hold the mouse pointer over a folder. This option doesn't affect the display of file-size information when you hold the mouse pointer over a file: File-size information for a file is always displayed.

■ Using Simple Folder view in the Folders Explorer bar. Simple Folder view displays only folders you've expanded in the Folders Explorer bar rather than displaying the full list of files.

■ Displaying the contents of system folders (such as the %Windir% folder and the Program Files folder) instead of hiding them.

■ Displaying the full path in the Address Bar (when you have the Address Bar displayed) and the title bar of a Windows Explorer window instead of just displaying the folder's name. Displaying the full path makes it easier to see which subfolder you're viewing.

■ Turning off the caching of thumbnails—the mini versions of graphics files used for Thumbnails view. By default, caching is on, and Windows XP Professional saves the thumbnails for all the graphics in a folder in a hidden file named Thumbs.db in that folder. Turning off caching saves disk space but forces Windows XP Professional to create the thumbnails again the next time you open the folder in Thumbnail view.

■ Toggling the display of hidden files and folders on and off.

■ Displaying or hiding extensions for file types registered with Windows XP Professional. By default, these extensions are hidden. This option isn't as clean-cut as it seems. See "Customizing File Types," later in this chapter, for a discussion of file types and extensions.

■ Displaying or hiding protected operating system files. These files are hidden by default.

■ Opening each folder window in a separate process instead of in the same process. Using separate processes should reduce the risk of Windows Explorer crashing, but doing so requires more RAM. The default setting is to open each folder window in the same process.

■ Remembering each folder's view setting, allowing you to customize the view used for each folder.

■ Reopening Explorer windows when you log on to the same folders you had open when you logged off (the Restore Previous Folder Windows at Logon check box). By default, Windows XP Professional doesn't do this.

■ Displaying an entry for Control Panel in the My Computer window. By default, Windows XP Professional doesn't.

■ Displaying encrypted files and compressed files in a different color to make them stand out. This option is on by default in Windows XP Professional.

■ Displaying an information pop-up when you hold the mouse pointer over an item on the desktop.

■ Using Windows XP's Simple File Sharing permissions rather than Windows XP Professional's full set of permissions. This option applies only to standalone and workgroup computers and is on by default for them.

Click the Restore Defaults button to restore the default settings for the options on this tab.

Searching for Files and Folders

Windows XP's Search Companion provides powerful search capabilities for finding files and folders that match criteria you specify. Search Companion has two search modes, Standard (the default) and Advanced. Standard mode uses a step-by-step interface that leads you through entering your criteria. Advanced mode dispenses with the steps, letting you search more quickly. The first time you use Search Companion, try its default settings to see how well they suit you. After that, you may well want to use only Advanced mode.

If you already have a Windows Explorer window open when you want to start searching, click the Search button on the Standard Buttons toolbar to launch Search Companion. Alternatively, choose File | Search. If you don't have a Windows Explorer window open, choose Start | Search. Windows XP Professional opens a Search Results window with Search Companion displayed.

Searching in Standard Search Mode

By default, Search Companion launches in Standard mode, which starts by asking you to choose what you want to search for: Pictures, Music, or Video; Documents; All Files and Folders; or Computers or People. The step-by-step search procedures are easy, but it's worth understanding the following:

- Searching for All Files and Folders gives you the most flexibility in specifying search criteria. Clicking this link puts you into Advanced mode, discussed in "Searching in Advanced Mode," later in this chapter.

- Searching for "pictures" makes Search Companion search for files in a wide variety of picture formats, including JPEG (JPG), GIF, BMP, and TIF.

- Searching for "music" files makes Search Companion search for files in various audio formats including WMA, MP3, RealAudio (RAM), WAV, and others.

- Searching for "video" files makes Search Companion search for files in assorted video formats including MPEG and AVI.

- Searching for Computers or People lets you choose between searching for a computer on your network and searching your Address Book for people.

- For most of the Standard mode process, Search Companion displays a Back button that you can use to return to the previous step and make a different choice. When there's no Back button, you can double-click the Search button on the Standard Buttons toolbar to reset Search Companion.

After a successful search, Search Companion in Standard mode displays links for telling it you've finished searching, making future searches faster (by using Indexing Service, discussed in the next section), refining the current search, and starting a new search. You can open a found file by double-clicking its filename in the list, and you can open the folder that contains one of the found files by right-clicking the filename and choosing Open Containing Folder from the shortcut menu.

Customizing Search Companion's Behavior

You can customize Search Companion's behavior in the following ways by clicking the Change Preferences link and using the links on the resulting screen:

- Turn off the animated character (for Standard mode) or choose a different animated character.

- Switch Search Companion to Advanced mode by choosing Change Files and Folders Search Behavior | Advanced.

- Turn off Search Companion for Internet searches by choosing Change Internet Search Behavior | With Classic Internet Search.

- Change your default Internet search engine by choosing Change Internet Search Behavior and working on the resulting screen.

- Turn Balloon Tips and AutoComplete off or on.

- Turn on Indexing Service to speed up your searches. Using Indexing Service can make a big difference if you have a large number of files to search. Indexing Service builds and updates an index of your computer's files and contents when your computer has processor cycles to spare. By consulting the resulting catalogs, Search Companion can return search results faster.

Note *If your computer stores a large number of documents, you may want to configure Indexing Service to speed up its operations. You can launch Indexing Service from Search Companion by choosing Change Preferences | With Indexing Service | Change Indexing Service Settings. See "Configuring Indexing Service" in Chapter 39 for a discussion of how to configure Indexing Service.*

Searching in Advanced Mode

In Advanced mode, you can specify a comprehensive range of search criteria: all or part of the filename, one or more words or phrases in the file, where to search, when the file was created, last accessed, or last modified, and its size. Figure 8-5 shows Search Companion in Advanced mode with each of its three collapsible sections (When Was It Modified?, What Size Is It?, and More Advanced Options) expanded. The two sections shown in the figure appear in the same Search Companion pane, but we've split it up so that it doesn't take up a whole page in the book.

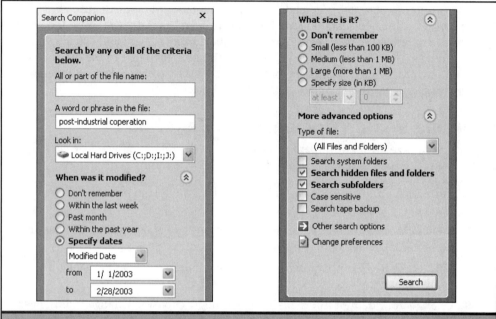

Figure 8-5.   *In Advanced mode, Search Companion lets you specify a wide range of search criteria.*

Most of the Advanced search options are easy to understand, but there are some subtleties to power-searching:

- When choosing criteria, include only those you're sure of. You'll find files faster by entering more general criteria and sorting or refining those results than by trying to be too specific and searching for criteria that get no matches.

- When specifying all or part of the filename, enter the most distinctive part of the filename. Include the extension if you're sure what it is.

- Use the wildcard **?** to represent one character and the wildcard ***** to represent any number of characters. (Use multiple question marks to represent one character each.)

- If you include the file extension in the All or Part of the File Name text box, Search Companion searches for files that have exactly that name. If you don't specify the extension or use wildcards, Search Companion searches for files whose names include the text you specify. For example, searching for **Project.doc** finds only the file named Project.doc. Searching for **Project** finds files with names such as Management Projects 2003.mdb and Executive Assistant Project File.xls as well as Project.doc.

■ When you specify multiple words (without a file extension) in the All or Part of the File Name text box, Search Companion treats them as an AND condition and searches for words that contain all the words. To create an OR condition, separate the search terms with semicolons (;).

■ Use the Case Sensitive check box for searching for case-sensitive words or phrases in the file. It's seldom worth searching for case-sensitive filenames.

■ By default, the When Was It Modified? options search by the date the file was last modified. To search by the date the file was created or the date it was last accessed, select the Specify Dates option button, choose Accessed Date or Created Date in the drop-down list, and specify the time period.

■ Don't select the Search System Folders check box or the Search Hidden Files and Folders check box when searching for documents unless you store your documents in your system folders. Use these search options only when searching for system files.

■ Select the Search Tape Backup check box only when you have to search a tape backup. Searching tapes takes far longer than searching local or networked drives.

■ Searching My Computer searches all hard drives, floppy drives, and removable media (including any CDs or DVDs in drives).

■ To search multiple drives or folders, type them into the Look In text box, using semicolons to separate them.

As with Standard mode, you can open a found file by double-clicking its filename in the list, and you can open the file that contains one of the found files by right-clicking the filename and choosing Open Containing Folder from the shortcut menu.

Customizing File Types

Like previous versions of Windows, Windows XP Professional maintains a table of registered file types. Each file type is associated with a specific file extension and a specific action in a specific application, so when you double-click a file of a registered file type, Windows XP Professional knows what action to take.

For example, if Microsoft Excel is installed on your computer, the XLS file extension is associated with the Microsoft Excel Worksheet file type. That file type is associated with the Open action in the Microsoft Excel for Windows application. So when you double-click a file that has the XLS file extension, Windows XP Professional opens the file in Excel.

How File Types and File Extensions Work

File types and extensions greatly increase the power and flexibility of Windows XP, but they bring with them some problems and subtleties that you need to understand, whether you choose to customize them or merely to use them. Windows XP Professional stores information on file types, file extensions, and their associations in the Registry. Windows XP Professional supplies some associations by default, and applications you install add their own associations or commandeer existing associations.

You can change file types and associations manually if necessary by working in the Folder Options dialog box, as described in this section. The most likely reason for needing to do so is that some installation routines steal associations from their current owners without consulting you. When this happens, you may need to return the associations to the previous application.

A *file extension* is the portion of the filename written after the last period in the filename. If that seems convoluted, it's because filenames in Windows XP Professional can include other periods, because the period character is permitted in filenames. So only the final period denotes the file extension. A file extension can be up to 200 characters long, but most extensions are three or four characters. For example, Microsoft Word documents use the DOC file extension, screensavers use the SCR file extension, MP3 files use the MP3 file extension (after which they're named), and web pages use the HTM or HTML file extension.

Files don't have to have file extensions, but in Windows, most files do have file extensions so that they're associated with a file type. If you double-click a file that doesn't have an extension, or that has a file type that isn't registered, Windows XP Professional prompts you with the Open With dialog box to choose an application to open the file.

A file extension can be associated with only one file type at a time so that Windows XP Professional knows which action to take for that file type. A file type can have any number of file extensions associated with it.

To specify the file type for a file, include the appropriate extension in the filename, either by typing it or choosing the file type in the Save As dialog box. Most applications automatically add a suitable file type if you don't explicitly specify one.

You can determine a file's file type in any of the following ways:

- By examining the file's entry in the Type column in Details view in a Windows Explorer window.

- By checking the Type of File readout on the General tab of the Properties dialog box for a file.

- By recognizing the icon used for the file. This may not be definitive because multiple file types can use the same icon. But it may be close enough for everyday work.

- By double-clicking the file and seeing which application (if any) Windows XP Professional opens it in. Again, this may not be definitive because many applications open various file types. And if the file is a script, executable, or malware, you may get unexpected or unpleasant results.

Making Windows XP Professional Display All File Extensions

By default, Windows XP Professional hides the file extensions for all registered file types. Windows XP Professional displays the extension for any file whose file extension indicates an unregistered file type.

There are three reasons for hiding file extensions:

- Many users don't really need to view file extensions most of the time.

- By hiding file extensions, Microsoft can make it much harder for users to inadvertently change a file's file extension by renaming it. When you rename a file with file extensions hidden, Windows XP Professional automatically adds the file's previous file extension to the new filename. By contrast, when you rename a file with file extensions displayed, you have to add the file extension to the new filename. (Windows XP Professional warns you if you change or omit the file extension.)

- Displaying file extensions for items such as the links on the Start menu spoil the looks of the Windows XP Professional interface.

Unfortunately, hiding file extensions also has bad effects:

- It's harder to tell what file type a file is (as discussed earlier).

- If you turn on the display of most file extensions, but others remain hidden (as discussed next), malicious hackers can exploit this inconsistency by sending you a file whose file extension is hidden but which appears to have a file extension denoting a safe file type. For example, the script file Your Salary Review.doc.js would appear to be called Your Salary Review.doc, which would suggest it's a Microsoft Word document file. Scripts can severely damage your data, application, and system files.

To display the file extensions for most file types, clear the Hide File Extensions for Known File Types check box on the View tab of the Folder Options dialog box (choose Tools | Folder Options from a Windows Explorer window). Clearing this check box makes Windows XP Professional display all file extensions except for those of shortcuts, URLs, script files, and some other special file types. Table 8-5 lists these file types.

Most of these file types appear in the Registered File Types list on the File Types tab of the Folder Options dialog box. You can force a file type to display its extension by selecting it in the list, clicking the Advanced button, and selecting the Always Show Extension check box in the resulting Edit File Type dialog box.

Some of these file types (for example, LNK and SCF) don't appear in the Registered File Types list. To force unlisted file types to display their extension, you need to create the file type first. To do so, click the New button on the View tab of the Folder Options dialog box. Enter the file extension in the Create New Extension dialog box and click the Advanced button. Windows Explorer automatically selects the appropriate file type

File Extension	Associated File Type (Default)
JOB	Task Object (a Task Scheduler job file)
JS	JScript Script File
JSE	JScript Encoded Script File
LNK	Shortcut File (including the links on the Start menu)
SCF	Windows Explorer Command File
SHB	Shortcut into a Document
URL	Internet Shortcut
VBE	VBScript Encoded Script File
VBS	VBScript Script File
WSF	Windows Script File

Table 8-5.   *File Extensions That You Have to Force Windows XP Professional to Display*

in the Associated File Type drop-down list. Click the OK button to finish creating the extension. You can then force the file type to always display its extension as described in the previous paragraph.

An easier way to display hidden file extensions is to use X-Setup (www.xteq.com/ products/xset). Choose Appearance | Files&Folders | Files | Show/Hide File Extensions.

Changing the Application That Opens a File Type

To change the application that Windows XP Professional uses to open any given file type, follow these steps:

1. Display the Open With dialog box (Figure 8-6) in either of these ways:

   - On the File Types tab of the Folder Options dialog box, select the file extension in the Registered File Types list box and click the Change button.

   - On the General page of the Properties dialog box for a file with the file extension you want to affect, click the Change button.

2. If the application you want to use is listed in the Programs list box, select it. If not, use the Browse button to locate it, or use the Look for the Appropriate Program on the web link to connect to the web and display Microsoft Application Search's information about the file type and file extension.

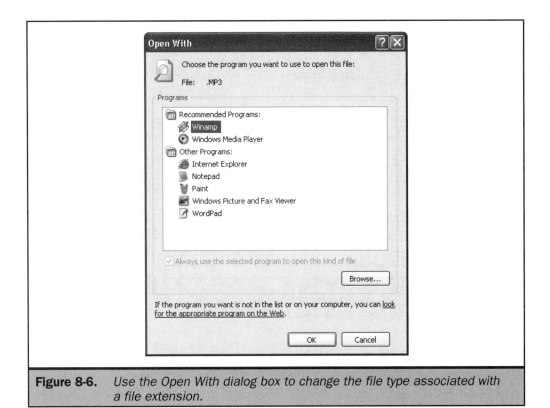

Figure 8-6.   *Use the Open With dialog box to change the file type associated with
a file extension.*

To restore the application previously used for the file type, select the file type in the
Registered File Types list box on the File Types tab of the Folder Options dialog box
and click the Restore button. (The File Types tab displays the Restore button in place of
the Advanced button when you change the application used for a file type. After you
use the Restore button, the File Types tab displays the Advanced button again.)

Editing a File Type to Change Its Behavior

As well as changing the application that Windows XP Professional uses to open any
given file type, you can change the action associated with a file type.

To change the action, select the file type in the Registered File Types list box on the
File Types tab of the Folder Options dialog box and click the Advanced button to display
the Edit File Type dialog box (Figure 8-7).

From the Edit File Type dialog box, you can do the following:

- Change the name of the file type and the icon Windows XP Professional displays
  for the file type.

- Apply a different existing action to the file type by selecting the action in the
  Actions list box and clicking the Set Default button.

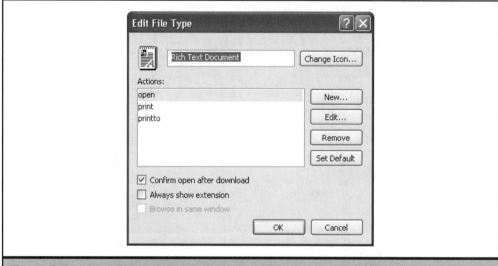

Figure 8-7.   *Work in the Edit File Type dialog box to change the name, icon, or associated action of a file type.*

■ Remove an existing action from the list in the Actions list box. Doing so removes the action from the File menu and the shortcut menu for the file type.

■ Edit an existing action to change what it does by clicking the Edit button and working in the Editing Action for Type dialog box. The controls in the Editing Action for Type dialog box are the same as those in the New Action dialog box, discussed in the next paragraph.

■ Create a new action for the file type. To do so, click the New button and work in the New Action dialog box. Enter the name for the action in the Action text box with an ampersand (&) before the letter you want Windows XP Professional to use as the access key. (For effect, each access key on the File menu or shortcut menu needs to be unique.) Enter the path and name of the application to use in the Application Used to Perform Actions text box. You can browse to the application's executable or type in the path and filename in double quotation marks. Add any parameters needed to make the application perform the action. If the application will need to use DDE (as some older applications do), select the Use DDE check box and enter the DDE details in the additional section of the New Action dialog box that Windows XP Professional displays.

■ If you will download files of this file type, select or clear the Confirm Open after Download check box as appropriate. If you want files of this file type to play automatically, clear this check box. Otherwise, leave it selected.

■ Select the Always Show Extension check box to force Windows XP Professional to always display the file extension for this file type.

- If the Browse in Same Window check box is available, select it to cause files of this file type to open in the current window instead of launching a new window.

Configuring AutoPlay

As discussed in Chapter 1, Windows XP Professional includes a version of AutoPlay that's significantly improved over the AutoPlay feature found in earlier versions of Windows. Windows XP's AutoPlay has two major improvements:

- AutoPlay applies not only to CDs and DVDs but also to other removable media, including CompactFlash, SmartMedia, and MemoryStick cards, Zip and other removable disks, and hot-pluggable drives.
- You can configure AutoPlay separately for different drives.

AutoPlay is enabled by default. To turn it off, or to configure it to take a specific action, follow these steps:

1. Open a My Computer window (Start | My Computer) and issue a Properties command for the drive you want to configure. Windows XP displays the Properties dialog box for the drive.

2. On the AutoPlay tab (shown on the left in Figure 8-8), select the content type in the drop-down list: Music Files, Pictures, Video Files, Mixed Content, Audio CD, or DVD Movie. Windows XP Professional displays the available actions in the Actions group box.

3. In the Actions group box, select the Select an Action to Perform option button and the action you want Windows XP Professional to perform for this type of content, or select the Prompt Me Each Time to Choose an Action option button. The actions vary depending on the type of content. For example, for the Pictures content type, you can choose among Copy Pictures to a Folder on My Computer, View a Slideshow of the Images, Print the Pictures, Open Folder to View Files, and Take No Action.

4. Repeat steps 2 and 3 for the other content types you'll use in this drive.

5. Close the Properties dialog box and repeat steps 1–4 for each other drive you want to configure AutoPlay on.

You can also configure AutoPlay more informally by using the dialog box that Windows XP Professional displays when you insert a medium on which AutoPlay can be used in a drive on which you haven't configured AutoPlay or you've configured AutoPlay to prompt you each time to choose an action for the content type the medium contains. (The screen on the right in Figure 8-8 shows an example of this dialog box for a DVD movie.) Choose the action you want to perform and select the Always Do the Selected Action check box if you want Windows XP Professional to perform it every time.

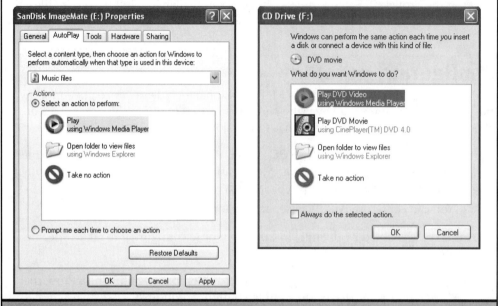

Figure 8-8. *You can configure AutoPlay either on the AutoPlay tab of the Properties dialog box for the drive in question (left) or in the dialog box that Windows XP Professional displays when you insert a medium on which AutoPlay can be used (right).*

Summary

This chapter has discussed how to use Windows Explorer and customize its behavior. It has talked about what files and folders are and how to compress them and drives, how to use views effectively, how to search for files and folders using Search Companion, how to customize file types and harness the power they offer, and how to configure AutoPlay.

The next chapter discusses how to install and uninstall applications.

Chapter 9

Installing and Uninstalling Applications

This chapter covers how to install and uninstall applications on Windows XP Professional. It starts by discussing which applications Windows XP Professional can run and the levels of permission required to install and uninstall applications. (You may be unable to install or uninstall any applications.) This chapter addresses how to install and uninstall applications manually and what you need to know about IntelliMirror, the Microsoft server-based technology that domain administrators can use to automate the installation and uninstallation of applications on networked computers. The chapter then details how to run and close applications and how to specify Compatibility mode options for applications that won't run without them. It explains your options for running Windows applications that won't run even in Compatibility mode and for running non-Windows applications on Windows XP Professional. Finally, this chapter discusses how to configure error reporting for both Windows XP itself and the applications you run on it.

Which Applications Can Windows XP Professional Run?

One of Microsoft's goals in designing Windows XP Professional was to make it run as many as possible of the 32-bit applications developed for Windows 2000, Windows NT, and Windows 9x. To help it run applications designed for earlier versions of Windows, Windows XP Professional includes a feature called *Compatibility mode,* which mimics the older version of Windows specified so that an application designed for a particular version of Windows can run on Windows XP as though it were running on that other version of Windows. Windows XP Professional also can run many 16-bit Windows applications (applications written to the Win16 application programming interface or API), 32-bit applications written to run on the Win32s extensions for 16-bit Windows, and DOS applications.

Windows XP Professional can't run applications designed for operating systems (OSes) other than Windows or DOS. For example, it can't run applications designed for Linux or Mac OS without using emulation software.

Which Applications Can You Install? Can You Install *Anything*?

Depending on how your installation of Windows XP Professional is configured, you may be able to install any applications you want to, any applications the administrators decide to provide you with, or no applications at all.

Domain: Administrators Usually Control What You Install

In some companies, administrators install the applications they've deemed necessary, and then lock down the computers tightly to prevent users (let's assume *you*) from installing any applications on them. In such companies, administrators typically provide comprehensive support when problems occur because they haven't allowed you enough latitude to cause a problem on your own. Administrators may restrict you from installing applications to make their own lives easier (if you can't break the computer, the administrator won't need to fix it) or because of corporate policy. Corporate policy may be dictated by compliance with standards like the Health Insurance Portability and Accountability Act (HIPAA), the need to maintain a secure environment for business reasons, or the laudable desire to keep the administrators sane and functional.

In other companies, administrators pursue a more laissez-faire philosophy, whereby they install the company-approved applications, but then let you install further applications themselves as you find necessary.

These administrators often provide only limited support when problems occur: If they can solve the problem without breaking a sweat, they do so. But if the problem proves less tractable, they simply wipe your computer's configuration and replace it with the company-approved default configuration. This approach provides two benefits for the administrators. First, the computer is back up and running in minimal time. Second, because you then have to apply each of your desktop settings manually (and perhaps restore key files from a backup), you're unlikely to install unsuitable applications cavalierly in the future. (This type of rapid replacement assumes your data files and user profile are kept on the network or at least are regularly backed up to a network location.)

Whether they pursue tight control or looser control of the computers they're responsible for, sensible administrators let roving users (such as roaming technicians or sales reps) install extramural printers on their portable computers so that they can print vital documents while they're in the field.

Workgroup: Computer Administrator Users Can Install Applications

If you're not in a domain environment or if you run your company's domain, you should be able to install any applications. In almost all cases, you need to be a Computer Administrator user to install applications on Windows XP Professional. This is because Limited users don't have sufficient user permissions to create files in the folders where most installation routines need to create them.

When a non–Computer Administrator user (let's assume _you_) launches an installation routine designed for Windows XP Professional, Windows 2000, or Windows NT, Windows XP Professional notices the problem and displays the Install Program As Other User dialog box. This dialog box tells you you're likely to need administrator rights to install the application, and invites you to supply a Computer Administrator user name and password. If you can do so, you can complete the installation. If not, you can cancel the installation with no harm done. Or you can attempt to complete the installation under your own credentials—but installation will usually fail, with a message such as "The system administrator has set policies to prevent this installation."

In some cases, Limited users *can* start installation routines designed to run on Windows 9*x* without Windows XP Professional noticing. But, in most cases, these installation routines won't be able to complete satisfactorily.

Preparing to Install an Application

Before you install an application, it's a good idea to close any other applications you're running. In most cases, installing an application doesn't disrupt any other applications that are running, but conflicts remain possible. More of a problem is that some installation routines require you to reboot your computer to complete the installation, which means you need to close all running applications anyway (or have them closed automatically for you). Worse, some badly designed installation routines reboot your computer without consultation.

Caution *In a standalone or workgroup configuration that uses Fast User Switching, make sure no other user is logged on to the computer in a disconnected session. Restarting the computer will lose all work they haven't saved.*

You may also want to create a System Restore point manually before installing an application. The most widely used installers, such as the Windows Installer, InstallShield, and WISE automatically create a restore point for you before installing and uninstalling an application. But if you don't know which installer an application uses, create a restore point manually to make certain there is one. When you create a restore point manually, you can give the restore point a descriptive name that enables you to identify the restore point more easily than an automatically named restore point.

Tip *Don't install more than one application or one suite of related applications (for example, Microsoft Office) at once, because, if you find your computer is unstable after installing multiple applications, it'll be harder to establish which application is to blame. Install one application or suite of applications at a time, and check that the application or applications run correctly before installing anything else.*

Installing Applications Manually

The easiest way to install an application manually is to launch the application's installation routine from the installation medium or the distribution medium. If the application is distributed on a CD or DVD, AutoPlay usually launches either the installation routine itself or an introductory screen that includes a link to the installation routine. If you've turned off AutoPlay for the device involved or if you downloaded the application, you can run the installation routine by double-clicking its filename in a Windows Explorer window or by entering the filename (and path, if necessary) in the Run dialog box.

Note *You may need to use Compatibility mode for the installation routine for an application designed for Windows 9x or other old versions of Windows, as well as for the application itself. See "Using Compatibility Mode to Run Legacy Applications," later in this chapter, for a discussion of Compatibility mode.*

You can also launch the installation routine for an application by using the Add/ Remove Programs Wizard. This method offers no real advantage over starting installation manually. The Add/Remove Programs Wizard helps you find the application's installation routine, but it may suggest installing the wrong application—in which case, you're better off starting installation manually.

To start an installation routine by using the Add/Remove Programs Wizard, follow these steps:

1. Choose Start | Control Panel | Add or Remove Programs to display the Add/ Remove Programs window. (Or enter **appwiz.cpl** in the Run dialog box.)

2. Click the Add New Programs button.

3. Click the CD or Floppy button and follow the wizard's prompts to locate the file. The wizard automatically locates installation files with names such as install.exe and setup.exe, as well as names that include setup.exe. But if the file has a strange name, you may need to use the wizard's options for locating it manually. By default, the Browse dialog box displays only installation routines with names it recognizes. To make it display all executable files, select the Programs item in the Files of Type drop-down list. To make it display other file types, select the All Files item.

After you launch the installation routine, follow through the options it presents. These will depend on which optional components the application includes and how many options the designers of the installation routine decided to let you configure. Most installation routines include accepting a license agreement, entering an installation key, choosing an installation location for the application, and waiting while the files are copied and configured.

Note *If Windows XP Professional's AppCompat database contains details of any known compatibility issues with an application you're installing, Windows XP displays a dialog box warning you of these issues.*

As mentioned earlier in this chapter, you may need to restart Windows XP Professional before you can use the application you just installed. Start the application by clicking the item it added to the Start menu. Check that the application (or suite of applications) works correctly before proceeding with your work.

By default, the Start menu highlights the entries for freshly installed applications so that they pop out at you, and it displays a New Programs Installed pop-up over the All Programs button. The Start menu stops displaying these notices when you use the applications. To turn off this notification, clear the Highlight Newly Installed Programs check box on the Advanced tab of the Customize Start Menu dialog box. (See "Customizing the Start Menu" in Chapter 7.)

By default, most Windows installation routines follow Microsoft's guidelines and install their files in the Program Files folder. If you run out of space there, you can temporarily redirect the Program Files folder to another folder by changing the ProgramFilesDir value entry in the HKEY_LOCAL_MACHINE\SOFTWARE\Microsoft\Windows\CurrentVersion subkey of the Registry. After installing the application, restore your previous ProgramFilesDir location.

Removing Applications Manually

You learned in the previous section that the Add/Remove Programs Wizard is barely useful for installing applications. But for uninstalling applications, this wizard is usually a great help. This is because, while some applications include a link to their uninstallation routine on the submenu they add to the Start menu, most don't, and few users want to dig out the application's distribution CD to uninstall the application. If you installed the application across the network, you may well not have access to the CD in any case.

As with installing an application, close all running applications before uninstalling an application. This is because conflicts could occur with applications you're running and because you may need to restart Windows XP Professional after the installation. In a standalone or workgroup configuration that's using Fast User Switching, make sure no other user is logged on to the computer. (Otherwise, Windows XP warns you that removing the application may not work if another user is running it.) Again, as with installation, create a System Restore restore point manually in case the uninstallation routine doesn't create one automatically and the uninstallation creates problems from which you want to recover using System Restore.

Uninstalling 32-Bit Applications

To uninstall a 32-bit application, follow these steps:

1. Choose Start | Control Panel | Add or Remove Programs to display the Add/Remove Programs window with the Change or Remove Programs tab foremost. (Or enter **appwiz.cpl** in the Run dialog box.)

2. Select the entry for the application in the Currently Installed Programs list box. To find the applications you want, you can use the Sort By list to sort the installed applications by name, size, frequency of use, or date last used.

3. Depending on the components and installation/uninstallation routine used by the application you choose to remove, it displays a single Change/Remove

button or two buttons, a Change button and a Remove button. Click the Change/Remove button or the Remove button.

4. If you clicked the Change/Remove button, the uninstallation routine walks you through the steps of specifying whether to change the installation (for example, removing some components from it) or to remove it altogether. If you clicked a Remove button, the uninstallation routine confirms the removal with you.

5. After uninstalling an application, the uninstallation routine may need to restart Windows XP Professional. Sometimes you may prefer to start Windows XP manually—for example, after making some other changes to its configuration.

You should be able to remove all 32-bit applications by using this procedure, provided you're a Computer Administrator user or your domain administrator hasn't prevented you from uninstalling any applications. However, most 16-bit Windows applications and DOS applications aren't listed in the Add or Remove Programs window. You need to uninstall such programs manually, as described in the next subsection.

Uninstalling 16-Bit Applications

To uninstall a 16-bit application, check for an uninstallation routine. If the application appears on its own submenu on the Start menu, check that submenu for an uninstallation option. If there isn't one, check the application's program files folder for an executable file or a batch file with a name such as uninst.exe or remove.bat. (If you don't know where this folder is, check the target location of the shortcut from which you run the application.) Some applications launch their uninstallation routine from the same setup.exe or install.exe file used to install them. The readme file or Help file for the application may contain instructions for uninstalling it—either giving you the name and location of an uninstallation routine or a list of the files and folders you need to delete manually.

You might also need to remove entries from initialization files, such as autoexec.bat, system.ini, or win.ini. Because Windows XP Professional stores all its permanent configuration information in the Registry, rather than in these initialization files, the files contain far fewer entries than they did in 16-bit versions of Windows, so finding the commands you need to remove is easier than it used to be. And, if you happen to remove the wrong commands, you're unlikely to cause Windows XP any serious problems.

Before deleting files and folders manually or removing entries from initialization files, create a System Restore point, in case you don't like the results you get.

Installing and Uninstalling Applications Using IntelliMirror

In a corporate setting, administrators are unlikely to spend time slogging from computer to computer installing applications manually. Instead, they're likely to use an application-deployment solution to install applications automatically across the network.

In a network that uses Windows domains, the tool administrators are most likely to use is IntelliMirror. *IntelliMirror,* a set of technologies included in Windows 2000 Server and Windows.NET Server, integrates with Active Directory and Group Policy to provide automated installation and uninstallation of applications to client computers across the network.

This section discusses what you as a user of a client PC need to know about installation and uninstallation via IntelliMirror, and what you'll typically see when they take place on your computer.

In networks that use Windows XP Professional clients or Windows 2000 Professional clients but that aren't built with Windows domains, administrators can use a variety of tools to deploy applications automatically to clients. Two widely used packages are PowerQuest DeployCenter and Norton Ghost Corporate Edition.

Publishing and Assigning Applications

In a domain setting, administrators can provide applications to you in either of two ways: publishing or assigning.

- When an administrator *publishes* an application to you, they make it available for installation by you. You then install it from the Add New Programs page in the Add/Remove Programs window.

- When an administrator *assigns* an application, Windows XP Professional installs the application automatically without your direct intervention. The administrator can assign an application either to you or to your computer. When the administrator assigns an application to you, Windows XP Professional adds shortcuts to the application to your Start menu the next time you log on. When you try to run the application, Windows XP Professional installs it. Depending on the extent to which the administrator has automated the installation, you may see the full set of installation messages and options, an abbreviated set, or none at all. When the administrator assigns an application to your computer, Windows XP Professional installs the application automatically the next time you restart Windows XP. Either way, the installation process should be straightforward from your point of view, with Windows XP Professional masking any configuration labors the administrator has performed in the background to make the application install correctly for the domain's client computers.

An administrator can also associate an assigned application or a published application with one or more file extensions. When you try to open a file with one of those extensions, IntelliMirror causes Windows XP Professional to install the application for you.

Removing Applications

As well as installing applications via IntelliMirror, administrators can remove application via IntelliMirror. The IntelliMirror term for "remove" is simply *remove.*

When an administrator removes an application, they can choose whether to uninstall it from the computer or leave it on the computer. For example, an administrator might remove an application they've published so that it's no longer available to you if you haven't yet installed it. But if you have installed it, it remains on your computer and you can continue to use it. Or an administrator might remove an application they've assigned that's been installed on your computer. In this case, the administrator would specify that the application be uninstalled.

When an administrator specifies that an application be uninstalled from your computer via IntelliMirror, IntelliMirror removes it automatically. If the application has been assigned or published to you, when you log on, you see a Please Wait dialog box that says "Removing managed software" and the name of the application. When this dialog box disappears, the application will have been uninstalled. If the application has been assigned to your computer, Windows XP Professional removes it after the next restart.

Running an Application

Once you've installed an application, you can run it by clicking its shortcut on the Start menu or on the Quick Launch toolbar, double-clicking its shortcut on the Desktop (or in a Windows Explorer window), or by entering its name (and path, if necessary) in the Run dialog box (Start | Run). The Run dialog box is useful mostly for running items for which you don't want to create a shortcut in an easily accessible location, but it can be convenient for applications in your path and whose filenames you know. For example, instead of choosing Start | All Programs | Accessories | Calculator, you could enter **calc** in the Run dialog box.

As discussed in Chapter 5, you can run an application automatically at startup in any of several ways: by adding a shortcut for the application to your Startup folder (\Documents and Settings*Username*\Start Menu\Programs\Startup) or to the All Users Startup folder, by using a startup script, or by starting the application as a service. In a domain environment, you may be restricted from using scripts or reconfiguring services, but you're likely to be able to manipulate your Startup folder.

Specifying the Window Size for an Application

To change the size at which an application runs, display the Properties dialog box for the shortcut from which you start the application and choose Normal Window, Minimized, or Maximized in the Run drop-down list on the Shortcut tab.

Running an Application Under Different Credentials

If you're a Limited user, you may need to run an application under a different user account than your own to make it work. For example, you might need to run an application under the credentials of an administrator. You can do so in either of two ways:

- If you need to use the other credentials only once or only occasionally, run the application by right-clicking its shortcut and choosing Run As from the shortcut menu. Windows XP Professional displays the Run As dialog box (Figure 9-1) so that you can specify the credentials.

- If you need to use the other credentials every time or most of the times you run the application, click the Advanced button on the Shortcut page of the Properties dialog box for a shortcut to the application. In the Advanced Properties dialog box, select the Run with Different Credentials check box. When you go to run the application from that shortcut, Windows XP displays the Run As dialog box so that you can specify the credentials.

Closing an Application

Most applications use the standard File | Exit command. Other applications place the Exit command on a differently named menu. Issuing an Exit command this way is usually the easiest way to close an application.

Figure 9-1. *Use the Run As dialog box to run an application under another user's credentials when your account doesn't have sufficient permissions.*

You can also close an application by pressing ALT-F4, clicking the Close button (the × button) on its window, or issuing a Close command from the application's control menu, title bar, or Taskbar button.

If an application crashes or (euphemistically) "stops responding," you can close it from Task Manager. Follow these steps:

1. Launch or activate Task Manager. (For example, right-click the notification area and choose Task Manager from the shortcut menu.)

2. Select the entry for the application on the Applications tab. This tab lists all applications that Windows XP Professional is aware of running, together with their status: Running or Not Responding.

Note *If you need to close an application from Task Manager, make sure it's listed as Not Responding. (If the application is listed as Running, make sure it doesn't have a dialog box displayed, but hidden behind another application, that's preventing you from working in the application.) Give the application a minute or so to finish performing any task it's currently working on (for example, a macro) that might be causing Windows XP to list it as Not Responding. If Windows XP itself is responding slowly to your commands, give the application longer still before deciding it has crashed.*

3. Click the End Task button. If the application is running properly, Windows XP Professional simply closes it. If a problem has occurred with the application, Windows XP displays the End Program dialog box to warn you about the consequences of forcing its closure. Figure 9-2 shows the Applications tab of Task Manager with WordPad not responding and the resulting End Program dialog box for WordPad.

4. Click the End Now button. Windows XP Professional closes the application and displays a dialog box that offers you the opportunity to share the details of the problem with Microsoft. Click the Send Error Report button or the Don't Send button, as appropriate.

If Task Manager can't close the application, close all other applications you're running and restart Windows XP Professional.

Note *Windows XP Professional includes a command-line utility named taskkill.exe, which you can use to end a task process that's stopped working. taskkill.exe is normally used by administrators when Task Manager isn't available—for example, when they're connecting remotely to a computer via Telnet to administer it. In most cases, using Task Manager is much easier. But if you must use taskkill.exe, use the tasklist.exe utility to display a list of tasks with their associated process ID (PID) numbers so that you know which PID to end with taskkill.exe.*

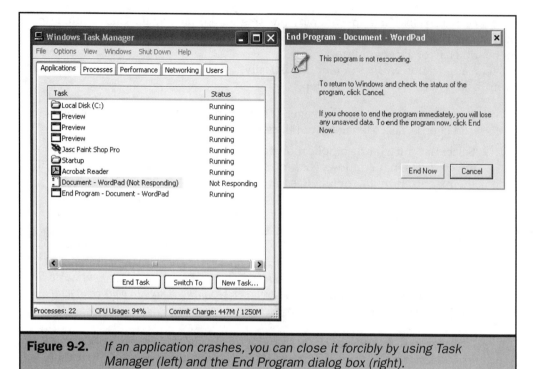

Figure 9-2.   *If an application crashes, you can close it forcibly by using Task Manager (left) and the End Program dialog box (right).*

Using Compatibility Mode to Run Legacy Applications

Windows XP Professional's Compatibility mode provides a way of running applications that aren't designed to work with Windows XP and whose design prevents them from running successfully on Windows XP without special settings. Compatibility mode mimics the software environment of the previous version of Windows you specify and lets you change display settings that may interfere with the application.

Applications may require Compatibility mode for any of several reasons. Here are some examples:

- Windows XP Professional uses a different folder structure than some earlier versions of Windows. For example, Windows XP stores user-specific data in the user profile, which is under the Documents and Settings folder for the user account. Older versions of Windows stored user-specific data in other locations, such as in the Windows folder itself.

- Some Windows 95 applications check specifically to make sure the OS is Windows 95. The programmers' aim was to prevent problems arising from the user trying to run the application on Windows 3.*x* or Windows for Workgroups with Win32s extensions. At the time, such checking was a good idea. But this meant some of these applications wouldn't run on later versions of Windows.

■ Some applications are designed to exploit the feebly protected memory model of Windows 9*x* or to access hardware resources directly.

For some applications, Windows XP Professional sets Compatibility mode options automatically when you install and run the applications. (Windows XP gets the information needed to do this from its AppCompat database, which is one of the items Windows Update updates automatically if you let it. The AppCompat database is stored in the %systemroot%\AppPatch folder.) For other applications, you need to set Compatibility mode options manually. You can choose the version of Windows whose environment you want Windows XP Professional to emulate—Windows 95, Windows 98, Windows NT 4, or Windows 2000—whether to restrict the display to 256 colors, to use 640×480 resolution, and to disable visual themes (which may prevent the application's controls form displaying correctly).

In some cases, you might apply Compatibility mode options manually to an application to which Windows XP Professional has already automatically applied Compatibility mode options. When this happens, Windows XP Professional layers the Compatibility mode options you specify on top of the existing options, using both.

For many applications that require Compatibility mode, you need only choose the appropriate environment, but the display options can be useful for older and more demanding software.

You can set Compatibility mode either by using the Program Compatibility Wizard (Start | All Programs | Accessories | Program Compatibility Wizard) or by working on the Compatibility tab of the Properties dialog box (Figure 9-3) for the application. The wizard lets you test your Compatibility mode choices before applying them to the program, but the Compatibility tab gives you quicker access to the choices.

How to Tell Whether an Application Is 32 Bit or 16 Bit

If you're running a legacy Windows application, you may not be sure whether it's a 32-bit application or a 16-bit application. You can find out in either of the following two ways:

■ Display the Properties dialog box for the application's executable file (this is probably in a subfolder of the Program Files folder, unless you installed it somewhere idiosyncratic). If the dialog box includes a Version tab, the application is 32 bit. If there's no Version tab, the application is 16 bit.

■ When the application is running, check the Processes page of Task Manager to see if there's an entry for WOWEXEC.EXE above the entry for the application. If there's an entry, it's a 16-bit application. If not, it's 32 bit. WOWEXEC.EXE is the Windows on Windows executable used for running 16-bit programs. The easiest

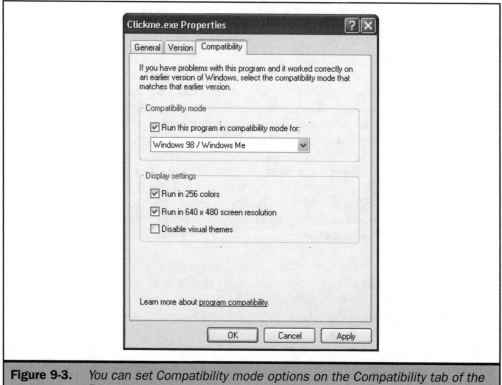

Figure 9-3.   *You can set Compatibility mode options on the Compatibility tab of the Properties dialog box for an application.*

way to identify the process for a running application is to right-click the application on the Applications page of Task Manager and choose Go to Process from the shortcut menu.

Building Your Own Compatibility Modes

If you can't get an application to run in any of the preset Compatibility modes Windows XP Professional provides, you can create your own custom Compatibility modes. This is mostly an administrator activity, but because you might need to create Compatibility modes to get a vital but recalcitrant application to run, I'll steer you quickly in the right direction.

Download the Microsoft Windows XP Application Compatibility Toolkit from the MSDN web site (msdn.microsoft.com/downloads) and install the Toolkit on your computer. The easiest way to find the Toolkit is to search for it.

The Application Compatibility Toolkit contains the following tools:

- **Application Verifier Tool** Use this tool to test an application's compatibility with Windows XP Professional. You can choose which aspects of the way an application runs the Application Verifier Tool should log.

- **Compatibility Administration Tool** Use this tool to examine the entries in Windows XP's compatibility database, to disable existing entries for applications that don't work as they should, and to create custom entries for applications that aren't covered or for applications for which you've disabled the existing entries.

- **PageHeap** Use this tool together with a debugger to test an application for heap-related bugs, corruptions, and memory leaks.

- **QFixApp** Use this tool to apply compatibility layers and fixes to an application.

Running Windows Applications That Won't Run in Compatibility Mode

If Windows XP Professional knows it can't run an application, even in Compatibility mode, it blocks the application from running and advises you of the problem. Other applications fail on their own without Windows XP Professional blocking them.

If you can't run a vital Windows application on Windows XP Professional—even after trying all the possible Compatibility mode settings—install the version of Windows the application needs and run the application from there. You can install the version of Windows either under a PC-emulation application (as described in the next section) or as a dual-boot arrangement. See Chapter 4 for instructions on installing an older version of Windows after Windows XP Professional.

Running Non-Windows Applications

Occasionally, you may need to run non-Windows applications on your computer—for example, Linux applications. You can do this either by dual-booting your computer with the OS these applications require or by using PC-emulation software to run that OS on top of Windows XP Professional.

The best-known PC-emulation applications are Virtual PC (www.connectix.com) and VMWare (www.vmware.com). You can also get Macintosh emulators, such as SoftMac 2000/XP (www.emulators.com) and Executor (www.ardi.com) but, at this writing, Mac emulators work only with older versions of Mac OS and the applications designed for those versions of Mac OS, not for Mac OS X and applications designed for it.

The advantages of emulation are that it works surprisingly well and it can save you considerable money over having to buy one or more additional computers. The disadvantages are that performance tends to be disappointing, because the OS that's being emulated involves a large amount of work for the OS doing the emulating, and most emulation applications support only a limited range of hardware. These limitations make emulation a better solution for running a small number of business applications or the occasional vital utility than for running demanding consumer applications, such as games, multimedia applications, or video-editing applications.

Configuring Error Reporting for Windows XP Professional and Applications

Windows XP Professional includes built-in functionality for reporting errors that occur in Windows XP itself and in applications that run on it. By reporting errors (via the Internet), you help Microsoft identify problems that need fixing in Windows XP Professional and its compatibility.

Microsoft doesn't promise to fix all the errors reported—many million people use Windows XP Professional, so that would be too ambitious. So, if you choose to report an error, understand that a personalized solution won't come winging its way to you as a result. But if enough users report the same error, chances are that, sooner or later, Microsoft will release a patch for it via Windows Update.

To configure error reporting for Windows XP and the applications you're running, display the System Properties dialog box (WINDOWS KEY–BREAK). Click the Error Reporting button on the Advanced page to display the Error Reporting dialog box (shown on the left in Figure 9-4). This dialog box lets you choose between disabling error reporting (with the choice of still having Windows XP Professional notify you when critical errors occur) and enabling error reporting for Windows XP itself, for the applications you're running, or for both. The default setting is to report errors for both Windows XP Professional and applications.

Note   *In a domain environment, an administrator may set error-reporting options through Group Policy. For example, an administrator might create a list of applications for which Windows XP Professional should never report errors.*

If you choose to enable error reporting for applications, you can specify how to handle different applications by clicking the Choose Programs button and working in the Choose Programs dialog box (shown on the right in Figure 9-4). You can choose between reporting errors for all applications (the default setting) or only the applications listed in the upper list box. In the lower list box, you can specifically include applications from having their errors reported. This option is useful if you continue to use an application with a known, but nonfatal, bug. It's particularly useful if that application is a custom application—for example, one developed by and for your company—that Microsoft has nothing to do with.

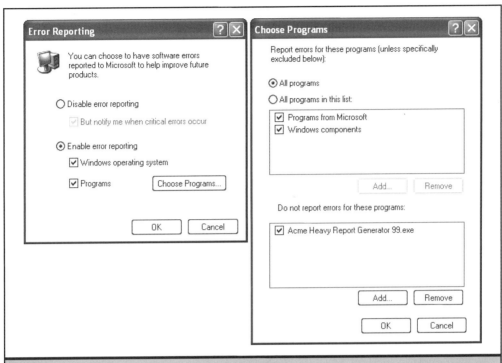

Figure 9-4. *Configure error reporting in the Error Reporting dialog box (left) and the Choose Programs dialog box (right).*

Summary

This chapter has discussed how to install and uninstall applications on Windows XP Professional, both manually and by having them deployed to you or your computer by a domain administrator. The chapter has covered how to run applications, using Compatibility mode as necessary, and the possibilities for running applications that won't run on Windows XP Professional. It also has explained how to configure error reporting for Windows XP and the applications you run.

The next chapter covers how to add hardware to your computer and how to troubleshoot hardware problems.

The
Complete
Reference

Chapter 10

Adding and Configuring Hardware

This chapter discusses how to add hardware to your computer and configure it to work properly. It starts by discussing what device drivers are, what they do, and why stable and functional drivers are vital to running Windows XP Professional successfully. The chapter covers how to add and remove hardware, and how to use Device Manager to manage the devices on your computer. It outlines considerations for installing and configuring certain classes of hardware devices. The chapter then explains your options for managing devices remotely (if your responsibilities extend that far). Finally, it shows you how to use hardware profiles to let you switch effortlessly between different hardware configurations of the same computer (for example, a laptop you use both docked and undocked).

If you're in a tightly managed corporate environment, you may be limited to installing the occasional hot-pluggable device. If so, much of this chapter will be beyond your permissions. In a less tightly managed environment, you'll probably be able to install some hardware, and install, update, and remove device drivers as necessary—and perhaps work with profiles as well.

Understanding What Device Drivers Are and What They Do

To use a hardware device, Windows XP Professional needs a suitable *device driver*—a software component that tells Windows XP what the device is and how to communicate with it.

The Windows XP Professional CD contains drivers for many hardware devices that were available when your copy of Windows XP was finalized. (Many manufacturers provided Microsoft with Windows XP Professional–compliant drivers for their hardware and software.) So that you needn't keep supplying your Windows XP CD when you need a driver, most of these drivers are installed on your computer in the Cabinet file driver.cab, which is stored in the %systemroot%\Driver Cache\i386 folder. Windows Update includes drivers for new devices and updated drivers for old devices. You can download other drivers from the web manually (for example, from manufacturers' web sites) or you can use Windows XP's features for searching the web for device drivers for hardware that you install or whose driver you ask to update.

Because drivers are necessary for the operating system (OS) to communicate with the hardware, the OS runs the drivers in a privileged location so that they can perform their duties. Badly written drivers can cause conflicts with the OS or even cause it to crash.

Most drivers are written (programmed) by third parties rather than by Microsoft. Most are written by the companies that create the hardware devices or by companies that work with them. In earlier versions of Windows, Microsoft hasn't successfully implemented quality control on drivers, which contributed to stability problems in those versions of Windows.

To avoid this problem, in Windows XP, Microsoft has implemented a system of quality control for the drivers. Windows XP Professional checks that each driver you install is signed with a digital signature that confirms the driver has been tested as being compatible with Windows XP Professional and the driver hasn't been tampered with. (By tampering with a driver, a malefactor could introduce rogue code onto a computer to damage the computer or compromise its security.) This checking and signature don't prove the driver doesn't contain any bugs, but they do prove it has achieved a certain standard of functionality and it hasn't changed since then.

So it's important to make sure the drivers you install on Windows XP are stable and high quality. It's almost never worth using beta drivers except on a test computer (if you have one). If you have legacy hardware, sometimes you may need to use unsigned drivers. If you do, you'll know about it: When you start to install a driver that's not signed, Windows XP warns you it's not signed and it could be dangerous.

Adding and Removing Hardware

This section discusses how to add and remove hardware devices from your computer, starting with the easiest type of devices—hot-pluggable devices.

Working with Hot-Pluggable Devices

Hot-pluggable devices are those you can plug in or unplug while Windows XP Professional is running, and have Windows XP load or unload the appropriate driver automatically. FireWire, USB, and PC Card devices are hot pluggable. Windows XP can sometimes detect serial devices (for example, serial modems) and automatically load drivers for them, but such devices aren't normally considered hot pluggable.

Note *FireWire is the most widely used term for hardware that uses the Institute of Electrical and Electronics Engineers (IEEE) 1394 high-speed serial bus. Apple popularized the term FireWire, which has stuck. Sony uses the term "iLink" for IEEE 1394. Many PCs include one or more FireWire ports. If your computer doesn't have any FireWire ports, you can probably add them via a PCI card or a PC Card. PC Card is a standard for small-sized, easily removable devices, typically used with portable computers. The 16-bit version of the PC Card standard was called PCMCIA, which is the acronym for Personal Computer Memory Card International Association. Many people still use the term PCMCIA to refer to PC Card devices.*

Adding Hot-Pluggable Devices

The first time you add a hot-pluggable device to your computer, the notification area displays a Found New Hardware pop-up that mentions the type of connection the device uses (for example, USB Device). Windows XP then examines the device and displays a second notification area pop-up that gives the name of the device (for example, Compaq_WL100_11Mbps_Wireless_PC_Card).

If you don't have sufficient permissions to install the device, Windows XP displays a Found New Hardware dialog box (Figure 10-1) so that you can specify the user name and password of a user who does. If you can't do so, it terminates with a Hardware Installation dialog box stating that you don't have the security privileges required to install the hardware and suggesting you either get an administrator to install it for you or log on as an administrator yourself. The notification area then displays a Found New Hardware pop-up telling you "A problem occurred during hardware installation. Your new hardware might not work properly."

If you supply a user name and password with enough privileges, installation continues. If Windows XP Professional finds a driver for the device in its driver cache, it installs the driver automatically. If not, and if your computer has an Internet connection available, Windows XP Professional searches for a suitable driver on the Windows Update site, and (if it finds one) downloads the driver automatically and installs it.

If neither driver.cab nor Windows Update (if available) produces a driver, Windows XP Professional launches the Found New Hardware Wizard so that you can provide the driver. See "Using the Found New Hardware Wizard and Add Hardware Wizard," later in this chapter, for an overview of this wizard.

Removing Hot-Pluggable Devices

In theory, you should be able simply to unplug all hot-pluggable devices. But, in reality, you need to stop some hot-pluggable devices before you remove them. To stop a device, click the Safely Remove Hardware icon in the notification area and choose the Safely Remove item for the device from the pop-up menu. (The Safely Remove Hardware icon

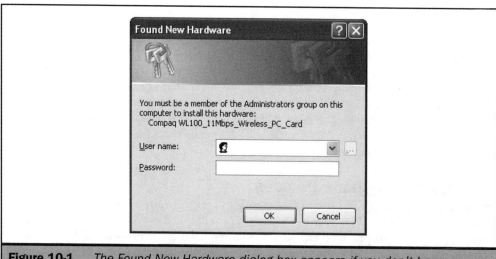

Figure 10-1.   *The Found New Hardware dialog box appears if you don't have permission to install this type of hardware. Enter an appropriate user name and password to proceed.*

shows a green arrow pointing to the left over a gray slab—a PC Card, but it's hard to recognize.)

If the device doesn't have an entry on the Safely Remove Hardware menu, you can simply unplug the device from the computer.

Once you remove the device, Windows XP Professional unloads its driver automatically.

Working with Other Devices

Beyond hot-pluggable devices, which are Plug and Play (PnP) devices by definition, the world of hardware devices roughly breaks down into other PnP devices and devices that aren't PnP.

PnP is a standard for automating the installation and configuration of hardware devices. PnP requires the following:

- The OS must support PnP. Windows XP does.

- The hardware device must support PnP and must respond to the events defined for the PnP standard.

- The hardware device must tell the OS its identification (the device type, version, and manufacturer), the resources it needs, and the drivers it needs.

- The computer's BIOS must support PnP. Because PnP has been around for several years now, all but the oldest computers that can run Windows XP have BIOSes that support PnP.

Most ISA devices don't support PnP. All FireWire, USB, and PC Card (PCMCIA) devices support PnP. Almost all AGP and PCI devices support PnP.

If a device supports PnP, you should be able to install it in your computer and configure it with minimal effort. Devices using buses that don't expose external ports on the computer are almost always not hot-pluggable. For example, the PCI bus and AGP bus on most computers use slots accessible only by opening the computer, which you can't safely do while the computer is running. So PCI cards and AGP cards aren't hot pluggable. But they're almost always PnP, which means you can shut down your computer, install a PCI card or an AGP card, boot Windows XP, and have the OS recognize the hardware device automatically and configure it automatically, if Windows XP has or can find a suitable driver for the device.

If Windows XP can't find a suitable driver for a new hardware device, it displays the Found New Hardware Wizard to let you provide or specify the driver you want to use.

If Windows XP Professional doesn't find a new hardware device you added to the computer, you can use the Add Hardware Wizard to tell Windows XP the device is there and what it is.

Using the Found New Hardware Wizard and Add Hardware Wizard

When Windows XP Professional can't find a driver for a new hardware device it's discovered, it displays the Found New Hardware Wizard to walk you through the process of identifying the device.

On the What Do You Want the Wizard to Do? page (Figure 10-2), choose between the Install the Software Automatically option button (the default) and the Install from a List or Specific Location option button. The automatic option is useful if you have a driver for the device on a CD, DVD, or floppy but you don't know exactly what the driver is named. The manual option is useful when you have a driver in a known location on a hard drive or you know where the driver is located on a removable medium (CD, DVD, or floppy) and prefer not to have Windows XP search for it.

Letting the Found New Hardware Wizard Search for the Driver

If you select the Install the Software Automatically option button, load the removable medium that contains the driver, and then click the Next button. The wizard searches for the driver. If the wizard finds the driver, it loads it. If not, the wizard searches the Windows Update site for a driver if an Internet connection is available. If this step

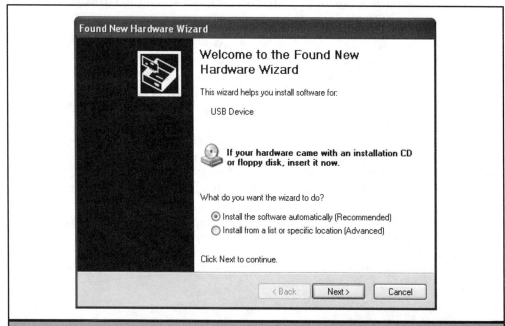

Figure 10-2.   *The Found New Hardware Wizard lets you choose between specifying a driver for the device manually or having Windows XP Professional search for a driver automatically.*

yields no driver, the wizard displays the Cannot Install This Hardware page. From here, you can either finish the wizard or return to the start of the wizard to specify the driver to use. Either way, select or clear the Don't Prompt Me Again to Install This Software check box, which controls whether the Found New Hardware Wizard keeps finding the device and prompting you to install a driver for it. This check box is selected by default.

Specifying the Driver or Its Location Manually

If you select the Install from a List of Specific Location option button, choose how to proceed on the Please Choose Your Search and Installation Options page (Figure 10-3). The default setting is the Search for the Best Driver in These Locations option button, which lets you choose whether to search removable media and whether to search a specific location you designate.

Alternatively, you can select the Don't Search. I Will Choose the Driver to Install option button and use the options on the Hardware Type page and the Select the Device Driver You Want to Install for This Hardware pages of the wizard to specify the driver:

- On the Hardware Type page, select the category of device you're installing—for example, Display Adapters, Modems, or Network Adapters. If the list box

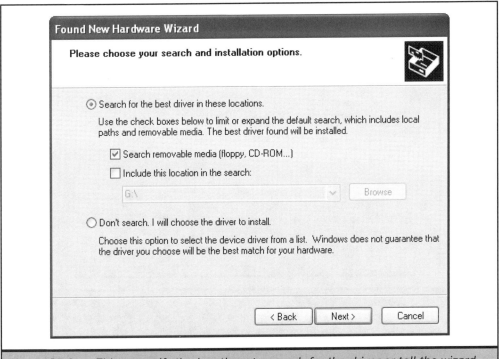

Figure 10-3. *Either specify the locations to search for the driver or tell the wizard you'll choose it manually.*

doesn't contain an entry for the type of hardware you're installing, select the Show All Devices entry at the top of the list.

Note *The wizard often takes several minutes to complete the search when you select the Show All Devices entry.*

■ On the Select the Device Driver You Want to Install for This Hardware page (Figure 10-4), select the device's manufacturer in the Manufacturer list box and the device's model in the Model list box. If you have a driver on a removable medium or on disk, click the Have Disk button and use the resulting dialog boxes to identify the driver.

If you specify a driver that isn't digitally signed, the wizard displays a warning in the second Select the Device Driver You Want to Install for This Hardware dialog box. If you proceed, it displays the Hardware Installation dialog box (Figure 10-5) to deliver the warning more directly, spelling out that the driver may "impair or destabilize the correct operation of your system either immediately or in the future." If you're certain

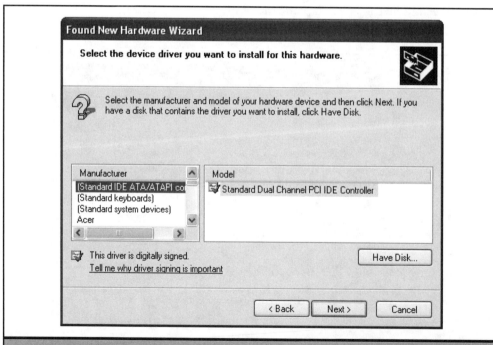

Figure 10-4. *From the Select the Device Driver You Want to Install for This Hardware page of the Found New Hardware Wizard, either specify the device's manufacturer and model or click the Have Disk button to supply a driver you have on a removable medium or on disk.*

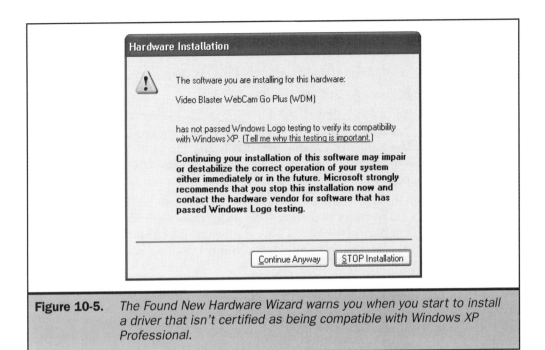

Figure 10-5. *The Found New Hardware Wizard warns you when you start to install a driver that isn't certified as being compatible with Windows XP Professional.*

you want to use this driver, click the Continue Anyway button. Otherwise, click the STOP Installation button and seek out a driver that has passed compatibility testing.

Once you specify the driver and settle any doubts the wizard raises about it, the wizard installs the driver. If installing the device involves replacing any existing files with replacements that are older than they, the wizard displays the Confirm File Replace dialog box to make sure you want to do so. In most cases, it's best to keep the latest files, unless you know for certain you need the older files.

The installation of the device drivers may also raise dialog boxes for configuring the device itself. Deal with these as necessary.

When the wizard finishes, check that the hardware is functional.

Using the Add Hardware Wizard

To force Windows XP to recognize a new hardware device you've installed, run the Add Hardware Wizard by clicking the Add Hardware link in the See Also pane from the Printers and Other Hardware screen in Control Panel (Start | Control Panel | Printers and Other Hardware) or by entering **hdwwiz.cpl** in the Run dialog box.

If you have the driver for the device on a removable medium, insert it in the appropriate drive. Then click the Next button on the wizard's Welcome screen to force a search for new hardware.

If the wizard finds the device, it leads you through choosing the driver to use for the device. This procedure is substantially the same as the procedure for the Found New Hardware Wizard, discussed in the previous section.

If the wizard can't find any new hardware, it displays the Is the Hardware Connected? screen to double-click that you've connected the hardware. Follow these steps:

1. Choose the Yes, I Have Already Connected the Hardware option button.

2. On the The Following Hardware Is Already Installed on Your Computer screen, select the Add a New Hardware Device item.

3. On the The Wizard Can Help You Install Other Hardware page, select the Install the Hardware That I Manually Select from a List option button. (The alternative is to let the wizard search for the device. Given that it has already searched once and failed to find the device, searching again is a waste of time.)

4. On the From the List Below, Select the Type of Hardware You Are Installing page, select the category of device. (This page is essentially the same as the Hardware Type page of the Found New Hardware Wizard.) If the list box doesn't contain an entry for the type of hardware you're installing, select the Show All Devices entry at the top of the list.

5. On the Select the Device Driver You Want to Install for This Hardware page, select the device or specify the location of another driver (see the previous section for details). Then follow through the rest of the installation.

Managing Devices Locally Using Device Manager

Device Manager provides a centralized graphical interface for managing hardware devices. You can use Device Manager to manage devices on your local computer and to view devices on remote computers. Device Manager can't manage devices on remote computers.

Displaying Device Manager

You can display Device Manager in any of the following ways:

■ Click the Device Manager button on the Hardware page of the System Properties dialog box.

■ Run devmgmt.msc from the Run dialog box. (This file is located in the %systemroot%\system32 folder, but you shouldn't need to specify the path when running it.)

> **Tip** *You may sometimes want to run Device Manager in the Administrator context without logging on as Administrator. Doing so is quicker than logging the current user account off and logging on again. This also has the advantage of limiting the number of applications and services run in the Administrator context, which can open your system to outside attack. To run Device Manager in the Administrator context from the current user account, use a runas command in the Run dialog box: runas /user:administrator "mmc.exe devmgmt.msc"(note that there's a space before "devmgmt" there). Enter the Administrator password in the command-prompt window that Windows XP Professional displays.*

■ Run Device Manager from its entry under System Tools in Computer Management.

If you use Device Manager frequently, you might also want to put an entry for Device Manager in a custom management console. See "Creating Custom Consoles" in Chapter 42 for a discussion of creating custom consoles.

If you don't have sufficient privileges to uninstall devices, change device properties, or work with device drivers, Windows XP displays a Device Manager dialog box telling you so. When you dismiss this dialog box, Windows XP displays Device Manager. You can then examine entries in Device Manager, but you can't make any changes. Device Manager removes the commands for taking actions with devices and drivers from its menus, toolbars, and shortcut menus, and it disables command buttons in the Properties dialog boxes for the devices.

Viewing Information in Device Manager

Device Manager is easy to use. Figure 10-6 shows two examples of Device Manager with its full set of toolbar buttons and menus. These screens are for the same computer (named Accelerated). The left screen shows the Devices by Type view, which Device Manager displays by default. The right screen displays the Resources by Type view.

Table 10-1 lists the views Device Manager provides and discusses their uses.

For a device that's configured and working correctly, Device Manager displays a generic icon representing the type of device—a loudspeaker icon for a sound-related item such as a sound card or codec, a monitor icon for a monitor, and so on. For a device that's not configured correctly or not working, Device Manager displays a yellow question mark with an exclamation point superimposed on it. For a device that's disabled, Device Manager displays a red cross on the icon for the device.

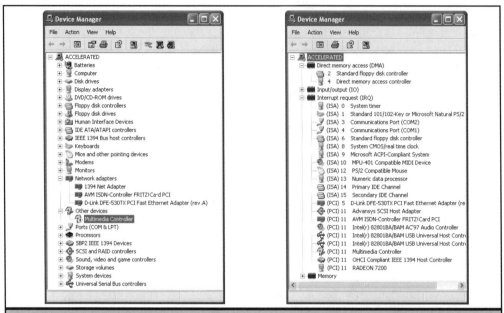

Figure 10-6.   *Use Device Manager to examine and manipulate hardware devices; it offers several views, including Devices by Type (left) and Resources by Type (right).*

View	Description and Use
Devices by Type	Device Manager's default view. Shows an alphabetical list of device types. Useful for quickly locating a device by type and for seeing which devices have configuration problems.
Devices by Connection	Shows an alphabetical list of connections. Useful for seeing which devices are connected to which connection. For example, you can quickly see which devices are connected to the PCI bus.
Resources by Type	Shows an alphabetical list of resources in categories such as Direct Memory Access, Input/Output, Interrupt Request, and Memory. Useful for seeing which devices are using which resources—for example, for getting a list of IRQ assignments.
Resources by Connection	Shows an alphabetical list of resources (in categories such as those previously mentioned) sorted by the devices connected to them. Useful for seeing which resources are being used by the devices on a certain connection.

Table 10-1.   *Device Manager Views and Their Uses*

Displaying Hidden and Disconnected Devices

By default, Device Manager hides some devices it figures you probably don't need to see: the Non-Plug and Play Drivers category, the NT APM/Legacy Support category, some networking items such as WAN Miniports (if you have them), and a few other items. You can toggle the display of these devices on and off by choosing View | Show Hidden Devices.

To display devices installed on your computer but not currently connected, create an environment variable named devmgr_show_nonpresent_devices and set its value to 1. The easiest way to create an environment variable is to work in the Environment Variables dialog box, as discussed in "Working with Environment Variables" in Chapter 11. You can also create this environmental variable by using a set command in a command-prompt window:

```
set devmgr_show_nonpresent_devices = 1
```

Once you've created this environment variable, display Device Manager and choose View | Show Hidden Devices.

Installing and Rolling Back Device Drivers

To check or change the driver a device is using, double-click a device to display its Properties dialog box, and then click the Driver tab to display it. The Driver tab (Figure 10-7 shows an example) provides basic details on the driver and buttons for displaying details, updating the driver, reverting to the previous driver, and uninstalling the driver.

Clicking the Update Driver button launches the Hardware Update Wizard, which walks you through the process of checking for or providing a new driver and installing it. Many of the screens in the Hardware Update Wizard are almost identical to those in the Add Hardware Wizard and Found New Hardware Wizard.

If updating a driver produces unsatisfactory results, you can *roll back* (revert to) the previous driver by clicking the Roll Back Driver button. In a great improvement on earlier versions of Windows, Windows XP Professional stores both details of the previous driver and the driver itself, so Windows XP Professional can easily restore the previous driver.

If you want to remove the device from your computer, click the Uninstall button and choose the OK button in the Confirm Device Removal dialog box that Windows XP displays. Clicking the Uninstall button has the same effect as, and has no advantage over, issuing an Uninstall command directly from Device Manager.

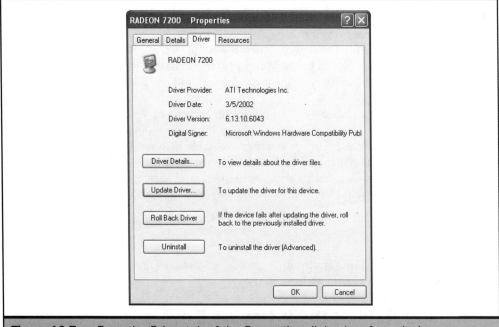

Figure 10-7. *From the Driver tab of the Properties dialog box for a device, you can check the driver, update it, roll it back to the previous driver, or uninstall the driver.*

Printing and Saving Configuration Information

Device Manager lets you print any of the following reports by choosing Action | Print and choosing the report type in the Print dialog box:

- **System Summary** A moderately detailed summary of your system's configuration, broken down into sections such as Disk Drive Info, IRQ Summary, DMA Usage Summary, Memory Summary, and IO [I/O] Port Summary.

- **Selected Class or Device** A detailed listing for the specific device or class of device selected.

- **All Devices and System Summary** A summary of your system's configuration, together with the detailed listing for each device. This report tends to waste paper, making it a good candidate for saving to a text file.

Device Manager doesn't let you save a report directly to disk instead of printing it. To save a report to disk, create a printer entry that prints to a text-only file (see "Setting Up a Text-Only Printer for Printing to a File" in Chapter 12) and print to that printer.

Disabling and Enabling Devices

To disable a device, select its entry in Device Manager and issue a Disable command from the toolbar, the Action menu, or the shortcut menu. Windows XP Professional displays a confirmation dialog box warning you that disabling the device will cause it to stop functioning. Click the Yes button if you're sure you want to proceed. Windows XP disables the device and marks its icon with a red cross.

If you have multiple hardware profiles on your computer, you have a choice of disabling a device either for the current hardware profile or for all hardware profiles. To set these options, double-click the entry for a device to display its Properties dialog box, and then select the appropriate setting in the Device Usage drop-down list on the General tab of the Properties dialog box.

To enable a device that's been disabled, select its entry and issue an Enable command from the toolbar, the Action menu, or the shortcut menu.

Uninstalling a Device

To uninstall a device, select its entry in Device Manager and issue an Uninstall command from the toolbar, the Action menu, or the shortcut menu. Windows XP Professional displays the Confirm Device Removal dialog box. Click the OK button if you're sure you want to proceed. Windows XP uninstalls the device and removes its entry from Device Manager.

Changing Resource Use

In most cases, Windows XP Professional automatically allocates to hardware devices the system resources they need: interrupt requests (IRQs), input/output (I/O) base addresses, memory addresses, and Direct Memory Access (DMA) channels. If you used earlier versions of Windows with hardware that required manual assignment of such resources, you'll remember that allocating resources could be hard work. In particular, there was considerable competition for IRQs for two reasons. First, various devices came preconfigured to use the same IRQ. (For example, many sound cards and some network cards wanted IRQ 5.) Second, on a busy computer, there sometimes weren't enough IRQs for all the devices.

Such problems are relatively rare these days because Advanced Configuration and Power Interface (ACPI), which is implemented on most modern system boards, lets multiple PCI devices share IRQs. In most cases, this sharing works well, but sometimes you may find that having a particular device share an IRQ causes conflicts. When this happens, assign the device its own IRQ.

Sometimes, you need to allocate resource use manually for legacy devices that use the ISA bus. To allocate resources, display the Properties dialog box for the device and work on the Resources tab. Figure 10-8 shows the Resources tab for an ISA network adapter, together with the Edit Input/Output Range dialog box, which you use for changing the I/O Range resources assigned to the device.

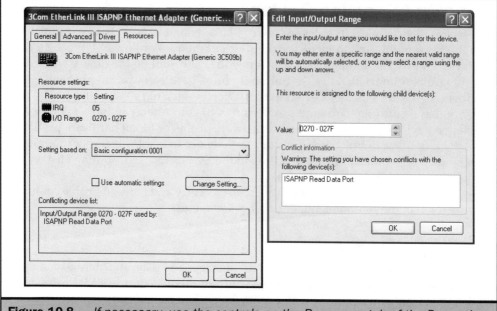

Figure 10-8. *If necessary, use the controls on the Resources tab of the Properties dialog box for a device, and the associated Edit dialog box, to change the system resources it uses.*

To change the settings, follow these steps:

1. Clear the Use Automatic Settings check box if it's currently selected.
2. Choose the configuration to change in the Setting Based On drop-down list.
3. Choose the resource setting to change in the list box.
4. Click the Change Setting button and work in the resulting Edit dialog box.

Scanning for Hardware Changes

To force Device Manager to scan your computer for hardware changes, such as devices you've added or reconfigured, but that haven't yet shown up in Device Manager, issue a Scan for Hardware Changes command from the toolbar, the Action menu, or the shortcut menu.

Considerations for Particular Devices

Windows XP Professional can install and configure many—perhaps most—devices without problems. This section briefly discusses installation and configuration considerations for CD and DVD drives, monitors, and modems, each of which deserves comment.

CD and DVD Drives

On the Properties tab of the Properties dialog box for a CD drive or DVD drive, you can choose whether to use digital CD audio or analog audio for the CD. If the drive supports digital output and has a suitable driver, digital audio should give you better audio quality than analog audio. You can also set the volume for CD audio on this tab. (If you prefer, you can set the CD audio volume through the Control Panel's Volume applet.)

On the DVD Region tab of the Properties dialog box for a DVD drive, you specify the DVD region for the drive to use. DVDs divide the world into eight encoding regions. To play a DVD encoded for a region, your DVD drive needs to be set to the correct regional encoding. You can change the encoding setting only a few times for a drive before it becomes locked, so don't change it precipitately.

Monitors, Multiple Monitors, and DualView

The following subsections discuss monitor-related issues.

Install the Correct Driver for Your Monitor

Windows XP Professional may assign the Plug and Play Monitor driver to your monitor. You may be able to improve video performance and color matching by manually supplying a driver written specifically for your model of monitor.

Troubleshooting Display Problems

The Troubleshooting tab of the Properties dialog box for a monitor and graphics card (click the Advanced button on the Settings page of the Display Properties dialog box to display this dialog box) contains two settings for troubleshooting display problems:

- The Hardware Acceleration slider controls the graphics acceleration features Windows XP uses. You can drag the slider to any setting between Full acceleration and None. The readout under the slider lists the features this setting disables. For example, the third setting from the left disables DirectDraw and Direct3D accelerations, cursor accelerations, and advanced drawing accelerations.

- The Enable Write Combining check box controls whether Windows XP uses *write combining,* a feature for transferring more information at once from the graphics card to the monitor. Turning off write combining can eliminate some display problems.

Configuring Multiple Monitors on a Desktop PC

If your computer's system board supports multiple monitors and you have two or more graphics cards (AGP, PCI, or a mixture) that are supported by Windows XP Professional and that can work with each other, you may be able to use multiple monitors with Windows XP. Using multiple monitors provides you with more screen area to work in and can make life much easier on busy desktops.

In theory, installing a second graphics card and monitor is simple but, in practice, keep these points firmly in mind:

- Set up one monitor at a time. *Don't* set up both at once.

- When you boot your computer after installing the second graphics card and monitor, the display may appear on the second monitor, rather than the first. You may be able to change this in your computer's BIOS. You may not be able to change it at all.

- You may need to run the Add Hardware Wizard to recognize the second graphics card.

- With some system boards and PCI graphics cards, multiple monitors may work only when specific cards are in specific PCI slots. If your first arrangement doesn't work, be prepared to try the graphics card or cards in different PCI slots.

- On the Settings tab of the Display Properties dialog box, drag the monitor icons around so they reflect the physical arrangement of your monitors. Select the monitor you want to work with by clicking its icon or by using the Display drop-down list.

- If you have an AGP card, use that connection for your primary monitor. For this monitor, select the Use This Device As the Primary Monitor check box. The primary monitor can display DirectX applications full-screen and can use all DirectX accelerations, while the secondary monitors can't.

- For each other monitor, select the Extend My Windows Desktop onto This Monitor check box.

Configuring Multiple Monitors on a Laptop PC

If your laptop PC has a graphics card that supports Windows XP Professional's DualView feature, you can use DualView to create a multiple-monitor configuration on your laptop PC's screen and an external monitor attached to your laptop's external graphics port. Connect the external monitor and see if the Settings tab of the Display Properties dialog box shows two monitors. If it does, configure them as described in the previous section. Your laptop's built-in display is the primary monitor.

If your laptop's external graphics port is turned off, you need to turn it on before DualView will work.

Modems

PCI modems, USB modems, and PC Card modems are PnP. Windows XP Professional usually detects and installs them automatically. When adding a serial modem, you may have to run the Add Hardware Wizard.

If the modem you add is the first for your computer, and you haven't already specified your location and phone dialing options, Windows XP displays the Location Information dialog box followed by the Phone and Modem Options dialog box so you can provide this information.

Managing Devices Remotely

To view and manage devices on a remote computer for which you have access permissions, XP provides the following options:

- You can use Computer Management's Action | Connect to Another Computer command to connect to another computer. From here, you can display the computer's devices in Device Manager, but you can't change their configuration.

- If you have an account on the remote computer and it's set up to accept Remote Desktop connections, you can use Remote Desktop Connection to connect to the computer. Once you've connected to it, you can run Device Manager on that computer and manage it locally. (Alternatively, if you have another remote-connection technology, you can use that instead.)

- If you don't have an account on the remote computer, but you can persuade a user of that computer to send you a Remote Assistance request or accept an unsolicited offer of Remote Assistance, you can connect to that computer. If you can then persuade that user to grant you control of the computer, you can run Device Manager on that computer and manage it.

- If the computer is running the Telnet service, you can connect to it via Telnet. (See Chapter 34 for a discussion of Telnet.)

Using Hardware Profiles for Different Configurations

This section discusses how to use hardware profiles to manage computers with two or more different hardware configurations. By using hardware profiles, you can move quickly from one hardware configuration to another hardware configuration without needing to disable, reenable, or reconfigure devices.

When to Use Hardware Profiles

Hardware profiles are most useful for laptop computers used with different hardware configurations. For example, you might use your laptop computer in a docked configuration in the office (perhaps with an external monitor or second monitor, an external keyboard and mouse, and a printer attached) and in its basic configuration on the road. If you took your laptop home from work, you might even plug it into another type of docking station connected to a different set of hardware.

Hardware profiles can also be useful for desktop computers used with substantially different configurations. For example, your company might have a workstation on a mobile cart that's wheeled from room to room, as necessary, and plugged into different network connections. This type of use is rarer than the laptop use previously described, but it happens. If this happens to you, you can benefit from using hardware profiles.

If your computer connects to a domain, you probably won't be permitted to create hardware profiles for yourself or configure the profile options to use when Windows XP Professional starts. If you need hardware profiles, an administrator will configure them for you. But you'll be able to choose the profile to use when you boot Windows XP.

Understanding the Default Hardware Profile

Each computer contains a default hardware profile called Profile 1 that Windows XP Professional creates when you install the OS. In this default profile, all the devices installed on the computer are enabled (unless they're disabled because they're not working or you've disabled them manually).

Creating a Profile

To work with hardware profiles, display the Hardware Profiles dialog box (Figure 10-9) by clicking the Hardware Profiles button on the Hardware tab of the System Properties dialog box (WINDOWS KEY–BREAK).

Figure 10-9. *Use the Hardware Profiles dialog box to create, modify, and delete profiles, and to specify how Windows XP Professional should handle profiles when it starts.*

Before creating a new profile, you may want to rename Profile 1 for clarity. Select it, click the Rename button, enter the new name in the Rename Profile dialog box, and then click the OK button.

To create a new profile, select the profile on which you want to base the profile. (At first, the only profile available is the default profile.) Then click the Copy button. In the resulting Copy Profile dialog box, enter the name for the new profile and click the OK button to create the profile. The profile then appears in the Hardware Profiles dialog box.

Choosing Which Profile to Use at Startup

As long as there's only one hardware profile, Windows XP Professional boots into it by default without consulting you. When you create one or more additional hardware profiles, Windows XP displays a menu of profiles at boot time so that you can choose which to use.

You can configure the order in which the profiles are listed on the menu by using the ↑ and ↓ buttons. The first profile on the menu is the default profile.

In the Hardware Profiles Selection group box, you can choose between having Windows XP Professional wait for you to select a hardware profile and having Windows XP automatically boot the first profile listed if you don't select a profile within the specified timeout. The default timeout is 30 seconds, but you may well want to change it.

Changing the Properties for a Profile

To change the properties for a profile, select the profile and click the Properties button to display the Properties dialog box for the profile (Figure 10-10).

If the profile is for a portable computer, select the This Is a Portable Computer check box and select the option button corresponding to the docking state the profile represents.

Select the Always Include This Profile As an Option when Windows Starts check box if you want to make sure Windows XP Professional always includes this profile on the Profiles menu. Otherwise, if Windows XP is certain this profile doesn't apply to the computer's current configuration, it may omit this profile from the Profiles menu.

Enabling and Disabling Devices in a Profile

Once you've created a new profile, set up the hardware as it will be when you use the computer in this profile. For example, dock your laptop and make sure the full set of devices is plugged into the dock or directly into the laptop; or undock your computer and unplug any extraneous peripherals. Then restart Windows XP Professional, select the new profile from the Profiles menu, and use Device Manager to enable any currently disabled devices you'll need in this profile and to disable any currently enabled devices you won't need. As mentioned earlier in this chapter, you can choose between disabling the device in the current hardware profile and disabling the device in all hardware

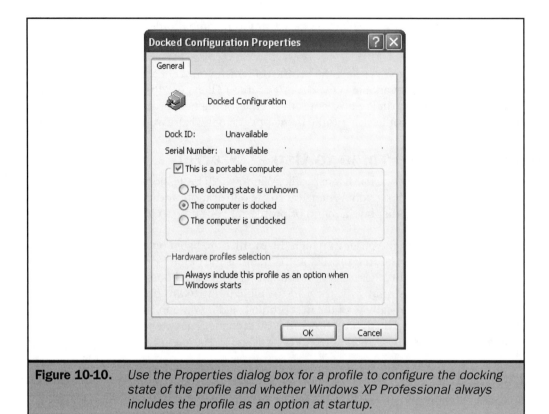

Figure 10-10. *Use the Properties dialog box for a profile to configure the docking state of the profile and whether Windows XP Professional always includes the profile as an option at startup.*

profiles. In most cases, you'll want the former setting. But if a device driver goes rogue, you may want to disable it in all hardware profiles immediately.

Beyond the devices physically present in the configuration, you may also want to disable one or more devices to improve performance on your computer. For example, if your laptop has a built-in network adapter that seems to consume large amounts of power, you might choose to disable it when you're using the laptop on battery power.

Summary

This chapter has discussed how to add hardware to your computer and reconfigure it when that hardware doesn't work correctly. It has also covered how to create and use hardware profiles for different configurations of the same computer.

The next chapter shows you how to tune Windows XP Professional for optimum performance.

The
Complete
Reference

Windows XP

Chapter 11

Tuning Windows XP Professional for Optimum Performance

203

This chapter discusses the tools that Windows XP Professional provides for managing events, logging crashes, and monitoring and improving the performance of the operating system. It covers using Event Viewer to examine the events that occur on your computer and using Dr. Watson to log data about crashes. It discusses how to use Task Manager and the Performance tool to monitor performance, and it suggests ways to improve system performance. Last, it covers how to create, change, and delete environment variables.

Managing Events

In Windows XP Professional, as in the physical world, an event takes place when something occurs. Events have differing importance, seriousness, and types. By logging events so that you can examine them when things go wrong, you can identify problems with your computer's configuration.

Windows XP Professional's Events and Log Files

Table 11-1 lists the five types of events that Windows XP Professional can log.

Table 11-2 lists the three log files of events that Windows XP maintains in the %Windir%\system32\config folder.

Event	Explanation
Error	Something went significantly wrong. For example, a service or a driver failed or some data was lost.
Warning	An anomaly or lesser problem occurred that may develop into a larger problem. For example, the backup browser stopped, or the time provider was unable to find a domain controller to use as a time source.
Information	A component (such as a driver or a service) executed successfully.
Success Audit	A user succeeded in accessing a resource that's being audited.
Failure Audit	A user tried and failed to access a resource that's being audited. Failure Audit events can indicate unauthorized attempts to access a computer or (more mundanely) that the user has forgotten their password.

Table 11-1. *Types of Event That Windows XP Professional Can Log*

Log	Filename	Contents
Application	appevent.evt	Details of events that occur in the applications running on the computer. These events are designed by the application's developers.
System	sysevent.evt	Details of events that occur in Windows XP but that aren't considered security related. For example, a network adapter might stop working, a print job might fail, or a service might be successfully started.
Security	secevent.evt	Details of security-related events, such as logons and logoffs, policy change events, and auditing (if applied).

Table 11-2. *Windows XP Professional's Event Logs, Filenames, and Contents*

For each event, Windows XP Professional records the following:

- The date and time the event occurred.
- The service or process that reported the event.
- The category into which the event falls. The Security log usually assigns a category, such as Logon/Logoff, to events, whereas many of the events in the Application log and the System log are assigned to the None category.
- The computer on which the event occurred and the user account involved. The user account may be a human user's account or the System account, which is used for running many system services.
- The Event ID (a numeric code that you can use to look up information about the event).
- The description of the event (in English—more or less).

Running Event Viewer

Windows XP's tool for examining events is Event Viewer (Figure 11-1), a Microsoft Management Console (MMC) snap-in. You can run Event Viewer either on its own or as part of another console.

You can run Event Viewer on its own in any of the following ways:

- Choose Start | Control Panel | Performance and Maintenance | Administrative Tools | Event Viewer.

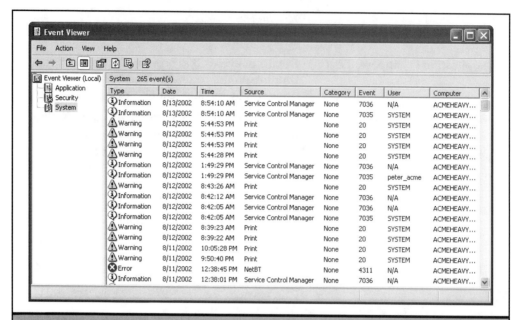

Figure 11-1. *Event Viewer lets you examine the events in the Application log, Security log, and System log.*

- Enter **eventvwr.exe** in the Run dialog box.
- If you've customized the Start menu to display Administrative Tools, choose Start | Administrative Tools | Event Viewer or Start | All Programs | Administrative Tools | Event Viewer as appropriate.

You can also run Event Viewer from its entry under the System Tools category in the Computer Management console. Or you can add Event Viewer to another custom console you create.

Reviewing Events

To review events, double-click the appropriate log in the left pane in Event Viewer to open it in the right pane. By default, Event Viewer displays the events sorted in descending order by date, so the most recent events are listed first. You can sort the events by clicking the column headings: Click a column heading once for an ascending sort, and click again for a descending sort.

Note *In a domain environment, you probably won't be able to access the Security log, but you should be able to access the Application log and System log. The red circle with the X on the Security log in Figure 11-1 indicates that access to that log is denied to the user currently logged on.*

You can customize the columns displayed in Event Viewer by choosing View | Add/Remove Columns and working in the resulting Add/Remove Columns dialog box. This dialog box also lets you rearrange the order in which the columns appear. You can also rearrange the order of the columns by dragging the column headings in the Event Viewer window.

You can open a new view of a log by issuing a New Log View command from the Action menu or the shortcut menu for the log. Event Viewer opens a new view of the log, adding a new entry with a name such as System (2) or Application (2) to the left pane. (You can change the display name—for example, for clarity—by working on the General page of the Properties dialog box for the log file.) You can then sort the different views of the log in different ways so that you can quickly toggle from one view to another by clicking the appropriate entry in the left pane.

You can filter events by issuing a View | Filter command from the menu bar or the shortcut menu for a log and working on the Filter tab of the Properties dialog box (shown on the left in Figure 11-2) for the log. The filtering options are largely self-explanatory: You can choose which event types to filter for; specify the event source, category, or event ID, user account, or computer involved; and specify a range of dates.

You can search for events that meet specific criteria by issuing a View | Find in Local *Log* command from the menu bar or the shortcut menu for a log and working in the

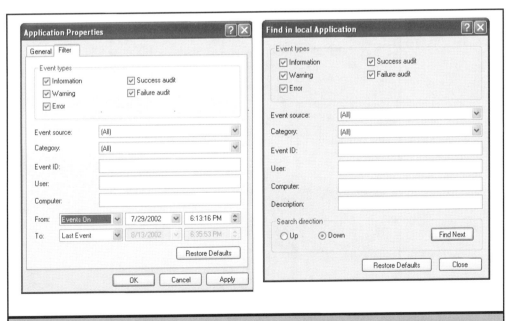

Figure 11-2.   *To find the events you need to examine, you can use the options on the Filter tab of the Properties dialog box for the log (left) to filter the events shown. Or you can use the Find in Local Log dialog box (right) to search for events that match specific criteria.*

Find in Local *Log* dialog box. (Here, *Log* is the name of the log involved.) The right screen in Figure 11-2 shows the Find in Local Application dialog box. You can specify search criteria including event types, event source, category, event ID, user account, computer and description. You can also choose whether to search up or down.

Once you've found an event you want to examine, double-click its entry to open the event's Event Properties dialog box. Figure 11-3 shows an example.

From the Event Properties dialog box, you can take the following actions:

- Use the ↑ button and the ↓ button to navigate to the previous event or next event.

- Click the Copy Event Details button to copy all the event's details to the Clipboard (for example, so that you can paste it into another application).

- If a link appears in the Description text box, and you have a functional Internet connection, click the link to open a browser window to Microsoft's Help and Support Center, where you can search for further information on the event, its implications, and how to deal with it.

- If the Bytes option button and the Words are available, use them to switch the view of the data between bytes view and words view.

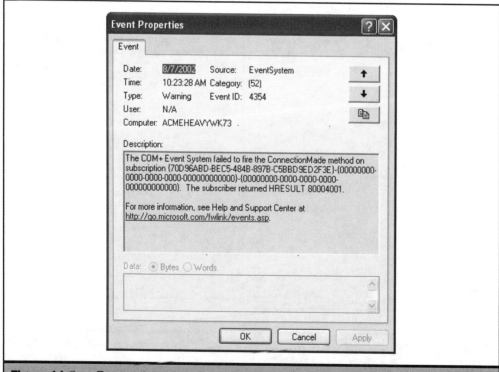

Figure 11-3.   *To examine an event in detail, open its Properties dialog box.*

Managing Your Event Log Files

Because events occur all the time, the event logs grow quickly, even when nothing has actually gone wrong on your computer. By default, Windows XP Professional sets a default size of 512KB for each log file and lets newer events overwrite older events when a log file reaches its maximum size.

If you administer your computer, you can change the maximum size for log files so that the files retain more or less information. You can also configure what Event Viewer does when the files grow beyond their allotted space, and you can clear the log. In a domain environment, log file size and behavior are usually administered centrally, and if you're not an administrator, you won't be able to see or affect the log size or behavior.

To choose settings for a log file, select it in the left pane of Event Viewer and issue a Properties command from the Action menu or shortcut menu. Event Viewer displays the General tab of the Properties dialog box for the log. Figure 11-4 shows an example

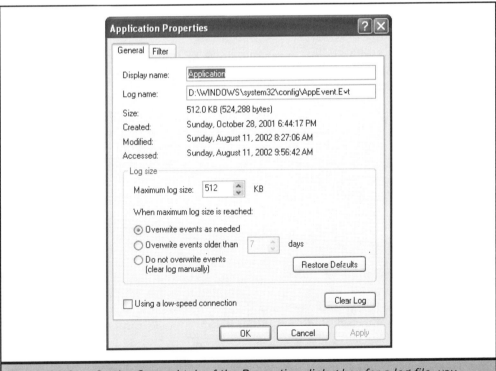

Figure 11-4. *On the General tab of the Properties dialog box for a log file, you can set a maximum size for the file and specify how Windows XP Professional should behave when the maximum size is reached.*

of the Properties dialog box for the Application log on a standalone computer. On a computer attached to a domain, the Clear Log button and the controls in the Log Size group box will usually be unavailable. You'll probably be able to change the display name for the log, but that's about it. But because you can change the name directly in the left pane of Event Viewer, it's not worth displaying the Properties dialog box for.

Specify the maximum size in the Maximum Log Size text box (the minimum size is 64KB) and choose among the Overwrite Events As Needed option button, the Overwrite Events Older Than *N* Days option button, and the Do Not Overwrite Events (Clear Log Manually) option button:

- **Overwrite Events As Needed**   The default setting. Windows XP Professional overwrites the oldest events first.

- **Overwrite Events Older Than *N* Days**   Limits Windows XP to overwriting events older than the specified number of days. If the log file grows to its maximum size within that timeframe and there are no events old enough to overwrite, Windows XP ceases writing events to the log file until you make space available. So if you use this setting, increase the maximum log file size to allow plenty of room.

- **Do Not Overwrite Events**   Stops Windows XP from overwriting events. When the log file reaches its maximum size, Windows XP ceases writing events to it. If you use this setting, remember to clear your log file regularly.

You can clear a log file by clicking the Clear Log button. Before doing so, it's a good idea to save the log file's contents by issuing a Save Log File As command from the Action menu or shortcut menu for the log file. Give the log file a descriptive name (rather than just "Application," "Security," or "System") so that when you reopen it, it'll be differentiated in the left pane of Event Viewer from the current logs.

Alternatively, after opening a saved log file (by issuing an Open Log File command from the Action menu or shortcut menu for Event Viewer itself or for any log), you can change its display name by clicking its name twice (two separate clicks, not a double-click) in the left pane and typing in the resulting edit box.

To export an event log to a file so that you can import it into a spreadsheet or database, issue an Export List command from the Action menu or shortcut menu. In the Export List dialog box, you can choose among tab-delimited text, comma-delimited text (CSV), tab-delimited Unicode text, and comma-delimited Unicode text formats. You can also choose to export only the selected rows rather than the whole event log.

Collecting Debugging Information with Dr. Watson

Windows XP Professional includes a debugging tool called Dr. Watson that you can use when you're having a serious problem with an application running on Windows XP or with Windows XP itself. Unless you have experience in debugging applications, you'll typically use Dr. Watson to collect debugging information that you then send to the software sleuths in the relevant support department. Because the files Dr. Watson produces range from large to huge, you'll usually need to compress them and submit them via FTP rather than attach them to e-mail messages (large attachments jam e-mail servers).

By default, Windows XP Professional is set to launch Dr. Watson when an *unhandled error* occurs—an error that the error-handlers in the application or in Windows XP itself are unable to deal with. To check this setting, open Registry Editor (see Chapter 40) to the HKLM\SOFTWARE\Microsoft\Windows NT\CurrentVersion\AeDebug key of the Registry and check the Auto value entry and the Debugger value entry. An Auto value of 1 means that Windows XP launches the debugger automatically. A Debugger value that includes drwtsn32 (for example, drwtsn32 –p %ld –e %ld –g) means that Dr. Watson is configured as the debugger. If you have permission to change the Registry, you can edit these value entries. But you can also set Dr. Watson to run automatically by entering **drwtsn32 –i** in the Run dialog box, which tends to be easier.

To capture more data with Dr. Watson, download the debug symbols from www.microsoft.com/ddk/debugging/symbols.asp and create a new system variable named _NT_SYMBOL_PATH with the value %systemroot%\symbols. (See "Working with Environment Variables," later in this chapter, for information on creating environment variables.)

When Dr. Watson is configured to run automatically like this, it saves information about each crash to the Documents and Settings\All Users\Application Data\Microsoft\Dr Watson\drwtsn32.log file. This is a text file, so you can view it with a text editor (such as Notepad) or word processor.

Dr. Watson has a minimal GUI (Figure 11-5) with which you can configure it to save the information you want.

Table 11-3 describes the configuration options for Dr. Watson.

Monitoring Performance

This section discusses two tools that Windows XP Professional provides for monitoring your system's performance and identifying problems: Task Manager and Performance.

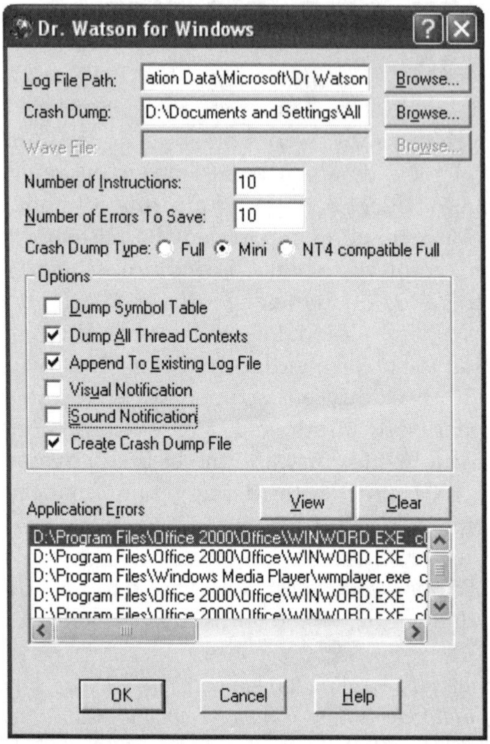

Figure 11-5. *Configure Dr. Watson to save the error information you want and to display the appropriate notification.*

Using Task Manager

As you saw in Chapter 9, you can use Task Manager to close an application or a process that has stopped responding (in other words, crashed) and to see whether an application is 32 bit or 16 bit. As you'll see later, Computer Administrator users on standalone or workgroup computers can also use Task Manager to see which processes other users are running, to log off those users, and to switch quickly to a disconnected session.

As you'll gather from that, Task Manager isn't primarily designed for monitoring performance. But it includes features that give you a quick overview of how your system is running. So it's a good way of getting an idea of whether all is well or whether you should use Performance to investigate further.

To launch Task Manager, right-click the notification area and choose Task Manager from the shortcut menu. (Alternatively, enter **taskmgr** in the Run dialog box.)

Option	Explanation
Log File Path	Specifies the folder in which Dr. Watson saves the crash data. If you change this folder, make sure the system has permission to write data to it.
Crash Dump Folder	If you select the Create Crash Dump File check box, specify the folder in which Dr. Watson should create it. Make sure the system has permission to write to this folder and that there's enough space for the type of dump you want to create.
Wave File	Specifies the sound file for Dr. Watson to play when an error occurs. Select the Sound Notification check box to enable this text box.
Number of Instructions	Specifies the number of instructions that Dr. Watson disassembles before and after the current program counter (the point at which a thread of instructions has reached) for a thread dump. The default setting is 10.
Number of Errors to Save	Specifies the maximum number of errors to save in the log file. When it reaches this number, Dr. Watson discards the oldest error to make space for each new error. The default setting is 10, which keeps the log file to a modest size.
Crash Dump Type	The option button selected controls the type of crash dump created: Full, Mini, or NT4 Compatible Full. If you're working with a support engineer, he will tell you which type of crash dump to create.
Dump Symbol Table	Controls whether Dr. Watson includes the symbol table (the memory address and name of each symbol) in the dump. Including the symbol table makes the log file much bigger, so it's best not to use this option unless the support engineer requests it.
Dump All Thread Contexts	Controls whether Dr. Watson logs all the threads in the application that suffered the crash or just the thread involved.
Append to Existing Log File	Controls whether Dr. Watson appends each crash log to the existing file or overwrites the existing file.
Visual Notification	Controls whether Dr. Watson displays a dialog box notifying you that an error has occurred and been logged.
Sound Notification	Controls whether Dr. Watson plays a sound file after a crash. You specify the file in the Wave File text box.
Create Crash Dump File	Controls whether Dr. Watson creates a crash dump file or just logs the error.

Table 11-3.   *Dr. Watson Configuration Options*

The Performance tab of Task Manager displays the following:

- The current CPU (processor) usage shows you what percentage of the available processor cycles are being used moment-by-moment. It's normal for processor usage to spike briefly to a high percentage when you launch an application. But if processor usage stays at 100 percent for more than a few seconds, the system is probably overloaded.

- The CPU usage history shows you how high the processor usage has been for the last few minutes. Use this readout to see whether processor usage has been consistently high. If your computer has dual processors, you'll see two readouts, as in Figure 11-6. If your computer has one processor, you'll see a single readout.

- The PF Usage readout shows you how much of the paging file is in use.

- The Page File Usage History shows you how much of the paging file has been in use for the last few minutes. Use this readout to track trends in paging file usage.

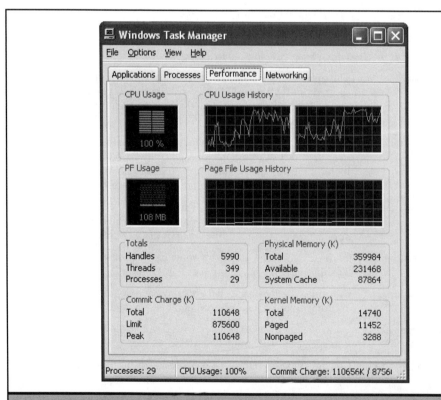

Figure 11-6. *Use the Performance tab of Task Manager to assess CPU and page file usage and to identify problems. This figure shows two boxes for CPU Usage History because this is a dual-processor computer.*

■ The Totals, Physical Memory, Commit Charge, and Kernel Memory group boxes show more detailed information on the resources available and how much has been used.

If CPU usage or page file usage stays high for a while, display the Processes tab of Task Manager and see which processes are consuming most CPU cycles and virtual memory:

■ To see which processes are using most CPU cycles, double-click the CPU column heading to perform a descending sort by it. Figure 11-7 shows an example in which HelpCtr.exe (Help and Support Center, the topmost item in the list) is using nearly half of the available CPU cycles.

■ To see which processes are using most virtual memory, choose View | Select Columns to display the Select Columns dialog box. Select the Virtual Memory Size check box and click the OK button. (Add other performance measures as well if you like.) Then perform a descending sort by the VM Size column heading.

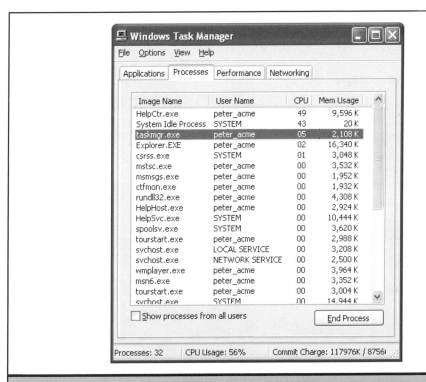

Figure 11-7.   *Use the Processes tab of Task Manager to see which processes are using most CPU cycles and virtual memory.*

Use the Applications tab of Task Manager to see if any application is not responding. If any is, use the End Task button to terminate it.

Using Performance

If Task Manager doesn't show you as much information as you need, use Windows XP's Performance tool. Performance can monitor a wide variety of *performance objects* (such as the processor, hard disk, or memory), each of which has a variety of *performance counters* (measures of how an aspect of that performance object is performing).

Performance incorporates System Monitor and Performance Logs and Alerts. System Monitor provides real-time monitoring of your system's performance, while Performance Logs and Alerts provides a way of examining your system's performance history. By using the two together, you can analyze your system's performance.

Run Performance in any of the following ways:

- Choose Start | Control Panel | Performance and Maintenance | Administrative Tools | Performance.

- Enter **perfmon.msc** in the Run dialog box to start Performance with System Monitor selected.

- If you've chosen to display the Administrative Tools menu on the Start menu or All Programs menu, choose Administrative Tools | Performance.

Using System Monitor

When you launch System Monitor, it monitors a default set of performance counters (look ahead to Figure 11-8), including memory pages per second, average disk queue length, and the percentage of processor time being used.

System Monitor largely avoids menus in favor of toolbar buttons and keyboard shortcuts. (There's a minimal shortcut menu that you can display by right-clicking anywhere in the System Monitor details pane.) Table 11-4 summarizes the toolbar buttons and keyboard shortcuts.

Toolbar Button	Keyboard Shortcut	Effect
New Counter Set	CTRL-E	Creates a new counter set
Clear Display	CTRL-D	Clears the display
View Current Activity	CTRL-T	Switches the display to show current activity

Table 11-4. *System Monitor Toolbar Buttons and Keyboard Shortcuts*

Toolbar Button	Keyboard Shortcut	Effect
View Log Data	CTRL-L	Displays the Source tab of the System Monitor Properties dialog box
View Graph	CTRL-G	Switches the display to Graph mode
View Histogram	CTRL-B	Switches the display to Histogram mode
View Report	CTRL-R	Switches the display to Report mode
Add	CTRL-I	Displays the Add Counters dialog box
Delete	DEL	Deletes the selected counter
Highlight	CTRL-H	Highlights the selected counter in the display
Copy Properties	CTRL-C	Copies the properties of the selected object
Paste Counter List	CTRL-V	Pastes the counter list
Properties	CTRL-Q	Displays the General tab of the System Monitor Properties dialog box
Freeze Display	CTRL-F	Freezes the display, stopping updates
Update Data	CTRL-U	Updates the display; available only when you've frozen the display
Help	F1	Opens the System Monitor help file

Table 11-4. *System Monitor Toolbar Buttons and Keyboard Shortcuts* (continued)

These are the main actions you can take with System Monitor:

- Change view among Graph view (the default view), Histogram view, and Report view. Histogram view uses bars rather than lines, which can make it easier to track specific counters. Report view provides a textual display of the counters, which makes it easier to track exact values.

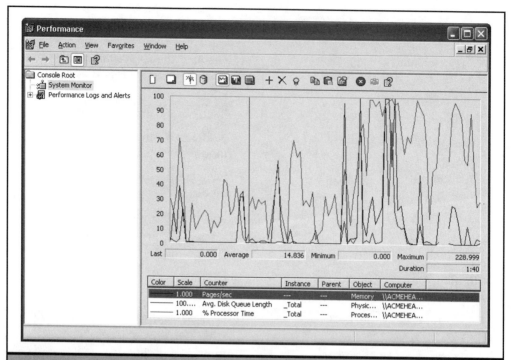

Figure 11-8. *In its default configuration, System Monitor tracks a small set of performance counters.*

- Add further performance counters to System Monitor by issuing an Add Counters command. Use the Add Counters dialog box (see Figure 11-9) to specify the computer to monitor (typically the computer you're using), the performance object (for example, Processor, Memory, Cache, or Paging File), and the specific counter. Click the Explain button in the Add Counters dialog box to display a window explaining the selected counter.

- Delete a selected counter by clicking the Delete button or pressing DEL.

- Freeze the display by clicking the Freeze button. Update the frozen display by clicking the Update Data button.

- Clear the display by clicking the Clear Display button.

- Configure the display and its contents by working on the five tabs of the Properties dialog box.

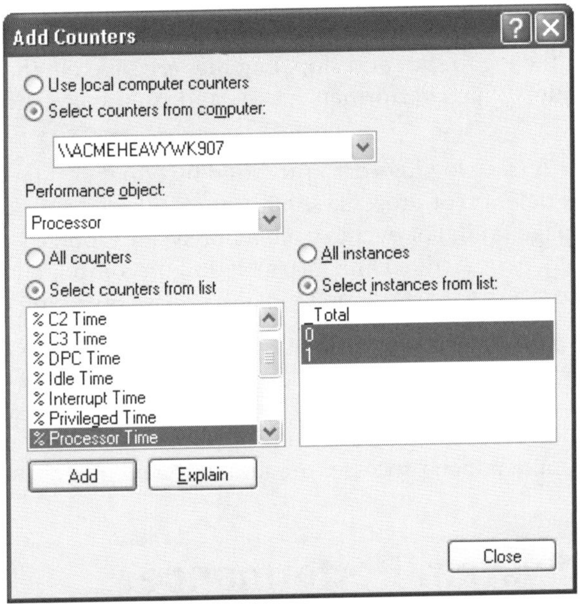

Figure 11-9. *Use the Add Counters dialog box to add performance counters to System Monitor.*

Using Performance Logs and Alerts

Performance Logs and Alerts lets you log data on performance objects and performance counters, view the resulting logs, and set alerts so Windows XP Professional can warn you when a threshold you specify has been reached.

Typically, you'll need to be an administrator to use Performance Logs and Alerts. If you're not an administrator, you'll need an administrator to grant you Full Control access to the HKLM\SYSTEM\CurrentControlSet\Services\SysmonLog\Log Queries key in the Registry on your computer and the right to start or configure services on the computer.

In a domain environment, you may find that the Performance Logs and Alerts service hasn't been installed on your computer. If this is the case, an administrator needs to install it. They can do this by opening Performance Logs and Alerts in Performance, which causes Windows XP Professional to install the Performance Logs and Alerts service automatically.

To display Performance Logs and Alerts, double-click the Performance Logs and Alerts item in Performance. Performance Logs and Alerts displays its subcomponents: Counter Logs, Trace Logs, and Alerts. You can then create the following by using the commands on the shortcut menus for these subcomponents:

- **Counter Logs**   A counter log logs data collected by the counters you set up. You can add both performance objects and performance counters to the counter log, choose sampling intervals, choose a log file type (for example, a comma-delimited text file that you could import into a spreadsheet), and arrange a schedule for the log to start and stop. Log files are saved in the %systemdrive%\ PerfLogs folder, which Performance Logs and Alerts offers to create if it doesn't exist.

- **Trace Logs**   A trace log logs data provided by either system events (such as the creation and deletion of processes and program threads, disk input and output, TCP/IP, or page faults) or events from a nonsystem source (such as the NTLM security protocol or Active Directory's NetLogon component). You can arrange a schedule for the log to start and stop and choose buffering options for the log.

- **Alerts**   An alert lets you specify one or more performance counters to watch, the schedule on which to watch them, and the action to take when one of the thresholds is reached. For example, you might set an alert to send you a network message when your computer is running short on available memory so that you can examine which processes are taking the memory.

Improving System Performance

If your computer seems to be running more slowly than it used to, follow the advice in this section to try to improve performance. The actions you can take include reducing the number of applications and services you run, minimizing the number of visual effects you're using, configuring foreground processor scheduling, choosing suitable settings for your paging file, maintaining your hard disks in good condition, and keeping Windows updated.

Lightening the Load of Applications and Services

To improve performance, run as few applications and services as is viable.

Even in a tightly controlled domain environment, you should be able to start and close applications. Reduce the number of applications that you run at the same time. Similarly, if you work with large files (for example, large graphics, audio file, video files, or publications), don't leave files open unnecessarily, because they consume memory and system resources.

Watch out for applications configured to run automatically when you log on to Windows XP Professional. As discussed in Chapter 5, applications can be run in a variety of ways at startup or logon, including via your Startup folder or the All Users Startup folder, via scripts, or as services. If you don't administer your computer, you may not be able to affect scripts or services directly. But you should be able to close unnecessary applications manually immediately after logon.

If you do administer your computer, shut down any services that you don't need to run. Because services lurk in the background and seldom advertise their presence, it can be easy to forget that you're running them even if your computer is creaking under the burden.

Check your notification area for applications that you don't need to be running at the moment.

Minimizing Visual Effects

To improve graphics performance, reduce the number of visual effects Windows XP Professional is using. To do so, follow these steps:

1. Click the Settings button in the Performance group box on the Advanced tab of the System Properties dialog box (WINDOWS KEY–BREAK) to display the Performance Options dialog box.

2. On the Visual Effects tab (shown on the left in Figure 11-10), choose either the Adjust for Best Performance option button or the Custom option button:

   ■ The Adjust for Best Performance option button turns off all the visual effects. Doing so optimizes performance, but the Windows XP interface looks less attractive. (The Adjust for Best Appearance option button turns on all the effects. The Let Windows Choose What's Best for My Computer option button applies a set of effects customized roughly to the speed of your processor and the capability of your graphics card. For any computer that isn't almost antiquated, this option turns on most or all effects.)

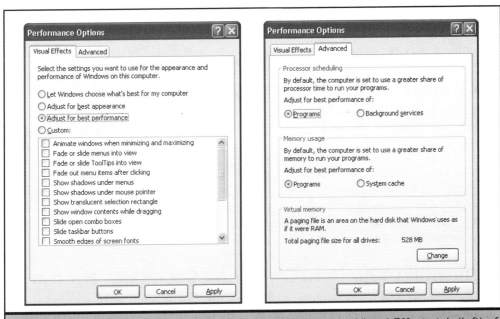

Figure 11-10. *Reduce the number of visual effects on the Visual Effects tab (left) of the Performance Options dialog box. Configure foreground processor scheduling on the Advanced tab (right).*

■ The Custom option button lets you turn on and off the visual effects manually by using their check boxes. By using this option, you can remove wasteful effects (such as Animate Windows when Minimizing and Maximizing, Show Window Contents While Dragging, and all the options whose names include the word "slide") while keeping effects that make a significant difference to the GUI (such as Smooth Edges of Screen Fonts and Use Visual Styles on Windows and Buttons).

3. Click the Apply button to see the effect of the settings you've chosen. Experiment with the visual effects settings until you find a reduced set of visual effects that looks good enough for long-term use.

Leave the Performance Options dialog box open for the next step.

Configuring Foreground Processor Scheduling

On the Advanced tab of the Performance Options dialog box (shown on the right in Figure 11-10), select the Programs option button in the Processor Scheduling group box and the Programs option button in the Memory Usage option button. The former causes Windows XP Professional to assign more slices of processor time to the foreground application, which makes it more responsive. The latter cause Windows XP to allocate more memory to applications rather than to system cache.

These two settings are the default settings for Windows XP Professional, so you shouldn't need to change them. But it's worth making sure that someone hasn't misconfigured your computer out of ignorance, incompetence, or malice. (The Background Services setting and the System Cache setting are good for servers.)

Memory and Paging File Settings

Make sure that your computer has enough RAM. Though Windows XP Professional will run with 64MB or 96MB RAM, 128MB is the practical minimum for running Windows XP Professional effectively with an application or two open. If you run multiple large applications, as most people do, get 256MB or more.

However much RAM you have, make sure that your paging file is set to a suitable size. Microsoft recommends setting the paging file to 1.5× the amount of RAM in your computer, but if your paging file usage is frequently or continually very high, you may need to increase the size of the paging file. See "Configuring the Paging File" in Chapter 39 for details on how to configure the paging file.

Defragmenting Your Hard Disks and Checking for Errors

Fragmentation can significantly decrease the performance of your hard disks, and errors on the disks can cause file corruption and data loss. To help keep your computer running as fast and smoothly as possible, regularly defragment your hard disks and check them for errors, as discussed in "Optimizing Disk Performance" in Chapter 39.

Turning Off Your Screensaver

If you want to improve performance when you're not using your computer, turn off your screensaver. As discussed in "Applying a Screensaver" in Chapter 7, screen savers are unnecessary these days. If you need your screen blanked or your computer locked after a certain period of inactivity, set Windows XP to blank it or lock it.

Keeping Windows XP Professional Updated

Use Windows Update to keep Windows XP updated with patches, security fixes, and improvements. See "Using Windows Update" in Chapter 6 for details.

Working with Environment Variables

Sometimes you'll need to set environment variables. (For example, if you need to display hidden and disconnected devices in Device Manager, you'll need to create an environmental variable, as discussed in "Displaying Hidden and Disconnected Devices" in Chapter 10.) Environmental variables are strings of text that provide information about system items such as drives, paths, or filenames.

There are two types of environment variables:

- System environment variables apply to the whole installation of Windows XP and to all users. Only administrators can create, change, and delete system environment variables.

- User environment variables apply only to the current user (let's assume that's *you*). You can create, change, and delete your user environment variables.

To work with environment variables, click the Environment Variables button on the Advanced tab of the System Properties dialog box (WINDOWS KEY–BREAK) and work in the Environment Variables dialog box (Figure 11-11).

To create a new user variable or system variable, click the New button in the User Variables group box or the System Variables group box (if it's available to you) and enter the details in the New User Variable dialog box (also shown in Figure 11-11) or the New System Variable dialog box.

To edit an existing environment variable, double-click it (or select it and click the Edit button) and work in the Edit Variable Name dialog box.

To delete an environment variable, select it and click the Delete button. Windows XP Professional doesn't confirm the deletion. If you delete an environment variable by mistake, you can recover it by using the Cancel button to close the Environment Variables dialog box. (Doing so also loses any other changes you've made in the dialog box.)

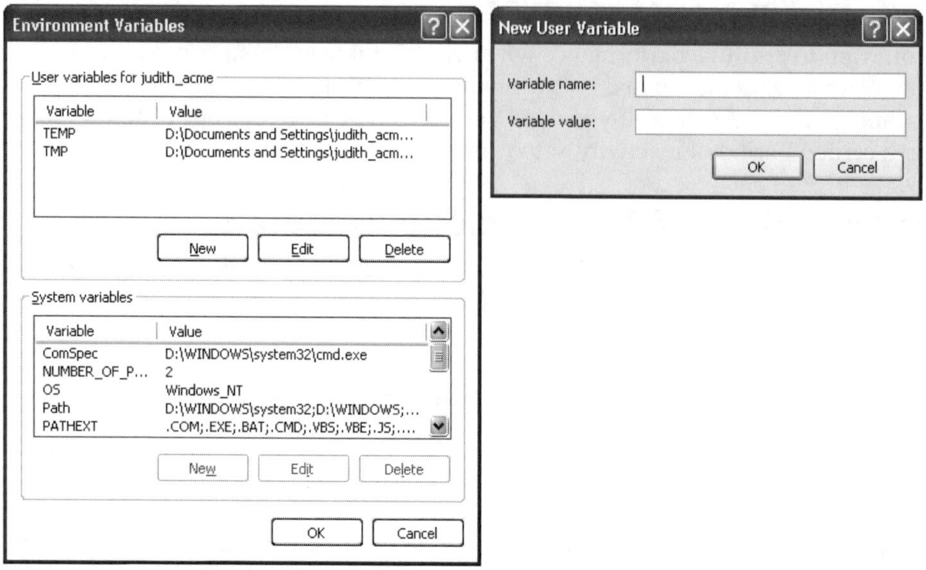

Figure 11-11. *From the Environment Variables dialog box, you can create new environmental variables, or edit or delete existing variables.*

Summary

This chapter has discussed how to use Event Viewer to examine the events that occur on your computer, how to use Dr. Watson to collect debugging information, and how to use Performance Monitor. It has also covered the main ways of improving system performance. Finally, it has shown you how to work with environment variables.

The next chapter discusses how to configure and manage printing.

The
Complete
Reference

Chapter 12

Configuring and
Managing Printing

225

T his chapter discusses how to set up and manage printing on your computer. If your computer attaches to a domain, you probably use network printers administered by the domain administrator. You can also use one or more local printers installed on your computer, either instead of or in addition to network printers. (For example, you might need a local printer to print confidential documents away from the maddening horde.)

In a domain environment, you're unlikely to share a printer connected to your computer with other users or to use a printer shared by another user's computer, so this chapter doesn't discuss those topics. See "Sharing Printers and Connecting to Shared Printers" in Chapter 27 for information on how to share printers with Windows XP Professional.

Setting Up Printers

This section discusses how to set up local printers, printers shared on the network, and Internet printers. A *local printer* is a printer attached to your computer. A *printer shared on the network* is a printer being shared by a server computer or by a dedicated print server device. (A workgroup computer can also share a printer with other computers in a workgroup. "Sharing a Printer" in Chapter 27 discusses how to set up such printer sharing.) An *Internet printer* is a printer that's attached to a computer, attached to a server computer, or attached to a print server, and that's being shared across an Internet connection.

Setting Up a Local Printer

Windows XP Professional usually detects a new local printer that you attach to your computer. When it detects the printer, Windows XP searches for a suitable printer driver, loads it automatically, and displays a pop-up to let you know the printer is installed and available. If Windows XP can't find a suitable driver, it launches the Found New Hardware Wizard to let you provide the driver to use.

If Windows XP Professional fails to detect the printer, choose Start | Control Panel | Printers and Other Hardware | Add a Printer to launch the Add Printer Wizard. Follow through the choices the wizard presents. The key choices are as follows:

- On the Local or Network Printer page, select the Local Printer Attached to This Computer option button.

- On the Select a Printer Port page, either select an existing port in the Use the Following Port drop-down list or select the Create a New Port option button and use the Type of Port drop-down list to specify the details. If your computer has a single parallel port, it's likely to be LPT1.

- Assign a name to the printer. The wizard suggests a default name based on the printer's make and model, but you may want to make the name more descriptive.

If you plan to share the printer (as discussed in "Sharing a Printer" in Chapter 27), keep the printer name short enough that the full printer name (including the computer's name and all backslashes required) is 31 characters or less.

■ If you already have another printer installed on your computer, choose whether to make the new printer the default.

■ Choose whether to share the printer with other users. (Again, see "Sharing a Printer" in Chapter 27.)

You can also launch the Add Printer Wizard by double-clicking the Add Printer item in the Select Printer group box that appears in common Print dialog boxes.

Setting Up a Network Printer

The procedure for setting up a network printer is a little different, depending on whether your computer is part of a domain or a workgroup. Either way, take the following steps, and then move to the appropriate subsection.

1. Launch the Add Printer Wizard by choosing Start | Control Panel | Printers and Other Hardware | Add a Printer.

2. On the Local or Network Printer page, select the A Network Printer, or a Printer Attached to Another Computer option button.

Setting Up a Network Printer in a Domain Environment

To set up a network printer in a domain environment, follow these steps:

1. On the Specify a Printer page, select the Find a Printer in the Directory option button.

2. Click the Next button. Windows XP Professional displays the Find Printers window. Figure 12-1 shows the Find Printers window after a successful search for printers.

3. Use the fields on the Printers tab, the Features tab, and the Advanced tab to specify details of the printers you're searching for. For example, you might search for printers in a specific location by using the Location field on the Printers tab. Or you might search for color printers by selecting the Can Print Color check box on the Features tab. Alternatively, leave all the fields clear to search for all the printers you're allowed to see.

4. Click the Find Now button. The list box at the bottom of the Find Printers window displays the list of printers found.

5. Select the printer to which you want to connect, and then click the OK button.

6. If this isn't the first printer you've added, choose whether to make this your default printer. Then close the wizard.

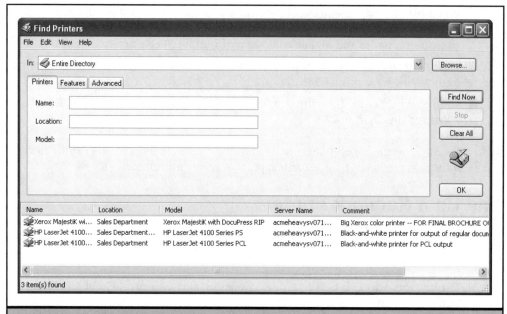

Figure 12-1. *Use the Find Printers window to search for printers in a domain environment.*

 If you know the full path to a network printer, you can set the printer up quickly by entering the path and printer name in the Run dialog box and clicking the OK button. Windows XP Professional sets up the printer automatically and displays a window showing the print queue for the printer.

Setting Up a Network Printer in a Workgroup

To set up a network printer in a workgroup, follow these steps:

1. On the Specify a Printer page, select the Browse for a Printer option button if the printer you're trying to add is connected to the network and active.

   ■ Use the Connect to This Printer option button if you know the name of the printer and the computer it's connected to. Enter the path and name.

   ■ Use the Connect to a Printer on the Internet or on a Home or Office Network option button if you know the URL for a shared printer. (See the next section.)

2. If you selected the Browse for a Printer option button, the wizard displays the Browse for Printer page (Figure 12-2).

3. Drill down to the printer and select it.

4. If this isn't the first printer you've added, choose whether to make it your default printer. Choose whether to print a test page, and then close the wizard.

Setting Up an Internet Printer

Windows XP Professional can also print to a printer that's shared on the Internet. For example, your company might share one or more printers on the Internet, so employees working on the road or at remote offices could print reports at the main office. Because sharing a printer on the Internet can represent a security threat to the company's network, shared printers are likely to be both tightly managed and of limited capabilities. You can also set up a printer on a home network for sharing if necessary.

You can set up an Internet printer in either of two ways. The more formal way is to follow these steps:

1. On the Specify a Printer page, select the Connect to a Printer on the Internet or on a Home or Office Network option button. Enter the printer's URL in the text box.

2. When prompted, enter your user name and password for the printer.

3. If the wizard prompts you to install a driver for the printer, do so.

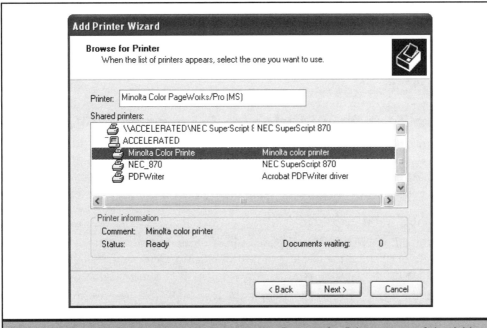

Figure 12-2. *Select the shared printer on the Browse for Printer page of the Add Printer Wizard.*

The other way to set up an Internet printer is to follow these steps:

1. Use a web browser to connect to the home page for the server that controls the printer you want to add. Browse to the URL http://*server*/Printers, where *server* is the IP address or name of the server.

2. On the Printers page displayed, click the link for the printer.

3. In the Printer Actions list on the printer's page, click the Connect link. Again, you may need to install a driver for the printer.

Setting Up a Printer for Printing to a File

By printing a document to a file, you can create a file you or someone else can use to produce a printout without needing an application that can read the original document. This capability is useful when you need to transfer files to other people in a printable condition. For example, you might need to send a print file to someone at a remote office so that they could print the document. Or you might need to have a print shop run out a high-quality color document for you.

You can print to a file from any printer by selecting the Print to File check box in the Print dialog box that most applications display when you issue a Print command. But if you need to print to a file frequently, you can set up a printer so that it always prints to a file. Doing this eliminates the chance of your forgetting to select the Print to File check box when printing.

To set up a printer to always print to a file, create the printer entry as usual. Then display the Properties dialog box for the printer and select the FILE port in the list box on the Ports page.

To indicate a printer is set to print to a file, Windows XP Professional adds a disk to the printer's icon.

Setting Up a Text-Only Printer for Printing to a File

If you need to save text-based output from an application, but the application you're using offers only a Print command, create a generic text-only printer and print the output to a file for that printer.

To add a generic text-only printer, follow these steps:

1. Run the Add Printer Wizard.

2. Select the Local Printer Attached to This Computer option button on the Local or Network Printer page. Clear the Automatically Detect and Install My Plug and Play Printer check box.

3. Select the FILE: (Print to File) item in the Use the Following Port drop-down list on the Select a Printer Port page.

4. On the Install Printer Software page, select Generic in the Manufacturer list box and Generic/Text Only in the Printers list box.

When you print to a file for this printer, Windows XP creates a text file that you can then open using any text editor (for example, Notepad) or word processor.

Deleting a Printer Entry

You can delete a printer entry by selecting it and issuing a Delete command—for example, pressing DEL or clicking the Delete This Printer link in the Tasks list. Windows XP Professional confirms the deletion. When it removes the printer entry, Windows XP keeps the printer driver on your computer in case you need to set up the printer entry again.

Managing Your Printers and Print Server

This section discusses how to manage printers and your print server. The *print server* is the software that controls printing on your computer.

The Properties dialog box for a printer contains a large number of options for configuring the printer. If the printer is installed locally or if you administer the printer, you'll be able to set all or most of these options. If you use a network printer administered by others, you probably won't be able to set *any* of the options. But you should be able to use the two command buttons on the General tab of the Properties dialog box: the Print Test Page button and the Printing Preferences button.

To display the Properties dialog box for a printer, select it on the Printers and Faxes screen, and then click the Set Printer Properties link in the Printer Tasks list. Alternatively, issue a Properties command from the File menu or the shortcut menu for the printer.

Because of this, this section discusses the printing options by functionality, starting with the functions you'll be able to use, even in a tightly controlled domain environment, rather than listing them all in order.

One topic this section doesn't discuss is sharing a printer. See Chapter 27 for information on sharing a printer.

Note   *The options this section discusses are those for a typical laser printer. If you have an inkjet printer or another type of printer, your printer may offer further options. Typically, you access these options on extra tabs in the Properties dialog box for the printer. (Other printers come with custom configuration software.)*

Changing Your Default Printer

By default, Windows XP Professional makes the first printer you install your default printer. When you install another printer, Windows XP asks if you want to make that printer your default printer.

To change the default printer when you're not running the Add Printer Wizard, select a printer you want to use as the default and issue a Set As Default Printer command from the File menu or the shortcut menu. You may be able to change your default printer in a domain environment.

Printing a Test Page

To print a test page, click the Print Test Page button on the General page of the Properties dialog box. You should be able to do this in a domain environment.

Changing Printer Preferences

To set printing preferences, display the Printing Preferences dialog box by taking one of the following actions:

- Click the Select Printing Preferences link in the Printer Tasks list on the Printers and Faxes screen.

- Issue a Printing Preferences command from the File menu or the shortcut menu on the Printers and Faxes screen.

- Click the Printing Preferences button on the General tab of the Properties dialog box for the printer.

- When printing, click the Preferences button in the common Print dialog box that appears when you issue a Print command from most applications.

The tabs of the Printing Preferences dialog box contain options for specifying print layout, page order, the number of document pages to print on each sheet of paper, paper quality, and so on. (If you administer the printer, you can choose the default settings for these options by clicking the Printing Defaults button on the Advanced tab of the Properties dialog box and working in the resulting Printing Defaults dialog box.)

You may well be able to set your printing preferences in a domain environment. But you're unlikely to be able to take any of the actions discussed in the following sections.

Setting the Printer's Name, Location, and Comment

The General tab of the Properties dialog box contains fields containing the printer's name, details of its location, and any comment the administrator has applied to the printer. If you administer the printer, you can change these fields. In a domain environment, you normally won't be able to change these fields.

The General tab also contains details of the printer model and its features (including its speed, resolution, and whether it can print in color).

Enabling Bidirectional Support

This option applies to local printers only—and only to local printers that provide bidirectional support. *Bidirectional support* lets the printer notify the computer of events, such as the toner running low or the paper jamming.

To enable bidirectional support, select the Enable Bidirectional Support check box on the Ports tab of the Properties dialog box for the printer. If the printer doesn't provide bidirectional support, Windows XP makes this option unavailable.

Creating, Configuring, and Deleting Printer Ports

You may occasionally need to create, configure, or delete printer ports. To do so, you work on the Ports tab of the Properties dialog box for the printer.

In most cases, you'll seldom need to add a port, even on printers you administer. Devices that need custom ports often have setup routines that create and configure the necessary port automatically.

The type of port you're most likely to need to add is a TCP/IP port, which lets you print to a print device connected to the network. To do so, click the Add Port button, select the Standard TCP/IP Port item in the Printer Ports dialog box, and click the New Port button. Windows XP Professional launches the Add Standard TCP/IP Printer Port Wizard, which leads you through the steps of supplying the IP address of the print device and creating a port that connects to it. The wizard checks the connection to the port and tells you whether it's working.

Another reason you may want to create a port is to redirect print jobs from a printer that's temporarily not working. To do so, select the Local Port item in the Printer Ports dialog box, click the New Port button, and enter the UNC name of the printer in the Enter a Port Name dialog box—for example, \\acmeheavysv071\laserjet. Print jobs to the dysfunctional printer will be rerouted to the printer you specify.

When you delete a port, Windows XP confirms the deletion.

To configure a port, select its entry and click the Configure Port button. The options available for configuring a port depend on the port type. Figure 12-3 shows two examples of the types of dialog box you may see. The left screen shows the Configure PrintServer dialog box for a Linksys print server. The right screen shows the Configure LPT Port dialog box for a parallel port.

Creating Multiple Printer Entries for a Printer

By creating multiple printer entries for a printer, you can print to that printer with different sets of options far more quickly and conveniently than by changing a slew of configuration options manually from one print job to the next. For example, you could set up one printer entry for high-quality color printing and another for draft-quality monochrome printing. Or you could create printer entries with different availability times or priorities.

To create a second (or subsequent) printer entry, install the printer by using the Add Printer Wizard as you did before. On the Use Existing Driver page, select the Keep Existing Driver option button. On the Name Your Printer page, give the printer a name different from the first printer entry. Add a comment explaining what the printer is set up for.

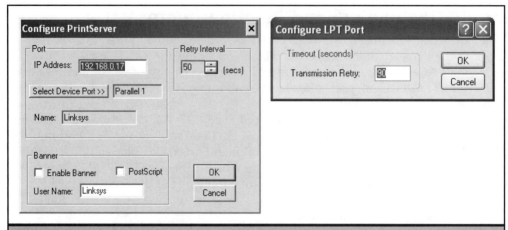

Figure 12-3.   *The configuration options available for a printer port depend on the port type. There are two examples: a print server and a conventional parallel port.*

Limiting the Times a Printer Is Available

You can limit the times a printer is available by selecting the Available From option button on the Advanced tab of the Properties dialog box for the printer, and then specifying the start time and finish time in the text boxes.

Configuring Spooling

By default, Windows XP Professional *spools* documents you print, which means it saves the print jobs quickly to disk and then feeds them from there to the printer more slowly across the printer's cable. This arrangement normally works well. Its main point is to enable the application from which you're printing to finish dealing with the print job sooner than it could if it were to send the print job directly to the printer. The disadvantage to spooling is it takes up disk space. If that disk space is local (as it will be for a local printer), you stack up many print jobs, and your hard disk is short of space, spooling might cause problems.

If you need to turn off spooling (you won't normally need to), select the Print Directly to the Printer option button on the Advanced tab of the Properties dialog box for the printer. You may want to do this if you suspect spooling is causing errors with printing.

If you suspect spooling of causing mischief, you can also try using the Start Printing after Last Page Is Spooled option button instead of the Start Printing Immediately option button. By delaying the start of printing until the whole document has been spooled, makes sure the entire document is ready for the printer. This can help eliminate some printing problems.

To learn or change the location of your spool folder, visit the Advanced tab of the Print Server Properties dialog box. (See "Configuring Print Server Properties," later in this chapter.)

Applying a Color Profile

For a color printer, Windows XP Professional uses a *color profile* to match color output to the colors it's supposed to have. Windows XP applies a color profile automatically from those it has available (in the %systemroot%\system32\spool\drivers\color folder), but you can apply a different color profile manually if you choose.

To apply a color profile, select the Manual option button, and then click the Add button and use the Add Profile Association dialog box to select the profile. Use the Set As Default button to set a color profile as your default.

Configuring Printer Pooling

If you have two or more printers of the same type, you can pool them to create a printer pool. The *printer pool* is represented by a single printer entry in Windows XP. When people print to that printer entry, the print jobs are distributed among the printers in the pool, according to which printers are available. Pooling thus enables you to balance the printing load among two or more printers.

To set up pooling, install both or all the printers that will participate in the pool. Select the Enable Printer Pooling check box on the Ports tab of the Properties dialog box for each printer and select the appropriate ports in the Print to the Following Port(s) list box.

When you print to pooled printers, you can't control which printer prints your print job, so you need to check each printer for your printout. Unless the pooled printers are located in different locations, this shouldn't be difficult.

Setting Printer Priority

If you set up multiple printer entries for the same printer, you can assign them different priorities by using the Priority text box on the Advanced tab of the Properties dialog box. The default priority is 1, the lowest setting. The highest priority is 99. Jobs from the printer entry with the highest priority take precedence in the print queue over jobs from printer entries with lower priorities.

Using a Separator Page

Separator pages are useful for keeping print jobs separate, particularly on busy network printers. A separator page usually contains brief details of the job and the user or computer who printed it. Some organizations prefer not to use separator pages because they waste paper.

To use a separator page with your print jobs, click the Separator Page button on the Advanced tab of the Properties dialog box. Then use the resulting Separator Page Properties dialog box to specify the path and filename to the page.

You'll find several separator page files in the %Windir%\system32 folder. Separator page files are small text files given the SEP extension. If you know the appropriate printing codes, you can create your own separator page files in Notepad.

Choosing Other Advanced Options

The Advanced tab of the Properties dialog box for a printer also contains the following options:

- The Hold Mismatched Documents check box causes Windows XP Professional to hold in the print queue any documents that don't match the printer setup. Doing this can help avoid misprinted documents.

- The Print Spooled Documents First check box makes Windows XP print fully spooled documents before partly spooled documents with higher priorities. Using this setting can streamline printing.

- The Keep Printed Documents check box controls whether Windows XP retains the spooled files on disk after printing them. Select this check box temporarily if you need to keep the spooled files so you can print jobs again quickly. Don't leave this check box selected for a long time because all the spooled files will choke up your disk.

- The Enable Advanced Printing Features check box controls whether Windows XP enables advanced printing features for the printer. Advanced printing features include features such as printing different numbers of document pages per sheet of paper and printing pages in orders other than page order.

Configuring Print Server Properties

As well as configuring your printers, you can configure your print server, the software that controls printing on your computer. To do so, choose File | Server Properties from the Printers and Faxes window and work in the resulting Print Server Properties dialog box.

For a printer you manage, you should be able to use all the print server controls. In a domain environment with network printers, however, you can probably use only these few controls:

- **Forms page**   Choose between Metric units and English units.
- **Drivers page**   View the properties of a driver on the Drivers tab.
- **Advanced page**   Use the Show Informational Notifications for Local Printers check box and the Show Informational Notifications for Network Printers.

You'll probably need to ask an administrator to adjust any other controls. The Print Server Properties dialog box contains four tabs:

- The Forms tab contains details of the forms set up for printing. You can create new forms based on existing forms and delete existing custom forms. You can choose between metric units of measurement and English units (in other words, inches).

- The Ports tab lists the existing ports on the print server. You can configure these ports, delete them, and add new ports.

- The Drivers tab lists the drivers installed for the printers. You can check the properties of a driver, remove it, replace it, or add another driver.

- The Advanced tab contains nine options, discussed in Table 12-1.

Option	Explanation
Spool Folder	The folder in which Windows XP Professional stores spooled files when printing. You can change the spool folder by typing the path to a different folder. For best performance, move the spool folder to a volume other than your system volume.
Log Spooler Error Events	Whether Windows XP Professional enters printer-related error events in the System log.
Log Spooler Warning Events	Whether Windows XP Professional enters printer-related warning events in the System log.
Log Spooler Information Events	Whether Windows XP Professional enters printer-related information events in the System log.
Beep on Errors of Remote Document	Whether the computer running the print server beeps when there's an error in printing a document sent by a remote computer.
Show Informational Notifications for Local Printers	Whether Windows XP Professional displays information pop-ups in the notification area when it's printing a job on a local printer or a standalone network printer.
Show Information Notifications for Network Printers	Whether Windows XP Professional displays information pop-ups in the notification area when it's printing a job on a printer connected to another computer.

Table 12-1. *Options on the Advanced Tab of the Print Server Properties Dialog Box*

Option	Explanation
Notify when Remote Documents Are Printed	Whether Windows XP Professional notifies remote users when their documents have printed.
Notify Computer, Not User, when Remote Documents Are Printed	(Available only when the Notify when Remote Documents Are Printed check box is selected.) Whether Windows XP Professional sends a notification to the computer from which the print job was sent, rather than to the user (who may have moved to a different computer).

Table 12-1.   *Options on the Advanced Tab of the Print Server Properties Dialog Box* (continued)

Printing a Document

To print a document, issue a Print command by choosing File | Print or pressing CTRL+P (the standard keystroke for Print) or an equivalent keystroke. The application displays the Print dialog box, of which Figure 12-4 shows an example. Select the printer to use, specify any further options, and click the Print button.

Many applications also include a Print button on a toolbar. This button typically prints the document with default settings without displaying the Print dialog box for you to check and change settings.

You can print a document directly from Windows Explorer by dragging the document to the icon for a printer (for example, in the Printers and Faxes window or on your Desktop). You can also print some documents by right-clicking their icon and choosing Print from the shortcut menu or (in Windows Explorer) the File menu.

While a document is being spooled, is waiting in the print queue, or is being printed, Windows XP Professional displays a printer icon in the notification area. You can hover the mouse pointer over this icon to get a quick readout of how many documents you have "pending" or double-click the icon to display a window showing the print queue. (If you have documents pending for multiple printers, Windows XP opens a window to show each queue.)

Printing When Offline

If you use a local printer rather than a network printer, you can put the printer offline and queue up jobs for it. This capability is useful both when you're offline from the printer and when you're online but want to hold print jobs till later.

To put a local printer offline, issue a Use Printer Offline command from the File menu or the shortcut menu from the Printers and Faxes screen. To put the printer back online, issue a Use Printer Online command from the File menu or the shortcut menu.

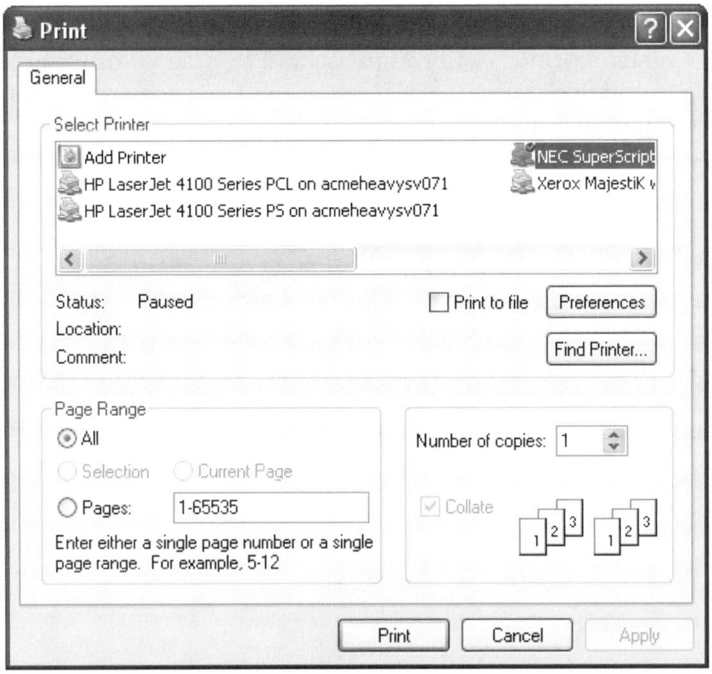

Figure 12-4. *Choose options for printing your document in the Print dialog box.*

Managing Print Jobs and Print Queues

Before a print job you've sent to the printer gets printed, you can manipulate it in the print queue (if you have permission). To do so, double-click the print queue for the printer by double-clicking the printer icon in the notification area.

From the print queue window's Document menu or the shortcut menu for a print job, you can take the following actions:

- Pause and resume print jobs.
- Restart a print job so it prints again from the beginning.
- Cancel a print job.
- Change the properties of a print job (for example, you can change the job's priority or apply a schedule to it).

For a local printer or a printer you control, you can easily manage the jobs in the print queue. For a network printer, your domain administrator is likely to have restricted you to managing the jobs you printed. Almost certainly, you'll be able to cancel your own print jobs. You may also be able to pause and resume them.

If you administer a printer, you can pause and resume all printing, or cancel all print jobs, from the printer's entry on the Printers and Faxes screen by issuing commands from the File menu or the shortcut menu.

Summary

This chapter has discussed how to install, configure, and troubleshoot printers.

This is the end of the first part of the book, which has dealt with installing and configuring Windows XP Professional.

The next part of the book shows you how to use Windows XP Professional for work and communications. The next chapter covers how to use the Windows XP interface effectively.

The
Complete
Reference

Windows XP

Part II

Working and Communicating

The Complete Reference

Chapter 13

Using the Windows XP Interface Effectively

This chapter discusses how to work effectively with the Windows XP interface. It starts by describing how to log on and log off in both a domain environment and a workgroup or standalone environment. The chapter shows you how to put Windows XP into standby and hibernation and how to exit Windows XP. It then covers the essential maneuvers for navigating the Windows XP interface. The chapter then covers how to get help by using Help and Support Center and context-sensitive help, and it outlines what the Remote Assistance feature is for. Last, it explains how to manage files and folders.

This chapter assumes the computer you're using is connected to a Windows domain, but it also discusses the Fast User Switching feature that Windows XP Professional provides for standalone computers and workgroup computers.

Logging On and Logging Off

To start work on Windows XP Professional, you *log on*, identifying yourself to the computer and (in a domain environment) to the servers that run the domain. At logon, Windows XP Professional authenticates you in the appropriate security context. For a domain computer, Windows XP Professional checks that you're permitted at the current time to log on to the computer you're trying to use and you supplied the correct password to prove your identity. For a standalone or workgroup computer, Windows XP checks that you have an account on the computer, your password matches the stored password, and you're allowed to log on at this time. (A Computer Administrator user can specify that another user only use the computer during certain hours.)

Windows XP Professional offers two different logon mechanisms: the Log On to Windows dialog box and the Welcome screen. The Log On to Windows dialog box is used for logging on to Windows networks but can also be used on standalone computers and workgroup computers. The Welcome screen is used only for logging on to standalone computers and workgroup computers that use the Fast User Switching feature: it can't be used to log on to a domain-based Windows network.

Logging On to a Domain

When your computer connects to a domain, only one user can log on at a time. This is for security and performance reasons. For logging on to a domain, Windows XP Professional always uses the Log On to Windows dialog box.

To log on to a domain, enter your user name and password in the Log On to Windows dialog box (Figure 13-1).

You'll probably have to press CTRL-ALT-DEL to display the Log On to Windows dialog box. Most administrators use the administration option that requires users to press CTRL-ALT-DEL for security reasons. Otherwise, malefactors can create a facsimile of the Log On to Windows dialog box and its background screen and use the fake to capture the user names and passwords of users who log on.

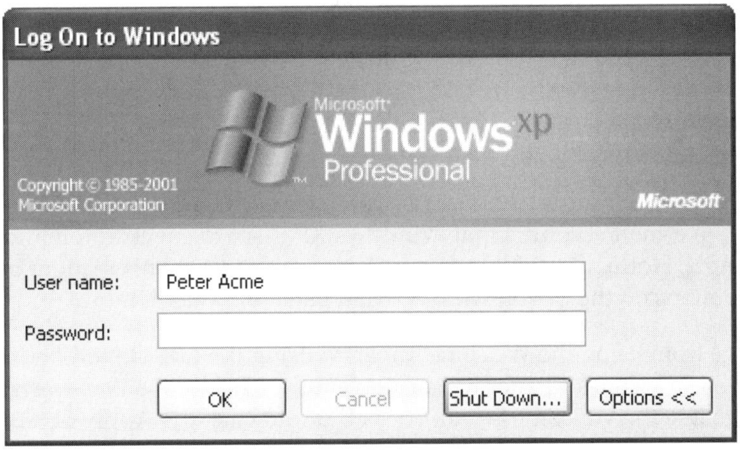

Figure 13-1.   *The Log On to Windows dialog box*

By default, the Log On to Windows dialog box displays the name of the last user to log off as a convenience. Because displaying this user name is also a security threat, many administrators suppress the display of the user name—so even if you were the last person to log off, you still need to enter your user name manually.

Clicking the Options button toggles the display of a Shutdown button, which you can click to display the Shut Down Windows dialog box.

Logging Off from a Domain

To end your user session on a computer connected to a domain, you log off. To do so, choose Start | Log Off and click the Log Off button in the Log Off Windows dialog box.

Before you log off, it's best to save all unsaved work in the applications you have open and close those applications manually. If you don't save your work, Windows XP prompts you to save it as it closes the applications automatically.

Logging On via the Welcome Screen

The Welcome screen is used by default for Windows XP Professional running on standalone computers and workgroup computers. This is because these computers are automatically configured to use Windows XP's Fast User Switching feature. The Welcome screen lists in alphabetical order the user accounts set up on the computer, except for the Administrator account, which it lists only if you force it to. (See "Forcing Windows XP to Display the Administrator Account on the Welcome Screen" in Chapter 27 for details of how to do this.)

The Welcome screen also displays basic data about any users currently logged on:

- It displays *Logged On* for a user who has a disconnected session with no applications running.

- It displays *N programs running* (where *N* is the number) for a user who has a disconnected session with applications running.

- It displays the number of unread e-mail messages the users have waiting for them in e-mail accounts that Windows XP is set to check automatically (for example, Hotmail or MSN accounts). You can remove this readout by using the options on the Logon\Unread Mail page of Tweak UI.

To change from using the Welcome screen to using the Log On to Windows dialog box, choose Start | Control Panel | User Accounts | Change the Way Users Log On or Off. Clear the Use the Welcome Screen check box and click the Apply Options button. When you clear the Use the Welcome Screen check box, Windows XP automatically clears the Use Fast User Switching check box and makes it unavailable, because Fast User Switching works only when the computer uses the Welcome screen.

If you set Windows XP Professional up on a standalone or workgroup computer with only one user, and you don't assign that user a password, Windows XP automatically logs the user on. You can prevent the automatic logon by assigning that user a password or by using the technique described in "Setting Up a User Account to Log On Automatically" in Chapter 5.

Logging Off with Fast User Switching Enabled

To log off a computer that's using Fast User Switching, choose Start | Log Off and click the Log Off button on the Log Off Windows screen.

Troubleshooting Welcome Screen Logon Problems

The Welcome screen simplifies the process of logging on to Windows XP for standalone and workgroup computers. But it's not able to convey the subtleties of restrictions administrators can place on user accounts. If the user account has expired, been disabled, or has time restrictions outside which the present moment falls, the Welcome screen prompts you for a password rather than telling you what the actual problem is. Because the password isn't the problem, entering the correct password doesn't let you use the account: Windows XP simply prompts you for the password again.

So if you implement account restrictions on a standalone or workgroup computer, use the Log On to Windows dialog box rather than the Welcome screen. If you need to use Fast User Switching, you have to use the Welcome screen. Explain the account restrictions to the users affected, including why supplying their correct password won't work.

Chapter 27 discusses how to manage user accounts on a standalone or workgroup computer.

Switching Users

If your computer isn't connected to a domain, you can use Windows XP's Fast User Switching feature. *Fast User Switching* enables two or more users to be logged on to the computer at the same time: one using it in what's termed the *active session* and the others not using it, but with their user sessions still running (*disconnected sessions*). Instead of logging out, the active user can *switch users* to disconnect their user session and leave it running in the background.

To switch users, choose Start | Log Off and click the Switch User button on the Log Off Windows screen. Windows XP disconnects your user session and displays the Welcome screen so that another user can log on or resume a disconnected session of theirs.

If you're a Computer Administrator user, you can switch to another disconnected session from Task Manager. On the Users tab of Task Manager, right-click the account's user name and choose Connect from the shortcut menu. If there's a password, enter it in the Connect Password Required dialog box.

By default, Windows XP's screen saver disconnects the active session and, when interrupted, displays the Welcome screen. To prevent the screen saver from disconnecting the active session like this, clear the On Resume, Display Welcome Screen check box on the Screen Saver tab of the Display Properties dialog box. Windows XP then resumes the active session when you move the mouse or press a key after the screen saver has been launched.

When a user's session is disconnected, either by the user issuing a Switch User command or by Windows XP starting the screen saver, the user's applications keep running and their files stay open. This introduces various complications to Windows XP:

- The applications and files open in a disconnected user session take up RAM, so a computer needs more RAM to run well with Fast User Switching. 128MB is adequate for Windows XP with moderate applications and without Fast User Switching. For Fast User Switching, you need 256MB or more, depending on how many disconnected user sessions the computer will sometimes have.

- The applications in a disconnected session are usually left running, rather than being suspended, so they consume some processor cycles. A busy application in a disconnected session can slow or hamstring the active session.

- Any files the disconnected user had open in their session remain open, and any unsaved changes remain unsaved. What happens if the active user tries to open the same file depends on the sophistication of the application involved. Some applications prevent the active user from opening the file because it's open already. Other applications let the active user open the file and save changes, thereby trashing the other user's changes.

- When an application in the active session requires common hardware resources that an application in a disconnected session has been using, the application in the disconnected session must release those resources. For example, if the active session starts playing audio, it needs to use the sound card, even if an application in a disconnected session has been using the sound card.

■ An application in a disconnected session can still use shared resources such as an Internet connection. If a user in a disconnected session is performing a large download, watching streaming video, or listening to streaming audio, little bandwidth may be available to the user in the active session.

■ If the active user is a Computer Administrator user, he can log off users in disconnected sessions. Any user not prevented from shutting down the computer can shut down the computer together with those disconnected sessions. Either way, any unsaved work in any disconnected session will be lost.

Turning Fast User Switching On and Off

To turn Fast User Switching on or off, follow these steps:

1. When turning Fast User Switching off, make sure no disconnected user session is running. (See "Checking Who's Logged On and Which Applications They're Running," next, for a discussion of how to do this.)

2. Choose Start | Control Panel | User Accounts | Change the Way Users Log On or Off.

3. Select or clear the Use Fast User Switching check box and click the Apply Options button.

If you can't turn Fast User Switching on even though your computer's not connected to a domain, it may be because you have only 64MB RAM. Add more RAM and try again.

Checking Who's Logged On and Which Applications They're Running

To see which other users are logged on in disconnected sessions, view the Users tab of Task Manager. Only if you're a Computer Administrator user can you see other user sessions in Task Manager—if you're a Limited user or the Guest user, you see only your own user session.

If you're a Computer Administrator user, you can take three other actions from here:

■ You can log other users off by selecting their entry on the Users tab, clicking the Logoff button, and clicking the Yes button in the confirmation message box that Windows XP displays. Logging a user off forces all the applications they have open to close and loses them any unsaved work, so this isn't an action to take lightly.

■ You can send a message to users by selecting their entry on the Users tab, clicking the Send Message button, and entering the details in the Send a Message dialog box. (Press CTRL-ENTER to start a new line and CTRL-TAB to type a tab.) The users receive this message when they resume their disconnected session or when they next log on (if someone else terminates their disconnected session).

■ You can see the processes another user is running by viewing the Processes tab of Task Manager and selecting the Show Processes from All Users check box. For ease of viewing, sort the list of processes by the User Name column by clicking the column heading. Some applications are easy to identify from their process names. For example, Explorer's process name is explorer.exe, Internet Explorer's is IEXPLORE.EXE, Excel's is EXCEL.EXE, Word for Windows' is WINWORD.EXE, and Task Manager's is taskmgr.exe. Other process names are more cryptic. There's no direct way to trace a process back to its application: You need to be able to determine the application from the process name.

Locking the Computer

Instead of logging out, you can lock your computer to prevent unauthorized use. Locking works differently when the computer is using Fast User Switching and when it isn't.

To lock your computer, press WINDOWS KEY–L. If the computer is connected to a domain, or if it's a standalone or workgroup computer configured not to use Fast User Switching and the Welcome screen, Windows XP displays the Unlock Computer dialog box (Figure 13-2). You can resume your session by entering your password and clicking the OK button. An administrator can unlock the computer by logging on with their credentials.

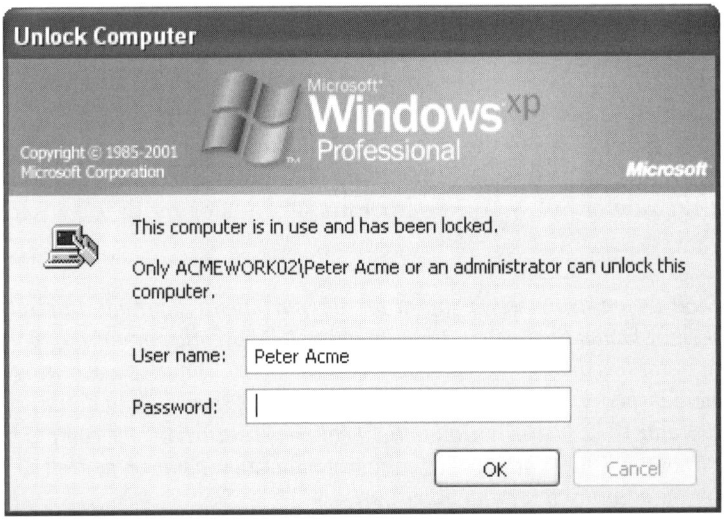

Figure 13-2. *When you lock a computer that's not using Fast User Switching, Windows XP displays the Unlock Computer dialog box.*

If the computer is configured to use the Welcome screen and Fast User Switching, Windows XP displays the Welcome screen. Any user can then log on as usual.

Putting Windows XP into Standby or Hibernation

If your computer's hardware supports standby or hibernation, you can put it into standby or hibernation instead of shutting it down. In *standby,* the computer essentially goes to sleep, but it still keeps data stored in RAM. In *hibernation,* the computer writes the contents of RAM to a file on the hard disk. Doing so takes up more space on your hard disk (as much space as you have RAM), but the contents of RAM are retained if the computer loses power. Standby is good for shorter periods of inactivity. Hibernation is mostly used for laptop computers being run on battery power.

To put your computer into Standby mode, choose Start | Turn Off Computer | Stand By.

If your computer supports hibernation, and hibernation is enabled, choose Start | Turn Off Computer | Hibernate.

Exiting Windows XP

To exit Windows XP on a computer that's connected to a domain, or is a standalone or workgroup computer not using the Welcome screen, choose Start | Shut Down. In the Shut Down Windows dialog box, select Shut Down and click the OK button.

To exit Windows XP on a computer that's using the Welcome screen, choose Start | Turn Off Computer. On the Turn Off Computer screen, click the Turn Off button.

You can also display the Shut Down Windows dialog box or the Turn Off Computer screen by issuing an ALT-F4 command when the Desktop is active.

Windows XP powers down the computer if it can. If not, Windows XP displays a screen telling you it's safe to turn off the computer. Press the power button. (You may need to hold the power button down for four seconds or more to switch off some computers.)

Note *If the Shut Down item doesn't appear on the Start menu, your administrator has denied you the Shut Down the System right by using a local policy or a group policy. If your administrator has done so, it's probably because your computer is running services other users need or performing a role such as sharing a fax server. (If in doubt, check with your administrator.) The power button will, of course, still turn off the computer, but turning it off without exiting Windows XP properly may cause damage, as well as incurring the wrath of the administrator and other users.*

Using the Windows Security Dialog Box

If Windows XP seems to stop responding to the keyboard and the mouse, try pressing CTRL-ALT-DEL. This key combination should display the Windows Security dialog box. This dialog box contains command buttons for locking the computer, logging off, shutting down, changing your password, launching Task Manager, and canceling the display of the dialog box (for when you've invoked it by mistake or unnecessarily).

Navigating the Interface

If you've used any previous version of Windows or any other recent graphical user interface (GUI), you'll quickly grasp the essentials of Windows XP's interface. This section discusses the basic concepts and keystrokes you need to know.

These are the main elements of the Windows XP GUI:

- The *Desktop* is the background area on top of which you do your work. You can place shortcuts, files, and folders on the Desktop for quick access. You can customize the Desktop, as discussed in "Customizing the Desktop" in Chapter 7.

- The *Start button* displays the Start menu, which contains links to the user-level applications installed on Windows XP. (The Start menu doesn't contain links for system applications that Windows XP itself uses.) The top of the Start menu displays the full name of the current user.

- The *taskbar* lets you access the applications you're running by clicking their Taskbar buttons: one click displays the application window, another click minimizes it. By default, the taskbar displays a button for each application window, but it groups related buttons onto group buttons when the taskbar starts to become full. You can configure the taskbar's grouping behavior as discussed in "Customizing the Taskbar and Notification Area" in Chapter 7.

- The *notification area* (or *system tray*) provides a clock (by default) and quick-access icons, and displays reminders and information pop-ups as required. You can customize the notification area's behavior as discussed in "Customizing the Taskbar and Notification Area" in Chapter 7.

Windows XP's GUI is designed to be navigated primarily with the mouse, but you can navigate with the keyboard as well. Table 13-1 lists the keystrokes for basic navigation.

 You can add further Windows keystrokes by using the Windows Keyboard Enhancer Program (www.copernic.com/winkey).

WORKING AND COMMUNICATING

Keystroke	Action
Desktop Keystrokes	
WINDOWS KEY	Display or hide the Start menu.
CTRL-ESC	Display or hide the Start menu.
WINDOWS KEY–B	Move the focus to the notification area.
WINDOWS KEY–BREAK	Display the System Properties dialog box.
WINDOWS KEY–D	Perform a Show the Desktop command.
WINDOWS KEY–E	Open a My Computer window in Windows Explorer.
WINDOWS KEY–F	Open a Search Results window in Windows Explorer and launch Search Companion.
WINDOWS KEY–CTRL-F	Open a Search Results window in Windows Explorer and launch Search Companion in Search for Computer mode.
WINDOWS KEY–F1	Open Help and Support Center.
WINDOWS KEY–L	Lock the computer.
WINDOWS KEY–M	Minimize all open windows.
WINDOWS KEY–SHIFT-M	Restore windows minimized by a WINDOWS KEY-M command.
WINDOWS KEY–R	Open the Run dialog box.
WINDOWS KEY–TAB	Move the focus to the next Taskbar button. (Press ENTER to activate the application.)
WINDOWS KEY–SHIFT-TAB	Move the focus to the previous Taskbar button. (Press ENTER to activate the application.)
WINDOWS KEY–U	Launch Utility Manager.
TAB	Move to the next control.
SHIFT-TAB	Move to the previous control.
Windows Explorer Keystrokes	
BACKSPACE	Move up one level.
ALT-ENTER	Display the Properties dialog box for the selected object.
ALT-D	Select the address in the Address bar (when displayed).
F4	Open the Address list.

Table 13-1.   *Keystrokes for Navigating the Windows XP GUI*

Getting Help

You can get help in Windows XP in several ways: from Help and Support Center, from context-sensitive help mechanisms, and from Remote Assistance. The following sections discuss these options briefly.

Using Help and Support Center

Help and Support Center is the primary help tool for Windows XP. Help and Support Center improves greatly on previous Windows help tools by integrating content from Help files stored on the local hard drive with web-based help, including automatic searching of the Microsoft Knowledge Base (support.microsoft.com), a huge support resource used by Microsoft's support technicians for answering user questions.

Choose Start | Help and Support to display the Home page of Help and Support Center (Figure 13-3). You can open multiple Help and Support Center windows at the same time if you want to look up multiple topics at the same time.

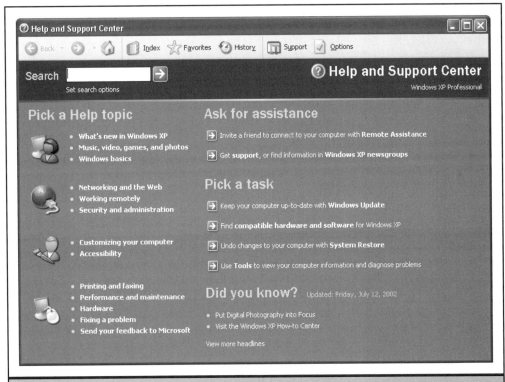

Figure 13-3.   *Help and Support Center's Home page gives you quick access to the various help topics and help tools available in Windows XP.*

As you can see in the figure, Help and Support Center is essentially a web browser customized for help content. The primary means of navigation are links on the help pages and a toolbar.

The Home page presents a couple of dozen links to help topics and tools. You can click a link to open a topic in the Pick a Topic list, follow one of the links in the Ask for Assistance list, choose a specific task in the Pick a Task list, or follow one of the links in the Did You Know? area, which Help and Support Center automatically updates with the latest content from Microsoft if an Internet connection is available. Your OEM or your network administrator may have customized the Did You Know? area to provide custom help content rather than the latest information from Microsoft.

Navigating with the Navigation Bar

To navigate Help and Support Center, you use the *navigation bar*, a toolbar that contains basic navigation buttons (Back, Forward, and Home) and buttons for accessing the Help Index, your help Favorites, your help History (a list of the help pages you've viewed), the Support home page, and the Options page.

Searching for Help Topics

To search for Help topics, enter the term in the Search text box and click the Search button:

- If you enter multiple search terms, the search engine searches for hits with both (or all) terms (a Boolean AND) and for hits with fewer of the terms or only one of the terms. It presents the results with hits for the most terms first.

- You can use the Boolean search operators AND, OR, NOT, and NEAR to make your query more specific.

- Search terms aren't case-sensitive, so you can enter them in all lowercase if you find that quicker.

The help engine searches its local files and (if an Internet connection is available) online resources, such as the Microsoft Knowledge Base, and presents the matches it finds in the Search Results pane in the following categories:

- The Suggested Topics area lists help topics from the local help files that contain keyword matches for your search terms. Help and Support Center lists Suggested Topics by the presentation of the content: Pick a Task, or Overviews, Articles, and Tutorials.

- The Full-Text Search Matches area lists help topics from the local help files in which one or more of your search terms appears in the help topic's body text, rather than as one of the help topic's keywords. Full-text matches are worth examining after you've exhausted the Suggested Topics.

■ The Microsoft Knowledge Base area lists results from the Microsoft Knowledge Base. By default, these results are full-text search matches rather than keyword matches, so they may cover a wide range of topics. They're also likely to contain advanced information. If you find the Knowledge Base's results helpful, you may prefer to search it directly by opening support.microsoft.com in your web browser rather than by using the Help and Support Center's busy interface.

To display a topic, click its link in the Search results pane. To toggle the view between only the topic and the full Help and Support Center view, click the Change View button.

Once you've performed a search, you can search within the search results by selecting the Search within Previous Results check box that Help and Support Center displays under the Search text box. If you've been browsing a topic, you can confine your search to that topic area by selecting the Search Only *Topic_Name* check box under the Search text box.

Using Help Favorites

Help favorites give you quick access to pages you want to visit again.

■ To add a topic to your help favorites, click the Add to Favorites button. Help and Support Center creates a favorite with the page's current name.

■ To access, rename, or delete a favorite, click the Favorites button and work in the Favorites pane. Help and Support Center sorts favorites automatically by name, so you may want to apply a name that starts with low numbers to any help topic you want to appear at the top of the Favorites pane.

Configuring Search Options and Display Options

By default, *Help and Support Center* limits the results to 15 per category and displays a search highlight on the matching words. You can customize Help and Support Center's search behavior by choosing Options | Set Search Options and working on the Set Search Options Screen. Here you can change the number of results per category; toggle the search highlight on and off; turn off searching of Suggested Topics, Full-Text Search Matches, or Microsoft Knowledge Base; or configure searching for Full-Text Search Matches and the Microsoft Knowledge Base. For example, you can choose to match similar words in full-text searching and choose whether to search for any of your search terms, all of the words, the exact phrase, or the Boolean phrase in the Microsoft Knowledge Base.

You can customize the Help and Support Center display by choosing Options | Change Help and Support Center Options. The Help and Support Center Options screen lets you toggle the display of Favorites and History on the navigation bar; choose whether to display some text labels, all text labels, or no text labels on the navigation bar; and choose among Small, Medium, and Large fonts for displaying help content.

Adding Content to Help and Support Center

You can customize the help available in Help and Support Center by choosing Options | Install and Share Windows Help and working on the resulting Install and Share Windows Help screen. From this screen, you can take the following actions:

- Share the help available on your computer with other users on your network.

- Install on your computer help content from another computer, from a CD, or from a disk image. This works only for the Windows XP or Windows.NET operating systems (OSs) and help files compiled for them.

- Uninstall extra help you've installed on this computer.

- Switch from the help for one OS to the help for another OS. This feature is primarily useful for technical support staff who need to support multiple OSs (for example, Windows XP Professional and Windows XP Home Edition) from the same computer. By switching to the help for the OS the customer is using, a support technician can avoid suggesting remedies included only in other OSs they support.

This option is only in Windows XP Professional, not in Windows XP Home Edition. For example, you can install the Windows XP Home help files on Windows XP Professional, but not the other way around.

Accessing the Troubleshooters

Windows XP includes a dozen or so troubleshooters for leading you through the steps of diagnosing and fixing common hardware and software problems. To access the troubleshooters, go to the Help and Support Center home page and choose Fixing a Problem | Troubleshooting Problems | List of Troubleshooters. Then click the link for the troubleshooter you want to start.

Getting Context-Sensitive Help

Windows XP includes context-sensitive help you can summon in the following ways:

- Press F1 to receive context-sensitive help on the item you're currently wrestling with.

- Click the ? button in a dialog box so Windows XP displays a hefty question mark attached to the mouse pointer, and then click the control in the dialog box about which you'd like to learn more. If the relevant help file contains information linked to the control, Windows XP displays a ScreenTip containing the help information. (If there's no linked information, Windows XP either displays a ScreenTip telling you so or displays no ScreenTip at all.)

Using Remote Assistance

Remote Assistance is a feature introduced in Windows XP that lets one user (termed the *novice*) receive help from another user (termed the *expert*) across a network or Internet connection. You can send a Remote Assistance invitation to request help from an expert or an expert can make you an unsolicited offer of Remote Assistance. (The latter feature is available only in Windows XP Professional in domain configurations.)

Chapter 33 discusses how to use Remote Assistance.

Managing Files and Folders

This section explains the basics of managing files and folders in Windows Explorer. If you've used Windows Explorer in a previous version of Windows, chances are you'll be familiar with most of these topics.

Creating a New Folder

You can create a new folder on your Desktop or in any folder in which you have permission to create files and folders.

Choose File | New | Folder or right-click open space and choose New | Folder from the shortcut menu. Type in the edit box to replace the default name (for example, New Folder) Windows XP assigns to the folder it creates, and then press ENTER or click elsewhere to apply the new name.

Creating a File

You can create some basic document types from a Windows Explorer window by choosing the file type from the New submenu on the File menu or the shortcut menu. But, normally, you create files from within an application by using the Save As command, rather than creating them in Windows Explorer.

Renaming a File

To rename a selected file or folder, issue a Rename command from the File menu or the shortcut menu, click the Rename This File link or the Rename This Folder link in the File and Folder Tasks pane, or press F2. Windows XP displays an edit box around the object's name. Type the new name and press ENTER or click elsewhere in the window to apply the name.

Deleting a File or Folder

To delete a file or folder, select it and issue a Delete command in any of the following ways:

- Click the Delete This File link or the Delete This Folder link in the File and Folder Tasks pane.

- Issue a Delete command from the File menu or the shortcut menu.
- Press DELETE.

You can also delete a file or folder by using the Delete command or the Erase command in a command-prompt window.

What happens when you delete a file or folder depends on where it's stored:

- If the file or folder is stored on a local hard drive, Windows XP places it in the Recycle Bin, which is a holding area for files and folders you've told Windows XP to delete. You can recover objects from the Recycle Bin until you empty the Recycle Bin or it becomes so full that Windows XP must delete some of its contents to make room for further items.

- If the file or folder is stored on a networked drive, on a floppy disk, or on a removable disk, Windows XP deletes it.

- If the file or folder is stored on a read-only medium (such as a CD-ROM) or in a folder in which you don't have permission to delete objects, Windows XP displays the Error Deleting File or Folder dialog box after you confirm the deletion.

By default, Windows XP always confirms the deletion of the file or folder or its removal to the Recycle Bin. You can turn this confirmation off, as described in "Configuring the Recycle Bin" in Chapter 7.

When you delete a folder, you delete all its contents as well.

To delete a file or folder stored on a local drive without putting it in the Recycle Bin, hold down SHIFT while issuing the Delete command.

You can also delete a file or folder by dragging it to the Recycle Bin. If the file or folder is stored on a local hard drive, Windows XP places the file in the Recycle Bin without confirmation. But if the file is located on any other drive, so that it will be deleted rather than placed in the Recycle Bin, Windows XP asks you to confirm the deletion.

Recovering a File or Folder from the Recycle Bin

To recover a file or folder from the Recycle Bin, double-click the Recycle Bin to open it in a Windows Explorer window. Then select the item or items you want to restore and issue a Restore command from the File menu, the shortcut menu, or by clicking the Restore This Item link or the Restore the Selected Items link in the Recycle Bin Tasks panel.

If an item you're restoring will overwrite another object of the same name, Recycle Bin warns you of the problem so that you can decide whether to proceed.

To empty the Recycle Bin, right-click its icon on the Desktop and select Empty Recycle Bin from the shortcut menu. If you have the Recycle Bin open, issue the Empty Recycle Bin command from the File menu or the shortcut menu (with no object selected) or click the Empty the Recycle Bin link in the Recycle Bin Tasks pane.

Copying and Moving Files and Folders

You can copy a file or folder in any of the following ways:

- Select the file or folder, click the Copy This File link or Copy This Folder link in the File and Folder Tasks pane or choose Edit | Copy to Folder, and use the Copy Items dialog box to specify the destination folder for the copy.

- Right-drag the file or folder to the destination folder and choose Copy Here from the shortcut menu.

- Drag the file or folder to a folder on a different drive. This technique can be awkward because dragging to a folder on the same drive moves the file instead of copying it, so you need to remember the drives involved.

- Select the file or folder, issue a Copy command from the Edit menu, from the shortcut menu, or by pressing CTRL-C, select the destination folder, and issue a Paste command from the Edit menu, from the shortcut menu, or by pressing CTRL-V.

- Issue a Copy command or an Xcopy command in a command-prompt window.

- Select the file or folder and choose the destination folder from the Send To menu on the File menu or the shortcut menu. (You can add locations to the Send To menu as described in "Customizing the Send To Menu" in Chapter 7.)

You can move a file or folder in any of the following ways:

- Select the file or folder, click the Move This File link or Move This Folder link in the File and Folder Tasks pane or choose Edit | Move to Folder, and use the Move Items dialog box to specify the destination folder.

- Right-drag the file or folder to the destination folder and choose Move Here from the shortcut menu.

- Drag the file or folder to a folder on the same drive.

- Select the file or folder, issue a Cut command from the Edit menu, from the shortcut menu, or by pressing CTRL-X, select the destination folder, and issue a Paste command from the Edit menu, from the shortcut menu, or by pressing CTRL-V.

- Issue a Move command in a command-prompt window.

If the copy or move operation will overwrite a file or folder in the destination folder that has the same name as a file or folder you're copying or moving, Windows XP displays the Confirm File Replace dialog box so that you specify whether to replace the file or folder. Click the Yes button, the Yes to All button, the No button, or the Cancel button as appropriate. To issue a No to All command, hold down SHIFT and click the No button.

WORKING AND
COMMUNICATING

Figure 13-4.   *The Advanced Attributes dialog box contains check boxes for controlling archiving, indexing, compression, and encryption.*

Checking the Attributes of a File

You can check the attributes of a file either by displaying its Properties dialog box (issue a Properties command from the File menu or the shortcut menu) and the Advanced Attributes dialog box or by using a Windows Explorer window with Details view customized to display the Attributes column. If you have the appropriate permissions, you can change the attributes by using the Properties dialog box and Advanced Attributes dialog box.

The Properties dialog box for a file shows the following attributes:

- The General tab contains check boxes for the Read-Only attribute and the Hidden attribute.

- The Summary tab contains a variety of information fields depending on the type of file. For example, a Word document file has different information fields than a WMA audio file.

The Advanced Attributes dialog box (Figure 13-4) contains check boxes for the attributes covering archiving, indexing, compression, and encryption.

Summary

This chapter has explained how to log on to and log off from Windows XP, and has discussed how logging on and off differs in a domain environment and a workgroup or standalone environment. It has shown you how to put Windows XP into standby or hibernation (if your computer supports standby or hibernation) and how to lock Windows XP when you leave your computer. You've also learned how to navigate the Windows XP interface; how to get help; and how to create, delete, copy, and move files and folders.

The next chapter discusses how to run applications, how to print, and how to fax.

The Complete Reference

Chapter 14

Running Applications, Printing, and Faxing

This chapter discusses how to run the applications installed on your computer, briefly recaps how to print documents, and shows you how to send and receive faxes.

Running Applications

This section briefly explains the ways of running applications in Windows XP.

Running an Application from the Start Menu

You should be able to run most user-level applications installed on your computer by using the shortcuts on the Start menu. These shortcuts are created by default when most applications are installed.

Shortcuts for applications that you run frequently will automatically migrate to the variable portion of the left column of the Start menu. To make sure an application's shortcut always appears on the Start menu, pin it there, as described in "Adding and Removing Start Menu Items" in Chapter 7.

 Normally, Windows XP closes the Start menu when you launch an application from it. To keep the Start menu open so that you can launch multiple applications, hold down SHIFT *as you click a shortcut on the Start menu.*

Running Applications from the Run Dialog Box

If an application has no shortcut on the Start menu, you can run it by entering its name in the Run dialog box and clicking the OK button. (This assumes the folder containing the application is in your path. If it's not, you'll need to type the path to the application as well.)

If you've run the application from the Run dialog box before, you can choose its entry from the drop-down list, either by clicking the arrow button and scrolling down to the entry or by *typing down* (typing enough of the beginning of the command to identify the entry uniquely) so that Windows XP selects the entry automatically.

Running an Application from the Quick Launch Toolbar

If you use the Quick Launch toolbar, customize it so that it contains the shortcuts you need and drag them into the most useful order—for example, so the shortcuts you use most frequently appear on the section of the Quick Launch toolbar that's always displayed.

 If you hide the Quick Launch toolbar, and then redisplay it, Windows XP sorts its entries alphabetically.

Running an Application from the Desktop

To access shortcuts on the desktop, use the desktop toolbar (see "Desktop Toolbar" in Chapter 7) or right-click the notification area and issue a Show the Desktop command. Alternatively, assign shortcut keys to your desktop shortcuts.

You can create additional shortcuts by using the techniques described in "Creating Shortcuts" in Chapter 7. For example, right-drag a file to the desktop and choose Create Shortcuts Here from the shortcut menu that Windows XP displays.

Running an Application Using a Shortcut Key

You can also run an application by using a CTRL-ALT-*letter* shortcut key assigned to a link on the Start menu or a shortcut on the desktop. This technique works for links on the most-recently used part of the Start menu and on the All Programs menu. It doesn't work for links to folders.

To create or edit such a shortcut key, display the Shortcut tab of the Properties dialog box for the link or shortcut, click in the Shortcut Key text box, and press the letter you want to use. (Windows XP adds the CTRL-ALT automatically to the shortcut key, so you needn't press these keys when creating the shortcut.)

In a domain environment, you may be unable to change the shortcut key assigned to a Start-menu link for an item. In this case, create a shortcut on the desktop for the application by right-clicking the Start menu item and choosing Send To | Desktop (Create Shortcut). Then create a shortcut key to that shortcut instead.

Running an Application from Its Program File

Alternatively, you can run an application by double-clicking its program file. However, because most program files are buried deep in the Program Files folder structure, you'll need to do some navigation before you can double-click the program file.

Running an Application from an Associated File Type

Double-click a file to open it in the application associated with its file type. If the application is already open, Windows XP normally uses that instance of the application rather than launching a new instance. If the application isn't open, Windows XP launches it.

Opening a File in an Application Other Than That Associated with Its File Type

To open a file in an application other than the application associated with the file's file type, issue an Open With command from the File menu or the shortcut menu and choose the application from the Open With submenu. To choose an application other than those listed, select the Choose Program item and use the Open With dialog box to specify the application. To add an entry for this application to the Open With submenu, select the Always Use the Selected Program to Open This Kind of File check box.

Running Applications on Startup

As discussed in Chapter 5, you (or an administrator) can run applications on startup by using the Startup folders or a startup script or by starting the application as a service. As discussed in Chapter 11, applications and services launched automatically at startup can sap a computer's performance. If your computer is lagging, you should reduce the number of applications and services launched automatically.

But if your computer has a fast processor, a fast hard disk, and plenty of memory to keep Windows XP Professional and all the applications you need running continuously, you can save time by launching all the applications at startup. For example, if you consistently use Lotus Notes, Microsoft Word, Microsoft Excel, and Illustrator throughout your workday, you might as well launch them all automatically at startup for speed and convenience.

Printing

This section assumes you've already connected to the printer or printers you'll be using. If not, look back to Chapter 12 for a discussion of how to connect to a printer.

Printing a Document from an Application

To print a document, follow these steps:

1. Open the document in a suitable application.
2. Use Print Preview (File | Print Preview in most applications) to check that the document is ready for printing.
3. Issue a Print command by choosing File | Print or pressing CTRL-P (the standard keystroke for Print) or an equivalent keystroke. The application displays the Print dialog box in which you can choose options for printing your document. Note that the options that are available vary depending on the application you are working in. Figure 14-1 shows two examples of the Print dialog box.
4. Select the printer to use.
5. Specify any further options, such as a range of pages or a subsection of the document.
6. Click the Print button.

Many applications also include a Print button on a toolbar for printing the document with default settings without displaying the Print dialog box.

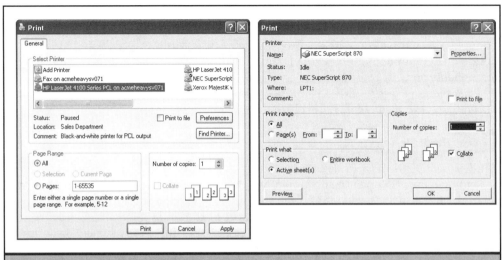

Figure 14-1. *The Print dialog box on the left is used by applications such as Notepad and WordPad. The Print dialog box on the right is used by Microsoft Excel.*

Printing a Document from Windows Explorer

You can print a document directly from Windows Explorer by dragging the document to the icon for a printer (for example, in the Printers and Faxes window or on your desktop). You can also print some documents by right-clicking their icon and choosing Print from the shortcut menu or (in Windows Explorer) the File menu.

 As mentioned in Chapter 12, you can put a local printer offline (by issuing a Use Printer Offline command from the File menu or the shortcut menu from the Printers and Faxes window) and queue up jobs for it. You can then put the printer back online (by issuing a Use Printer Online command) when you're ready to print the jobs.

Sending and Receiving Faxes

For sending faxes, Windows XP Professional can use faxes shared on a Windows network—for example, fax modems installed on a computer running Windows 2000 Server or Windows.NET Server and shared using Fax Service. Windows XP Professional also includes faxing capabilities strong enough for most individual use and for much small-office use.

When your computer is connected to a domain, you're likely to use a dedicated fax server or shared faxes running on Windows 2000 Server or Windows.NET Server. However, if only a few people require faxing from their computers (as opposed to faxing hard copies of documents), but those people need full fax capabilities, administrators may set them up with fax modems attached directly to their computers. Similarly, if you need to be able to send faxes when not connected to a domain (for example, when traveling with a laptop) or if you use Windows XP Professional on a standalone computer, you'll need a fax modem and Windows XP Professional's fax components on your computer.

This section explores the possibilities Windows XP Professional offers for faxing. Depending on your situation, it's likely that only some of the subsections will apply to you.

Overview of Faxing

Windows XP treats the action of sending a fax as a form of printing. The normal way of sending a fax is to open the document you want to send, issue a Print command, and select the fax printer to use in the Print dialog box. When you click the OK button or Print button to close the Print dialog box and proceed, Windows XP invokes the Send Fax Wizard, which walks you through the process of specifying the recipient, fax number, and message, adding a cover page, and so on.

Windows XP makes the Send Fax Wizard available when you install a fax modem on your computer—either a local fax modem or a fax modem shared by a server. The Send Fax Wizard is available even without your installing Windows XP's other fax components.

Windows XP Professional also includes the following fax components, which you have to install before you can use them. In a domain environment, you'll typically need to get an administrator to install these components for you.

Windows XP uses the following fax components:

- **Fax Configuration Wizard** Walks you through configuring basic settings for sending and receiving faxes on your fax modem.
- **Fax Console** Manages the faxes you send and receive
- **Fax Cover Page Editor** This is a basic application for creating and customizing fax cover pages.
- **Fax Monitor dialog box** Shows you what's happening when Windows XP is sending or receiving a fax. By default, Windows XP displays the Fax Monitor dialog box when a fax is being sent or received, but you can display it all the time if you so choose.

These tools are largely the same in Windows XP Professional as in Windows 2000 Server and Windows.NET Server. But the fax components in the server OSs have additional capabilities and include the Microsoft Fax Service Manager component, which includes management features such as fax routing and the logging of fax activity.

If you install faxing on your computer, you'll be able to run Fax Console, Fax Monitor, and Fax Cover Page Editor on your computer. If you send faxes through a shared fax, these components will be run on the computer sharing the fax.

Connecting to a Shared Fax

To connect to a shared fax, add it in the same way as you add a printer:

1. Click the Add a Printer link in the Printer Tasks list in the Printers and Faxes window to start the Add Printer Wizard.

2. On the Local or Network Printer page, select the A Network Printer or a Printer Attached to Another Computer option button.

3. The easiest way to enter the name of the fax is to search for the fax in the directory by using the Find Printers window. But if you know the path to the fax, you can enter it manually instead.

4. If you already have one or more printers (or faxes) set up on this computer, choose whether to use this fax as your default printer. (You probably won't want the fax as the default.)

Sending a Fax

The basic steps for sending a fax are largely the same on both a shared fax and a local fax:

1. Open the document, get it ready, and issue a Print command to display the Print dialog box.

You can fax a scanned image from the Photo Printing Wizard by selecting the fax in the What Printer Do You Want to Use? list on the Printing Options page of the wizard.

2. Select the appropriate fax entry in the Print dialog box.

3. To change the quality of the fax, click the Preferences button and choose Normal or Draft on the Fax Properties tab of the Printing Preferences dialog box. Close the Printing Preferences dialog box.

4. Accept the settings in the Print dialog box (for example, click the Print button). Windows XP launches the Send Fax Wizard.

Note *The first time you go to send a fax, Windows XP runs the Fax Configuration Wizard to get standard information about you. Figure 14-3 in "Installing and Configuring the Fax Components," later in this chapter, shows the Sender Information page you'll see.*

5. On the Recipient Information page of the wizard (Figure 14-2), enter the recipient or recipients. You can either type in each name and phone number or add recipients from your Address Book. (If the recipient's Address book entry has no fax number or multiple fax numbers, the wizard warns you of the problem.) Select the Use Dialing Rules check box if you want Windows XP to supply such country, area, or long-distance codes as needed from your current location.

WORKING AND
COMMUNICATING

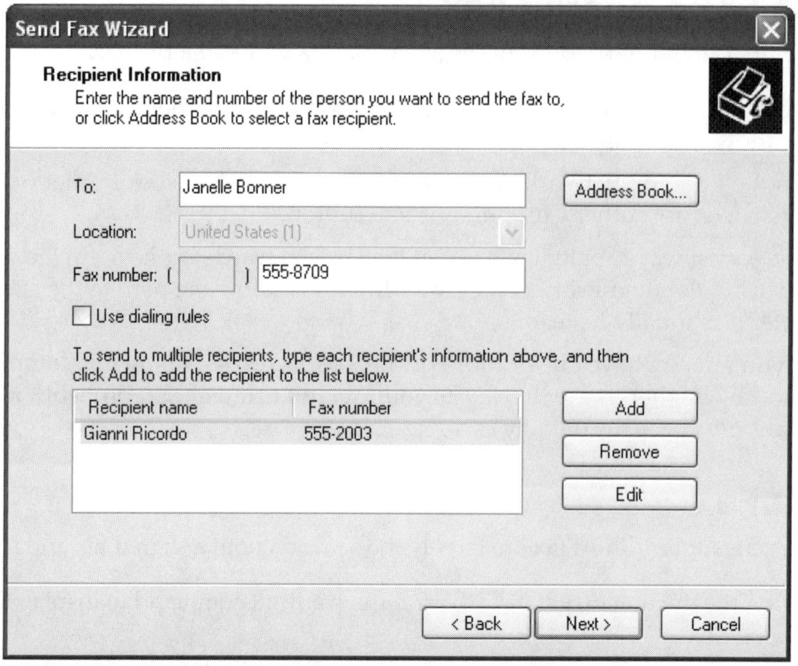

Figure 14-2. *On the Recipient Information page of the Send Fax Wizard, enter the recipient or recipients and their fax numbers.*

6. On the Preparing the Cover Page page of the wizard, specify whether you want to use a cover page template. If you do, choose the template to use, and then enter the subject line and note text.

Note *To adjust your sender information, click the Sender Information button on the Preparing the Cover Page page and work in the resulting Sender Information dialog box. This dialog box contains the same fields as the Sender Information page of the Fax Configuration Wizard. If you've run the Fax Configuration Wizard, the data in the Sender Information dialog box will be as you entered it. If you haven't run the Fax Configuration Wizard, you can enter the data in the Sender Information dialog box instead. To make Windows XP retain the data for future faxes you send, make sure the Use the Information for This Transmission Only check box is cleared.*

7. On the Schedule page of the wizard, specify when to send the fax (by choosing the Now option button, the When Discount Rates Apply option button, or the Specific Time in the Next 24 Hours option button) and designate the fax priority: High, Normal, or Low.

- Which of a fax server's capabilities you can use depends on which permissions the administrator has given you. You'll most likely have permission to submit low-priority and normal-priority faxes. If the administrator hasn't given you permission to submit high-priority faxes, you won't be able to use the High priority setting.

- The fax's administrator sets the hours for discount-rate faxing through Fax Console. ("Using Fax Console to Administer Faxes," later in the chapter, explains how to do this.)

8. If you're using a shared fax, on the Delivery Notification page of the wizard, specify whether and (if so) how Fax Service should notify you of the success or failure in sending the fax. Choose the Don't Notify option button, the Pop Up a Message on This Machine option button, or the E-mail Message option button. For the last, specify the e-mail address to use.

   - Which of the notification options are available to you depends on how the administrator has configured Fax Service.

   - On this page, you may also be able to choose to receive a single receipt for a fax transmitted to multiple recipients (instead of one receipt for each recipient). You may be able to choose to receive a copy of the sent fax so that you can tell which fax the notification refers to. (This option may not be available.)

Tip *If you want to fax a brief message to someone rather than fax an existing document, you can fax just a cover sheet. This means confining your message to a subject line and a note field, but if that works for you, it's quick and effective. To send only a cover sheet, choose File | Send a Fax from Fax Console or enter **fxssend.exe** in the Run dialog box.*

Receiving Faxes Through a Shared Fax

If you use a shared fax to send faxes, chances are good you'll use a shared fax to receive incoming faxes as well. How you receive faxes will depend on how the administrator has configured the shared fax. The administrator can configure Fax Service Manager to route incoming faxes via e-mail to their recipients, to store them in a folder and notify recipients, or to print them on a specified printer.

Installing and Configuring the Fax Components

If you have a fax modem, and Windows XP Professional's fax components aren't installed on your computer, install them by clicking the Set Up Faxing link in the Printer Tasks list in the Printers and Faxes window (Start | Control Panel | Printers and Faxes). You'll need to provide your Windows XP Professional CD or installation source.

After installing the fax components, you need to configure them. To help you do so, Windows XP Professional runs the Fax Configuration Wizard the first time you launch Fax Console or the Send Fax Wizard.

The first time anyone runs the Fax Configuration Wizard on your computer, it collects both standard information about the sender and general information about the fax modem and the phone numbers to identify with it.

For each user, the wizard collects the information on the Sender Information page (Figure 14-3). This information is self-explanatory and optional—you can send faxes without entering it—but if you need to include cover sheets, entering the information here can save you time later.

The first time you run the Fax Configuration Wizard on your computer, it displays the Select Device for Sending or Receiving Faxes page (Figure 14-4). On this page, you choose which of your available fax devices to use (if you have more than one device), whether to use it for sending and receiving, and (if you use it for receiving) whether to use automatic answering after a specified number of rings or manual answering.

If you configured the fax device to send faxes, the Fax Configuration Wizard displays the Transmitting Subscriber Identification (TSID) page, on which you can enter a TSID up to 20 characters long to identify yourself, your business, or simply your fax number. The TSID is displayed to the recipient of the fax so they can tell whom it's coming from.

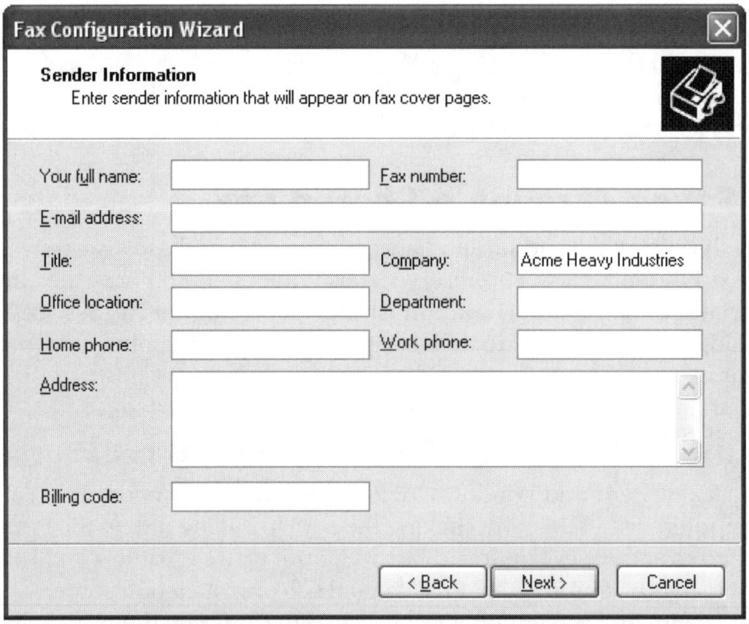

Figure 14-3.   *Enter your standard sender information for fax cover pages on the Sender Information page of the Fax Configuration Wizard.*

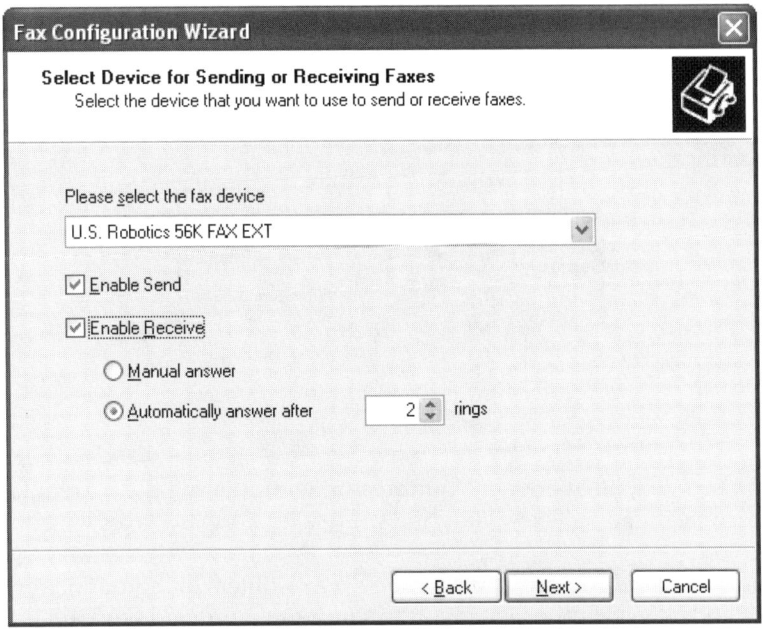

Figure 14-4. *Specify the device to use for sending faxes on the Select Device for Sending or Receiving Faxes page of the Fax Configuration Wizard.*

If you configured the fax device to receive faxes, the Fax Configuration Wizard displays the Called Subscriber Identification (CSID) page, on which you can enter a CSID of up to 20 characters long to provide information. The CSID is displayed to someone who sends you a fax so that they can check they've sending it to the right number, person, or place.

Finally, if you configured the fax device to receive faxes, the Fax Configuration Wizard displays the Routing Options page, on which you tell Fax Services what to do with incoming faxes. Your options are to print the fax on an available printer or to store an extra copy in a folder you specify (or both). Whether you select either option (or both), Fax Services stores a copy of the fax in Fax Console's archive.

Note *Windows XP's Fax Service doesn't support automatically routing faxes to a mailbox. To get faxes to a mailbox, you need to send them as e-mail attachments.*

Using Fax Console to Administer Faxes

If you're running Fax Service on your computer, you use Fax Console (shown next) to administer faxing. The Fax Console provides Incoming, Inbox, Outbox, and Sent Items folders to organize faxes. Run Fax Console by choosing Start | All Programs | Accessories | Communications | Fax | Fax Console. (Alternatively, enter **fxsclnt.exe** in the Run dialog box.)

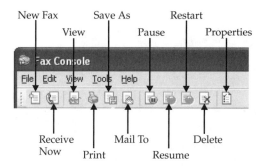

The Fax Console toolbar contains buttons for manipulating the current fax. You can pause and resume outgoing faxes, view and print faxes, forward faxes via e-mail, delete faxes, and so on.

To configure your fax device, choose Tools | Fax Printer Configuration (or right-click the Fax item and choose Properties from the shortcut menu) and work on the five tabs of the resulting Properties dialog box. The following paragraphs summarize the configuration options available:

- **General tab** Set or change the Name, Location, and Comment information for the fax. Check the capabilities of the fax (for example, its maximum resolution). Set printing preferences (paper size, image quality, and landscape or portrait orientation).

- **Sharing tab** If your fax device is shareable (many aren't), configure sharing options on this tab.

- **Devices tab** Configure a fax device by selecting it in the list box, clicking the Properties button, and working in the resulting Properties dialog box. The Send page lets you control whether the fax device is used for sending faxes, set the device's TSID, and specify whether to include a banner in faxes, the number of retries, the retry interval, and the hours for discount-rate faxing. The Receive tab lets you control whether the fax device is used for receiving, set its CSID and answer mode, and specify whether to print received faxes or store an extra copy in a designated folder. The Cleanup tab lets you specify whether to delete failed faxes automatically and (if so) their stay of execution.

- **Tracking tab** Choose whether Fax Service should display a progress readout in the notification area when a fax is being sent or received, and whether it should display alerts for the success or failure of incoming and outgoing faxes. Choose whether Fax Service should automatically display Fax monitor when a fax is being sent or received. Click the Configure Sound Settings button and work in the Sound Settings dialog box to specify whether Fax Service plays a sound when the fax line rings, when a fax is received, when a fax is sent, and when a faxing error occurs.

■ **Archives tab**   Choose whether to archive incoming and outgoing faxes, and (if so) the folders in which to archive them.

If you prefer to work with a subset of the available options, you can run the Fax Configuration Wizard again by choosing Tools | Configure Fax.

Receiving Faxes

If you've set Fax Service to receive faxes automatically, Fax Service automatically answers the phone after the specified number of rings.

If you've opted to receive faxes manually, choose File | Receive a Fax Now from Fax Console or click the Answer Now button in Fax Monitor.

Creating Fax Cover Pages

If you've installed the Windows XP fax components, you can create custom fax cover pages by using Fax Cover Page Editor. (If not, you're stuck with the cover pages that whoever administers the fax you're sharing has provided for you.)

To run Fax Cover Page Editor, choose Start | All Programs | Accessories | Communications | Fax | Fax Cover Page Editor. Alternatively, enter **fxscover.exe** in the Run dialog box or choose Tools | Personal Cover Pages from Fax Console, and then click the New button in the Personal Cover Pages dialog box.

Fax Cover Page Editor is straightforward to use. These are the main points:

■ Each cover page template has to include several required fields, such as the sender's name and the recipient's name. Use the Insert menu's submenus to add the fields you require.

■ To add unchanging text, click the Text button on the Drawing toolbar. To format selected text or fields, choose Format | Font.

■ To align objects, evenly space them horizontally or vertically, center them on the page (again, horizontally or vertically), or change the front-to-back order of layered objects, use the commands on the Layout menu.

The quickest way of creating a cover page template is to edit one of the canned templates Fax Service provides.

Using Fax Monitor

When you have the Windows XP fax components installed on your computer, Fax Service displays the Fax Monitor dialog box (Figure 14-5) by default when it's sending

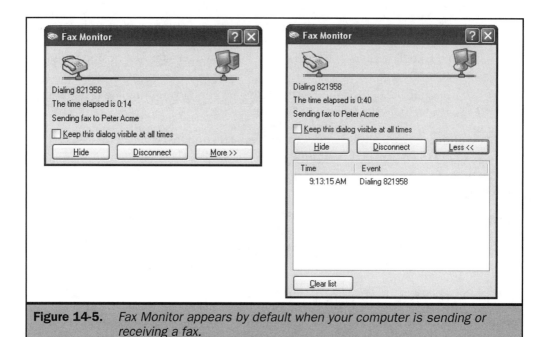

Figure 14-5.   *Fax Monitor appears by default when your computer is sending or receiving a fax.*

or receiving a fax to show you what's happening. You can launch Fax Monitor manually at any time by choosing Tools | Fax Monitor from Fax Console.

You can toggle between the standard size and expanded size of the Fax Monitor dialog box by clicking the More button and the Less button. The Fax Monitor dialog box also offers buttons for disconnecting the current connection, answering an incoming call manually, clearing the current list of faxes, and hiding the dialog box.

Summary

This chapter has discussed how the various ways of running the applications on your computer and has shown you how to print documents from them or from Windows Explorer. It has covered how to send and receive faxes both by using fax devices shared on a network and by installing, configuring, and using Windows XP Professional's fax components locally.

The next chapter explains how to use Windows Media Player for audio and movies.

The Complete Reference

Chapter 15

Using Windows Media Player for Audio and Movies

his chapter discusses how to use Windows Media Player to listen to audio (including music), tune into Internet audio, and watch movies. Because Windows Media Player is designed to be straightforward to operate, this chapter is short and concentrates mainly on understanding Windows Media Player's many configuration options, rather than on the easy-to-grasp controls of the interface.

Windows Media Player is included in the retail version of Windows XP Professional and in most original equipment manufacturer (OEM) versions of it. But because Windows Media Player is one of the components the Department of Justice and the Dissenting States have forced Microsoft to make removable from Windows XP Professional, your OEM may have omitted Windows Media Player from the version of Windows XP Professional you have. If so, abandon this book and consult the documentation for whichever media player your OEM has chosen to include with it.

Running Windows Media Player

Choose Start | Windows Media Player or Start | All Programs | Windows Media Player to start Windows Media Player.

Using Full Mode and Skin Mode

Windows Media Player has two main modes: Full mode and Skin mode. At first, Windows Media Player runs in Full mode by default.

By default, in *Full* mode, Windows Media Player hides the window frame and menu bar to produce an irregular, somewhat streamlined shape (Figure 15-1). You can display the hidden items by moving the mouse pointer over where the title bar or menu bar would appear. You can toggle this hiding behavior on and off by clicking the Show Menu Bar/Auto Hide Menu Bar button, the button at the left end of the gray bar along the top of the Windows Media Player window. You can also choose Show Menu Bar, Hide Menu Bar, or Auto Hide Menu Bar from the View | Full Mode Options menu.

By default, Windows Media Player displays its taskbar, the panel at the left side that contains buttons for navigating among Windows Media Player's pages. You can toggle the display of the taskbar by clicking the narrow button in its right side or by choosing View | Full Mode Options | Hide Taskbar. If you hide the taskbar, you can switch to a different page of Windows Media Player by choosing it from the View | Taskbar menu.

In *Skin* mode, Windows Media Player takes up less space and displays only play controls. You can access further commands from the shortcut menu. To switch to Skin mode, click the Switch to Skin Mode button, choose View | Skin Mode, or press CTRL-2. You can apply skins from the Skin Chooser page in Full mode. Figure 15-2 shows two examples of skins.

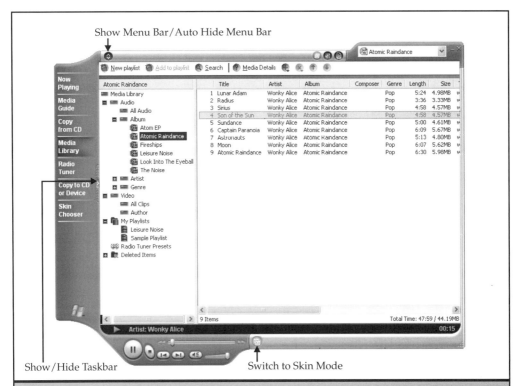

Figure 15-1. *Windows Media Player's default configuration for Full mode hides the window frame and menu bar, and it displays the Taskbar panel.*

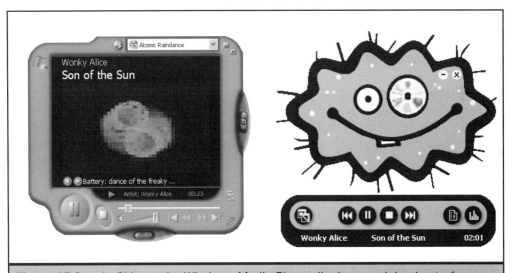

Figure 15-2. *In Skin mode, Windows Media Player displays a minimal set of controls. You can apply skins that produce very different looks.*

To return to Full mode, click the Switch to Full Mode button, choose Switch to Full Mode from the shortcut menu, or press CTRL-1.

Operating Windows Media Player via the Keyboard

Windows Media Player is largely designed to be operated with the mouse, and its GUI has self-explanatory play controls, volume controls, and controls for the graphical equalizer (View | Now Playing Tools | Show Equalizer and Settings) and sound effects. But you can also perform basic operations from the keyboard. Table 15-1 lists the main keypresses for Windows Media Player.

 If you use Windows XP Professional without Service Pack 1, your computer may not be able to enter Standby mode when Windows Media Player is paused. Stop Windows Media Player before trying to enter Standby.

Action	Keypress
Play or pause a file	CTRL-P
Stop playback	CTRL-S
Increase the volume	F10
Decrease the volume	F9
Mute the sound	F8
Display the video full screen	ALT-ENTER
Switch to skin mode	CTRL-2
Switch to full mode	CTRL-1
Eject the CD or DVD drive	CTRL-E
Search your computer for media files	F3

Table 15-1.   *Keypresses for Controlling Windows Media Player*

Preventing Windows Media Player from Starting in Media Guide

By default, when you launch Windows Media Player in Full mode, it displays the Media Library page and populates it with the latest content from the WindowsMedia.com site. For most users, this is a waste of bandwidth. To prevent Windows Media Player from displaying the Media Library page and downloading content, clear the Start Player in Media Guide check box on the Player Settings tab of the Options dialog box.

Configuring Automatic Updates and Internet Options

It's a good idea to keep Windows Media Player up to date with the latest updates and patches to keep it as functional and secure as possible. (For example, the original version of Windows Media Player that shipped with Windows XP Professional had several bugs that could be exploited by attackers. In June 2002, Microsoft issued a major security patch for Windows Media Player.)

In the Automatic Updates group box on the Player tab of the Options dialog box, choose the frequency with which Windows Media Player should check for updates and specify whether Windows Media Player should download codecs (coder/decoder software) when you try to play an audio stream for which you don't have a suitable codec installed.

Note   *Microsoft distributes some Windows Media Player updates via Windows Update. In a domain environment, the administrator may coordinate all updates centrally via Software Update Services. If you control updates, you can check manually by choosing Help | Check for Player Updates from Windows Media Player.*

In the Internet Settings group box on the Player tab, make sure the Allow Internet Sites to Uniquely Identify Your Player check box is selected so Windows Media Player works with audio servers to optimize the playback of streaming audio. Select the Acquire Licenses Automatically check box if you want Windows Media Player to download automatically or generate a license for audio files you download that need licenses.

Listening to and "Copying" CD Audio

You can listen to a CD by loading it in your CD drive or DVD drive. If the drive is configured to use AutoPlay, Windows Media Player starts playing the CD automatically. If not, click the Copy from CD page, and then click the Play button.

Windows Media Player lets you "copy" audio from CD to disk so you can listen to it without the CD. To "copy" audio, you click the Copy Music button on the Copy from

CD page. (If Windows Media Player hasn't retrieved the track names for the CD from the WindowsMedia.com web site, as it does by default if an Internet connection is available, click the Get Names button.)

Configuring Settings for "Copying" Audio

You can configure the settings for "copying" audio on the Copy Music tab of the Options dialog box. These are the essentials:

- Windows Media Player doesn't literally copy the audio. Instead, it extracts (*rips*) it from CD and encodes it in a compressed audio format. Windows Media Player's default format is Windows Media Audio (WMA), but it can also encode to the widely used MP3 format if you add a third-party MP3 encoder. The easiest way to find a third-party MP3 encoder that snaps in to Windows Media Player is to click the MP3 Information button on the Copy Music tab and follow the links in the resulting browser window. (You'll need to pay for the encoder. You can also find free third-party standalone MP3 encoders at sites such as www.mp3.com and www.musicmatch.com.)

- The greater the compression, the worse the audio sounds. Experiment with the Copy Music at This Quality slider to find a setting that sounds good to you.

- The Protect Content check box controls whether Windows Media Player applies a digital license to the audio files you create from CD. This license restricts the files to being played on the computer on which you create them. If you use licenses, you need to back them up so you can restore them.

- Click the Change button to change the location to which Windows Media Player copies audio. Click the Advanced button and use the File Name Options dialog box to specify how Windows Media Player names the audio files.

Windows Media Player automatically adds files you "copy" to your Media Library. From there, you can play them individually, by album, or in playlists you create.

Applying Visualizations to Audio

The Now Playing page of Windows Media Player displays visualizations (visual effects to accompany audio) by default. You can control them using the controls under the visualization or the View | Visualizations submenus. You can add visualizations to Windows Media Player's list by using the Add button on the Visualizations tab of the Options dialog box.

Visualizations don't usually work correctly for analog playback from CD drives—only for digital playback.

Listening to Internet Radio

Internet radio includes both online broadcasts by commercial and public radio stations and webcasts by smaller stations or individuals who don't broadcast on the air. To listen to Internet radio, click the Radio Tuner tab on the taskbar and use the controls on the Radio Tuner page to search for and select stations.

 In a domain environment, the administrator may have chosen to prevent you from using Internet radio in order to conserve bandwidth on the Internet connection and, perhaps, to help prevent you from being distracted from your work.

The controls on the Radio Tuner page are straightforward. You can browse the available stations; use the Advanced search options to search by language, callsign, band, speed, and so on; and maintain a My Stations list of stations for quick access.

 You won't be able to save radio presets if Internet Explorer is set to use the Block All Cookies, High, or Medium-High privacy setting, because these settings block the cookies necessary for saving presets. You can change this setting to Medium, Low, or Accept All Cookies on the Privacy tab of the Internet Options dialog box if you have permission.

Configuring Your Connection Speed

Windows Media Player uses your connection speed to determine the quality of audio and video streams you request. By default, the Detect Connection Speed option button on the Performance page of the Options dialog box is selected, letting Windows Media Player automatically detect the connection speed when you request a stream. Sometimes you may need to specify a particular connection speed by selecting the Choose Connection Speed option button and picking the speed from the drop-down list. For example, you might need to specify a slow connection speed to prevent Windows Media Player from downloading high-quality streams that choke your Internet connection.

Configuring Buffering for Streaming Media

Windows Media Player uses buffering to ensure the continuity of the audio or video stream, storing a few seconds' worth of data so it can ride out brief interruptions in the stream. Windows Media Player's default is to use automatic buffering settings. You may want to specify a longer buffering time manually if default buffering doesn't produce uninterrupted streams.

Caution *If you change between Full mode and Skin mode while streaming media, Windows Media Player rebuffers the stream. This is a bug. The only workaround is not to change mode while streaming.*

Streaming Protocol	Outbound TCP	Inbound TCP	Outbound UDP	Inbound UDP
UDP	1755	—	1755	1024–5000 (one or more ports in this range)
TCP	1755	1755	—	—
HTTP	80	80	—	—

Table 15-2.   *Ports That Windows Media Player Requires Open for Streaming Media Using UDP, TCP, and HTTP*

Configuring Network Protocols

On the Network Protocols tab of the Options dialog box, you can select the network protocols to use for streaming audio and video content. You can also use the options in the Proxy Settings group box to configure proxy settings for protocols that use a proxy server. In a domain environment, you'll probably need to consult an administrator about these settings.

Getting Streaming Content Through a Firewall

If you're not able to play streaming media content from the Internet using Windows Media Player at work, it's most likely because your company's firewall doesn't let the data packets pass on the appropriate ports. Table 15-2 lists the ports Windows Media Player needs to have open for streaming media using User Datagram Protocol (UDP), Transmission Control Protocol (TCP), and Hypertext Transfer Protocol (HTTP).

 If you're using Internet Connection Sharing (ICS) or Internet Connection Firewall (ICF), you won't be able to use audio or video streams using User Datagram Protocol (UDP). Try selecting the Multicast check box, the TCP check box, and the HTTP check box on the Network tab of the Options dialog box. If the media server requires UDP, you won't be able to stream the media while using ICS or ICF.

Watching Videos and DVDs

To watch a video file, open it from the Media Library page, by double-clicking it in a Windows Explorer window, or by clicking its link on a web page.

Choose View | Full Screen or press ALT-ENTER to display the picture full screen. Press ALT-ENTER to reduce the full-screen display back to a window.

Configuring Video Acceleration

You can choose rough grades of video acceleration by using the Video Acceleration slider on the Performance page of the Options dialog box. This slider has three positions: Full (using the video mixing renderer and overlays), Some (using the video mixing renderer, but not using overlays), and None (using neither). For tighter control, click the Advanced button and work in the Video Acceleration Settings dialog box, which lets you set these options and others manually. This dialog box also lets you specify the size of the video window and (if you have a DVD decoder installed) choose whether to use the video mixing renderer and overlays for that too. If you have both hardware and software decoders, you can choose which to use.

Adding a DVD Decoder to Windows Media Player

Before you can play DVDs with Windows Media Player, you need to add a third-party DVD decoder to it (unless your PC already has one installed). The easiest way to find a DVD decoder that'll work is to search for DVD in Help and Support Center, and then follow the resulting If You Do Not Have a DVD Decoder link. This link brings you to a page that lists the available DVD decoders compatible with Windows XP Professional.

Once you've installed a compatible decoder, you can play a DVD either from AutoPlay or by choosing the DVD drive from the Play | DVD or CD Audio submenu.

If your DVD decoder stops working (after having worked fine before) or Windows Media Player doesn't recognize DVDs, the problem may be that your media library contains invalid entries. Rebuild it as described in "Rebuilding Your Media Library," later in this chapter.

Building Your Media Library and Configuring Access to It

To provide quick access to multimedia files, Windows Media Player builds and maintains a database of the multimedia files on your computer. Windows Media Player may prompt you to search your computer for multimedia files. Alternatively, choose Tools | Search for Media Files to start the search manually. In the Search for Media Files dialog box (shown in Figure 15-3 with its advanced search options displayed), specify which drives or folders to search. In the Advanced Search Options group box, specify the minimum sizes for audio files and video files to include, whether to add files smaller than these sizes when you play them, and whether to include your system folders in the search.

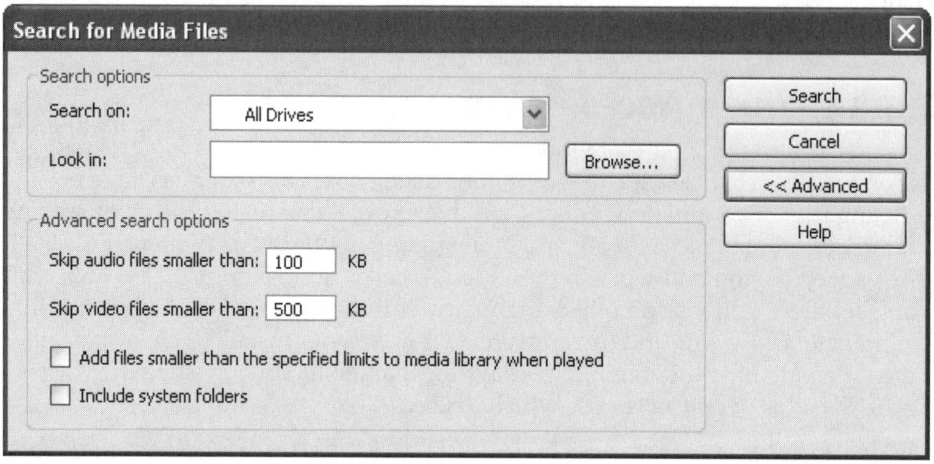

Figure 15-3. *In the Search for Media Files dialog box, choose which drives and folders to search for multimedia files.*

Windows Media Player gathers details of the multimedia files it finds and adds them to the database. You can access this database on the Media Library page of Windows Media Player, which categorizes the files into Audio and Video. You can browse the Audio category by All Audio, Album, Artist, and Genre, and the Video category by All Clips and Author. The Media Library page also lets you create playlists and access the playlists you've created.

Caution *Windows Media Player shares your media library with all users of the computer. This behavior is mostly convenient in a home setting, because it reduces the likelihood of multiple users copying the same CDs to the hard disk, thus filling it up. And on many home computers, users keep multimedia files in folders that other users can access. But this behavior can cause problems on a computer used by multiple users in a business setting, because files one user adds to the media library may well not be available to other users (for example, if the files are stored in a network folder or a redirected folder). If a file isn't available to you, Windows Media Player offers you the chance to browse for it or to remove it from the media library. If you remove the file from the media library, though, it will no longer be there for the user who can access it.*

Configuring Access to Your Media Library

By default, Windows Media Player allows other applications on your computer read-only access to your media library. You can change this setting by selecting the No Access option button or the Full Access option button in the Access Rights of Other Applications group box on the Media Library tab of the Options dialog box.

Also by default, Windows Media Player allows Internet sites no access to your media library. In the unlikely event that you need Internet sites to be able to access your media library, you can change this to read-only access or full access by selecting the appropriate option button in the Access Rights of Internet Sites group box on the Media Library tab.

By default, Windows Media Player automatically adds to your media library any audio file you buy online (and download to your computer). To keep these files out of your media library, clear the Automatically Add Purchased Music to My Library check box on the Media Library page.

Rebuilding Your Media Library

The media library contains static links rather than dynamic links, so if you move any of your multimedia files, Windows Media Player won't be able to play them from the links in the media library. If only a few links are affected, you may want to delete them manually. But if many of your multimedia files have moved, you may need to rebuild your media library to make it useful.

To rebuild your media library, follow these steps:

1. Export all the still-functional playlists you don't want to lose.

2. Exit Windows Media Player.

3. Display hidden files and folders in Windows Explorer if they're currently hidden.

4. Delete the wmplibrary_v_0_12.db file in the %allusersprofile%\Application Data\Microsoft\Media Index folder. (*%allusersprofile%* is the system variable for the Documents and Settings\All Users folder.)

5. Restart Windows Media Player. It creates a new media library file.

6. Choose Tools | Search for Media Files to search your computer for your multimedia files in their new locations.

7. Use the File | Import Playlist to Media Library command to import any playlists you saved.

Configuring File Types and Devices

The options on the File Types tab and the Devices tab are typically less useful in a business setting. Here are brief details:

■ Use the File Types tab to specify which file types Windows Media Player is associated with. Using this tab is quicker than working with the File Types tab of the Folder Options dialog box. You need to be logged on as an administrator to reassign file types.

■ The Devices tab lets you configure the CD or DVD drives and portable audio devices (for example, an MP3/WMA player) you use with Windows Media Player. For a CD or DVD drive, you can choose between digital and analog playback, digital and audio copying, and whether to use error correction for playback and copying. Use the Add button to add a portable audio device.

> **Note** *Choosing digital or analog playback in Windows Media Player overrides the corresponding setting for the CD or DVD drive in Device Manager.*

Summary

This chapter has provided the essential information you need to use Windows Media Player's key features effectively. It has discussed how to use Windows Media Player for CD audio and audio files, how to listen to Internet radio stations, and how to watch video files and DVDs. It has shown you how to build your media library, how to configure access to it, and how to destroy and rebuild your library if it gets corrupted. Along the way, the chapter has explained how to troubleshoot frequently occurring problems with Windows Media Player.

The next chapter covers how to use Messenger and NetMeeting for real-time chat and application-sharing.

The Complete Reference

Windows XP

Chapter 16

Using Real-Time Chat, Application Sharing, and Collaboration

W indows XP includes two applications for real-time chat, collaboration, and application sharing. *Windows Messenger*—the Windows XP version of MSN Messenger—is positioned prominently in the Windows XP user interface. *NetMeeting*, an older communications tool, is hidden until you invoke it.

Both Windows Messenger (hereafter "Messenger") and NetMeeting can be useful for work and play. This chapter discusses how to configure the applications and use them for real-time chat and application-sharing. The next chapter discusses how to use them for audio-conferencing and video-conferencing.

Because NetMeeting and Messenger offer many of the same collaboration features, this chapter discusses most of their features together. Most of the collaboration commands are the same in NetMeeting and Messenger. Where they're different, this chapter points out the differences.

Instant Messaging for Work and Play

Instant messaging started as a consumer application, but it has been adopted enthusiastically by a large number of businesses whose employees need real-time communication with each other and with people at other companies. *Text-based chat* provides quick and effective communication at minimal cost of bandwidth, so it works well even over the slowest connections (for example, dial-up connections).

Note   *Some companies use consumer-grade real-time communications software (such as Messenger and NetMeeting, both discussed in this chapter) for business communications. However, other companies use commercial-grade real-time communications software instead for their business communications. Commercial-grade software typically offers security enhancements, management features, and logging capabilities that consumer-grade software doesn't offer.*

Loosely speaking, communication can be either synchronous or asynchronous. *Synchronous communication*—literally, communication that happens at the same time—requires both or all participants to communicate at the same time, in real time. For example, telephone calls, video-conferencing, and fistfights are forms of synchronous communication. By contrast, *asynchronous communication* is communication that doesn't happen in real time. E-mail, voicemail, and FedEx are examples of asynchronous communication.

Instant messaging combines several of the advantages of synchronous communication with asynchronous communication. Instant messaging is initially synchronous, in that both or all participants in a conversation need to be online at the same time to connect. But once a conversation has been established, you can let it lapse and revive it as necessary, keeping it going asynchronously if you want to. You can have multiple instant-messaging windows open at the same time, each of which can contain a conversation with one or more people. You can add audio or video to one of the conversations, while maintaining text-based communication in the others. You can transfer files to or receive files from participants in each conversation. And you can share applications with one or more users in a conversation or even let them control your computer.

Instant messaging has plenty of disadvantages to accompany its advantages. First, if the person you want to communicate with isn't online or has chosen not to be available to you, you won't be able to communicate with them via instant messaging. Second, if the instant-messaging software they're using is incompatible with yours, you won't be able to communicate with them even when they're online and prepared to communicate with you. Third, instant messaging can be a severe time-waster, combining the worst features of hanging around the water-cooler or coffee-machine with some of the less attractive aspects of the Internet. Fourth, while text-based chat requires minimal bandwidth, greedier aspects of instant messaging (such as audioconferencing and videoconferencing) can make bandwidth disappear as rapidly as cookies left unattended in the lunchroom. File transfer alone can bring a T1 Internet connection to its knees.

In a domain environment, the administrator will typically restrict instant-messaging applications to a short list of company-approved purposes that limit the amount of time you can waste on instant messaging and the amount of damage you can do by using its capabilities. You may well be able to use text-based chat (although some companies prevent workers from using instant messaging at all). You may be allowed to use application-sharing to brainstorm with colleagues—for example, in remote offices. You're much less likely to be allowed to use file transfer, and if you are allowed to use it, you may be allowed to transfer only small files. You'll probably be allowed to use audioconferencing and videoconferencing only if you can demonstrate a convincing business need. You probably won't be allowed to let remote users take control of your computer via instant-messaging applications. And you may be able to use instant messaging only within your corporation or to contacts outside the corporate firewall as well.

This chapter and the next chapter discuss how to use all these features—if you have permission to do so.

How Messenger and NetMeeting Compare to Each Other

Messenger and NetMeeting have large areas of overlap. Both offer text chat, audio and video conversations, file transfer, whiteboarding, application sharing, and remote control capabilities. NetMeeting has been included in versions of Windows for several years now. Messenger is much newer and is essentially a replacement for NetMeeting.

Messenger is controlled centrally by Microsoft's .NET Messenger Service or by another communications system, such as Exchange Server. All Messenger communications are organized through .NET Messenger Service or the other communications system, which means when you use Messenger, your actions are effectively being tracked all the time. This means .NET Messenger Service or the other communications system knows who your contacts are, when you converse with them, whether you use audio and video, which files you transfer back and forth, and so on. The way Messenger is designed, this constant monitoring is necessary for its features to work—but for some users, the monitoring raises privacy concerns.

For such users, NetMeeting provides a more discreet and controllable communications client. By contrast, if you use a computer in a domain, the network administrators are not only entitled, but are more or less obliged to monitor your actions anyway.

In this context, the privacy implications of Messenger fade into the general background of workplace surveillance. And, in any case, the administrators may well have restricted the actions you can take with Messenger to reduce the chance of your embarrassing either yourself or your company.

Messenger is a vital component of Windows XP's Remote Assistance feature, which lets one user help another across a network or Internet connection while maintaining a high level of security. (See Chapter 33 for a discussion of what Remote Assistance is and how to use it.)

NetMeeting originally tied into the Internet Locator Server (ILS) system for finding contacts running NetMeeting and compatible software. Since then, however, Microsoft has transmuted ILS into the Microsoft Internet Directory for .NET Messenger Service. NetMeeting can use the Microsoft Internet Directory only by activating Messenger—which means you might as well be using Messenger in the first place. However, you can use NetMeeting to establish direct connections to other users whose IP address, computer name, or phone number you know. In a domain, your company may run its own messaging servers to enable you to connect easily to colleagues. If you don't use audio and video in your NetMeeting calls, you can encrypt the data you send and receive for text chat, file transfer, and collaboration activities.

Note *One capability this chapter doesn't discuss, but which you might like to know about sometime, is NetMeeting's Remote Desktop Sharing feature. Remote Desktop Sharing lets you access your own Desktop remotely and securely across a network connection or an Internet connection. Remote Desktop Sharing isn't as useful or as easy to use as the Remote Desktop feature built into Windows XP Professional, but you may want to investigate it if you need to access a computer running Windows XP Home. (Windows XP Home doesn't include Remote Desktop.) You could also use Remote Desktop Sharing to connect to your Windows XP Professional computer if your administrator prevented you from using Remote Desktop—except that the administrator will almost certainly prevent you from using Remote Desktop Sharing as well. If you're allowed to use Remote Desktop Sharing, choose Tools | Remote Desktop Sharing to activate this feature.*

Configuring Messenger

This section discusses how to configure Messenger. Many of the configuration options are straightforward, but others are more subtle than they appear. So this section discusses each of the options briefly to make sure you understand them. To make the information easier to find, it presents the options in categories by function.

Note *Microsoft is developing Messenger rapidly, so the Messenger interface may have changed since this book went to press. However, the basics described in this section seem likely to remain the same.*

You can configure some of Messenger's options while offline, but to choose other options, you need to sign either into Messenger Service using your .NET Passport or into your other communications services by using your account for that service.

Changing Your Display Name

Start your configuration of Messenger by checking to see if Messenger is displaying a suitable name for you. By default, Messenger uses the contents of the First Name field of your .NET Passport or the name assigned to your communications account as your display name. You can change this in the My Display Name text box (or the My .NET Messenger Service Display Name text box, depending on the version of Messenger) on the Personal tab of the Options dialog box (Figure 16-1). For example, you might want to add your last name to your first name or use a nickname instead.

WORKING AND COMMUNICATING

Figure 16-1.   *Make sure your display name is correct on the Personal page of the Options dialog box.*

Publishing Your Phone Numbers

You can have Messenger display up to three phone numbers for you: home, work, and mobile. Choose Tools | Publish My Phone Numbers to display the Phone tab of the Options dialog box, and then enter the numbers in the My Home Phone text box, the My Work Phone text box, and the My Mobile Phone text box. Make sure the My Country/Region Code drop-down list shows the correct country or region. (Messenger picks up the country or region code from your Windows XP phone options. If you haven't set phone options, Windows XP may prompt you to do so.)

These phone numbers then appear in the Properties dialog box for a contact. To display this Properties dialog box, right-click the contact and choose Properties from the shortcut menu.

Changing the Font and Font Size Messenger Uses for Your Text

To change the font for your display text (the text you write), display the Change My Message Font dialog box in either of the following ways:

- Click the Change Font button on the Personal tab of the Options dialog box.
- Click the Font button in a Conversation window (or choose Edit | Change Font).

The Change My Message Font dialog box limits you to a small selection of "sensible" font sizes—between 8 points and 16 points. Each Messenger user can change the relative size of text displayed by Messenger by choosing View | Text Size and selecting the size (Smallest, Smaller, Medium, Large, or Largest) from the submenu. Don't use the tight script fonts because they tend to be illegible even at the Largest setting.

Showing or Suppressing Emoticons

By default, Messenger displays *emoticons* (graphical symbols such as ☺) when you type the appropriate text sequence. To toggle emoticons on and off, select or clear the Show Graphics (Emoticons) in Instant Messages check box in the My Message Text area of the Personal tab of the Options dialog box.

Preventing Messenger from Running Automatically and Opening Your Internet Connection

By default, Messenger is configured to sign you into Messenger Service as soon as you log onto Windows XP and to keep you signed in until you sign out manually or log off XP. This default behavior works well if you have a persistent Internet connection and you want to run Messenger all the time so that people can contact you.

To prevent Messenger from running automatically and signing you on when you log onto Windows, clear the Run This Program when Windows Starts check box in the General area of the Preferences tab of the Options dialog box (Figure 16-2).

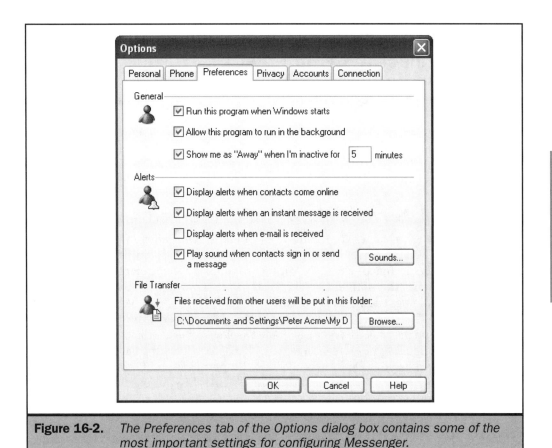

Figure 16-2. *The Preferences tab of the Options dialog box contains some of the most important settings for configuring Messenger.*

Preventing Messenger from Running in the Background

By default, Messenger is configured to keep running in the background and to keep you signed into the Messenger Service after you close the Messenger window. This behavior enables you to communicate with your contacts and receive messages, calls, files, Remote Assistance invitations, and so on from them even if the Messenger window isn't open. However, keeping Messenger running when you're using it with .NET Messenger Service also keeps your Internet connection open, which may be a problem if you have a dial-up connection. Keeping Messenger open also lets Messenger Service and your contacts monitor your presence online.

When you first close the Messenger window, Messenger displays a pop-up in the notification area to warn you it's still running. But once you've dismissed the pop-up and told it not to reappear, it's easy to forget Messenger is running in the background.

To prevent Messenger from running in the background, clear the Allow This Program to Run in the Background check box in the General area of the Preferences tab of the Options dialog box.

Preventing Messenger from Signing You In When You Connect to the Internet

Even if you've manually signed out of Messenger, and then closed your Internet connection, Messenger automatically signs you in the next time you establish the Internet connection.

By default, Outlook Express causes Messenger to sign you in when you run Outlook Express. To change this behavior, choose Tools | Options in Outlook Express to display the Options dialog box, clear the Automatically Log On to Windows Messenger check box in the General area on the General tab, and then click the OK button.

Choosing the Interval Before You're Marked As "Away"

By default, Messenger changes your status from Online to Away after you've been inactive for five minutes. You can adjust the length of time by changing the value in the Show Me As "Away" when I'm Inactive for *NN* Minutes text box on the Preferences tab of the Options dialog box. Alternatively, you can clear the Show Me As "Away" when I'm Inactive for *NN* Minutes check box to turn this option off. If you do so, Messenger changes your status to Away when you've been inactive for the number of minutes specified in the Wait text box on the Screen Saver page of the Display Properties dialog box—the length of inactivity required for your screen saver to kick in. (To display the Display Properties dialog box, right-click your Desktop and choose Properties from the shortcut menu.)

If you use no screen saver and clear the Show Me As "Away" check box, Messenger never changes your status to Away.

Choosing Alerts for Contacts, Messages, and E-mails

The four options in the Alerts section of the Preferences tab of the Options dialog box let you choose whether to display alerts for the following events:

- When one of your contacts comes online
- When you receive an instant message
- When you receive an e-mail message on your Hotmail or MSN account
- When one of your contacts signs in or sends you a message

Most people find being alerted they've received an instant message helpful. Opinion is split on the value of the other alerts.

If you use the alerts, you can specify the sounds used for each of the alerts. To do so, click the Sounds button and work with the Messenger events in the Program Events list box on the Sounds tab of the Sounds and Audio Devices Properties dialog box. See "Customizing System Sounds" in Chapter 7 for details.

Changing the Folder into Which Transferred Files Are Placed

By default, Messenger places files you receive via file transfer in your \My Documents\ My Received Files\ folder. To make Messenger put the files somewhere else, click the Browse button in the File Transfer area of the Preferences tab of the Options dialog box and use the resulting Browse for Folder dialog box to specify the folder.

Maintaining Your Allow List and Block List

The Privacy tab of the Options dialog box (Figure 16-3) provides a My Allow List list box and a My Block List list box for keeping your lists of those contacts who may and may

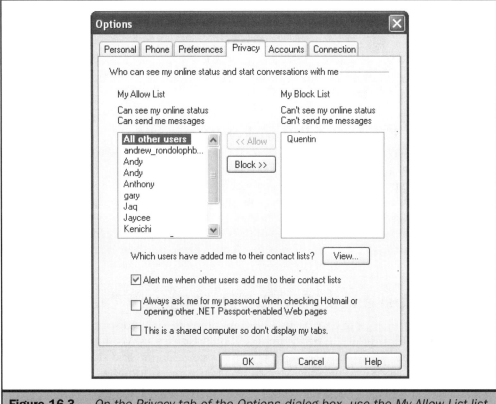

Figure 16-3. *On the Privacy tab of the Options dialog box, use the My Allow List list box and the My Block List list box to manage which contacts may and may not view your status and contact you.*

not see your online status and send you messages. You can shift one or more selected contacts from one list box to the other by using the Allow button or the Block button. The All Other Users entry appears by default in the My Allow List list box, letting all Messenger users other than those listed check your status and send you messages. If you need privacy from everyone except the contacts you specifically allow to contact you, move the All Other Users item to the My Block List list box.

Checking Whose Contact Lists You're On

To see which other users have added you to their contact lists, click the View button on the Privacy tab of the Options dialog box. Messenger displays a dialog box that shows whose contact lists you appear on. Use this information to identify forgotten friends or to block users as appropriate. You can also right-click a user's name and choose Add to Contacts from the shortcut menu to add that user to your contact list or choose Properties to display information about the user. (If the user is already one of your contacts, the Add to Contacts item will be unavailable.)

To make sure Messenger always warns you when another Messenger user adds you to their contact list, verify the Alert Me when Other Users Add Me to Their Contact Lists check box on the Privacy tab is selected. (This check box is selected by default.) You'll see what happens as a result of this setting in "Add a Contact when They Add You to Their Contact List," later in this chapter.

Keeping .NET Passport under Control

One of .NET Passport's features is to automatically log you into .NET Passport–enabled Web sites once you've successfully logged into .NET Passport during a Windows XP session. If you're in the habit of leaving your computer running and accessible to other people while you're still logged in, it may be a good idea to select the Always Ask Me for My Password when Checking Hotmail or Opening Other .NET Passport–Enabled Web Pages check box on the Privacy tab of the Options dialog box. (This check box is cleared by default.) When this check box is selected, each time you try to access a .NET Passport–enabled page, Internet Explorer will demand your password.

Preventing Messenger from Displaying Your Tabs

To prevent Messenger from displaying your tabs along the left side of the Messenger window, select the This Is a Shared Computer So Don't Display My Tabs check box on the Privacy tab of the Options dialog box. After you sign out and sign back in again, or after someone else signs in using Messenger from your Windows XP user account, Messenger doesn't display the tabs. It also removes the Show Tabs command from the Tools menu so that the user can't display tabs by using this command.

Removing tabs prevents other users who are using Messenger from your Windows XP account from seeing which tabs you have installed and which tabs you're using. At this writing, the services available on the tabs are few and relatively uncontroversial. But as (or if) more companies and, perhaps, government departments provide services via extensions that appear as tabs in Messenger, hiding the tabs to prevent other users from accessing them will become more important.

 Under normal circumstances, you shouldn't let anybody else use your user account. (If you administer the computer, set up each other user with their own account and make temporary users use the Guest account.) The exception is if you use an account that's deliberately shared for administrative purposes.

Setting Messenger Up to Use a Communications Service

As mentioned earlier in this chapter, Messenger can use either the .NET Messenger Service (which uses .NET Passport) or another communications service (for example, Exchange Server's instant messaging service) as its primary logon. To specify which service to use, display the Accounts tab of the Options dialog box (shown on the left in Figure 16-4).

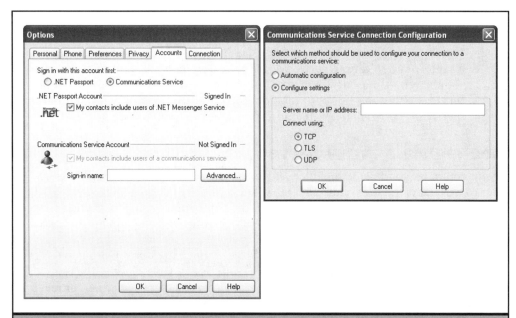

Figure 16-4.   *On the Accounts tab of the Options dialog box (left), choose whether Messenger should log on to the .NET Messenger Service or another communications service first. If necessary, use the Communications Service Connection Configuration dialog box (right) to configure the settings for your communications service.*

To sign into your communications service first, follow these steps:

1. Select the Communications Service option button.

2. If you'll also use .NET Messenger Service to reach some contacts, select the My Contacts Include Users of .NET Messenger Service check box.

3. Enter your sign-in name for the communications service in the Sign-in Name text box.

4. If your communications service doesn't use automatic configuration based on your sign-in name, click the Advanced button to display the Communications Service Connection Configuration dialog box (shown on the right in Figure 16-4). Select the Configure Settings options button and specify the server name or IP address and the protocol to use.

To sign into .NET Messenger Service first, follow these steps:

1. Select the .NET Passport option button.

2. If you also use a communications service, select the My Contacts Include Users of a Communications Service option button.

3. Enter your sign-in name for the communications service in the Sign-in Name text box.

4. If your communications service doesn't use automatic configuration based on your sign-in name, click the Advanced button to display the Communications Service Connection Configuration dialog box. Select the Configure settings and specify the server name or IP address and the protocol to use.

Connecting via a Proxy Server

If your computer connects to the Internet via a proxy server, you may need to check your configuration on the Connection tab of the Options dialog box (Figure 16-5). If you connect to the Internet directly from the computer you're using, or if you connect via a small network that uses Internet Connection Sharing, you shouldn't need to worry about the controls on this page.

The key control on this tab is the I Use a Proxy Server check box. Once you select this check box, Messenger makes all the other controls available. Specify the type of proxy server in the Type drop-down list. Enter the server's name in the Server text box. Correct the port number from the default that Messenger enters in the Port text box if applicable.

If you specify a SOCKS Version 5 proxy server, you'll need to enter your user name in the User ID text box and your password in the Password text box.

Connecting to the Internet through ICS (with or without ICF correctly configured) is considered a "direct connection (no firewall)" by Messenger.

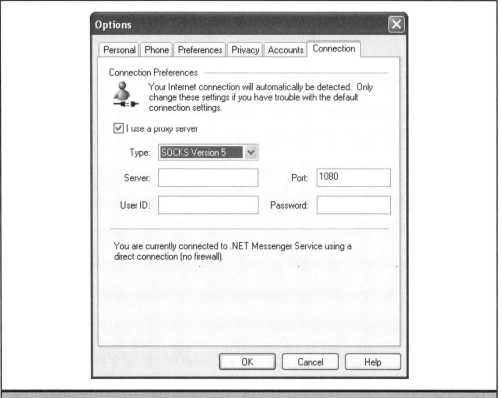

Figure 16-5. *If you use a proxy server to connect to the Internet, specify the details on the Connection tab of the Options dialog box.*

Displaying Messenger Always on Top of Other Windows

If you want Messenger always to appear on top of other applications, so that it's always visible when you're working in Windows, choose Tools | Always on Top from the main Messenger window.

Troubleshooting Messenger Configuration and Connection Issues

This section discusses how to troubleshoot three of the more frequent configuration and connection issues that surface with Messenger. These issues involve error messages about your display name, Messenger redialing your dial-up Internet connection when you don't want it to, and Messenger being blocked by firewalls.

"The Display Name You Chose Was Invalid"

If you get the error message "The display name you chose was invalid. Please choose another display name and try again," this usually means you've stepped on a trademark or another word Microsoft is sensitive to on its own account or has been sensitized to by another company. For example, if you try to call yourself "Microsoft," Messenger will object. When you dismiss the error message box, Messenger resets your display name to its previous value.

You might also have entered an offensive word Microsoft has decided to block. At this writing, the list of words is a little uneven, but you can probably guess most of them.

Messenger Keeps Redialing Your Internet Connection After You've Closed the Messenger Window

If Messenger keeps redialing your Internet connection after you've closed the Messenger window with the intention of exiting Messenger, chances are Messenger is configured to run in the background. Because it's not immediately apparent either that it's Messenger doing the dialing or that Messenger is still running after you've closed the Messenger window (unless you scrutinize the notification-area icon), this problem can be confusing at first.

To prevent this from happening, clear the Allow This Program to Run in the Background check box in the General area of the Preferences tab of the Options dialog box. Closing the Messenger window then signs you out of Messenger Service and exits Messenger.

ICF or Another Firewall Blocks Messenger

If you find Internet Connection Firewall (ICF) or another firewall is blocking Messenger connections, you may need to open ports manually through the firewall. These are the ports Messenger uses for communicating:

Service	TCP Port	UDP Port
Incoming voice call (computer to computer)	6901	6901
Voice (computer to phone)	—	6801, 6901, 2001–2120
Receiving files	6891–6900	—

In most cases, ICF doesn't cause Messenger any problems because the two have been taught to communicate with each other: Messenger negotiates with ICF the ports it needs to have open, and ICF opens them by implementing the appropriate services. If you want to examine the ports, display the Advanced Settings dialog box for the external ICS interface and look at the services called msmsgs running on the Services page. Figure 16-6 shows an example in which several computers are connecting via ICS and using Messenger through ICF.

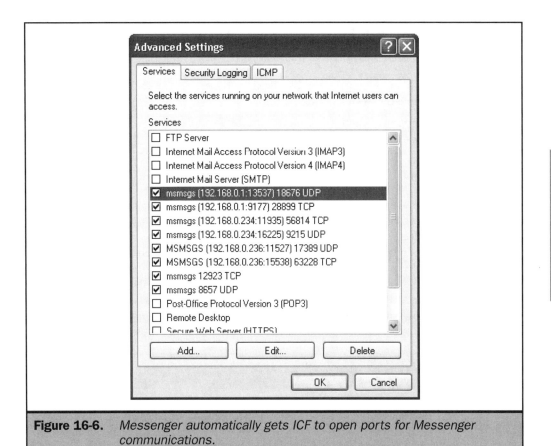

Figure 16-6. *Messenger automatically gets ICF to open ports for Messenger communications.*

Note   *See "Securing Your Internet Connection with ICF" in Chapter 35 for a discussion of how to configure ICF and open ports in it.*

Creating and Managing Your Contact List

Before you can easily establish a conversation with anyone in Messenger, you need to add one or more contacts to your contact list. You can do this in any of three ways:

■ Using their e-mail address or .NET Passport sign-in name

■ Searching for them in a directory

■ Adding them to your contact list when they add you to their list

The next three subsections discuss these possibilities. The subsections after those discuss how to block, unblock, and delete contacts.

Adding a Contact by Their Sign-in Name

To add a contact by their sign-in, take these steps:

1. Run the Add a Contact Wizard by clicking the Add a Contact item in the I Want To list or choosing Tools | Add a Contact.

2. On the first page of the wizard, select the By E-mail Address or Sign-in Name option button and click the Next button.

3. On the Please Type Your Contact's Complete E-mail Address page of the wizard, enter the contact's e-mail address and click the Next button.

If the person has a .NET Passport, Messenger displays a page like the one in Figure 16-7, telling you the contact has been added to your contact list and, if the person isn't using Messenger, Messenger Service will send them an e-mail encouraging them to start using it. If the person doesn't have a .NET Passport, Messenger displays a page telling you it couldn't add the person to your contact list, but offers to send them an e-mail encouraging them to sign up for a .NET Passport and start using Messenger. In either case, you can add a message of your own to the boilerplate message to encourage the person to take the message seriously. Add at least your real name and other identifying information in case the person doesn't recognize your e-mail address.

Figure 16-7. *If a contact has a .NET Passport, you can add them to your contacts list in Messenger with minimal effort.*

Adding a Contact by Searching for Them

If you don't know the e-mail address or .NET Passport sign-in name of the contact you want to add to your contact list, run the Add a Contact Wizard and choose the Search for a Contact option button on its first page. The wizard displays the Type Your Contact's First and Last Name page. Enter as much accurate information about the contact as possible, including city or state if they're in the United States, and choose which directory to search through in the Search for This Person At drop-down list. For example, if you're using .NET Messenger Service, you can choose the Hotmail Member Directory.

If the search is successful, the wizard displays a Search Results list, from which you can choose the person who seems to match. So far, so good—but if you searched using the Hotmail Member Directory, the wizard next displays a page apologizing for not being able to add the person to your contact list because of the Hotmail privacy policy and telling you it will send them an e-mail instead. Again, you can customize the e-mail to make sure the person knows who you are and (perhaps) so that they have more motivation to respond positively to the invitation.

Adding a Contact When They Add You to Their Contact List

The third way of adding a contact pops up when another Messenger user adds you to their contact list. If you have the Alert Me when Other Users Add Me to their Contact Lists check box on the Privacy page of the Options dialog box selected, Messenger displays the Windows Messenger dialog box shown next when another user adds you to their contact list.

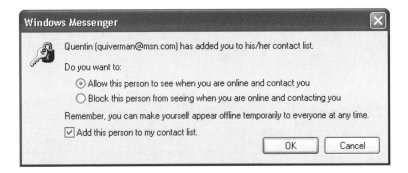

From here, you can select either the Allow This Person to See when You Are Online and Contact You option button or the Block This Person from Seeing when You Are Online and Contacting You option button. If you choose to allow the person to add you as a contact, select or clear the Add This Person to My Contact List check box, as appropriate, before clicking the OK button to close the dialog box.

If you choose to block the person, Messenger clears the Add This Person to My Contact List check box—but you can select it if you want to add the person to your contact list but block them at present. Whether you add the person to your contact list or not, you get added to their contact list, but you appear permanently in the Not Online group. To contact the contact, you'll need to unblock them—you can't send messages to a contact you've blocked.

Blocking or Unblocking a Contact

You can block a contact by issuing a Block command from a Conversation window or the main Messenger window:

- Click the Block button in a Conversation window. If the conversation contains multiple people, Messenger displays a menu of people you can block; select the right one. If the conversation contains just the two of you, Messenger knows whom to block. Your conversation is then effectively ended, although the Conversation window remains open.

- Right-click a contact in the main Messenger window and choose Block from the shortcut menu.

When you've blocked someone, they can't check your online status, view your phone numbers, or send you messages until you unblock them. To unblock someone, you can use one of three options:

- Click the Unblock button in a Conversation window in which you've blocked that contact.

- Right-click the contact in the main Messenger window and choose Unblock from the shortcut menu.

- Display the Privacy tab of the Options dialog box (Tools | Options), select the contact in the My Block List option button, click the Allow button, and close the dialog box.

Deleting a Contact

You can delete a contact by right-clicking their entry in the main Messenger window and choosing Delete Contact from the shortcut menu. Messenger displays a message box to confirm the deletion in case you've clicked hastily.

Connecting with Messenger

You can establish a connection with another Messenger user from the main Messenger window in any of the following ways:

■ Double-click the contact's name in the Online category.

■ Right-click the contact's name in the Online category and choose Send an Instant Message from the shortcut menu.

■ Click the Send an Instant Message link in the action pane (the I Want To list). Messenger displays the Send an Instant Message dialog box. Select the contact on the My Contacts page and click the OK button. (This way of establishing a connection is so much more clumsy than the others that it's seldom worth using.)

■ If the Messenger user isn't one of your contacts, click the Send an Instant Message link in the action pane to display the Send an Instant Message dialog box. Click the Other tab to display the Other page and enter the person's e-mail address in the text box. If, by the time you're reading this, Messenger has been made interoperable with other instant-messaging services, select the appropriate service in the Service drop-down list. Then click the OK button. Messenger opens a Conversation window addressed to that user.

| Caution | *When you use the Other page in the Send an Instant Message dialog box, Messenger doesn't verify the address until you try to send a message. If you've made a mistake with the address or if the person isn't online at the time, Messenger tells you the message couldn't be delivered to the recipient.* |

In the Conversation window that Messenger has opened, enter your opening message in the text box and click the Send button to send it. Messenger transmits the message to your contact.

If your contact is receiving alerts, Messenger displays a pop-up telling them your display name and the text of the message (or the first part of it, if the message is long). If your contact isn't receiving alerts, Messenger opens a minimized Conversation window and flashes its Taskbar button in a contrasting color to their color scheme to attract their attention.

Once your contact clicks the pop-up or the minimized Conversation window, the conversation is up and running. Figure 16-8 shows the beginning of a conversation in a Conversation window. You can add another contact to an existing conversation by clicking the Invite Someone to This Conversation link in the I Want To list.

The Conversation window is easy to use because it includes buttons or links for most of the commands it offers. We'll examine most of the features throughout the rest of this chapter and in the next chapter.

The status line at the top of the Conversation window displays any warnings. For example, it may tell you "Chris may not reply because his or her status is set to Busy" if Chris has set his or her status to Busy. The status bar at the bottom of the window tells you when someone in a conversation with you is typing a message in the Conversation window so that you can avoid getting your chat out of sync.

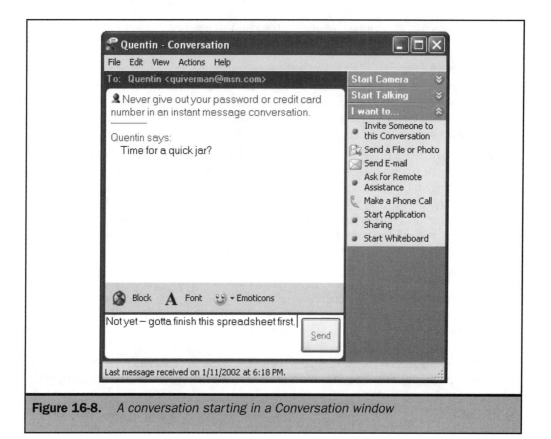

Figure 16-8. *A conversation starting in a Conversation window*

Entering Emoticons in Your Messages

You can enter emoticons in your messages using either the mouse or the keyboard:

- With the mouse, click the Emoticons button in the Conversation window and choose the emoticon from the drop-down pane. This pane shows the most common emoticons, but not all that Messenger supports.

- With the keyboard, type the text sequence for the emoticon. If you can remember the text sequence, entering it in a message is much quicker than using the mouse. For a list of the text sequences for emoticons, click the Emoticons button in the Conversation window and choose the ... button to display an Internet Explorer window with the Messenger Help screen listing the text sequences.

Ending a Conversation

To end a conversation, click the Close button on its Conversation window or choose File | Close from the Conversation window.

Ending a Messenger Session

How you can end a Messenger session depends on whether you've left Messenger configured to keep running in the background or you've decided to take control over it.

If you've prevented Messenger from running in the background (by clearing the Allow This Program to Run in the Background check box in the General area of the Preferences tab of the Options dialog box), you can close Messenger by clicking the Close button on the Messenger window or by choosing File | Close.

If you've allowed Messenger to run in the background, you can close Messenger only by clicking (or right-clicking) the Messenger icon in the notification area and choosing Exit from the shortcut menu.

Regardless of whether you've allowed Messenger to run in the background, you can sign out of Messenger Service by choosing File | Sign Out from the main Messenger window or by clicking the Messenger icon in the notification area and choosing Sign Out from the shortcut menu. You can then sign back in by clicking the link in the main Messenger window (if you have it displayed) or by clicking the Messenger icon in the notification area and choosing Sign In from the shortcut menu.

Changing Your Status

By default, Messenger sets your status to Online once you connect to Messenger Service. Messenger changes it to Away after the length of inactivity specified on the Preferences page of the Options dialog box (if you've selected the Show Me As "Away" when I'm Inactive for *NN* Minutes check box) or the length of inactivity it takes for your screen saver to kick in. Messenger changes your status to Offline when you sign out of Messenger Service.

When you're signed into Messenger Service, you can change your overt status by clicking your entry at the top of the main Messenger window and choosing the status you want (Online, Busy, Be Right Back, Away, On the Phone, Out to Lunch, or Appear Offline) from the resulting menu. You can also change your status by clicking (or right-clicking) the Messenger icon in the notification area, selecting the My Status item on the menu, and choosing the status from the submenu.

Using Groups to Sort Your Messenger Contacts

If you have a lot of contacts, you may find Messenger's default Online/Offline grouping doesn't show you all the contacts you need to see at any given time. Instead, you can create and populate custom groups so that you can sort your contacts by categories as needed.

To work with groups, choose Tools | Sort Contacts By | Groups from the main Messenger window. Messenger displays the default groups: Coworkers, Family, Friends, and Other Contacts. You can then drag your existing contacts into the appropriate group or create new groups for your contacts by using the Add a Group command on the Tools | Manage Groups submenu. Messenger adds a new group that you can then rename.

Alternatively, you can use the Rename a Group submenu to rename one of the existing groups or the Delete a Group submenu to dispose of a group.

To return your contacts to the Online and Offline categories, choose Tools | Sort Contacts By | Online/Offline.

Transferring Files with Messenger

File transfer with Messenger is easy—provided you're allowed to perform it.

In a domain environment, your administrator may have decided to block file transfer for any (or all) of a variety of reasons that may include the following:

- Unfettered file transfer encourages users to squander bandwidth by transferring files unnecessarily.

- Many of the files transferred via file transfer between instant-messaging clients have traditionally been illegal copies of copyrighted files—for example, MP3 files or video files.

- Other files transferred via file transfer between instant-messaging clients have been entirely legal files that may bother your company for other reasons. For example, if you transfer pornographic files using your company's software or connection, the company could be sued on sexual-harassment grounds.

- File transfer to people outside the company may threaten the company's security.

An ISP may have blocked file transfer to protect its bandwidth or to reduce its liability.

Note   *If you need to transfer to your colleagues files larger than will go through your mail server, your administrator may make an area on an FTP site available to you.*

Even if your administrator or your ISP doesn't block file transfer, Messenger has two limitations you should know about:

- Messenger can transfer only one file at a time to a person in a conversation. This means if you want to transfer a number of files to the same person, you'll need to be at your computer so that you can send them one by one, instead of being able to stack them as you can with NetMeeting.

- If you're in a Messenger conversation with multiple people, you can send a file to only one of them in a file-transfer operation. You can then start another transfer to send the same file to another person in the conversation, but you're effectively transferring the file twice, so if all other things are equal, the transfer will take twice as long. (A form of multicast distribution would be better, in which you upload the file once to a server that distributes copies of it to each of the people you've designated as recipients.)

You can get around the second limitation by using a compression utility, such as the limited Zip-file functionality built into Windows XP (or, better, a more powerful compression utility such as WinZip) to create an archive file, and then send the archive as the single file. However, it's not a good idea to send colossal files over any but the fastest of connections because you can waste a huge amount of time if the file transfer gets broken off for any reason and you have to restart it from the beginning.

Send a File with Messenger

Messenger makes it easy to send a file to somebody you're in a conversation with. Start by clicking the Send a File or Photo link in the Conversation window or choosing File | Send a File or Photo.

Note *One of the ways in which an administrator may prevent file transfer is by choosing firewall settings that block file transfers. Even if the Messenger features for file transfer appear to be working, you might not be able to transfer files at all, either because the firewall at your end is blocking the transfers or because a firewall at the would-be recipient's end of the connection is blocking the transfers.*

If only one other person is in the conversation with you, Messenger knows to whom you want to send the file or photo. If there's more than one other person, Messenger displays the Send a File dialog box, which lists the contacts in the conversation so that you can select which of them should receive the file. Once you've selected the contact, Messenger opens a new Conversation window with just that contact, thus keeping the details of the file transfer out of the original Conversation window.

Messenger then displays the Send a File to *Contact's Name* dialog box. Select the file and click the Open button, and the contact receives a notice in the Conversation window telling them you want to send them a file. The notice contains an Accept link and a Decline link. If the contact chooses the Accept link, Messenger starts the file transfer and keeps both you and the recipient informed of its progress. If the contact chooses the Decline link, you get a notice telling you they declined the transfer.

If you're not already in a conversation with the person to whom you want to send the file, you can start the file-transfer process by clicking the Send a File or Photo link in the Action pane of the main Messenger window or choosing Action | Send a File or Photo. Messenger displays the Send a File dialog box, in which you specify the contact or other person. Messenger then opens a Conversation window and displays the Send a File to *Contact's Name* dialog box. The process then continues as described earlier.

Tip *Another way of starting a file transfer is to drag a file from your Desktop or an Explorer window and drop it on a contact in the main Messenger window.*

Receive a File with Messenger

If you read the previous section, you'll have had no difficulty working out what happens when someone sends you a file with Messenger: If you're in a conversation with them, you get a notice in the Conversation window inviting you to accept or decline the file transfer. If you're not in a conversation with them, you get a screen pop to bring your attention to the new Conversation window that's flashing on your taskbar. Click the Accept link or the Decline link, as appropriate.

Messenger places files by default in your My Documents\My Received Files folder. You can change this by using the Browse button on the Preferences tab of the Options dialog box (Tools | Options).

Troubleshoot File Transfers with Messenger

File transfers with Messenger are usually easy unless someone has actively taken steps to prevent you from transferring files. This section describes the problems you may encounter.

Before we start, remember Messenger's limitations: you can transfer only one file at a time to each contact—you can't stack up multiple file transfers to the same person the way you can with NetMeeting. And you can perform a maximum of ten file transfers at a time.

Can Transfer Only One File at a Time

If Messenger doesn't let you start further file transfers after you've got one going, the problem is likely to be that your firewall is configured with only one port open for file transfers.

For file transfer, Messenger uses ports 6891–6900. If only port 6891 is open, you'll be able to perform only one file transfer—either inbound or outbound—at a time. If you have access to your firewall, check its configuration and open more ports in the range 6891–6900, if possible. (If you don't have access to the firewall, ask the administrator responsible for it, but be warned they may have deliberately restricted the number of files you can transfer.)

If the problem isn't with your firewall, it may be with your ISP. In this case, find out whether your ISP is blocking transfers. If necessary, ask your ISP to open more ports.

Can't Send Files from Behind ICF

If you can't send files from an ICS client that connects through a connection protected with ICF, ports 6891–6900 (discussed in the previous subsection) probably aren't open. If you can configure ICF, add entries to the Services page of the Advanced Settings dialog box to open these ports for Messenger file transfers. (See the section "Opening Ports Manually on ICF" in Chapter 35 for details on opening ports.)

Can't Send Files from Behind a Corporate Firewall or Personal Firewall

If you're using Messenger from behind a corporate firewall, you may not be able to send files because ports 6891–6900 are closed. If your administrators have deliberately closed these ports, you'll probably have a hard time persuading them to reopen the ports for file transfer. However, if the ports are open but transfers still aren't working, suggest diffidently the administrators configure the TCP ports so the sockets on them remain open for an extended period of time. (If the sockets time out quickly, Messenger file transfers may get interrupted.)

You may experience similar problems when using Messenger behind a personal firewall. However, you have a better chance of reconfiguring a personal firewall than a corporate firewall.

Can't Send Files from Behind a NAT Device

If the NAT device through which Messenger is connecting to the network doesn't support Universal Plug and Play (UPP), Messenger won't be able to perform file transfers through it. Either upgrade the NAT device (for example, by flashing it with an update) or use an alternate means of file transfer.

Setting Up and Configuring NetMeeting

To use NetMeeting, set it up and configure it as described in this section.

Note *If you're unable to set up NetMeeting, it's most likely because an administrator has prevented you from using NetMeeting. Alternatively, an administrator may allow you to use NetMeeting, but may configure NetMeeting for automatic setup. The administrator may also have prevented you from accessing any or all of the tabs in the Options dialog box, which contain most of NetMeeting's configuration options.*

Because Windows XP doesn't provide any interface items for NetMeeting, NetMeeting offers to create them when you run it. Launch NetMeeting by entering **conf** in the Run dialog box. The first time you launch NetMeeting like this, it runs its Setup Wizard, which walks you through setup and basic configuration of NetMeeting.

These are the key points in the setup and configuration process:

■ NetMeeting forces you to enter text in the First Name text box, the Last Name text box, and the E-mail Address text box. Each entry can be any text (the e-mail address doesn't have to resemble an e-mail address), but you have to enter *some* text. The Location text box and the Comments text box are optional. NetMeeting uses the information you enter to identify you to other NetMeeting users. You can change these settings on the General tab of the Options dialog box (Tools │ Options).

- You needn't specify a directory server. However, in a domain environment, NetMeeting suggests port 389 on the domain controller. This is the port used for Active Directory traffic on a Windows 2000 Server or Windows.NET Server domain controller and for Lightweight Directory Access Protocol (LDAP) traffic on Exchange Server.

- In a standalone or workgroup configuration, NetMeeting suggests Microsoft Internet Directory. Because Microsoft has effectively dismantled Microsoft Internet Directory, there's no point in choosing this setting. Make sure the Log On to a Directory Server when NetMeeting Starts check box is cleared. You can change this setting on the General tab of the Options dialog box. If you choose to log on to a directory server, you can prevent NetMeeting from listing your name on it by choosing the Do Not List My Name in the Directory check box either during setup or on the General tab of the Options dialog box.

- The connection speed you specify for NetMeeting controls the audio and video compression NetMeeting uses. NetMeeting offers the following settings: 14,400 bps Modem (a 14.4 Kbps modem); 28,800 bps or faster modem (a 28.8 Kbps, 33.6 Kbps, or 56 Kbps modem); Cable, xDSL, or ISDN; or local area network (LAN). You can change this setting by clicking the Bandwidth Settings on the General tab of the Options dialog box and working in the Network Bandwidth dialog box.

> **Note** *Even if you're using NetMeeting on a LAN, you may be unable to get fast video because an administrator may limit the amount of bandwidth NetMeeting's audio and video features can consume. The administrator would impose this restriction to prevent you from hogging network bandwidth.*

- NetMeeting runs the Audio Tuning Wizard during setup to tune your speaker volume and microphone settings. You can run the Audio Tuning Wizard at any time by choosing Tools | Audio Tuning Wizard to accommodate changes or adjustments to your sound hardware. From the Audio tab of the Options dialog box (shown on the left in Figure 16-9), you can also adjust silence detection manually; enable or disable full-duplex audio, auto-gain, automatic microphone-volume adjustment, and DirectSound; and choose a specific codec for audio compression by clicking the Advanced button and working in the Advanced Compression Settings dialog box (shown on the right in Figure 16-9). If your computer doesn't have a sound card, or if an administrator has prevented you from using audio (to save bandwidth) or configuring audio, NetMeeting hides the Audio tab.

After you finish setup, NetMeeting runs itself. Figure 16-10 shows the main NetMeeting window with labels.

After NetMeeting starts, you can choose further settings in the Options dialog box (Tools | Options). The settings you'll most likely need to change immediately after setup are those on the Video tab (discussed in the next section) and those on the Security tab (discussed in the section after next).

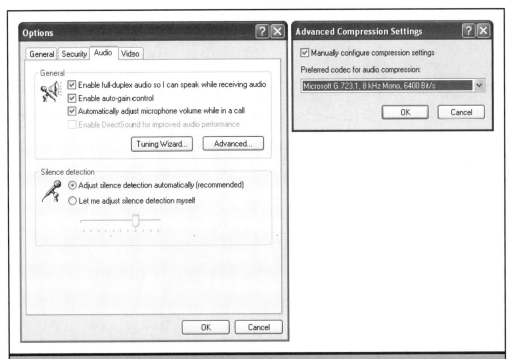

Figure 16-9.   *You can configure NetMeeting's audio settings during setup or on the Audio tab of the Options dialog box (left). To choose a specific codec for audio compression, click the Advanced button and work in the Advanced Compression Settings dialog box (right).*

Note   *The* Advanced Calling *button on the General tab of the Options dialog box displays the Advanced Calling Options dialog box, which contains settings for specifying a gatekeeper or a gateway through which to make conferencing calls. You're likely to use a gatekeeper or gateway only in a domain setting, in which case an administrator will usually configure these settings for you. The administrator will also usually either disable the options in the Advanced Calling Options dialog box, so you can't change them yourself, or simply disable the Advanced Calling button, so you can't display the dialog box.*

Choosing Video Options for NetMeeting

These are the main options on the Video tab of the Options dialog box (Figure 16-11):

- Whether to automatically send video and receive video at the start of each call. Unless you have an extremely fast connection, it's usually best not to send and receive video until you've established the call. An administrator can prevent you from sending video, receiving video, or both.

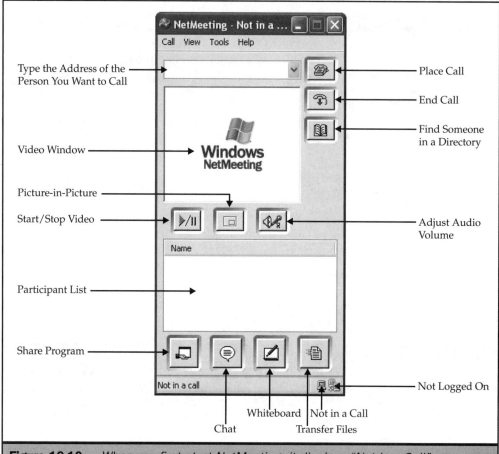

Type the Address of the Person You Want to Call

Video Window

Picture-in-Picture

Start/Stop Video

Participant List

Share Program

Place Call

End Call

Find Someone in a Directory

Adjust Audio Volume

Not Logged On

Whiteboard   Not in a Call

Chat   Transfer Files

Figure 16-10.   *When you first start NetMeeting, it displays "Not in a Call" in the title bar.*

- The image size to send: Small, Medium, or Large. (Your camera may support only some of these sizes.) The next chapter discusses the formats these sizes represent and the resolutions they use.

- Whether you prefer to receive faster video or better-quality video. You're trading frame rate (the speed) against image quality here.

- Which video capture device you want to use. If you have only one video camera attached to your computer, NetMeeting selects it by default. Depending on the type of video camera, you may be able to choose further options by clicking the Source button and the Format button to display configuration dialog boxes for it.

- Whether to display your video preview (what your camera is displaying) as a mirror image or as what the camera actually sees.

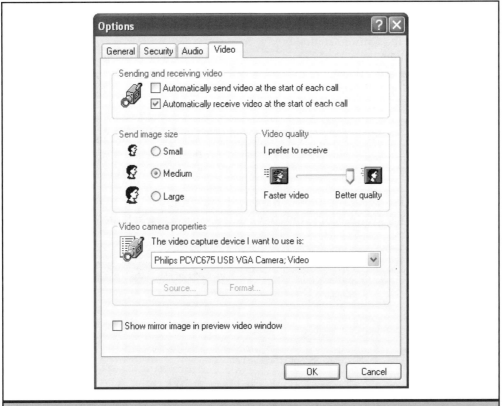

Figure 16-11. *The Video tab of the Options dialog box lets you specify the size and quality of video you send and receive.*

Choosing Security Options for NetMeeting

In NetMeeting, you can secure data-only calls—calls that don't include audio or video. NetMeeting can encrypt the data transmitted from one computer to another. It can also use digital certificates to authenticate users' identity. (See Chapter 21 for a discussion of what digital certificates are and where to get them.)

 In a domain environment, an administrator can choose security settings for NetMeeting calls. The administrator can force you to use security on all calls. The administrator can also disable the security settings so that you can't make secure calls.

NetMeeting's default setting is not to secure even data-only calls, so if you want to use NetMeeting's security features, you need to set them manually. The easiest way to secure your data-only calls is to select the I Prefer to Make Secure Outgoing Calls check box and the I Prefer to Receive Secure Incoming Calls. Accept Only Secure Incoming Calls when I'm Not in a Meeting check box in the General group box on the Security tab (Figure 16-12) of the Options dialog box.

There's no downside to making secure outgoing calls. The only downside to setting NetMeeting to accept only secure incoming calls is that NetMeeting will automatically reject any incoming calls that don't use security, so you won't know the callers have been trying to reach you.

 Even if you choose to make secure outgoing calls, you can override this setting by using the Place a Call dialog box, as you'll see shortly. Similarly, if you choose not to make secure outgoing calls, you can make secure calls by using the Place a Call dialog box.

For secure calls, use the options in the Certificate group box on the Security tab to specify the digital certificate you want to use for security. The default setting is the Use

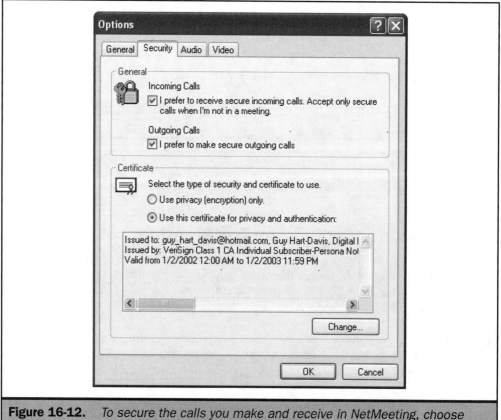

Figure 16-12. *To secure the calls you make and receive in NetMeeting, choose options and specify a certificate on the Security tab of the Options dialog box.*

Privacy (Encryption) Only option button, which uses NetMeeting's built-in digital certificate to encrypt the data transmitted between your NetMeeting client and the client it's communicating with. If you have a digital certificate of your own that you want to use, select the Use This Certificate for Privacy and Authentication option button. NetMeeting automatically selects the first certificate in your private certificate store and displays its name in the list box in the Certificate group box. To change the certificate, click the Change button and select the certificate in the Select Certificate dialog box.

Making and Receiving Calls with NetMeeting

You can make a call by entering the IP address or computer name in the Type the Address of the Person You Want to Call text box and clicking the Place Call button. (You can also use the Place a Call dialog box, as described next.)

To place a call to an address or a number you've called recently, use the drop-down list in the main NetMeeting window or in the Place a Call dialog box. This list, which is called the *History Call Log*, stores the last 100 addresses or numbers you've called successfully.

Tip   *You can remove the evidence of the NetMeeting calls you've placed by removing the entries from the Address box in the New Call dialog box. To do so, run the Registry Editor (see Chapter 40), navigate to the HKEY_CURRENT_USER\Software\Microsoft\ Conferencing\UI\CallMRU key, and remove any namen or addrn entries you wouldn't want other people to see. Alternatively, edit the entries to show different names or addresses.*

Making a Secure Call from the Place a Call Dialog Box

If you've chosen not to make secure outgoing calls by default, you can make a secure call by clicking the Place Call button (with nothing entered in the Place Call text box) or choosing Call | New Call to display the Place a Call dialog box. Select the Require Security for This Call (Data Only) check box. Similarly, if you've chosen to make secure outgoing calls by default, you can clear the Require Security for This Call (Data Only) check box when you need to make a nonsecure call.

Accepting a Call

When someone places a call to you, NetMeeting displays the NetMeeting – Incoming Call dialog box, of which Figure 16-13 shows three examples. The topmost example shows a call without security; the dialog box shows an Accept button and an Ignore button. The middle example shows a call with security; the dialog box shows a Details button as well. The bottom example shows the information you see when you click the Details button: the information from the certificate used for encryption or authentication.

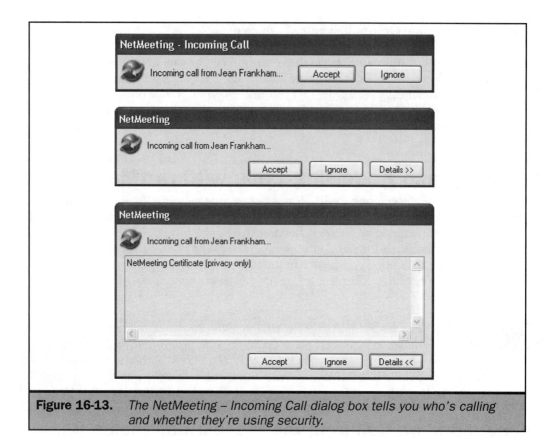

Figure 16-13.   *The NetMeeting – Incoming Call dialog box tells you who's calling and whether they're using security.*

Click the Accept button to accept the call or the Ignore button to reject it. If the call is secure, you can click the Details button to display details of the digital certificate the caller is using for encryption and authentication.

Adding Another Person to a Call

You can add another person to a NetMeeting call by placing a call to them once you've established the first call. Unlike Messenger, which lets you create multiple two-person text-chat calls at the same time, NetMeeting lets you have only one ongoing call. Any further people you call during a call are added to it.

Removing Someone from a Call

If you started the call, you can remove a participant from it by right-clicking their entry in the Participant List and choosing Remove from Meeting from the context menu.

Determining Whether an Incoming Call Is Secure

If you've chosen not to receive only secure calls, you can tell whether an incoming call is secure by seeing if the Incoming Call dialog box includes a Details button. If it does, the call is secure. Click the Details button to display information on the certificate the caller is using for security and authentication. (They may be using only the NetMeeting certificate for security. If so, you won't be able to see who the caller is.)

Automatically Accepting Calls

You can set NetMeeting to automatically accept calls by choosing Call | Automatically Accept Calls. This option can be useful when you're expecting an incoming call at a time when you may be out of your office briefly.

In a domain environment, an administrator may prevent you from automatically accepting calls.

Hanging Up a Call

To end a call, click the End Call button or choose Call | Hang Up. If you started the call, hanging up ends the whole call, so NetMeeting displays a confirmation dialog box to that effect before it hangs up. If you're just one of the participants in a call with two or more other people, NetMeeting hangs up your connection immediately, leaving the other participants in the call to continue without you.

Troubleshooting Connections in NetMeeting

This section discusses two problems with connections in NetMeeting: you get a message saying you're unable to connect to the user, and you're unable to establish NetMeeting connections through a firewall.

You're Unable to Connect to the User

When trying to establish a connection to another NetMeeting user, you may get the message "User did not accept your call" or "User is unable to accept NetMeeting calls."

Normally these messages mean pretty much what they say: "User did not accept your call" means either the user explicitly rejected your call or they didn't respond to it (for example, because they weren't there) and NetMeeting timed it out. "User is unable to accept NetMeeting calls" typically means the user either isn't connected to the Internet or they are connected, but not running NetMeeting.

However, these messages sometimes indicate your installation of NetMeeting has become damaged. If you get these messages consistently for every user you try to connect to, try uninstalling and reinstalling NetMeeting.

You're Unable to Connect Through a Firewall

If your computer connects to the Internet through a firewall, you may be able to run NetMeeting without problems—or you may run into various kinds of problems, depending on how the firewall is configured and what its capabilities are.

For NetMeeting to work fully, the firewall needs to be configured to pass through primary TCP connections (on ports 389, 522, 1403, 1720, and 1731) and secondary UDP connections (on dynamically assigned ports in the range 1024 to 65535). NetMeeting uses port 1720 for the H.323 call setup protocol, which dynamically negotiates a TCP port for the call. Then the audio call control protocol, using port 1731, and the H.323 call setup protocol (still using port 1720) negotiate User Datagram Protocol (UDP) ports from the range of available, dynamically assignable ports for the Real-Time Protocol (RTP), which runs on top of UDP. NetMeeting uses two ports on either side of the firewall for streaming audio and video.

Table 16-1 shows a breakdown the IP ports NetMeeting uses and what it uses them for.

If your firewall can handle the TCP connections but not the UDP connections, NetMeeting will provide basic functionality but no audio or video.

If your firewall can't virtualize internal IP addresses or can't virtualize them on-the-fly, you'll be able to establish outgoing NetMeeting connections through the firewall, but you won't be able to receive incoming connections from computers located outside the firewall.

Port	Use	Protocol
389	Internet Locator Server	TCP
522	User Locator Server	TCP
1503	T.120	TCP
1720	H.323 call setup	TCP
1731	Audio call control	TCP
Dynamic	H.323 call control	TCP
Dynamic	H.323 streaming	RTP over UDP

Table 16-1. *NetMeeting's IP Ports and Their Uses*

Using Chat in NetMeeting

Unlike Messenger, NetMeeting doesn't automatically open a chat window the moment you establish a call; instead, it lets you decide what you want to do: chat with text, voice, or video (or all three); share applications to collaborate on projects; transfer files to each other; or use the Whiteboard to brainstorm.

 **Note**   *In a domain environment, an administrator can prevent you from using NetMeeting's chat features.*

To chat with the people in your call, click the Chat button. NetMeeting displays a Chat window (Figure 16-14) on each participant's computer.

Most of the chat features are easily grasped: you type the message in the text box and click the Send Message button to send it. By default, NetMeeting sends the message to every participant in the call, but you can choose to send a private message to a particular participant by using the Send To drop-down list. These messages appear in gray font and with "[private]" on the recipient's computer and "[private to *participant's name*]" on the sender's (and don't appear in the other participants' Chat windows).

You can paste text into the Chat text box, but if it's too long, it'll be truncated. On most versions of NetMeeting, you can paste in 900 to 1,000 characters. NetMeeting doesn't warn you if you paste in more characters than the buffer can hold—it just goes ahead and truncates the extra characters without warning.

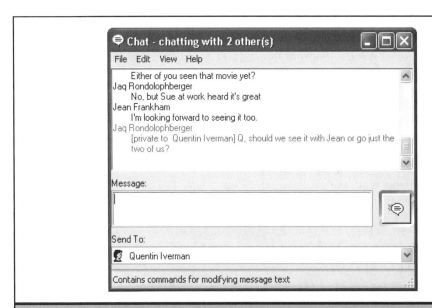

Figure 16-14.   *NetMeeting's Chat window provides modest, but effective, chat features, including the capability to send private messages to individual participants.*

You can save a chat session at any time by choosing File | Save As. NetMeeting displays the Save As dialog box. Specify the filename and location, choose the file type (either HTM or HTML chat files or TXT or DOC text files), and click the Save button. Once you've saved a chat session, you can save later versions of it (for example, when further chat has occurred) by choosing File | Save.

When you close the Chat window, NetMeeting prompts you to save unsaved changes to Chat.

Using Whiteboard with NetMeeting and Messenger

Whiteboard provides a virtual whiteboard for brainstorming and planning during your conferences. It combines ease of use with enough power to be useful for a variety of purposes.

Whiteboard has advantages and disadvantages compared to sharing an application. The main advantages are that Whiteboard is designed for brainstorming, so it provides suitable tools, and it's optimized for use over networks, so it will run at an acceptable speed even over dial-up connections. By contrast, sharing a fatter application can make modem connections seem frustratingly slow because more information needs to be transferred.

Another advantage is that you can use Whiteboard as a kind of sandbox (a secure environment): although you're working with other people on your computer (and on theirs at the same time), none of you can take any action on anyone else's computer. By contrast, if you're sharing an application, the other people can take actions in it you might not want. For example, if you're sharing a VBA-enabled application, another user might execute some VBA code. If you're sharing an Explorer window, another user could delete some of your files. If you were watching, you'd see them perform the deletion, but you might not be quick enough to prevent it.

Whiteboard's main disadvantage is that its capabilities are limited compared to most applications you might want to share: Whiteboard is essentially a version of Microsoft Paint with a couple of twists and with collaboration features added. These features are pretty solid: you can create multiple pages on Whiteboard, you can unsynchronize a page so that you can work on it without other people interfering, and you can lock Whiteboard to stop anybody damaging the work your collaboration has achieved so far. But if you want to collaborate on tasks such as editing text or manipulating a graphic, Whiteboard won't get you far. For operations such as those, you'll need to share an application.

Differences Between Whiteboard in NetMeeting and Messenger

Whiteboard is largely the same in Messenger as in NetMeeting. This is because Messenger borrows Whiteboard directly from NetMeeting. But there are two crucial differences.

- NetMeeting lets multiple people participate in a Whiteboard session, whereas Messenger lets only two people participate. Having only two people in a collaboration lets you work faster over a slow connection, but it greatly limits the amount of collaboration you can achieve at once.

■ Whiteboard in Messenger works only with Windows XP, not with earlier versions of Windows. Whiteboard in NetMeeting, on the other hand, works with all known versions of 32-bit Windows for desktop computers, with a few limitations. (For example, NetMeeting isn't 100-percent compatible with ICS. This can cause problems with collaboration.)

So Messenger gives you greater ease of use, but NetMeeting gives you more flexibility. As discussed earlier in this chapter, you can establish secure connections with NetMeeting, whereas Messenger connections must go through .NET Messenger Service or your communications service.

 You can run Messenger and NetMeeting at the same time, but you can't run their sharing features at the same time.

Whiteboard Basics

To start a Whiteboard session in a NetMeeting conference, click the Whiteboard button in the main NetMeeting window. Alternatively, choose Tools | Whiteboard or press CTRL-W. NetMeeting opens Whiteboard on all the computers in the conference without prompting any of the other users in the conference.

 NetMeeting 3.x includes two versions of Whiteboard: the regular version, which you invoke by using the commands just described, and a Whiteboard 2.x version that's compatible with NetMeeting 2.x and NetMeeting 1.x, which you can invoke by choosing Tools | Whiteboard (1.0–2.x). Whiteboard 2.x offers almost all the same features as Whiteboard 3, but its menu configuration and interface are a little different. This section discusses Whiteboard 3. In a domain environment, an administrator may prevent you from using Whiteboard 2.x while allowing you to use Whiteboard 3. (The administrator would implement this restriction to reduce the amount of bandwidth NetMeeting takes.)

To start a Whiteboard session from Messenger, click the Start Whiteboard link in the I Want To list or choose Actions | Start Whiteboard. (You can take either of these actions from an existing conversation or from the main Messenger window to establish a new conversation.) If you issue one of these commands from the main Messenger window or in a Conversation window that contains two or more other participants, Messenger displays the Start Whiteboard dialog box to let you pick the contact or other person with whom to start the Whiteboard session. If you issue one of these commands in a Conversation window in which there's only one other person, Messenger starts the Whiteboard session with that person.

If you've used Paint, Whiteboard's drawing tools should seem familiar and straightforward. Figure 16-15 shows the Whiteboard window with a brainstorming session in progress. Figure 16-16 shows the Whiteboard toolbar buttons and navigation buttons with labels.

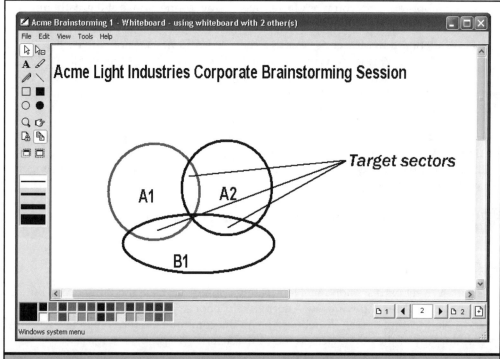

Figure 16-15.   *NetMeeting's Whiteboard is Microsoft Paint bulked up with collaboration tools.*

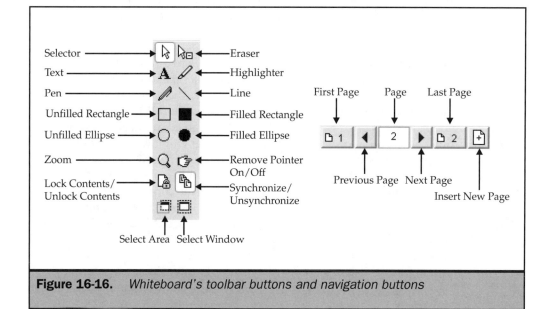

Figure 16-16.   *Whiteboard's toolbar buttons and navigation buttons*

Most of these tools are self-explanatory. For example, to select an item, you click the Selector button so that the mouse pointer changes to the Selector arrow, and then click the item you want to select. To erase an item, you click the Eraser button so that the mouse pointer changes to the Eraser arrow, and then click the item you want to erase.

Some of the tools, such as Lock Contents and Unsynchronize, aren't so obvious. The next sections discuss these tools.

If you start Whiteboard from Messenger, Messenger also displays the Sharing Session toolbar, shown next, from which you can easily start Whiteboard or application sharing, and from which you can quickly close your sharing session.

WORKING AND
COMMUNICATING

Working with Text

Once you've placed an object on the page in Whiteboard and finished creating it, you can move it or apply basic formatting to it, but you can't otherwise edit it. This is a particular problem with text, which tends to need editing much more than visual elements do.

 Whiteboard 2.x (in NetMeeting) lets you edit the text in a text box. For whiteboarding involving serious amounts of text, you may want to use Whiteboard 2.x rather than Whiteboard 3 because of this capability. If you choose, and if your administrator lets you, you can run Whiteboard 2.x and Whiteboard 3 at the same time, but doing so risks causing confusion. To perform group editing on text, share a text editor (such as Notepad) or a word processor (such as WordPad).

To add text to the current page, click the Text button. The mouse pointer changes to an insertion point. Click the page at the point where you want the upper-left corner of the text to appear. NetMeeting displays a text box with a flashing cursor. Type the text for the text box, pressing ENTER to break lines as necessary or create paragraph breaks. When you've finished working in the text box, click the Selector button to deselect the text box. (Alternatively, click to start another text box.)

To format the text in a text box, right-click the text box, choose Font from the shortcut menu, and then use the Font dialog box to specify the formatting. (Alternatively, select the text box by clicking in it. Then choose Tools | Font to display the Font dialog box.)

All the text in any given text box has to have the same formatting, so you needn't select any text before applying formatting—selecting the text box is enough. This means you need to use a different text box for each text element that requires different formatting.

Because you can't edit text once you've finished creating its text box, it's easiest to create each paragraph—in some cases, each line—as a separate text box.

The Whiteboard is primarily a means of assembling information. It's not a great means of exchanging text or graphical information. However, you *can* copy a text box or a graphical object from the Whiteboard and paste it into another application. For a text box, you get just the text without the formatting. For a graphical object, you get the whole object, including color.

To exchange larger amounts of text, send it via chat or via file transfer (if you're permitted to use these tools).

| Note |

The Edit | Select All command lets you quickly select all the objects on a Whiteboard page. This command is primarily useful for copying all the contents of a page to another page. (You can also use it to delete all the objects from a page, but the Edit | Clear Page command is quicker and more convenient.) Copying all the contents of a page works only for Whiteboard: If you paste what you've copied into another application, you get only the contents of the first text box on the page.

Adding, Deleting, and Synchronizing Pages

Whiteboard lets you create multiple pages in the same file, so you can create several drafts of the work in progress or let each member of the conference work on a separate page to brainstorm different approaches.

Take these actions to work with pages:

- To insert a page after the current page, click the Insert New Page button, press CTRL-+ (CTRL and the plus key), or choose Edit | Insert Page After. To insert a page before the current page, choose Edit | Insert Page Before.

- To navigate from one page to another, use the navigation buttons and the Page text box. (In NetMeeting versions before NetMeeting 3, choose Edit | Page Sorter and use the Page Sorter dialog box.)

- To delete a page, choose Edit | Delete Page or press CTRL-- (CTRL and the minus key).

- To clear the current page, choose Edit | Clear page or press CTRL-DEL.

By default, Whiteboard synchronizes the pages, so all participants in the conference see the changes being made: when one participant makes a change to a page that's being synchronized, Whiteboard displays that page on the other participants' Whiteboard windows as well. By unsynchronizing a page, you can work on it without the changes you make being automatically displayed to the other participants, but they can still access the page manually and see the changes you're making.

To unsynchronize a page, click the Unsynchronize button. When you're ready to synchronize the pages again, click the Synchronize button.

Moving and Copying Information

To move an item, use the Selector to select it, and then drag the item to where you want it to appear. To move two or more items at the same time, select the first item, hold down CTRL, select each of the other items, and then drag them to the new location.

To move one or more items from one page to another, select the item or items, cut them from the page they're on, and paste them onto the other page. Alternatively, copy the items and paste copies onto the other page.

If one object overlaps another, issue a Bring to Front command or Send to Back command from the shortcut menu or the Edit menu to specify which object should appear on top of the other.

Copying an Application Window into Whiteboard

You can paste either an application window or a selected area of the screen into Whiteboard:

- To paste an application window, click the Select Window button or choose Tools | Select Window, and then click the window you want to paste.

- To paste an area of the screen, click the Select Area button or choose Tools | Select Area, and then use the resulting crosshair to select the area of the screen.

For either command, Whiteboard displays an information message box explaining the command until you tell it to desist. Whiteboard then hides itself so that you can make your selection. It then pastes the window or selected area in at the upper-left corner of Whiteboard.

 Graphics such as screenshots contain much more information than text, lines, and simple graphical shapes, so they take much longer to transfer over a slow or moderate-speed connection.

Locking Whiteboard

Any user can lock Whiteboard to prevent other people from making further changes to its contents. Once you've locked it, you can make changes, whereas others can only save or print Whiteboard.

To lock Whiteboard, click the Lock Contents button on the toolbar or choose View | Lock Contents. To unlock Whiteboard, click the Unlock Contents button that replaces the Lock Contents button.

You can't lock Whiteboard when another user has an object open that requires locking. For example, a text box is locked until the user currently working in it removes the focus from it. So when someone's working in a text box, you can't lock Whiteboard. If you try, NetMeeting displays a Lock message box warning you "Another Whiteboard has one or more objects locked on this page" or "Cannot lock the Whiteboard, the object has focus on another computer." To release the lock, you need to get the user with the locked object to remove the focus from that object.

You also can't lock Whiteboard when it's not synchronized. When Whiteboard isn't synchronized, the Lock Contents button is dimmed and unavailable. When you synchronize Whiteboard, it makes the Lock Contents button available.

Saving Whiteboard

You can save the contents of Whiteboard by using the File | Save command and the resulting Save As dialog box. Once you've saved a file, you can save later versions to the same file by reissuing the File | Save command, or you can save later versions in separate files by using the File | Save As command and specifying a new filename, as with most applications.

NetMeeting 3.x Whiteboard files use the NMW file format. Whiteboard, in earlier versions of NetMeeting, uses the WHT file format. The NMW file format is compatible with T126—one of the T.120 standards that cover the data-sharing element of a multimedia teleconference. This means you can open NMW files in other whiteboarding applications if you have any.

If you haven't saved the contents of Whiteboard when you close the Whiteboard window or exit NetMeeting or Messenger, Whiteboard prompts you to save the contents. NetMeeting also prompts you to save the contents if you have Whiteboard open with unsaved contents when you join a new conference.

Opening a Saved Whiteboard File

You can open a saved Whiteboard file by issuing an Open command (File | Open or CTRL-O) from Whiteboard or by double-clicking the file in an Explorer window or on the Desktop.

Sharing an Application—or Your Desktop— Using NetMeeting or Messenger

NetMeeting and Messenger both let you share either one or more applications, or your whole desktop with other people in a meeting or call. This capability is useful for working together on documents, demonstrating how to use software, and similar tasks.

NetMeeting's and Messenger's application-sharing features are almost identical, so this section discusses them together. Where there's a difference between NetMeeting's and Messenger's implementation of a feature, or when one application has a feature the other does not, this section points it out. The key difference is that Messenger lets you share applications with only one other person, whereas NetMeeting lets you share applications with multiple people.

Advantages, Disadvantages, and Dangers of Application Sharing

Application sharing has good points and bad points in roughly equal amounts. On the plus side, you can work together with one person (with NetMeeting or Messenger) or more people (with NetMeeting), and only one of you needs to have the shared application or applications installed on your computer. You can chat with the people in the meeting or call about the sharing. (If only one other person is in the call, you can use audio and video as well as chat to discuss what you're sharing, but you need a LAN connection or a broadband Internet connection.) And you can share only the display of the application or of your desktop, or you can share the display and allow others to control the application or your desktop. If you choose to share control, you can allow requests for control automatically for convenience or screen each one manually for security.

The minus side of application sharing involves security and performance. Sharing an application without allowing control is relatively safe, provided you don't let the participants in the meeting or the call see anything you don't want them to see. But allowing control of a shared application, let alone your desktop, raises major security issues because another participant may take actions you don't want before you can prevent them from doing so.

So before you allow control of a shared application, sit back and assess the risks involved. The more limited the capabilities of the application you let other users control, the less damage they can do—intentionally or otherwise. Balance against that the actions you need to be able to take in the application together. For example, if you're creating a text document, consider whether you need to use Word or whether WordPad—or even Notepad—would do. Will you just be editing text together or will you need to use features such as revision marks? Does Word's VBA functionality pose a threat? Remember that most applications use common dialog boxes (such as the Open dialog box and the Save As dialog box) that include commands for creating, renaming, and deleting folders, and for deleting and renaming files, as well as commands for copying or cutting both files and folders.

Before you allow control of your desktop, ask yourself why you're sure it's safe to do so. Unless you're certain of the good will and the skills of the other person or people, don't do it.

Administrative Control of Application Sharing

Because application sharing can pose a severe threat to the security of your computer, Windows XP lets administrators control application sharing through policies. An administrator can do the following:

■ Prevent you from using application sharing at all.

■ Prevent you from sharing any applications yourself, while allowing you to view and share applications or desktops others are sharing.

- Prevent you from sharing your desktop, while allowing you to share individual applications.

- Prevent you from sharing command-prompt windows (because other users can launch applications and take other actions from a command prompt) and Windows Explorer windows (because other users can take many actions from a shared Windows Explorer window).

- Prevent you from allowing control of an application or the desktop you've shared.

- Prevent you from sharing an application or your desktop in true color. (True color consumes large amounts of bandwidth and is seldom necessary.)

Sharing an Application

To share an application, take one of the following steps:

- In NetMeeting, display the Sharing window by choosing Tools | Sharing, clicking the Share Applications button in the main NetMeeting window, or pressing CTRL-S.

- In Messenger, issue a Start Application Sharing command from the I Want To list or the Actions menu in a Conversation window or in the main Messenger window. Messenger establishes the connection, displays the Sharing Session toolbar, and displays the Sharing window.

Figure 16-17 shows the Sharing window with some sharing underway (so that you can see all the controls more clearly). Because I've allowed control of the applications (again, to make the controls easier to see), NetMeeting has replaced the Allow Control button with the Prevent Control button, its counterpart.

To share an application, select it in the Share Applications list box and click the Share button. To stop sharing an application, select it and click the Unshare button. To stop sharing all the applications you're sharing, click the Unshare All button.

Sharing Your Desktop

To share your desktop, select the Desktop item in the Share Applications list box and click the Share button. (You'll need to stop sharing any previously shared applications first.) To stop sharing your desktop, click the Unshare button or the Unshare All button.

Sharing in True Color

To share the application in true color, select the Share in True Color check box. Sharing an application in true color is a bad idea unless everyone with whom you're sharing the application is on the same network or has a broadband Internet connection *and* you need to use true color.

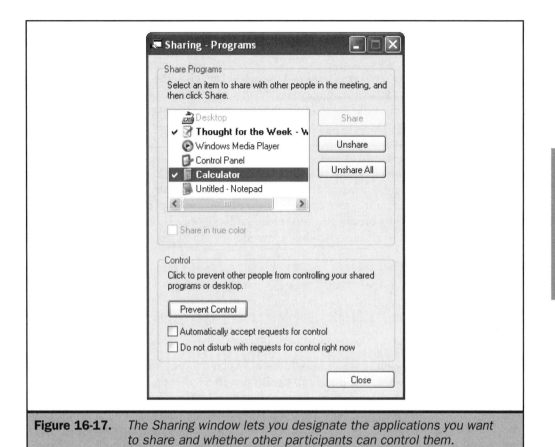

Figure 16-17. *The Sharing window lets you designate the applications you want to share and whether other participants can control them.*

For example, if you're collaborating on tweaking a photograph in Photoshop or another graphics editor, you might need true color to see what you're doing. For other applications, such as working together on documents, spreadsheets, presentations, or programming, you'll do better to let NetMeeting or Messenger reduce the color to a depth more practical for the speed of the connection. In some cases, you may see noticeable dithering as NetMeeting or Messenger reduces the color. In other cases, you may see false colors—for example, pinks instead of whites. Unless you're doing highly detailed work, these minor display imperfections probably won't bother you.

Allowing Control of the Shared Application or Desktop

If you choose (and your administrator permits), you can allow the other participants in the call or meeting to take control of the shared application or Desktop. As discussed earlier in this chapter, allowing control presents a real security risk to the integrity of data on your computer. But if you trust the other participant or participants in the meeting to do nothing bad or incompetent with the shared application, you may decide to allow control.

To allow control of all the applications you're sharing, click the Allow Control button. Once you've clicked it, you can choose whether to automatically accept requests for control. The default setting is *not* to automatically accept requests for control. If you leave this setting, when someone requests control of a shared application, NetMeeting or Messenger notifies you and lets you accept or deny the request. This manual evaluation of requests for control gives you better security than automatic acceptance of requests, but it makes the process of working together in the shared application slower.

When you're sharing control of an application via NetMeeting, things can get hectic if several people are trying to input changes at the same time. If you need to calm things down and give yourself a break, you can select the Do Not Disturb with Requests for Control check box in the Sharing window. Anyone who then requests control gets a message box saying you're "busy right now."

Note	*In NetMeeting, any application you choose to share is shared with all the other computers you're conferencing with. You can't limit sharing to one or more specific computers. In Messenger, you can share only with one other computer at a time.*

The shared window displays the name of the participant sharing an application or their Desktop, so it's usually easy enough to see which computer any given application is running on. Any unshared applications positioned in front of the shared applications' windows appear as blanked-out areas. Because you won't see this problem on applications you're sharing, make sure the windows you're sharing are clear of obstruction. The classic candidates for being in the way are the NetMeeting application window, the Sharing window, and (in Messenger) the Sharing Session window. Figure 16-18 shows a shared Applications window with the Sharing Session window at the upper-left corner to illustrate the problem.

When you allow control of an application, you have control of it by default. Other participants in the meeting or the call see a window titled *Yourname's* Applications – Controllable. They can request control by double-clicking in the shared window or choosing Control | Request Control. If you haven't selected the Automatically Accept Requests for Control check box in the Sharing window, you then get a Request Control dialog box with an Accept button and a Reject button so that you can decide whether to grant the request or refuse it.

If another participant gets control of the applications one way or another, they can release it by choosing Control | Release Control.

If you're sharing from NetMeeting with two or more other people, they can use the Control | Forward Control submenu to forward control of the applications to a specified participant.

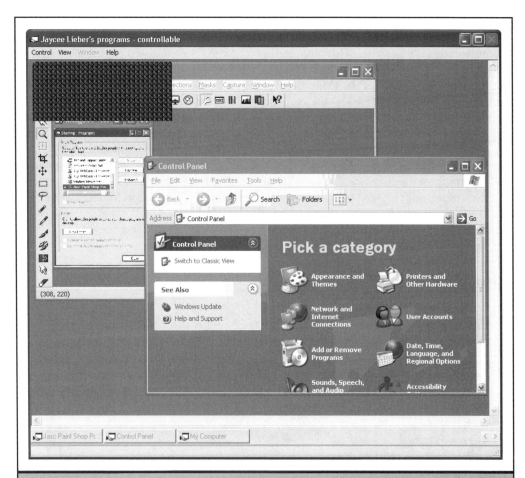

Figure 16-18. *The shared applications appear in an applications window like this on the other computer's screen; the Desktop appears blanked out if it's not being shared, and unshared applications can obscure the shared applications.*

Transferring Files with NetMeeting

NetMeeting lets you transfer files during your calls and conferences. However, in a domain environment, an administrator can prevent you from sending or receiving files via NetMeeting. The administrator can also permit you to send files but they can specify a maximum size.

Before Receiving Files

Before you receive any files with NetMeeting, change your received files folder—the folder in which NetMeeting places files you receive via file transfer. By default, this folder is the Program Files\NetMeeting\Received Files folder. This isn't a great place for it because Windows XP hides the contents of the Program Files folder by default and the same folder is used by each NetMeeting user, which gives the users access to each other's files. (That said, there's some good news on this front—NetMeeting is smart enough not to overwrite an existing file in the received files folder that has the same name as a new incoming file. Instead, it renames the incoming file with *Copy*(n) *of* at the beginning of the filename, where *n* is the lowest unused number.)

To change your received files folder, click the Transfer Files button (or choose Tools | File Transfer or press CTRL-F) to display the File Transfer window. Then choose File | Change Folder, use the resulting Browse for Folder dialog box to select the folder to use, and click the OK button to close the dialog box and set the folder.

Sending Files via File Transfer

To send files with NetMeeting, display the File Transfer window by clicking the Transfer Files button (or choosing Tools | File Transfer or pressing CTRL-F). The File Transfer window with some files being transferred, is shown here:

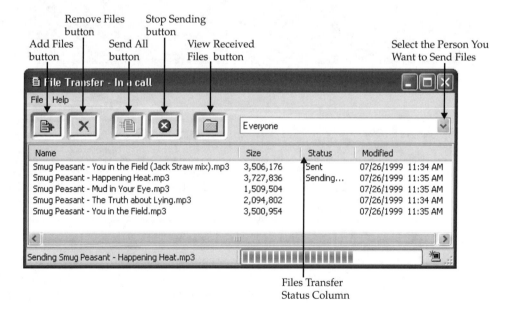

To send files to another user, you add this user to the File Transfer window, specify who the files are going to, and send them. Here's what to do:

- To add the files, you can drag them from your Desktop or from an Explorer window to the File Transfer window, but usually it's easier to click the Add Files button (or choose File | Add Files) and use the resulting Select Files to Send dialog box to select the files to send.

- To specify the recipient, select their entry in the Select the Person You Want to Send Files drop-down list. The default selection is Everyone.

- To send all the files in the File Transfer window, click the Send All button (or right-click a file and choose Send All from the shortcut menu, or choose File | Send All). To send just one file, right-click it and choose Send a File from the shortcut menu. Alternatively, select the file and choose File | Send.

To stop sending a file, click the Stop Sending button on the toolbar in the File Transfer window or choose File | Stop Sending. NetMeeting displays a message box confirming the cancellation.

Caution   *If you try to send a shortcut, NetMeeting sends the file itself. This happens by design rather than by accident, on the assumption that the location the shortcut points to will probably not be available to the recipient. This is largely true if you're sending the shortcut to someone remote, but may well not be true if you're both on the same LAN or wide area network (WAN). The exception to this rule is when the shortcut is a URL: NetMeeting transfers URLs as they are.*

Receiving Files via File Transfer

When NetMeeting detects an incoming file, it displays a file transfer window giving the file's name, who it's coming from, and the progress of the file transfer. Figure 16-19 shows an example of this window.

You can choose to accept or delete the incoming file while it's being transferred. Clicking the Accept button closes the file transfer window, preventing you from seeing the details of the rest of the transfer operation. You may want to leave the file transfer window open so that you can see what's happening. When NetMeeting has received the whole file, the file transfer window makes the Open button available and displays a Close button in place of the Accept button. You can click the Open button to open the file, but usually it's best to virus-check it first. This is because clicking the Open button issues an Open command for the file's real file type, which may not be the same as the file type that its extension claims. So if the file is a script file or an executable masquerading as, say, a JPG, issuing the Open command executes the script or runs the executable.

Note   *If you receive multiple files, NetMeeting displays a window for each, cascading them across your screen. You don't need to acknowledge one file transfer to receive the next.*

To examine the files you've received (and perhaps to virus-check them), choose File | Open Received Folder from the File Transfer window to look at these files (for example,

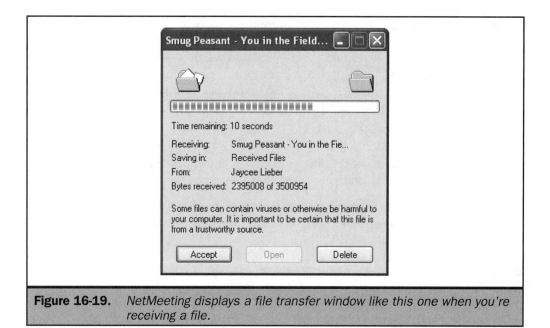

Figure 16-19.   *NetMeeting displays a file transfer window like this one when you're receiving a file.*

to virus-check them). NetMeeting opens a Windows Explorer window and displays the contents of your received files folder in it.

If you don't want to accept the incoming file, click the Delete button. NetMeeting terminates the inbound transfer and cancels any other inbound transfers from the same source.

Summary

This chapter has discussed how to configure Messenger and NetMeeting and use them for chat, application-sharing, whiteboarding, and file transfer. You've learned the advantages and disadvantages of Messenger and NetMeeting for each task, which of the two applications to use when, and how to get the best out of both of them.

The next chapter discusses how to use Messenger and NetMeeting for audioconferencing and videoconferencing.

Chapter 17

Audioconferencing
and Videoconferencing

This chapter discusses how to use Messenger and NetMeeting for audioconferencing and videoconferencing. The chapter assumes you've read the previous chapter, which discussed the basic configuration requirements for Messenger and NetMeeting.

As mentioned in the previous chapter, in a domain environment, you probably won't be able to use Messenger's or NetMeeting's audioconferencing or videoconferencing capabilities unless you have a business need to do so. This is because both take significant amounts of bandwidth that your company may prefer to keep for other purposes. Videoconferencing takes much more bandwidth than audioconferencing, but even audioconferencing takes a huge amount more bandwidth than text-based chat.

Note	*Your company may be reluctant to let you use instant messaging because of security concerns. Some companies have experienced security problems with instant-messaging clients such as AIM and Yahoo Messenger.*

Hardware for Audioconferencing and Videoconferencing

To use audioconferencing or videoconferencing, you need to have the appropriate hardware:

- **Sound Hardware**   You need a sound card that can handle full-duplex audio (sending and receiving audio at the same time), a microphone, and either speakers or headphones, depending on whether you want anybody around you to be able to hear the other end of conversations you have. If your sound card can manage only half-duplex audio, you won't be able to send and receive audio at the same time, which makes conversations stilted and difficult.

- **Video Hardware**   You need a camera connected to your computer. For Messenger and NetMeeting, even a modest webcam can provide high-enough resolution. Messenger supports only one resolution: Quarter Common Intermediate Format (QCIF: 176×144 pixels). NetMeeting can use three different resolutions, the highest of which is Common Intermediate Format (CIF: 352×288 pixels). Most webcams can manage 640×480 resolution and have no problem providing CIF, let alone QCIF.

- **Network or Internet Connection**   You need an Internet connection or a network connection to the person you're communicating with. Audio conferencing is usually intelligible over a 28.8 Kbps connection, but it benefits greatly from a faster connection. Video conferencing is usually unsatisfactory at speeds less than two-channel ISDN (128 Kbps); again, a faster connection improves it considerably. The speed of the throughput is limited by the slower end of the connection, so if the person you're communicating with has a slower connection than you, that speed will control the quality of the audio and video transmitted.

In a domain environment, you probably won't have much influence over the speed of your network or Internet connection: you'll share the company's network and its Internet connection with other users. If performance is disappointing and you're able to put enough weight behind your complaints, the administrator might allocate more bandwidth or a higher priority to your traffic.

In a domain environment, you probably won't get to have much input on hardware choice. But whether you're in a domain, a workgroup, or on your own, you should be able to reposition your audio and video hardware for best effect, and you'll benefit from putting a few moments into getting their positions right. These are the main points:

- Position the microphone so that it'll clearly pick up your voice but not your breath-stream. For most people, this means the microphone shouldn't be right in front of your mouth, but rather off to the side of your mouth or near your throat. Not having the microphone in front of your face will probably make you look better on video, too.

- If you're using speakers, make sure their output won't be picked up by the microphone. If you're in a cubicle or an open office, headphones are likely to prove more satisfactory, although they may not improve your looks on video.

- Place the camera with care and check the image it's producing—particularly that the lighting is adequate. You'll probably find a camera angled slightly down from the top of your monitor gives a more flattering result than one angled up from the desk for an under-the-chin and up-the-nostrils shot. You'll also have fewer problems with overhead lighting. If the camera has zoom and focus controls, use them.

Limitations of Messenger and NetMeeting

With Messenger and NetMeeting, you can have audio and video conversations with only one other person at a time—you can't have an audio and video conversation with two or more other people. You're also limited to having only one audio conversation (or audio-and-video conversation) at a time. You can keep one or more other text-only conversations going while having an audio or video conversation.

Windows Messenger (the version included in Windows XP Professional) can send audio and video only to Windows Messenger, not to versions of MSN Messenger (versions of Messenger that run on older versions of Windows, on the Mac, on the Pocket PC, and on other devices).

Conferencing with Messenger

This section discusses how to make voice and video calls with Messenger. Messenger makes it as easy as possible to add voice and video to your existing conversations, so this section is relatively short.

 If you're interested in making PC-to-phone calls with Messenger, see the section "Make PC-to-Phone Calls with Messenger" in the middle of the chapter for details on how to get started.

Running the Audio and Video Tuning Wizard

If you haven't configured Messenger to use your audio and video hardware, run the Audio and Video Tuning Wizard to set up the hardware. If you don't run the wizard, it springs into action when you try to add audio or video (or both) to a call. This can be awkward if you're midway through a conversation at the time.

To run the Audio and Video Tuning Wizard, choose Tools | Audio Tuning Wizard. The wizard walks you through the steps of selecting the camera, previewing the image, positioning your microphone and speakers, and testing your speaker volume and microphone sensitivity.

If the wizard detects any obvious problems, such as a total lack of input from the microphone, it notifies you so that you can fix them and try again.

 If your environment for using Messenger changes (for example, it gets noisier or quieter), or you change your hardware or move the hardware around, run the Audio and Video Tuning Wizard again to retune your settings.

Holding a Voice Conversation

You can start a voice conversation from scratch or add voice to an existing conversation. Here's how to do so:

- To start a voice conversation from scratch, click the Start a Voice Conversation link in the action pane and use the Start a Voice Conversation dialog box to select the contact on the My Contacts page or the Other page. Messenger displays a pop-up telling your contact you're sending them an invitation.

- To add voice to an existing conversation, click the Start Talking button in the Conversation window or choose Actions | Start Talking.

In the Conversation window, your contact sees an announcement that you want to have a voice conversation with them. The announcement contains an Accept link and a Decline link they can click to respond to the invitation.

If your contact chooses the Accept link, Messenger sets up the audio channel between you. You can then talk to each other. Use the Speakers control to control the speaker volume and the Microphone control to adjust the microphone sensitivity. The Speakers control is linked to the master volume control for Windows XP. For example, if you use the Volume icon in the notification area to adjust the volume, you'll see the Speakers control reflect this change. Similarly, the Microphone control is linked to the microphone control for recording.

To end a voice conversation, click the Close button on the Conversation window or choose File | Close. To end the voice part of the conversation but continue chat (and other tools such as program sharing), click the Stop Talking button or choose Actions | Stop Talking.

Note   *Even though Messenger leaves the Invite Someone to This Conversation link available when you're in a voice or voice-and-video call, you can't add another person to the call. If you choose this link, Messenger adds a message telling you so to the text in the Conversation window.*

Holding a Voice and Video Conversation

As with voice, you can start a voice and video conversation from scratch or add voice and video to an existing conversation. Here's how to do so:

■ To start a voice and video conversation from scratch, click the Start a Video Conversation link in the action pane (if necessary, click the More item at the bottom of the initial I Want To list and select the link from the continuation of the list). Then use the Start a Video Conversation dialog box to select your contact. Again, Messenger shows your contact a pop-up telling them you want to see and be seen.

■ To add voice and video to an existing conversation, click the Start Camera button in the Conversation window or choose Actions | Start Camera.

In the Conversation window, your contact sees an announcement saying you want to have a video and voice conversation with them. The announcement contains an Accept link and a Decline link they can click to respond to the invitation.

Note   *You can't have a video conversation in Messenger without using voice as well.*

If the other person chooses the Accept link, Messenger sets up the audio and video channels between them and you. Figure 17-1 shows an ongoing voice and video conversation.

Figure 17-1. *A voice and video conversation in Messenger*

When you're sending video, Messenger offers two options you can access either from the View menu or from the menu Messenger displays when you click the Options button below the video window. These are the options:

- The Stop Sending Video command stops transmitting video without tearing down the video connection between you and the other party. This is a toggle setting, so you issue the same command again to restart video. Stopping the video momentarily like this is useful for recovering from a bandwidth crunch or taking a time out to scratch yourself in an embarrassing place without the camera betraying you.

- The Show My Video As Picture-in-Picture command toggles your video preview on and off.

To end a voice and video conversation, click the Close button on the Conversation window or choose File | Close. To end the voice and video part of the conversation but continue using other tools (for example, chat and Whiteboard), click the Stop Camera button or choose Actions | Stop Camera. (Stopping the camera also stops the audio.)

Troubleshooting Conferencing with Messenger

This section discusses some of the most common problems with audio and video on Messenger: the microphone slider in the Conversation window not behaving as it should, Messenger audio suffering from feedback or echo, and Messenger not supporting your digital-video camcorder or your analog TV tuner adapter.

Microphone Slider in the Conversation Window Seems Not to Work

If the Microphone slider in the Conversation window seems not to adjust the recording volume, Messenger's microphone setting may be associated with Windows XP Professional's microphone control for playback rather than for recording.

To change the association, open the volume control by clicking the Advanced Volume Controls link in the See Also task list on the Sounds, Speech, and Audio Devices page in Control Panel (select Start | Control Panel, and then click the Sounds, Speech, and Audio Devices link). The volume control goes by various names, depending on your audio hardware: It may be called Master Volume, Play Control, or something else.

Choose Options | Properties to display the Properties dialog box, select the Recording option button in the Adjust Volume For group box, and click the OK button. Windows XP Professional switches the volume control display to that of the recording control's and (in most cases) changes the name of the window to something like Recording Control or Record Control. (Again, the name depends on your hardware and software.)

At this point, you might feel you need to adjust the microphone settings in the window. Do so if you feel like it; but if not, just close the Recording Control window (or whatever it's called on your computer). This little rigmarole should have associated the Messenger Microphone slider with the microphone control for recording.

Microphone Slider Moves When You Move the Speaker Slider

If you find that moving the Speaker slider to adjust the volume of a call causes the Microphone slider to move as well, rest assured this is normal behavior because of the automatic gain control, which attempts to equalize sound volume. Messenger doesn't let you turn off the automatic gain control.

Messenger Delivers Feedback or Echo

If you get echoing or feedback on your Messenger audio calls, download the Messenger fix that contains the Acoustic Echo Cancellation (AEC) update from the Microsoft Support web site (support.microsoft.com). At this writing, AEC works only with USB cameras that use Microsoft USB audio, but Microsoft may have improved the fix by the time you read this—so it's worth checking the Microsoft Support Web site even if your camera doesn't match that description. (Search for "Windows Messenger" and "Acoustic Echo Cancellation.")

Windows XP Professional doesn't include AEC, so Messenger needs to implement AEC itself. Messenger's Options dialog box doesn't give you an option for turning AEC on and off, but the I Am Using Headphones check box on the Select the Microphone and Speakers You Want to Use page of the Audio and Video Tuning Wizard turns off AEC.

 If AEC doesn't work with your hardware, try repositioning your microphone and speakers to reduce or eliminate the feedback or echo. Alternatively, use headphones instead of speakers.

Messenger Doesn't Support Your DV Camcorder or Analog TV Tuner Adapter

If Messenger doesn't support your digital video camcorder or analog TV tuner adapter, download the Messenger fix that contains the AEC update, as described in the previous section. This fix includes support for digital video camcorders and analog TV tuners (although AEC itself doesn't work with them).

Making PC-to-Phone Calls with Messenger

As mentioned at the beginning of this chapter, you can also use Messenger to make calls from your PC to a regular phone. For PC-to-phone calls, Messenger uses .NET Voice Services—another component in the plethora of .NET services.

To use .NET Voice Services, you need to sign up with a voice service provider (VSP)—a company that provides telephony services compatible with .NET Voice Services.

 At press time, .NET Voice Services doesn't work through Network Address Translation (NAT), including Internet Connection Sharing (ICS) and many wireless network systems, so you can use it only on a PC that has a direct connection to the Internet. Microsoft is working to upgrade .NET Voice Services to work with NAT—so check to see if they've finished.

Choosing Your Voice Service Provider

The first step in making PC-to-phone calls with Messenger is to choose your VSP. The way Messenger is set up, you can use only one voice service provider at a time, so do your homework before signing up with one.

The easiest way to sign up for a VSP is to click the Make a Phone Call link in the Action pane or choose Actions | Make a Phone Call. Messenger displays the Phone window, checks that your computer has a suitable connection to the Internet (in other words, no NAT at this writing), and offers you a Get Started Here button. Click it, and Messenger displays the Select a Voice Service Provider window with links to providers. Investigate the providers, choose the one that best meets your needs, sign up for it, and buy some minutes to use. (If you get a message that tells you your voice service account information is temporarily unavailable and invites you to click a link to check .NET Service status, wait for a while, and then try again.)

Once you've signed up for a VSP, its name appears in the Phone window. Figure 17-2 shows an example.

Making a Call

To make a call, display the Phone window by clicking the Make a Phone Call link in the Action pane or choose Actions | Make a Phone Call. Specify the country and the phone number, and then click the Dial button.

To call a contact, you can click the Contacts icon and use the resulting Make a Phone Call dialog box to select the contact. The Phone window phone number drop-down list displays the contact's numbers for you to choose the right one.

For the recipient, the call appears to be a regular incoming call on their telephone, except that because of the analog-to-digital and digital-to-analog conversions, the quality is much lower than the quality of a regular voice call.

Changing Your Voice Service Provider

To change to a different VSP, you need to cancel your existing VSP account, so it's not a change to make on the spur of the moment.

To change your VSP, choose Tools | Change Voice Service from the Phone window. Messenger connects to your VSP, which walks you through the process of canceling your account. You can then sign up for a new account with another VSP by clicking the Get Started Here button in the Phone window.

Figure 17-2. *The Phone window lists your VSP and provides basic controls for making PC-to-phone calls via your Internet connection.*

Conferencing with NetMeeting

This section discusses how to make two-person voice and video calls with NetMeeting. As you'll remember from the previous chapter, NetMeeting can make secure data-only calls, but all calls involving voice and video are insecure.

Running the Audio Tuning Wizard

If you've added your audio and video hardware to your computer since you set up NetMeeting, run the Audio Tuning Wizard to make sure NetMeeting knows which hardware you want to use and has the speaker and microphone levels set sensibly.

Holding an Audio Conversation

If you have functioning audio hardware on your computer, all you need to do to start an audio conversation with another user is place an insecure call to them. (By default, NetMeeting sets up audio on insecure calls.)

To change the audio levels, click the Adjust Audio Volume button to make NetMeeting display the audio controls, shown in Figure 17-3, in place of the participant list. You can then select or clear the Mute/Unmute Microphone check box to mute or unmute the microphone, drag the Adjust Microphone Volume slider to adjust the microphone sensitivity, select or clear the Mute/Unmute Speakers check box to mute or unmute the speakers, and drag the Adjust Speaker Volume slider to adjust the speaker volume.

Holding a Video Conversation

If you've selected the Automatically Send Video at the Start of Each Call check box and the Automatically Receive Video at the Start of Each Call check box in the Sending and Receiving Video group box on the Video page of the Options dialog box, NetMeeting automatically starts sending and receiving video when you establish a connection to another NetMeeting user.

 Although you can set NetMeeting to start video automatically at the beginning of each call, it's usually better to start video manually once you've established the call and ascertained that audio works correctly. This is because, if you get a low-bandwidth connection at either end, trying to use video will prevent you from using audio to determine the problem and decide how to deal with it, so you'll have to fall back on text chat.

If you haven't chosen to send video automatically, you can start sending it by clicking the Start Video/Stop Video button (the leftmost of the three buttons under the video window) or by choosing Tools | Video | Send once you've set up an insecure call.

To display the video image you're sending as a picture-in-picture miniature on the lower-right corner of the video window, click the Picture-in-Picture button or choose View | Picture-in-Picture.

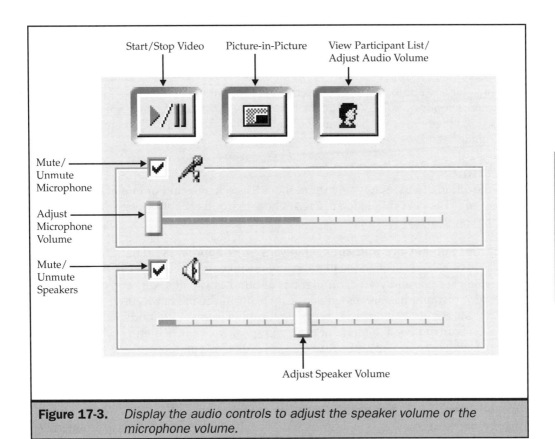

Start/Stop Video   Picture-in-Picture   View Participant List/
Adjust Audio Volume

Mute/
Unmute
Microphone

Adjust
Microphone
Volume

Mute/
Unmute
Speakers

Adjust Speaker Volume

Figure 17-3. *Display the audio controls to adjust the speaker volume or the microphone volume.*

To view the video image you're sending at its full size (instead of at the picture-in-picture size), choose View | My Video.

To stop and start receiving video, right-click the video picture and select Pause from the shortcut menu or choose Tools | Video | Receive.

You can't change the size of the video image being sent to you, but you can change the size at which NetMeeting displays it on your computer. To do so, right-click the video window, select the Window Size item from the shortcut menu, and choose 100%, 200%, 300%, or 400% from the submenu. (Alternatively, choose Tools | Video | Window Size and choose the size from the submenu.) The bigger you make the image, the grainier it'll be, but increasing the size by a modest amount can make a small image easier to see.

Tip *To capture a still image of the video being sent to you, right-click the video picture and choose Copy from the shortcut menu. Then paste the image into a graphics program such as Paint.*

Troubleshooting Audio Problems in NetMeeting

This section discusses how to troubleshoot the most common audio problems in NetMeeting. The section breaks these problems down into two basic categories: First, you can't get any audio. Second, you can get audio, but it sounds bad.

Troubleshooting audio problems in NetMeeting is often difficult because it can be hard to tell whether the problems are being caused at your end of the connection or at your contact's end.

No Audio

This subsection discusses how to troubleshoot the lack of sound or loss of sound in NetMeeting. The next subsection discusses how to troubleshoot assorted problems with the sound you're getting.

Check the Sound Card and Your Speakers or Headphones   First, choose Tools | Options and check to see that the Options dialog box includes an audio tab. If you don't see one and your computer has a sound card that's working, chances are an administrator has prevented you from using audio in NetMeeting.

Make sure your sound card is working for other audio and your speakers or headphones are plugged in (and, for powered speakers, switched on). Make sure the volume hasn't been muted at the Play Control or the Volume Control.

If you have two or more sound cards, make sure NetMeeting has selected the right one. To change the sound card NetMeeting is using, run the Audio Tuning Wizard.

Turn off Other Audio Sources   If you're not able to get audio in NetMeeting, turn off any other audio source you're using. For example, if you're listening to an Internet radio station, playing back MP3 files, or ripping a CD and listening to it, you may be unable to get audio in NetMeeting at the same time.

Set the Sample Rate Conversion Quality to Best   With some versions of NetMeeting and some hardware, you may need to set Sample Rate Conversion Quality to the Best setting to enable audio with NetMeeting.

For example, in Windows XP, follow these steps:

1. Choose Start | Control Panel | Sounds, Speech, and Audio Devices | Sounds and Audio Devices to display the Sounds and Audio Devices Properties dialog box.

2. Click the Advanced button in the Sound Play group box on the Audio tab to display the Advanced Audio Properties dialog box.

3. On the Performance tab, move the Sample Rate Conversion Quality slider to the Best setting.

 The Performance tab of the Advanced Audio Properties dialog box doesn't appear for some sound cards.

Start NetMeeting Fully Before Accepting an Incoming Call   If you accept an incoming call while you're starting up NetMeeting and before it has fully started up, you may be unable to use audio or video during the call. This happens when NetMeeting on your computer hasn't started up enough to respond to incoming request for a connection using the H.323 protocol. The calling computer takes this lack of response to mean that your version of NetMeeting can't handle H.323. It then attempts to establish a connection using T.120, which your computer (which has probably fully started NetMeeting by now) accepts.

If you run into this problem, disconnect the call and establish it again.

Proxy Server Ports 1720 and 1731 Must Be Open   If you're connecting through a proxy server, and everything else seems okay but you're unable to get audio, check whether ports 1720 and 1731 are open. (Ask your server administrator if necessary.) NetMeeting needs these ports to be open on the proxy server to send audio.

Audio Sounds Bad

This subsection discusses problems that may make the audio in NetMeeting sound bad and what, if anything, you can do about them.

Too Much Background Noise   If you're using NetMeeting in a noisy environment, your microphone may be picking up too much background noise for it to convey your voice clearly. Reduce the background noise, if possible, or reposition the microphone so that it picks up less of the noise. Run the Audio Tuning Wizard to retune the microphone.

Audio Quality Is Low   Several problems can cause low-audio quality, including lack of processing power, lack of bandwidth, and poor microphone placement or tuning. If you have an older computer, minimize the demands on it by quitting any applications you don't need to have running while you're using NetMeeting. Similarly, if you have limited bandwidth, prevent other applications from using it for the duration. Check for obvious deficiencies in the positioning of your microphone and run the Audio Tuning Wizard to see if it can tune the microphone better.

If your computer is permanently incapable of producing quality audio, you may need to invest in a new sound card. If your computer is a laptop, consider using USB speakers or USB headphones to bypass an underperforming sound card you can't replace or try an external sound card such as the Sound Blaster Extigy.

Audio Is Inaudible   The microphone may be too far from the sound source (for example, your voice) or its record volume may be set too low. Try moving the microphone nearer to the sound source or using the Audio Tuning Wizard to increase the record volume. If necessary, do both.

Audio Is Distorted   The microphone may be too close to the sound source (for example, your voice) or its record volume may be turned up too high. Try moving the microphone further away or using the Audio Tuning Wizard to reduce the record volume (or do both).

If the volume is satisfactory but you're getting annoying static on plosives and fricatives, try moving the microphone out of your breath-stream. Position the microphone to the side of your mouth or nearer your throat.

Audio Is Choppy   Choppy audio may indicate several different problems. Of these, the most likely is that your sound card can't handle full-duplex audio satisfactorily. If this is the case, drop back to half-duplex audio by clearing the Enable Full-Duplex Audio So I Can Speak while Receiving Audio check box in the General group box on the Audio tab of the Options dialog box (Tools | Options).

You may also need to turn off DirectSound. To do so, clear the Enable DirectSound for Improved Audio Performance check box in the General group box on the Audio tab of the Options dialog box.

Next most likely is that NetMeeting isn't getting the bandwidth to transfer audio. Unless you can increase the bandwidth on your connection (for example, by adding a second ISDN channel or another modem to a multilink connection), the only way to improve matters is to stop any other applications using that bandwidth. Turn off the Internet radio station and any stock tickers, stop any automatic checking of e-mail, and so on.

Audio Has Echoes   Echoes in NetMeeting audio usually means the person you're talking to has gotten their speakers too close to their microphone for the current sensitivity of the microphone. You might also have done this yourself because you won't usually notice the problem.

The cures are simple enough: put more distance between the microphone and the speakers; turn down the speaker volume; decrease the gain on the microphone (either manually or by running the Audio Tuning Wizard); or use headphones instead of speakers.

Audio and Other NetMeeting Features Suffer from Lack of Bandwidth   If you have a low-bandwidth Internet connection (for example, a modem connection), you're probably already painfully aware of its limitations. But because of the demands that audio and video place on your bandwidth, you may need to be even more careful than usual when using NetMeeting. For example, you may be unable to get decent audio quality while receiving files or video. In this case, you'll need to decide where your priorities lie.

If both you and the person you're talking to have fast connections that normally deliver speedy uploads and downloads, the problem may be with one of your Internet service providers (ISPs). Some ISPs throttle back greedy applications at times of heavy demand. You're more likely to have this happen to you if you're trying to transmit a large video picture as well as audio.

If you're using NetMeeting on an internal network, don't assume that anything like the full bandwidth of the network will be available to you. You will be contending with other users for network bandwidth in any case, and an administrator may have restricted the amount of bandwidth you can consume.

Application sharing demands a surprising amount of bandwidth. In particular, moving a shared program window on the Desktop requires NetMeeting to transmit a large amount of information. If you're collaborating over a low-bandwidth connection, expect audio to suffer at times like this.

Network Bandwidth Is Set Too High   As mentioned in the previous chapter, the Network Bandwidth dialog box lets you specify the approximate speed of the connection you're using for your NetMeeting calls. Your choices are 14400 bps Modem; 28800 bps or Faster Modem; Cable, xDSL or ISDN; and Local Area Network. NetMeeting uses this setting to determine the rate at which to send audio and video. If you specify a faster connection than you're using, NetMeeting will try to send too much information, which can result in a choppy or broken signal.

To fix this problem, display the Network Bandwidth dialog box (choose Tools | Options to display the Options dialog box. Then click the Bandwidth Settings button on the General tab) and choose a lower bandwidth setting.

Even Half-Duplex Audio Doesn't Work Properly   If you find even half-duplex audio doesn't work properly, chances are ambient noise on the full-duplex end is holding open the receive channel on the half-duplex end of the call, thus preventing it from sending. Reduce ambient noise and run the Audio Tuning Wizard at the full-duplex end to eliminate this problem.

Troubleshooting Video Problems in NetMeeting

This section discusses how to troubleshoot video problems in NetMeeting. These problems range from not getting any video to not getting satisfactory video.

Video Image Is Jerky

Jerky video is pretty much a fact of life when you're videoconferencing over limited-bandwidth connections, so the first order of business is to get your expectations in line with reality.

Here are the basics. None of them should surprise you:

- NetMeeting adjusts its frame rate depending on the bandwidth available at both ends of the connection. If you have a T1 line, but the person at the other end has a V.90 dial-up connection (which gives 33.6 Kbps upstream), you'll get a slow frame rate because that's all the other person's connection can send. Likewise, they'll get a slowish frame rate because, even though your connection can supply a high frame rate, their connection can't receive any faster than 56 Kbps.

- In general, the smaller the video image, the higher the frame rate you get.

- If bandwidth isn't a problem and the video camera supports a high frame rate, *and* your computer's video hardware is up to scratch (less a problem these days than it used to be), you should be able to get SQCIF or QCIF up to 30 frames per second (fps), which gives smooth movement but a small picture. You'll be lucky to get CIF above 15 fps because each frame contains four times as much information as QCIF.

> **Note**
>
> *Because NetMeeting doesn't support video overlay mode, your CPU is involved in all video you send and receive via NetMeeting. So to get a high frame rate in NetMeeting, your computer needs to be running at a decent speed. Generally speaking, this, too, is less of a problem these days than it used to be in the late twentieth century. If your computer is powerful enough to run Windows XP Professional at a decent speed, it should be able to handle NetMeeting's video demands.*

Change Your Video Device

When you change the video device on the Video tab of the Options dialog box, you may need to close the Options dialog box and reopen it to force the Send Image Size group box to list the image sizes the video device provides.

Poor-Quality Video or Wrong Colors in Video Window

If the video quality is wretched, or if the wrong colors appear in parts of the video window, either you've chosen a larger video image size than your bandwidth and computer can handle or you've set the image quality too low. (A third possibility is that the video camera's subject isn't well enough lit, but this problem tends to be easier to diagnose.)

If you've chosen too large an image size, decrease it and close any superfluous applications. If you've set too low an image quality, increase the I Prefer to Receive slider setting in the Video Quality group box on the Video page of the Options dialog box. (By default, NetMeeting chooses the Faster Video setting when you specify 28.8 Kbps bandwidth.)

Black Screen in Video Window

If the video window in NetMeeting is showing a black screen, try the following:

■ If you have two or more video-capture devices, make sure NetMeeting is set up to use the correct one. (Use the The Video Capture Device I Want to Use Is drop-down list in the Video Camera Properties group box on the Video tab of the Options dialog box.)

■ Once you're sure the video-capture device is right, check the video format you're using to make sure it's a format NetMeeting supports.

■ Make sure the video-capture device isn't set to use video overlay mode. NetMeeting doesn't support video overlay mode. (Video overlay mode lets the video-capture device bypass the processor and send video directly to memory on the video-capture card. Generally, video overlay mode is a good idea—but only if the application involved supports it.)

You Can't Disconnect and Reconnect Video Camera During a Call

NetMeeting doesn't support disconnecting and reconnecting video sources during a call, so if you disconnect your camera, and then reconnect it (or connect another camera),

NetMeeting probably won't display the new image. If you need to change your camera or reconnect it for other reasons (for example, to untangle its cable), end the call, adjust the camera, and then establish a new call.

Summary

This chapter has discussed how to use Messenger and NetMeeting for audioconferencing and videoconferencing, and how to troubleshoot some of the problems that are most likely to occur.

The next chapter covers how to use Windows XP Professional on a laptop.

WORKING AND
COMMUNICATING

Chapter 18

Using Windows XP Professional on a Notebook PC

This chapter discusses the major considerations for using Windows XP Professional on a notebook PC, from configuring power-management options specific to notebook PCs to using offline files and the Briefcase feature. Because Windows XP tends to refer to notebook PCs as "laptops," this chapter uses the term "laptop" rather than "notebook PC."

Where these considerations apply more or less exclusively to laptops, this chapter discusses them in detail. Where the considerations apply to both laptops and desktops, this chapter refers you to the relevant discussion in other chapters in this book.

Configuring Power Management Options for Laptops

If you use your laptop away from a power outlet, battery management quickly becomes a prime concern. To make your battery (or batteries) last as long as possible, configure power-management options as discussed in this section. Typically, you'll need administrator-level rights to the computer to set power options. Otherwise, you'll be able to access the Power Options Properties dialog box and change the settings, but Windows XP Professional will display a Power Policy Manager Unable to Set Active Policy dialog box telling you that access is denied when you try to apply the settings. So if your administrator doesn't grant you sufficient rights to configure power options, badger them for the rights so that you can configure these important settings.

To configure power options, display the Power Options Properties dialog box in any of the following ways:

- Choose Start | Control Panel | Performance and Maintenance | Power Options.
- Click the Power button on the Screen Saver tab of the Display Properties dialog box.
- Enter **powercfg.cpl** in the Run dialog box.

Power Schemes Tab

On the Power Schemes tab (Figure 18-1) of the Power Options Properties dialog box, choose settings for turning off the monitor and hard disks, for the system to stand by, and for the system to enter hibernation. If Windows XP recognizes your computer as a laptop, it lets you choose different settings for Plugged In and Running on Batteries configurations. Choose shorter times in the Running on Batteries column to reduce your computer's power consumption to a minimum.

Alarms Tab

On the Alarms tab (Figure 18-2) of the Power Options Properties dialog box, choose whether Windows XP should use a low battery alarm, a critical battery alarm, both, or neither.

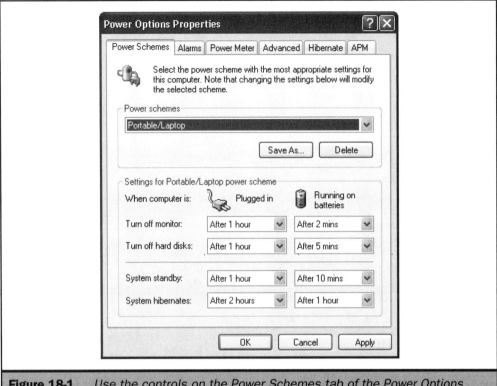

Figure 18-1. *Use the controls on the Power Schemes tab of the Power Options Properties dialog box to minimize your laptop's power demands when it's running on batteries.*

Here's what you need to know about the battery alarm settings:

- The low battery alarm and critical battery alarm are triggered by the battery level reported to Windows XP reaching the designated level. (Sometimes a laptop's hardware display of battery power may show a different percentage level than Windows XP's software display.)

- You can't set a low battery alarm power percentage that's less than the critical battery alarm power percentage. You can set the low battery alarm and the critical battery alarm to use the same power percentage, but in practice, it makes little sense to do so.

- For either the low battery alarm or the critical battery alarm, you can set an alarm action by clicking the appropriate Alarm Action button and working in the resulting Alarm Actions dialog box. Figure 18-3 shows the Low Battery Alarm Actions dialog box. You can choose whether Windows XP notifies you via sound, via a display message, or both. Choose the action the computer should take

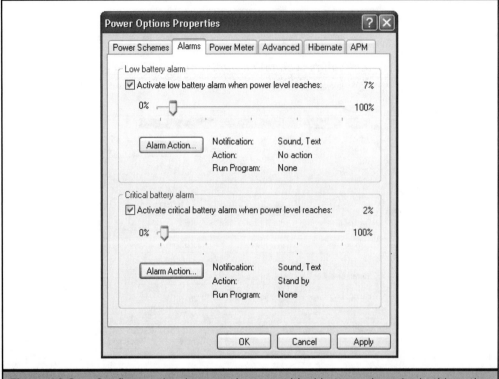

Figure 18-2. Configure a low battery alarm or critical battery alarm (or both) on the Alarms tab of the Power Options Properties dialog box.

(Stand By, Hibernate, or Shut Down) when the alarm is triggered, and whether Windows XP should force the standby or shutdown if an application stops responding; or specify an application to run when the alarm is triggered.

■ If you choose to run an application when one of the battery alarms is triggered, the account under which the application is run must have a password and the Task Scheduler service must be running. (See Chapter 41 for a discussion of scheduling tasks and using the Task Scheduler service.)

Power Meter Tab

The Power Meter tab of the Power Options Properties dialog box displays details of the power remaining in the computer's battery or batteries. If the computer has two or more batteries, this display is useful for seeing how much power is left in each battery. If the computer has only one battery, you can get a readout of the battery's remaining power more easily by hovering your mouse pointer over the Power icon in the notification area. (To display the Power icon, select the Always Show Icon on the Taskbar check box on the Advanced tab of the Power Options Properties dialog box.)

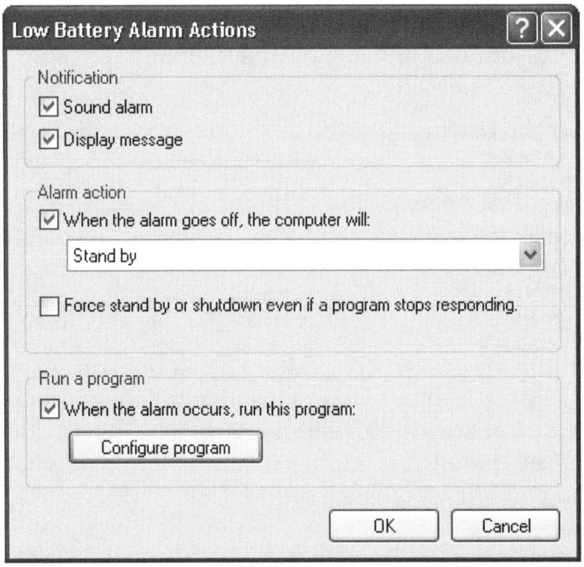

Figure 18-3. *In the Low Battery Alarm Actions dialog box (shown here) and the Critical Battery Alarm Actions dialog box, you can configure the actions that Windows XP takes when the battery level reaches the low or critical level.*

Using Windows XP's Power-Control Features

If your laptop's processor includes power-control features such as SpeedStep or PowerNow, Windows XP Professional automatically reduces the processor speed when the laptop is running on battery power. Windows XP Professional doesn't provide user-interface controls for manipulating the processor speed, but you can gain some control by editing the Registry. See "Controlling SpeedStep or PowerNow Processors" in Chapter 40 for details.

Using ClearType and DualView

ClearType is a display technology for LCD screens that uses a technique called *sub-pixel rendering* (illuminating or turning off part of pixels rather than full pixels) to produce a smoother effect on the fonts displayed onscreen. Some people like the effect ClearType produces, others don't; but it's worth trying on your computer to see if it suits you. Most modern LCD screens can use ClearType, while some older ones don't benefit from it.

To turn ClearType on or off, follow these steps:

1. Click the Effects button on the Appearance tab of the Display Properties dialog box to display the Effects dialog box.

2. Select or clear the Use the Following Method to Smooth Edges of Screen Fonts check box.

3. If you select this check box, select ClearType in the drop-down list. If you don't like the effects that ClearType produces, try Standard smoothing instead, or turn smoothing off.

4. Close the Effects dialog box and the Display Properties dialog box.

DualView is an implementation of Windows XP Professional's multiple-monitor capability for laptop PCs. Because you can't install multiple graphics cards in a laptop PC the way you can in a desktop PC, DualView uses a laptop's external graphics port instead to drive a second monitor. By connecting an external monitor to this graphics port, you can extend your desktop on to it.

See "Configuring Multiple Monitors on a Laptop PC" in Chapter 10 for a discussion of how to use DualView.

Using Offline Files

Windows XP Professional's Offline Files feature lets you store copies of network files and folders on your local PC so that you can take them with you and work with them when you're not connected to the network. When you reconnect your computer to the network, Windows XP Professional synchronizes your cached copies of the files with the original files on the network.

Note *Offline Files can also be useful for speeding up your work when your computer is connected to the network but only via a slow connection. For example, if you're working from a remote office via a dial-up connection, you'll be able to improve performance by working with offline versions of files and then synchronizing your changes rather than working directly with files across the dial-up connection.*

This section uses the term *Offline Files* (with the initial capital letters) to refer to the Offline Files feature that enables you to use files when offline. It uses the term *offline files* (all lowercase) to refer to the files that are made available by using the Offline Files feature.

To use Offline Files, the files first need to be made available offline. In most cases, you'll need to be (or to get) an administrator to do this. In a domain environment, the administrator will normally make this change by using a Group Policy setting rather than making it directly on your computer.

In a domain environment, administrators can control the Offline Files feature extensively by using Group Policy settings. For example, they can prevent you from using Offline Files at all; or they can permit you to use Offline Files but prevent you from configuring any of its settings. They can force you to have certain files available when you're offline, they can force encryption on the offline files, and so on. This section mentions many of the settings that administrators can impose so that you know why you may not be able to use an option that's described here.

If you use offline files in a standalone or workgroup configuration, make sure that Fast User Switching is switched off. When Fast User Switching is on, the Offline Files feature doesn't work.

Offline Files works with any computer running an operating system that supports file sharing using server message block (SMB). This includes computers running Windows 9x, Windows NT 4 (Workstation or Server), Windows 2000 (Professional or Server), Windows XP (Professional or Home Edition), and Linux with Samba.

Enabling and Configuring Offline Files

To enable Offline Files, select the Enable Offline Files check box on the Offline Files tab (Figure 18-4) of the Folder Options dialog box (Tools | Folder Options from a Windows Explorer window displaying a local drive). In a domain environment, you'll need to be

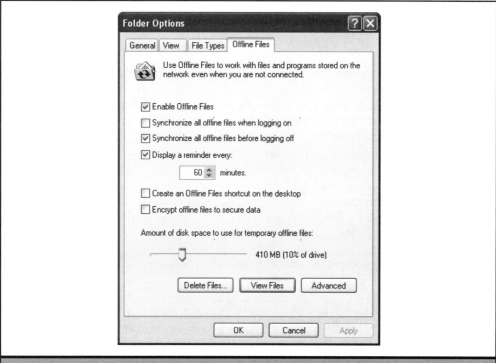

Figure 18-4. *Enable the Offline Files feature and configure settings for it on the Offline Files tab of the Folder Options dialog box.*

an administrator or have equivalent privileges to do this. If the Enable Offline Files check box is dimmed and unavailable, you'll know that you need to get an administrator to do this for you.

You also need to be an administrator to select or clear the Encrypt Offline Files to Secure Data check box and adjust the Amount of Disk Space to Use for Temporary Offline Files slider. Again, the administrator is likely to apply these settings through Group Policy rather than directly on your computer. In the original version of Windows XP Professional, choosing a setting of 0 percent of disk space produces an "Incorrect Function" error message if you try to make files available offline. Service Pack 1 fixed this problem.

> **Note** *As mentioned earlier, in a domain environment, an administrator can prevent you from changing any Offline Files settings at all.*

You can use encryption only for files stored on a volume formatted with NTFS. The "temporary offline files" description is a little oblique. This isn't space to hold the files that you decide to make available offline: Windows XP Professional takes up space for those as required. This space is for files that an administrator decides will be made available to you—for example, application files or information resources that you'll need for your computer to run successfully when offline. You don't have any say in making these files available or rejecting them.

Once an administrator has enabled Offline Files, you'll be able to choose the following:

- Whether to synchronize all offline files when logging on, when logging off, both, or neither. This choice isn't as clear-cut as it appears. Synchronizing at logon performs a quick synchronization at logon, not a full synchronization, so you won't necessarily have the latest versions of files. Selecting the Synchronize All Offline Files before Logging Off causes Windows XP Professional to perform a full synchronization, as you'd expect. Clearing this check box doesn't cause Windows XP Professional to skip synchronization at logoff: It just causes Windows XP Professional to perform a quick synchronization when you log off instead of a full synchronization. So don't expect to be able to log off in moments and scramble into a taxi for the airport by clearing the Synchronize All Offline Files Before Logging Off check box.

> **Note** *In a domain environment, an administrator can force synchronization to occur when you log on, when you log off, or both.*

- Whether and (if so) at what interval to display a reminder in the notification area that you're working offline. This option is convenient if you sometimes work offline when in the office and connected to the network. When you're away from the office, you'll usually be pretty clear that you're working offline, and the reminder won't have much value.

■ Whether to create an Offline Files shortcut on the desktop for quick access to your Offline Files folder. Such a shortcut is useful for manipulating your offline files. Normally, though, you'll access your offline files through your applications in exactly the same way as when you're online. For example, if you work with the Word document z:\users\public\Requirements.doc when online, you can access the document using the same path when working offline—you don't need to go through the Offline Files folder, because Windows XP Professional makes the document available using its network path.

You can click the Delete Files button to delete your offline copies of all the files that you've chosen to make available. See "Deleting Offline Files," later in this chapter.

Note   *If your offline-files cache becomes corrupted so that you can't synchronize files, you may need to reinitialize the cache. This is a drastic step: Reinitializing the cache deletes all your offline files and resets the database, so you lose any changes that you've made in your offline files. To reinitialize the cache, hold down* CTRL *and* SHIFT *and click the Delete Files button on the Offline Files tab of the Folder Options dialog box. Then restart Windows XP Professional.*

You can click the View Files button to display a Windows Explorer window to the Offline Files Folder. By displaying this folder in Details view, you can see each file's file type, its synchronization status (for example, File Is Synchronized, Only Local Copy Exists, or Local Copy Has Been Modified), its availability (for example, Always Available for a file you've pinned, Temporarily Available for a file an administrator has specified you should have available offline), the status of the server on which the file is located (Online or Offline), the location of the file, its size, and when it was last modified.

Note   *In a domain environment, administrators can prevent you from accessing the Online Files folder directly. If they do this, you can access the files only through their network locations.*

You can click the Advanced button to display the Offline Files – Advanced Settings dialog box (shown on the left in Figure 18-5). This dialog box lets you specify how your computer behaves when it loses the connection to another computer on the network. You can use different behavior for specific computers by clicking the Add button and using the Offline Files – Add Custom Action dialog box (shown on the right in Figure 18-5) to add individual computers to the Exception List list box.

The Never Allow My Computer to Go Offline option is confusingly named, because if your computer's network connection (or the computer to a networked computer with which your computer is working) is lost, your computer has no choice but to go offline. What this option means is that your computer isn't allowed to go into a state in which it uses offline files: When the network connection to a computer is lost, the files on that computer are as inaccessible to you as if the Offline Files feature had never been invented.

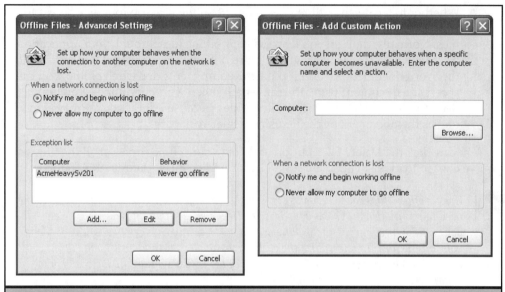

Figure 18-5. In the Offline Files – Advanced Settings dialog box (left), specify what your computer should do when the connection to a certain computer is lost, and use the Offline Files – Add Custom Action dialog box (right) to add exceptions for given computers.

Note *In a domain environment, administrators can specify how Windows XP Professional behaves when a server becomes unavailable to you. For example, they can choose the Work Offline to make sure that the offline files are available to you when you lose contact with the server.*

File Types You Can't Make Available Offline

By default, Windows XP Professional prevents you from using various file types offline, such as MDB and LDB files (Microsoft Access database files and their locking files). An administrator can use a Group Policy setting to override the file types that can't be used offline or to add other file types to them.

Note *The error "Unable to make filename available offline. Files of this type cannot be made available offline" means that you've asked Windows XP Professional to make available offline a file of a file type that Windows XP Professional's default settings or your administrator's Group Policy settings don't allow you to use offline. For example, you might have tried to make a Microsoft Access database file available offline. By default, Windows XP Professional completes synchronization even when such errors occur. (The file that raised the error message isn't synchronized.) You can change this behavior by editing the Registry as described in "Making Synchronization Manager Pause on Errors" in Chapter 40.*

Where Offline Files Are Stored

Windows XP Professional stores your offline files and folders and data about the locations and permissions of the original files on the network in the %systemroot%\ CSC folder. (CSC is the abbreviation for *client-side caching*, the technical term for Offline Files.) This folder is shared among all users of the computer. If this folder is stored on an NTFS volume, only administrators can access the contents of this folder directly through Windows Explorer. (On a FAT32 volume, all users can access the CSC folder. But even if the volume uses FAT32, Windows XP Professional maintains the NTFS permissions set on the files.)

Normally you won't need to access the contents of the CSC folder directly: Instead, you'll work with the files in the network locations in which they're apparently still stored, or you'll access the files through your Offline Files folder.

Making Files and Folders Available Offline

Once you've enabled the Offline Files feature on your computer (or had an administrator enable it for you), designate the files and folders that you want to make available when you're offline. To do so, issue a Make Available Offline command from the File menu or the shortcut menu for the file or folder. Making a file or folder available offline like this is called *pinning* the file or folder.

Note *The first time you issue a Make Available Offline command, Windows XP Professional runs the Offline Files Wizard, which walks you through configuring the main options for the Offline Files feature: whether to automatically synchronize offline files when you log on and off (the wizard lumps the two options together in one check box), whether to enable reminders, and whether to create a desktop shortcut to your Offline Files folder. If you've chosen settings already, as described in the previous section, you shouldn't need to choose them again. If you clear the Automatically Synchronize the Offline Files when I Log On and Log Off My Computer check box in the wizard, the wizard doesn't change your settings for the Synchronize All Offline Files when Logging On check box and the Synchronize All Offline Files before Logging Off check box on the Offline Files tab of the Folder Options dialog box.*

If you issued the Make Available Offline command for a folder that contains subfolders, Windows XP Professional displays the Confirm Offline Subfolders dialog box, shown next, so that you can choose whether to make the subfolders available too. In many cases, you'll want to do so. But if some of the subfolders contain large amounts of material that you don't need, you may prefer to make only those subfolders you need available offline.

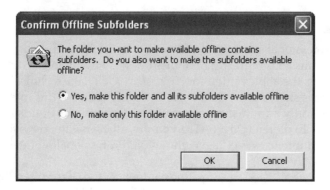

 If you make available offline a folder that contains no subfolders, Windows XP Professional doesn't ask you whether you want to make available offline any subfolders than are subsequently created in that folder. But when subfolders are created, it does make them available offline. In a domain environment, an administrator can force Windows XP Professional to always make subfolders available offline when their parent folder is available offline.

Windows XP Professional displays the Synchronizing dialog box as it copies the files or folders to your Offline Files cache.

Caution *If your My Documents folder has been redirected to a network location, you may not be able to avoid synchronizing subfolders of the My Documents folder as well. This is because of a bug in the original version of Windows XP Professional that was fixed in Service Pack 1.*

Synchronizing Offline Files

This section discusses the process of synchronizing your offline files. Windows XP Professional makes this process as straightforward as possible, but there are some subtleties that you need to understand.

How Synchronization of Offline Files Works

How Windows XP Professional synchronizes offline files with their network counterparts depends on whether an offline file has changed, its network counterpart has changed, or both have changed. Here are the details:

- If a file on the network has remained unchanged, but your offline copy has changed, Windows XP Professional replaces the original with your offline copy.

- If a file on the network has changed, but your offline copy has remained unchanged, Windows XP Professional updates your offline copy with the new original.

- If a file on the network has changed and your offline copy has changed, you have to decide whether to overwrite the network file with your offline copy or vice versa. See "Resolving File Conflicts," later in this chapter, for details.

- If a file on the network has been deleted, and your offline copy has changed, you can choose whether to delete your offline copy or save it to the network.

- If a new file has been created in a folder that you've marked to have available offline, Windows XP Professional copies it to your offline files.

- If you've created a new file in your offline folder, Windows XP Professional copies it to the corresponding network folder.

- If you've deleted a file in your offline files folder by using conventional deletion techniques, and the corresponding file on the network is unchanged, Windows XP Professional deletes the network file.

- If you've deleted a file in your offline files folder, but someone else has changed the corresponding file on the network, Windows XP Professional doesn't delete the network file.

Full Synchronization and Quick Synchronization

Windows XP Professional supports both full synchronization and quick synchronization. *Full synchronization* synchronizes all the offline files in your local cache with the files on the network share. *Quick synchronization* checks that all the offline files in your local cache are complete, and completes any that aren't complete, but doesn't check that the offline files in your local cache are up to date with the files on the network share. (Offline files in your local cache can be incomplete if you open a document from an automatically cached folder for the first time. Offline Files creates an entry for the file in your Offline Files database, but it doesn't copy the whole file until you synchronize.)

Choosing When Offline Files Are Synchronized

Windows XP Professional can synchronize files in the following ways:

- At logon or logoff
- When your computer is idle
- At times specified in a synchronization schedule
- When you issue a Synchronize command manually
- When a network connection becomes available again after having been unavailable

The following subsections discuss how to configure and use synchronization.

Note *In a domain environment, administrators can use Group Policy settings to specify synchronization of all offline files at logon, at logoff, or when a computer is put into standby or hibernation.*

WORKING AND
COMMUNICATING

Displaying the Synchronization Settings Dialog Box   To configure synchronization settings for offline files, display the Items to Synchronize dialog box by choosing Tools | Synchronize from a Windows Explorer window. Click the Setup button to display the Synchronization Settings dialog box. Then use the options described in the following subsections to configure synchronization settings for logon and logoff, for when your computer is idle, or to schedule synchronization.

Configuring Synchronization Settings for Logon and Logoff   The Logon/Logoff tab (Figure 18-6) of the Synchronization Settings dialog box lets you specify synchronization settings for individual network connections. Follow these steps:

1. Select the connection in the When I Am Using This Network Connection drop-down list.

2. Select the check boxes for the appropriate offline files and offline Web pages in the Synchronize the Following Checked Items list box.

3. Select the When I Log On to My Computer check box or the When I Log Off My Computer check box as appropriate. Remember that selecting the logon option

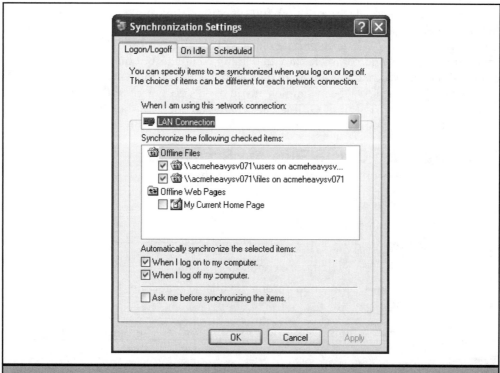

Figure 18-6.   *If you choose to synchronize offline files when you log on or log off, use the settings on the Logon/Logoff tab of the Synchronization Settings dialog box to fine-tune your choices.*

produces a quick synchronization; selecting the logoff check box produces a full synchronization at logoff; and clearing the logoff check box produces a quick synchronization at logoff.

4. Select the Ask Me before Synchronizing the Items check box if you want Synchronization Manager to confirm synchronization before performing it.

Repeat the procedure for other network connections as applicable.

Configuring Synchronization Settings for when Your Computer Is Idle   The On Idle tab (shown on the left in Figure 18-7) of the Synchronization Settings dialog box lets you specify synchronization settings for individual network connections when your computer is idle. On-idle synchronization is a quick synchronization rather than a full synchronization. Follow these steps:

1. Select the connection in the When I Am Using This Network Connection drop-down list.

2. Select the check boxes for the appropriate offline files and offline Web pages in the Synchronize the Following Checked Items list box.

3. Select the Synchronize the Selected Items while My Computer Is Idle check box.

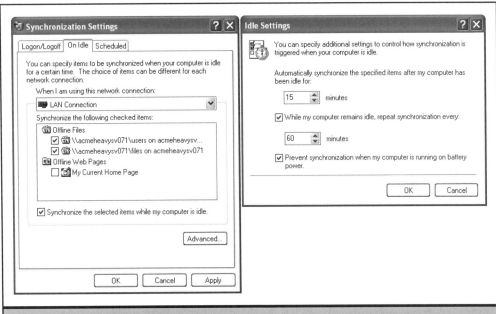

Figure 18-7.   *You can configure synchronization settings when your computer is idle by using the controls on the On Idle tab (left), and you can configure what idleness is and how the Synchronization Manager should respond to it using the Idle Settings dialog box (right).*

WORKING AND COMMUNICATING

4. To specify what constitutes idleness and how frequently Synchronization Manager repeats synchronization while the computer remains idle, click the Advanced button and work in the Idle Settings dialog box (shown on the right in Figure 18-7). This dialog box also lets you choose whether to prevent synchronization from occurring when the computer is running on battery power.

Repeat these steps for other network connections as necessary.

Setting Up Scheduled Synchronization   If you prefer to have synchronization occur at specific times, work on the Scheduled tab of the Synchronization Settings dialog box. Scheduled synchronization is a full synchronization rather than a quick synchronization. Follow these steps:

1. Click the Add button to run the Scheduled Synchronization Wizard.

2. Use the controls on the page of the wizard shown in Figure 18-8 to specify the items you want to synchronize using a given network connection. Choose whether to have Synchronization Manager establish a network connection for you if necessary for the synchronization.

3. Follow through the remaining pages of the wizard to specify the time, frequency, and start date for the synchronization, and to assign a name to the synchronization schedule.

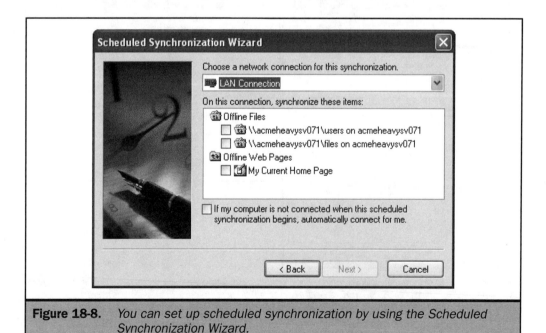

Figure 18-8.   *You can set up scheduled synchronization by using the Scheduled Synchronization Wizard.*

Repeat these steps to create synchronization schedules for other network connections as necessary.

From the Scheduled tab of the Synchronization Settings dialog box, you can also edit and delete existing synchronization schedules.

Synchronizing Offline Files Manually

You can synchronize your offline files manually at any time by choosing Tools | Synchronize from a Windows Explorer window and selecting the files, folders, or offline Web pages in the Items to Synchronize dialog box (Figure 18-9).

Typically, you'll want to synchronize all your offline files, and the Items to Synchronize dialog box automatically selects the check box for each item so that you can synchronize everything by accepting the default settings. However, if you have big folders, you may prefer to synchronize them manually on their own at a convenient time.

Note *Windows XP Professional automatically makes redirected folders available offline. As you'll remember from "Understanding Folder Redirection" in Chapter 7, an administrator can redirect your My Documents folder, Desktop folder, Application Data folder, My Pictures folder, and Start menu folder to network locations for ease of backup. If you have a roaming profile, all the folders in your user profile are redirected to the network.*

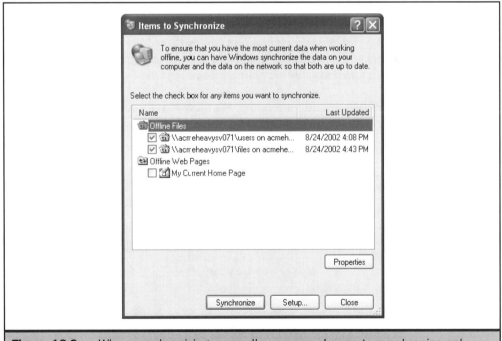

Figure 18-9. *When synchronizing manually, you can choose to synchronize only certain items in the Items to Synchronize dialog box.*

Resolving File Conflicts

When both the offline copy of the file and the version on the network share have changed, Synchronization Manager displays the Resolve File Conflicts dialog box so that you can choose which version of the file to use by selecting the Keep Both Versions option button, the Keep Only the Version on My Computer option button, or the Keep Only the Network Version option button. Select the Do This for All Conflicts check box if you want Synchronization Manager to take the specified action for all the offline files affected.

> *When both your offline version of a file and the online version of a file have been updated, you'll often need to keep both versions so that you can check which of them to keep or merge changes in the different versions of the file. If the files are in a format such as Microsoft Word, you may be able to use a compare-documents feature (for example, Tools | Track Changes | Compare Documents in Microsoft Word) to identify and merge changes from two documents into a fully updated version. But in many applications, you'll need to perform the comparison and update manually.*

Removing Offline Folders

If you no longer need access to a file or folder you've made available offline, issue another Make Available Offline command to tell Windows XP Professional to stop making the file or folder available.

Note   *It's usually a good idea to synchronize offline files before making a file or folder unavailable offline so that you don't lose any changes that you've made to the offline versions. However, if you don't want to keep any changes you've made to the offline versions, you won't need to synchronize before removing them.*

When you issue this command for a folder, Windows XP Professional displays the Remove Offline Folders dialog box (shown next) so that you can specify whether you want to stop making the folder's subfolders available offline.

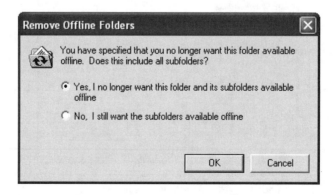

Reconnecting to Network Shares

When you're working offline because a network connection has been lost or the network resource has become unavailable, and the connection or resource becomes available again, Windows XP Professional checks the status of your offline files and the connection before automatically reestablishing the connection. Windows XP Professional doesn't automatically reestablish the connection if any of the following are true:

■ You have one or more offline files from that network share open on your computer.

■ One or more of your offline files from that network share contain changes that need synchronizing.

■ The network connection to the network share is a slow link (for example, a dial-up connection). The speed that Windows XP Professional considers a slow link is set by an administrator through Group Policy.

If any of these is true, Windows XP Professional keeps you working offline even though the network connection is available. Changes that you make to files located on the network share are saved to the offline copy of the file, which you'll then need to synchronize.

If none of the above considerations are true, Windows XP Professional automatically reestablishes the connection. If you open a file located on the network share, Windows XP Professional saves the changes both to the file itself and to the offline copy of the file.

Deleting Offline Files

You can delete files and folders from your Offline Files folder by opening your Offline Files folder and issuing Delete commands for the appropriate objects. Here's what happens:

■ When you delete files in a folder that you've pinned, the folder stays pinned. The next time you perform a full synchronization, Windows XP Professional caches all the files in the folder again.

■ When you delete a folder that you've pinned, or a file that you've pinned (as opposed to a file in a folder that you've pinned), you remove the pinning. To make the folder or file available offline again, you need to pin it again.

To delete your offline folders from your computer without affecting the originals of the files on the network, click the Delete button on the Offline Files tab of the Folder Options dialog box. Windows XP Professional displays the Confirm File Delete dialog box (Figure 18-10). To delete offline files that have been automatically cached (as opposed to files that you've pinned), choose the Delete Only the Temporary Offline Versions option button. To delete both offline files that have been automatically cached and files that you've pinned, select the Delete Both the Temporary Offline Versions and the Versions That Are Always Available Offline option button. Then click the OK button. Windows

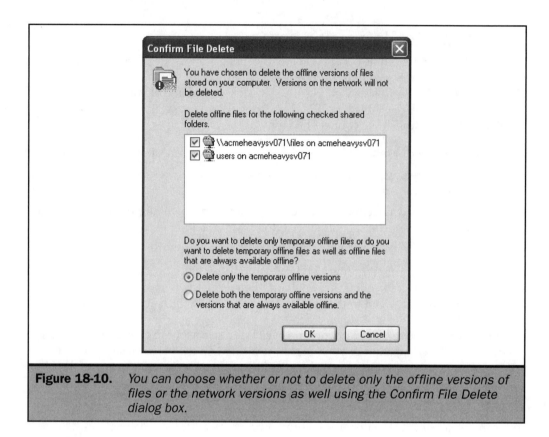

Figure 18-10.   *You can choose whether or not to delete only the offline versions of files or the network versions as well using the Confirm File Delete dialog box.*

XP Professional deletes the files and then displays a message box telling you how many files it has deleted and how much space they occupied.

Note   *In a domain environment, an administrator can specify that Windows XP Professional delete your offline copies of files when you log off. Windows XP Professional doesn't synchronize the files before deleting them, so you lose any changes that you've made to your local files. If you know that your administrator has chosen this setting, force synchronization before logging off from Windows XP Professional if you have offline changes that you don't want to lose.*

Using the Briefcase

If you can't use the Offline Files feature for whatever reason, try using Windows XP Professional's Briefcase feature instead. Briefcase is much less powerful than Offline Files, but it provides part of Offline Files's functionality with some extra flexibility. You can create one or more Briefcases, copy files to them, work with the copies away from the originals, and then update the originals with the copies (or vice versa, as appropriate) when you return to your desktop or network.

Note *Briefcase is included in both Windows XP Professional and Windows XP Home Edition, whereas Offline Files is included only in Windows XP Professional. Briefcase is installed in default configurations of Windows XP Professional and Windows XP Home Edition.*

Here's what you need to know to use Briefcase effectively:

- To create a Briefcase, issue a New | Briefcase command from the desktop's shortcut menu or from the File menu or the shortcut menu in a Windows Explorer window. Rename the Briefcase from its default name (New Briefcase) by using standard renaming techniques.

- To add files to the Briefcase, copy them there. Windows XP Professional displays the Updating Briefcase dialog box instead of the Copying dialog box when copying files to the Briefcase. The easiest way to copy files to a Briefcase you use often is to put a shortcut to the Briefcase on your Send To menu. (See "Customizing the Send To Menu" in Chapter 7 for instructions.)

- You can work with the files in the Briefcase by using standard Windows techniques. For example, to work with a Microsoft Excel workbook that's in the Briefcase, open it from Excel.

- The files in the Briefcase are sometimes called *child* files. The *parent* files are the files in their original locations (for example, on your computer or on the network). New files you create in the Briefcase are called *orphans*, because they don't have parent files.

Note *A file can become an orphan if you delete, move, or rename its parent. When this happens, you can either restore the parent to its previous place or name in order to update it or copy the orphan file to the parent's former location manually.*

- When you update the Briefcase, Windows XP doesn't copy orphan files, because they don't have parents that need to be updated. You need to copy orphan files from the Briefcase manually.

- When you delete a file from the Briefcase, Windows XP Professional puts it in the Recycle Bin as usual if it's stored on a local drive and deletes it if it's stored elsewhere. When you update the contents of the Briefcase, Windows XP Professional deletes the original copies of files deleted from the Briefcase.

- To update the files in the Briefcase, reconnect the computer containing the Briefcase to, or load the removable disk containing the Briefcase on, the computer or network that contains the original files. Then open the Briefcase in a Windows Explorer window and issue the Update All command from the Briefcase menu or click the Update All Items link in the Briefcase Tasks list. (You can also update only certain items by selecting them and choosing Briefcase | Update Selection.)

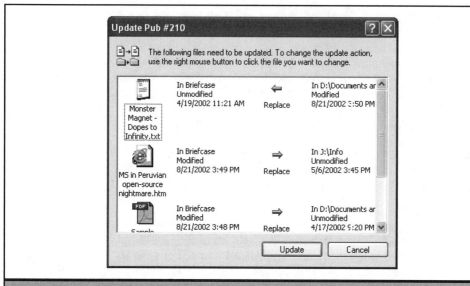

Figure 18-11.   *Check the details of the Briefcase files to be updated in the Update dialog box.*

In the Update dialog box (Figure 18-11), check the details of the files that will be affected by the Update operation, and choose a different action from the shortcut menu for a file if necessary. Then click the Update button to perform the Update operation.

■   To prevent a file in the Briefcase from being updated, split it from its original by issuing the Split from Original command from the Briefcase menu.

Using Compression

Laptop hard drives have finally grown to a decent capacity (as of this writing, 60GB laptop drives are available), but if you have an older laptop, it may have a hard drive small enough to keep you permanently short of space. Worse, because laptop hard drives are more expensive than desktop hard drives, it's often not worth replacing them, especially if doing so requires a technician's services. (Some laptops can accept a second hard drive—usually at the expense of a battery or a CD or floppy drive—but most cannot.)

To make the most of limited space on a laptop hard drive, use NTFS compression as discussed in "Using NTFS Compression" in Chapter 8. If you need to encrypt some of the files on your laptop, bear in mind that you can't use compression and encryption on the same files. Separate your files into folders (or, better, drives) that can be compressed and folders or drives that can be encrypted.

Using Encrypting File System

If you use Windows XP Professional on a laptop, you'll almost certainly want to protect some of your files against being read by anyone who steals the laptop or happens upon it out of your possession. To protect your files, encrypt them using Encrypting File System (EFS), as discussed in Chapter 19.

As mentioned in the previous section, you can't use both compression and encryption on the same files. If you need to use compression to pack all the files you require onto your laptop, segregate in a separate folder the files that must be encrypted.

Using Hardware Profiles

Because of its portability, you're more likely to use a laptop in different locations than you are a desktop computer.

If you use a laptop with different hardware configurations (for example, docked and undocked) or with different networks, use hardware profiles to simplify the process of switching from one hardware configuration to another. See "Using Hardware Profiles for Different Configurations" in Chapter 10 for details on how to create and use hardware profiles.

Connecting to a Wireless Network

If you use a laptop in a corporate setting, you may well need to use a wireless network connection—if you're lucky, one that lets you roam about the office from access point to access point. See Chapter 28 for a discussion of how to connect to wireless networks and how to use roaming.

Summary

This chapter has discussed the key considerations for using Windows XP Professional on a laptop. It has discussed how to configure power management options for laptops, apply ClearType, and use DualView. You've also seen how to configure and use Offline Files (if your administrator lets you) and use the Briefcase feature (if they don't). The chapter has also briefly mentioned four features discussed in other chapters that you may well need to use on a laptop: compression, Encrypting File System, wireless networks, and hardware profiles.

The next part of the book covers security, backup, and disaster recovery. It starts by discussing how to protect your data by using security and encryption.

WORKING AND COMMUNICATING

The Complete Reference

Part III

Security, Backup, and Disaster Recovery

Chapter 19

Protecting Your Data with Encrypting File System

This chapter discusses how to use Encrypting File System (EFS) to encrypt the files and folders you want to protect. EFS is a key security component of Windows XP Professional and isn't included in Windows XP Home Edition, whose users are assumed not to need such tight security. For anyone whose files need tight security, EFS provides a compelling reason to use Windows XP Professional rather than Windows XP Home Edition on a standalone or workgroup computer. In a domain environment, users will necessarily be using Windows XP Professional rather than Windows XP Home Edition, and an administrator is likely to decide when it's essential to use EFS and when it's not.

EFS is a powerful technology that can provide strong protection for your files—protection so strong that you yourself will never be able to decrypt the files again if you lose your encryption key and don't have a recovery plan. So you need to approach EFS with caution rather than bull-headed enthusiasm. You can implement EFS in moments—but don't implement EFS on a whim without understanding how to recover data and without putting a recovery plan in place, because you could seriously regret doing so.

When to Use Encrypting File System

In a domain environment, it's likely that an administrator will decide whether you need to use EFS or not, based on need and corporate policy. (A corporation's data might be safer if all its computers used EFS—but not if using EFS meant losing access to files that a user had encrypted by mistake or through malice.) If you get to choose whether to use EFS, weigh its pros and cons carefully before making your decision.

Use EFS to prevent other people from reading your files once they've managed to access them. EFS represents a secondary (or tertiary, or subsequent) line of defense for your files rather than the primary line of defense.

Your primary line of defense should be to prevent other people from accessing your files at all. To this end, take basic security precautions such as the following:

- Use a firewall to prevent unauthorized access to your computer from the Internet or other networks you connect to.
- Lock your computer in your office (if possible).
- Protect your computer with a bootup password.
- If multiple people use your computer, use user accounts to segregate users in their own space and keep them out of your files.
- Format your volumes with NTFS rather than FAT32 (let alone FAT).
- Store your files in folders whose permissions are fully locked down or which you otherwise tightly control.

You need to implement primary lines of defense such as these because EFS doesn't prevent other people from accessing your files if they have permission to access the folder that contains the files. EFS just encrypts the files so that they're not readable without being decrypted. Decryption should be very difficult, but if anyone determined enough can gain access to your files, they may be able to crack the encryption given considerable time and effort.

 In a domain environment, an administrator will usually use Group Policy to enable or disable EFS. In a workgroup environment, you can disable and reenable EFS through the Registry. See "Disabling and Reenabling EFS Through the Registry" in Chapter 40 for details.

Understanding the Basics of EFS

This section discusses the basics of Encrypting File System: what EFS does, how it works, and what limitations it has.

EFS uses keys to encrypt and decrypt data. As discussed earlier in this book, your user account has a unique security identifier (SID). That SID has a public key linked to it. EFS derives a key from the SID's public key and uses the resulting key to encrypt data. This key is required to decrypt the encrypted data, so user accounts with other SIDs can't decrypt your encrypted data. However, you can designate a *recovery agent*— a user authorized to decrypt your encrypted data. You can also allow specific other users to decrypt an encrypted file of yours by adding them to the access control list (ACL) for the file. Likewise, others can allow you to decrypt files they've encrypted with EFS.

EFS encrypts and decrypts files on-the-fly as you work with them. For example, if you've encrypted a workbook, you can open it directly from Excel as if it weren't encrypted: Windows XP Professional decrypts the data in the encrypted file and passes it to Excel, which displays the data in the clear.

By contrast, an external encryption solution such as Pretty Good Privacy (PGP; www.pgp.com) requires you to manually encrypt files you want to protect and manually decrypt files so that you can work with them.

Limitations of EFS

EFS works only on volumes formatted with NTFS, not on volumes formatted with FAT or FAT32. On NTFS volumes, you can encrypt either individual files or entire folders.

You can't encrypt any files that have the System attribute set. You can't encrypt any files in Windows XP Professional's %systemroot% folder.

You can't apply both compression and encryption to a file. In order to encrypt a compressed file, Windows XP Professional decompresses it first. When you try to compress an encrypted file, Windows XP Professional warns you that it'll need to decrypt the file. You can cancel the compression operation at this point.

SECURITY, BACKUP, AND DISASTER RECOVERY

Encrypting and Decrypting Files and Folders

As mentioned in the previous section, you can encrypt either individual files or folders. For security, always encrypt folders rather than files. Encrypting folders ensures that temporary files created in the current folder by applications as work are also encrypted rather than being stored unencrypted. By encrypting folders before creating any files in them, you can ensure that all the files you create are always encrypted.

Tip	*Because some applications store temporary files in the Windows XP Professional temp folders rather than in the current folder, it's a good idea to encrypt these folders as well. If you're not sure where these folders are, check the values of the %tmp% and %temp% environment variables in the Environment Variables dialog box (press WINDOWS KEY–BREAK to display the System Properties dialog box; then click the Environment Variables button on the Advanced tab). You may also want to encrypt your print spool folder, because unencrypted files in it could allow an attacker to access your data directly. (Alternatively, you can turn off print spooling as discussed in "Configuring Spooling" in Chapter 12. But doing so can slow down printing to a degree intolerable unless your need for security is paramount.)*

Applying Encryption

To apply encryption to a file or (preferably) a folder, follow these steps:

1. Click the Advanced button on the General tab of its Properties dialog box to display the Advanced Attributes dialog box.

2. Select the Encrypt Contents to Secure Data check box.

3. Click the OK button to close the Advanced Attributes dialog box, and then close the Properties dialog box.

When you apply encryption to a folder that contains subfolders, Windows XP Professional displays the Confirm Attribute Changes dialog box to ask whether you want to apply the change to only the folder or to its subfolders and files as well. Choose the Apply Changes to This Folder Only option button or the Apply Changes to This Folder, Subfolders and Files option button as appropriate. You'll usually want to apply the changes to the subfolders and files as well.

Tip	*If you find yourself needing to keep unencrypted files or subfolders inside encrypted folders, consider rearranging your folder structure so that you have separate branches of folders for encrypted files and unencrypted files. Keeping encrypted and unencrypted files separate will help you avoid leaving files unencrypted that should be encrypted.*

The first time you choose to encrypt a file that's not in an encrypted folder, Windows XP Professional displays the Encryption Warning dialog box shown in Figure 19-1 warning you that the file can become decrypted when modified and suggesting that you encrypt the parent folder as well. Choose the Encrypt the File and the Parent

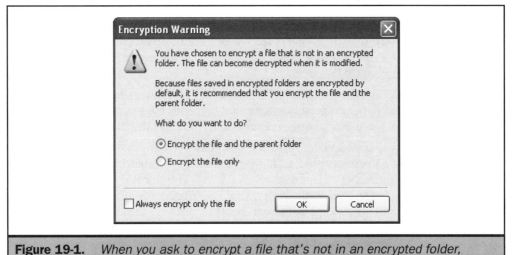

Figure 19-1.   *When you ask to encrypt a file that's not in an encrypted folder, Windows XP Professional displays the Encryption Warning dialog box offering to encrypt the parent folder as well.*

Folder option button or the Encrypt the File Only option button as appropriate. Whichever option you choose, you can select the Always Encrypt Only the File check box if you want to suppress this warning in future.

Removing Encryption

To remove encryption from a file or folder, clear the Encrypt Contents to Secure Data check box in the Advanced Attributes dialog box for the file or folder. When you issue this command for a folder, Windows XP Professional displays the Confirm Attribute Changes dialog box so that you can specify whether to apply the change only to the folder or to its subfolders and files as well.

Working with Encrypted Files and Folders

As mentioned earlier in this chapter, Windows XP Professional handles EFS encryption and decryption transparently. So you work with encrypted files in Windows Explorer or in applications just as you would work with unencrypted files. When you create a file in an encrypted folder, Windows XP Professional encrypts it; when you create a file in a folder that's not encrypted, Windows XP Professional doesn't encrypt it. When you back up encrypted files and folders to a backup application that supports EFS (for example, Windows XP's Backup Utility), the files and folders in the backup remain encrypted.

But there are a few subtleties to be aware of when you copy or move files:

■ If you copy or move an unencrypted file or folder into an encrypted folder, Windows XP Professional automatically encrypts the file or folder without displaying any notification.

■ If you copy or move an encrypted file or folder from an encrypted folder to a folder that's not encrypted but is located on a volume formatted with NTFS, Windows XP Professional preserves the encryption on the file or folder.

■ If you copy or move an encrypted file or folder from an encrypted folder to a folder that's not encrypted and is located on a volume formatted with a file system other than NTFS (for example, FAT32, FAT16, or FAT12), Windows XP Professional can't maintain the encryption. So Windows XP Professional displays the Encrypted File dialog box (shown next) so that you can choose whether to lose the encryption or cancel the copy operation or move operation.

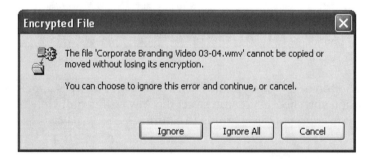

■ As mentioned earlier, you can't compress encrypted files and folders. If you try to compress an encrypted file or folder, Windows XP Professional warns you that it needs to decrypt the file or folder first.

 By default, encrypted files and folders appear in a different color in Windows Explorer windows. This display is controlled by the Show Encrypted or Compressed NTFS Files in Color check box on the View tab of the Folder Options dialog box. Encrypted files and folders are displayed in the default color in common Windows dialog boxes (for example, the common Open dialog box).

Sharing Encrypted Files and Folders with Others

Because files and folders you encrypt with EFS are encrypted using a key linked to your SID, other people can't use the files unless you specifically allow them to. Even then, each user whom you permit to use your encrypted files needs to have an EFS certificate.

The easiest way to create an EFS certificate is to encrypt a file or folder under your account. Doing so causes Windows XP Professional to create an EFS certificate automatically.

To allow another user to use a file that you've encrypted, follow these steps:

1. Display the Advanced Attributes dialog box for the file by clicking the Advanced button on the General tab of the Properties dialog box for the file.

2. Click the Details button to display the Encryption Details dialog box (Figure 19-2).

3. Click the Add button and use the Select User dialog box to specify the user or users to add to the Users Who Can Transparently Access This File list.

Using Others' Encrypted Files

To use files that another user has encrypted with EFS, supply that user with your EFS certificate and have them add you to their Users Who Can Transparently Access This File list for the appropriate file, as described in the previous section.

 You can use EFS on remote folders as long as the computer that contains them is in the same domain as your computer.

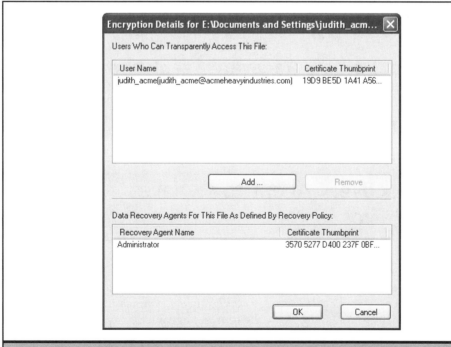

Figure 19-2. *Use the Encryption Details dialog box to specify other users who are allowed access to an encrypted file.*

SECURITY, BACKUP, AND DISASTER RECOVERY

Accessing Your Encrypted Files from Another Computer

You can access your encrypted files from a computer other than your regular computer if you install your EFS certificate on that computer. If you have a roaming user profile, your EFS certificate will be automatically available to any computer you're permitted to log on to. If not, install your EFS certificate on the computer manually.

Using the cipher Command

As you've seen, Windows XP Professional provides graphical tools for encrypting and decrypting files and folders. But it also provides a command-line tool: cipher. You need to use cipher for two encryption-related operations (which this section discusses). You can also use cipher for more extensive operations, although you're unlikely to need to do so unless you're administering computers that use EFS. This section doesn't discuss how to use cipher for those other operations, but you can view the help available for cipher by typing **cipher /?** at a command prompt.

Using cipher to Create a New Encryption Key

If you lose your encryption key and can't recover it, you'll need to create a new encryption key. This key won't let you decrypt data encrypted with your lost key, so you'll need to recover that data, as described in the next section. But the new key will let you encrypt new data.

To create a new encryption key, issue a **cipher /K** command.

Using cipher to Create a Recovery Agent Certificate

To create a recovery agent certificate, issue a **cipher /r:***path_and_filename* command, where *path_and_filename* is the path and base filename for the recovery agent certificates that cipher will create. cipher prompts you for a password and then creates one certificate file in the CER format and another in the PFX format.

Using a Recovery Agent to Recover Encrypted Files

Because EFS provides strong encryption, it's vital to be able to recover encrypted data if you lose your encryption key. Otherwise the files that you've so carefully protected will be carefully protected from you as well as everyone else.

If your computer is a member of a domain, you shouldn't need to worry about implementing a recovery policy. This is because Windows XP Professional automatically configures the domain administrator to be the recovery agent for computers that connect to the domain. In most cases, the domain administrator will designate other recovery agents so that all encrypted files will be easily recoverable.

If you use Windows XP Professional and EFS in a workgroup or a standalone situation, you need to set up a recovery agent in case you lose your encryption key.

 Here are two problems to be wary of. First, if you reinstall Windows XP Professional (for example, to recover from configuration problems), you'll need to import your EFS certificate before you can access your encrypted files. This is because each installation of Windows XP Professional creates a different SID for your account, and the EFS certificate for your new SID is different from the EFS certificate for your old SID. Second, if an administrator forces a password change on your computer, you won't be able to access your encrypted files without recovering them.

Setting Up a Recovery Agent

To set up a user account as a recovery agent, follow these steps:

1. Create a recovery agent certificate by using the **cipher /r** command (refer to "Using cipher to Create a New Encryption Key," earlier in the chapter). Copy the resulting files to removable media or a secure online folder and delete the original files from your computer.

2. Log off from your current user account and log back on using the user account that you want to make your recovery agent. You may well want to use the Administrator account.

3. Run the Certificates console and import the PFX file containing the recovery agent certificate to Certificates – Current User\Personal. Mark the key as exportable and select the Automatically Select the Certificate Store Based on the Type of Certificate option button.

4. Run **secpol.msc** to launch Local Security Settings. Expand the Security Settings\Public Key Policies item, select the Encrypting File System item, and issue the Add Data Recovery Agent command from the Action menu or the shortcut menu. Use the Browse Folders button on the Select Recovery Agents page of the Add Recovery Agent Wizard to open the CER file containing the recovery agent certificate.

Note   *Chapter 21 discusses how to use digital certificates.*

5. Run the Certificates console (still from the account you've just designated as your recovery agent), and export the recovery agent's certificate. Include the private key with the certificate, enable strong protection, and choose to delete the private key if the export is successful.

6. Store the recovery agent's certificate somewhere very safe away from your computer. If you lose the recovery agent's certificate as well as your certificate, you won't be able to decrypt your encrypted files.

SECURITY, BACKUP, AND DISASTER RECOVERY

You may be wondering why step 5 in the preceding list tells you to remove the recovery agent's certificate. That's because adding the certificate in step 4 is enough to make Windows XP Professional include the recovery agent's public key in any files you encrypt from now on. Once Windows XP Professional knows it should include the recovery agent's key, having the recovery agent's key on your computer is a security threat, because an attacker might be able to use the key to decrypt your encrypted files against your will.

Recovering Encrypted Files with Your Recovery Agent

If the worst comes to the worst, and you lose your encryption key, you'll need to use your recovery agent to recover your encrypted files. To do so, log on to the account you designated as your recovery agent and import the recovery agent certificate. You'll then be able to decrypt the encrypted files.

If you yourself have set up your encrypted files and your recovery agent, you probably won't have any problem determining which files to recover. If you've set up separate folder structures for your encrypted files and your unencrypted files, you can simply decrypt all the encrypted files.

If you don't know which files you need to recover, install the efsinfo.exe tool from the Support\Tools\Support.cab cabinet file on your Windows XP Professional CD. You can install this tool to a folder of your choice by selecting it and issuing an Extract command from the File menu or the shortcut menu. (Alternatively, you can install it with other support tools by running the SupTools.msi installer from the Support\Tools folder on the CD.)

Open a command-prompt window to the folder that contains the files you're interested in and run efsinfo.exe from the folder in which you installed it.

You can issue a plain **efsinfo** command (without any switches) to list the encryption state (Not Encrypted or Encrypted) for the files and folders in the current folder and the list of users who can decrypt the encrypted ones. Issue an **efsinfo /r /u** command to list the recovery agents as well. Issue an **efsinfo /r** command to list the recovery agents without the users. (For other switches, issue an **efsinfo /?** command.)

▌ Summary

This chapter has discussed how to use Encrypting File System to encrypt files and folders you want to protect on your computer. This chapter has shown you how EFS works and what its limitations are. You've learned how to encrypt and decrypt files and folders, how to work with encrypted files and folders, and how to share encrypted files and folders with other users. You've also learned how to implement a recovery policy to make sure that you don't get on the wrong end of the security that EFS provides.

The next chapter discusses how to work with local policies on your computer— should your domain administrator allow you to do so.

The
Complete
Reference

Windows XP

Chapter 20

Understanding Group Policy and Local Policies

This chapter discusses Group Policy and local policies and how they apply to your computer. The chapter starts by covering what Group Policy is, who sets it, and the effects you'll see at the user end. It then explains what local policies are, when they're used, and under what circumstances you can configure them yourself. Last, the chapter shows you how to see which policies are applied to a particular computer or user.

If you're using Windows XP Professional on a laptop in a domain environment, you may be able to work with local policies when you're not connected to the domain. If you're using Windows XP Professional on a desktop computer in a domain environment, and you have no administrative privileges, you're unlikely to be able to work much—if at all—with policies. However, you may benefit from understanding a little about how Group Policy works and what can be done with it.

Understanding Group Policy

Group Policy is a tool that can greatly simplify the administration of Windows XP Professional and Windows 2000 Professional computers in a domain environment. Group Policy works closely with Active Directory—the directory service used in Windows 2000 Server and Windows.NET Server domain-based networks—to implement settings (referred to as *policies*) on a group of computers. (Group Policy works only in a Windows 2000 Server or Windows.NET Server domain.)

To work with Group Policy, an administrator launches the Group Policy editor for the Windows 2000 Server or Windows.NET Server computer from the Active Directory Users and Computers applet or the Active Directory Sites and Services applet. Using the Group Policy Editor, the administrator can create *group policy objects* (GPOs) that contain groups of policies. The administrator can apply these GPOs to sites, domains, or organizational units. (An organizational unit [OU] is a subdivision of a domain.)

The Four Levels of Policy

Group Policy can be applied at three levels of Active Directory:

- At site level, Group Policy affects every computer that's part of each domain in the site.

- At domain level, Group Policy affects every computer in the domain.

- At OU level, Group Policy affects every computer in the OU. An OU can be nested inside another OU, so multiple OU levels of policy may apply to your computer.

Below Group Policy are local policies, discussed in the next section, forming a fourth level of policy.

The order in which the policy settings are applied to your computer are as follows:

- Local policy
- Group Policy at site level

■ Group Policy at domain level

■ Group Policy at OU level

■ Group Policy at a nested OU level (if there is one)

Figure 20-1 illustrates the layers of policy in the order in which they're applied to your computer.

For example, Group Policy includes a policy called Disable Internet Connection Wizard. This policy can be Not Configured, Enabled, or Disabled. When the policy is enabled, Windows XP prevents you from running the Internet Connection Wizard. An administrator might enable this policy at the site level to have the site's default configuration prevent users from running the Internet Connection Wizard. The administrator could then enable the policy for a particular OU whose users needed to be able to run the wizard (for example, for users who take laptops on the road and who

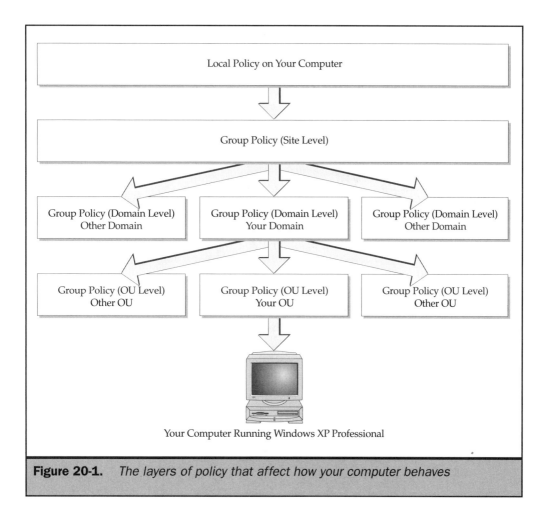

Figure 20-1.   *The layers of policy that affect how your computer behaves*

might need to set up an alternative Internet connection). The OU policy would override the site policy because the OU policy is applied after the site policy. (The site policy would already have overridden the local policy.)

Normally, the policy applied to a domain computer is inherited from the GPOs in the manner described in the previous paragraph. However, an administrator can block policy inheritance so that a computer doesn't inherit policies from one of the Group Policy levels.

Given that Group Policy is filtered through these different layers, and that inheritance may have been blocked, it can be hard to tell from viewing GPOs which settings apply to a particular user or computer. You might need to trace a setting back through each layer of policy to determine what setting it had. Windows XP includes an MMC snap-in called Resultant Set of Policy that automatically works out the net effect of GPOs on a particular user or computer. You can also use the Resultant Set of Policy snap-in on your local computer in a workgroup or standalone environment to see how the computer policies you've configured apply to a particular user. See "Checking Which Policies Apply to a User," later in this chapter, for instructions on using the Resultant Set of Policy snap-in and similar tools.

When Group Policy Is Applied

Group policy settings are applied during bootup and logon, at update intervals set by an administrator, or when an administrator or a user manually forces an update. (To force an update, issue a **gpupdate** command at a command prompt.)

Examples of Group Policy

An administrator can use Group Policy to automatically configure Windows XP Professional computers in a domain environment. Here are some examples of Group Policy:

- As you saw in Chapter 3, an administrator can use Remote Installation Services (RIS) to automate the installation of Windows XP Professional, and they can use IntelliMirror to publish, assign, and remove applications on top of Windows XP Professional.

- As you saw in Chapter 7, an administrator can redirect the My Documents, My Pictures, Application Data, Desktop, and Start Menu folders to network locations so that your documents and configuration information are automatically saved in a central location rather than on the local computer.

- An administrator can use Group Policy to control what appears on your desktop and whether you can change it.

- An administrator can use Group Policy to impose restrictions on the actions that you can take on a Windows XP Professional computer in a domain environment.

Preventing users from configuring their computers as they might like to is sometimes referred to as *change control*.

Using Local Policies

Local policies are essentially group policies defined on the computer itself. As you saw earlier in the chapter, local policies apply in a domain environment but are subordinate to the three layers of group policies: any setting applied through a local policy can be overturned by a corresponding policy at the site level, the domain level, or the OU level. On a standalone or workgroup computer, however, there are no GPOs, so the local policies directly control the computer and user environments.

Local policies are much less extensive than Group Policy. For example, you can't install Windows XP Professional through local policies—not that you should need to, given that your computer is running Windows XP Professional already. Nor can you install applications via local policies—a capability that would be much more useful than installing the OS itself.

That said, local policies provide an effective way to configure Windows XP Professional for multiple users on the same computer, apply desktop settings, and configure the helper applications that typically come with Windows XP (for example, Internet Explorer and Outlook Express). If you administer your computer, and multiple people use the computer, you may want to use local policies to outline the changes that users are and aren't allowed to make to the computer.

Local policies are broken down into two branches:

- **Computer Configuration branch**   Contains computer-related policies. These policies are applied near the end of the Windows XP bootup process, before any user logs on.

- **User Configuration branch**   Contains user-related settings. These settings are applied at logon for all users.

There's considerable overlap between the Computer Configuration branch and the User Configuration branch. For example, both Computer Configuration and User Configuration contain policies for Windows Messenger. Each contains a policy called Do Not Allow Windows Messenger to Be Run. When this policy is enabled (in other words, switched on), the user can't run Messenger. You can set the policy under either Computer Configuration or User Configuration. If you set the policy under both, with different settings, the Computer Configuration setting takes precedence over the User Configuration setting.

The settings that you can apply with local policies overlap to a large extent with Registry settings that you can change. But local policies have several advantages over the Registry: The interface is easier to use; you can't make mistakes as easily; and if you do make mistakes, the results are likely to be much less painful than mistakes involving the Registry might be.

Running the Group Policy Console

To work with local policies, you run the Group Policy console on your local computer. To launch the Group Policy console, choose Start | Run, enter **gpedit.msc** in the Run dialog box, and then click the OK button. Windows XP opens the Local Computer Policy object in the Group Policy console.

> **Note** *See Chapter 42 for a discussion of the Microsoft Management Console and how to work with it.*

Alternatively, you can add the Group Policy snap-in to another console. To do so, follow the procedure described in "Creating Custom Consoles" in Chapter 42. Open the console in author mode, and then use the Add/Remove Standalone Snap-in dialog box to add the Group Policy snap-in. In the Select Group Policy Object dialog box, specify Local Computer to work with Group Policy on your computer.

You can also work with Group Policy on another computer in either of two ways:

- Add the Group Policy snap-in to a console. In the Select Group Policy Object dialog box, click the Browse button and use the resulting Browse for a Group Policy Object dialog box and Select Computer dialog box to specify the remote computer. You'll need to provide suitable credentials for connecting to that computer. By adding the Group Policy snap-in multiple times, you can add an entry to the console for each remote computer you want to manage from the console.

- Issue a **gpedit.msc /gpcomputer:"***computername***"** command, where *computername* is the computer's name. Enclose the name in double quotation marks. This command opens a Group Policy console for the remote computer. You can't add further computers to the console.

Using the Group Policy Console

Figure 20-2 shows the Local Computer Policy object open in the Group Policy console. As you can see, both the Computer Configuration branch and the User Configuration branch contain a Software Settings folder, a Windows Settings folder, and an Administrative Templates folder.

To configure a policy, expand a branch until you reach the object that contains the policy. Then double-click the policy in the right pane to display a dialog box that contains the available choices for the policy.

The size and shape of this dialog box and (more importantly) its contents depend on which settings the policy offers and whether Windows XP provides an explanation

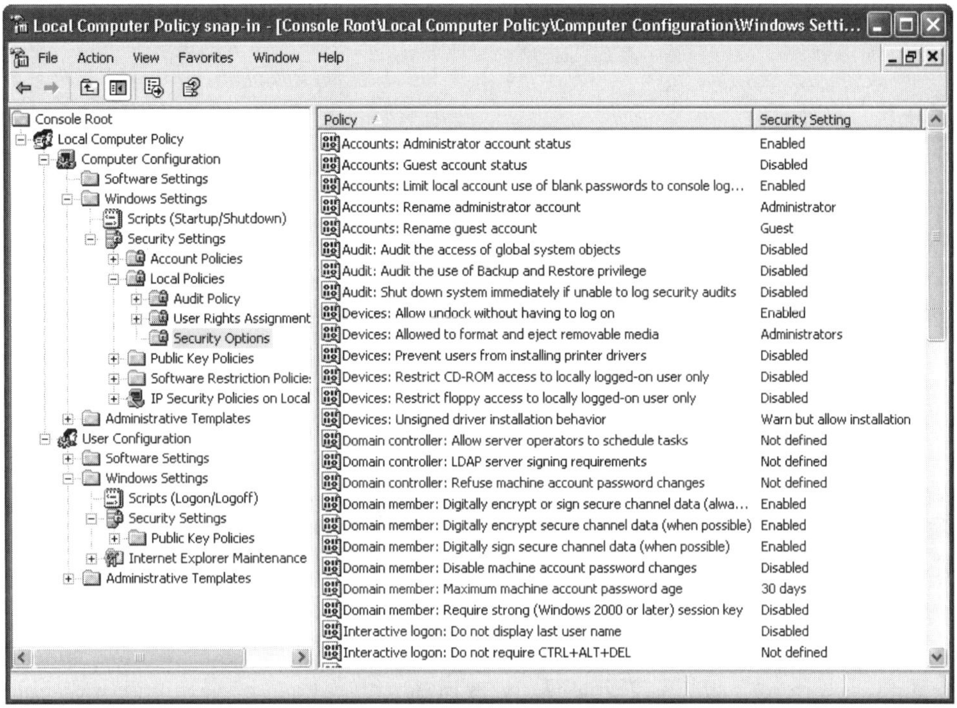

Figure 20-2.   *Use the Local Computer Policy object in the Group Policy console to configure policies on your local computer.*

for it. Many policies offer a choice of Not Configured, Enabled, or Disabled. When you select the Enabled option, Windows XP makes available any relevant options. The left screen in Figure 20-3 shows the Setting tab of the Prevent Access to Drives from My Computer Properties dialog box. When you select the Enabled option button, the dialog box makes available the Pick One of the Following Combinations drop-down list so that you can specify which drives to prevent the users from accessing directly. The right screen in Figure 20-3 shows the Explain tab of this Properties dialog box, which provides a text explanation of the policy.

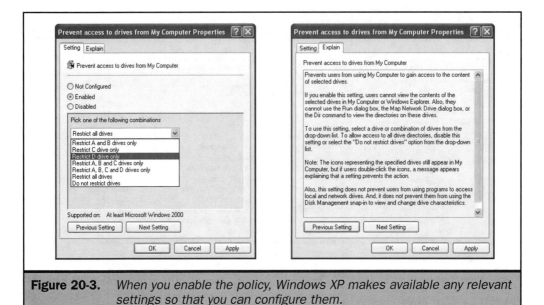

Figure 20-3.   *When you enable the policy, Windows XP makes available any relevant settings so that you can configure them.*

Other policies offer only Enabled and Disabled settings. For example, the Devices: Prevent Users from Installing Printer Drivers policy must be either enabled or disabled. The Properties dialog box for this policy is shown here:

Most of the Properties dialog boxes for the policies include a Previous Setting button and a Next Setting button that let you move easily to the next policy in the current folder without having to close and reopen the Properties dialog box.

Disabling Unused Parts of the Local Computer Policy Object

If you're not using the Computer Configuration settings or the User Configuration settings (or both), you can disable them. Disabling the settings means that Windows XP doesn't have to spend time applying them at bootup or logon. You can also disable the settings you're currently using if you want to stop using local policies for a while (for example, for troubleshooting odd phenomena that you suspect are the results of local policies).

To see which of the settings you're using, select the Local Computer Policy object and issue a Properties command from the File menu or the shortcut menu. Windows XP displays the Local Computer Policy Properties dialog box (Figure 20-4). Check the

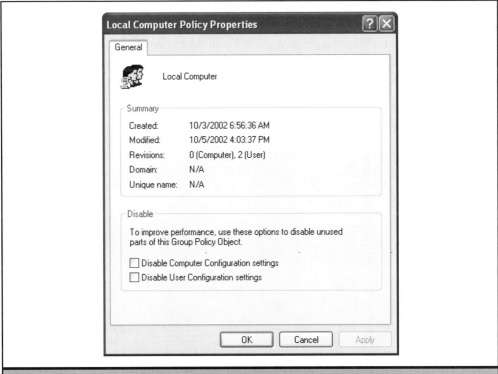

Figure 20-4. *In the Local Computer Policy Properties dialog box, you can check how many Computer Configuration policies and User Configuration policies you're using as well as disable either or both.*

SECURITY, BACKUP, AND DISASTER RECOVERY

Revisions readout in the Summary group box to see how many Computer Configuration policies and User Configuration policies you're currently using.

To disable one or both branches, select the Disable Computer Configuration Settings check box or the Disable User Configuration check box as appropriate.

Adding and Removing Administrative Templates

As you saw in the previous section, both the Computer Configuration branch and the User Configuration branch contain an Administrative Templates folder that contains templates of policies. You can change the collection of administrative templates by adding extra templates or removing the existing ones. For example, you might want to add another administrative template provided by Microsoft or a third party. (Administrators who need to apply large numbers of custom configuration settings—for example, to applications developed within their corporations—can even create their own administrative templates if necessary.)

Windows XP Professional comes with the six administrative templates listed in Table 20-1. Group Policy automatically loads four of these templates; the other two are for use with Internet Explorer Administration Kit (IEAK) rather than with Group Policy.

Filename	Location under Administrative Templates	Loaded by Default	Explanation
conf.adm	\Windows Components\ NetMeeting	Yes	Policies for the NetMeeting conferencing client.
inetres.adm	\Windows Components\ Internet Explorer	Yes	Policies for controlling Internet Explorer.
inetcorp.adm	N/A	No	Policies for controlling Internet Explorer through IEAK. Not used with Group Policy.

Table 20-1. *Windows XP Professional's Administrative Templates*

Filename	Location under Administrative Templates	Loaded by Default	Explanation
inetset.adm	N/A	No	Policies for controlling Internet Explorer through IEAK. Not used with Group Policy.
system.adm	Various locations	Yes	Almost all the policies that appear in the Local Computer Policy object that aren't contained by the other templates. (The exceptions are script policies, some security policies, and some Internet Explorer Maintenance policies.)
wmplayer.adm	\Windows Media Player	Yes	Policies for Windows Media Player. These appear only under User Configuration.

Table 20-1. *Windows XP Professional's Administrative Templates* (continued)

Each template's settings appear under both the Computer Configuration branch and the User Configuration branch unless otherwise noted.

Note *The administrative templates apply to both Administrative Templates folders—you can't load a different selection of templates in each folder.*

To change the collection of templates, follow these steps:

1. Select either Administrative Templates folder and issue an Add/Remove Templates command from the Action menu or the shortcut menu to display

the Add/Remove Templates dialog box (shown next). The dialog box displays the templates currently loaded in your Administrative Templates folders.

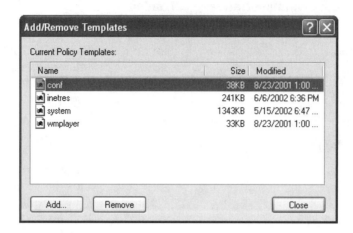

2. To remove an existing template, select it and click the Remove button.

3. To add another template, click the Add button and use the resulting Policy Templates dialog box to navigate to and select the template.

4. When you've made your selection of administrative templates, click the Close button to close the Add/Remove Templates dialog box.

Windows XP stores the files for administrative templates in the %systemroot%\inf folder. When you add an administrative template, Windows XP copies it from the inf folder to the %systemroot%\system32\GroupPolicy\Adm folder. When you remove the template, Windows XP deletes the copy in the Adm folder.

Filtering the Policies Displayed

To make it easier to find the policies you need, you can filter the policies displayed in the Group Policy console. Filtering works separately for the Computer Configuration\ Administrative Templates folder and the User Configuration\Administrative Templates folder. Follow these steps:

1. Select the Administrative Templates folder you want to affect.

2. Choose View | Filtering from the menu bar or the shortcut menu to display the Filtering dialog box (Figure 20-5).

3. To reduce the display to show only the policies that have been configured, select the Only Show Configured Policy Settings check box.

4. To reduce the display to show only the policy settings that can be managed from the Local Computer Policy object, select the Only Show Policy Settings that Can Be Fully Managed check box.

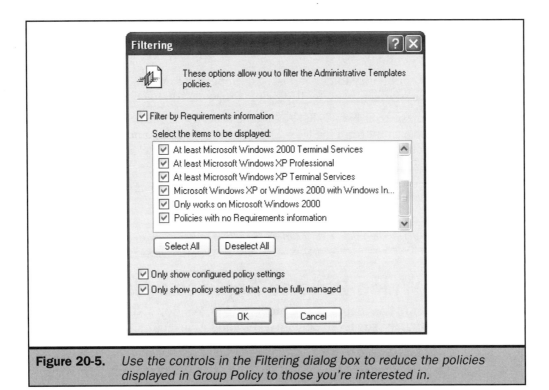

Figure 20-5.   *Use the controls in the Filtering dialog box to reduce the policies displayed in Group Policy to those you're interested in.*

5. If you're working on a remote computer that's running an older version of Windows, select the Filter by Requirements Information check box, and then use the check boxes in the Select the Items to Be Displayed list box to remove items that don't apply to the version of Windows running on that computer.

6. Click the OK button to close the Filtering dialog box and to apply your choices.

Exempting Some Users from User Configuration Policies

As discussed earlier in this chapter, the Computer Configuration policies are applied before any user logs on, and the User Configuration policies are applied at logon—for all users. But you can exempt certain users from the User Configuration policies by denying them the Read permission to the folder that contains the policy settings. To do so, configure your policies and then follow these steps:

1. If hidden files and folders are currently hidden, display them by selecting the Show Hidden Files and Folders option button on the View tab of the Folder Options dialog box (choose Tools | Folder Options from a Windows Explorer window).

2. Display the %systemroot%\system32 folder in a Windows Explorer window (for example, choose Start | Run, enter **%systemroot%\system32**, and then click the OK button).

3. Select the GroupPolicy folder and issue a Properties command from the File menu or the shortcut menu to display the Properties dialog box for the folder.

4. In the Group or User Names list box on the Security tab, select the group or user you want to exempt from the User Configuration policies, and then select the Deny check box in the Read row. Windows XP automatically clears any conflicting check boxes in the Allow column.

5. Click the OK button to close the Properties dialog box and apply your changes.

 If you chose to exempt the Administrators group, you'll need to restore this group's Full Control permission before they can work further with Group Policy.

Checking Which Policies Apply to a User

As discussed earlier in this chapter, a computer running Windows XP Professional can have GPOs applied at the site level, domain level, and OU level (or OU levels)—all on top of the local policies. To avoid needing to trace each policy from the local policies through these layers of GPOs in order to determine what the effective setting for a policy is, Windows XP Professional provides several tools: the View Group Policy Settings Applied tool in Help and Support Center, the gpresult command, and the Resultant Set of Policy snap-in. The following subsections discuss each in turn.

Using the View Group Policy Settings Applied Tool

The easiest way to see which settings are applied to your computer is to use the View Group Policy Settings Applied tool. Follow these steps:

1. Choose Start | Help and Support to launch Help and Support Center.

2. Click the Tools link in the Pick a Task list to display the Tools page.

3. In the Tools pane on the Tools page, click the Advanced System Information link to display the Advanced System Information page.

4. Click the View Group Policy Settings Applied link to display a summary of policy (Figure 20-6).

The bottom of the summary page includes links for saving the report to an HTML file (which you can then send to a support technician) and for running the Resultant Set of Policy tool.

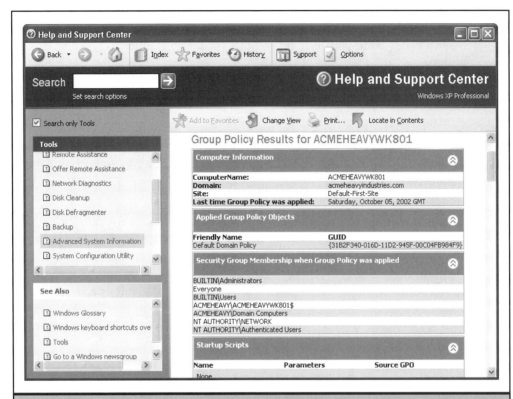

Figure 20-6.   *The Advanced System Information page in Help and Support Center provides a summary of the Group Policy settings applied to your computer.*

Using the gpresult Command

For a text-based readout of Resultant Set of Policy, issue a **gpresult** command at a command prompt. Either direct the result to a file or use the | more pipe (**gpresult | more**) to make the readout easier to view.

Using the Resultant Set of Policy Snap-in

The Resultant Set of Policy snap-in lets you check the policy settings applied to a particular computer or user by using an interface similar to that of the Group Policy console. In a domain environment, an administrator can also use Resultant Set of Policy to simulate the implementation of a policy. (In a workgroup or standalone configuration, you can't use this capability.)

To use the Resultant Set of Policy snap-in, follow these steps:

1. Open a blank MMC console (choose Start | Run, type **mmc**, and click the OK button).

2. Display the Add/Remove Snap-in dialog box by pressing CTRL-M or choosing File | Add/Remove Snap-in.

> **Note**   *You can also add the Resultant Set of Policy snap-in to an existing console.*

3. Click the Add button to display the Add Standalone Snap-in dialog box.

4. Select the Resultant Set of Policy snap-in and click the Add button. Windows XP launches the Resultant Set of Policy Wizard.

5. On the Mode Selection page, click the Next button. On a server, this page offers you the choice of Logging Mode or Planning Mode. On Windows XP Professional, only Logging Mode is available.

6. On the Computer Selection page, you'll usually want to leave the This Computer option button selected, as it is by default. However, if you have permissions to access another computer, you can select the Another Computer option button, click the Browse button, and use the resulting Select Computer dialog box to specify the computer.

7. The Computer Selection page also contains a check box that lets you restrict the Resultant Set of Policy Wizard to displaying only user policy settings rather than policy settings for the computer. Select this check box if appropriate.

8. On the User Selection page (Figure 20-7), choose whether to display policy settings for the current user (for example, yourself), display policy settings for another user (as shown in the figure), or display only computer settings (in other words, exclude user policy settings).

9. On the Summary of Selections page, verify your choices, and then click the Next button. The wizard checks the policies that apply to the user or computer and displays its final screen.

10. Click the Finish button to close the wizard. Windows XP returns you to the Add Standalone Snap-in dialog box.

11. Click the Close button to close the Add Standalone Snap-in dialog box.

12. Click the OK button to close the Add/Remove Snap-in dialog box. Windows XP returns you to the console, which displays a branch for the resultant set of policy that you created. The following illustration shows an example that includes both the Computer Configuration and User Configuration settings. Navigate to the policy you're interested in and check its setting.

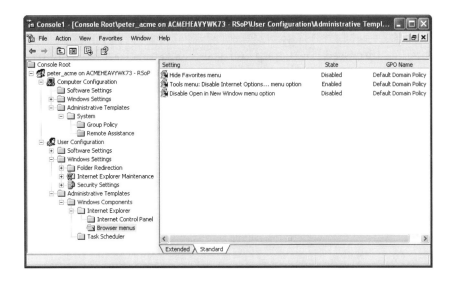

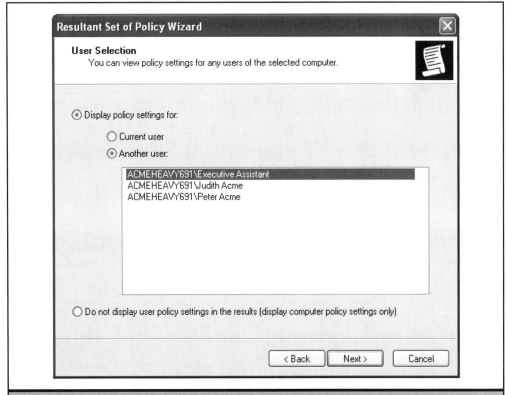

Figure 20-7. *On the User Selection page of the Resultant Set of Policy Wizard, choose which user to display the policy settings for.*

Summary

This chapter has discussed how Group Policy and local policies affect Windows XP Professional computers, how you can use local policies to configure a workgroup or standalone computer, and how to see which policies are applied to a particular computer or user.

The next chapter discusses what digital certificates are and how to use them to ensure the security of digital content.

Chapter 21

Understanding and Using Digital Certificates

This chapter discusses what you need to know about digital certificates to use them effectively with Windows XP Professional. It covers what digital certificates are, what you may want to use them for, and how to do so. The chapter talks about the types of digital certificates available, what they're for, and where to get them. This chapter also shows you the tools Windows XP Professional provides for working with certificates.

What Certificates Are and What They're For

Digital certificates are a way of proving identity in electronic communications, where physical identity documents such as business cards, passports, or physical tokens, such as access cards for secure rooms, are of little use. A *digital certificate* is a collection of identity information that's encrypted and signed with the digital signature of the certification authority that issued it. A digital certificate can identify an individual, a group of people, or an organization.

You can use a digital certificate for various purposes, such as adding a digital signature to e-mail messages, encrypting messages and attachments so that only the specified recipient can read them, and making sure signed messages you receive haven't been tampered with. Companies use digital certificates to establish the provenance of software and communications.

Although a digital certificate is (in theory) more or less impossible to forge, it can be borrowed, stolen, or shared easily. Microsoft describes the benefit of digital certificates as follows: "You can use digital certificates to verify that another person has a right to use a given identity." Note the phrasing: You don't know the other person *is* who the certificate says they are, but you do know the person has the right to *use* that identity—that is, if they haven't stolen the digital certificate.

A digital certificate typically contains at least the holder's name and e-mail address, and it may often contain much more information, such as age, address, and citizenship. (This causes some problems, as discussed in the next section.) The digital certificate includes details of the type of encryption used and of the holder's cryptographic keys.

Digital certificates are issued by certification authorities (CAs). You may also hear the term "certificate authority," but "certification authority" is more widely used.

Understanding Anonymity, Pseudonymity, and Identity

At this writing, digital certificates don't provide pseudonymity. *Pseudonymity* lets you provide a credential to prove you satisfy a requirement without providing your full identity. For example, say you need to prove you're over 21 to get into a bar. If you show a driver's license so that the doorman can see the photo matches and the date of birth is far enough in the past to make you old enough, you've used the driver's license as a credential to get in. You've effectively remained pseudonymous, because your identity is still disguised. But if the bar scans your driver's license and stores the information, you've been fully identified—and you may feel your privacy has been violated.

Using a digital certificate tends to be like having your driver's license scanned, only worse. A typical digital certificate bundles together a number of separate items of information. But you may want to share only one of those items of information with someone. For example, you might want to prove your identity (by name) without revealing your e-mail address. But with current digital certificates, you can't prove your identity without, at the same time, divulging the other information the certificate contains.

There's a strong argument for developing digital certificates that contain lesser amounts of information, or digital certificates from which you can choose to expose only a specific subset of information for any given transaction. For example, to access a secure extranet site, you might need to prove you worked for your company or you had demonstrated a certain level of trustworthiness. With a more flexible digital certificate, you could prove this fact without providing your full identity, e-mail address, position, and so on. With current digital certificates, you would need multiple certificates, each containing only the relevant items of information. From this portfolio of certificates, you could then present the certificate that provided the minimum amount of information necessary for a purpose.

Understanding the Basics of Public-Key Cryptography

In *public-key cryptography*, each key holder—let's assume *you*—has a key pair that consists of a public key and a private key. These keys are used to encrypt and decrypt data securely. You share your public key with the whole wired world, either directly (by sending the key to the recipient) or indirectly, via a public key infrastructure (PKI) that lets people look up your public key (or that of any other person or organization). You keep the private key to yourself.

The public key is used to encrypt messages and documents coming to you, and to authenticate and decrypt messages coming from you. Anything encrypted with your public key can only by decrypted using your private key. You also use your private key to encrypt outgoing messages and documents. Those messages and documents can be decrypted only by using your public key.

For mathematical reasons, neither key in the key pair can be inferred from the other key, so it's safe to publish your public key worldwide: nobody will be able to derive your private key from it. Assuming you keep your private key safe, anyone sending you a message encrypted with your public key can be sure you're the only person who will be able to decrypt it. But because *anyone* can get your public key, they need to encrypt the message with their private key to prove to you that it comes from them. You then decrypt the message using their public key (followed by your private key), and you've authenticated each other and communicated securely.

Both parties involved in a transaction secured by digital certificates have to trust the issuer of the digital certificates to have authenticated the other party closely enough for the needs of the transaction. The degree of authentication varies depending on the transaction being carried out. Here are some examples:

- To read an e-mail from a friend, you might settle for a digital certificate that gives only a modest degree of certainty that the person the message came from is actually the person you think they are.

- Before installing potentially dangerous software on your computer, you might demand a digital certificate deliver a high degree of certainty that the company named had signed the software and the software hadn't subsequently been tampered with.

- Before supplying sensitive information to a government agency, you'd most likely insist the agency identify itself beyond any reasonable doubt.

Digital certificates can be used within closed systems—for example, within a sealed corporate, military, or government system—but they're more widely used for authentication on the Internet. For digital certificates to work, a PKI needs to be in place for accessing public keys. Certification authorities need to supply digital certificates to individuals and organizations they've satisfactorily authenticated. Those individuals and organizations can then trust each other because both trust the certification authorities—either the certification authority that has issued their own certificate or a different certification authority their certification authority trusts.

Types of Digital Certificates

Various kinds of digital certificates are available, including the following:

- Corporate certificates identify companies or entities within them.

- Software developer certificates prove that software components come from the individual or company specified and that they haven't been tampered with since that individual or company signed them with the certificate. For example, Microsoft uses digital signatures to verify the authenticity of drivers for Windows XP Professional.

- Secure Sockets Layer (SSL) server certificates are used to secure the connections between web servers and web browsers. An SSL server certificate certifies that an SSL server belongs to a particular company.

- Wireless server certificates ensure the communications between wireless clients and wireless servers are private and secure.

- Personal certificates enable individuals (for example, *you*) to apply digital signatures to e-mail messages (to prove they come from you, rather than having been forged by someone else), to encrypt e-mail messages so that they can't be read if intercepted in transit, and to verify your identity to a remote computer.

Getting a Digital Certificate

The process of getting a digital certificate varies depending on the type of certificate you decide you want and the company you get it from. This section outlines the general steps involved.

Where to Get a Digital Certificate

There are three ways of getting a digital certificate:

- *From the company you work for.* Your company may run its own CA (perhaps as part of its internal security group) for issuing digital certificates to its departments and employees. (Other companies issue their own certificates through a third-party—for example, an outsourced security provider.) Windows 2000 Server and Windows.NET Server provide features for running a certification authority. See "Getting a Certificate from a Corporate CA," later in this chapter, for a brief discussion of the process involved.

- *From a commercial certification authority.* These include VeriSign, Inc. (www.verisign.com), GlobalSign NV (www.globalsign.net), and Thawte Certification (www.thawte.com), a VeriSign subsidiary. See "Getting a Certificate from a Commercial CA," later in this chapter, for a brief discussion of the process involved.

- *By using an application that enables you to create a digital certificate yourself.* For example, some versions of Microsoft Office ship with a program named SELFCERT.EXE, which you can use to create a digital certificate bearing any name you choose. Such a certificate is next to useless for authenticating identity—if *you* can create a certificate without any verification, so can anyone else—but it can be useful for practicing importing, exporting, and deleting digital certificates.

Getting a Certificate from a Corporate CA

If your company runs its own CA, you can request a digital certificate from it as follows:

- For a CA that's integrated into Active Directory, select the certificate store in the Certificates console and issue an All Tasks | Request New Certificate command from the Action menu or the shortcut menu. Windows XP Professional launches the Certificate Request Wizard, which walks you through the process of requesting the certificate.

- For a CA that's not integrated into Active Directory, use a web browser to open http://*server*/certsrv (substitute the server's IP address or name for *server*). On the resulting web page, follow the instructions for requesting a certificate.

Getting a Certificate from a Commercial CA

The requirements for getting a certificate depend on the type of certificate you want and the stringency the CA applies to checking your identity. In most cases, you start by visiting the CA's web site and filling in an online application form. Typically, you'll need to verify your e-mail address early in the process.

 For the latest list of certification authorities that Microsoft favors, click the Get Digital ID button on the Security tab of the Options dialog box (Tools | Options) in Outlook Express. Outlook Express opens a browser window to the Microsoft Office Assistance Center's list of certification authorities.

For some certificates, you may need to supply paper documents or visit a representative of the CA in person. For other certificates, you can supply enough verification online, either via a big-name agency (TRW, Equifax, or Experian for a personal certificate, and Dun & Bradstreet Financial Services or something similar for a business) or by submitting verifiable information, such as the details of your passport, driver's license, or identity card (if your country uses them).

For most certificates, you'll need to pay using a means of payment that helps verify your identity (for example, a credit card or debit card).

Creating a New RSA Exchange Key

If the process of creating the digital certificate involves generating a new RSA exchange key, as well it might, you're likely to see the Creating a New RSA Exchange Key Wizard spring into action. First, you'll see the Creating a New RSA Exchange Key dialog box shown in Figure 21-1.

Here, you can change the security level by clicking the Set Security Level button and using the second Creating a New RSA Exchange Key dialog box, shown in Figure 21-2, to specify the level of security.

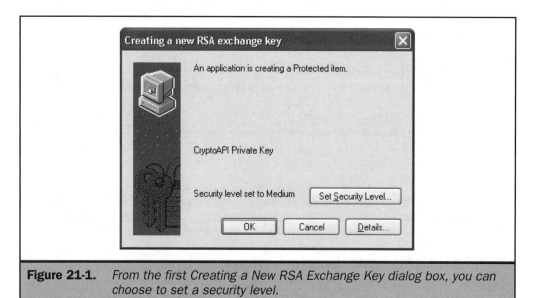

Figure 21-1.   *From the first Creating a New RSA Exchange Key dialog box, you can choose to set a security level.*

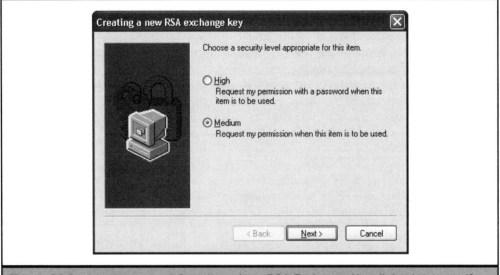

Figure 21-2. *In the second Creating a New RSA Exchange Key dialog box, specify the level of security you want.*

A *High* security level means you have to enter a password before Internet Explorer can supply the certificate when a site requests it. A *Medium* security level means Internet Explorer asks your permission before supplying the certificate, but you don't need to enter the password. A *Low* security level (not an option in the dialog box shown) means Internet Explorer supplies the certificate without consulting you when a site requests it.

If you chose the High security level, when you click the Next button, you see another screen of the Creating a New RSA Exchange Wizard, prompting you for the password. Enter it and click the Finish button.

 The certification process may offer to protect your private key. You probably don't want to accept this offer because it will prevent you from exporting your private key to archive it or to install it on another computer. In other words, you'll be able to use the digital certificate only on the computer on which you initially install it.

Keeping Your Digital Certificate Safe

If you didn't encrypt your private key, you should export a copy of the digital certificate to a floppy disk or other handy removable medium immediately and store it in a safe location off your premises. (See "Exporting a Digital Certificate," later in this chapter, for instructions.) If you don't have a secure deposit box at your bank, now might be the time to get one. You might also choose to further encrypt the file containing the digital certificate and store it in a secure online locker that you will be able to access easily, even if your computers are destroyed or stolen.

Managing Your Digital Certificates

Windows XP Professional stores your digital certificates in the Registry, from where applications that need them can use them. For example, Outlook, Outlook Express, and other e-mail applications use digital certificates both to sign outgoing messages and to encrypt and decrypt e-mail messages. Signing the messages verifies they come from you (or, rather, from someone with access to your digital certificate). Encryption prevents your outgoing messages from being read by someone who doesn't have the required private key and your incoming signed messages from being read by anyone who doesn't have your private key.

| Note | *Address Book includes a Digital IDs page (in the Properties dialog box for a contact) you can use to associate a digital certificate with an e-mail address for a contact. (Address Book and Outlook Express refer to digital certificates as digital IDs.)* |

Windows XP Professional provides two main tools for working with certificates: the Certificates console and the Certificates dialog box. The following subsections show you how to use these tools.

This section runs you through the maneuvers you're likely to perform with digital certificates: installing them, examining them, and removing them. You can take these actions from either the Certificates console or the Certificates dialog box.

Opening the Certificates Console

To open the Certificates console (Figure 21-3), run **certmgr.msc**. Alternatively, add the Certificates snap-in to a new MMC console or an existing MMC console opened in author mode. For example, you might choose to add the Certificates snap-in to Computer Management so that you could manage certificates along with almost everything else.

The Certificates console displays the certificates divided into the stores in which they're kept: Personal, Trusted Root Certificate Authorities, Enterprise Trust, Intermediate Certification Authorities, and so on. The stores appear in the left pane. Open a store to display its contents in the right pane.

Opening the Certificates Dialog Box

To open the Certificates dialog box, follow these steps:

1. Launch or activate Internet Explorer.

2. Choose Tools | Options to display the Internet Options dialog box.

3. On the Content tab, click the Certificates button to display the Certificates dialog box (Figure 21-4).

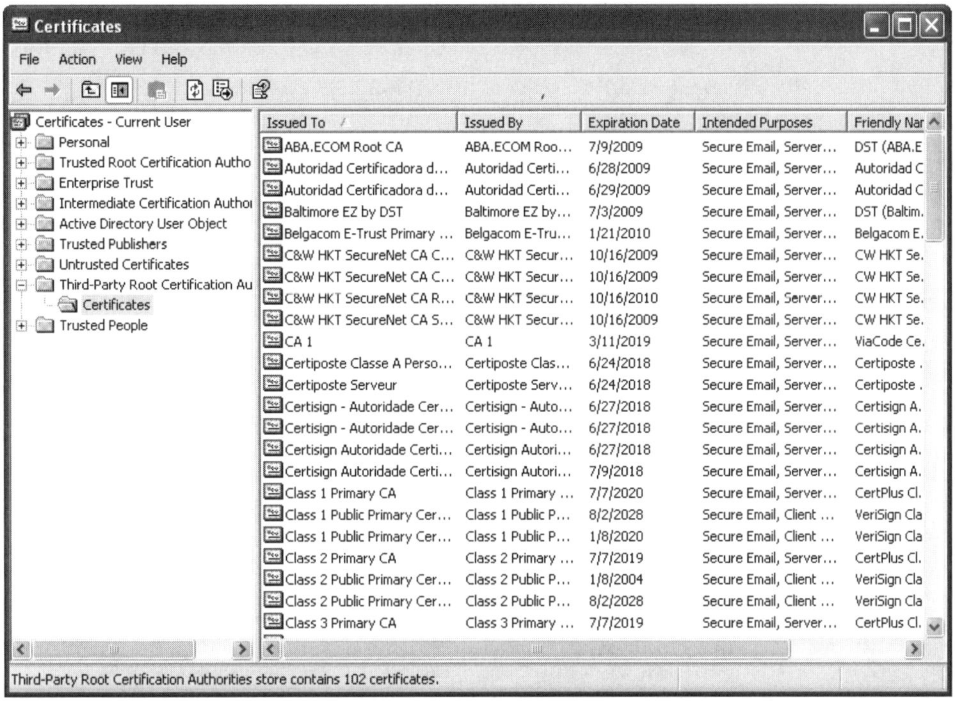

Figure 21-3. *You can access certificates by using the Certificates console or by adding the Certificates snap-in to another MMC console.*

The Certificates dialog box displays separate tabs for different categories of certificates.

Installing a Digital Certificate

When you apply for and download a digital certificate, some CAs automatically install it on your computer. Other times, you'll need to install your new digital certificate, or someone else's digital certificate, on your computer manually.

To install a certificate, follow these steps:

1. Launch the Certificate Import Wizard in one of the following ways:

   ■ In the Certificates dialog box, click the Import button.

   ■ In the Certificates console, select the store in which you want to place the certificate, and then issue an All Tasks | Import command from the Action menu or the shortcut menu.

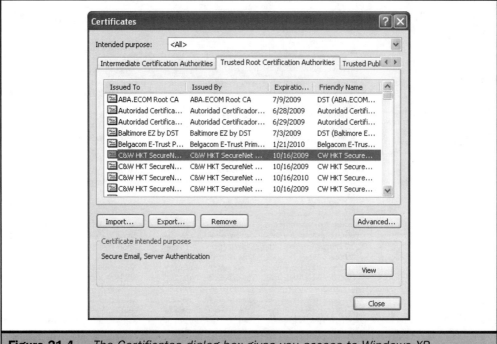

Figure 21-4.   *The Certificates dialog box gives you access to Windows XP Professional's features for managing digital certificates.*

- Double-click the certificate to open its Certificate dialog box, and then click the Install Certificate button on the General tab.

2. On the File to Import page, enter the filename of the certificate in the File Name text box, either by using the Browse button or by typing the path and filename manually. Note, the Files of Type drop-down list in the Open dialog box accessed from the Browse button defaults to X.509 Certificate (*.CER, *.CRT) and you'll have to change the setting if you want to import a type of certificate other than one of those types.

3. On the Certificate Store page (Figure 21-5), verify that Windows XP Professional has selected the right store for the certificate. If you started the Certificate Import Wizard from the Certificates console, the wizard suggests the store that was selected in the console. If you started the Certificate Import Wizard from the Certificates dialog box, Windows XP Professional selects the Automatically Select the Certificate Store Based on the Type of Certificate option button. If you leave this selected, Windows XP Professional assigns the certificate to the store that seems best suited for it. In most cases, Windows XP Professional makes the right choice, but in some cases, you may want to specify the certificate store manually. To do so, take the following steps:

Figure 21-5. *The Certificate Store page of the Certificate Import Wizard lets you specify manually which certificate store to place the certificate in or choose to let Windows XP Professional choose the store automatically.*

- Select the Place All Certificates in the Following Store option button. Windows XP Professional enables the Certificate Store text box and the Browse button.

- Click the Browse button to display the Select Certificate Store dialog box (shown in its two manifestations in Figure 21-6—with and without the physical stores displayed).

- To specify the store by category, select the store in the list box.

- To specify the physical store, select the Show Physical Stores check box. Windows XP Professional displays the physical stores (as in the version of the dialog box on the right). Expand the appropriate branch of the tree and select the subfolder. For most of the branches, your choice is Registry, Group Policy, or Local Computer.

- Click the OK button to close the Select Certificate Store dialog box and return to the Certificate Store page of the wizard.

4. On the Completing the Certificate Import Wizard page, double-click the summary of the choices you've made. If all is well, click the Finish button. The Certificate Import Wizard completes the import procedure and, if it's successful, displays a message box saying so.

Figure 21-6.   *In the Select Certificate Store dialog box, you can specify the category of store for the certificate or the physical store to use.*

Examining a Digital Certificate

One of the steps you're likely to take with many certificates is to examine them to see whether they're current and what they're supposed to be for.

For a brief list of a certificate's intended purposes, select the certificate in the list box in the Certificates dialog box or the right pane in the Certificates console, and then look at the purposes listed in the Certificate Intended Purposes group box.

For more detail, double-click the certificate. Windows XP Professional displays the Certificate dialog box, which contains details of the certificate on its three tabs: General, Details, and Certification Path.

General Tab Information

The General tab (Figure 21-7) contains information about the issuer of the certificate, the person or entity to which the certificate was issued, and the period for which the certificate is valid. If all is well with the certificate, the General tab also lists the purposes for which the certificate is intended—for example, "protects e-mail messages," "ensures the identity of a remote computer," or "protects software from alteration after publication." If there may be a problem with the certificate, the General tab gives a message such as "Windows does not have enough information to verify this certificate." If the Issuer Statement button on the General tab is available, you should be able to display information about the issuer of the digital certificate by clicking it.

Details Tab Information   The Details tab (Figure 21-8) contains details about the certificate: everything from its version, serial number, and algorithm to its public key and thumbprint. You can reduce the amount of information shown by making a

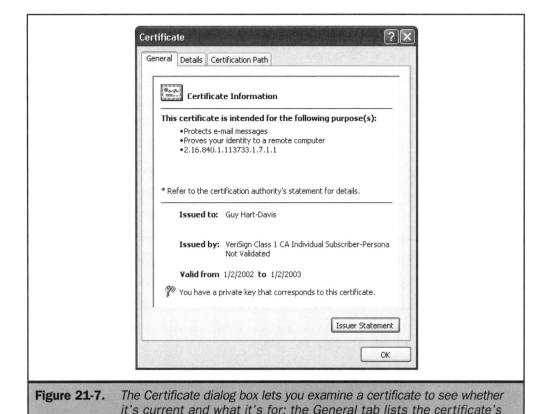

Figure 21-7. *The Certificate dialog box lets you examine a certificate to see whether it's current and what it's for; the General tab lists the certificate's purposes—or any problems with it—its issuer, and its validity period.*

selection—<All>, Version 1 Fields Only, Extensions Only, Critical Extensions Only, or Properties Only—from the Show drop-down list. To view the details of a field that won't fit in the Value column of the upper list box, select the field to make Windows XP Professional display it in the lower list box.

Certification Path Tab Information   The Certification Path tab (Figure 21-9) displays the hierarchy of certificates—from the certification authority ultimately responsible for this certificate to the holder of the certificate. You can view the certificate for one of the bodies higher in the hierarchy by selecting it and clicking the View Certificate button.

The Certificate Status box on the Certification Path tab displays the current status of the certificate—for example, "This certificate is OK" or "This certificate has expired or is not yet valid." (Strangely, Windows XP Professional can't distinguish between certificates that have expired and those whose validity period hasn't yet started.)

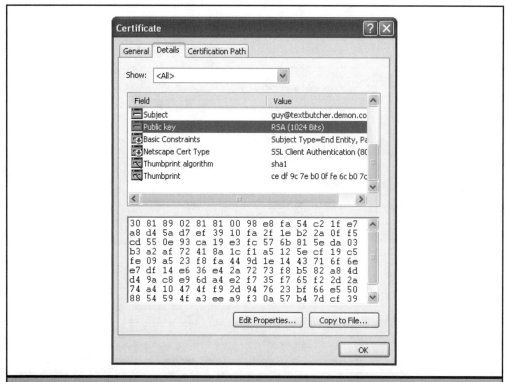

Figure 21-8. The Details tab lets you examine the details of the certificate, including its thumbprint, thumbprint algorithm, and public key.

Removing a Digital Certificate

If a certificate has expired or become untrustworthy, you may want to remove it, as described in this section. If a certificate has become less trustworthy than it used to be, instead of removing it, you may want to change the purposes for which you use it. The next section describes how to do that.

Caution *Before you remove a digital certificate, be aware of the consequences of doing so. If you remove one of your personal certificates, you'll no longer be able to decrypt data you encrypted using that certificate. For example, you'll neither be able to read any e-mail messages to others that you encrypted using that digital certificate nor read any e-mail messages others encrypted for you to read securely using that certificate. If you've used the digital certificate to authenticate yourself for web sites, you'll be unable to access those sites without authenticating yourself again (presumably using a different certificate). And if you remove the digital certificate for a certification authority, Windows XP Professional won't trust any digital certificates issued by lower-level certification authorities or by companies that, in turn, are authorized by that certification authority.*

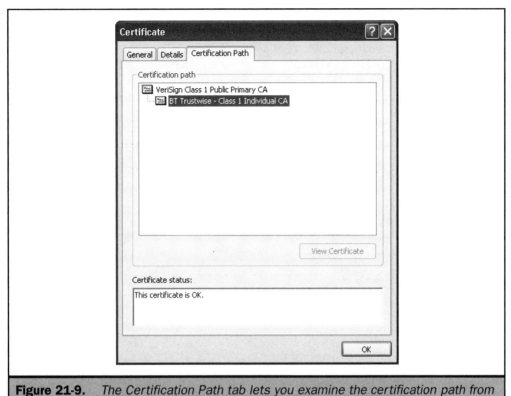

Figure 21-9. *The Certification Path tab lets you examine the certification path from the certification authority to the holder of the certificate.*

To remove a digital certificate, open the Certificates dialog box or the Certificates console, and then do the following:

- In the Certificates dialog box, select the certificate, and then click the Remove button.

- In the Certificates console, select the certificate, and then issue a Delete command from the Action menu, the shortcut menu, or the toolbar.

Windows XP Professional displays a Certificates dialog box to warn you of the consequences of removing the certificate and to confirm you want to proceed. Click the Yes button if you're sure you want to remove the certificate.

Changing a Digital Certificate's Friendly Name, Description, and Purposes

If you use digital certificates extensively, you can quickly accumulate many digital certificates. To help you keep your digital certificates recognizable, Windows XP

Professional lets you edit the friendly name (the descriptive name) and the description for a certificate. To do so, click the Edit Properties button on the Details tab of the certificate's Certificate dialog box to display the Certificate Properties dialog box. On the General tab (Figure 21-10), you can change the text in the Friendly Name text box and add a description in the Description text box.

On this tab, you can also specify the purposes for which you want to use the certificate by using the Enable All Purposes for This Certificate option button, the Disable All Purposes for This Certificate option button, or the Enable Only the Following Purposes option button. For the third option, use the check boxes to specify which purposes to use. You're limited to those purposes for which the certificate has been issued—you can't add purposes the certificate doesn't cover.

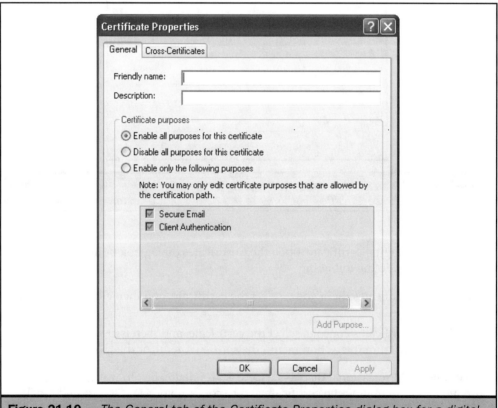

Figure 21-10. *The General tab of the Certificate Properties dialog box for a digital certificate lets you edit the friendly (descriptive) name and description for the certificate, and specify the purposes for which you want to use the certificate.*

Exporting a Digital Certificate

To export a digital certificate, open the Certificates dialog box or the Certificates console, and then launch the Certificate Export Wizard in one of the following ways:

- In the Certificates dialog box, select the certificate, and then click the Export button.

- In the Certificates console, issue an All Tasks | Export command from the Action menu or the shortcut menu.

These are the key steps of the Certificate Export Wizard:

1. The Export Private Key page may or may not offer you the choice of exporting the private key with the certificate. If the private key associated with the certificate isn't marked as exportable, Windows XP Professional won't let you export it. If you choose to export the private key, you have to enter a password to protect the private key. (You enter the private key later in the wizard, not

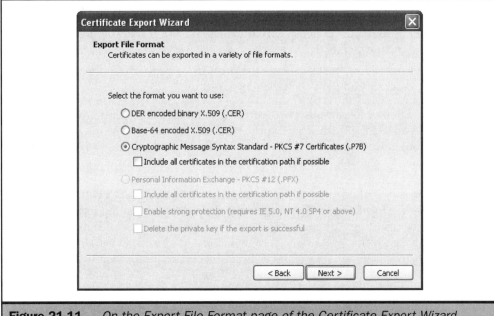

Figure 21-11.   *On the Export File Format page of the Certificate Export Wizard, choose the format in which to save the certificate file.*

immediately.) Make sure the password is strong if you need to protect it against being cracked.

2. The Export File Format page (Figure 21-11) lets you specify the format in which to export the digital certificate. These are your choices:

   ■ **DER Encoded Binary X.509**   A binary format best used for exporting a single certificate (rather than all the certificates in a certification path). The file uses a CER extension.

   ■ **Base64 Encoded X.509**   A textual representation of a DER encoded certificate. Use this format when you need to send a certificate to a computer running an OS other than Windows (for example, Linux). Like the DER Encoded Binary X.509 file, this file uses a CER extension.

   ■ **PKCS #7**   A file that contain all the certificates in the certification path. The file meets the Cryptographic Message Syntax Standard PKCS #7 created by RSA Security, Inc. The file uses a P7B extension.

   ■ **PKCS #12**   A file that contains all the certificates in the certificate path. The file meets the PKCS #12 standard, again created by RSA Security, Inc. With PKCS #12, you can use strong protection and you can choose to delete the private key after successfully exporting the certificate. Microsoft uses the extension PFX for PKCS #12 data, whereas Netscape uses the extension P12.

3. On the File to Export page, specify the filename and location under which to save the certificate file.

4. On the Completing the Certificate Export Wizard page, check the information you've entered, and then click the Finish button.

By default, Internet Explorer exports certificates in the DER Encoded Binary X.509 format. When you use the Certificate Export Wizard, you can change the certificate type easily enough. But you can also export a certificate by dragging its file from the Certificates dialog box to a folder. When you do so, Internet Explorer automatically uses the default format.

To change the default format, click the Advanced button in the Certificates dialog box and choose the format in the Export Format drop-down list in the Export Format group box in the resulting Advanced Options dialog box (Figure 21-12). If you use the PKCS #7 Certificates format, select or clear the Include All Certificates in the Certification Path check box to specify whether to include all the certificates or just the one you're exporting.

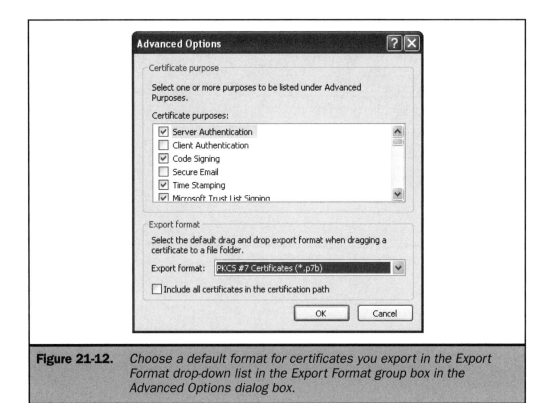

Figure 21-12. *Choose a default format for certificates you export in the Export Format drop-down list in the Export Format group box in the Advanced Options dialog box.*

Turning Off Automatic Updating of Root Certificates

By default, Windows XP Professional automatically updates the root certificates. In most cases, this is a good setting to use. However, in some circumstances, you may need to turn off the automatic updating of root certificates—for example, if your company's policy is to update root certificates manually to make sure all the company's computers are using the same certificates at the same time.

To turn off the automatic updating of root certificates, run the Windows Components Wizard (Start | Control Panel | Add or Remove Programs | Add/Remove Windows Components) and clear the Update Root Certificates check box. In a domain environment, an administrator may have prevented you from removing Windows components.

Summary

This chapter has discussed what digital certificates are, what they're for, and how to use Windows XP Professional's tools for working with them.

The next chapter covers how to audit permissions and security on Windows XP Professional.

Chapter 22

Auditing Events

This chapter discusses the capabilities Windows XP Professional provides for auditing events. Such auditing enables an administrator to track what's happening on a computer and identify possible security and performance issues.

To audit permissions and security, you need to be an administrator, either of a domain or of a standalone or workgroup computer. However, even if you're not an administrator, you may benefit from understanding what auditing is and what administrators can track by using auditing. You won't be able to see the auditing settings an administrator has applied to you.

In Windows XP Professional, auditing is applied through group policy settings, local policy settings, or both. In a domain environment, an administrator will typically configure auditing centrally by using group policy settings. In a standalone or workgroup environment, an administrator will use local policy settings to configure auditing.

Because auditing will usually be configured centrally in a domain, and this book assumes you're not a domain administrator, this chapter outlines what can be audited and the process of auditing rather than discussing every auditing setting in detail. The instructions this chapter provides for auditing are for working with local policies on a workgroup or standalone computer rather than group policies in a domain.

What Auditing Is

If you've ever submitted a tax return, you probably have a fair idea of what auditing is in the financial sense, even if the IRS has never descended on you. In the Windows XP Professional sense, auditing is substantially different—it's the tracking of the outcome of specific events that occur on the operating system (OS). For example, you can audit who logs on to a computer, who tries to log on but fails, and who shuts down or restarts a computer. You can also audit access to individual objects, such as files, folders, or printers. By auditing attempts to use printers, for example, you can determine which printers are more heavily used than others and which printers users are trying unsuccessfully to use.

As discussed in Chapter 20, group policies can be applied at the site level, at the domain level, and at the organizational unit (OU) level. By implementing auditing settings through group policy objects (GPOs) at the appropriate levels, an administrator can apply different auditing to different groups of users as necessary.

What You Can Audit

Windows XP Professional lets you audit nine different categories of events. Table 22-1 explains these events. For each event, you can choose a setting of No Auditing (the default setting), Success, or Failure.

Event Category	Explanation
Logon	Audits each successful or failed logon, logoff, or establishment of a network connection to the computer. These logons, logoffs, and network connections can be attempted by either users or processes (for example, services). Windows XP Professional doesn't log successful logons to a client computer if the domain controller is auditing successful account logon events (discussed next).
Account Logon	Audits each successful or failed logon to or logoff from a computer other than the computer used to validate the user account. For example, when a user attempts to log on to a client computer in a domain, the domain controller validates the user account. This generates an account logon event. A successful account logon event prevents a logon event from being written on the client computer.
Account Management	Audits each successful or failed change to a user account or group—anything from creating a new user account to deleting a group, from changing the password for a user account to modifying the permissions for a group.
Object Access	Audits each successful or failed attempt to access an object in the file system or Registry. For example, you can audit access to a folder, a printer, or a Registry key. After enabling auditing for object access events, you specify auditing separately for each individual object to which you want to apply auditing—in other words, enabling this item doesn't start Windows XP Professional auditing every object access.
Directory Service Access	Audits each successful or failed attempt to access an object in Active Directory. Directory service access events are similar to object access events (explained in the previous row of this table), but they apply to Active Directory objects rather than to file system or Registry objects. Again, after enabling auditing for directory service access events, you specify auditing separately for each individual object to which you want to apply auditing.
Policy Change	Audits each successful or failed attempt to change policies for user rights, auditing, or trust.

Table 22-1. *Events You Can Audit in Windows XP Professional*

Event Category	Explanation
Privilege Use	Audits each successful or failed attempt by a user to use a user right. For example, audit privilege use logs use of rights such as loading and unloading device drivers or creating a paging file. (To see the list of user rights, launch Local Security Settings by running **secpol.msc**, and then expand the Local Policies\User Rights Assignment branch.) Auditing privilege use doesn't apply to the following rights: Generate Security Audits, Bypass Traverse Checking, Debug Programs, Create a Token Object, Replace Process Level Token, Back Up Files and Directories, and Restore Files and Directories.
Process Tracking	Audits each successful or failed attempt to manipulate processes—for example, starting a process, stopping a process, or indirectly accessing an object.
System Events	Audits each successful or unsuccessful attempt to restart the computer or shut it down. Audits events that affect the system's security or the security log.

Table 22-1. *Events You Can Audit in Windows XP Professional* (continued)

When to Use Auditing

You can use auditing both as a precaution against system intrusion or unwanted changes in your system and to identify the cause of particular problems you experience when using your computer. For example, you could use auditing to find out what's causing system performance issues or which user (or process) is changing or deleting files in a particular folder.

As you saw in the previous section, Windows XP Professional enables you to audit many different aspects of the OS. By auditing every possible category of events, you can capture a huge amount of data about what's happening on the computer. However, the more you audit, the more data you need to go through to discover useful information. So, in most cases, it's best to limit your auditing to events that will produce smaller amounts of higher-quality information or help you solve a particular problem. For example, in many cases it's worth auditing failed account logon events, because these almost always indicate a problem. By contrast, while you *can* audit access to all your shared folders and their contents, there's little point in doing so unless you're trying to solve a problem with a given folder—in which case, you should confine the auditing to that folder so as not to capture irrelevant information.

Here are some examples of what you (or an administrator) may choose to audit:

- By auditing account logon events for failure, you can see who's trying to log on to a computer and failing to do so. Many repeated failed logon attempts may indicate someone trying to break a password with a password-cracking application. A few repeated failed logon attempts may indicate a user who has forgotten their password.

- By auditing account logon events at unusual hours (for example, when the office is closed) for success, you can detect an intrusion using a password that's been stolen or *socially engineered* (gleaned through trickery).

- By auditing the access events and change events of specific folders and files for both success and failure, you can see who is successfully making changes to folders or files you'd prefer them not to change and who is trying unsuccessfully to make such changes. Typically, you'll want to audit these events only when you've discovered a problem with changes being made. This is because, for any folder or file that's extensively used, auditing will produce a large amount of data you'll then need to sift through to find useful information.

- By auditing printer failure events, you can see which users are unable to print to printers they're supposed to be able to use. Conversely, you may need to audit printer success events to see who's overusing certain printers (for example, color printers or photo printers).

- By auditing the actions a specific user is taking, you can identify problems they're causing.

- By auditing administrative actions, you can keep a record of changes made to accounts and groups. This isn't the best way of tracking such changes, but it can be useful as a backup way of tracking them, particularly if several administrators are able to change the configuration of the same computer or group of computers.

Turning on Auditing

Before you can use auditing on your computer, you need to turn it on. Follow these steps:

1. Start the Local Security Settings console in any of the following ways:

   - Choose Start | Control Panel | Performance and Maintenance | Administrative Tools | Local Security Policy.

   - Choose Start | Administrative Tools | Local Security Policy or Start | All Programs | Administrative Tools | Local Security Policy.

   - Run **secpol.msc**.

2. Expand the Security Settings\Local Policies branch and select the Audit Policy folder. The Audit Policy folder is shown here with some settings chosen:

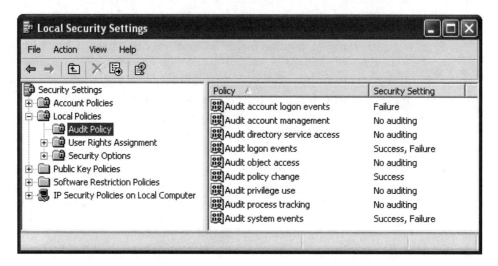

3. To set auditing for a policy, display the policy's Properties dialog box (an example of which is shown next) by double-clicking the policy's entry in the right pane or by selecting it and issuing a Properties command from the Action menu or the shortcut menu.

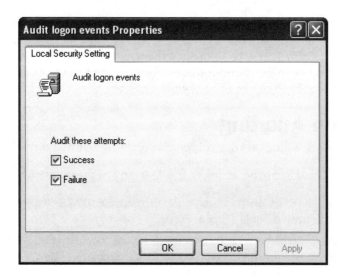

4. Select the Success check box, the Failure check box, or both.

5. Click the OK button to close the Properties dialog box.

6. Set auditing for other policies as appropriate, and then close the Local Security Policy console.

Once you've turned on auditing for any category of events other than object access events or directory service access events, Windows XP Professional begins auditing those events. To turn on auditing for object access, you also need to configure which objects to audit and which permissions to audit for them. To do so, follow the instructions in the following sections.

Before you can audit access to files and folders, however, your computer needs to be using regular file sharing rather than Simple File Sharing. This is because Simple File Sharing hides the Security tab of the Properties dialog box for files, folders, and other objects. As discussed earlier in the book, Windows XP Professional defaults to using Simple File Sharing in a standalone or workgroup configuration to simplify the process of sharing files and folders. In a domain configuration, Windows XP Professional always uses regular file sharing.

To turn off Simple File Sharing on a standalone or workgroup computer, follow these steps:

1. Open a Windows Explorer window.
2. Choose Tools | Folder Options to display the Folder Options dialog box.
3. On the View tab, clear the Use Simple File Sharing check box at the bottom of the Advanced Settings list box.
4. Click the OK button to close the Folder Options dialog box.

Auditing Access to Files and Folders

You can audit access to files and folders to see which users have accessed the files and folders, changed them, deleted them, or exercised other permissions on them.

To audit access to files and folders, follow these steps:

1. Open a Windows Explorer window to the file or folder you want to audit access to.
2. Select the file or folder and issue a Properties command from the File menu or the shortcut menu to display the Properties dialog box.
3. Click the Security tab to display it.
4. Click the Advanced button to display the Advanced Security Settings dialog box for the object.
5. Click the Auditing tab to display it. Figure 22-1 shows an example of the Auditing tab of the Advanced Security Settings dialog box with an auditing entry already in place.
6. To add an auditing entry, click the Add button. Windows XP Professional displays the Select User or Group dialog box.

SECURITY, BACKUP, AND
DISASTER RECOVERY

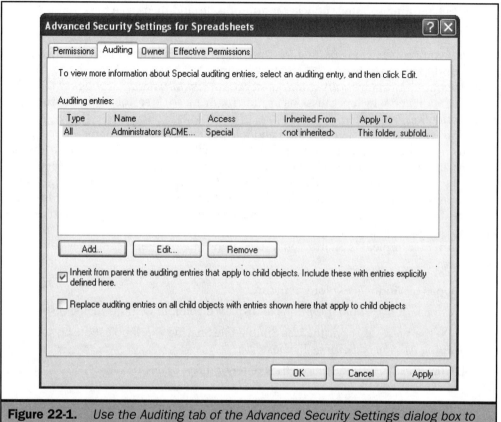

Figure 22-1. Use the Auditing tab of the Advanced Security Settings dialog box to apply auditing to an object or remove auditing from it.

7. Type in or browse to the user or group for which you want to create the auditing entry. You can audit the Everyone group if you want to, but often you're likely to prefer to limit the auditing to a smaller group of users or an individual user.

8. Click the OK button to display the Auditing Entry dialog box for the object (Figure 22-2).

9. In the Apply Onto drop-down list, specify the objects to which Windows XP Professional should apply the auditing. Table 22-2 explains your choices for a folder. They're not as self-explanatory as they might seem, because child objects can inherit auditing entries from their parent objects.

Figure 22-2. *Use the Auditing Entry dialog box to create an auditing entry for an object.*

Note *In many cases, you'll find the This Folder, Subfolders and Files item the most convenient, because it makes any new subfolders and files you create within the folder inherit the auditing applied to the parent folder. That means you needn't apply auditing to the subfolders and files manually unless you want them to have different auditing settings than their parent.*

10. Set up your auditing by selecting the check boxes in the Successful column and the Failed column for each permission you want to audit.

11. Select or clear the Apply These Auditing Entries to Objects and/or Containers Within This Container Only check box as appropriate. This confusingly named check box controls whether the auditing choices you apply to this folder have the same effect on the subfolders: when this check box is cleared, they do; when this check box is selected, they don't. For example, if you select the This Folder,

Apply Onto Setting	Current Folder	Subfolders in Current Folder	Files in Current Folder	Subsequent Subfolders	Files in Subsequent Subfolders
This Folder Only	✓	✗	✗	✗	✗
This Folder, Subfolders and Files	✓	✓	✓	✓	✓
This Folder and Subfolders	✓	✓	✗	✓	✗
This Folder and Files	✓	✗	✓	✗	✓
Subfolders and Files Only	✗	✓	✓	✓	✓
Subfolders Only	✗	✓	✗	✓	✗
Files Only	✗	✗	✓	✗	✓

Table 22-2. *Auditing Choices in the Apply Onto Drop-Down List*

Subfolders, and Files item in the Apply Onto drop-down list and leave this check box cleared, Windows XP Professional applies the auditing not only to this folder, its subfolders, and the files it contains, but to subsequent subfolders and the files they contain as well. When you select this check box, Windows XP Professional doesn't apply the auditing to the subsequent subfolders and the files they contain.

12. Click the OK button to close the Auditing Entry dialog box. Windows XP Professional returns you to the Advanced Security Settings dialog box.

13. Select or clear the Inherit from Parent the Auditing Entries that Apply to Child Objects. Include These with Entries Explicitly Defined Here check box. This check box controls whether the object for which you're setting auditing entries (for example, a folder) inherits from its parent folder any auditing entries that apply

to child objects. (Any auditing entries that apply only to the parent folder won't be inherited whether or not this check box is selected.)

14. Select or clear the Replace Auditing Entries on All Child Objects with Entries Shown Here that Apply to Child Objects check box. Selecting this check box (which is cleared by default) makes this object's auditing entries that apply to child objects override any corresponding entries set on the child objects. (As you'll remember from earlier in this chapter, auditing entries applied to child objects normally override any inherited auditing entries.)

15. Click the Apply button to apply the auditing entries and work further in the Advanced Security Settings dialog box, or click the OK button to apply the auditing entries and close the Advanced Security Settings dialog box.

Auditing Access to Printers

To audit access to printers, follow these steps:

1. Choose Start | Printers and Faxes or Start | Control Panel | Printers and Other Hardware | Printers and Faxes to open the Printers and Faxes folder.

2. Select the printer and issue a Properties command from the File menu or the shortcut menu to display the Properties dialog box.

3. Click the Security tab to display it.

4. Click the Advanced button to display the Advanced Security Settings dialog box.

5. Click the Auditing tab to display it.

6. Work as described in Steps 6–14 in the previous section to create auditing entries for the printer.

Auditing Access to the Registry

To keep track of Registry changes to a standalone or workgroup computer that has multiple computer administrator accounts configured, you can audit access to the Registry. To do so, follow these steps:

1. Run Registry Editor (Start | Run, **regedit**, OK).

2. Navigate to and select the key to which you want to apply the auditing.

Note *Because the Registry contains so many keys, you'll usually want to apply auditing to high-level subkeys (subkeys nearer to the root keys) rather than to subkeys further down the tree, and use inheritance to cascade the auditing to the subkeys lower down the tree. However, on other occasions, you may want to audit access to specific subkeys only.*

3. Issue a Permissions command from the Edit menu or the shortcut menu to display the Security tab of the Permissions dialog box for the key.

4. Click the Advanced button to display the Advanced Security Settings dialog box.

5. Click the Auditing tab to display it.

6. Work as described in Steps 6–14 of "Applying Auditing to a File or Folder," earlier in this chapter, to create auditing entries for the key.

Note *For a discussion of the Registry permissions you can audit, see Table 40-4 in Chapter 40.*

Auditing Backup and Restore

As mentioned earlier in the chapter, two of the privileges Windows XP Professional doesn't audit when you enable auditing of privilege use are the Back Up Files and Directories right and the Restore Files and Directories right. Instead, you need to enable auditing of backup and restore explicitly.

To audit backup and restore, follow these steps:

1. Launch the Local Security Settings console by running **secpol.msc**.

2. Expand the Local Policies branch and click the User Rights Assignment item to display its policies in the right pane of the console.

3. Double-click the Audit: Audit the Use of Backup and Restore Privilege item to display its Properties dialog box.

4. Select the Enabled option button. (This setting is disabled by default.)

5. Click the OK button to close the Properties dialog box.

6. Close the Local Security Settings console.

Reviewing Your Audit Entries

Turning on auditing for the appropriate events or permissions may capture the data you're seeking, but you'll need to review and analyze the data to get any value out of it. To review the data, run Event Viewer (discussed in detail in Chapter 11) and examine the Success Audit and Failure Audit items in your logs. Most events are added to the Security log. Figure 22-3 shows the Security log open in Event Viewer.

Note *If you audit many events, increase the size of your Security log so that you don't lose data.*

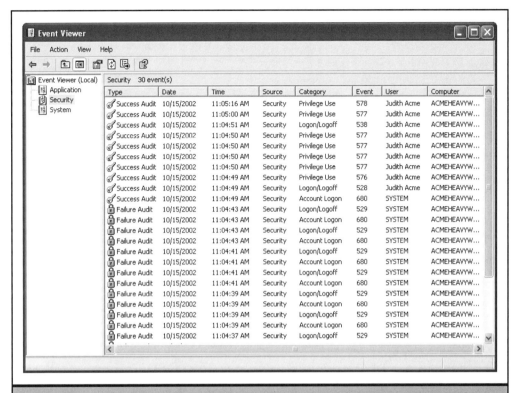

Figure 22-3. *Use Event Viewer to review the events you've been auditing.*

> **Tip** *You can export the contents of the selected event log to tab-delimited text or comma-delimited text format by issuing an Export List command from the Action menu or the shortcut menu. You can then import the resulting file into a spreadsheet or database to analyze it.*

Summary

This chapter has discussed how to audit events on computers running Windows XP Professional. In a domain environment, an administrator will most likely configure auditing centrally, but on a workgroup or standalone computer you administer, you may need to configure auditing yourself.

The next chapter explains how to back up your data, how to restore it, and how to use the System Restore and Automated System Recovery (ASR) features to recover from system problems.

Chapter 23

Using Backup, Restore, System Restore, and ASR

This chapter discusses how to use Windows XP Professional's features for protecting your computer against disaster. The chapter starts by covering how to use Backup Utility to back up your data so that you can restore it if necessary. The chapter then explains how to use the System Restore feature to maintain a set of known configuration checkpoints to which you can restore Windows XP Professional if configuration changes make it unstable or otherwise unsatisfactory. The chapter finishes by describing what Windows XP Professional's Automated System Recovery (ASR) feature is and how to use it to provide an effective mechanism for recovering from configuration disasters that render your computer inoperable.

The next chapter covers how to use the other tools Windows XP Professional provides for recovering from disaster.

Backup

If you're responsible for your own data, you need to back up your files so that you can restore them if anyone deletes them, your hard disk fails, or your computer gets lost or stolen. For backup, Windows XP Professional includes a backup utility named Backup Utility that meets many users' backup requirements. (If Backup Utility doesn't meet your requirements, get a third-party backup application and use that instead.) This section discusses how to use Backup Utility, what its limitations are, and which of them you can work around.

> **Note** *If you have a relatively small number of files, and you're prepared to reinstall your system files and applications after a disaster, you may choose not to use formal backup software and instead simply copy the files to a recordable CD.*

In a domain environment, an administrator is almost certain to back files up centrally for most of the domain's clients. To make the backup process simple, the administrator will probably make you store your data files on a file server, rather than on your local computer. As discussed in Chapter 8, the administrator may also configure Windows XP Professional to store your configuration files on a server, rather than storing them on your local computer. The administrator can then back up the configuration files as well. With all valuable files stored and backed up centrally, the administrator can replace the system volume with a standard configuration of Windows XP Professional and applications remotely by using Remote Installation Services (RIS) and IntelliMirror if your Windows XP Professional configuration gives trouble or stops working. In such a situation, you, as the user, shouldn't need to worry about backing up and restoring your data as long as you keep it all in approved locations on the network.

> **Note** *If you have Administrator privileges or Backup Operator privileges for a computer, you can back up and restore any files on it—even files that are normally protected from you, such as those in other users' private folders. If you're a Limited user, you can back up and restore only your own files.*

Backup Media

Backup Utility can back up your data to local hard drives, network drives, tape drives, or removable media such as Zip or Jaz disks.

Backup Utility can't back data up directly to a recordable CD unless you install packet-writing software, such as Roxio's DirectCD, on your computer. However, you can back up your data to a file on your hard drive, and then burn that file to a recordable CD. (Some other backup applications can back data up directly to a CD. This is one of the reasons why you might consider using another backup application instead of Backup Utility.)

Backing Up Your System

To back up your system, follow these steps:

1. Choose Start | All Programs | Accessories | System Tools | Backup to launch Backup Utility.

2. By default, Backup Utility starts in its wizard mode the first time you run it, so you see the Welcome to the Backup or Restore Wizard page.

   ■ Backup Utility's alternative to the Backup or Restore Wizard is Advanced mode, which is discussed later in this chapter. (This section assumes you're using the Backup or Restore Wizard.) To display Backup Utility in Advanced mode, click the Advanced Mode link.

   ■ To make Backup Utility launch in Advanced mode in the future, clear the Always Start in Wizard Mode check box.

3. On the Backup or Restore page, select the Back Up Files and Settings option button.

4. On the What to Back Up page (Figure 23-1), select the appropriate option button (see Table 23-1 for a list of options). If you select the Let Me Choose What to Back

What to Back Up Option	Explanation
My Documents and Settings	Backs up all the folders and files in your user profile: your configuration information and the contents of your My Documents folder and its subfolders.
Everyone's Documents and Settings	Backs up the user profile for each user account on the computer.

Table 23-1.   *What to Backup Options*

What to Back Up Option	Explanation
All Information on This Computer	A full backup, including an ASR disk. You can then recover your complete system by using ASR, as described later in this chapter. For this to work, the backup file must not be on an internal hard drive because ASR will delete it.
Let Me Choose What to Back Up	Enables you to select the folders and files to back up.

Table 23-1. *What to Backup Options* (continued)

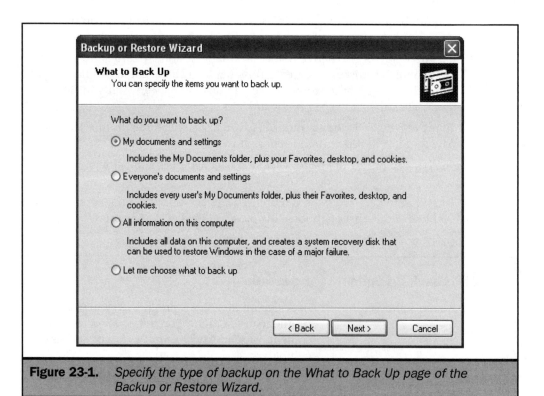

Figure 23-1. *Specify the type of backup on the What to Back Up page of the Backup or Restore Wizard.*

Up option button, use the Items to Back Up page (Figure 23-2) to select the drives, folders, and files to back up.

5. On the Backup Type, Destination, and Name page (Figure 23-3), specify the backup type and the location and filename for the backup. If your computer has a tape drive, you'll be able to choose it in the Select the Backup Type drop-down list. If not, your only option will be File.

6. On the Completing the Backup or Restore Wizard page, check the summary of the choices you've made. If necessary, use the Back button to return to an earlier page and change a setting.

7. Click the Finish button to perform a Normal backup with the choices you entered in the wizard. Alternatively, click the Advanced button to see other options for the backup. These options are discussed in the following subsection.

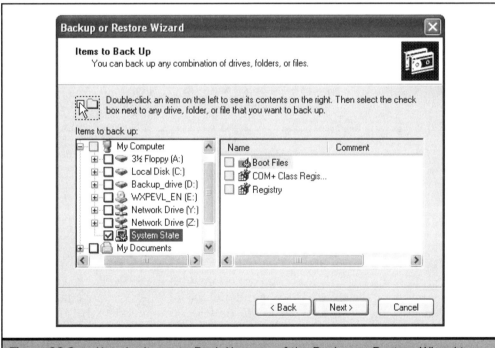

Figure 23-2. *Use the Items to Back Up page of the Backup or Restore Wizard to back up a custom set of folders and files.*

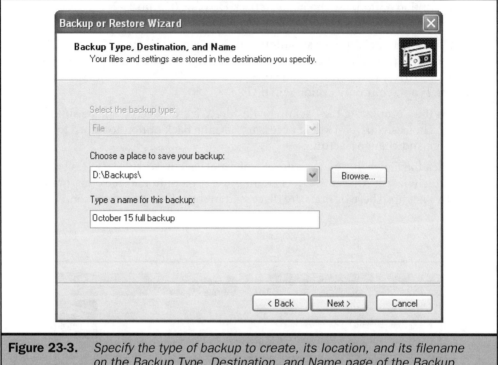

Figure 23-3. *Specify the type of backup to create, its location, and its filename on the Backup Type, Destination, and Name page of the Backup or Restore Wizard.*

Choosing Advanced Backup Options

By clicking the Advanced button on the Completing the Backup or Restore Wizard page, you can access four further pages of backup options. The following subsections discuss the choices these pages offer.

Choosing a Backup Type

On the Type of Backup page of the Backup or Restore Wizard, choose the type of backup you want to perform. The types of backup differ in the files they back up and the state in which they leave the *archive bit,* a tag on a file or folder that indicates whether it needs backing up (the archive bit is on, or set) or not (the archive bit is off, or cleared). Table 23-2 explains what the different types of backup do to the files and folders marked for the backup and to the archive bit.

These are the differences between differential backups and incremental backups:

■ Differential backups get bigger each day (and so need more disk space) because they include each file that has changed since the last full backup was performed. As a result, you can restore a computer by using the last full backup and the last differential backup.

Backup Type	What It Does	Archive Bit
Normal	Backs up each file and folder.	Cleared
Copy	Copies (not backs up) each specified file or folder.	Cleared
Differential	Backs up each file and folder changed since the last full backup.	Not Cleared
Incremental	Backs up each file and folder changed since the last full backup or incremental backup.	Cleared
Daily	Backs up each file and folder changed on the day the backup is run.	Cleared

Table 23-2.   *Backup Types*

■ Incremental backups include only the files that have changed since the last full backup or the last incremental backup—they're not cumulative. So to restore a computer, you need the last full backup and each incremental backup that has been created since that full backup.

Choosing Verification, Compression, and Shadow Copying

On the How to Back Up page of the Backup or Restore Wizard, you can choose whether to verify the data after backup (always a good idea), whether to use hardware compression (which is only available on some tape drives and other custom backup devices), and whether to disable volume shadow copy.

Volume shadow copy makes an immediate copy of the volume, and then backs up the copy rather than the volume itself. The advantage is that you can keep working with your applications and files even while the backup is occurring. The disadvantage is that volume shadow copy works only for NTFS volumes—it doesn't work for FAT volumes of any kind. Volume shadow copy is on by default.

Replacing the Existing Backup or Appending Data to It

On the Backup Options page of the Backup or Restore Wizard, you can choose whether to append the backup you're creating to an existing backup or to replace the existing backup. These choices apply only if the backup location contains an existing backup.

If you choose to replace the existing backup, you have the choice of selecting or leaving cleared the Allow Only the Owner and the Administrator Access to the Backup Data and to Any Backups Appended to This Medium check box. This check box lets you restrict access to the backup to the owner of the backup and administrators.

Scheduling the Backup to Run Later

On the When to Back Up page of the Backup or Restore Wizard, you can choose whether to run the backup now (the default) or create a schedule for the backup to run later. If you create a schedule, you need to specify the account under which the backup will run. This account must have a password.

Restoring Files from a Backup

When you need to restore files from a backup, follow these steps:

1. Choose Start | All Programs | Accessories | System Tools | Backup to launch Backup Utility. As before, Backup Utility starts in its Wizard mode by default, so you see the Welcome to the Backup or Restore Wizard page.

2. On the Backup or Restore page, select the Restore Files and Settings option button.

3. On the What to Restore page (Figure 23-4), open the backup file from which you want to restore files. Navigate to the folders and files to restore and select their check boxes.

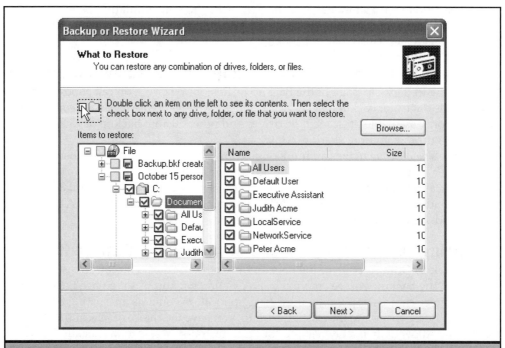

Figure 23-4. Select the folders or files to restore on the What to Restore page of the Backup or Restore Wizard.

4. On the Completing the Backup or Restore Wizard page, you can either click the Finish button to proceed with a basic restore (which restores the files to their original locations but doesn't replace existing files that have the same names as the files being restored) or click the Advanced button to choose advanced options. These options are discussed in the following subsection.

Choosing Advanced Restore Options

By clicking the Advanced button on the Completing the Backup or Restore Wizard page, you can access three further pages of restore options. The following subsections discuss the choices these pages offer.

Where to Restore Page

On the Where to Restore page of the Backup or Restore Wizard, choose whether to restore the files to their original location, to an alternate location, or to a single folder:

- Use the Original Location option when you need to restore one or more folders or drives and you're prepared to overwrite the current files with the files you're restoring.

- Use the Alternate Location option to restore the files or folders to a different folder without overwriting the current files. You can then work with the restored files and decide whether to replace the current files manually. Use the Alternate Location text box to specify the folder to use.

- Use the Single Location option to restore the files to a different location consisting of a single folder without overwriting the current files. Placing all the files in a single folder can be useful when you're restoring a few files from separate folders and keeping them together is more convenient than having them in separate folders. Use the Folder Name text box to specify the folder to use.

How to Restore Page

On the How to Restore page, choose what Backup Utility should do if the files you're restoring have the same names as files already in the specified location on your computer. Choose the Leave Existing Files option button, the Replace Existing Files if They Are Older than the Backup Files option button, or the Replace Existing Files option button as appropriate.

Advanced Restore Options Page

On the Advanced Restore Options page, select or clear the following check boxes as appropriate to the backup you're performing:

- The Restore Security Settings check box controls whether Backup Utility reapplies permissions and auditing settings to the files you're restoring. This check box is available only when you're restoring a backup made from an NTFS drive to an

NTFS drive. When available, this check box is selected by default, and you'll usually want to use it.

■ The Restore Junction Points, but Not the Folders and File Data They Reference check box controls whether Backup Utility restores junction points without restoring the folders and files they point to. A *junction point* is a physical cluster on your hard disk that references data stored in another location. You typically create a junction point by mounting a drive in an NTFS folder (see "Creating a Partition" in Chapter 39 for an explanation of mounting a drive). You won't usually need to use this option.

■ The Preserve Existing Volume Mount Points check box controls whether Backup Utility preserves any existing volume mount points on the volume or overwrites them with the data in the backup. This check box is selected by default. In most cases, it's best to try restoring the files and folders while preserving the mount points. If that doesn't work, you can try restoring the mount points from backup as well.

Using Backup Utility in Advanced Mode

Instead of having the Backup or Restore Wizard shepherd you through the process of selecting the files to back up, you can run Backup Utility in Advanced mode. The following subsections discuss the options Advanced mode offers.

Using the Four Tabs in Advanced Mode

Advanced mode contains four tabs and gives you direct access to the backup choices Backup Utility supports. These are the four tabs:

■ The Welcome tab (shown in Figure 23-5) provides quick access to the advanced form of the Backup Wizard, the advanced form of the Restore Wizard, and the Automated System Recovery Wizard. This tab also contains a link for switching Backup Utility back to Wizard mode.

■ The Backup tab provides controls for selecting the drives, folders, and files to back up, choosing the destination, and specifying the filename.

■ The Restore and Manage Media tab provides controls for selecting the items to restore and specifying where to restore them.

■ The Schedule Jobs tab provides a calendar. Select a date and click the Add Job button to start creating a scheduled backup. By setting up a schedule, you can perform your backups automatically at a convenient time, such as the early hours of the morning. (See Chapter 41 for a discussion of how to schedule tasks.)

Tip   *One item you'll often want to include in your backups is the System State item, which has its own item in the My Computer branch. On a computer running Windows XP Professional, the System State item includes the boot files, the COM+ class registration database, and the Registry.*

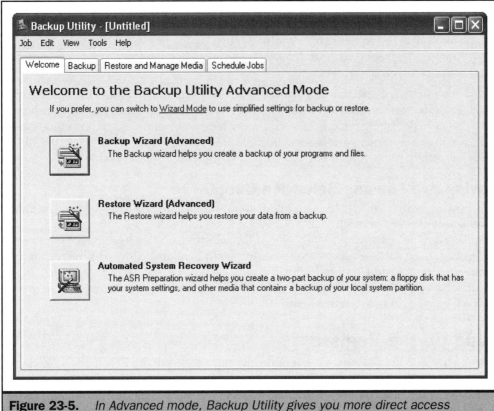

Figure 23-5. *In Advanced mode, Backup Utility gives you more direct access to its settings.*

Choosing Options in the Options Dialog Box

When working in Advanced mode, you can choose further options in the Options dialog box (Tools | Options). This dialog box contains the following five tabs:

- The *General* tab includes a selection of options, from choosing whether to verify the data after the backup finishes (a good idea) to specifying whether to back up the contents of mounted drives.

- The *Restore* tab offers the same choices as the How to Restore page of the Backup or Restore Wizard for controlling what Backup Utility does if the files you're restoring have the same names as files already in the specified location on your computer.

- The *Backup Type* tab lets you choose among Normal, Copy, Differential, Incremental, and Daily backups.

- The *Backup Log* tab lets you choose among creating a detailed backup log, a summary log (the default), and no log. To open a log, choose Tools | Report and select the report in the Backup Reports dialog box. Click the View button to open the report in your default text editor. Click the Print button to print the report to your default printer.

- The *Exclude Files* tab lets you adjust the list of files and folders Backup Utility automatically excludes from the backup. The default list includes your temporary files folder, Internet Explorer's temporary files, your client side cache (offline files), your paging file, your hibernation file, and other files and folders that would typically be a waste of backup space because you'll never need to restore them.

Saving and Loading Selection Scripts

After you select the folders, files, and items you want to include in a backup, you can save the selection by choosing Job | Save Selections and using the Save As dialog box to specify a name. (If you've already saved the selection, choose Job | Save Selections As instead to save the selection under a new name.) Backup Utility calls the resulting file a *selection script* and assigns it the .BKS extension.

To load a saved selection script, choose Job | Load Selections and use the Open dialog box to select the selection script.

Backing Up the Registry

You can back up the Registry as part of the system by selecting the System State check box on the Backup tab of Backup Utility in its Advanced mode. To back up the Registry on its own (rather than with the other components included in your system state), follow the instructions in "Backing Up and Restoring the Registry" in Chapter 40.

System Restore

System Restore is a semiautomatic recovery tool designed for recovery from problems such as configuration mishaps, system instability, and the installation of software that doesn't work as it should.

System Restore automatically creates snapshots of the configuration of your system files so that you can subsequently restore your computer to a specific configuration after trouble strikes. These snapshots are called *restore points* or *system checkpoints* and are stored on your hard drive in space System Restore automatically reserves. By default, System Restore keeps restore points for 90 days before deleting them automatically. If System Restore runs out of space, it deletes the oldest restore points to make space for newer restore points.

Running System Restore

You need to be an administrator to run System Restore. If you try to run System Restore as a nonadministrator, Windows XP Professional displays a System Restore dialog box explaining that you don't have sufficient security privileges to restore your system and suggesting you contact your administrator.

To run System Restore, choose Start | All Programs | Accessories | System Tools | System Restore. You can also launch System Restore by running %systemroot%\ system32\Restore\rstrui.exe. However, because you'll need to specify the path, using the Start menu is usually faster and easier. Figure 23-6 shows System Restore's home page.

Administrators have tight control over System Restore. An administrator can do the following:

- Turn off System Restore to prevent you from using it.
- Turn on System Restore and prevent you from configuring it.
- Turn off System Restore but allow you to configure it (if you're an administrator).

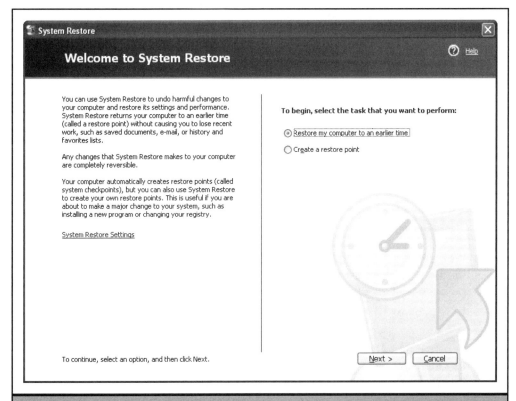

Figure 23-6. *System Restore's minimalist interface hides powerful capabilities for recovering from configuration problems.*

What System Restore Protects

System Restore protects your system files, your application files, and your Start menu shortcuts and links. System Restore doesn't protect your data files. To protect your data files, back them up by using Backup Utility or another backup application. System Restore doesn't protect backup files created using Backup Utility either.

To see details of the files, folders, and file types System Restore excludes, run %systemroot%\system32\Restore\filelist.xml.

Creating System Restore Points Automatically and Manually

In its default configuration, Windows XP Professional automatically creates the following restore points (whether you're an administrator or not):

- The first time you boot Windows XP Professional after installation.

- Every 24 hours of calendar time. If the computer isn't running, Windows XP Professional creates the restore point as soon as possible after the scheduled time when it's running. You can change the interval for automatically creating restore points based on calendar time by editing the RPGlobalInterval DWORD value in the HKLM\Software\Microsoft\WindowsNT\CurrentVersion\ SystemRestore key. This value entry specifies the interval in seconds. The default is 86,400 seconds—24 hours.

Tip *You can also make Windows XP Professional create restore points at intervals while your computer keeps running. This capability is useful for critical computers you leave running most of the time. To create these session-interval restore points, change the RPSessionInterval value entry in the HKLM\Software\Microsoft\WindowsNT\ CurrentVersion\SystemRestore key from its default setting of 0 (which creates no restore points) to the number of seconds for the interval. For example, you might specify 7,200 seconds to create a session-interval restore point every two hours. You can create session-interval restore points either in addition to or instead of calendar-interval restore points.*

- When you restore your system to an earlier or later restore point using System Restore. (You can restore to a later restore point if restoring to an earlier restore point doesn't give the results you need.)

- When you use Backup Utility to restore your system.

- When you install or uninstall an application that uses an installation routine of which System Restore is aware. Examples include InstallShield and Windows Installer.

- When you install some device drivers—particularly device drivers that aren't digitally signed.

You can also create restore points manually at any time if you're an administrator. You can assign a descriptive name to restore points you create, thus making them easier to identify than the automatically named restore points. Suitable times for creating restore points include just before you make configuration changes, just before you install an application that may not use an installer compatible with System Restore, or just before you install a driver you don't entirely trust.

To create a restore point, follow these steps:

1. Choose Start | All Programs | Accessories | System Tools | System Restore to launch System Restore.

2. Select the Create a Restore Point option button and click the Next button to display the Create a Restore Point screen.

3. Enter the description for the restore point. You needn't add the date and time to the description because System Restore does so automatically.

4. Click the Create button.

5. On the Restore Point Created screen, click the Close button to close System Restore.

Restoring Windows XP Professional to a Restore Point

To restore Windows XP Professional to a restore point, follow these steps:

1. Choose Start | All Programs | Accessories | System Tools | System Restore to run System Restore.

2. Select the Restore My Computer to an Earlier Time option button and click the Next button to display the Select a Restore Point screen (Figure 23-7).

3. Select the restore point to use by clicking a date shown in boldface on the calendar control, and then selecting the restore point in the list box.

 The calendar control shows available restore points only for the month currently displayed, not for any days included in the calendar from the previous month or the next month. To see the restore points available for another month, display that month in the calendar control.

4. Click the Next button to display the Confirm Restore Point Selection screen.

5. Check the details of the restore point you chose, close any other applications you're running, and click the Next button to perform the restoration.

6. After your computer reboots, check to ensure Windows XP Professional is running properly. If it isn't, use System Restore to restore Windows XP Professional either to its previous state (undoing the restoration) or to an earlier restore point.

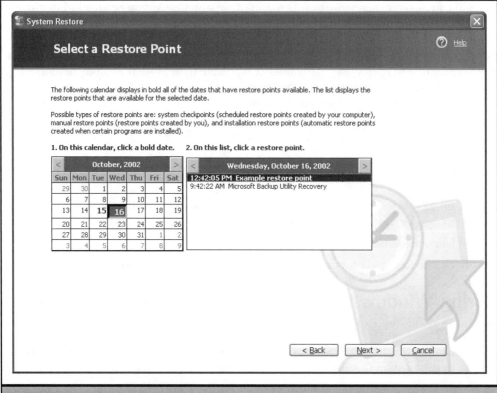

Figure 23-7. *Select the restore point on the Select a Restore Point screen.*

Configuring and Turning Off System Restore

You can change the amount of space System Restore is allowed to take up on your hard drive. You can also turn off System Restore for any drives that don't need it. You can even turn off System Restore for all drives. The latter is an extreme step that's almost never wise. (The exception is when your computer is flat out of disk space and you can't afford the 200MB or more System Restore requires on your system volume.)

An administrator may have prevented you from configuring System Restore. If they've done so, the System Restore Settings link won't appear on the System Restore home page, and the System Restore tab won't appear in the System Properties dialog box.

System Restore's default setting is to reserve 12 percent of each hard drive larger than 4GB and 400MB of each hard drive smaller than 4GB. On large hard drives, this much space is often more than necessary, and you can reduce the amount allocated. The less space you allow System Restore, the fewer restore points it can keep, so you may need to experiment to find the optimum setting for your computer.

It's best to run System Restore only on drives that contain system files and application files, and turn System Restore off for drives that don't contain system files. In most typical configurations, this means running System Restore only on your system drive. However, if your application files are stored on a different drive than your system files (for example, because your system drive is too small to contain both), you should run System Restore on the drive that contains the applications as well.

To change the amount of space System Restore can take up, follow these steps:

1. Press WINDOWS KEY–BREAK to display the System Properties dialog box, and then click the System Restore tab to display it (Figure 23-8). Alternatively, open System Restore and click the System Restore Settings link on the System Restore home page to display the System Restore tab of the System Properties dialog box.

Note   *The controls on the System Restore tab of the System Properties dialog box vary depending on whether the computer has a single hard-drive volume or two or more volumes. The computer shown in Figure 23-8 has two hard-drive volumes, which causes Windows XP Professional to display the Available Drives list box and the Settings button. If your computer has only one hard-drive volume, the System Restore tab displays a Disk Space Usage slider instead of the Available Drives list box and the Settings button. You use this slider to set the amount of hard disk space System Restore can take up.*

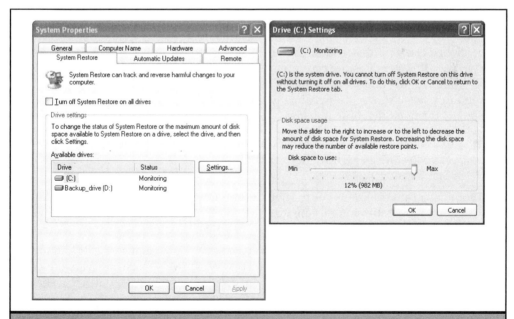

Figure 23-8. *Use the System Restore tab of the System Properties dialog box (left) to configure or turn off System Restore. Use the Settings dialog box (right) to configure settings for one of multiple drives.*

SECURITY, BACKUP, AND
DISASTER RECOVERY

2. To turn off System Restore entirely, select the Turn Off System Restore on All Drives check box or the Turn Off System Restore check box. (The Turn Off System Restore check box appears on computers that have only one hard-drive volume.) As mentioned earlier in this section, turning off System Restore entirely is seldom recommended.

3. To configure System Restore for a drive, select the drive in the Available Drives list box and click the Settings button. Windows XP Professional displays the Settings dialog box for the drive.

   ■ The controls in the Settings dialog box vary depending on whether the drive is a system drive.

   ■ The right screen in Figure 23-8 shows an example of the Settings dialog box for a system drive. The Settings dialog box for a nonsystem drive includes a Turn Off System Restore on This Drive check box.

4. Use the Disk Space to Use slider to specify how much space System Restore may use. Or, if appropriate, select the Turn Off System Restore on This Drive check box to disable System Restore for the drive. If your computer has only one drive, use the corresponding controls on the System Restore tab of the System Properties dialog box.

5. If your computer has multiple drives, configure System Restore settings for them, too.

Deleting Restore Points

As mentioned earlier in this section, System Restore automatically deletes restore points after 90 days. If System Restore runs out of disk space before then, it deletes the older restore points so that it has space to store new restore points.

You can't delete restore points directly through Windows Explorer, but you can manipulate them in the following ways:

   ■ To delete all restore points except the last, run Disk Cleanup and select the System Restore check box. (See "Disk Cleanup" in Chapter 39 for a discussion of disk cleanup.)

   ■ To delete all restore points, turn off System Restore. This isn't recommended, because if you turn off System Restore, you'll find it more difficult to recover from configuration mishaps.

   ■ To reduce the time System Restore keeps restore points, reduce the RPLifeInterval value in the HKLM\Software\Microsoft\WindowsNT\CurrentVersion\ SystemRestore key in the Registry from 7,776,000 seconds (90 days) to a shorter period.

Automated System Recovery (ASR)

ASR is a tool for automatically recovering your system after a disastrous failure. ASR is intended to be a last resort for restoring a system after all other troubleshooting steps and recovery techniques have failed. ASR is the last step before reinstalling Windows XP Professional manually from scratch. You *can* use ASR to recover from lesser problems, but doing so is often a bad idea and can have unintended consequences.

 See "Overview of Windows XP Professional's Recovery Tools" in the next chapter for a discussion of Windows XP Professional's other recovery tools and when to use each of them.

ASR is included only in Windows XP Professional—Microsoft chose not to include it in Windows XP Home Edition. This is presumably as much because users might try to use it when they shouldn't as because Microsoft requires a major feature to differentiate Windows XP Professional from Windows XP Home Edition.

 In a domain environment, your data files and your configuration files may all be stored on the network so that an administrator can easily back them up. In such a situation, you may not need to use ASR at all. Instead, if your Windows XP Professional configuration is damaged, an administrator may restore the system volume with a standard configuration remotely by using Remote Installation Services (RIS) and IntelliMirror.

How ASR Works

ASR backs up the contents of your system volume to a large archive file and saves a small amount of vital configuration information to a floppy disk. After disaster has struck and you've exhausted all other recovery options, you boot from your Windows XP Professional CD into a special ASR mode. You supply your floppy disk and tell Windows XP Professional where to find the ASR backup.

The archive file can be stored on a removable medium or on a hard disk. Because the backup contains all the files on the system volume, it will be large—typically anywhere from a little over 1GB to many gigabytes. The backup medium needs to be large enough to contain the archive file. A recordable DVD, a backup tape, or an external hard drive are all suitable.

If you plan to store your ASR backup file on a hard disk, keep the following points in mind:

- The backup file must be stored on a volume other than the system volume. If the backup file is stored on the system volume, the file will be overwritten when ASR attempts to restore the system volume to its former state. ASR formats the partition, and then creates the junction points and directory structure on it from the information on the ASR floppy disk.

■ While you can store the ASR backup file on a different volume on the same internal hard disk that contains your system volume, storing the file on a different hard disk is a better idea. This is for two reasons. First, any hardware problem that affects the system volume (for example, bad sectors or a corrupted partition table) may also affect other volumes on the same drive. This may prevent you from recovering from your ASR backup set. Second, your backup file will be safer if it's kept away from your computer. An external hard drive or a network drive can provide this flexibility together with plenty of space to back up your entire system volume.

Caution	*It's vital to understand that ASR is anything but a panacea for system problems and data loss. ASR does not back up your entire system. ASR will not help you recover from the loss, corruption, or accidental deletion of data files unless you've stored them on your system volume. So use ASR to protect your system files, but back up your data files regularly as well.*

Making an ASR Backup Set

For ASR to represent the optimal recovery solution for an otherwise unmitigated disaster, you'll need to keep your ASR backup set up to date. This means running the ASR Wizard regularly and frequently. You may not need to update your ASR backup set as frequently as you perform backups, because your system configuration is likely to change less frequently than your data files do. However, by establishing a schedule and sticking to it, you can ensure ASR will restore your system to a usable state.

Restoring your computer to a long-ago configuration of Windows XP Professional may be better than having to reinstall the operating system (OS) manually from scratch. This is because the restored version of the OS will include all the applications and updates you've installed and any data files you've created on your system volume. But you'll need to repeat any installations, updates, or configuration changes you'd made since you created the ASR backup set.

To make your ASR backup set, follow these steps:

1. Prepare a floppy disk and either a suitable removable medium or enough hard disk space on a volume other than the system volume to contain the backup file. The floppy doesn't need to be blank because the files ASR saves to it are tiny. But be sure to use a floppy that doesn't contain any files you currently need because you should store the floppy safely away from your computer.

2. Choose Start | All Programs | Accessories | System Tools | Backup to launch Backup Utility.

3. If the Backup or Restore Wizard runs, click the Advanced Mode link to switch Backup Utility to Advanced mode.

4. On the Welcome tab of Backup Utility, click the Automated System Recovery Wizard button.

5. On the Backup Destination page of the wizard, select the destination for the backup file. As mentioned earlier in the chapter, don't save the backup file to the system volume.

6. Finish the wizard and allow the backup to complete. Backup Utility displays the Backup Progress dialog box while the backup is running.

7. When prompted, insert the floppy disk so that Backup Utility can copy the ASR initialization files to it.

8. When the ASR backup is complete, close Backup Utility. Label the floppy disk and the removable medium (if you're using one) and store them in a safe location.

Running ASR to Restore Your System Volume

To restore your system volume using ASR, follow these steps:

1. Insert the Windows XP Professional CD in your CD drive.

2. Unless your computer is configured to try to boot from the floppy drive, insert the ASR floppy disk in the floppy drive.

3. If your ASR backup is on a removable medium, load the medium or have it ready to load.

4. Restart your computer and boot from the CD to start the Windows XP Professional setup routine.

5. Once the boot from the CD is underway, insert the ASR floppy disk if you didn't do so before.

6. Press F2 when Windows Setup prompts you to press that key to start ASR.

7. If Windows Setup prompts you to supply your ASR backup file, do so. Otherwise, leave ASR to restore your computer. The restoration process is essentially an automated installation augmented with files from your ASR backup. Toward the end of the restoration process, Backup Utility launches and displays the Restore Progress dialog box to show you what's happening. Figure 23-9 shows an ASR restore in action.

8. You may need to press F3 to reboot your computer manually.

9. Backup Utility reboots the computer after completing the restoration. If your computer will try to boot from the floppy disk, remove it from the floppy drive.

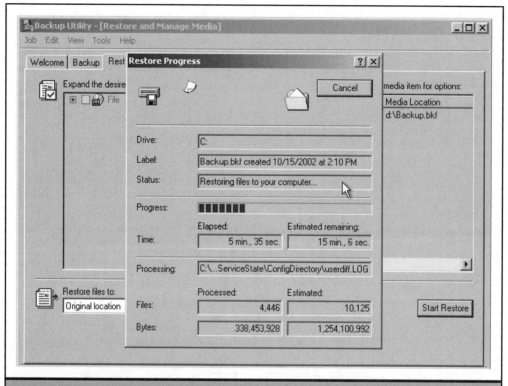

Figure 23-9.   *An ASR restore starts in Windows Setup's text mode. Backup Utility then launches and displays the Restore Progress dialog box.*

Replacing a Lost ASR Floppy Disk

If you lose your ASR disk, you won't be able to run ASR. But you can create a replacement ASR disk as follows:

1. Run Backup Utility in Advanced mode.

2. Click the Restore and Manage Media tab to display it.

3. Open the ASR backup file

4. Expand the drive containing the system files to display the %systemroot%\ Repair folder.

5. Select the asr.sif check box and the asrpnp.sif check box.

6. Select the Single Folder item in the Restore Files To drop-down list.

7. Enter **a:** in the Alternate Location text box.

8. Click the Start Restore button.

9. Click the OK button in the Confirm Restore dialog box.

10. If Backup Utility warns you that the target file system does not support some of the features of the original file system, click the OK button. This message occurs if your system volume uses NTFS: the floppy disk uses FAT-12, which doesn't support NTFS permissions.

Summary

This chapter has discussed how to use backup and restore, the System Restore feature, and ASR to preempt disaster and (in the case of ASR) to recover from disasters of a particular type.

The next chapter continues the theme of disaster by discussing how to recover from other types of disasters by using Windows XP Professional's other recovery tools.

SECURITY, BACKUP, AND
DISASTER RECOVERY

The
Complete
Reference

Chapter 24

Recovering
from Disaster

This chapter discusses the tools that Windows XP Professional provides for recovering from disaster. These tools include System Configuration Utility, Last Known Good Configuration, and Recovery Console.

This chapter builds on the previous chapter, which discussed how to use Backup Utility to back up data and restore it, how to use the System Restore feature to prepare for and recover from some configuration problems, and how to use the Automated System Recovery (ASR) feature as a last resort for fixing severe configuration problems.

Overview of Windows XP Professional's Recovery Tools

Windows XP Professional provides an extensive set of tools for recovering from disasters. Table 24-1 lists typical problems you may experience with Windows XP Professional in escalating order, showing which recovery tool or technique is appropriate to each problem. The following sections discuss the tools in more detail, referring you to other chapters as appropriate.

When This Problem Occurs	Use This Recovery Tool or Technique
A data file has been deleted or lost, or has become damaged or corrupted.	Backup Utility
Installing a new device driver has caused a problem.	Device Driver Roll Back
Installing a new application has caused a problem.	Uninstall the application
An application's files have become corrupted or have been deleted.	Reinstall the application
Installing an application has made your system unstable.	System Restore
Installing a driver has made your system unstable.	System Restore
A device driver seems to make your system unstable or prevent features from working.	Disable the device

Table 24-1. *Windows XP Professional's Recovery Tools by Problem*

When This Problem Occurs	Use This Recovery Tool or Technique
Windows XP boots and starts but then runs unstably.	System Configuration Utility and Clean Boot
Windows XP won't start fully.	Last Known Good Configuration
Windows XP won't boot.	Recovery Console
Windows XP won't boot, and using Recovery Console doesn't help.	Parallel installation of Windows XP
Windows XP won't boot because files or the file system are damaged.	Automated System Recovery
Windows XP doesn't boot and ASR doesn't work.	Reinstall Windows XP

Table 24-1. *Windows XP Professional's Recovery Tools by Problem* (continued)

Backing Up Your Files Using Backup Utility

As discussed in "Backup" in Chapter 23, Windows XP's Backup Utility (or another backup application) should be your first line of defense against losing data files. By backing up your files regularly and frequently, you can ensure that you have up-to-date backups from which you can replace any files that get deleted, lost, damaged, or corrupted.

Rolling Back a Device Driver

Sometimes installing a new device driver (even an approved driver that you've downloaded via Windows Update) may make your computer unstable. When this happens, or if you suspect it has happened, use Windows XP's roll-back capability to revert to the driver you were previously using for the device. See "Installing and Rolling Back Device Drivers" in Chapter 10 for instructions.

Uninstalling and Reinstalling Applications

If an application you install seems to make Windows XP Professional unstable, try uninstalling the application to see if doing so removes the problem. If it does, the problem is most likely related to the application. See "Removing Applications Manually" in Chapter 9 for instructions on uninstalling both 32-bit applications and 16-bit applications.

If an application starts to run erratically, the problem may be that one or more of the application's files have been (or have become) corrupted. When this happens, you may be able to repair the corrupted files manually (for example, by replacing individual corrupted files with fresh versions of the same files). In other cases, you may need to reinstall the application. To reinstall an application, uninstall it, and then run its installation routine again.

Using System Restore

If Backup Utility, device driver roll back, and uninstalling and reinstalling an application (as appropriate) won't fix a problem your computer is experiencing, it's probably time to turn to System Restore. See "System Restore" in Chapter 23 for details on how to return your computer to one of the system checkpoints Windows XP has created automatically or to a restore point you've created manually.

Using System Configuration Utility and Clean Boot

System Configuration Utility is a tool for modifying the configuration with which your computer boots. Use System Configuration Utility to overcome boot problems and startup problems when the problems are not so severe as to prevent Windows XP from booting and you from logging on. Briefly, you use System Configuration Utility to perform a clean boot (a boot with as few drivers and services as possible) and then gradually add drivers and services until the problems reoccur. After identifying the offending driver or service, you remove it from your normal configuration.

Note *You need to be an administrator to make changes with System Configuration Utility.*

To start System Configuration Utility, run **msconfig**. You shouldn't need to specify the path, but if you do, it's %systemroot%\PCHEALTH\HELPCTR\Binaries.

System Configuration Utility is a powerful tool with an interface that looks more difficult to use than it actually is. System Configuration Utility's interface contains six tabs: General, SYSTEM.INI, WIN.INI, BOOT.INI, Services, and Startup. The General tab of System Configuration Utility is shown in Figure 24-1.

Here's a brief overview of what the six tabs do:

- The General tab provides overall control of the options on the other five tabs. The three main option buttons let you switch between three configurations: a normal configuration that loads all your device drivers and services, a diagnostic configuration that loads a basic set of drivers and services, and a custom

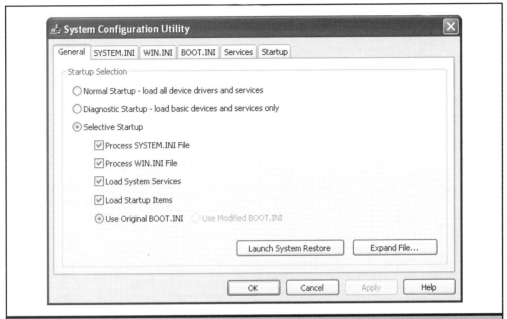

Figure 24-1.   *Use System Configuration Utility to troubleshoot configuration problems by turning off initialization files, drivers, services, and applications that may be destabilizing Windows XP.*

configuration (the Selective Startup option button) that lets you specify which of the options on the other five tabs to enable and which to disable.

■ The SYSTEM.INI tab (shown in Figure 24-2) and WIN.INI tab (which looks similar) let you choose which categories of entries or which individual entries in the system.ini and win.ini file to run. Use these tabs to find out which entries in the system.ini file and the win.ini file are causing problems. You do this by disabling categories or individual entries and rebooting your computer to test the effects of the changes. You can rearrange the order in which the entries are processed, because the order can make a difference to the result. You can also edit individual entries if necessary.

■ The BOOT.INI tab provides a GUI for editing the boot.ini file. See "Editing Your boot.ini File with System Configuration Utility," later in this chapter, for details.

■ The Services tab (shown in Figure 24-3) lets you see which services are running and disable them as necessary. The Hide All Microsoft Services check box lets you focus on third-party services.

■ The Startup tab lets you see which items are set to run automatically at startup. You can enable or disable these items as appropriate.

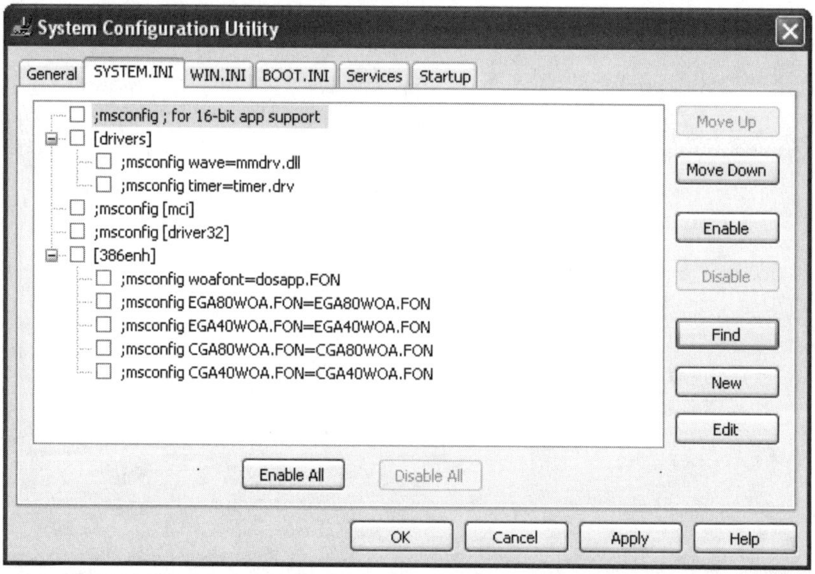

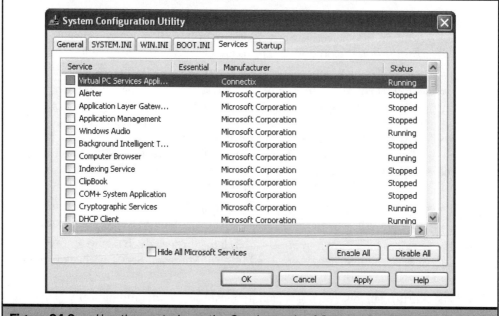

Figure 24-2.   Use the controls on the SYSTEM.INI tab to disable categories or entries in the system.ini file that may be causing problems.

Figure 24-3.   Use the controls on the Services tab of System Configuration Utility to disable services that may be causing startup problems.

Troubleshooting with System Configuration Utility

To use System Configuration Utility to track down the driver, service, or startup application that's making Windows XP unstable, perform a clean boot and then gradually add groups of drivers, services, and startup applications until the problem manifests itself again. Once you've narrowed the problem down to the drivers, the services, or the startup applications, work with the members of that group to identify the offender. For example, if the problem reoccurs when you include the services, work with the individual services on the Services tab to see which service is causing the problem.

Close all applications except System Configuration Utility, and then follow these general steps:

1. Perform a clean boot by selecting the Selective Startup option button on the General tab and clearing the four check boxes below this option button. Click the OK button, and then click the Restart button in the System Configuration dialog box that Windows XP displays.

2. System Configuration Utility forces a reboot. When Windows XP restarts and you log back on, System Configuration Utility displays the dialog box shown next to warn you that it's running. Click the OK button. You may want to select the Don't Show This Message or Launch the System Configuration Utility when Windows Starts check box.

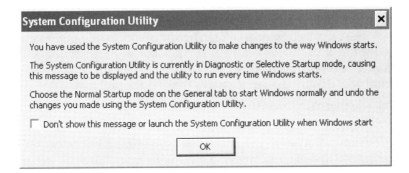

3. Use your computer for a while as normally as possible to see if it's stable in this clean boot configuration.

- If Windows XP runs stably, select the Process SYSTEM.INI File check box on the General tab, click the OK button, and allow System Configuration Utility to reboot the computer. Go to the next step.

- If Windows XP doesn't run stably, you may need to choose other boot options. See "Editing Your boot.ini File with System Configuration Utility," later in this chapter.

4. Check whether Windows XP runs stably after processing the system.ini file.

- If Windows XP runs stably, select the Process WIN.INI File check box on the General tab, click OK, and allow System Configuration Utility to reboot the computer. Go to the next step.

- If Windows XP doesn't run stably, the system.ini file probably contains the problem item. Clear all the check boxes on the SYSTEM.INI tab except the first and try booting with that. If all is well, select the second check box and try booting with that. Repeat the process until you identify the problem.

5. Check whether Windows XP runs stably after processing the win.ini file.

   - If Windows XP runs stably, select the Load System Services check box on the General tab, click OK, and allow System Configuration Utility to reboot the computer. Go to the next step.

   - If Windows XP doesn't run stably, the win.ini file probably contains the problem item. Clear all the check boxes on the WIN.INI tab except the first and try booting with that. If all is well, select the second check box and try booting with that. Repeat the process until you identify the problem.

6. Check whether Windows XP runs stably after loading system services.

   - If Windows XP runs stably, select the Load Startup Items check box on the General tab, click the OK button, and allow System Configuration Utility to reboot the computer. Go to the next step.

   - If Windows XP doesn't run stably, one of the system services is probably causing the instability. On the Services tab, click the Disable All button to disable all services. Click the Essential column heading twice to bring the essential services to the top of the list. Select the first check box and try booting with that. If all is well, select the second check box and try booting with that. Repeat the process until you identify the service that's causing the problem.

7. Check whether Windows XP runs stably after loading startup applications.

   - If Windows XP runs stably, your problem has mysteriously disappeared. Problems do mysteriously disappear sometimes, but they don't inspire confidence in the operating system. Update your antivirus software and run it. Check your disks as discussed in Chapter 39, and increase the frequency of your backups.

   - If Windows XP doesn't run stably, one of the startup applications is probably causing the instability. On the Startup tab, click the Disable All button to disable all startup applications. Select the first check box and try booting with that. If all is well, select the second check box and try booting with that. Repeat the process until you identify the startup application that's causing the problem.

8. When you find the offending item, remove it from your configuration. Select the Normal Startup option button on the General tab and click the OK button. After System Configuration Utility reboots your computer, make sure that Windows XP runs stably.

Editing Your boot.ini File with System Configuration Utility

The BOOT.INI tab of System Configuration Utility (Figure 24-4) provides a graphical interface for checking and editing your boot.ini file.

From the BOOT.INI tab, you can take the following actions:

■ In the [operating systems] section of the file in the list box, select the boot entry you want to affect and then click the Check All Boot Paths button, the Set As Default button, the Move Up button, or the Move Down button, as appropriate.

■ Change the value in the timeout text box to change the length of time for which Windows XP displays the boot menu at bootup.

■ Use the check boxes in the Boot Options group box to apply boot options to the selected boot entry. Table 24-2 explains these boot options. (Refer to Table 5-1 in Chapter 5 for a discussion of the main elements of a boot.ini file.)

Once you've used the controls on the BOOT.INI tab to change your boot.ini file, System Configuration Utility selects the Use Modified BOOT.INI option button on the General tab to apply your changes.

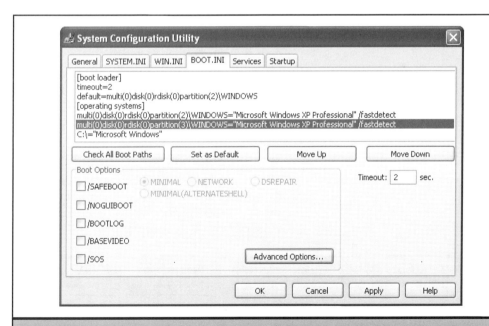

Figure 24-4. *Windows XP warns you that you're using Diagnostic mode or Selective Startup mode. Windows XP then starts System Configuration Utility unless you prevent it from doing so.*

SECURITY, BACKUP, AND
DISASTER RECOVERY

Boot Parameter	Explanation
/safeboot:minimal	Boots Windows XP in Safe mode.
/safeboot:network	Boots Windows XP in Safe mode with network support.
/safeboot:dsrepair	Boots Windows XP in Safe mode for restoring Active Directory. Don't use this setting with Windows XP Professional.
/safeboot:minimal(alternateshell)	Boots Windows XP in Safe mode with a command-prompt interface instead of the normal Explorer shell.
/bootlog	Logs the boot process in %systemroot%\ntbtlog.txt. Use the log to determine which drivers loaded successfully and which failed.
/noguiboot	Boots Windows XP without displaying the splash screen and graphics after the text-mode part of the boot process. (This part of the boot process normally uses the standard VGA video driver. Windows XP then switches to the video driver you've loaded.)
/basevideo	Forces Windows XP to use the standard VGA video driver instead of your regular video driver. Use this parameter to troubleshoot problems you suspect are caused by your video driver.
/sos	Makes Windows XP display the names of drivers as it loads them. Use this parameter together with the /bootlog parameter to see which drivers are causing problems.

Table 24-2. *Boot Parameters from System Configuration Utility's BOOT.INI Tab*

Using Last Known Good Configuration

Last Known Good Configuration is a tool for recovering from Registry changes or other damage to system files that prevents Windows XP from booting fully. Last Known Good

Configuration restores Windows XP to the last configuration in which it booted fully. To do this, Last Known Good Configuration uses configuration data from the latest ControlSet key (one of ControlSet001, ControlSet002, or ControlSet003) in the HKLM\ SYSTEM\ key in the Registry.

Because Last Known Good Configuration returns Windows XP to the configuration in which it last booted successfully, you'll need to reinstate any configuration changes you made after that boot. This usually won't be too much of a problem, because one or more of those configuration changes is likely what's prevented Windows XP from booting fully.

To use Last Known Good Configuration, start or restart Windows XP as follows:

- If your computer has a multiboot configuration, press F8 when Windows XP displays the Please Select the Operating System to Start screen.

- If you don't have a multiboot configuration, press F8 while the computer is restarting.

From the Windows Advanced Options menu (Figure 24-5), select the Last Known Good Configuration item and press ENTER.

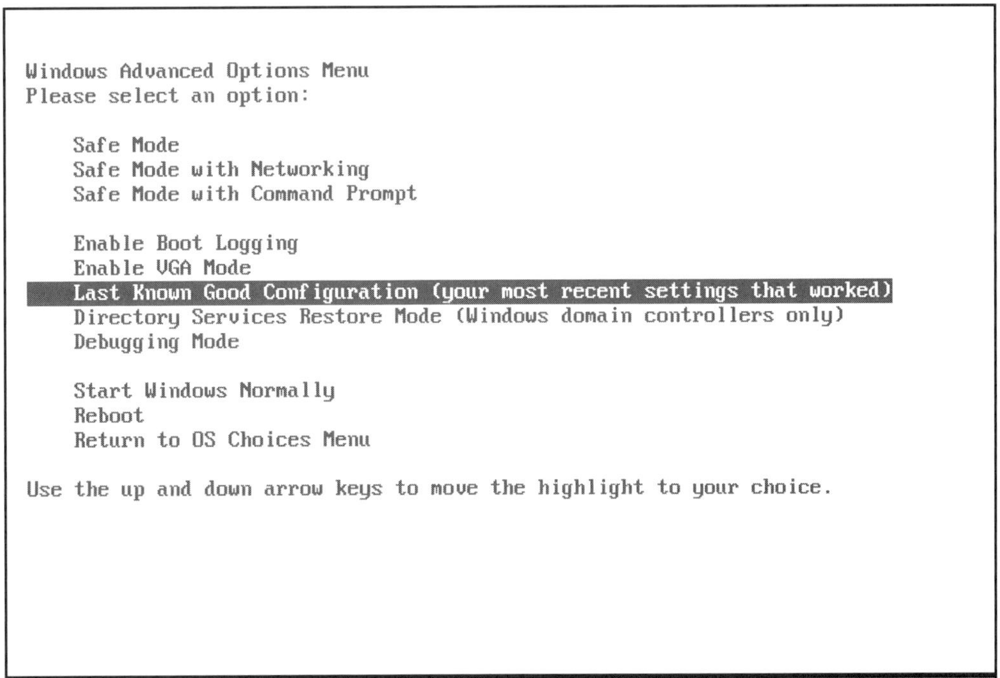

```
Windows Advanced Options Menu
Please select an option:

    Safe Mode
    Safe Mode with Networking
    Safe Mode with Command Prompt

    Enable Boot Logging
    Enable VGA Mode
    Last Known Good Configuration (your most recent settings that worked)
    Directory Services Restore Mode (Windows domain controllers only)
    Debugging Mode

    Start Windows Normally
    Reboot
    Return to OS Choices Menu

Use the up and down arrow keys to move the highlight to your choice.
```

Figure 24-5. *Use Last Known Good Configuration to recover from configuration changes that prevent Windows XP from booting fully.*

Recovering with Recovery Console

Recovery Console is a command-line tool for fixing configuration problems when Windows XP won't boot fully and—usually—when using Last Known Good Configuration has failed to solve the problem. To use Recovery Console, boot to Recovery Console either from the Windows XP CD or (if you've installed Recovery Console on your hard disk) from the Windows Advanced Options menu.

Recovery Console supports a limited number of commands. With these commands, you can fix many configuration problems.

 You need to be an administrator to install and use Recovery Console.

Installing Recovery Console on Your Hard Drive

By installing Recovery Console on your hard drive before trouble strikes, you can make Recovery Console available even when you don't have your Windows XP CD in hand. However, you may not always be able to boot to Recovery Console from your hard disk (for example, if files have been corrupted on your hard drive), so having the Windows XP CD available is a good idea.

To install Recovery Console on your hard drive, insert your Windows XP CD in your CD drive and run *cd***:\i386\winnt32.exe /cmdcons**, where *cd* is the drive letter assigned to your CD drive. In the Windows Setup dialog box that asks if you want to install Recovery Console, click the Yes button.

Booting to Recovery Console

You can boot to Recovery Console from your hard drive (if you've installed Recovery Console, as described in the previous subsection) or from your Windows XP CD.

Booting to Recovery Console from Your Hard Drive

If you've installed Recovery Console on your hard drive, select the Microsoft Windows Recovery Console item when Windows XP displays the Please Select the Operating System to Start screen.

Booting to Recovery Console from Your Windows XP CD

To boot to Recovery Console from your Windows XP CD, follow these steps:

1. Insert your Windows XP CD in the CD drive.

2. Restart the computer and boot from the CD. (You may need to change BIOS settings to boot from the CD.)

3. At the Welcome to Setup screen, press R to select the Recovery Console option.

Logging On to Recovery Console

When Recovery Console starts, it briefly offers you the chance to press ENTER to load a nonstandard keyboard for the Recovery Console session.

After booting to Recovery Console, you'll see the Recovery Console login screen (shown in Figure 24-6 after a successful logon), which lists the Windows installations available on the computer and asks which you want to log onto. In the figure, there's only one installation, but if you have a multi-boot configuration, you'll see an entry for each Windows NT-based OS that Recovery Console has recognized.

Type the number for the Windows installation you want to log on to and press ENTER. Type the administrator password (and press ENTER) when Recovery Console prompts you for it. If the password is correct, Recovery Console displays a command prompt from which you can use the commands discussed in the next section.

 You can enter the password for any administrator account on the computer. For example, in a standalone or workgroup configuration, you can enter the password of any computer administrator user.

To exit Recovery Console, issue an exit command.

SECURITY, BACKUP, AND DISASTER RECOVERY

```
Microsoft Windows XP(TM) Recovery Console.

The Recovery Console provides system repair and recovery functionality.

Type EXIT to quit the Recovery Console and restart the computer.


1: C:\WINDOWS

Which Windows installation would you like to log onto
(To cancel, press ENTER)? 1
Type the Administrator password: ****
C:\WINDOWS>_
```

Figure 24-6. *In Recovery Console, log on to the Windows installation you're trying to repair.*

Using Recovery Console Commands

Recovery Console supports a couple dozen of commands. Some of these are commands you'll be familiar with if you've worked with DOS. Others are specific to Recovery Console. Many of the commands have effects that you can't undo, so use them with due care and consideration.

Table 24-3 lists the Recovery Console commands.

Command	Explanation
attrib	Changes the attributes of a file or folder. For example, use an **attrib –r** command to remove the read-only attribute from a file or folder.
batch	Loads the specified batch file.
bootcfg	Configures and repairs boot files. See "Rebuilding Your Boot Configuration with bootcfg," later in this chapter.
cd	Changes to the specified folder (same as chdir).
chdir	Changes to the specified folder (same as cd).
chkdsk	Checks the specified drive and displays the results of the check. For example, **chkdisk c:** checks the C: drive.
cls	Clears the screen of its current contents.
copy	Copies the specified item or items to the specified destination.
del	Deletes the specified item or items (same as delete).
delete	Deletes the specified item or items (same as del).
dir	Lists the contents of the specified folder or (with no folder specified) the current folder.
disable	Disables the specified service or driver. See "Preventing a Service from Running," later in this chapter.
diskpart	Used without parameters, loads the disk partition manager. This is the same partition manager shown in Figure 2-1 and discussed in "Partitioning the Drive and Choosing the Installation Partition" in Chapter 2. You can also use diskpart from the command line with parameters, but, almost always, using the interface is easier.

Table 24-3.   *Recovery Console Commands*

Command	Explanation
enable	Enables the specified service or driver to run using the specified start type. See "Preventing a Service from Running," later in this chapter.
exit	Exits Recovery Console and restarts your computer.
expand	Extracts a compressed file from a cabinet (.CAB) file.
fixboot	Writes a replacement boot sector onto the specified partition.
fixmbr	Repairs the master boot record (MBR) on the boot partition or the specified partition.
format	Formats or reformats the specified drive.
help	Lists the commands available in Recovery Console.
listsvc	Lists the services and drivers available and their startup setting (Boot, Auto, Manual, System, or Disabled)
logon	Logs you on to another Windows installation. You need to supply an administrator's password to log on successfully.
map	Lists the currently mapped drive letters and the devices they're mapped to. For hard disks, it shows the partitions as well.
md	Creates a folder with the specified name (same as mkdir).
mkdir	Creates a folder with the specified name (same as md).
more	Displays the specified text file on screen (same as type). This is not the |more pipe you can use in command-prompt windows in Windows XP to display information one screenful at a time. Recovery Console automatically displays one screenful of information at a time when a command returns more than a screenful.
net use	Maps the specified network share to the specified drive letter. See "Mapping a Network Drive with net use," later in this chapter.
rd	Deletes the specified folder (same as rmdir).
ren	Renames the specified file or folder to the specified name (same as rename).

Table 24-3. *Recovery Console Commands* (continued)

SECURITY, BACKUP, AND
DISASTER RECOVERY

Command	Explanation
rename	Renames the specified file or folder to the specified name (same as ren).
rmdir	Deletes the specified folder (same as rd).
set	Displays the environment variables used by Recovery Console and lets you set variables.
systemroot	Changes folder (and drive, if necessary) to the %systemroot% folder.
type	Displays the specified text file on screen (same as type).

Table 24-3.   *Recovery Console Commands* (continued)

What You Can and Can't Access from Recovery Console

By default, Recovery Console is limited to accessing the following areas of the file system:

- The root directory for each volume (for example, C: and D: hard drive volumes)
- The %systemroot% folder and its subfolders
- Removable media such as floppy disks and CD-ROMs
- Network shares that you map by using the net use command

By default Recovery Console can't access other folders than these. For example, you can't access the Documents and Settings folder or the Program Files folder. Recovery Console also can't write to the floppy drive or to a removable disk. To change these default settings, you need to apply policy settings and then use set statements in Recovery Console.

Using set Statements to Configure the Recovery Console Environment

Recovery Console uses four environment variables that control whether you can take certain actions in Recovery Console. These environmental variables are disabled by default, so they need to be enabled before you can use them. To enable the variables, you can use Group Policy (if you're a domain administrator) or local policies (if you administer your own computer).

To enable environment variables through local policies, follow these steps:

1. Open the Local Security Settings console by running **secpol.msc**, choosing Start | Control Panel | Performance and Maintenance | Administrative Tools | Local Security Settings, or choosing Start | All Programs | Administrative Tools | Local Security Settings.

2. Expand the Local Policies branch and select the Security Options item to display its policies in the right pane of the console.

3. Double-click the Recovery Console: Allow Floppy Copy and Access to All Drives and Folders item to display its Properties dialog box.

4. Select the Enabled option button to enable the policy.

5. Click the OK button to close the Properties dialog box.

6. Close Local Security Settings.

Tip *The Local Policies\Security Options policies also include a policy named Recovery Console: Allow Automatic Administrative Logon. This policy is disabled by default. You can enable it if you want any user to be able to log onto Recovery Console without providing an administrative password. However, because a user can wreak havoc by using Recovery Console incompetently or maliciously, using the automatic administrative logon option is seldom a good idea.*

Table 24-4 explains the Recovery Console environment variables.

Environment Variable	Explanation
AllowWildCards	Controls whether you can use wildcards (such as * and ?) in Recovery Console commands that support them.
AllowAllPaths	Controls whether you can access files and folders other than the defaults discussed in the previous subsection.
AllowRemovableMedia	Controls whether you can copy files and folders to removable media (for example, a floppy disk).
NoCopyPrompt	Suppresses confirmation when copying a file over an existing file.

Table 24-4. *Recovery Console Environment Variables*

The syntax for setting these environment variables is as shown below, where *environment_variable* is the environment variable and *parameter* is TRUE or FALSE:

```
set environment_variable = parameter
```

For example, the following commands turn on the use of wild cards and access to files and folders other than the defaults:

```
set allowwildcards = true
set allowallpaths = true
```

Rebuilding Your Boot Configuration with bootcfg

One problem that may prevent your computer from booting successfully is that your boot configuration has been corrupted or damaged. When this happens, use the Recovery Console bootcfg utility to repair your boot configuration.

Table 24-5 explains the main parameters for bootcfg, but it doesn't discuss the two most esoteric options, which are used to redirect the boot loader to a COM port for "headless administration" and to disable this feature.

Parameter	Explanation
/list	Displays a list of the entries currently in the boot menu.
/default	Displays a list of the entries currently in the boot menu so that you can specify the default. (The command prompts you to "select installation to add," but it makes the entry you specify the default.)
/add	Lets you add an installation to the boot menu. You enter a name (the "load identifier") and any OS load options (for example, you might use the **/fastdetect** parameter to turn off searching for serial mouses).
/rebuild	Scans the computer for installations you can add to the boot menu and prompts you to add them. As with the /add parameter, you enter a load identifier and any OS load options.
/scan	Scans the computer for installations and lists their %systemroot% folders.

Table 24-5. *Most Useful bootcfg Parameters*

Mapping a Network Drive with net use

The net use command lets you map a network share to a drive letter. The syntax for net use is as follows:

```
net use [\\server_name\share_name
/user:domain_name\username [password] | drive_letter: /d]
```

Table 24-6 explains the parameters for net use.

Preventing a Service from Running

As discussed in Chapter 43, a misconfigured service can prevent your computer from booting successfully. When this happens, you'll need to prevent the service to allow your computer to boot.

Use a **listsvc** command to display a list of services, then issue a **disable** command for the service you want to disable by using either the service name or the display name. (See Table 43-1 in Chapter 43 for a list of service names and display names.)

Note *You can also use the disable command to disable a driver from loading.*

Parameter	Explanation
server_name	The server to connect to
share_name	The network share to connect to
domain_name	The domain for validating the user's credentials
username	The user account to use for connecting to the network share
password	The password for the user account. You can omit the password in the command and enter it when prompted instead.
drive_letter	The drive letter to map to the network share

Table 24-6. *net use Command Parameters*

To enable a service or a driver, use an **enable** command with the appropriate parameter: service_auto_start, service_boot_start, service_system_start, or service_demand_start.

Recovery Using Parallel Installation

If you're not able to recover using Recovery Console, the next step is to create a parallel installation of Windows XP Professional, boot that installation, and use it to repair the damage to your main installation.

A parallel installation is useful for recovering from Registry damage. For example, by booting to a parallel installation and mounting the Registry in the damaged installation, you can repair the damaged installation. After repairing the installation, you can boot back into it.

Recovery Using ASR

If you're unable to recover your installation of Windows XP Professional by using the tools described so far in this chapter, try using ASR. "Automated System Recovery" in Chapter 23 discusses how to use ASR to recover from a system problem, including the pitfalls that can prevent ASR from working correctly.

Recovery Using Reinstallation

If you're unable to recover your installation of Windows XP Professional by using all the other recovery tools listed in Table 24-1, and ASR has failed (or you hadn't created an ASR backup set), you'll probably need to reinstall Windows XP to recover from the problem.

In a domain environment, an administrator will probably reinstall Windows XP Professional for you by using an automated setup routine or Remote Installation Services.

Summary

This chapter has discussed the tools that Windows XP Professional provides for recovering from disaster. You've learned how—and when—to use System Configuration Utility,

Last Known Good Configuration, and Recovery Console to fix Windows XP configuration problems.

This is the end of the third part of the book. The following part discusses how to use Windows XP Professional on a local area network (LAN). Chapter 25, the first chapter in this part, shows you how to configure network connection and access network drives.

SECURITY, BACKUP, AND DISASTER RECOVERY

The
Complete
Reference

Part IV

Using Windows XP Professional on a LAN

Chapter 25

Configuring Network Connections and Accessing Network Drives

491

W hether your Windows XP Professional computer is part of a Windows domain or a smaller network, you'll almost certainly need to access drives on other computers to get your work done. For example, in a domain environment, an administrator is likely to encourage (or force) you to store your files on networked drives on file servers so that the administrator can easily back up everyone's files. In a workgroup environment, you'll often need to work with files stored on your colleagues' computers or they'll need to work with files stored on your computer.

This chapter discusses how to configure network connections, from renaming them, to enabling and disabling them, to including them in network bridges. The chapter also describes how to access network drives and how to configure advanced network properties.

In a domain environment, an administrator may have prevented you from carrying out most (or perhaps all) of the activities described in this chapter. To make you aware of the things you may be unable to do, the chapter starts with a discussion of the options a network administrator can set to restrict the actions you can take with network connections.

Note	*In a domain environment, you're unlikely to share drives or folders on your computer with other computers on the network. By contrast, in a workgroup setting, you may well want to share drives or folders. See Chapter 27 for a discussion of the options that Windows XP Professional offers for sharing drives and folders in a workgroup.*

Administrative Control of Network Connections in a Domain

Which of the activities described in the chapter you can perform depends on how an administrator has configured your copy of Windows XP Professional. Because networking is one of the major focuses of Windows XP Professional and network problems can cause major headaches for administrators, your network's administrator is likely to exercise tight control over their network. As with many other aspects of Windows configuration, the administrator will use Group Policy to configure networking settings and what you can do with them.

Group Policy includes more delicately nuanced settings for configuring permissions for network connections than this chapter can reasonably attempt to discuss. In a domain environment, Windows XP Professional automatically prevents nonadministrators from taking some actions with network connections. An administrator can implement further restrictions, some of which apply only to computer administrators (for actions that nonadministrators are prevented from taking) and others that apply to both computer administrator users and nonadministrators.

These are the general restrictions you're likely to see in a domain environment:

- If you're a user (rather than an administrator), you won't be able to enable or disable LAN components. You may be able to view the properties for a LAN connection, but you won't be able to change them. A domain administrator can prevent administrators from enabling and disabling LAN components as well.

- You may be able to rename LAN connections (for example, to assign a descriptive name to a connection so that it's easier to identify).

- An administrator can prevent you from viewing and changing the properties of a LAN connection.

- An administrator can prevent you from displaying the status icon for a connection in the notification area or from displaying the Status dialog box for a connection.

- An administrator can remove the Entire Network item from the My Network Places folder to prevent you from trying to browse the entire network (because doing so might waste network bandwidth or encourage you to try connecting to resources that you're not supposed to connect to).

- An administrator can remove the Map Network Drive command and the Disconnect Network Drive command from the Tools menu and from the shortcut menus that would include these commands. They might do this to prevent you from changing your existing drive mappings.

- You may or may not be able to access the New Connection Wizard, the wizard used for creating network and Internet connections.

 In a workgroup, an administrator can prevent workgroup computers from appearing in the Computers Near Me view in My Network Places. They might implement this restriction to discourage you from trying to establish extra connections to computers in your workgroup.

Working with Network Connections

Windows XP Professional's main tool for working with network connections is the Network Connections folder. Depending on how Windows XP Professional is configured, you can access the Network Connections folder in any of the following ways:

- Choose Start | Connect To | Show All Connections.
- Choose Start | Network Connections.
- Choose Start | Control Panel | Network and Internet Connections | Network Connections.

Figure 25-1 shows a Network Connections folder that contains three dial-up connections, one Incoming Connections item (you can only have one of these), two LAN connections, and one VPN connection. One of the LAN connections is for an Ethernet

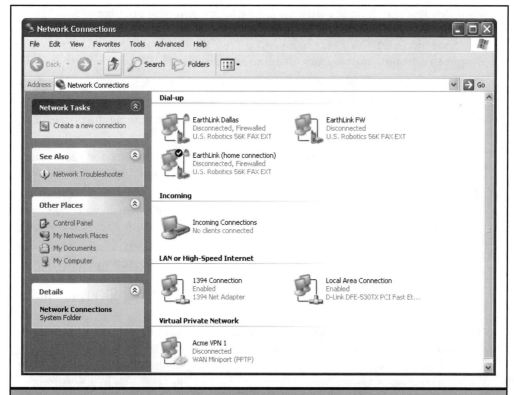

Figure 25-1.   *The Network Connections folder is Windows XP Professional's main tool for working with network connections.*

card; the other LAN connection is for a FireWire card (identified as 1394 Connection) because FireWire can be used to connect computers to each other, as well as to connect peripherals to a computer.

Using Details View to Display More Information

By default, Windows XP Professional opens the Network Connections folder in Tile view, which displays a brief summary of information on each connection: the connection's name, its status (for example, Disconnected, Firewalled for a dial-up connection, or Enabled for a LAN connection), and the device used.

You can switch to other views by using the View button, View menu, or View submenu on the shortcut menu as usual. Only Details view is useful, as it provides more information than Tile view, including the phone number or host address of the connection and the user account or system account that owns the connection. You can customize the selection of columns by right-clicking a column heading and using the resulting drop-down menu to toggle a column on and off. You can rearrange the order of the columns by dragging a column heading to the left or right.

Renaming Network Connections

If your administrator permits you to rename network connections, you may want to assign descriptive names so that you can easily distinguish two or more connections of the same type. For example, if you have multiple dial-up connections for the same ISP for different cities, you might assign each a name that included its city, so that they're immediately identifiable.

To rename a selected connection, issue a Rename command from the File menu or the shortcut menu, press F2, or click the connection's name twice with a short pause between the clicks. Edit the name and press ENTER.

Changing the Properties for a Network Connection

If an administrator permits you to change the properties for a network connection, select the connection and issue a Properties command from the File menu or the shortcut menu to display its Properties dialog box. Figure 25-2 shows the General tab and the Authentication tab of the Properties dialog box for a typical Local Area Connection.

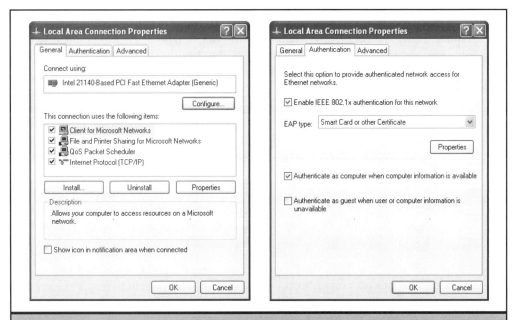

Figure 25-2. *Choose protocols and configure their settings on the General tab (left) of the Properties dialog box for a network connection; choose authentication options on the Authentication tab (right).*

On the General tab, you can take the following actions:

■ Click the Configure button to display the Properties dialog box for the network adapter used for the connection. The settings available in this dialog box depend on the adapter. For a Fast Ethernet adapter, for example, you can often choose whether it uses 100BaseTx Full Duplex mode, 100BaseTx Half Duplex mode, 10BaseT Full Duplex mode, 10BaseT Half Duplex mode, or Auto-Negotiation mode. (Full duplex sends and receives data at the same time. Half-duplex sends and receives separately.)

■ Enable or disable a network client, a service, or a protocol for the connection by selecting or clearing its check box in the This Connection Uses the Following Items list box.

■ Install a new network client, service, or protocol by clicking the Install button, using the Select Network Component Type dialog box to choose among Client, Service, and Protocol, and working in the resulting dialog box. Installing a networking component in this way installs it for all connections, not just for the connection from which you're working.

Note *You'll need to be a computer administrator to install or remove network components for a LAN connection.*

■ Uninstall a currently installed network client, service, or protocol by selecting it in the This Connection Uses the Following Items list box, clicking the Uninstall button, and then clicking the Yes button in the resulting dialog box. Uninstalling a networking component removes it from all connections, not just from the connection you're working on.

■ Configure a network client, service, or protocol by clicking the Properties button and working in the resulting Properties dialog box. (Only some components have configurable properties.) For example, if you use the NWLink IPX/SPX/NetBIOS Compatible Transport Protocol, you might need to set the internal network number or specify the frame type and network number for the connection.

■ Select the Show Icon in Notification Area when Connected check box to display a notification-area icon for the connection. This icon can be helpful because it lets you see when data is being transferred across the connection and because it provides quick access to the Status dialog box for the connection.

On the Authentication tab of the Properties dialog box for a Local Area Connection, you can choose options for authenticating your computer on the network:

■ *Enable Network Access Control Using IEEE 802.1X check box* Controls whether Windows XP Professional uses port-based network access control on this connection. If you select the check box, select the type of Extensible Authentication Protocol (EAP) to use in the EAP Type drop-down list. For the default selection,

Smart Card or Other Certificate, you can click the Properties button and use the Smart Card or Other Certificate Properties dialog box to specify whether to use a smart card or a certificate.

- *Authenticate As Computer when Computer Information Is Available check box*   Controls whether Windows XP Professional tries to authenticate the computer to the network when no user is logged on.

- *Authenticate As Guest when User or Computer Name Is Unavailable*   Controls whether Windows XP Professional tries to authenticate the computer as a guest when no user information or computer information is available. Guest users have severely limited privileges on almost all networks, but they can usually take a few actions.

On the Advanced tab of the Properties dialog box for a Local Area Connection, you can turn Internet Connection Firewall (ICF) on and off. See "Securing Your Internet Connection with ICF" in Chapter 36 for a discussion of ICF.

Disabling and Reenabling a Network Connection

If an administrator permits you to disable and reenable network connections, you can do so easily from the Network Connections folder:

- To disable a network connection, select it and issue a Disable command from the File menu or the shortcut menu.

- To reenable the connection, select it and issue an Enable command from the File menu or the shortcut menu.

Bridging Network Connections

Windows XP Professional includes a feature for creating a network bridge to connect two network segments so that the computers on the segments can all communicate with each other.

You're highly unlikely to need to bridge networks in a domain environment—an administrator will do any bridging necessary, and they'll almost certainly use dedicated bridge hardware for the task rather than a computer running Windows XP Professional. In fact, in a domain environment, an administrator can—and may well—prevent you from installing and configuring a network bridge. This setting applies only when the computer is connected to the network on which the computer receives Group Policy updates. So you might be able to bridge network connections on your work laptop at home when you're unable to bridge connections in the office.

In a small-office network or a home-office network, however, network bridging can be useful and effective. In such a situation, you're most likely to need to bridge two networks of different types. This is because, if all the computers are networked using the same technology, it's much easier to connect them all in a single network than to create two separate networks and bridge them. However, if your network segments are of different types, bridging makes sense. A computer is connected to each network using a suitable network adapter (for example, a FireWire card and a Fast Ethernet card) for each network. That computer then passes packets from each network segment to the other.

For example, suppose you have a handful of computers in your home office, all located close to one another, and you need the fastest affordable connection among them. You might choose to implement FireWire or USB 2.0 because both offer much greater speed than Fast Ethernet but are much less expensive than Gigabit Ethernet. To connect this network to the Fast Ethernet network you use for the computers in the other rooms of your house or apartment, you could bridge the networks at a computer that you leave on, for example, your ICS host. Bridging the two networks lets the computers on the FireWire network see the computers on the Fast Ethernet network, and vice versa.

| **Note** | *A software network bridge has the disadvantage that the computer running the bridge must keep running the whole time any of the computers on the separate network segments need to communicate with each other.* |

Another different network type you may want to bridge is a wireless network, so that you have a network that's part wired Ethernet (Fast or regular) and part wireless. You can do this as well with Windows XP Professional. But before you do, make sure you can't do the same thing more simply by using a wireless access point that includes a bridge to Fast Ethernet. Many wireless access points have this capability because it's so popular.

To bridge two networks, follow these general steps:

1. Decide which computer you'll implement the bridge on. This computer will need to be running all the time any computer on either network segment needs to communicate with any computer on the other network segment. This computer will also have to devote some computing power to forwarding the traffic.

2. Install a second network adapter of the appropriate type in that computer if necessary.

3. Connect the computer to both networks and make sure that both network connections are working.

4. In the Network Connections folder, select the icons for the connections you want to bridge.

5. Issue a Bridge Connections command from the Advanced menu or the shortcut menu.

6. Windows XP Professional displays the Network Bridge message box as it bridges the connections. Windows XP Professional then adds a Network Bridge category to the Network Connections folder, adds to it an icon for the bridge, and moves the bridged connections to this category.

You can bridge more than two network segments at the same time, but usually it's best to start by bridging two segments, and then add further segments as necessary

After you've set up the bridge, things work a little differently:

- The computer hosting the bridge forwards all IP packets from each network segment to the other segment.

- The network adapters in the bridge share an IP address.

- To configure the bridged adapters, you work with the bridge rather than with the network adapters. The exception is when you need to remove a network adapter from the bridge: right-click the network adapter and choose Remove from Bridge from the shortcut menu.

- You can disable the bridge by issuing a Disable command from the File menu or the shortcut menu.

- You can delete the bridge by issuing a Delete command from the File menu or the shortcut menu and choosing the Yes button in the Confirm Connection Delete dialog box.

Configuring Network Bindings and Provider Order

If you administer your own computer, you'll also be able to set the order in which network services use available network connections and the order in which your computer accesses them. Choose Advanced | Advanced Settings to display the Advanced Settings dialog box, which opens with the Adapters and Bindings tab (shown on the left in Figure 25-3) displayed. (The Advanced Settings command isn't available to users who aren't administrators and, in a domain environment, a domain administrator can make the command unavailable to administrators as well.)

Configuring Network Bindings

In the Connections list box, you can change the order in which network services access the available connections. Normally, you'll need to change the order only if you have two or more LAN connections, as in the previous figure, which shows the computer's Ethernet connection under the name Local Area Connection and the FireWire connection under the name 1394 Connection. Make sure that the network connection you want services to use first appears at the top of this list. In the example, because I'm not using the 1394 Connection for networking, I've moved it to below the Local Area Connection, which is used for networking.

What you're more likely to need to do on the Adapters and Bindings tab of the Advanced Settings dialog box is change the order in which bindings are used for a connection or unbind one or more protocols from a connection. For example, you might unbind TCP/IP from the File and Printer Sharing service to prevent people from remotely accessing the files and printers you're sharing.

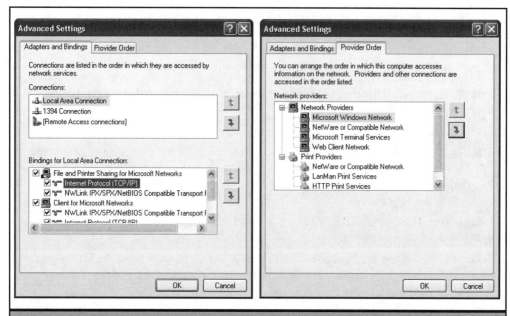

Figure 25-3. On the Adapters and Bindings tab (left) of the Advanced Settings dialog box, you can configure the order in which Windows XP Professional uses network connections and the bindings that each connection uses. On the Provider tab (right), you can change the order in which Windows XP Professional uses network providers and print providers.

To change binding order or unbind a protocol, follow these steps:

1. Select the connection in the Connections list box. Windows XP Professional displays the bindings for the connection in the Bindings For list box.

2. To change the binding order, select an item and use the ↑ button or the ↓ button to move it to its new position.

3. To unbind a protocol, clear its check box.

Configuring Provider Order

The Provider tab of the Advanced Settings dialog box (shown on the right in Figure 25-3) contains controls for changing the order in which Windows XP Professional uses network providers and print providers. By moving the primary provider to the top of the list, you can increase the speed at which your computer accesses data on the network. For example, you might move the Microsoft Windows Network item to above the Microsoft Terminal Services item in the Network Providers list.

Accessing Network Drives

This section discusses how to access network drives so that you can work with their contents. In many cases, you'll want to establish permanent connections to network drives, because then you can always access them when you're using your computer. When you map a network drive to a drive letter, Windows XP Professional maintains a connection to the network drive so that you can quickly access it. In other cases, you may be unable to map a network drive to a drive letter. This section discusses alternative maneuvers you may be able to perform.

When mapping a drive, you can choose whether to create a persistent mapping, so that Windows XP Professional tries to reestablish the connection each time you log on, or to create a temporary mapping that lasts only until the end of your current user session. In most cases, you'll use persistent mappings so that you can always get at your documents.

In a domain environment, an administrator is likely to set up all the drive mappings you'll supposedly need. After doing this, an administrator may remove the Disconnect Network Drive command (to prevent you from disconnecting any of the mappings) and the Map Network Drive command (to prevent you from creating any new mappings) from the Windows Explorer interface. An administrator may also have removed the Entire Network item and the Computers Near Me item from the My Network Places folder to limit the amount of browsing that you can do.

As you've seen earlier in this book, the names of network drives typically start with two backslashes (\\), which preface the name of the server sharing the drive. This naming scheme is called the Universal Naming Convention (UNC). For example, in the UNC path \\acmeheavysv071\users, the server is named acmeheavysv071 and the shared folder is named users.

Connecting a Network Drive

You can connect a network drive either by issuing a Map Network Drive command, and then specifying the drive to connect to, or by browsing to the drive, and then issuing a Map Network Drive command. The following subsections discuss these options.

Creating a Network Drive Mapping by Using the Map Network Drive Command

To create a network drive mapping by using the Map Network Drive command, follow these steps:

1. Open a Windows Explorer window. (For example, choose Start | My Network Places.)

2. Choose Tools | Map Network Drive to display the Map Network Drive dialog box (Figure 25-4).

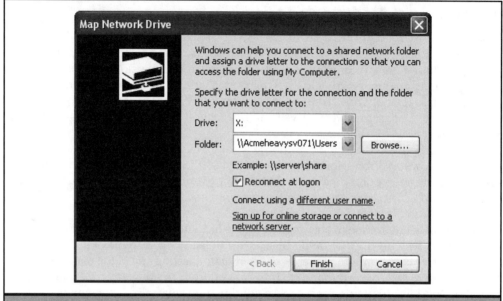

Figure 25-4.   The Map Network Drive dialog box lets you map a shared folder to a drive letter under either your current user account or another user account.

3. Click the Browse button and use the resulting Browse for Folder dialog box to select the folder that you want to map to the drive. (Alternatively, type the path to the folder in the Folder text box.)

4. To make Windows XP Professional reestablish the network drive each time you log on, leave the Reconnect at Logon check box selected, as it is by default. If you want the drive mapping to last only for the current session, clear this check box.

5. If you need to use credentials to access the network drive other than the credentials under which you're currently logged on, click the Connect Using a Different User Name link. In the resulting Connect As dialog box, enter the user name and password to use for accessing the network drive, and then click the OK button to close the Connect As dialog box.

6. Click the Finish button. Windows XP Professional establishes the network drive mapping.

Creating a Network Drive Mapping for the Current Drive

To create a network drive mapping for the current drive or folder, follow these steps:

1. Open a Windows Explorer window.

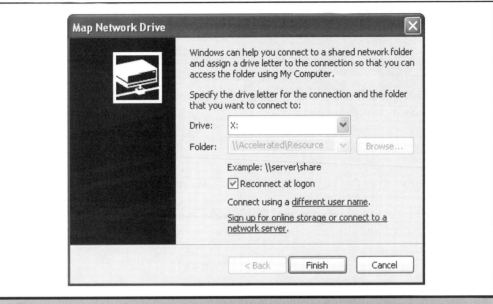

Figure 25-5.   *Use the Map Network Drive dialog box to assign a drive letter to a shared network folder, so that you can access it more quickly in future.*

2. Browse to the network drive or folder by using whichever means you prefer. For example, click My Network Places and use the My Network Places window to browse to the network drive or folder you want to connect.

3. Right-click the drive or folder and choose Map Network Drive from the shortcut menu. Windows XP Professional displays the Map Network Drive dialog box with the path already entered in the Folder dialog box (Figure 25-5).

4. Click the Finish button.

Connecting to a Network Share by Using the Run Dialog Box

If an administrator has removed the Map Network Drive command from the Windows Explorer interface, you may still be able to connect to a network share by browsing to it through the network. If an administrator has also removed the Entire Network item and the Computers Near Me item from My Network Places, finding network locations will be harder. But you may still be able to connect to a network share by entering its path in the Address Bar in a Windows Explorer window or in the Run dialog box.

You may also be able to map a drive letter to the shared folder by using the subst command at a command prompt. The basic syntax for subst is as follows:

```
subst drive_letter: path
```

For example, the following command assigns the drive letter *M* to the shared folder \\acmeheavysv071\users:

```
subst m: \\acmeheavysv071\users
```

To see which drives you've mapped with subst, enter a subst command without any parameters.

To disconnect a drive you've mapped with subst, use the /d parameter. For example, the following command disconnects the M: drive:

```
subst m: /d
```

Drive-letter mappings you create with subst last only until the end of the current user session.

Disconnecting a Network Drive

You can disconnect a network drive in either of the following ways:

- In a My Computer window, select the drive and issue a Disconnect command from the File menu or the shortcut menu. Windows XP Professional disconnects the drive without confirmation.

- In a Windows Explorer window, choose Tools | Disconnect Network Drive to display the Disconnect Network Drives dialog box (Figure 25-6). Select the drive or drives to disconnect and click the OK button.

When you disconnect a drive on which you have files open, Windows XP Professional warns you that data may be lost. Choose the No button in the warning dialog box, close the files, and then disconnect the drive.

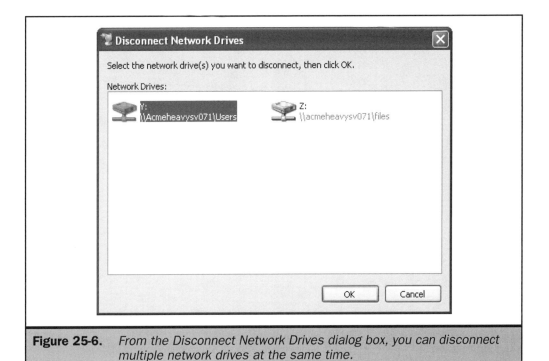

Figure 25-6.   *From the Disconnect Network Drives dialog box, you can disconnect multiple network drives at the same time.*

Summary

This chapter has discussed how to configure network connections and access network drives. You've also learned about the control that administrators can exercise over network connections.

The next chapter discusses how to configure and troubleshoot TCP/IP connections.

Chapter 26

Configuring and Troubleshooting TCP/IP Connections

507

This chapter discusses how to configure and troubleshoot TCP/IP connections. TCP/IP is Windows XP Professional's preferred protocol for network and Internet communications, so fully functional TCP/IP communications are vital to most Windows XP Professional network activities. For example, every time you access the Internet from Windows XP Professional, you're using a TCP/IP connection. You're also likely to be using TCP/IP every time you access a file on a server or check your e-mail.

This chapter assumes that you're less interested in the details of how and why TCP/IP works than in how to make it perform everyday tasks —and how to troubleshoot TCP/IP when it doesn't work. However, to configure and troubleshoot TCP/IP, you need to understand the basics of how TCP/IP works. So this chapter briefly explains IP addresses, public and private addressing, DHCP and static addressing, DNS, WINS, and APIPA, along the way.

Much of this chapter discusses command-line TCP/IP utilities. Run these utilities from the command prompt (Start | All Programs | Accessories | Command Prompt or Start | Run, **cmd**, OK). You can stop most of the command-line utilities by issuing a Cancel command (CTRL-C). You can pause most of these command-line utilities by pressing PAUSE.

Configuring TCP/IP Connections

To configure TCP/IP, open the Internet Protocol (TCP/IP) Properties dialog box by following these steps:

1. Open the Network Connections folder by choosing Start | Connect To | Show All Connections, Start | Network Connections, or Start | Control Panel | Network and Internet Connections | Network Connections, depending on how your Start menu is configured.

2. Select the connection you want to affect (for example, your Local Area Connection item), and issue a Properties command from the File menu or the shortcut menu. (Alternatively, click the Change Settings of This Connection link in the Network Tasks pane.)

Note *If, when you display the Properties dialog box for the network connection, Windows XP Professional displays a Local Network dialog box telling you that "Some of the controls on this property sheet are disabled because you do not have sufficient privileges to access or change them," you'll know that an administrator has prevented you from configuring the properties for the connection. In this case, you probably won't be able to configure TCP/IP.*

3. Double-click the Internet Protocol (TCP/IP) item in the This Connection Uses the Following Items list box to display the Internet Protocol (TCP/IP) Properties dialog box.

■ For a LAN connection, which is what you're most likely to configure, the This Connection Uses the Following Items list box appears on the General tab of the Properties dialog box.

■ For a dial-up connection, which offers fewer TCP/IP options, this list box appears on the Networking tab of the Properties dialog box.

Figure 26-1 shows two screens of the Internet Protocol (TCP/IP) Properties dialog box. When the Obtain an IP Address Automatically option button is selected, the dialog box contains a General tab and an Alternate Configuration tab, as shown on the left. When the Use the Following IP Address is selected, Windows XP Professional hides the Alternate Configuration tab, as shown on the right.

Note *If the Advanced button on the Internet Protocol (TCP/IP) Properties dialog box is unavailable, an administrator has prevented you from configuring advanced TCP/IP properties.*

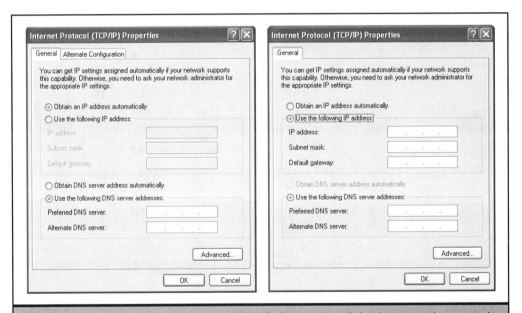

Figure 26-1. *The Internet Protocol (TCP/IP) Properties dialog box contains two tabs when the computer is set to obtain an IP address automatically (left) and one tab when the computer has a specific IP address (right).*

Understanding the Basics of TCP/IP

TCP/IP is the abbreviation for the Transmission Control Protocol/Internet Protocol suite of protocols. (Because the full name is such a mouthful, almost everyone uses the abbreviation.) Table 26-1 lists the protocols in the TCP/IP suite that you're most likely to encounter.

Abbreviation	Protocol Name	Usage
ARP	Address Resolution Protocol	Resolving IP addresses to physical addresses
FTP	File Transfer Protocol	Transferring files from one computer to another
HTTP	Hypertext Transfer Protocol	Managing communications between a web browser and a web server
ICMP	Internet Control Message Protocol	Providing network control and management functions
IMAP	Internet Mail Access Protocol	Accessing, storing, and managing incoming e-mail messages on a server
IP	Internet Protocol	Forwarding data packets from one destination to another
POP	Post Office Protocol	Accessing incoming e-mail messages on a server
SMTP	Simple Mail Transfer Protocol	Transferring e-mail messages from one server to another
SNMP	Simple Network Management Protocol	Monitoring and managing computers and devices on a network
TCP	Transmission Control Protocol	Providing reliable delivery of data
Telnet	Telnet	Connecting to a remote computer to issue commands on it
UDP	User Datagram Protocol	Transferring data (often used in streaming audio and video)

Table 26-1. *Major TCP/IP Protocols*

By default, Windows XP Professional installs TCP/IP and binds it to any network adapter installed in your computer, so you probably won't need to install TCP/IP. But you may well need to configure it.

IP Addresses

In a TCP/IP network, each computer is identified by an IP address. Each *IP address* contains 32 bits, which are typically arranged in four eight-bit segments called *octets* and are represented as four groups of numbers with periods between them—for example, 198.45.24.162 or 10.0.0.1. This format is called *dotted-decimal notation.* Depending on the network class, the first one, two, or three octets are used to indicate the network address, and the remaining octets are used to indicate the host address within that network.

Three main classes of IP addresses are used for networks: Class A, Class B, and Class C. (There's also a Class D that's used for multicast rather than for networks, and a Class E that's reserved for experimentation.) Table 26-2 summarizes the details for Class A, B, and C networks.

Each IP address has to be unique on the network to which the computer is attached; otherwise, it wouldn't be possible to identify any computer definitely. For example, each computer directly connected to the Internet has a unique IP address, which is why an individual user's activities on the Internet or web can be tracked. The IP address may be assigned permanently, so that the computer always has the same address (a *static* IP address), or it may be assigned temporarily from a pool of available IP addresses when the computer establishes a dial-up connection to the Internet (a *dynamic* IP address). IP addresses on the Internet are called *public* IP addresses.

Most computers on corporate networks don't connect to the Internet directly—instead, they connect through a shared connection. In this case, the device sharing the

USING WINDOWS XP PROFESSIONAL ON A LAN

Address Class	Network Octets	Host Octets	Number of Networks	Number of Hosts	Used For
A	1	3	127	16,777,216	Huge networks, such as IBM, General Electric, or MIT
B	2	2	16,384	65,535	Medium-sized networks
C	3	1	2,097,152	254	Small networks

Table 26-2.   *Class A, B, and C IP Network Details*

connection has the public IP address. Computers within the network have *private* IP addresses from one of three ranges of private addresses:

Private IP Address Range	Used For
10.0.0.0–10.255.255.255	Large networks
172.16.0.0–172.31.255.255	Medium-sized networks
192.168.0.0–192.168.255.255	Small networks and home networks, including ICS

Private addresses are valid only within private networks—you can't use a private address on the Internet—so these three address ranges take care of the vast majority of computers connected to corporate networks of any size. Probably the most widely used of the private addresses is 192.168.0.1, which is used by many Network Address Translation (NAT) devices and by every computer that's running Microsoft's Internet Connection Sharing (ICS) feature.

Subnet Masks

A Class A, Class B, or Class C network can be divided into subnetworks or subnets. A *subnet* is a group of computers that can communicate with each other without routing because the computers can reach each other without the packets needing to cross a router. Traffic within a subnet gets to its destination more quickly than traffic that has to cross one or more routers, and the router has correspondingly less work.

A subnet uses a subnet mask to identify which computers are on the same subnet. The *subnet mask* tells the IP software which parts of the IP address need to match for the computers to be on the same subnet.

 On a small- or home-office network, you'll almost always need the subnet mask 255.255.255.0.

Default Gateway

The *default gateway* is the router that your computer uses to access other networks. You'll need to specify your default gateway only if you use a static IP address rather than DHCP, which is discussed next.

Understanding DHCP and Static Addressing

IP addresses can be assigned automatically or manually. Windows XP Professional's default configuration as a network client is to receive an IP address automatically from a Dynamic Host Configuration Protocol (DHCP) server or DHCP allocator. Windows 2000 Server and Windows.NET Server each include a DHCP server. Windows XP Professional's ICS feature includes a DHCP allocator, a smaller version of the server, and many NAT devices designed for SOHO use have DHCP built in.

The *DHCP server* maintains a pool of available addresses. When a client applies to the DHCP server for an address, the server assigns one of the addresses that's available. This assignment is called a *lease* and may last as long as the client needs the IP address or only for a specified period of time. When a client leaves the network, the DHCP server reclaims the address and restores it to the pool. By using DHCP, an organization can use IP addresses more efficiently than by allocating a static IP address to each computer. For example, if, at most, only two-thirds of a company's computers ever connect to the network at the same time, the company can get by with one-third fewer IP addresses by using DHCP. DHCP also simplifies management—for example, a DHCP server won't assign an invalid IP address to a client, whereas a network administrator might assign an invalid address through a slip of the finger or a slip of the mind.

The disadvantage to using DHCP is that a computer is likely to receive a different IP address each time it joins the network. This makes it more difficult to identify a computer by its IP address. For example, if the computer with the IP address 172.16.1.144 has committed a networking transgression, the administrator will have to look up the IP address assignments to see which physical computer (or user) is at fault. To make the identification process easier, many administrators assign a static IP address to the more important (or more troublesome) computers on the network, and then use DHCP to automatically assign IP addresses to the smaller fry.

For computers configured to get an IP address via DHCP, Windows XP Professional includes a fallback mechanism of an alternate TCP/IP configuration. See "Falling Back on the Alternative Configuration and APIPA," later in this chapter.

To use DHCP, select the Obtain an IP Address Automatically option button on the General tab of the Internet Protocol (TCP/IP) Properties dialog box. To specify a static IP address, select the Use the Following IP Address option button and enter the IP address, subnet mask, and default gateway in the text boxes.

Normally, you'll use only one default gateway. However, in some circumstances, you may need to add further default gateways. Click the Advanced button on the General tab of the Internet Protocol (TCP/IP) Properties dialog box to display the Advanced TCP/IP Settings dialog box, and then work with the controls in the Default Gateways group box.

Configuring DNS and WINS

IP addresses are a great way for computers to identify one another, but most humans find it much easier to remember a name than an IP address. TCP/IP uses several means of resolving names to IP addresses: Domain Name System (DNS), Windows Internet Naming System (WINS), the HOSTS file, and the LMHOSTS file. Of these, you're far most likely to use DNS, but we'll examine the others briefly as well.

Configuring DNS

DNS is Windows XP Professional's default method of name resolution. To resolve a name via DNS, Windows XP Professional queries its primary DNS server. (If the primary DNS server is unavailable, Windows XP Professional queries its alternate DNS server.) The DNS server checks the *domain namespace,* a distributed database that contains mappings of domain names and host names to IP addresses and that runs on DNS servers. If the server finds a match for the address, either in its own copy of the database or in the database on another DNS server it queries, the server returns the information to the client. If the server can't find a match, it returns a DNS error.

If your computer is set up to use DHCP, it'll probably get its DNS server address automatically as well. The Obtain DNS Server Address Automatically option button on the General tab of the Internet Protocol (TCP/IP) Properties dialog box will be selected.

If your computer won't get DNS server addresses automatically, select the Use the Following DNS Server Addresses option button and enter the IP addresses of the primary DNS server and alternate DNS server in the text boxes. If you have further DNS servers to add, click the Advanced button and use the Add button on the DNS tab of the Advanced TCP/IP Settings dialog box (Figure 26-2). Use the ↑ button and ↓ button to arrange the DNS servers into order: the first is your primary DNS server, and the second is your alternate DNS server.

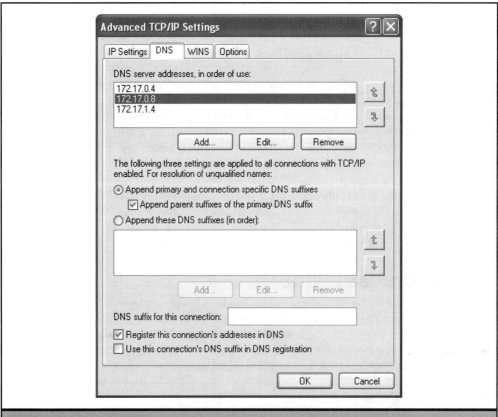

Figure 26-2.   *If necessary, use the DNS tab of the Advanced TCP/IP Settings dialog box to add further DNS servers.*

You'll rarely need to change your computer's DNS suffix manually. However, if you do need to, follow these steps:

1. Display the System Properties dialog box (WINDOWS KEY–BREAK).

2. Click the Change button on the Computer Name tab to display the Computer Name Changes dialog box (shown on the left in Figure 26-3).

3. Click the More button to display the DNS Suffix and NetBIOS Computer Name dialog box (shown on the right in Figure 26-3).

4. Enter the new suffix in the Primary DNS Suffix of This Computer text box.

5. If you want Windows XP Professional to automatically change the suffix if you move your computer to another domain, make sure the Change Primary DNS Suffix when Domain Membership Changes check box is selected.

6. Click the OK button to close each of the dialog boxes in turn.

Configuring WINS

WINS is a database that contains the mappings of computers' NetBIOS names to IP addresses. If you look at Figure 26-3, you'll notice that the DNS Suffix and NetBIOS Computer Name dialog box displays the NetBIOS computer name. The NetBIOS name is related to your computer's DNS name. If your computer's name is 15 characters or

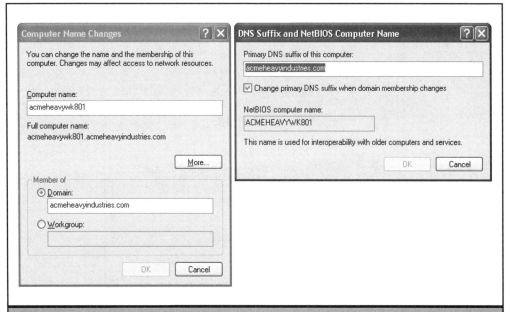

Figure 26-3. *If you need to change your computer's DNS suffix manually, display the DNS Suffix and NetBIOS Computer Name dialog box (right) from the Computer Name Changes dialog box (left).*

less, the NetBIOS name is the same as the computer's DNS name; if the computer's name is more than 15 characters, the NetBIOS name is a shortened version of the DNS name.

WINS is primarily used by older computers and services that can't use DNS to resolve a computer's DNS name. However, WINS can also be useful for looking up computers on remote networks.

To add one or more WINS servers, click the Advanced button on the General tab of the Internet Protocol (TCP/IP) Properties dialog box, and then click the Add button on the WINS tab (Figure 26-4) of the Advanced TCP/IP Settings dialog box.

Understanding the HOSTS File and the LMHOSTS File

The *HOSTS* file is a text file that contains a table of mappings of IP addresses to host names. The HOSTS file is used when DNS is unavailable or can't return the required information. To work with the HOSTS file, open the %systemroot%\system32\drivers\ etc\hosts file in a text editor, such as Notepad, and add to it the necessary IP addresses and host names.

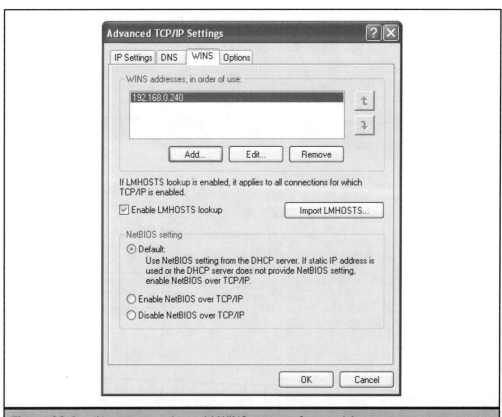

Figure 26-4. *You may need to add WINS servers for resolving computer names on remote networks.*

Like the HOSTS file, the *LMHOSTS* file is a text file that contains a table of mappings. Unlike HOSTS, LMHOSTS contains mappings of computers' NetBIOS names to IP addresses. The LMHOSTS file is used when DNS is unavailable or can't return the required information. To create a LMHOSTS file, open the %systemroot%\system32\ drivers\etc\lmhosts.sam file in a text editor, such as Notepad. Add to the file the necessary IP addresses and NetBIOS names, and then save the file in the same location, but under the name lmhosts with no extension.

Falling Back on the Alternate Configuration and APIPA

If your computer is configured to request an IP address via DHCP, and no DHCP server is available, you're not stuck, because Windows XP Professional includes an alternate TCP/IP configuration. This feature is mostly intended to cover you when your computer either is attached to a different network than its usual network or isn't attached to a network at all. For example, if you use a laptop at work, you might take it home and connect it to your home network. If your home network doesn't have a DHCP server, your computer won't be able to obtain an IP address as it does when attached to the office network. The alternate configuration provides an alternate IP address for such times.

By default, Windows XP Professional uses a feature called Automatic Private IP Addressing (APIPA) for the alternate configuration. APIPA allows a computer to automatically assign itself an IP address from a special private range (169.254.0.1–169.254.255.254) when it can't contact a DHCP server within a specified period of time. Windows XP Professional uses APIPA to derive the IP address, and then applies it, together with the subnet mask 255.255.0.0. (APIPA doesn't provide a gateway, a DNS server, or a WINS server.) Windows XP Professional then checks that no other device on the network is using that IP address. If the IP address is already in use, Windows XP Professional derives another IP address, applies it, and checks it, repeating the process (up to ten times, if necessary) until it has an IP address that's unique on the network. Windows XP Professional uses this IP address for the time being, but checks every five minutes to see if a DHCP server has become available on the network. When a DHCP server becomes available, Windows XP Professional requests an IP address from the server and changes to that IP address.

The best thing you can say about APIPA is that it works—after a fashion. The initial negotiation of the IP address can take time, and the repeated checks for the DHCP server detract from network performance. In many cases, configuring a static alternate IP address is more effective.

To set the alternate TCP/IP configuration, display the Alternate Configuration tab (Figure 26-5) of the Internet Protocol (TCP/IP) Properties dialog box. (The Alternate Configuration tab isn't available if your computer has a static IP address assigned to it.)

To use APIPA, make sure the Automatic Private IP Address option button is selected. To assign a static IP address, select the User Configured option button and enter the details of the address in the text boxes: the IP address, the subnet mask, the default gateway, the preferred and alternate DNS servers, and the preferred and alternate WINS servers.

Figure 26-5. *If your computer gets its IP address from a DHCP server, you can specify an alternate configuration on the Alternate Configuration tab of the Internet Protocol (TCP/IP) Properties dialog box for when the DHCP server isn't available.*

   If you have a small network or home network that usually connects to the Internet through ICS or another NAT device that provides DHCP, you may want to configure static IP addresses in the alternate configuration for times when the ICS computer or NAT device is down. By configuring static addresses, you can provide backup connectivity without the overhead required by APIPA's constant checking for the return of a DHCP server.

To check whether your computer is using APIPA, issue an **ipconfig /all** command at a command prompt. If the readout shows Yes on the Autoconfiguration Enabled line and the IP address is in the range 169.254.0.1–169.254.255.254, your computer is using APIPA.

Setting a DHCP Class ID

An administrator can set up DHCP to support different classes of PCs that use DHCP. The administrator can then assign to each class a suitable priority and length of DHCP lease (for example, a short lease for dial-up connections, a longer lease for local connections). An administrator can specify the class ID on a computer running Windows XP Professional by using the ipconfig command (discussed in "Checking and Changing TCP/IP Configuration with ipconfig," later in this chapter).

To display a list of available DHCP class IDs for a particular adapter, issue an **ipconfig /showclassid** command with the name of the adapter—for example:

```
ipconfig /showclassid "Local Area Connection"
```

To display a list of all DHCP class IDs, issue an **ipconfig /showclassid *** command. To set a DHCP class ID, issue an **ipconfig /setclassid** *adapter classID* command, where *adapter* is the network adapter and *classID* is the DHCP class ID. For example:

```
ipconfig /setclassid "Local Area Connection" "Default BOOTP Class"
```

To remove the current DHCP class ID from an adapter, issue an **ipconfig /setclassid** *adapter* command without specifying a class ID:

```
ipconfig /setclassid "Local Area Connection"
```

Using Windows XP Professional's TCP/IP Utilities

This section discusses the utilities that Windows XP Professional provides for testing and troubleshooting TCP/IP connectivity: ipconfig, ping, pathping, tracert, route, arp, netstat, and hostname. The following section outlines a troubleshooting methodology for TCP/IP connections that uses these utilities.

Tip *Some of the TCP/IP utilities return more information than will fit in the command-prompt window. You can deal with this in two ways. Either use the | more pipe to limit output to one screenful at a time, and press SPACEBAR to display the next screen. Or redirect the output to a file by entering a greater-than sign (>) and the filename and path. For example, the **ipconfig /all >%userprofile%\config\config1.txt** command saves the output of the **ipconfig /all** command to a file named config1.txt in the config folder in the current user's profile folder. To save only part of the output from a command, select it in the command-prompt window, press ENTER to copy it to the Clipboard, and then paste it into a text editor (for example, Notepad) or word processor. You can then save the file as normal.*

Checking and Changing TCP/IP Configuration with ipconfig

ipconfig is a command-line tool for displaying information on your computer's IP configuration and changing the configuration.

The syntax for ipconfig is as follows:

```
ipconfig [/all] [/renew [adapter]] [/release [adapter]]
[/flushdns] [/displaydns] [/registerdns]
[/showclassid adapter] [/setclassid adapter [ClassID]]
```

You can use a plain **ipconfig** command to display brief configuration information for all network adapters on the computer. Figure 26-6 shows an example for a computer that has an Ethernet LAN connection and a dial-up connection (listed as PPP Adapter). Table 26-3 explains the parameters for ipconfig.

Note   *The /release, /renew, and /showclassid parameters use an optional* adapter *argument that specifies the name of the network adapter on which to perform the command. If you omit the* adapter *argument, ipconfig performs the command on all available network adapters. The easiest way to get the correct name for an adapter is to issue one of the ipconfig commands that shows information (for example,* **ipconfig /all***) and check the resulting output. You can use the * wildcard to enter the rest of the adapter name quickly. For example, instead of typing* **"Local Area Connection"** *(including the double quotation marks), you could type* **Lo***.

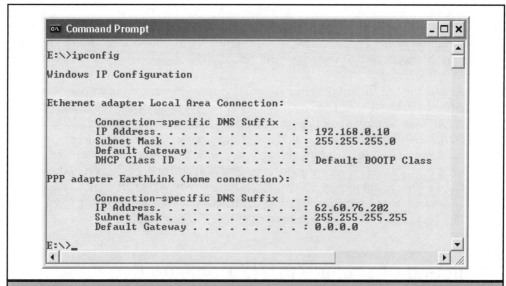

Figure 26-6.   *Use a plain ipconfig command to return brief configuration information on all network adapters.*

Parameter	Explanation
/all	Displays all TCP/IP configuration information for all network adapters.
/release [*adapter*]	Releases the DHCP configuration and discards the IP address for the specified adapter or for all adapters.
/renew [*adapter*]	Renews the DHCP configuration for the specified adapter or for all adapters.
/displaydns	Displays the information held in the DNS resolver cache, which is used to resolve frequently queried names without needing to query the DNS servers.
/flushdns	Removes the information from the DNS resolver cache (see the previous item).
/registerdns	Starts the manual dynamic registration of DNS names and IP addresses.
/showclassid [*adapter*]	Displays the DHCP class ID for the specified adapter or for all adapters. See "Setting a DHCP Class ID," earlier in the chapter.
/setclassid *adapter* [*ClassID*]	Sets the DHCP class ID for the specified adapter to the specified class ID. See "Setting a DHCP Class ID," earlier in the chapter.

Table 26-3.   *Parameters for the ipconfig Command*

Using ping to Check Whether a TCP/IP Connection Is Working

If your computer seems unable to contact another computer across a TCP/IP network connection, use the ping (Packet InterNet Groper) command to check that the connection is functioning. ping works by sending ICMP Echo Request messages to the destination and analyzing the replies it receives.

The syntax for ping is as follows:

```
ping [-t] [-a] [-n count] [-l size] [-f] [-i TTL] [-v TOS] [-r count] [-s count]
 [[-j host-list] | [-k host-list]]  [-w timeout] target_name
```

As you can see, the only required parameter is *target_name,* which specifies the IP address or host name of the computer from which you're requesting the ICMP replies. The first line of the following example pings Osborne's server. The rest of the example shows the status, the replies received, and the summary.

```
C:\>ping osborne.com

Pinging osborne.com [198.45.24.162] with 32 bytes of data:

Reply from 198.45.24.162: bytes=32 time=184ms TTL=238
Reply from 198.45.24.162: bytes=32 time=184ms TTL=238
Request timed out.
Reply from 198.45.24.162: bytes=32 time=186ms TTL=238

Ping statistics for 198.45.24.162:
    Packets: Sent = 4, Received = 3, Lost = 1 (25% loss),
Approximate round trip times in milli-seconds:
    Minimum = 184ms, Maximum = 186ms, Average = 184ms
```

This basic usage of ping is effective for checking that a TCP/IP connection is available and effective. If you don't receive the "Reply from" packets, you'll know that there's a problem with the network connection. Table 26-4 explains the other responses you may see from ping.

To deal with the error messages, you need to use the –w and –i parameters. Table 26-5 explains these parameters and the other optional parameters that ping supports.

ping Error Message	Explanation
ping request could not find host *hostname*	Windows XP Professional was unable to resolve the destination host name. This message may indicate a problem with your network's DNS servers or WINS servers or your ISP's DNS servers.

Table 26-4.   *ping Error Messages and Their Meanings*

ping Error Message	Explanation
Request timed out	ping received no reply within the specified timeout period. (The default timeout period is four seconds.) Increase the timeout period by using the –w parameter and try again.
Destination host unreachable	ping is unable to establish a local or remote route to the destination host. There may be a problem with your computer's routing table or the router's routing table.
TTL expired in transit	ping wasn't able to reach the destination within the specified number of hops. Try using the –i parameter to increase the hop count. If a larger hop count still returns this message, you may have a routing loop. Use tracert (discussed later in this chapter) to check for a routing loop.

Table 26-4.   *ping Error Messages and Their Meanings* (continued)

Parameter	Explanation
target_name	The IP address or host name of the destination computer.
–t	Sends ping packets until the user issues a stop command. Press CTRL-C to stop the ping command. Press CTRL-BREAK to interrupt ping and display statistics on the operations it's performed so far. (After displaying the statistics, ping resumes its uncompleted operations.)
–a	Resolves the IP address to its host name.
–n *count*	Specifies the number of echo requests to send. The default is four requests.
–l *size*	Specifies the number of bytes to include in the echo request's data field.
–f	Sets the Don't Fragment flag in the echo requests. This flag tells routers not to fragment the request messages.

Table 26-5.   *Parameters for the ping Command*

Parameter	Explanation
–i *TTL*	Specifies the Time to Live (TTL) for the echo requests—the number of hops the messages are allowed to traverse before expiring. The default TTL setting for Windows XP Professional computers is usually 128. You can set a TTL of up to 255, but doing so may make ping take a long time to complete.
–v *TOS*	Specifies the Type of Service (TOS) to use in the IP header of the echo request. The default setting is 0. Valid values are 0–255.
–r *count*	Records the route taken by the echo request. Valid values are 1–9.
–s *count*	Enables time-stamping for the echo request and the echo reply request. Valid values are 1–4.
–j *host-list*	Specifies that ping use a loose source route along the *host list,* which is a list of up to nine IP addresses separated by spaces. A *loose source route* means that packets are allowed to travel through other routers while traveling from one specified router to the next.
–k *host-list*	Specifies that ping use a strict source route along the host list. A *strict source route* means that the packets have to travel from one specified router to the next without going through other routers along the way.
–w *timeout*	Specifies the longest time (in milliseconds) to wait for a reply before timing it out. The default is 4,000 milliseconds (four seconds).

Table 26-5.   *Parameters for the ping Command* (continued)

Using pathping to Check a TCP/IP Route

If the replies you receive to ping requests indicate that your connection is losing packets along the way, you can use the pathping command to try to identify the router that's causing the problem. *pathping* is essentially an adaptation of ping that checks each hop along the route to a destination and displays statistics on the number of replies it receives from each router.

The syntax for pathping is as follows:

```
pathping [-g host-list] [-h maximum_hops] [-i address] [-n] [-p period]
[-q num_queries] [-w timeout] [-P] [-R] [-T] [-4] [-6] target_name
```

Table 26-6 explains the parameters for pathping. Note that these parameters are case-sensitive, so the –p parameter is distinct from the –P parameter.

Parameter	Explanation
target_name	Specifies the IP address or host name of the destination computer.
–g *host-list*	Uses a loose source route along the host list. See the –j entry in Table 26-5, earlier in the chapter, for an explanation of the host list and a loose source route.
–h *maximum_hop*s	Specifies the maximum number of hops to use. The default setting is 30.
–i *address*	Specifies the source address to use.
–n	Suppresses the resolution of addresses to host names. Using this parameter can make pathping return results more quickly.
–p *period*	Specifies the number of milliseconds to wait between pings. The default setting is 250 milliseconds. Don't send pings at ultrashort intervals because doing so can cause network congestion.
–q *num_queries*	Specifies the number of echo requests to send to each router along the path.
–w *timeout*	Specifies the longest time (in milliseconds) to wait for a reply before timing it out. The default is 3,000 milliseconds (three seconds).
–P	Checks to see if the path supports the Resource Reservation Protocol (RSVP).

Table 26-6.   *Parameters for the pathping Command*

Parameter	Explanation
–R	Checks to see if each router on the path supports RSVP. You'll need this parameter only if you're testing a path for Quality of Service (QoS).
–T	Checks to see if the routers on the path support Layer 2 priority capability. This parameter is also used for QoS.
–4	Uses Internet Protocol version 4 (IPv4).
–6	Uses Internet Protocol version 6 (IPv6).

Table 26-6. *Parameters for the pathping Command* (continued)

Here's an example of pathping in action. To keep the lines from being too long to read easily in the book, the example uses the –n parameter, which suppresses the resolution of IP addresses to host names.

```
E:\>pathping -n yahoo.com

Tracing route to yahoo.com [64.58.79.230]
over a maximum of 30 hops:
  0   62.60.75.138
  1   194.176.218.114
  2   194.176.218.246
  3   194.176.218.44
  4   194.176.220.189
  5   194.176.220.190
  6   166.63.211.193
  7   206.24.226.99
  8   206.24.238.34
  9   216.33.98.218
 10   216.35.210.126
 11   64.58.79.230

Computing statistics for 275 seconds...
                Source to Here    This Node/Link
Hop   RTT       Lost/Sent = Pct   Lost/Sent = Pct   Address
  0                                                 62.60.75.138
                                  0/ 100 =   0%     |
  1   153ms     0/ 100 =   0%     0/ 100 =   0%     194.176.218.114
                                  0/ 100 =   0%     |
```

```
 2  170ms      0/ 100 =  0%     0/ 100 =  0%   194.176.218.246
                               0/ 100 =  0%    |
 3  191ms      0/ 100 =  0%     0/ 100 =  0%   194.176.218.44
                               0/ 100 =  0%    |
 4  188ms     10/ 100 = 10%     8/ 100 =  8%   194.176.220.189
                               0/ 100 =  0%    |
 5  179ms      0/ 100 =  0%     0/ 100 =  0%   194.176.220.190
                               0/ 100 =  0%    |
 6  169ms      0/ 100 =  0%     0/ 100 =  0%   166.63.211.193
                              18/ 100 = 18%    |
 7  249ms      0/ 100 =  0%     0/ 100 =  0%   206.24.226.99
                               0/ 100 =  0%    |
 8  256ms      0/ 100 =  0%     0/ 100 =  0%   206.24.238.34
                               0/ 100 =  0%    |
 9  254ms      0/ 100 =  0%     0/ 100 =  0%   216.33.98.218
                               0/ 100 =  0%    |
10  247ms      0/ 100 =  0%     0/ 100 =  0%   216.35.210.126
                               0/ 100 =  0%    |
11  244ms      0/ 100 =  0%     0/ 100 =  0%   64.58.79.230

Trace complete.
```

The first part of pathping's output lists the hops in the route to the destination. (This is the same information that you'll get by using the tracert command.) pathping then displays the Computing statistics for *NN* seconds message while it collects and processes information from the routers in the list and the links between the routers. pathping then displays the results by hop, showing the number of packets lost out of the number of packets sent.

The output line with the hop number and the router's address shows the loss rate for that router. For example, the router at hop 4 is losing packets, most likely because it's overloaded.

The output line with the vertical bar in the Address column between the addresses in each hop shows whether packets are being lost on the link between the routers. For example, the link at hop 6 is losing packets, most likely because of congestion.

Using tracert to Trace a TCP/IP Route

The *tracert* (trace route) command returns the path taken to the specified destination. tracert lets you see which connections are involved in the path, where any unexpected delays are happening, or the point at which an attempted connection fails. However, for most purposes, pathping is more informative than tracert.

tracert uses the following syntax:

```
tracert [-d] [-h maximum_hops] [-j hostlist] [-w timeout] target_name
```

Table 26-7 explains the parameters for tracert. You'll recognize most of them from ping and pathping.

Here's an example of the output for a basic tracert command with no parameters except *target_name*:

```
C:\>tracert demon.net

Tracing route to demon.net [193.195.224.1]
over a maximum of 30 hops:

1     *         *         *         Request timed out.
2   390 ms   109 ms     59 ms   war1-15.router.demon.net [194.159.180.1]
3    68 ms    65 ms    137 ms   war1-176.router.demon.net [194.159.180.69]
4    82 ms    77 ms     77 ms   finch-161.router.demon.net [194.159.36.34]
5    78 ms    77 ms     71 ms   finch-162.router.demon.net [194.159.36.67]
6    78 ms    77 ms     77 ms   11-finch-16.access.demon.net [194.159.253.32]
7   111 ms    95 ms     89 ms   finch-gap-if0.router.demon.net [195.173.56.3]
8    82 ms    89 ms     77 ms   finch-staff1.server.demon.net [193.195.224.1]

Trace complete.
```

Parameter	Explanation
–d	Suppresses the resolution of addresses to host names. Using this parameter can make tracert return results more quickly, but it makes the results less informative.
–h *maximum_hops*	Specifies the maximum number of hops to use. The default setting is 30.
–j *hostlist*	Specifies that tracert use a loose source route along the host list. The host list is a list of up to nine IP addresses separated by spaces. A loose source route means that packets are allowed to travel through other routers while traveling from one specified router to the next.
–w *timeout*	Specifies the longest time (in milliseconds) to wait for a reply before timing it out. The default is 4,000 milliseconds (four seconds). When tracert doesn't receive a reply, it displays a row of asterisks for the router.
target_name	Specifies the IP address or host name of the computer to which you're tracing the route.

Table 26-7. *Parameters for the tracert Command*

Using route to View and Modify the Routing Table

The route command lets you examine and modify the entries in your computer's IP routing table. By examining and changing these entries, you may be able to identify and solve a routing problem that's preventing your packets from reaching their destinations. route uses the following syntax:

```
route [-f] [-p] [command [destination] [mask netmask] [gateway]
[metric metric]] [if interface]]
```

Table 26-8 explains the parameters for route.

Parameter	Explanation
–f	Deletes from the routing table any entry that's not a host route (a route with the netmask 255.255.255.255), the loopback route (with the destination 127.0.0.0 and the netmask 255.0.0.0), or a multicast route (with the destination 240.0.0.0 and the subnet mask 240.0.0.0).
–p	Creates a persistent route when used with the add command. Displays a list of persistent routes when used with the print command. This parameter isn't used with other commands.
command	Runs the specified command: add to add a route, change to modify a route, delete to delete one or more routes, and print to print one or more routes.
destination	Specifies the route's destination: an IP network address, an IP address for a host route, or a setting of 0.0.0.0 for the default route.
mask *netmask*	Specifies the subnet mask for the route's destination. If you omit this parameter, route uses 255.255.255.255 as the subnet mask.
gateway	Specifies the gateway to use to reach the addresses specified by the route's destination and the subnet mask. You can enter an IP address or a name that can be resolved to an IP address via DNS, HOSTS, or LMHOSTS.
metric *metric*	Specifies the *integer cost metric* (an integer value from 1 to 999) for the network route. The *metric* is a measure of route efficiency, with a lower value representing a more efficient and faster route.

Table 26-8. *Parameters for the route Command*

Parameter	Explanation
if *interface*	Specifies the index of the interface to use to reach the destination. Use a route print command to return a list of interfaces and their indexes. You can enter the interface index either as a decimal number (which is usually easier) or as a hexadecimal value preceded by 0x. If you omit this parameter, route chooses the interface according to the gateway address.

Table 26-8. *Parameters for the route Command* (continued)

For example, you can use a **route print** command to return the contents of the routing table, including the list of interfaces and their indexes. The following command returns the routing entries that start with 172:

```
route print 172.*
```

The following command adds a persistent route to the destination 193.237.129.165 with the subnet mask 255.255.0.0 and the next hop address 158.152.1.222:

```
route -p add 193.237.129.165 mask 255.255.0.0 158.152.1.222
```

Note *The error message* Route: bad gateway address netmask *means that the destination and subnet mask you've entered produce an invalid combination. For example, you might have entered a destination that's more specific than its subnet mask. When you see this error message, change the destination or subnet mask accordingly.*

The following command deletes all routes that begin with 224 by using the * wildcard:

```
route delete 224.*
```

Using arp to View and Modify the ARP Cache

The Address Resolution Protocol (ARP) cache contains a table of IP addresses and their corresponding physical addresses for each Ethernet or Token Ring network adapter on your computer. The *arp* command lets you view the entries in the ARP cache and modify them if necessary.

arp uses the following syntax:

```
arp [-a [inetaddr] [-N ifaceaddr]] [-d inetaddr [ifaceaddr]]
[-s inetaddr etheraddr [ifaceaddr]]
```

Note | *arp also has a –g switch that's identical to the –a switch. I've removed this switch from the syntax for simplicity, but you may see it used occasionally.*

Table 26-9 explains the parameters for arp. Note that the –N parameter is case-sensitive.

Parameter	Explanation
inetaddr	Specifies an IP address, expressed in dotted-decimal notation.
ifaceaddr	Specifies an IP address, expressed in dotted-decimal notation, representing a network interface.
etheraddr	Specifies the physical address of an Ethernet adapter, expressed in hexadecimal and separated by hyphens—for example, 00-01-02-14-d5-f3.
–a [*inetaddr*]	Lists, if no *inetaddr* argument is supplied, the ARP cache table for all network interfaces. If *inetaddr* is supplied, lists the ARP cache table for the specified IP address.
–a –N *ifaceaddr*	Lists the ARP cache table for the specified interface.
–d *inetaddr* [*ifaceaddr*]	Deletes the entry that has the IP address specified by *inetaddr*. When used with *ifaceaddr*, deletes the entry specified by *inetaddr* from the interface specified by *ifaceaddr*. Enter * for *inetaddr* to delete all entries from the interface specified by *ifaceaddr*.
–s *inetaddr etheraddr* [*ifaceaddr*]	Creates a new static entry in the ARP cache. The entry resolves the IP address specified by *inetaddr* to the physical address specified by *etheraddr*. You can use the *ifaceaddr* parameter to add the entry to a specific interface's ARP table.

Table 26-9. *Parameters for the arp Command*

USING WINDOWS XP
PROFESSIONAL ON A LAN

Using netstat to Return Network Statistics

The *netstat* command provides a wealth of statistics about network connections and what's happening on them. netstat uses the following syntax:

```
netstat [-a] [-e] [-n] [-o] [-p protocol] [-r] [-s] [interval]
```

Table 26-10 explains the parameters for netstat.

Parameter	Explanation
–a	Lists all active TCP connections together with the TCP ports and UDP ports on which the computer is currently listening.
–e	Shows the statistics for Ethernet including the following: bytes received and sent, unicast and nonunicast packets received and sent, discarded packets, errors, and unknown protocols. You can use **netstat –e –s** to divide the statistics by protocol, which can give you a better view of what's happening.
–n	Lists all active TCP connections, but lists the connections by IP address rather than resolving the host names. This makes for a more compact display.
–o	Lists all active TCP connections, including the process ID (PID) for each connection. You can then use tasklist.exe or Task Manager to see which process is responsible for a PID associated with a connection that's causing trouble.
–p *protocol*	Lists the connections for the specified protocol. Use **tcp** for TCP, **udp** for UDP, **tcpv6** for TCP version 6, or **udpv6** for UDP version 6. You can use –p with –s to list statistics by protocol. In this case, use **tcp** for TCP, **udp** for UDP, **tcpv6** for TCP version 6, **udpv6** for UDP version 6, **icmp** for ICMP, **icmpv6** for ICMP version 6, **ip** for IP, and **ipv6** for IP version 6.
–r	Displays the IP routing table. (netstat –r is the same as route print.)
–s	Lists statistics by protocol. You can use –s with –p to display specific protocols.
interval	Makes netstat refresh the interval at the specified number of seconds. To stop netstat, press CTRL-C. If you omit *interval*, netstat doesn't repeat.

Table 26-10. *Parameters for the netstat Command*

Using the hostname Command to Return the Computer's Host Name

The *hostname* command provides a quick way to return the host name of the current computer from a command prompt. This command takes no parameters: just enter **hostname** at a command prompt.

 Another way of checking the host name of the computer is to display the System Properties dialog box (WINDOWS KEY–R) and check the Full Computer Name readout on the Computer Name tab. The host name is the first part of this name.

Troubleshooting TCP/IP Connections

This section presents a methodology for troubleshooting TCP/IP connections. As you'll see, most of the utilities discussed in the previous section play a role.

Use Help and Support Center's Network Diagnostics

Start your troubleshooting by running the Network Diagnostics in Help and Support Center to see if it can diagnose the problem. Follow these steps:

1. Choose Start | Help and Support to open a Help and Support Center window.

2. Click the Tools link in the Pick a Task list to display the Tools screen.

3. Click the Network Diagnostics link in the Tools pane to display the Network Diagnostics screen.

4. Click the Set Scanning Options link to display the Options screen.

5. In the Actions list, make sure the check boxes for the appropriate options are selected:

   - The *Ping* check box controls whether Network Diagnostics uses the ping command to check connectivity. Because ping reveals a large amount of connectivity information, using ping is a good idea.

   - The *Connect* check box controls whether Network Diagnostics checks that the remote computers specified in your configuration are running the networking services you're trying to contact them for. For example, this option checks that your DHCP server is running a DHCP service. (By contrast, ping checks only that the computer at the DHCP server's address is responding to ping packets.)

   - The *Show* check box controls whether Network Diagnostics includes basic information in the report it shows you.

   - The *Verbose* check box controls whether Network Diagnostics includes the output of commands it used in the report it shows you. For example, if Network

Diagnostics pings the DHCP server, verbose output lets you examine the output of the ping command. This can help you identify problems without needing to run further commands yourself.

■ The *Save to Desktop* check box controls whether the Save to File button saves the report to your desktop, as well as to the %systemroot%\pchealth\helpctr\system\netdiag folder. The copy on the desktop is redundant but easier to access, either for reference or for e-mailing to a support technician.

6. In the Categories list, make sure that the check boxes for the appropriate categories are selected: Network Clients, Network Adapters, Domain Name System (DNS), Dynamic Host Configuration Protocol (DHCP), Default Gateways, Internet Protocol Address, and Windows Internet Naming Service (WINS). After selecting the appropriate check boxes, click the Save Options button to save your selection of options for future use.

7. Click the Scan Your System link to start the scan. Depending on the options you've chosen, the scan will probably take a minute or two to complete. Network Diagnostics then displays a summary of its findings. Figure 26-7 shows part of a summary in Help and Support Center's reduced view. In this example, all the items tested seem to be working.

8. Expand the entries for any items marked FAILED to see what the problem is.

If the problem is related to a TCP/IP configuration item, you may need to troubleshoot the problem by using the command-line utilities, as described in the following subsections.

Check Your TCP/IP Configuration

Open a command-prompt window and issue an **ipconfig** command to return your computer's TCP/IP configuration information. For example, the following command returns configuration information for all network adapters:

```
ipconfig /all
```

Check the following:

■ Check that the computer's host name is set to what you expect it to be. A misconfigured host name might cause communications problems.

■ Check that the IP address seems to be right for your network. On a corporate network, you may need to ask an administrator about the address range used. On a small network using NAT and DHCP, the IP address will usually be in the 192.168.*x.x* range. On a small network using ICS, the IP address must be in the 192.168.0.*x* range.

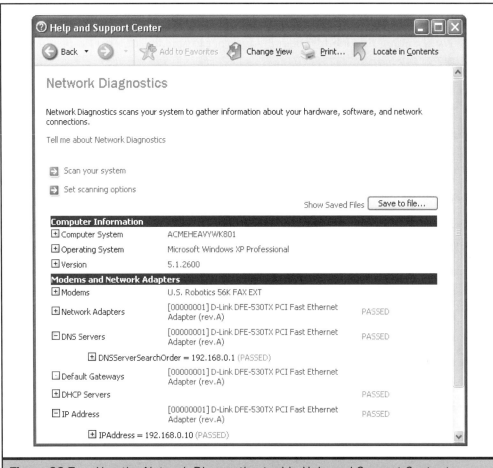

Figure 26-7. *Use the Network Diagnostics tool in Help and Support Center to perform a quick check of your system's network configuration.*

- If the IP address starts with 169.254, your computer is configured to obtain an IP address through DHCP but hasn't been able to reach a DHCP server, so it has assigned itself an IP address using APIPA. You may need to use an ipconfig / release command to release the binding on a specified adapter and an ipconfig / renew command to create a new binding. For example, the following commands release and renew the Local Area Connection item:

```
ipconfig /release "Local Area Connection"
ipconfig /renew "Local Area Connection"
```

■ Check the subnet mask. If it's set to 0.0.0.0, it probably means that TCP/IP is configured with a static address that's already in use elsewhere on the network. Try changing the IP address in the Internet Protocol (TCP/IP) Properties dialog box.

Check Your Computer's Connectivity

If your TCP/IP configuration seems to be okay, use ping to test whether your computer can communicate with other computers on the network. Follow these steps:

1. If you didn't use an ipconfig command in the previous section to display your TCP/IP configuration information, run one now so that you have the information it returns. Keep this information handy, by printing it, writing it, copying it to a file, or simply leaving the output displayed in a second command-prompt window.

Note *Using an ipconfig command has a second benefit: it checks your loopback address and your IP address for you, by using ping behind the scenes. You could check these manually by using a **ping 127.0.0.1** command (for the loopback address) and a **ping IP_address** command (where IP_address is the IP address shown in the ipconfig output), but you don't need to. Pinging the loopback address successfully proves that TCP/IP is installed correctly on your computer. Pinging your computer's IP address successfully proves that your computer's routing table is working, because TCP/IP forwards the packets to the loopback address.*

2. Ping the default gateway by the IP address shown in the ipconfig output to make sure that it's working.

   ■ If you can't ping the default gateway, there may be a problem with your network adapter, network cable, with the hardware that connects your computer to the gateway, or with the gateway itself.

   ■ If you know the IP address of another local computer, try pinging that. If the ping is successful, the problem may lie with the gateway.

   ■ If you can't ping another local computer, use an **arp –a** command to display the contents of your ARP cache. Use **arp –d** commands to delete suspect entries. You can also flush the arp cache by issuing an **netsh interface ip delete arpcache** command. (*netsh* is a scripting tool that we haven't examined in this chapter.) netsh deletes the entries and returns a laconic "OK."

   ■ If working with your ARP cache doesn't help, investigate your network adapter, network cable, and (if you have access to them), the network hardware.

Note *Two other things to check at this point are TCP/IP filtering and IPSec. Wrongly applied TCP/IP filtering can cripple your TCP/IP connections. See "Applying TCP/IP Filtering" in Chapter 30 for a discussion of how to apply TCP/IP filtering correctly to your network connections. Likewise, IPSec can prevent communications, because IPSec policy may block ping packets. See Chapter 30 for a discussion of IPSec.*

3. If you can ping your default gateway successfully, ping a remote host by its IP address. (You'll need to know the remote host's IP address to do this—so if you're reading this section ahead of time, find out and note the IP address of a remote host to ping. If you're reading this section while troubleshooting, ask a colleague to ping a remote host by name and tell you the IP address shown on the replies.)

4. If you can ping a remote host successfully by IP address, ping it by its host name. If you can do so, name resolution in working.

   ■ If you can't do so, there may be a problem with your DNS server. Try pinging the DNS servers shown by ipconfig to check that they're running.

   ■ If your DNS servers seem to be functioning, try using tracert or route to trace the path to a remote host. You may also want to try pathping to detect where a connection is losing packets.

5. If a remote connection seems to hang, you may be able to identify the problem by issuing a **netstat –a** command and examining the activity on your TCP and UDP ports.

Summary

This chapter has discussed how to configure TCP/IP connections and the tools that Windows XP Professional provides for working with them. You've seen how to troubleshoot TCP/IP connections when they don't work correctly. Along the way, you learned the basics of how TCP/IP works.

The next chapter explains how to use Windows XP Professional in workgroup configurations in your home or your small office.

USING WINDOWS XP PROFESSIONAL ON A LAN

Chapter 27

Managing Windows XP Professional at Home or in SOHO

This chapter discusses considerations for using Windows XP Professional at home or in a small-office or home-office (SOHO) setting. The main difference between "small-office" use and corporate use is that a small office uses a workgroup configuration rather than a domain configuration.

This chapter starts by mentioning the key ways in which Windows XP Professional behaves differently in a workgroup than when it's connected to and controlled by a Windows domain. The chapter then shows you how to set the computer's name, description, and workgroup, how to turn Fast User Switching on and off, and how to share folders using both Simple File Sharing and regular file sharing. The chapter discusses how to share printers, how to manage local users and groups, and how to configure Outlook Express for security and effectiveness.

Key Differences Between Workgroup and Server Configurations

As mentioned earlier in the book, Windows XP Professional is designed to connect to a Windows domain running on Windows 2000 Server or Windows.NET Server. When you connect Windows XP Professional to a domain like this, you can administer the computer centrally.

In a standalone or workgroup environment, Windows XP Professional behaves differently in these key ways:

- By default, Fast User Switching is enabled. Fast User Switching lets users *disconnect* a session and leave it running in the background rather than logging off.

- By default, each user account you create during Windows Setup is a Computer Administrator account. Until you restrict the user accounts, each user has wide-ranging permissions on the computer and can administer it.

- By default, Windows XP Professional uses Simple File Sharing rather than regular file sharing with NTFS's full set of permissions.

- No group policies apply because no domain is available to supply them. You can configure the computer by applying local policies.

Setting the Computer's Name, Description, and Workgroup

A *workgroup* is a collection of computers that have the same workgroup name set. You create a workgroup by telling Windows XP that the computer is a member of a workgroup. (By contrast, the process of setting up a domain is formal and explicit.)

In a workgroup, each computer needs to have a unique computer name. This name is used to identify the computer on the network. Each computer also has a text description to help users identify the computer. (The description can be left blank.)

The easiest way to set the computer's name, its description, and workgroup is by using the Network Setup Wizard, which walks you through the process. A bug in the Network Setup Wizard makes it suggest the workgroup name MSHOME rather than any workgroup name already set, so if you run the Network Setup Wizard again, you'll need to enter your workgroup name again to prevent the wizard from changing the workgroup to MSHOME.

You can also change the computer's description on the Computer Name tab of the System Properties dialog box. To change the computer's name or workgroup, click the Change button and use the controls in the Computer Name Changes dialog box.

After changing the computer's name or workgroup, you need to restart Windows XP.

Turning Fast User Switching On and Off

As mentioned earlier in the book, Fast User Switching works only on standalone computers and computers attached to workgroups. You can't use it on computers connected to a domain for security reasons. To use Fast User Switching, you need to use the Welcome screen as well.

To apply Fast User Switching, follow these steps:

1. Choose Start | Control Panel | User Accounts | Change the Way Users Log On or Off to display the Select Logon and Logoff Options page of Control Panel.

2. Select the Use Fast User Switching check box. If the Use the Welcome Screen check box is cleared, select it too.

3. Click the Apply Options button.

When you turn off Fast User Switching, you need to make sure that no other user is logged on.

 Tip *Don't use Fast User Switching unless you need it. Using Fast User Switching increases the amount of memory that Windows XP needs (because applications and files open in disconnected sessions require memory) and may reduce performance.*

"Client" and "Server" Roles in a Workgroup

Most workgroups use a peer-to-peer configuration in which many or all of the computers in the workgroup provide services to each other. For example, say you have a workgroup with five computers, of which one computer shares folders, one computer shares a printer, and another shares an Internet connection. Those three computers are providing services. Each computer in the workgroup acts as a client when it accesses services that other computers are providing.

Windows XP handles the roles of client and server seamlessly. If you split the resources you're sharing among several computers, you shouldn't need to configure performance options on them differently than you would for a workstation. However, if you dedicate one of the computers in the workgroup to providing all services, and don't use it as a workstation, you should change its performance options, as described in the next section, to improve its performance as a server.

For a computer that's sharing folders, you can apply caching settings for offline files, as discussed in the section after next.

Choosing Appropriate Performance Options

As discussed in "Improving System Performance" in Chapter 11, the Advanced tab of Windows XP's Performance Options dialog box lets you adjust processor scheduling either for running applications or for providing background services. Similarly, you can adjust memory usage for best performance of either applications or system cache.

If your Windows XP Professional "server" is acting as both a server and a workstation, select the Programs option buttons in the Processor Scheduling group box and the Memory Usage group box on the Advanced tab of the Performance Options dialog box. But if your "server" isn't used as a workstation, select the Background Services option button in the Processor Scheduling group box and the System Cache option button in the Memory Usage group box. Changing these settings will improve the computer's performance in delivering services to the other computers on your network.

Choosing Caching Settings for Offline Files

As discussed in "Using Offline Files" in Chapter 18, Windows XP Professional can cache copies of network folders and files on your local PC so that you can take them with you and work with them when you're not connected to the network.

When Windows XP Professional is hosting the network drive, you can configure caching settings for the folders you're sharing. By default, Windows XP Professional lets users cache the content of shared folders so that they can work with that content when they're offline (or when the computer containing the folder is offline, which, in effect, amounts to the same thing). You can allow or deny this caching. If you choose to allow it, you can specify the type of caching the folder provides.

Windows XP Professional supports three types of caching: manual caching of documents, automatic caching of documents, and automatic caching of applications and documents. The following subsections explain these types of caching.

Manual Caching of Documents

Manual Caching of Documents is the default setting for shared folders. When you choose this setting, users need to instruct Windows XP manually to cache a shared folder. The advantage of manual caching is that users will not cache the shared folder unless they need to. This reduces the likelihood that multiple users will modify copies of the same file while offline (although, if each user manually caches the file, they can still do so), causing synchronization conflicts when they reconnect to the shared folder. It also reduces the number of accesses to the folder.

Automatic Caching of Documents

The Automatic Caching of Documents setting makes Windows XP cache an offline copy of each file a user opens from the shared folder. These files are then available to the user when they're offline (or the shared folder is). Any files the user doesn't open while connected to the shared folder are not available when the user is offline.

Automatic Caching of Programs and Documents

The Automatic Caching of Programs and Documents setting makes Windows XP cache the files users open from the folder so that users can not only run them when offline but also run them in offline mode while online. That's right—Windows caches copies of the files on the users' local drives, and the users run them from there even when they're connected to the network.

This arrangement reduces network traffic considerably, because once the files have been cached on the users' hard drives, the users access them locally rather than across the network. But if the users change the files—if multiple users change the same file— all sorts of synchronization conflicts will occur.

Microsoft recommends that when you use this option you make the files in the shared folder read-only. That way, users can't change the files, so they will never need to write changes back to the folder and there will never be any synchronization conflicts. So you should use this option only for files that will be useful to the users in a read-only condition, such as documentation files and programs run from the network. Don't use this option for documents users need to edit.

By default, Windows XP allows manual caching of files in the shared folder. To disable caching, or specify automatic caching, follow these steps:

1. Issue a Properties command from the File menu or the shortcut menu to display the Properties dialog box for the folder.

2. Click the Caching button on the Sharing tab. Windows XP displays the Caching Settings dialog box (Figure 27-1).

3. To turn off caching, clear the Allow Caching of Files in This Shared Folder check box.

4. To change the type of caching allowed, choose Manual Caching of Documents, Automatic Caching of Programs and Documents, or Automatic Caching of Documents from the Setting drop-down list.

5. Click the OK button to close the Caching Settings dialog box.

Figure 27-1.   *If users will need offline access to this folder, specify caching in the Caching Settings dialog box.*

Sharing a Folder on the Network

As you saw earlier in this book, you can share a folder with all other users of your computer by placing the folder in the Shared Documents folder. The Shared Documents folder has permissions set so that other users of the computer can access its contents.

To share folders with users of other computers on your network, you have to set permissions to allow them to access the folders. How you do so depends on whether Windows XP Professional on your computer is using Simple File Sharing.

The following subsections discuss the three categories of permissions that Windows XP Professional uses and how share permissions work. After that, you'll see how to proceed under Simple File Sharing and regular file sharing.

Understanding the Three Categories of Permissions

Windows XP Professional uses three categories of permissions: share permissions, folder permissions, and special permissions.

Share Permissions

Share permissions are the basic level of permission, providing only three permissions: Full Control, Change, and Read. You can apply share permissions to NTFS, FAT, and FAT32 volumes. Share permissions are good for sharing folders without much effort, but they don't give you granular control over which actions a user can take with the shared folder and its contents.

Folder Permissions

Folder permissions are the next level of permission, providing six permissions: Read, Write, Read & Execute, Modify, List Folder Contents, and Full Control. You can set folder permissions only on volumes that use NTFS; FAT and FAT32 don't support folder permissions. Despite their name, folder permissions apply to files as well.

Special Permissions

Special permissions are the finest grade of permission, providing 14 permissions that you can set to define precisely which actions a user can take with a shared folder or file. Each folder permission consists of a set of special permissions. For example, the Write folder permission consists of the following special permissions: Create Files/Write Data, Create Folders/Append Data, Write Attributes, Write Extended Attributes, Read Permissions, and Synchronize.

How Permissions Work

Permissions work as follows:

- You assign share permissions to a folder (or drive) and folder permissions or special permissions to a folder or a file. For that folder or file, you specify which users or groups of users can take which categories of actions. For example, you can specify permissions so that the Everyone group (which contains all users of the computer) can view the contents of a folder and read the files it contains but not make any changes to them.

- You can assign permissions for a folder or file to individual users, groups of users, and automated system processes. Usually, it's best not to manually restrict the permissions assigned to system processes: If you deny the appropriate permissions to a system process, you may prevent Windows XP from taking actions that it needs to.

- By default, a child object (a file or subfolder) inherits permissions from its parent folder (the folder that contains it). For example, say you have a folder named "Jane's Presentations" to which you assign permissions. If you create a folder named "Feedback" within the Jane's Presentations folder, it automatically inherits all the permissions you set for Jane's Presentations. The same goes if you create a text file in the Jane's Presentations folder or the Feedback folder. You can turn off inheritance, and you can explicitly deny an allowed permission.

- A permission can be either *allowed* or *denied*. Both allowance and denial can be explicit (applied directly) or implicit (received through inheritance).

- Permissions build on each other. If a user has permissions as a member of two different groups (for example, the Users group and the Administrators group), the more extensive set of permissions applies.

In a standalone or workgroup configuration, Windows XP Professional's default security model is wide open. Each user created during setup is automatically made a Computer Administrator user, which gives them access to every folder and file on the computer. If you want to give individual users some privacy, you need to do some work with permissions.

Understanding Share Permissions

Windows XP's simplest level of permissions is share permissions. Share permissions work on FAT, FAT32, and NTFS volumes and are the class of permissions used by Simple File Sharing. You can also set share permissions manually once you've turned off Simple File Sharing.

Table 27-1 explains share permissions.

Implementing Permissions via Simple File Sharing

Simple File Sharing hides the complex permissions that NTFS makes possible and reduces their possible permutations to five different levels of sharing (see Table 27-2). Under Simple File Sharing, you can set up file sharing only on folders, not on individual files.

The problem with Simple File Sharing is that unless you understand the relatively complex sharing produced by each possible arrangement of the sharing controls, you may inadvertently share folders with users you don't want to be able to access them.

Windows XP Professional's default sharing arrangement in a standalone or workgroup environment is Level 2 sharing on each user's My Documents folder and its subfolders, and Level 3 sharing on the Shared Documents folder and its subfolders. When you run the Network Setup Wizard, it applies Level 4 sharing to each computer's Shared Documents folder to make it accessible to network users.

Permission	Explanation
Full Control	The user or group can perform any action on the shared folder and its contents, including assigning permissions to other users.
Change	The user or group can read and open files, execute executable files, and modify and delete files. The user or group cannot assign permissions.
Read	The user or group can read and open files and execute executable files, but cannot modify or delete files.

Table 27-1.   *Share Permissions*

Level	Description	Applies To	Full Control	Change	Read-Only	How to Apply It
1	Private	My Documents folder and subfolders only	Owner, System account			Select the Make This Folder Private check box or choose the Yes, Make Private button after applying a password to your account by using the User Accounts tool.
2	Almost Private	My Documents folder and subfolders only (applied by default)	Owner, System account, all Computer Administrator users of this computer			To reapply manually, clear the Make This Folder Private check box and the Share This Folder on the Network check box.
3	Shared with Other Users of This Computer	Shared Documents folder and its subfolders only (applied by default)	Owner, System account, all Computer Administrator users of this computer		Limited users, Guest user	Move the folder to the Shared Documents folder.
4	Shared on the Network (Read-Only)	Any folder other than the Program Files folder and the Windows folder	Owner, System account, all Computer Administrator users of this computer		Limited users, Guest user, remote users	Select the Share This Folder on the Network check box. Make sure the Allow Network Users to Change My Files check box is cleared.
5	Shared on the Network (Full Control)	Any folder other than the Program Files folder and the Windows folder	Owner, System Account, all Computer Administrator users of this computer, all remote users	Limited users, Guest user		Select the Share This Folder on the Network check box and the Allow Network Users to Change My Files check box.

Table 27-2.   *Sharing Levels under Simple File Sharing*

When Simple File Sharing is on, Windows XP hides the Security tab of the Properties dialog box for a file and a folder. For a folder, it displays a simplified version of the Sharing tab that provides no advanced settings.

 Under Simple File Sharing, a file always has the same permissions as its parent folder unless you've used a utility such as cacls or xcacls to change the file's permissions manually or you've used a MOVE command to move a file from one folder to another folder on the same drive but with different permissions.

Sharing a Folder under Simple File Sharing

To share a folder or drive on the network when your computer is using Simple File Sharing, you must first enable remote access to your computer. You can do so in either of the following ways:

- Run the Network Setup Wizard by choosing Start | All Programs | Accessories | Communications | Network Setup Wizard. Follow the wizard's prompts. Among its other actions, the wizard enables network file sharing on your computer.
- Click the If You Understand the Security Risks but Want to Share Files Without Running the Wizard, Click Here link on the Sharing tab of the Properties dialog box for a folder. (This link appears there only until you run the Network Setup Wizard.) Select the Just Enable File Sharing option button in the Enable File Sharing dialog box that Windows XP then displays.

Once you've enabled remote access, you can share a folder under Simple File Sharing by using the "share on the network" technique. Follow these steps:

1. In a Windows Explorer window, select the folder and issue a Sharing and Security command from the shortcut menu or the File menu to display the Sharing tab of the Properties dialog box (Figure 27-2) for the folder.

Note *If you haven't yet run the Network Setup Wizard to connect the computers on your network, you must either run the wizard (by clicking the Network Setup Wizard link in the dialog box) or click the If You Understand the Security Risks but Want to Share Files Without Running the Wizard, Click Here link. Then select the Just Enable File Sharing option button in the Enable File Sharing dialog box, and then click the OK button.*

2. Select the Share This Folder on the Network check box.

3. Enter in the Share Name text box the name under which the file should appear on the network. The share name can be the same as the folder name, but it can't contain commas or semicolons.

4. Shorten any long name to 12 characters or less if Windows 9x or Windows NT 4 computers will need to be able to access it.

5. The Allow Other Users to Change My Files check box controls whether other users can change your files. This check box is cleared by default.

■ Not allowing other users to change your files gives those users the following permissions: Read & Execute, List Folder Contents, and Read. They don't get the Modify permission or the Write permission. (This is Level 4 sharing.)

■ Allowing other users to change your files gives those users the Full Control permission. (This is Level 5 sharing.)

6. Click the OK button. Windows closes the Properties dialog box and shares the folder with the degree of permissions you specified.

Windows Explorer displays a folder icon with an open hand under it to indicate that a folder is shared.

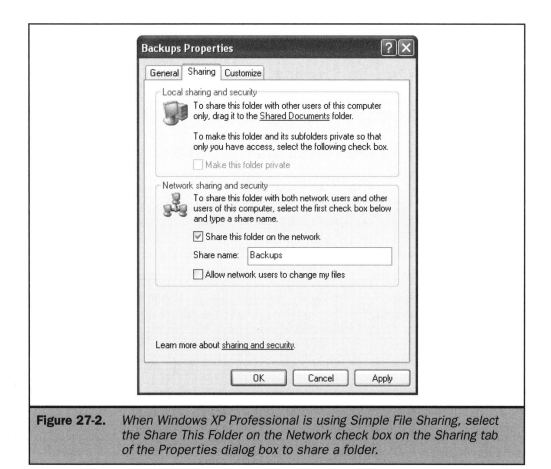

Figure 27-2. *When Windows XP Professional is using Simple File Sharing, select the Share This Folder on the Network check box on the Sharing tab of the Properties dialog box to share a folder.*

Making Your Private Folders Truly Private

If your computer is using Simple File Sharing, your first action should be to make your private folders truly private by applying Level 1 sharing to them. To do so, display the Sharing page of the Properties dialog box for your My Documents folder and select the Make This Folder Private check box.

If your user account isn't protected with a password, Windows XP displays a Sharing dialog box prompting you to create a password. Do so. If you don't, your privacy is worthless.

You can also make your private folders private by applying a password to your user account using the User Accounts tool and selecting the Yes, Make Private button when Windows XP prompts you to make the folders private.

Moving a Private Folder

When you move a private folder (a folder using Level 1 sharing) to a folder that isn't private, the moved folder takes on the sharing level of its new parent folder. If you want to keep the folder private, you need to turn off Simple File Sharing and set permissions for the folder manually.

Turning Off Simple File Sharing

To turn off Simple File Sharing, clear the Use Simple File Sharing check box on the View tab of the Folder Options dialog box.

Sharing a Folder Under Regular File Sharing

As you saw earlier in this chapter, Simple File Sharing reduces the sharing process to a couple of easy choices. But for finer control, you may prefer to assign permissions manually. By doing so, you can allow some users access to folders but keep other users out of them. Or you can allow some users to make changes but restrict other users to reading the folders.

To assign permissions manually, turn off Simple File Sharing on the View tab of the Folder Options dialog box, and then follow these steps:

1. In a Windows Explorer window, select the folder and issue a Sharing and Security command from the shortcut menu or the File menu to display the Sharing tab of the Properties dialog box (Figure 27-3) for the folder.

2. Select the Share This Folder option button to enable the controls in the Share This Folder group box.

3. Enter the name that you want users to see for this shared folder in the Share Name text box. The default setting is the name of the folder.

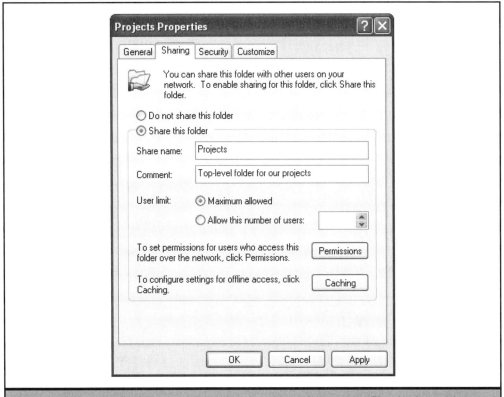

Figure 27-3.   *When Windows XP Professional is using regular file sharing, select the Share This Folder option button on the Sharing tab to share the folder, and then select further options as appropriate.*

4. In the Comment text box, enter any comment that you want Windows to display for the shared folder. For example, you might enter a comment that explains what type of files the folder contains.

5. In the User Limit area, select the Allow This Number of Users option button and specify the number of users in the Users text box if you want to restrict the number of users who can access the shared folder at once. The default setting is the Maximum Allowed option button, which lets up to 10 users access the shared folder at the same time. You might want to restrict the number of users of a folder for any of several reasons:

■ To prevent multiple users from opening the same file in an application that doesn't use file locking. (Set Windows XP to allow one user.)

■ To make sure the computer doesn't suffer too heavy a demand at any time. For a moderately fast computer on a Fast Ethernet network, handling requests for 10 light to moderate users shouldn't cause problems.

■ To make sure that an application licensed only for a limited number of concurrent users can't be accessed by more than that number of users at once.

6. Set permissions for the folder as described in the next section.

7. If you need to specify whether users can cache the contents of the folder, or how they can cache the contents, set caching for the folder as described in "Choosing Caching Settings for Offline Files," later in this chapter.

8. Click the OK button to close the Properties dialog box and apply the sharing you specified to the folder.

To stop sharing a folder, select the Do Not Share This Folder option button on the Sharing tab of its Properties dialog box and click the Apply button.

To set specific permissions for a folder you're sharing, follow the instructions in the next section and the section after that.

Setting Share Permissions for an Object

After turning off Simple File Sharing, you can set share permissions for a folder by working from the Sharing tab of the Properties dialog box. (Refer to Table 27-1, earlier in this chapter, for an explanation of share permissions.)

To set share permissions, take the following steps:

1. Display the Sharing tab of the Properties dialog box for the folder by issuing a Sharing and Security command from the shortcut menu or the File menu.

2. Click the Permissions button to display the Permissions dialog box for the folder (Figure 27-4).

3. Remove any existing permissions that are too extensive:

■ For example, if the Everyone group has the Full Control permission for the object, you'll probably want to remove it. It's possible to do this by selecting the Everyone item in the Group or User Names list box and clicking the Remove button, but you'll probably want the Everyone group to have *some* permissions. Instead, select the Everyone item (which will probably be selected by default, as in the example) and clear the Allow check box for the Full Control item in the Permissions list box.

■ Allow the Change permission if you want users to be able to change and delete files (or the folder itself); if not, clear this check box.

■ Allow the Read permission if you want users to be able to list, open, and run the files and folders.

4. Add permissions for other groups.

- Click the Add button to display the Select Users or Groups dialog box.

- Choose the user or group as usual to add it to the Group or User Names list box in the Permissions dialog box.

- With the name still selected (as it should be after Windows adds it), select the appropriate Add check boxes and Deny check boxes to specify permissions for the user or group.

5. Add further users and groups as necessary, and assign permissions to them.

6. When you've finished assigning permissions, click the OK button to close the Permissions dialog box and apply the specified permissions.

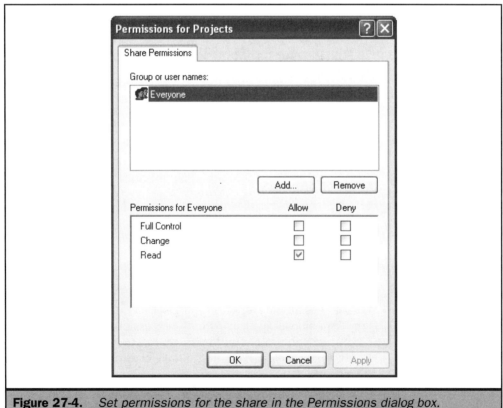

Figure 27-4. *Set permissions for the share in the Permissions dialog box.*

Setting Folder Permissions and Special Permissions for an Object

Apart from the share-level permissions, which you can apply only to folders, you can apply folder permissions and special permissions to both files and folders, provided that they're stored on a drive formatted with NTFS rather than FAT or FAT32. Despite their name, all the folder permissions apply to files as well as folders, except for the List Folder Contents permission, which applies only to folders.

Table 27-3 explains the folder permissions.

Folder permissions give you fair control over the actions that users can take with files and folders. They're adequate for most day-to-day sharing and restrictions.

As you can see from Table 27-3, most of the folder permissions encompass multiple actions. Each of these actions is implemented via individual *special permissions*. You can use these special permissions for fine control over your files and folders. Table 27-4 explains the special permissions.

Permission	Folder: User Can...	File: User Can...
Read	View the contents of the folder.	Open a document file. Run an executable file.
Write	Create a new file or subfolder in the folder.	Append data to an existing file.
Read & Execute	View the contents of the folder. Traverse the folder.	Open a document file. Run an executable file.
Modify	View the contents of the folder. Traverse the folder. Delete the folder. Delete subfolders in the folder.	Open a document file. Run an executable file. Delete a file.
List Folder Contents	View the contents of the folder.	Not applicable.
Full Control	User has all the above permissions. User can also change permissions and take control of files, folders, and resources.	User has all the above permissions. User can also change permissions and take control of files.

Table 27-3. *Folder Permissions*

Permission	Folder: User Can...	File: User Can...
Traverse Folder/ Execute File	Change folders through a folder (even if the user does not have rights to view the contents of the folder being traversed). Applies only when the user has been denied the Bypass Traverse Checking user right in the Group Policy snap-in in Windows XP Professional or Windows XP Server.	Execute (run) a file.
List Folder/ Read Data	Display the contents of a folder.	View the contents of a file.
Read Attributes	Display the folder's attributes.	Display the file's attributes.
Read Extended Attributes	Display the folder's extended attributes (if any). Extended attributes are defined by some programs.	Display the file's extended attributes.
Create Files/ Write Data	Create files in the folder.	Create a new file. Change the content of an existing file.
Create Folders/ Append Data	Create folders in the folder.	Append data to an existing file (add data to its end). User cannot change, delete, or overwrite existing data in the file.
Write Attributes	Modify the folder's attributes.	Modify the file's attributes.
Write Extended Attributes	Create extended attributes for the folder.	Create extended attributes for the file.
Delete Subfolders and Files	Delete subfolders from the folder. You can grant this permission without granting the Delete permission.	Delete files from the folder.

Table 27-4. *Special Permissions for Folders and Files*

Permission	Folder: User Can...	File: User Can...
Delete	Delete the folder.	Delete the file.
Read Permissions	View the permission list for the folder.	View the permission list for the file.
Change Permissions	Change permissions for the folder.	Change permissions for the file.
Take Ownership	Take ownership of the folder. If you're the owner of a file or folder, you can always change permissions on it.	Take ownership of the file.
Synchronize	Used only for multithreaded, multiprocess programs. Allows a thread to wait on the handle for the folder and synchronize with another thread.	Used only for multithreaded, multiprocess programs. Allows a thread to wait on the handle for the file and synchronize with another thread.

Table 27-4.   *Special Permissions for Folders and Files* (continued)

Each folder permission is a set of special permissions. Table 27-5 shows which special permissions each folder permission has.

You'll find that most of the breakdown of the special permissions into the file and folder permissions makes a lot of sense. For example, the folder Read permission includes the List Folder/Read Data permission, the Read Attributes special permission, the Read Extended Attributes special permission, the Read Permissions special permission, and the Synchronize special permission.

However, if you just scanned through Table 27-5, you may have noticed one thing that seems puzzling: the List Folder Contents folder permission has exactly the same special permissions as the Read & Execute folder permission. This is correct—they *do* have the same special permissions—but there's a slight difference in the way the permissions are inherited. The Read & Execute folder permission is inherited by both files and folders, whereas the List Folder Contents folder permission is inherited by folders but not by files.

Special Permission	Full Control	Modify	Read & Execute	List Folder Contents	Read	Write
Traverse Folder/ Execute File	Yes	Yes	Yes	Yes	No	No
List Folder/ Read Data	Yes	Yes	Yes	Yes	Yes	No
Read Attributes	Yes	Yes	Yes	Yes	Yes	No
Read Extended Attributes	Yes	Yes	Yes	Yes	Yes	No
Create Files/ Write Data	Yes	Yes	No	No	No	Yes
Create Folders/ Append Data	Yes	Yes	No	No	No	Yes
Write Attributes	Yes	Yes	No	No	No	Yes
Write Extended Attributes	Yes	Yes	No	No	No	Yes
Delete Subfolders and Files	Yes	No	No	No	No	No
Delete	Yes	Yes	No	No	No	No
Read Permissions	Yes	Yes	Yes	Yes	Yes	Yes
Change Permissions	Yes	No	No	No	No	No
Take Ownership	Yes	No	No	No	No	No
Synchronize	Yes	Yes	Yes	Yes	Yes	Yes

Table 27-5.   *How Folder Permissions Map to Special Permissions*

Note   *If a user is a member of two groups that have different permissions, the user gets the more extensive set of permissions. For example, all users of the computer are members of the Everyone group, so they get the (minimal) rights assigned to that group. Some users—preferably not all users—are also members of the Administrators group, so those users get the many rights assigned to that group on top of the rights assigned to the Everyone group.*

Special permissions are sometimes referred to as atomic *permissions, because they're the smallest parts into which permissions are broken up. Folder permissions, each of which group several special permissions together, are referred to as* molecular *permissions. When you mix permissions, you get* compound *permissions.*

Applying Folder Permissions to a File or Folder

To apply folder permissions to a file or folder, follow these steps:

1. Open an Explorer window and navigate to the folder or file to which you want to apply permissions.

2. Select the file or folder and issue a Properties command from the shortcut menu or the File menu to display the Properties dialog box.

3. Click the Security tab to display it (Figure 27-5).

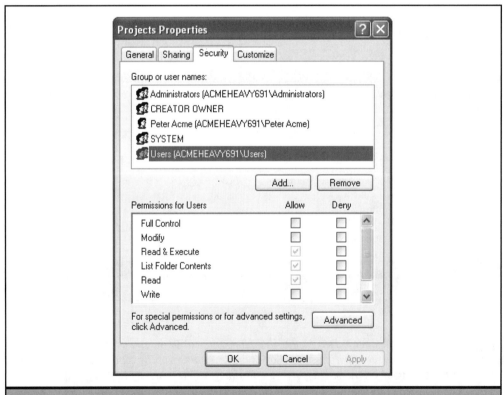

Figure 27-5. *Use the Security tab of the Properties dialog box for the file or folder to apply folder permissions. This is the Security tab for a folder.*

4. In the Group or User Names list box, select the name of the user or group you want to work with. To add another user or group, click the Add button, and then use the Select Users or Groups dialog box to select the user or group.

5. In the Permissions list box, select the Allow check boxes or the Deny check boxes to specify the permissions you want to set for the selected user or group.

> **Tip** *If a permission is explicitly allowed, its Allow check box in the Permissions list box on the Security tab of the Properties dialog box for the file, folder, or drive is selected. If a permission is explicitly denied, its Deny check box is selected. If the check box is shaded, the user or group has inherited the permission. You can override an inherited permission by selecting the opposite permission. For example, if the Permissions list shows that a user has inherited an Allow permission, click the Deny check box to override the inherited permission.*

6. If necessary, apply special permissions (as described in the next section), specify auditing (as discussed in Chapter 22), or view the effective permissions for the file or folder (as described in the section after next).

7. Click the Apply button to apply the permissions while leaving the Properties dialog box open, or click the OK button to apply the permissions and close the Properties dialog box.

Applying Special Permissions

You can use special permissions to exert finer control over which users can take which actions with which files or folders.

To apply special permissions to a file or folder, follow these steps:

1. From the Security tab of the Properties dialog box for the file or folder, click the Advanced button. Windows XP displays the Advanced Security Settings dialog box. Figure 27-6 shows the Permissions tab of this dialog box, which lists the permission entries for the file or folder.

2. To change an existing permission entry, follow these steps:

   ■ In the Permission Entries list box, select the permission entry you want to change.

   ■ Click the Edit button. Windows displays the Permission Entry dialog box (shown in Figure 27-7) showing the existing permissions for the object.

   ■ Select the Allow check boxes for the permissions you want to allow, and the Deny check boxes for the permissions you want to deny. Click the Clear All button to clear all existing permissions.

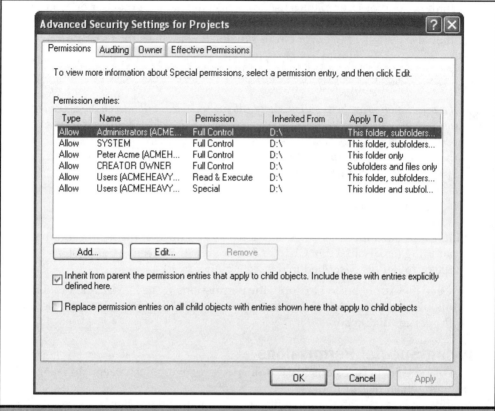

Figure 27-6.   *To apply special permissions, work from the Permissions tab of the Advanced Security Settings dialog box.*

- If the Apply These Permissions to Objects and/or Containers within This Container Only check box is available, select it if you want to apply the permission to the selected objects and all applicable child objects.

- Click the OK button to close the Permission Entry dialog box and enter the new permission entry on the Permissions tab of the Advanced Security Settings dialog box.

3. To create a new permission entry, follow these steps:

- Click the Add button and use the Select User or Group dialog box to specify the user or group. Windows XP then displays the Permission Entry dialog box.

- Select one of the choices in the Apply Onto drop-down list: This Folder Only; This Folder, Subfolders and Files; This Folder and Subfolders; This

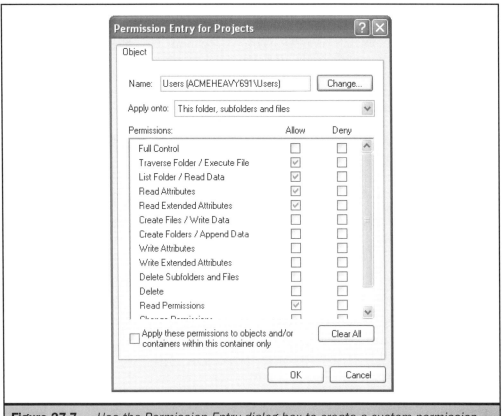

Figure 27-7.   *Use the Permission Entry dialog box to create a custom permission for the file or folder.*

Folder and Files; Subfolders and Files Only; Subfolders Only; or Files Only.

- Specify the permissions as discussed in step 2, then close the Permission Entry dialog box.

4. To remove an existing permission, select it in the Permission Entries list box and click the Remove button.

Note   *The Remove button isn't available when a permission has been inherited from another folder.*

5. To prevent permissions for an object from being affected by inheritance, clear the Inherit from Parent the Permission Entries That Apply to Child Objects. Include These with Entries Explicitly Defined Here check box. (This check box

is selected by default.) When you clear this check box, Windows XP displays the Security dialog box (an example of which is shown next) asking whether you want to copy the permissions from the parent object to the child object. Remove the permissions inherited from the parent so that you can specify all permissions explicitly for this object, or cancel the action. Click the Copy button to copy the permissions as they are (so that you can then edit them), or click the Remove button to remove the permissions.

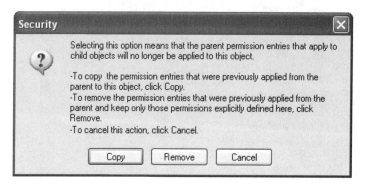

6. To reset existing permissions on child objects so that they inherit permissions from their parent objects, select the Replace Permission Entries on All Child Objects with Entries Shown Here That Apply to Child Objects check box.

7. Click the Apply button to apply the permissions you've changed to the appropriate objects.

8. Apply further permissions as necessary, or take further steps such as those outlined in the next sections. When you've finished, click the OK button to close the Advanced Security Settings dialog box.

Taking Ownership of an Object

If you revoke too many permissions, you can easily get yourself into the situation where you can neither access a file (or folder) nor change its permissions because you've revoked your permission to take either action. This is frustrating, but you can fix it by using the Owner attribute of the file or folder to reassign permissions.

Each object has an Owner attribute. This attribute lets the user or group in question assign permissions, even if they can't access the object. When a user creates an object, Windows XP automatically assigns them the Owner attribute. When Windows XP itself creates an object, such as the system files it creates when it boots, it assigns the Owner attribute to the Owner user and the Owners group for the computer.

So if you're the owner of the object, you can reassign permissions for the object to get it back into circulation. If you're not the owner, but you are a Computer

Administrator user, you can take ownership of the object so that you can reassign permissions.

To take ownership, follow these steps:

1. Select the object and issue a Properties command from the shortcut menu or the File menu to display the Properties dialog box.

2. Click the Security tab to display it.

3. Click the Advanced button to display the Advanced Security Settings dialog box.

4. Click the Owner tab to display it (Figure 27-8).

5. In the Change Owner To list box, select the name of the user or group to whom you want to switch ownership of the object.

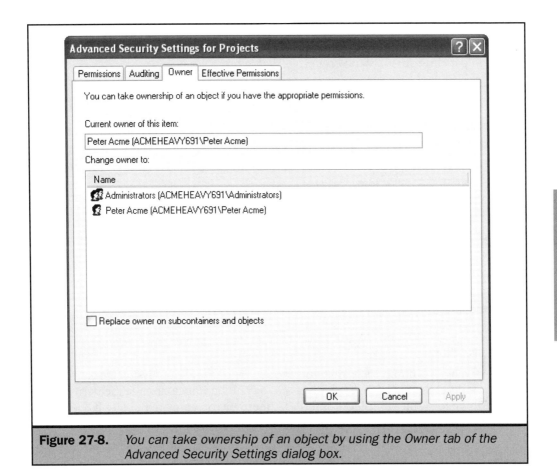

Figure 27-8.   *You can take ownership of an object by using the Owner tab of the Advanced Security Settings dialog box.*

6. If the object is a folder, you can select the Replace Owner on Subcontainers and Objects check box to apply the change to subfolders and files as well.

7. Click the OK button to apply the change and close the Advanced Security Settings dialog box.

You can now assign permissions to the object as usual. Start by assigning permissions that will allow you to access the object.

Viewing Effective Permissions

Given the number of permissions that Windows XP supports, the various ways in which you can apply them to folders and files, and the fact that permissions accumulate, it can become hard to be sure which users and groups have which permissions for a particular file or folder.

To find out which permissions are in effect for a file or folder, follow these steps:

1. Select the object and issue a Properties command from the shortcut menu or the File menu to display the Properties dialog box.

2. Click the Security tab to display it.

3. Click the Advanced button to display the Advanced Security Settings dialog box.

4. Click the Effective Permissions tab to display it (Figure 27-9).

5. Click the Add button and use the Select User or Group dialog box to specify the user or group. Windows XP then displays the effective permissions in the Effective Permissions list box.

6. Click the OK button to close the Advanced Security Settings dialog box.

Applying Permissions Effectively

As you've seen already in this chapter, you can apply permissions to folders (including drives), files, users, and groups.

To set the minimal amount of permissions and get the most effect, follow these basic guidelines:

- Assign permissions to groups rather than to individual users. Doing so takes less effort.

- Arrange your folders so that you can set appropriate permissions for a folder at (or near) the top of the folder tree and have inheritance cascade the permissions down to all the subfolders and files. Inheritance is your friend. Use it. Don't waste time setting separate permissions folder by folder the whole way down a folder tree. The result will probably be confusing—even to you.

- Never assign special permissions if you can achieve the same effect more simply with folder permissions. Before assigning any special permissions, be clear why any individual user needs special permissions that others don't.

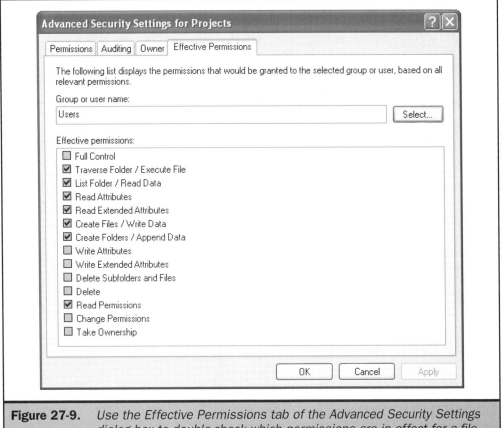

Figure 27-9.   *Use the Effective Permissions tab of the Advanced Security Settings dialog box to double-check which permissions are in effect for a file or folder.*

- Use Allow permissions to achieve most of the sharing you need. Use Deny permissions to remove a few rights that a user receives through group membership.

Managing Shared Files and Folders with the Shared Folders Tool

To see which files and folders you're sharing, and which users are using them, open a Computer Management window and use the Shared Folders feature:

- The Shares item lists the folders that your computer is sharing, their path, the share type (for example, Windows), the number of client connections, and any comment applied to the folder.

■ The Sessions item lists the user sessions in shared folders, the computer the user is using, the connection type, the number of open files, the length of time they've been connected, the idle time, and whether they're connected as a guest. You can end a selected user's session by issuing the Close Session command from the Action menu or the shortcut menu. You can close all sessions by issuing the Disconnect All Sessions command from the Action menu or the shortcut menu.

■ The Open Files item lists the shared files that other users have open, the user name, the connection type, the number of locks on the file, and the mode in which the file is open (for example, Read). Note that the list may include the parent folder of each open user file. You can close a selected file by issuing the Close Open File command from the Action menu or the shortcut menu. You can close all open files by issuing the Disconnect All Open Files command from the Action menu or the shortcut menu.

Sharing Printers and Connecting to Shared Printers

In a home or SOHO environment, you're likely to need to share a local printer—attached to your computer—with other users. Or you may need to connect to a printer that another user is sharing.

Sharing a Printer

You can share a local printer in either of two ways:

■ When setting up the printer with the Add Printer Wizard, select the Share Name option button on the Printer Sharing page. Assign the name by which you want to share the printer on the network.

■ Open the Printers and Faxes screen (Start | Printers and Faxes). Select the printer and issue a Sharing command from the shortcut menu or File menu to display the Sharing tab of the Properties dialog box. Select the Share This Printer option button and enter a name in the Share Name text box.

Setting Permissions on a Shared Printer

Table 27-6 explains the permissions Windows XP offers for printers.

When you share a printer as described in the previous subsection, Windows XP automatically assigns the permissions shown in Table 27-7.

Permission	Explanation
Print	You can print to the printer.
Manage Printers	You can administer the printer.
Manage Documents	You can manage documents in the print queue.
Read Permissions	You can see which printer permissions are assigned to which users and groups.
Change Permissions	You can change permissions for the printer.
Take Ownership	You can take ownership of the printer from its current owner.

Table 27-6.   *Printer Permissions*

As you can see, these permissions are extensive. In some workgroups, you may well want to restrict the permissions for some groups. To change the permissions, issue a Properties command for the printer, and then work on the Security tab of its Properties dialog box and in the Advanced Security Settings dialog box.

Connecting to a Shared Printer

To connect to a shared printer, use the method described in "Setting Up a Network Printer in a Workgroup" in Chapter 12.

Group	Print	Manage Printers	Manage Documents	Read Permissions	Change Permissions	Take Ownership
Administrators	Allow	Allow	Allow	Allow	Allow	Allow
Creator Owner			Allow	Allow	Allow	Allow
Everyone	Allow			Allow		
Power Users	Allow	Allow	Allow	Allow	Allow	Allow

Table 27-7.   *Default Permissions Assigned to a Shared Printer*

Managing Local Users and Groups

This section discusses how to manage local users and groups. You'll need to do this only if you're using Windows XP Professional in a standalone or workgroup environment. If you're in a domain environment, chances are your computer will be managed from a server in the domain.

If you're the sole user of a standalone computer running Windows XP Professional, you probably won't need to do much user or group management. However, you may benefit from understanding the tools involved.

Windows XP Professional's User Accounts Tools

Windows XP Professional includes two very different tools for managing user accounts:

■ The User Accounts tool (Figure 27-10) is a simplified graphic tool that provides an easy way to create, delete, and configure user accounts on Windows XP Professional. The User Accounts tool is Windows XP Professional's default in a standalone or workgroup configuration; it isn't available in a domain configuration. To run the User Accounts tool, choose Start | Control Panel | User Accounts.

■ The User Accounts dialog box is a more succinct tool for creating, deleting, and configuring user accounts. The User Accounts dialog box gives you more control over accounts but less hand-holding than the User Accounts tool does. In a domain configuration, Windows XP Professional provides the User Accounts dialog box to administrators by default; in a standalone or workgroup configuration, Windows XP Professional hides the User Accounts dialog box. To launch the User Accounts dialog box, run **control userpasswords2**. If you'll need to use the User Accounts dialog box frequently, create a shortcut to it. Figure 27-11 shows both of the tabs in the User Accounts dialog box.

For basic tasks, you can use either the User Accounts tool or the User Accounts dialog box. In most cases, using the User Accounts tool is easier, because this tool is specifically designed for use on a standalone or workgroup computer and prevents you from choosing settings that may turn out unsuitable.

For some tasks, however, you must use the User Accounts dialog box—for example, to set up a user account to log on automatically (as discussed in "Setting Up a User Account to Log On Automatically" in Chapter 5), to force users to press CTRL-ALT-DEL to log on, or to remove a .NET Passport from a user account.

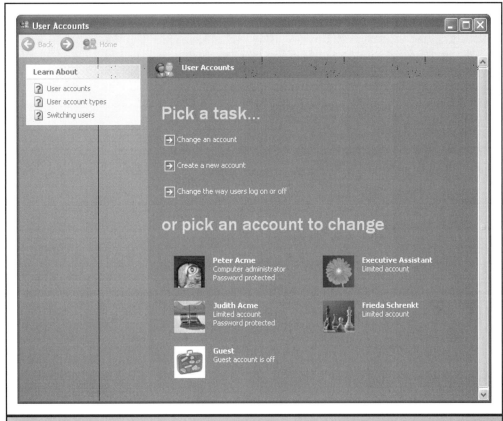

Figure 27-10. *The User Accounts tool puts a simplified graphical interface on account management and restricts you to performing basic account management.*

Creating a User Account

To create a user account on a standalone or workgroup computer, do one of the following:

- Click the Create a New Account link in the Pick a Task link in the User Accounts tool and follow the resulting screens.

- Click the Add button in the User Accounts dialog box and follow through the steps of the Add New User Wizard.

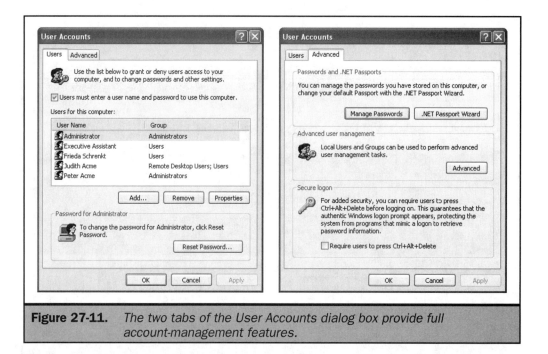

Figure 27-11.   *The two tabs of the User Accounts dialog box provide full account-management features.*

   If you've managed to set up Windows XP Professional with only the Administrator account, Windows XP forces you to create another Computer Administrator account before allowing you to create a Limited account.

Table 27-8 explains the four types of user accounts that Windows XP Professional suggests you use on a standalone or workgroup computer.

Protecting Your User Accounts

Here are notes about protecting your user accounts against intrusion:

- Always protect every user account with a password.
- You can't assign a password to the Guest account by using the User Accounts tool, but you can assign one by using the User Accounts dialog box.
- Because Windows XP automatically creates the Administrator account and the Guest account, these accounts are a favorite target of malicious hackers. You can rename these accounts by opening the Local Security Settings console (run **secpol.msc**), expanding the Local Policies\Security Options branch, and then using the Accounts: Rename Administrator Account policy and the Accounts: Rename Guest Account policy. Renaming the accounts makes them harder for malefactors to access.

Account Type	Explanation
Administrator	This is the default administrator account that Windows XP creates automatically on the computer. By default, this account stays hidden; you use this account to administer the computer only when a problem has occurred and Windows XP needs to start in Safe mode. This account doesn't appear on the Welcome screen unless you force Windows XP to display it (see "Forcing Windows XP to Display the Administrator Account on the Welcome Screen," later in this chapter).
Computer Administrator	An administrator account with full privileges on the computer. When you create user accounts at the end of Windows Setup, Windows XP automatically makes them Computer Administrator accounts. You can change these accounts to Limited accounts as necessary.
Limited user	An account with restricted privileges. Limited users can change their passwords, change various desktop settings, work with files they create, and view files in the Shared Documents folder. Limited users can't take any administrative actions and in most cases can't install or remove applications.
Guest	An account with severely restricted privileges designed for use by those who don't need even a Limited account. Windows XP creates the Guest account by default but disables the account, so you need to activate the account before anyone can use it.

Table 27-8. *Windows XP's User Accounts for Standalone and Workgroup Computers*

USING WINDOWS XP
PROFESSIONAL ON A LAN

- Keep the Guest account turned off except for when a guest user actually needs to use it.

- In a domain environment, an administrator can force users to use passwords. On a standalone or workgroup computer, you can set the password policies explained in Table 27-9 by opening the Local Policies\Security Options branch in the Local Security Settings console (run **secpol.msc**), but the policies apply only when the user uses passwords. For example, if a user account has no password, requiring a minimum password length has no effect. However, if the user of that account goes to create a password, it must meet the length requirement.

Policy	Explanation
Enforce Password History	Prevents users from reusing their old passwords. You can specify how many old passwords Windows XP should remember.
Minimum Password Length	Passwords must include at least the specified number of characters.
Password Must Meet Complexity Requirements	Passwords must include a mixture of letters, numbers, and symbols.

Table 27-9. *Password Policies in Local Security Settings*

- Never change a user's password manually unless you must. If you force a password change, the user loses all their stored passwords, all their certificates, and access to files encrypted with EFS. Instead, encourage users to change their passwords frequently and to use strong passwords.

Changing the Properties of a User Account

After creating a user account, you can change its properties as necessary. For example, if a user gets married or divorced, you might need to change their user name. If a Limited user proves responsible and needs wider powers, you might need to change their account to a Computer Administrator account.

You can change a user account's properties from either the User Accounts tool or the User Accounts dialog box:

- In the User Accounts tool, click the account name to display the What Do You Want to Change about *Username's* Account? page. Click the appropriate link. For example, to change the user's name, click the Change the Name link.

- In the User Accounts dialog box, click the Properties button to display the Properties dialog box for the user, and then work with the controls on its two tabs (Figure 27-12).

Deleting a User Account

You can delete a user account easily from the User Accounts tool or from the User Accounts dialog box:

- In the User Accounts tool, click the account name to display the What Do You Want to Change about *Username's* Account? page. Click the Delete the Account link.

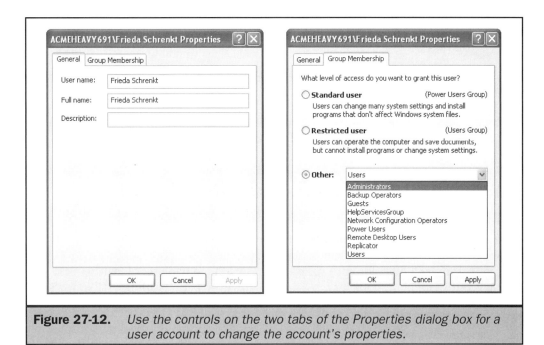

Figure 27-12.   *Use the controls on the two tabs of the Properties dialog box for a user account to change the account's properties.*

- In the User Accounts dialog box, select the account on the Users tab and click the Remove button.

Before deleting a user account, save all the data that you'll need from the account. If you use the User Accounts tool to delete the account, it offers you the choice of keeping the user's files. These files are the contents of the My Documents folder (and its subfolders) and the desktop—nothing else. To save other items, such as the user's Address Book, Outlook Express messages, or Favorites, run the Files and Settings Transfer Wizard before deleting the account.

Forcing Windows XP to Display the Administrator Account on the Welcome Screen

By default, Windows XP doesn't display the Administrator account on the Welcome screen. This is because you should seldom need to use the Administrator account. The Administrator account appears on the Welcome screen only when Windows XP starts in Safe mode following a problem (or you force a start in Safe mode).

You can force Windows XP Professional to display the Administrator account—or another specified account—on the Welcome screen. To do so, run Registry Editor and create a new DWORD value entry named Administrator in the HKLM\SOFTWARE\

Microsoft\Windows NT\CurrentVersion\Winlogon\SpecialAccounts\UserList key. Assign a value entry of **1** to display the account.

> **Note** *See Chapter 40 for a discussion of how to run Registry Editor and work in the Registry.*

You can also use this technique in reverse to hide a user account that would normally appear on the Welcome screen. Create a DWORD value entry with the user account name and assign the value **0** to hide the account.

Configuring Outlook Express for Security and Effectiveness

Outlook Express is bundled with most distributions of Windows XP Professional (your OEM may have chosen not to include Outlook Express). As freeware already installed on your computer, Outlook Express is compelling: it has a wide set of features and enough configuration options for most needs. However, because Outlook Express's default security model is open enough to enable malefactors to cause problems, you must secure Outlook Express.

This section discusses the main considerations for configuring Outlook Express as a secure and effective mail client in a small business or home business. You'll see how to choose virus-protection options, send and receive secure e-mail, transfer other e-mail accounts to Outlook Express, create rules for managing mail and news, and understand when to use multiple identities with Outlook Express.

Choosing Virus-Protection Options

Viruses can wreak havoc on your computer in moments. To prevent them from doing so, use effective antivirus software and ensure that the options in the Virus Protection area of the Security tab of the Options dialog box (Figure 27-13) have appropriate settings.

The Select the Internet Explorer Security Zone to Use list lets you choose which of Internet Explorer's security zones Outlook Express uses. The default setting is the Restricted Sites Zone option button, which increases your security but may prevent Outlook Express from taking some actions. Instead, you can choose the Internet Zone option button, which reduces your security but makes it less likely that you'll lose any functionality.

The Warn Me When Other Applications Try to Send Mail As Me check box controls whether Outlook Express displays a warning when another application tries to send e-mail using your Outlook Express identity. This may happen when you use Remote

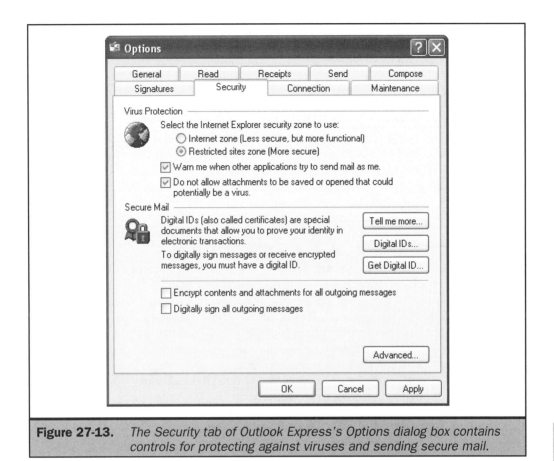

Figure 27-13.   *The Security tab of Outlook Express's Options dialog box contains controls for protecting against viruses and sending secure mail.*

Assistance to send an e-mail invitation (see Chapter 33) or when you use an automated mailto form from Internet Explorer (for example, a form on a web page).

The Remote Assistance action is harmless—beneficial, even—and the automated form's action should be harmless, too. The reason for the warning is that many macro viruses use Outlook Express or Outlook itself to send e-mail, controlling Outlook Express or Outlook from another program via the Windows Automation feature. For example, the Melissa macro virus and the I Love You virus used Microsoft Word to control the e-mail program.

The Do Not Allow Attachments to Be Saved or Opened That Could Potentially Be a Virus check box controls whether Outlook Express refuses attachments that might be viruses or contain viruses. This option is well intended but only marginally effective. The problem is that although this feature undeniably protects you from some viruses, it has a high ratio of false positives. For example, if someone sends you a Word document or Excel workbook with even the tiniest of toolbar, menu, or keystroke customizations,

Outlook Express treats the document or workbook as if it contains macros that might threaten your computer. Even if you know that the document is harmless, Outlook Express prevents you from using it.

Sending and Receiving Secure E-mail

Outlook Express supports using digital certificates (which it called *digital IDs*) to send and receive secure e-mail. You configure default options for using digital certificates on the Security tab of the Options dialog box and the Advanced Security Settings dialog box (which you reach from the Security tab of the Options dialog box). You can then change those options on any message you send. For example, you can choose to digitally sign all messages on the Security tab but then remove digital signing from an individual message you send.

Encrypting All Messages and Attachments

To encrypt all outgoing messages and attachments, select the Encrypt Contents and Attachments for All Outgoing Messages check box. If you prefer to apply encryption manually to individual messages that need it, clear this check box.

Because you have to have a digital certificate for every recipient to whom you want to send encrypted messages, you may prefer to apply encryption manually. However, if you have digital certificates for many or most of your correspondents, this option is viable, because Outlook Express warns you when you're sending a message or attachment to someone whose digital certificate you don't have. You can then choose whether to send the message without encryption or cancel sending it.

Digitally Signing All Outgoing Messages

To apply a digital signature to all your outgoing messages so that the recipients can be sure it's you that messages come from, select the Digitally Sign All Outgoing Messages check box on the Security page of the Options dialog box. If you have a digital certificate, there's no downside to this option.

Choosing Advanced Security Settings

If you're planning to send encrypted messages or digitally signed messages, check the default settings in the Advanced Security Settings dialog box (Figure 27-14).

Encrypted Messages Area Options

In the Encrypted Messages area of the Advanced Security Settings dialog box, you can use the Warn on Encrypting Messages with Less Than This Strength drop-down list to adjust the minimum level of encryption you'll tolerate. The default setting is 168 bits, which is the strongest level of security Outlook Express supports. If you find yourself frequently getting warnings that you're using a shorter key length—for example, "only" 128 bits—lower this setting to avoid receiving warnings unnecessarily.

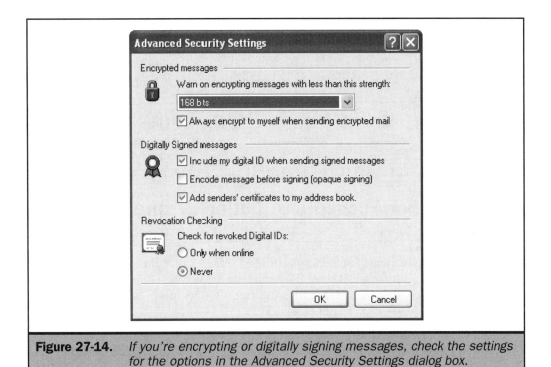

Figure 27-14.   *If you're encrypting or digitally signing messages, check the settings for the options in the Advanced Security Settings dialog box.*

Select the Always Encrypt to Myself when Sending Encrypted Mail check box if you want to keep an encrypted copy of the message. This copy is encrypted with your digital certificate, *not* with the message recipient's digital certificate, so that you can read it later.

Digitally Signed Messages Area

The Include My Digital ID when Sending Signed Messages check box controls whether Outlook Express sends your digital certificate with each digitally signed message you send. Sending the digital certificate is useful because it means a recipient who doesn't have your public key already can verify that the message is from you (and subsequently encrypt messages they send to you) without having to go through the public-key infrastructure to find your public key. If the recipient already has your public key, sending the digital certificate is redundant. But because digital certificates are compact, sending one unnecessarily wastes only a small amount of bandwidth.

The Encode Message Before Signing (Opaque Signing) check box controls whether Outlook Express encodes your digitally signed messages in such a way as to protect the digital signature from tampering. This is generally a good idea, except that if the recipient's e-mail program doesn't support S/MIME, they won't be able to read the message. Use this option with care. It's not selected by default.

The Add Senders' Certificates to My Address Book check box controls whether Outlook Express automatically adds to your Address Book the certificates of people who send you digitally signed messages. For most people, it's a good idea to use this option, which is selected by default.

Revocation Checking Area

The two option buttons in the Revocation Checking area—the Only when Online option button and the Never option button—let you specify when to check that the digital IDs other people are using are still valid and haven't been revoked. If you're feeling security conscious, select the Only when Online option button.

Transferring Other Accounts to Outlook Express

Outlook Express includes strong features for importing e-mail messages and news messages from other mail applications. For example, Outlook Express can import messages from the following e-mail applications: Eudora Pro or Eudora Light versions up to 3.0; Microsoft Exchange; Microsoft Internet Mail; Microsoft Outlook; Microsoft Outlook Express version 4, 5, or 6; Microsoft Windows Messaging; Netscape Communicator; and Netscape Mail versions 2 and 3.

You'll find these features on the File | Import submenu:

- To import messages, issue a File | Import | Messages command and follow through the pages of the Outlook Express Import Wizard.

- To import mail settings, choose File | Import | Mail Account Settings and work on the pages of the Internet Connection Wizard.

Note   *If you can't import your settings for a mail or news account, display the settings in your old mail or news application. Write down the settings and set up a new account in Outlook Express manually by choosing Tools | Accounts to display the Internet Accounts dialog box, clicking the Add button, and then choosing Mail or News (as appropriate) from the resulting menu to start the Internet Connection Wizard.*

- To import news settings, choose File | Import | News Account Settings and work on the pages of the Internet Connection Wizard.

Importing Addresses into Address Book

Outlook Express is closely integrated with Windows XP's Address Book applet. When migrating to Outlook Express, you can also import your address data from the old address book into Address Book. How you do so depends on your old address book application.

The easiest address book format to import is the Windows Address Book (WAB) format, which is the same format that Address Book uses. To import a WAB, choose File | Import | Address Book (WAB), and then select the address book file.

Address Book can directly import entries in formats including Eudora Pro or Eudora Light address books, the LDAP Data Interchange Format (LDIF), Microsoft Exchange Personal Address Book, Microsoft Internet Mail for Windows 3.1 Address Book, Netscape Address Book, and Netscape Communicator Address Book. To import one of these, choose File | Import | Other Address book to display the Address Book Import Tool dialog box, select the appropriate format, and then click the Import button. You then specify the file to import.

If your address book is in a format other than those listed in the previous paragraph, use an Export command from the address book's application to export the address book data as a text file in comma-separated values (CSV) format. To import the file into Address Book, follow these steps:

1. Choose File | Import | Other Address Book to display the Address Book Import Tool dialog box.

2. Select the Text File (Comma Separated Values) item and click the Import button.

3. Choose the address book file in the first CSV Import dialog box.

4. Specify the field mapping in the second CSV Import dialog box (shown on the left in Figure 27-15) and the Change Mapping dialog box (shown on the right in Figure 27-15).

The easiest way to create a new Address Book entry is from a message in Outlook Express. You can start a new entry in either of the following ways:

■ Right-click a message header in the preview pane and choose Add Sender to Address Book from the shortcut menu.

■ In a message window for a message you've received, right-click an e-mail address in the From, To, or Cc areas and choose Add to Address Book from the shortcut menu.

Because the resulting Address Book entry contains little more than the e-mail address, it's a good idea to immediately add to the entry any other information you know about the person associated with the address.

Creating Rules for Mail and News Management

Outlook Express includes strong features for managing mail and news automatically. For example, you can filter incoming messages so as to alert you to important messages, place less important messages in a folder so that you can deal with them later, and automatically delete spam and other unwanted or offensive messages. You can also

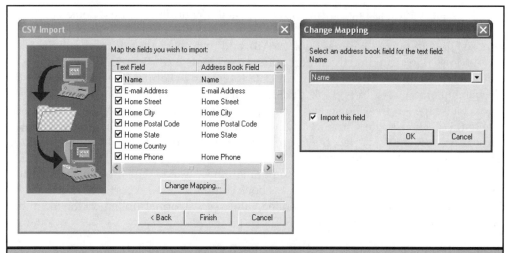

Figure 27-15. *When importing an address book stored in a CSV text file, use the CSV Import dialog box and the Change Mapping dialog box to specify which field in the text file maps to which field in Address Book.*

maintain a list of blocked senders—people from whom you never want to receive messages.

The commands for creating and managing rules and blocking senders are on the Tools | Message Rules submenu. The choices on this submenu display the three tabs (Mail Rules, News Rules, and Blocked Senders) of the Message Rules dialog box (Figure 27-16), which provide access to the tools for managing mail, news, and blocked senders.

When to Use Multiple Identities with Outlook Express on Windows XP

Outlook Express supports multiple identities for mail and news accounts. An *identity* is essentially a miniature user profile—a user profile that applies to Outlook Express and Address Book rather than to Windows XP as a whole. Outlook Express creates your main identity when you first run Outlook Express, and you can create further identities as needed.

 In a domain environment, an administrator can prevent you from creating and changing identities. But given that you're unlikely to use Outlook Express in a domain environment, this restriction shouldn't bother you too much.

Figure 27-16. *Use the three tabs of the Message Rules dialog box to create rules for managing mail and news and for blocking senders.*

In Windows 9*x*, Outlook Express identities were useful because in many cases, multiple users in small-office or home settings would use the same user account instead of each maintaining a separate user account. Outlook Express identities provided an effective way of maintaining separate mail accounts within the same Windows user account. You can protect an identity with a password to keep other users out of your e-mail.

By contrast, Windows XP contains strong multiuser features (as you've seen throughout this book) that enable you to keep each user's data firmly separated from any other user's data. So in Windows XP, you should create a user account for each separate user rather than have multiple users share the same user account. (There are exceptions to this rule, but only a few.) Each user can then use Outlook Express within their user account using the main identity.

However, if you need to access multiple separate categories of mail accounts from within the same user account, you may want to use identities to help you keep the categories separate. For example, you might maintain a business identity and a personal identity so that you can keep your business e-mail separated from your personal e-mail.

These are the main commands for creating and using identities:

- To create an identity, choose File | Identities | Add New Identity.

- To manage identities, choose File | Identities | Manage Identities and work in the Manage Identities dialog box. This dialog box contains controls for creating and deleting identities, setting the properties for identities, and choosing which identity to use when starting an application.

- To switch from one identity to another, choose File | Switch Identities, select the identity, and click the OK button.

- To log an identity off, choose File | Switch Identity | Log Off.

- To import messages from an identity (for example, before deleting the identity), choose File | Import | Messages | Outlook Express 6. In the Import from OE6 dialog box, select the Import Mail from an OE6 Identity option button, select the identity, and click the Next button.

Summary

This chapter has discussed considerations for using Windows XP Professional at home or in a small-office or home-office (SOHO) setting. You've seen how to share files and printers, set permissions, manage local users and groups, and choose key configuration options for Outlook Express.

The next chapter shows you how to configure and use wireless network connections.

Chapter 28

Configuring and Using Wireless LAN Connections

This chapter discusses how to configure and use wireless network connections. The chapter starts by covering the basics of wireless networks, because you need to know a little about how they work in order to configure Windows XP to connect to them. A large part of the basics involves security, because wireless network security is major concern for administrators, and the security measures they take affect how you access the network. The chapter then shows you how to discover which wireless networks are available, how to configure connections to them, and how to connect to them.

Understanding the Basics of Wireless Networks

This section discusses the basics of wireless networks: the 802.11a and 802.11b standards that define current wireless networking, the different types of wireless networks you'll typically encounter, the speed and range of wireless networks, and the security features that administrators typically implement.

802.11a and 802.11b

Wireless networks are built around the Institute of Electrical and Electronics Engineers (IEEE) 802.11a and 802.11b standards. 802.11b is also called WiFi.

At this writing, 802.11b networks have been in operation for several years and are widely used. 802.11a equipment is new to the market and is used mostly where higher data transmission rates are essential. While 802.11a's speed provides an obvious incentive to upgrade, 802.11a isn't interoperable with 802.11b, so an upgrade involves considerable expense to replace 802.11b equipment with 802.11a equipment. Some OEMs sell access points that include both 802.11a and 802.11b capability. These access points enable companies to use both 802.11a and 802.11b client hardware at the same time.

The Appeal of Wireless Networks

The appeal of wireless networks lies not in their data transmission rates (which, as you'll see, are significantly lower than those of modern wired networks) but in the ease and speed with which they can be set up (particularly small wireless networks) and the flexibility they confer.

Because wireless networks require no cables to connect the clients to the access points, they can be set up with minimal effort and minimal or no damage to the building. Creating a small wireless network involves little more than setting up the access point, installing a wireless network adapter in each computer that will use the network, and configuring the adapters and access point to communicate with each other. You don't need to drill holes in walls to run cables through or attach cables to baseboards the way you do for a wired network. This makes wireless networks suitable for locations you're not allowed to modify (for example, many rented premises that weren't built with networks in mind). Wireless networks are also great for setting up temporary networks (for example, at a trade show).

Because the computers in a wireless network aren't tethered by a network cable, you can move them easily from one point to another while staying connected to the network. For example, in an office, you can take your laptop over to a colleague's desk so that you can work with him, or to a conference room for a meeting. At home, you can work in the kitchen or in front of the TV instead of in the den. In many wireless networks that use multiple access points, you can roam from one access point to another without losing your connection to the network.

Types of Wireless Networks

Generally speaking, there are two separate categories of wireless network that use 802.11b and 802.11a technology:

- **Wireless Metropolitan Area Networks (WMANs)**   Cover part of a metropolitan area with a wireless cloud. Wireless network clients with the correct authorization can access the network from any point covered by the wireless cloud. At this writing, WMANs are being deployed to provide high-speed Internet access to network clients. WMANs are also used by large companies, college campuses, and other bodies that need to provide network access over a larger area than a LAN covers. Most WMANs use 802.11b technology.

- **Wireless Local Area Networks (WLANs)**   Cover a smaller area than WMANs. WLANs cover the same area as an equivalent wired LAN—anything from a room to a few buildings. Some WLANs are connected to wired LANs so that they are effectively extensions of those LANs. Other WLANs stand alone. The following subsections present three examples of typical WLAN configurations, starting with the smallest type.

Ad-Hoc (Computer-to-Computer) WLANs

Computer-to-computer (or *peer-to-peer*) or *ad-hoc WLANs* connect a handful of computers (perhaps only two) directly to each other without using an access point. You might use an ad-hoc WLAN to connect a pair of computers quickly and simply while on the road. You might also use an ad-hoc WLAN to set up a temporary network while in a meeting with colleagues with whom you needed to collaborate on a project or exchange data. Figure 28-1 shows a simple ad-hoc WLAN.

Wireless-Only WLANs

In a small network (for example, a small-office network or a home-office network), a WLAN may be used as the main network connection for all computers. The disadvantage of the WLAN's slower data transmission rates are more than offset by the speed and convenience with which the WLAN can be set up and the flexibility the WLAN confers.

Such a small WLAN will typically use only a few access points—perhaps even one, if the geographical area encompassed by the network and the number of clients it must support are both small enough for a single access point to cover. Some wireless access

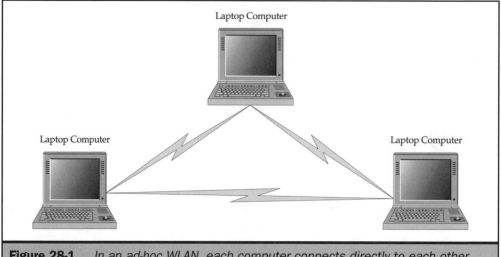

Figure 28-1.   *In an ad-hoc WLAN, each computer connects directly to each other computer without using an access point.*

points have features such as Internet routers and printer servers built in, allowing you to minimize the number of devices needed to run the network.

Figure 28-2 shows a wireless-only WLAN such as might be used in a small-office network. This WLAN uses a single access point that includes a print server and router, thus providing an Internet connection and print services to the wireless clients.

Wireless WLANs Attached to Wired LANs

Perhaps the most common WLAN scenario is a WLAN attached to a wired LAN to provide mobile clients with wireless connectivity to the wired LAN. One or more access points are used to provide wireless coverage of the area in which mobile clients will require connectivity. The WLAN is connected to the wired LAN via a bridge. Mobile clients attached to the WLAN enjoy essentially all the same amenities that clients attached to the wired LAN enjoy. The main difference is that mobile clients connect at a lower speed but are free to move around.

Figure 28-3 shows a WLAN attached to a wired LAN. To fit on the page, the figure shows a small network with two access points, but the principles remain the same for larger networks.

In a corporate network, a WLAN is likely to be used as an extension or a backup to the wired network. Users provided with wireless-equipped laptops can connect to the network anywhere in the area covered by the WLAN. Similarly, in a school, a WLAN might be used to provide connectivity to computers that are wheeled from one classroom to another.

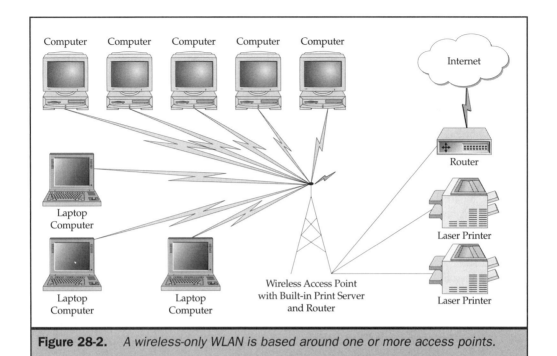

Figure 28-2.   *A wireless-only WLAN is based around one or more access points.*

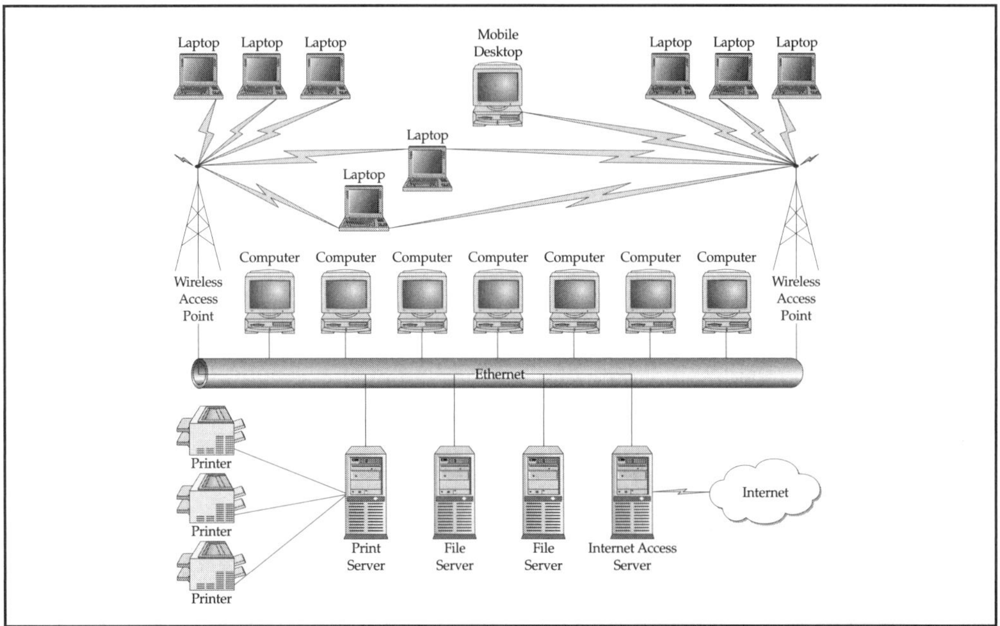

Figure 28-3.   *A WLAN is often connected to a wired LAN so that mobile clients can connect to the wired LAN.*

A wireless bridge can also be used for connecting two buildings that have a direct line of sight. The wireless bridge can provide a fast connection between the buildings, can be set up quickly, and requires neither telephone lines nor planning permission for installing cables between the buildings.

Speed and Range

802.11b equipment uses the 2.4 GHz frequency band and can manage data rates up to 11 Mbps—a little faster than regular Ethernet (10 Mbps), but around a tenth of the speed of Fast Ethernet (100 Mbps). 802.11a equipment, introduced after 802.11b, uses the 5 GHz frequency band and can manage data rates up to 54 Mbps—around half the speed of Fast Ethernet.

These are maximum speeds: depending on the distance your computer is located from the access point; how many obstructions are in the way; how many other computers are using the access point; and atmospheric conditions, you may experience much lower data rates (for example, 5.5 Mbps, 2.4 Mbps, or 1.1 Mbps for 802.11b equipment), as the wireless network adapter and access point negotiate the most workable data rate for the strength of the connection.

Like the speed, the range of wireless networks depends on obstructions and environmental conditions. For example, in ideal conditions, a typical 802.11b wireless access point may offer an outdoor range of 550m and an indoor range of 115m. But in practice, the effective maximum range will frequently be far less—perhaps 100m outdoors and 35m indoors. A very small office may be able to make do with one access point, but any office larger than that will require multiple access points to provide full coverage with reasonably fast data rates to its mobile clients.

Roaming

In many WLAN implementations, mobile clients can roam from one access point to another without losing their connection, just as cellphone users can move from cell to cell while carrying on a conversation.

Roaming allows operations such as file transfer or checking e-mail to continue in the background even as the computer is in motion from one location to another—for example, when you're walking from your office to the conference room at the other end of the building. In other implementations, a client must disconnect from one access point before connecting to another.

Wireless Network Security

WLANs tend to be a headache for network administrators, because such networks are inherently insecure. In a typical WLAN, the area covered by the access points extends beyond the confines of the office building in all directions: outward, upward, and downward. This means that someone outside in the parking lot, or someone several floors higher or lower in an office building, could easily tap into the network if it's not properly secured.

The following subsections discuss the security mechanisms that network administrators typically use to secure their WLANs. If you're using a WLAN that someone else administers, you'll benefit from understanding these security mechanisms, because they're likely to affect the way you connect to the network. If you're planning to install a WLAN in your office or home, you should implement most of these security mechanisms yourself to secure your network from intrusion.

As you'll see, securing a WLAN has two main components: preventing unauthorized users from connecting to the network and securing the data that travels across the WLAN and to any wired network the WLAN is connected to. We'll start with the mechanisms for preventing unauthorized connections.

Choosing Access Point Locations

An administrator can position wireless access points so as to minimize the area covered by the WLAN outside the company's premises. For example, it's usually a bad idea to position the access points at the corners of a building, because they'll cover a wider area outside from there.

In an ideal layout, access points would be positioned so that they delivered strong and reliable coverage throughout the office or building but no coverage outside it. In practice, it's seldom possible to achieve this: Usually, getting adequate coverage to the perimeter of the WLAN involves positioning the access points so that they also cover some areas outside the office or building as well. You'll most likely experience this problem when positioning access points for a home or small-office WLAN as well.

Even more important for most administrators is ensuring that unauthorized users or departments don't attach wireless access points of their own to the network. Because wireless access points are inexpensive and easy to install, there's a temptation for users to install them so that they too can enjoy a wireless connection to the network. Users are unlikely to implement effective security measures on such access points, so these represent a severe security risk to the company's network. By using wireless equipment with powerful directional antennas, hackers can tap into a wireless network from more than a dozen miles away if there's a line of sight. Or hackers can just hang out in the coffee shop in the middle of a business district with a wireless-equipped device (for example, a laptop or Pocket PC) and see how many wireless networks they can access. Once attached to the network, they can either attack it from the inside or simply enjoy the amenities (for example, a fast Internet connection), diversions, and secrets it offers.

Anecdotes of the number of WLANs that hackers have been able to access while performing "war drives" in major urban areas suggest that up to 50 percent of WLANs don't implement even basic security. Given that many of these WLANs belong to companies that should know better than to leave them open, it seems likely that users have installed unauthorized access points and failed to secure them.

USING WINDOWS XP PROFESSIONAL ON A LAN

Note *Some test WLANs are left deliberately unsecured as "honeypots" to gauge the frequency of hacking attempts and the goals behind them.*

If you're planning to install a WLAN of your own, make sure any access point you purchase supports 128-bit Wired Equivalent Privacy (most do) and has flashable firmware that can easily be upgraded with patches and security enhancements.

Disabling SSID Broadcasts

Besides extending the network beyond the location's physical boundaries, many wireless access points automatically broadcast their service set identifier (SSID) in their default configuration. SSID broadcasts essentially invite anyone within range to try to access the network.

Broadcasting the SSID can be useful in a public-access WLAN or (more likely) WMAN, but it represents a security risk in most corporate, small, and even home networks. So administrators typically turn off SSID broadcasts on access points in private networks. If you have a WLAN in your home or small office, you should turn off SSID broadcasts. To do so, use the configuration software that came with your access point.

Administrators also rename each access point's default SSID, because some major wireless OEMs assign SSIDs based on default strings that are well known to hackers, and change the default passwords (which are also well known). The administrators then share the access points' SSIDs with as few users as possible. You can take this step for a home or small-office WLAN as well.

Changing SSIDs and disabling SSID broadcasts is a basic security measure, but it's a good start. To access a WLAN via an access point that's not broadcasting its SSID, you need to know the SSID. Otherwise, you won't be able to locate the access point.

Using Access Lists

Most wireless access points let the administrator create an *access list* of network adapters that are allowed to connect to the WLAN. The access list contains the Media Access Control (MAC) addresses of the wireless network adapters. To connect to the WLAN, your computer's wireless network adapter must have one of the approved MAC addresses. Otherwise, you'll be denied access to the WLAN.

The Access List is a relatively weak security measure, because MAC addresses are transmitted in clear text. So an attacker who can intercept WLAN traffic (for example, by using a sniffer tool) can learn one or more approved MAC addresses. The attacker can then connect to the WLAN by spoofing (imitating) an approved MAC address.

This limitation doesn't make the Access List useless, but it does make the Access List only part of the solution for securing a WLAN. If you have a WLAN in your home or small office, see if the configuration software that came with your access point supports creating an access list. If it does, it will most likely provide you with the MAC addresses of the wireless adapters currently connected to the network.

Using Authentication

The next method that network administrators can use to secure their WLANs is authentication. 802.1*x* authentication, typically implemented using a Remote Authentication Dial-in User Service (RADIUS) server, checks each connection request against a database of users permitted to connect. This is a step you may be unable to take easily for a home or small-office WLAN.

To connect to a WLAN that's using authentication, you'll need to have the appropriate authentication settings.

Disabling DHCP

Many wireless routers use DHCP by default to automatically assign IP addresses to wireless clients that connect to the network. Automatically assigning IP addresses makes it easy for a client to connect—or for an attacker to connect.

To make connection more difficult for anyone unauthorized, an administrator can disable DHCP and assign a static IP address to each client that needs to connect. By changing the IP block used by the wireless router from one of the widely used default IP address blocks (such as the 192.168.0.0–192.168.0.255 block) to a different IP address block, an administrator can also make it more difficult for an attacker to supply a suitable static IP address. These are security measures you should be able to implement for a home or small-office WLAN as well.

   See "Understanding DHCP and Static Addressing" in Chapter 26 for an explanation of DHCP.

Using Wired Equivalent Privacy (WEP)

Once the user has been authenticated and has connected to the WLAN, it's important to keep the data being transmitted across the WLAN secure. The primary mechanism for keeping data secure on WLANs is Wired Equivalent Privacy (WEP), which is designed to give wireless networks the same level of security as a network cable. Wireless networking equipment typically supports either 64-bit WEP or 128-bit WEP. 64-bit WEP uses a 40-bit key (for example, five eight-bit ASCII characters), which provides minimal security. 128-bit WEP uses a 104-bit key (for example, 13 eight-bit ASCII characters), which provides moderate security.

However, a flaw in the WEP algorithm makes WEP traffic relatively easy to crack for someone who can intercept it and then analyze it. This problem makes WEP only one step toward securing a wireless network. This problem doesn't render WEP useless or mean that you shouldn't use it, but it does mean that you need to supplement WEP with other security measures.

For a home or small-office WLAN, you should definitely implement the strongest WEP that your hardware supports, because WEP may deter casual hackers. To implement WEP on your access point, use the configuration software provided with the access point. To implement WEP on your wireless clients, follow the instructions in "Configuring a WLAN Connection Manually," later in this chapter.

Using Virtual Private Networking

Because several of the security mechanisms discussed in the preceding subsections have flaws or weaknesses, an administrator may use virtual private networking for wireless network traffic. The administrator would implement a firewall between the wireless network and the wired network and configure this firewall to pass only VPN traffic to the wired network. Encrypting the VPN traffic with L2TP and IPSec would help prevent sniffing attacks from gathering any usable data that would enable the attacker to access the wired network.

Configuring and Using Wireless LAN Connections

The steps you'll need to configure a wireless LAN connection and connect to the network depend on how the network is configured. Most of the security mechanisms discussed in the previous section affect how you set up your wireless LAN connection and use it.

Connecting Automatically to a WLAN

If the WLAN to which you're connecting doesn't use security mechanisms, you'll be able to connect with minimal effort. The same is true if the WLAN does use security mechanisms but your computer is already configured to connect to the WLAN.

By default, Windows XP is set up to configure wireless network settings automatically. To this end, Windows XP automatically searches for available wireless networks when you install a hot-pluggable wireless network adapter (for example, a PC Card or USB adapter) or when you log on to a computer that has a wireless network adapter installed.

When Windows XP detects an available wireless network, it either displays a pop-up in the notification area telling you that "One or more networks are available" (as shown on the left in the following illustration) or connects to the network and displays a pop-up in the notification area showing the service set identifier (SSID) of the wireless network and the signal strength. The right screen in the following illustration shows an example in which the SSID is AcmeHeavyW01 and the signal strength is Very Good.

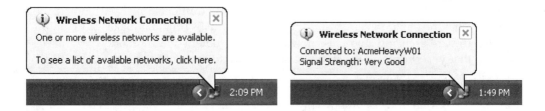

Note   *You can work with a wireless network connection from the Network Connections folder, but for most purposes working from the connection's notification area icon is faster and easier. As with other connections, the Show Icon in Notification Area when Connected check box on the General tab of the connection's Properties dialog box controls whether this icon is displayed. For wireless network connections, the icon is displayed by default.*

Configuring a WLAN Connection Manually

If your computer and access point aren't set up correctly to communicate automatically, the Wireless Network Connection icon in the notification area will display the message "Wireless connection unavailable." You'll need to configure the connection manually. To do so, follow these steps:

1. Click the Wireless Network Connection icon in the notification area to display the Connect to Wireless Network dialog box. The Available Networks list box will show no wireless networks at this point.

2. Click the Advanced button to display the Wireless Network Connection Properties dialog box (Figure 28-4).

3. Click the Add button to display the Wireless Network Properties dialog box (Figure 28-5).

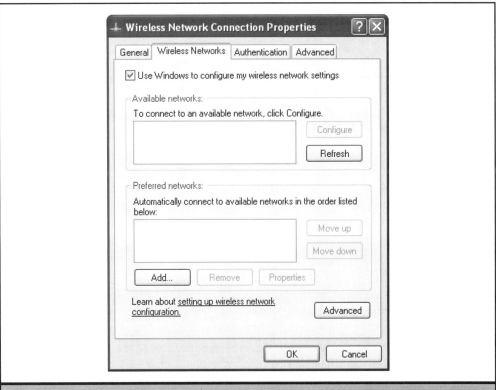

Figure 28-4.   *Create entries for wireless connections in the Wireless Network Connection Properties dialog box.*

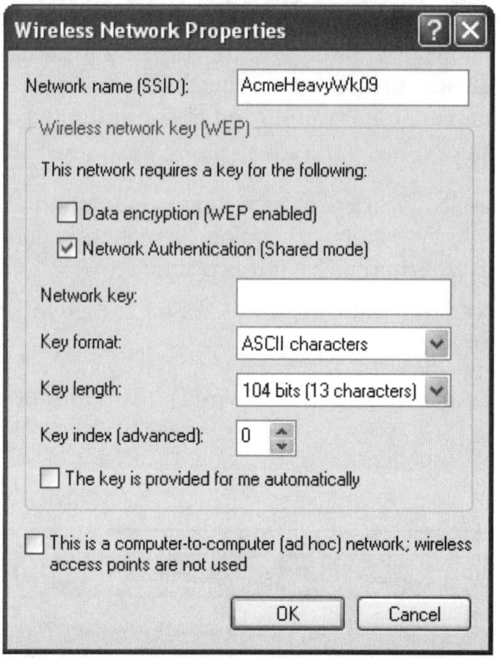

Figure 28-5. *Use the Wireless Network Properties dialog box to add a new wireless network to your Preferred Networks list and to configure WEP options for the connection.*

4. Enter the WLAN's SSID in the Network Name (SSID) text box. (If you don't know the SSID, ask your network's administrator. Get the WEP settings at the same time, because you'll need them for the next step.)

5. Choose WEP settings in the Wireless Network Key (WEP) group box. The settings you choose will depend on how your access point is configured, but these are the general principles:

■ Select the Data Encryption (WEP Enabled) check box if you need to use a WEP key. As you read earlier in this chapter, the WEP key is used to encrypt the data you transmit once you're connected to the network.

■ Select the Network Authentication (Shared Mode) check box if you need to use a network key to authenticate your computer to the network. (Shared mode simply means that you're using authenticating by using a key. Not using a key for authentication is called Open System mode.)

- If you selected either the Data Encryption (WEP Enabled) check box or the Network Authentication (Shared Mode) check box, you need to enter the key manually or select the The Key Is Provided for Me Automatically check box. For instance, the wireless network adapter on your computer may be able to provide the key automatically. If not, clear this check box. Type the key in the Network Key text box. (The WEP key is case sensitive.) Specify the key format (ASCII Characters or Hexadecimal Digits) in the Key Format drop-down list. Check that the Key Length drop-down list has automatically selected the correct item—the 104 Bits (13 Characters) item or the 40 Bits (5 Characters) item—for the length of key you typed. If your administrator has told you to use a key index, enter it in the Key Index drop-down list.

6. For a connection to an access point, make sure the This Is a Computer-to-Computer (Ad Hoc) Network; Wireless Access Points Are Not Used check box is not selected.

7. Click the OK button to close the Wireless Network Properties dialog box. Windows XP enters the SSID for the entry you created in the Preferred Networks list box.

8. Add further networks to the Preferred Networks list box as needed by repeating steps 3–7.

After adding your preferred networks to the Preferred Networks list, check the contents of the Available Networks list box. If one of the networks you've entered in the list is within range of your wireless network adapter, it may already have appeared in the Available Networks list box. Figure 28-6 shows an example. If so, select it and click the Configure button to connect to it. Clicking the Configure button displays the Wireless Network Properties dialog box. Because you've already configured the wireless network, you can close this dialog box immediately.

| **Note** | *The Wireless Network Connection Properties dialog box displays a skittle-like icon to represent an access-point network and a flat icon for an ad-hoc network. A circle around the top of the skittle or on top of the flat icon indicates that the connection is currently connected.* |

If no network has appeared in the Available Networks list box, click the Refresh button to force Windows XP to search for networks. If one appears, click the Configure button to connect to it. Again, you can close the Wireless Network Properties dialog box immediately if the network connection is successful.

If no network appears in the Available Networks list box even after you issue a Refresh command, you may need to take further steps. (You might also be out of range of all wireless networks, or the networks might not be operational.) First, specify which types of WLAN your computer should try to access. To do so, follow the instructions in the next subsection.

USING WINDOWS XP PROFESSIONAL ON A LAN

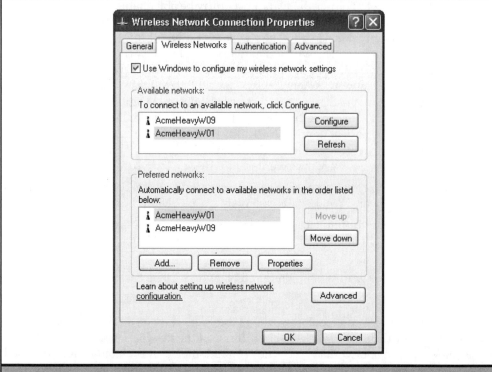

Figure 28-6. *When you've added wireless networks to your Preferred Networks list, they may appear in the Available Networks list box. You may need to issue a Refresh command to make them appear.*

Tip *If Windows XP is consistently unable to establish a wireless connection even though you've double-checked that all the settings are correct, here are three tricks you can try, in ascending order of severity. First, disable and reenable your wireless network adapter, or (if it's a PC Card or USB device) remove it and reinsert it. Second, log off Windows XP, and then log back on (or restart Windows XP, if you prefer). Third, delete the connection's entry from your Preferred Networks list and then create it again. The latter process is tedious, but it can help solve connection problems.*

Specifying Which Types of WLAN to Access

Windows XP lets you specify whether your computer tries to access WLANs based around access points (*infrastructure WLANs*), computer-to-computer WLANs, or both. If your computer isn't connecting to a wireless network, the reason may be that the computer is configured to try to access the other type of network. Even if your computer is connecting to the network it's supposed to, you may be able to improve performance by working with these settings.

To specify which types of WLAN your computer tries to access, follow these steps:

1. Click the Wireless Network Connection icon in the notification area to display the Connect to Wireless Network dialog box.

2. Click the Advanced button to display the Wireless Network Connection Properties dialog box.

3. Click the Advanced button to display the Advanced dialog box (shown next).

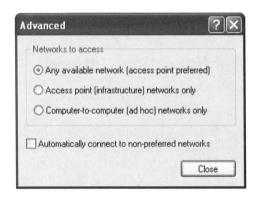

4. In the Networks to Access group box, choose which types of network to access by selecting the Any Available Network (Access Point Preferred) option button, the Access Point (Infrastructure) Networks Only option button, or the Computer-to-Computer (Ad Hoc) Networks Only option button.

   ■ The Any Available Network (Access Point Preferred) option button is the default and gives the most flexibility if you'll need to connect to both networks that use access points (infrastructure networks) and computer-to-computer networks (ad-hoc networks).

   ■ When you use only an infrastructure WLAN, select the Access Point (Infrastructure) Networks Only option button. This setting will prevent your computer from trying to establish ad-hoc WLANs with other wireless-equipped computers.

   ■ When you use only ad-hoc WLANs, select the Computer-to-Computer (Ad Hoc) Networks Only option button. Preventing your computer from searching for other networks will help establish your ad-hoc connections a little more quickly. You may also need to use this setting to establish an ad-hoc WLAN when you're in an area covered by an infrastructure WLAN. For example, if you need to set up an ad-hoc WLAN with a colleague at the airport, using this setting will prevent your computer from trying to connect to the airport's public-access WLAN.

5. Select the Automatically Connect to Non-Preferred Networks option button if you want Windows XP to be able to automatically connect to networks that aren't on your Preferred Networks list. This option is occasionally useful when you're connecting to a public-access WLAN. In general, however, it's better to connect manually to WLANs you don't normally access so that you know exactly which network you're connecting to.

6. Click the OK button to close the Advanced dialog box.

At this point, you should be ready to connect to a network if you haven't done so already. Click the Refresh button to force Windows XP to search for networks. If one appears, click the Configure button to connect to it. Again, you can close the Wireless Network Properties dialog box immediately if the network connection is successful.

Choosing Further Configuration Options

If you're still unable to connect to a network, you may need to take one or both of the following steps:

- Assign a static IP address to the connection manually. To do so, display the General tab of the Wireless Network Connection Properties dialog box and double-click the Internet Protocol (TCP/IP) item in the This Connection Uses the Following Items list box. In the resulting Internet Protocol (TCP/IP) Properties dialog box, select the Use the Following IP Address option button and enter the static IP address, subnet mask, and default gateway that your administrator provides you with. See "Understanding DHCP and Static Addressing" in Chapter 26 for more information.

- Change authentication options for the connection. To do so, display the Authentication tab of the Wireless Network Connection Properties dialog box and choose options as discussed in "Changing the Properties for a Network Connection" in Chapter 25.

Checking Your Signal Strength and Connection Speed

Windows XP uses five descriptive terms for signal strength: Excellent, Very Good, Good, Low, or Very Low. Generally, a Low signal strength provides a viable but slow connection. A Very Low signal strength means the connection is so weak that you're in danger of losing it. A signal strength of Good or better provides a reliable connection to the network at a reasonable speed.

To check the signal strength and speed at which you're connected, hover the mouse pointer over the Wireless Network Connection icon in the notification area until Windows XP displays a pop-up, as shown on the right in the following illustration. Alternatively, click the Wireless Network Connection icon in the notification area to display the Wireless Network Connection Status dialog box (shown on the left in the following illustration) and check the Signal Strength readout.

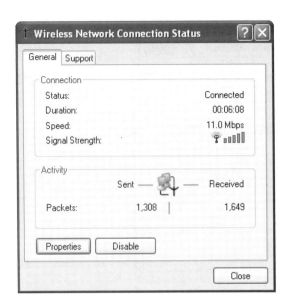

Listing All Available Networks

If multiple wireless networks are available for which you haven't specified a preferred connection order, Windows XP displays a notification area pop-up telling you that the networks are available. Click the pop-up to display the list of available networks.

You can also display the list of available networks by right-clicking the wireless network connection's notification area icon and choosing View Available Wireless Networks from the shortcut menu.

When you take either of the actions just described, Windows XP displays the Connect to Wireless Network dialog box (Figure 28-7). Select the network to which you want to connect, and then click the Connect button.

Setting Up an Ad-Hoc WLAN

Setting up an ad-hoc WLAN is straightforward. Follow these steps on each computer that will participate in the WLAN:

1. Click the Add button in the Wireless Network Connection Properties dialog box to display the Wireless Network Properties dialog box.

2. In the Network Name (SSID) text box, enter the SSID you want to assign to the WLAN. You get to choose this name. Make it distinctive so that outsiders won't be able to guess it.

3. If you choose to use WEP (which is a good idea), choose the same WEP settings on each computer. Remember that the WEP key is case sensitive.

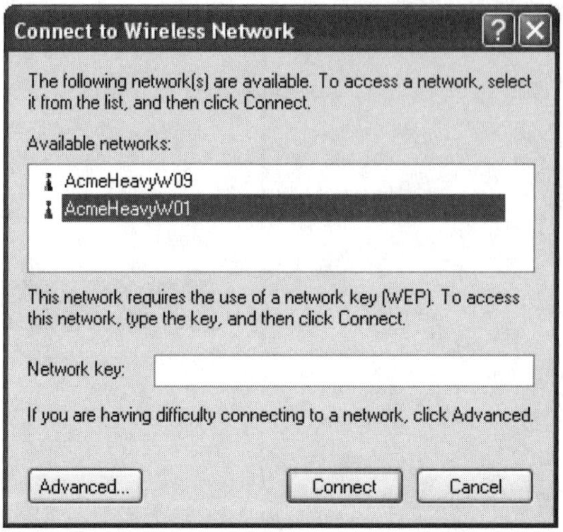

Figure 28-7.   *In the Connect to Wireless Network dialog box, choose the network you want to connect to. If necessary, enter the WEP key for the connection.*

4. Select the This Is a Computer-to-Computer (Ad Hoc) Network; Wireless Access Points Are Not Used check box.

5. Click the OK button to close the Wireless Network Properties dialog box.

Once you've completed these steps on each computer, they should be able to connect to each other.

If you'll be using only ad-hoc networks with this computer, select the Computer-to-Computer (Ad Hoc) Networks Only option button to improve performance.

Enabling and Disabling Your Wireless Network Connection

If you have sufficient permissions, you can disable your wireless network connection by right-clicking its notification area icon and choosing Disable from the shortcut menu. You can also disable the connection by opening the Network Connections folder, selecting the connection, and issuing a Disable command from the File menu or the shortcut menu.

Disabling the wireless network connection removes its icon from the notification area, so to reenable the connection, you need to work from the Network Connections folder. Select the connection and issue an Enable command from the File menu or the shortcut menu to reenable it.

Summary

This chapter has discussed how to configure and use a wireless network connection. You've learned the basics of how wireless local area networks (WLANs) work and the mechanisms that administrators use to secure them, and you've seen how these mechanisms affect the way that you configure wireless networking in Windows XP.

The next chapter discusses how to configure the additional networking components that Windows XP doesn't include in a default installation.

The
Complete
Reference

Chapter 29

Configuring
Additional Networking
Components

Thishis short chapter discusses the additional networking components Windows XP includes but doesn't install by default. These components include Universal Plug and Play (UPnP), Simple TCP/IP Services, Routing Services, Route Listening Service, Print Service for Unix, SNMP Service, and the venerable networking protocol NetBEUI.

If your computer is part of a domain, you're unlikely to be able to install and configure these networking components: an administrator will configure those components you need at the domain level. But if you administer your own computer, or your own small network, you may need to install and use some of the components. The following sections discuss what the components are and suggest when you might want to use them.

Installing Universal Plug and Play

Universal Plug and Play (UPnP) is a network service by which UPnP-compliant devices can communicate their presence on the network and the services they offer. Computers on the network can discover devices via UPnP. For example, Windows XP's Internet Connection Sharing feature (discussed in Chapter 35) uses UPnP to advertise its presence to other computers on the network. When a computer other than the ICS host receives notification of ICS, it displays a pop-up in the notification area to alert the user to the services the device is offering.

Caution   *The initial version of UPnP included in Windows XP included a buffer overrun bug that malicious hackers could exploit to either take control of a victim's computer or perform a denial-of-service attack on it. Windows XP Service Pack 1 includes the patch for this bug, so if you've installed Service Pack 1, you'll have taken care of the bug. If you haven't installed Service Pack 1, either do so or download the patch via Windows Update.*

To install UPnP, run the Windows Components Wizard, double-click the Networking Services item to display the Networking Services dialog box, and select the Universal Plug and Play item.

Installing and Configuring SNMP Service

Simple Network Management Protocol (SNMP) is a standard Internet protocol for collecting data about devices on a network and managing devices that support SNMP commands. For example, an administrator can use SNMP to connect remotely to a router or switch, monitor its configuration and performance, and change its settings.

Similarly, an administrator can use SNMP to monitor your computer if it has SNMP Service installed and running. If the SNMP management application the administrator is using requires the Windows Management Instrumentation (WMI), your computer also needs to have the WMI SNMP Provider tool installed.

 You're unlikely to need to install SNMP Service for a small network. Don't install SNMP service unless you're sure you need it, because SNMP can reveal your computer's user account names and routing information to outsiders.

To install SNMP, run the Windows Components Wizard, double-click the Management and Monitoring Tools item to display the Management and Monitoring Tools dialog box, and select the Simple Network Management Protocol check box. To install WMI SNMP Provider as well, select the WMI SNMP Provider check box in the Management and Monitoring Tools dialog box.

You can configure SNMP Service by running the Services console, double-clicking the SNMP Service entry, and working on the tabs of the resulting Properties dialog box. But you won't usually need to configure SNMP Service manually like this—in a domain environment, an administrator is likely to use Group Policy to configure SNMP Service centrally rather than configure each computer separately.

Installing and Configuring Simple TCP/IP Services

Simple TCP/IP Services are a group of services offered by most Unix-based operating systems. You may want to install these services if your network includes Unix or Linux computers. Otherwise, don't install them: they won't do you any good, and malefactors can exploit them for denial-of-service attacks on your network.

 You can't install the services in Simple TCP/IP Services individually, because Windows XP lumps them all together. Once you've installed these services, they're all enabled.

Table 29-1 explains the services included in Simple TCP/IP Services and the ports they use.

To install Simple TCP/IP Services, run the Windows Components Wizard, double-click the Networking Services item to display the Networking Services dialog box, and select the Simple TCP/IP Services item.

Windows XP configures Simple TCP/IP Services for Automatic startup. You can configure Simple TCP/IP Services for Manual startup by working in the Services console, as discussed in Chapter 43.

Service	Explanation	TCP Port	UDP Port
Character Generator	An implementation of the Chargen protocol (RFC 864). Chargen returns a specific character pattern (the 95 printing characters in the ASCII character set) to the sending computer. This service is used for troubleshooting line printers.	19	19
Daytime	An implementation of the Daytime protocol (RFC 867). Daytime returns a listing of the day of the week, month, day, year, current time (in HH:MM:SS format), and the time zone. For example: Friday, January 31, 2003 17:00:00–PST.	13	13
Discard	An implementation of the Discard protocol (RFC 863). Discard eliminates (simply gets rid of) any data received on the port it's listening to. Discard can be useful for debugging communications.	9	9
Echo	An implementation of the Echo protocol (RFC 862). Echo echoes (returns) any messages it receives and is used for testing and debugging communications.	7	7
Quote of the Day	An implementation of the Quote of the Day protocol (RFC 865). Quote of the Day returns a short message taken from the %systemroot%\system32\drivers\etc\ quotes file. You can edit this file in a text editor (for example, Notepad) to improve its miserable selection of quotes. Quote of the Day can be used for amusement or for troubleshooting communications.	17	17

Table 29-1. *Simple TCP/IP Services*

Installing RIP Listener

Routing Information Protocol (RIP) is a routing protocol used on TCP/IP networks. RIP keeps a list of the networks that are reachable and the number of hops needed to reach each network. (See the next Note for an explanation of hops.) Routers use RIP to build their routing tables after they're booted. Similarly, RIP Listener lets Windows XP listen to RIP messages and change its routing tables according to the information they contain.

You'll need to use RIP Listener in a small network only if you're using Windows XP to route packets to a remote network.

 A hop is a link between two computer systems that a data packet needs to traverse to get from its source to its destination. For example, if a packet travels from point A to point D via routers B and C, it has taken three hops: A to B, B to C, and C to D.

To install RIP Listener, run the Windows Components Wizard, double-click the Networking Services item to display the Networking Services dialog box, and select the RIP Listener item.

RIP Listener doesn't need any configuration, and Windows XP Professional configures it for Automatic startup. If necessary, you can change RIP Listener to Manual startup by working in the Services console, as discussed in Chapter 43.

Installing and Configuring Print Services for Unix

The Print Services for Unix component has two functions:

- It enables Windows XP to print to a printer attached to a Unix or Linux computer using line printer daemon (LPD).

- It enables Windows XP to provide print services to Unix or Linux computers.

If your computing setup includes Unix or Linux computers, you'll probably want to install Print Services for Unix so that you can share printers. If you have no Unix or Linux computers, you won't need Print Services for Unix.

To install Print Services for Unix, run the Windows Components Wizard and select the Other Network File and Print Services check box. In Windows XP Professional, this component contains only Print Services for Unix, so you don't need to drill down to the Details dialog box. (In Windows.NET Server, the Other Network File and Print Services component contains file and print services for the Mac as well. That's why the component has a more nebulous name than it seems to need in Windows XP Professional.)

To set up a Windows XP computer to print to a LPD printer, follow these steps:

1. Choose Start | Printers and Faxes to display the Printers and Faxes screen.

2. Click the Add a Printer link in the Printer Tasks list or issue an Add Printer command from the File menu or shortcut menu to start the Add Printer Wizard.

3. Select the Local Printer Attached to This Computer option button on the Local or Network Printer page. Make sure the Automatically Detect and Install My Plug and Play Printer check box is cleared.

4. Select the Create a New Port option button on the Select a Printer Port page. In the Type of Port drop-down list, select the LPR Port item. When you click the Next button, Windows XP displays the Add LPR Compatible Printer dialog box, shown here:

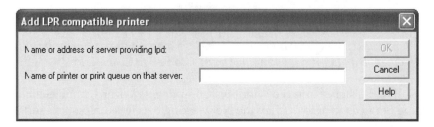

5. Enter the LPR server's host name or IP address and the name of the printer or print queue, and then click the OK button.

6. After Windows XP establishes communication with the printer, it offers you further options as applicable. After you finish the wizard, check that you can print to the printer.

After installing Print Services for Unix, you'll also be able to set up a Unix or Linux computer to print to a printer your Windows XP computer is sharing.

Installing and Configuring NetBEUI

NetBEUI (NetBIOS Extended User Interface) is an older networking protocol that was used by various OSs including Windows for Workgroups, OS/2, and Windows NT. NetBEUI uses the Network Driver Interface Specification (NDIS) to communicate with network adapters.

Compared to TCP/IP and IPX/SPX, NetBEUI has serious shortcomings. In particular, NetBEUI is nonroutable, so you can't use it across network segments— it's essentially useful only for small networks. However, you may need to install NetBEUI for compatibility with legacy applications.

Microsoft no longer supports NetBEUI but still includes NetBEUI on the Windows XP CD (in the \VALUEADD\MSFT\NET\NETBEUI\ folder). To install NetBEUI, copy the file nbf.sys to your %systemroot%\System32\Drivers\ folder and the file netnbf.nif into your %systemroot%\INF\ folder. Then take the following steps:

1. Display the Properties dialog box for the network connection on which you want to install NetBEUI.

2. Click the Install button on the General page to display the Select Network Component Type dialog box.

3. Select the Protocol item and click the Add button to display the Select Network Protocol dialog box.

4. Select the NetBEUI Protocol item in the Network Protocol list box and click the OK button.

Summary

This chapter has discussed how to install (and, where necessary, configure) the additional networking components Windows XP Professional includes. By using these components, you can cater to specific needs your network may have.

The next chapter shows you how to use IPSec and TCP/IP filtering to secure network traffic.

The Complete Reference

Windows XP

Chapter 30

Securing Network Traffic with IPSec and TCP/IP Filtering

This chapter discusses how to secure your network traffic using Internet Protocol (IP) Security (IPSec) and TCP/IP filtering. Windows XP Professional includes IPSec, but Windows XP Home Edition doesn't. Both operating systems include TCP/IP filtering.

In a domain environment, you're highly unlikely to be able to configure either IPSec or TCP/IP filtering yourself. As a result, you probably won't need to worry about IPSec and TCP/IP filtering—but you may benefit from knowing a little about these security mechanisms. If so, read the first section. If not, skip this chapter.

By contrast, in a standalone or workgroup environment in which you're a Computer Administrator user, you'll not only be able to apply and configure IPSec and TCP/IP filtering, but you're also likely to have a strong interest in doing so. In this case, read on.

What IPSec Is and What It Does

IPSec is a set of protocols and services for securing IP communications between two computers by encrypting data. On a local area network (LAN), IPSec can secure communications between computers communicating either as peers or as a client and server. Across a wide area network (WAN), IPSec can secure communications from router to router or from gateway to gateway. IPSec can also secure remote access connections—for example, across a dial-up connection.

The computers at each end of an IPSec connection need to have an IPSec policy assigned so that they can negotiate a secure connection for transferring data. The devices between the two computers typically don't need to support IPSec unless they're running Network Address Translation (NAT) or packet-filtering (for example, a firewall) that may interfere with the IPSec packets. IPSec assumes that the medium over which the data is passing isn't secure.

IPSec works on both wired and wireless networks. It's particularly useful for securing communications over wireless network connections, because the Wired Equivalent Privacy (WEP) algorithm intended to secure wireless network connections to a level equivalent to a wired network contains severe weaknesses that make it important to use an additional means of security.

Note   *Another possibility for securing data on internal network connections is virtual private networking. See "VPN Connections" in Chapter 31 for a discussion of virtual private networking.*

In most cases, a domain administrator will apply IPSec through Group Policy to the computers that need it. Depending on the company's need for or emphasis on security, this might include all computers or just a subset of computers that work with more sensitive data.

In a standalone or workgroup setting, you can apply IPSec through Local Security Policy. This chapter discusses how to do so. You can use IPSec on both internal and external network connections, but you'll typically want to use IPSec only on external network connections (such as remote-access connections) unless you believe that your network may be attacked from within.

 Local IPSec policies also apply to domain computers when they're disconnected from the domain. When the computer is connected to the domain, the global IPSec policies take precedence over the local policies.

Windows XP Professional's IPSec Components

Windows XP Professional uses three main components to implement IPSec: the IPSec Policy Agent, the IPSec driver, and Internet Key Exchange. This section discusses the IPSec Policy Agent in some detail and the other two components briefly. The following section, which covers how IPSec communications are established, illustrates what the IPSec driver and Internet Key Exchange do.

The IPSec Policy Agent runs as a service on Windows XP Professional. (You'll see it listed as IPSec Services if you open the Services item in Computer Management or load the Services snap-in in another MMC console.) The IPSec Policy Agent service starts automatically with Windows XP Professional and retrieves the appropriate IPSec policy for your computer:

- If your computer is part of a domain, the IPSec Policy Agent downloads the appropriate IPSec policy from Active Directory when Windows XP Professional starts. It caches this policy information in the Registry. While Windows XP Professional continues to run, the IPSec Policy Agent polls Active Directory at specified intervals for policy changes, again caching the policy information in the Registry. If Active Directory isn't available, the IPSec Policy Agent retrieves the last IPSec policy cached in the computer's Registry and uses that until Active Directory is available.

- If your computer isn't part of a domain, the IPSec Policy Agent retrieves the IPSec policy from your computer's Registry.

After retrieving the IPSec policy, the IPSec Policy Agent then sends to the IPSec driver the list of IPSec filters defined by the policy so that the IPSec driver knows which packets to filter and when. If no IPSec policy has been assigned to the computer, the IPSec Policy Agent waits for one to be assigned. (The service continues to run.)

How IPSec Communications Are Established

You can configure Windows XP Professional to always require IPSec for certain communications (and to refuse to communicate with computers that don't support IPSec) or request IPSec but allow unsecured communications with computers that don't support IPSec.

Once you've configured your computer to request or require secured communications for communicating with another computer, your computer automatically negotiates security with the other computer when an application needs to send data to that computer. The IPSec driver checks each inbound and outbound IP packet against the filters. When an outbound packet matches a filter, the IPSec driver transmits the packet or blocks it according to the rules set in the filter. The IPSec driver passes any packet that doesn't match a filter back to the TCP/IP driver for transmission or receipt. Similarly, the IPSec driver compares inbound packets to its filters. When a packet matches a filter, the IPSec driver takes the action specified in the filter.

When sending a packet requires a secure connection to be negotiated, the IPSec driver notifies Internet Key Exchange (IKE), which negotiates the secure connection.

The computers establish *security associations* (SAs) for the communications session. An SA combines the destination address for the communications, the security protocol used, and a *Security Parameters Index* (SPI)—a unique ID value that distinguishes this communications session from other secure communications session that the computer may be participating in. (For example, your computer may communicate securely with two or more other computers at the same time. The SPI values distinguish the various secure communications sessions.)

First, the computers establish a *main mode SA*, which details the trust relationship between the two computers, and a shared master key for authenticating and encrypting the session. For security, this key is worked out independently by each computer involved in the communication and is never transmitted across the network.

Note   *If the computers have communicated before via IPSec and have established a main mode SA whose key hasn't yet expired, they can reuse this main mode SA rather than negotiating a new main mode SA. You can force the computers to negotiate a new main mode SA for each communication by using a feature called Master Key Perfect Forward Secrecy, which is discussed later in this chapter.*

Second, the computers establish a pair of *quick mode SAs*: an inbound SA and an outbound SA. These SAs contain the SPI and the keys used to hash or encrypt the data.

On the sending computer, IKE then passes the cryptographic key to the IPSec driver. The IPSec driver uses the outbound SA to apply a hash to the outgoing packets to protect their integrity and (if the IPSec policy specifies encryption) encrypt the packets, and transmits the packets.

On the receiving computer, the IPSec driver uses the inbound SA to check the integrity of the packets and decrypt them if they're encrypted. The IPSec driver then passes the packets to the application for which they're destined.

How IPSec Protects Data in Transit

IPSec protects data in transit by using a variety of mechanisms, which the following list summarizes:

- IPSec can encrypt data before transmitting it so that unencrypted data can't be eavesdropped or *sniffed* in transit. (As you'll see later, encryption is optional.) Only the sending computer and receiving computer know the encryption key. The encryption keys are refreshed periodically (the refresh interval is configurable) to prevent an attacker from using a key they've intercepted earlier to attack a subsequent communications session.

- IPSec attaches a *checksum* (a piece of verification data) to each packet so that the recipient computer can ensure that the packet hasn't been modified in transit.

- IPSec authenticates the computers involved in a communications session to prevent the data packets from being redirected to a third party that could alter or monitor them. (This type of attack is called a *man-in-the-middle* attack.)

- IPSec uses several mechanisms—including preshared keys, public key digital certificates, or the Kerberos V5 authentication protocol—to ensure that the computers in a communications session are the computers they're supposed to be and that their identity hasn't been *spoofed* (imitated).

Other Protection IPSec Offers

Beyond these capabilities for protecting data in transit, IPSec offers two forms of protection for computers from network attacks:

- IPSec can use port blocking or protocol blocking to help prevent computers being incapacitated by *denial-of-service* (DoS) attacks. DoS attacks are attacks that attempt to flood the computer with deliberately malformed packets to which it tries to respond, thus preventing the computer from fulfilling its normal duties.

- IPSec can also help prevent application-layer attacks—attacks that try either to insert a virus into the network or to cause a fault with the operating system— because the IPSec filters block at the network layer any packets that don't meet their criteria. (See the next note for an explanation of the application layer and the network layer.)

| Note | *The* application layer *is the uppermost of the seven networking layers in the Open Systems Interconnect (OSI) networking model for computer-to-computer communications. Below the application layer are (in order) the presentation layer, session layer, transport layer, network layer, data link layer, and physical layer.* |

USING WINDOWS XP
PROFESSIONAL ON A LAN

Preparing to Use IPSec

IPSec is powerful technology and can provide effective security for networks of many different sizes. But before you deploy IPSec, make sure you understand it, need it, and you can meet its requirements. Otherwise, you can limit your communications without enjoying any appreciable benefit.

In particular, be aware of the following:

- Encrypting and decrypting data with IPSec increases the demands on your computer's processor and so decreases its performance. If you have a fast processor, this shouldn't be a problem. If you have a slower processor that's only just fast enough to run Windows XP Professional, using IPSec may make performance disappointing. In this case, one possibility is to get a network adapter that can handle the encryption so that the processor doesn't have to.

- If you implement IPSec incorrectly, you may prevent your computers from communicating with each other. Don't rush your implementation of IPSec: Plan your needs, create policies, test them, and apply them only when you're sure they work.

- Any device that filters traffic on your Internet connection will need IPSec filters in place in order to pass traffic secured with IPSec.

- IPSec isn't a panacea for communications security problems. To secure your communications, implement IPSec but also take other security measures, such as protecting your Internet connection with a properly configured firewall and reducing the number of services running on your computer.

Working with IPSec Policies

To work with IPSec policies on your local computer (as opposed to using Group Policy to configure IPSec policies in a domain environment), you use Local Security Policy. To launch Local Security Policy and display the IPSec policies, follow these steps:

1. Run **secpol.msc** or choose Start | Control Panel | Performance and Maintenance | Administrative Tools | Local Security Policy.

2. Select the IP Security Policies on Local Computer item to display the IPSec policies.

Note   *You can also add IP Security Policies on Local Computer to a custom console if you find doing so convenient.*

Using an Existing IPSec Policy

Windows XP includes three built-in IPSec policies that you can apply in their default configuration or modify to match your requirements. Microsoft states that it provides these three policies as examples and they're not intended for use as they ship, so in most cases it's best to modify the policies or create custom policies from scratch.

Table 30-1 lists Windows XP Professional's predefined IPSec policies and discusses the situations in which they can be used (preferably with modifications).

As you can see from the table, these policies are mutually exclusive. So you can apply only one policy to any given installation of Windows XP Professional at a time. Applying a policy is called *assigning* a policy. By default, Windows XP Professional doesn't have any IPSec policy assigned.

To assign an existing IPSec policy, display the IP Security Policies on Local Computer item in Local Security Settings (or another MMC console). Select the policy and issue an Assign command from the Action or shortcut menu. (You can also click the Assign This Policy button on the toolbar. It's the second button from the right in the default configuration.)

Policy Name	Typical Usage	Description
Client (Respond Only)	Client computer	If a server requests IPSec security, the client responds by using security on the port and protocol specified by the server. For other communications, the client doesn't use security.
Server (Request Security)	Server computer	The server requests security for IP traffic. However, if a client doesn't respond with security, the server allows unsecured communication to take place.
Secure Server (Require Security)	Secure server computer	The server requires security for IP traffic and prevents communication with any client that doesn't respond to requests for security.

Table 30-1.   *Windows XP Professional's Built-in IPSec Policies*

USING WINDOWS XP
PROFESSIONAL ON A LAN

Creating Custom IPSec Policies

You can create custom IPSec policies either from scratch or by modifying one of Windows XP's built-in policies. (If you already have custom policies, you can modify those too.) Windows XP Professional provides a wizard for creating custom policies, but it's easiest to start by modifying existing policies. The first subsection discusses how to modify an existing IPSec policy. The second subsection discusses how to create a custom policy from scratch.

Modifying an Existing IPSec Policy

To modify an existing IPSec policy, open Local Security Policy and display the IP Security Policies item. Select the policy and issue a Properties command from the Action menu, shortcut menu, or toolbar to display the Properties dialog box for the policy. (Alternatively, double-click the policy to display the Properties dialog box.) Then work as described in the following subsections.

Changing the Policy's Name, Description, and Refresh Interval

On the General tab of the Properties dialog box (Figure 30-1) for an IPSec policy, you can change the policy's name and description. The name and description both appear in the Local Security Settings window to help you identify the policy and understand its purpose. When you change a policy, edit the name and description to help you track the changes you've made.

If your computer connects to a domain, you can also change the interval at which Windows XP Professional polls Active Directory to see if it needs to update the local policy with any changes applied through Group Policy. If your computer doesn't connect to a domain, this setting doesn't have any effect. The default setting is 180 minutes, which is intended to provide reasonably prompt updates without causing undue network traffic or degrading server performance (as very short polling intervals might do).

*You can force Windows XP Professional to check Active Directory for IPSec policy updates (and other Group Policy updates) by issuing a **gpupdate** command in a command-prompt window.*

Changing Key Exchange Settings

To help keep your IPSec-secured sessions secure, you can tighten the key exchange settings for the policy. (You can also loosen the key exchange settings if you consider doing so advisable.)

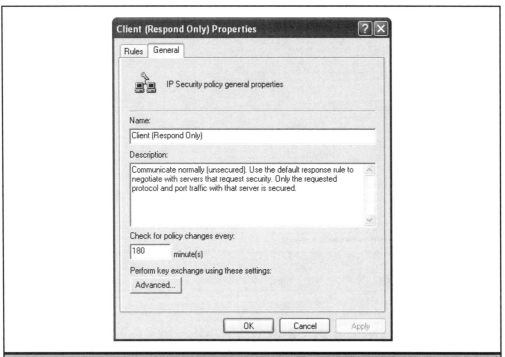

Figure 30-1. *From the General tab of the Properties dialog box for an IPSec policy, you can change the policy's name, description, interval for checking policy changes, and key exchange settings.*

To change your key exchange settings, click the Advanced button on the General tab of the Properties dialog box to display the Key Exchange Settings dialog box (Figure 30-2). This dialog box contains controls for the following:

- *Apply Master Key Perfect Forward Secrecy.*   This setting prevents Windows XP Professional from reusing a master key for a session. This setting forces Windows XP Professional to negotiate a new master key whenever it requires a new session key.

- *Increase or (preferably) decrease the interval at which Windows XP Professional authenticates and generates a new key.*   The default setting is 480 minutes (8 hours). Don't set a very short interval, because that can interrupt your communications sessions.

- *Force Windows XP Professional to authenticate and generate a new key after a specified number of sessions.*   The default setting is 0, which means that Windows XP Professional doesn't need to authenticate and generate a new key. If you apply Master Key Perfect Forward Secrecy, Windows XP Professional enters the value 1 in the Authenticate and Generate a New Key after Every *NN* Sessions text box and makes the text box unavailable.

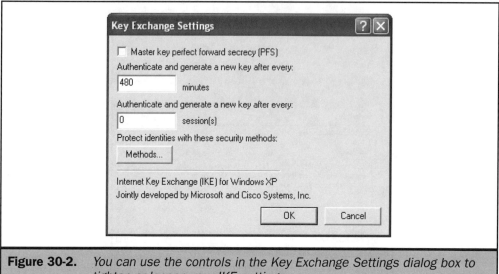

Figure 30-2.   *You can use the controls in the Key Exchange Settings dialog box to tighten or loosen your IKE settings.*

Changing Key Exchange Security Methods

You can change the key exchange security methods by clicking the Methods button in the Key Exchange Settings dialog box to display the Key Exchange Security Methods dialog box (shown on the left in Figure 30-3). From the Key Exchange Security Methods dialog box, you can take the following actions:

- Add a security method by clicking the Add button and defining it in the IKE Security Algorithms dialog box (shown on the right in Figure 30-3). See the discussion below of the integrity algorithm, the encryption algorithm, and the Diffie-Hellman group.

- Edit an existing security method by selecting its entry, clicking the Edit button, and working in the IKE Security Algorithms dialog box.

- Remove security methods or rearrange the order in which they're used. (The topmost method is used first.)

The IKE Security Algorithms dialog box lets you choose the integrity algorithm, the encryption algorithm, and the Diffie-Hellman group to use for IKE security. Here are brief explanations of these options:

- **Integrity Algorithm**   Message Digest 5 (MD5) uses a 128-bit key to compute the hash. Secure Hash Algorithm 1 (SHA1) uses a 160-bit key to compute the hash. So SHA1 provides stronger integrity than MD5.

- **Encryption Algorithm**   Data Encryption Standard (DES) uses a 56-bit encryption key, which provides relatively weak encryption by today's standards. (The U.S.

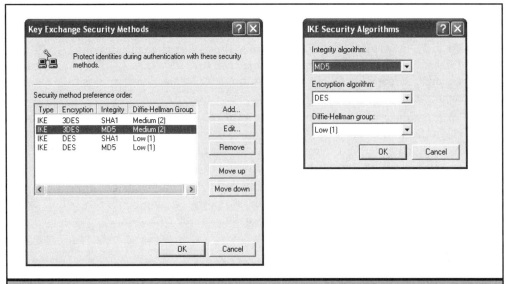

Figure 30-3. *Specify security methods in the Key Exchange Security Methods dialog box (left). Create new security methods or edit existing methods in the IKE Security Algorithms dialog box (right).*

government adopted DES in 1977, so it's done sterling service and is about due for retirement.) Triple DES (3DES) uses three 56-bit encryption keys to provide much stronger encryption. 3DES has two disadvantages: First, it requires more computational overhead than DES, so it may slow down performance on an older computer. Second, because 3DES is relatively new, not all operating systems support it. Windows XP Professional does (as you can see), but Windows 2000 requires Service Pack 2 or the High Encryption Pack to use 3DES. So depending on whom you're communicating with, you may need to use DES rather than 3DES.

■ **Diffie-Hellman Group**   The Low setting uses a 768-bit key. The Medium setting uses a 1024-bit key, which is much stronger. Use Medium for security and Low for slightly better performance. (Whitfield Diffie and Martin Hellman are famous encryption experts.)

Adding, Editing, and Removing IPSec Rules from a Policy

From the Rules tab of the Properties dialog box (Figure 30-4) for an IPSec policy, you can add new rules, edit existing rules, delete existing rules, or remove them temporarily from the policy.

These are the actions you can take:

■ To temporarily remove a rule from the policy, clear its check box in the IP Security Rules list box. To restore the rule to the policy, select its check box again.

- To delete a selected rule, click the Remove button and choose the Yes button in the confirmation dialog box.

- To add a new rule by using the Security Rule Wizard, make sure the Use Add Wizard check box is selected, and then click the Add button. Follow through the wizard's screens for specifying the settings for a rule. See "Settings for a Rule," next, for a discussion of the settings.

- To add a new rule the hard way, make sure the Use Add Wizard check box is cleared, and then click the Add button. Windows XP Professional displays the New Rule Properties dialog box. Use the controls on this dialog box's tabs to specify the settings you want to use for the rule.

- To edit an existing rule, double-click it (or select it and click the Edit button). Windows XP Professional displays the Properties dialog box for the rule. Use the controls on this dialog box's tabs to change the rule to meet your needs.

Settings for a Rule

As you saw a moment ago, you can create a new rule by using the Security Rule Wizard or the New Rule Properties dialog box, and you can edit a rule by working in its

Figure 30-4.   *You can create new rules, edit existing rules, or delete existing rules on the Rules tab of the Properties dialog box for an IPSec policy.*

Properties dialog box. This subsection discusses the settings that the wizard and the Rule Properties dialog box offer.

Authentication Methods   Specify which authentication method to use for the rule. Your choices are as follows:

- Kerberos V5, the default authentication protocol in an Active Directory domain. You can use Kerberos V5 within a domain or from one domain to another trusted domain. You can't use Kerberos V5 for Windows XP Professional computers that don't connect to a domain. Likewise, you can't use Kerberos V5 for computers running Windows XP Home Edition.

 You must make sure that the computers that need to communicate share a common authentication method. If not, they won't be able to negotiate secure communications.

- A certificate from a specified certification authority.
- A preshared key (a string of text you type).

Tunnel Setting   Specify whether the rule should use an IPSec tunnel. If the rule will use an IPSec tunnel, enter the IP address of the tunnel's endpoint. This must be a static IP address.

Connection Type   Specify whether to use the rule for all network connections, for LAN connections (internal connections), or for remote access connections.

IP Filter List   Specify the IP filter list to apply to the rule. You can edit or remove existing rules, or click the Add button and use the IP Filter List dialog box (Figure 30-5) to create a new filter list.

Filter Action   Specify the filter action to use for the rule. The easiest way to add a filter action is to make sure the Use Add Wizard check box is selected and click the Add button to launch the IP Filter Wizard, which walks you through the steps of creating a new IP filter. These steps are specifying the source IP address of the traffic, the destination address of the traffic, and the IP protocol type to filter. If the protocol is TCP or UDP, you also need to specify the source and destination ports for the traffic.

Instead of using the IP Filter Wizard to add a filter action, you can clear the Use Add Wizard dialog box and work on the three tabs of the Filter Properties dialog box; this dialog box gives you more direct control than the IP Filter Wizard. When editing a filter action, you use the Filter Properties dialog box.

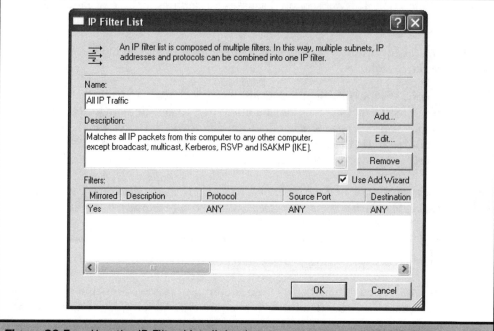

Figure 30-5.   *Use the IP Filter List dialog box to create a new list of IP filters or edit an existing list.*

Note *By default, the IP Filter Wizard creates mirrored filters—filters that also apply to packets that have the exact opposite source and destination addresses of those you specify. Mirrored filters are useful for two-way traffic between computers: the computer at the other end of the filter can communicate with you via the same filter by which you communicate with it. You can turn off mirroring on a filter by clearing the Mirrored check box on the Addressing tab of the Filter Properties dialog box.*

Choosing Security Methods for Dynamic Rules

For dynamic rules, you can specify which security methods IPSec should use when negotiating a connection with another computer. To do so, work on the Security Methods tab of the Edit Rule Properties dialog box, of which Figure 30-6 shows an example.

From the Security Methods tab, you can take the following actions:

■ Rearrange the existing security methods into a different order by using the Move Up button and the Move Down button.

■ Remove an existing security method by clicking the Remove button and confirming the action in the resulting dialog box.

■ Apply Session Key Perfect Forward Secrecy. Choosing this option forces IKE to negotiate new master keying material each time it needs a new session key instead of deriving the new session key from the current master key keying material. Session Key Perfect Forward Secrecy increases security at the cost of performance.

■ Add a new security method by clicking the Add button and working in the New Security Method dialog box.

■ Modify an existing security method by clicking the Edit button and working in the Modify Security Method dialog box.

The interface options for adding a new security method and modifying an existing security method are essentially the same: the Modify Security Method dialog box contains the same controls as the New Security Method dialog box (shown on the left in Figure 30-7). From these dialog boxes, you can choose the Encryption and Integrity option button, the Integrity Only option button, or the Custom option button.

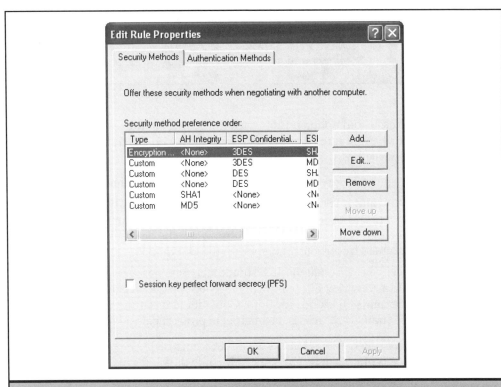

Figure 30-6. *Choose security methods for a dynamic rule on the Security Methods tab of the Edit Rule Properties dialog box.*

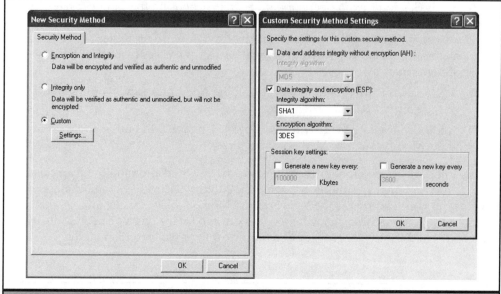

Figure 30-7. *Choose the security method in the New Security Method dialog box (left) or the Modify Security Method dialog box (not shown). Use the Custom Security Method Settings dialog box (right) to create a custom security method.*

If you choose the Custom option button, click the Settings button and use the controls in the Custom Security Method Settings dialog box (shown on the right in Figure 30-7) to define your custom settings:

- For integrity-only security, you can choose the integrity algorithm (MD5 or SHA1)

- For encryption and integrity, you can choose both the integrity algorithm (MD5, SHA1, or None) and the encryption algorithm (3DES, DES, or None). You may want to omit an IPSec encryption algorithm when the data being transferred is already encrypted by a protocol higher up the OSI model.

- You can specify how frequently IKE should generate new session keys by using the Generate a New Key Every *NN* Kbytes check box, the Generate a New Key Every *NN* Seconds check box, or both. Consider generating new session keys frequently for traffic that crosses the Internet to protect against known key attacks.

You'll notice that in the Custom Security Method Settings dialog box, data and address integrity without encryption is referred to as AH, while data integrity and encryption is referred to as ESP. AH is the abbreviation for Authentication Header; ESP is the abbreviation for Encapsulating Security Protocol. Because it doesn't use encryption, AH offers better performance than ESP, while ESP offers better security. Use AH when you need only authentication of your communications. When you need to be sure that your communications are protected from prying eyes, use ESP.

Creating a New IPSec Policy from Scratch

Once you've gotten the hang of working with Windows XP Professional's predefined IPSec policies, you may want to create your own IPSec policies from scratch. To create a policy, use the IP Security Policy Wizard to lay down the outline of the policy, and then use the dialog boxes and controls discussed earlier in this chapter to adjust its settings more closely.

Open Local Security Settings (for example, run **secpol.msc**) and expand the IP Security Policies on Local Computer item. Then issue a Create IP Security Policy command from the shortcut or Action menu to launch the IP Security Policy Wizard. Follow the steps, which are summarized here:

- Enter the name and description for the IP security policy. Make these as descriptive as possible. (You can change the name and description later if necessary.)

- Choose whether the policy should respond to incoming requests for secure communication by using the default response rule.

- If you choose to use the default response rule, specify the initial authentication method to use: Kerberos V5 (the Active Directory default), a certificate from a specified certification authority, or a preshared key.

Note   *Once you've defined IPSec policies that meet your needs, you can export them for use elsewhere by selecting the IP Security Policies on Local Computer item and issuing an All Tasks | Export Policies command from the Action or shortcut menu. Similarly, you can import policies by selecting the IP Security Policies on Local Computer item and issuing an All Tasks | Import Policies command from the Action or shortcut menu.*

Managing IP Filter Lists and Filter Actions

Earlier in this chapter, you saw how to create IPSec filters from within a policy you're working on. Windows XP Professional also lets you approach the IPSec process from the opposite direction: You can create global filters by working in the Manage IP Filter Lists and Filter Actions dialog box (Figure 30-8), and then apply them to policies you configure or create. To display the Manage IP Filter Lists and Filter Actions dialog box, issue a Manage IP Filter Lists and Filter Actions command from the Action or shortcut menu.

Getting IPSec Packets Past Firewalls

As discussed earlier in this chapter, routers and other networking devices simply pass along IPSec packets as they would any other type of packet—such devices don't need to know that the IPSec packets are hashed or encrypted as long as they can get the packets to their destination. But firewalls and Network Address Translation (NAT) devices

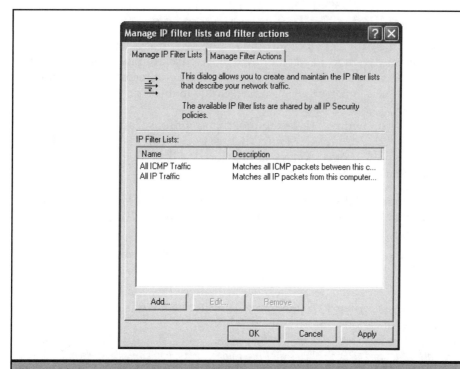

Figure 30-8. Use the Manage IP Filter Lists and Filter Actions dialog box to create and configure filters that aren't necessarily yet attached to IPSec policies.

cause problems with IPSec packets. (The next section discusses the problems that NAT devices cause.)

To get IPSec packets past your firewall, allow the following packets to pass:

- IP protocol 50 for ESP traffic
- IP protocol 51 for AH traffic
- UDP port 500 for IKE traffic

Why Network Address Translation Prevents IPSec Traffic

Briefly, NAT is a technology for sharing a single Internet connection among multiple computers. The NAT device, which can be implemented in either hardware or software, funnels Internet traffic from all the connected computers through its Internet connection, changing the IP addresses of the outgoing packets and the incoming packets as appropriate. (See "Network Address Translation" in Chapter 35 for a discussion of what NAT is and what it does.)

NAT stops IKE negotiation messages, because these messages contain encrypted IP addresses that NAT can't redirect to the appropriate internal or external address. If NAT changes the unencrypted address on an IKE packet, it invalidates the packet's integrity check value (ICV), so that the packet appears not to be authentic and is consequently rejected.

Applying TCP/IP Filtering

If you need to secure your own computer against attacks across your network or Internet connections, another weapon you can deploy is TCP/IP filtering. Windows XP lets you filter traffic by TCP ports, UDP ports, and IP protocols. (TCP/IP filtering is included in both Windows XP Professional and Windows XP Home Edition.)

Caution   *TCP/IP filtering doesn't block Internet Control Message Protocol (ICMP) packets.*

Windows XP's default setting is not to filter TCP/IP packets or IP protocols, so all IP traffic flows freely across your computer's network adapters unless a firewall (or IPSec filtering) catches it. TCP/IP filtering can be highly effective, but you need to apply it with great care, because if your filters stop the TCP/IP traffic you need them to let pass, you won't be able to communicate via the network.

Tip   *Download the current list of TCP/IP port assignments from www.iana.org/ assignments/port-numbers so that you have the latest information on which port is used for what.*

To use TCP/IP filtering, follow these steps:

1. Display the Properties dialog box for any network interface. For example, from the desktop, display the Network Connections window (Start | Connect To | Show All Connections), right-click the Local Area Network item, and choose Properties from the shortcut menu.

2. In the This Connection Uses the Following Items list box on the General tab of the Properties dialog box, select the Internet Protocol (TCP/IP) item and click the Properties button. Windows XP displays the Internet Protocol (TCP/IP) Properties dialog box.

3. Click the Advanced button on the General tab of the Internet Protocol (TCP/IP) Properties dialog box. Windows XP displays the Advanced TCP/IP Settings dialog box.

USING WINDOWS XP PROFESSIONAL ON A LAN

4. Click the Options tab, make sure the TCP/IP Filtering item is selected in the Optional Settings list box, and click the Properties button. Windows XP displays the TCP/IP Filtering dialog box (Figure 30-9).

5. Select the Enable TCP/IP Filtering (All Adapters) check box to enable TCP/IP filtering on your installation of Windows XP.

6. Set up filtering on TCP ports by selecting the Permit Only option button above the TCP Ports list box (instead of the Permit All Options dialog box, which is selected by default), clicking the Add button, and using the Add Filter dialog box to add (one by one) the list of TCP ports on which you want to allow traffic to pass. Use the Remove button to remove a selected TCP port from the list.

7. Set up filtering on UDP ports by selecting the Permit Only option button above the UDP Ports list box, clicking the Add button, and using the Add Filter dialog box to add (one by one) the list of UDP ports on which you want to allow traffic to pass. Use the Remove button to remove a selected UDP port from the list.

8. Set up filtering of IP protocols by selecting the Permit Only option button above the IP Protocols list box, clicking the Add button, and using the Add Filter dialog box to specify the IP protocols that you want to allow to cross your network adapters. Use the Remove button to remove a selected IP protocol from the list.

9. Close all four dialog boxes to apply your settings.

10. Restart Windows XP to make the TCP/IP filtering take effect.

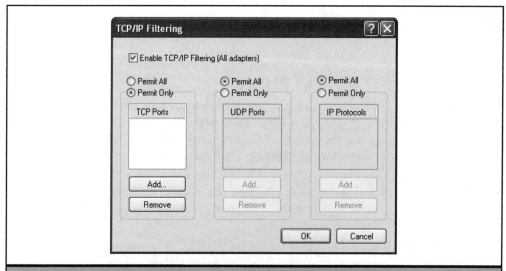

Figure 30-9.   Use the TCP/IP Filtering dialog box to apply filtering to TCP ports, UDP ports, or IP protocols.

After applying TCP/IP filtering, verify that your TCP/IP communications are working as they should do. If not, establish which other ports or protocols you need to allow to pass across your network adapters, and set TCP/IP filters accordingly.

Summary

This chapter has discussed what IPSec is, what it does, and how to apply it to your Windows XP Professional computer to secure your communications with other computers. It has also covered how to apply TCP/IP filtering to your network connections to further protect them.

This is the end of Part IV of the book. The next part of the book discusses how to use remote network connections with Windows XP Professional, starting with incoming network connections.

The Complete Reference

Part V

Using Remote Network Connections

The
Complete
Reference

Windows XP

Chapter 31

Configuring and Using Incoming Connections and VPN Connections

his chapter shows you how to configure incoming connections on your Windows XP
Professional computer and use them to connect remotely to your computer. The
chapter first covers direct connections to your computer via parallel ports or serial
ports, infrared ports, and direct dial-up connections. The chapter then discusses how
to create and use virtual private network (VPN) connections to connect securely to
a remote network across an insecure network (for example, the Internet).

Transferring Data via Direct Connections

Like several earlier versions of Windows, Windows XP supports connecting two
computers to each other via parallel-port cables, serial-port cables, and infrared links.
One computer acts as the host for the connection, and the other computer acts as the
guest. The guest can access shared folders and use shared resources (for example,
a printer) on the host, but the host can't access folders and resources on the guest
unless you reverse the two computers' roles.

This type of rudimentary network is useful for basic file transfer and sharing needs
when no conventional network connection is available—for example, when you move
from an old computer to a new computer and need to transfer a large amount of data
to the new computer, or if you're a business traveler on the road with a pair of computers
that need to communicate. But for most regular or long-term use, a conventional network
connection (one that uses a network card in each computer) is much more convenient
than a parallel, serial, or infrared connection. This is because a conventional network
connection gives you more flexibility: each computer can share resources and each can
access shared resources.

Tip
*You can also network Windows XP Professional computers via FireWire ports using
FireWire cables or via USB ports using USB cables. These types of network connections
can be useful for home-office, small-office, and workgroup configurations, but they're
limited by the lengths of the cables you can use. (For example, the maximum run of
FireWire cable is approximately 15 feet, so the computers need to be close together.)
Windows XP treats USB network connections and FireWire connections as full-fledged
network connections rather than as direct connections, so you configure these connections
as you do Ethernet connections rather than direct connections.*

Windows XP also supports incoming dial-up connections via devices such as
modems. Windows XP can accept only one incoming connection at a time, but even this
can be enough for modest networking needs—for example, collecting a few forgotten
files, or backing up a few new files, when you're on the road.

General Procedure for Setting Up Incoming Connections

This section explains the general procedure for setting up your computer to accept incoming connections. The following sections discuss the considerations for (in turn) parallel port, infrared, serial, and dial-up connections.

Incoming connections are a little difficult to get to grips with because of some quirks in the way that Windows XP implements them:

■ Instead of having a separate item for each different type of incoming connection (for example, an item for incoming dial-up connections and a separate item for incoming parallel-port connections), Windows XP lumps all incoming connections into an item named Incoming Connections. This item appears after you first set up an incoming connection by using the New Connection Wizard. You can then manipulate the Incoming Connections item further by running the New Connection Wizard again or by working in the Incoming Connections Properties dialog box.

■ Windows XP won't let you create a serial connection for the first incoming connection you set up.

■ The New Connection Wizard also includes an option for setting up a computer as the host for an incoming connection. You normally don't need to use this option unless you're setting up a serial connection.

■ It's not immediately apparent that the mechanisms for adding, configuring, and removing users for incoming connections affect not only incoming connections but also the user accounts for the computer as well.

To set up your computer to accept incoming connections, follow these steps:

1. Display the Network Connections window. For example, choose Start | Connect To | Show All Connections or choose Start | Control Panel | Network and Internet Connections | Network Connections.

2. Click the Create a New Connection link in the Network Tasks list to start the New Connection Wizard.

3. On the Network Connection Type page of the wizard, select the Set Up an Advanced Connection option button.

4. On the Advanced Connection Options page of the wizard, select the Accept Incoming Connections option button.

5. On the Devices for Incoming Connections page of the wizard (Figure 31-1), select the port or modem to use.

Figure 31-1. *Choose the port or modem to use on the Devices for Incoming Connections page of the New Connection Wizard.*

Note *To use a serial port for the connection, you need to finish this wizard and restart it. On the pages of the wizard, choose Set Up an Advanced Connection | Connect Directly to Another Computer | Host to reach the Connection Device page. On the Connection Device page, choose the serial port to which you've connected the serial cable—for example, Communications Port (COM1). Change the user permissions if necessary and then finish the New Connection Wizard. You'll then be able to connect via the serial port.*

6. On the Incoming Virtual Private Network (VPN) Connection page of the wizard, select the Do Not Allow Virtual Private Connections option button.

7. On the User Permissions page of the wizard (Figure 31-2), specify the users allowed to use this connection. Select a check box to permit one of the listed users to connect. Add a user by clicking the Add button, entering the user's details in the New User dialog box, and then clicking the OK button. Change a user's password by clicking the Properties button and working in the resulting Properties dialog box.

Figure 31-2. *Specify the users who can use the connection on the User Permissions page of the New Connection Wizard.*

> **Caution**   *Changes you make to accounts on the User Permissions page of the New Connection Wizard affect not just user permissions for direct connections but also user permissions for logging on. For example, using the Remove button to remove a user from the list on the User Permissions page also removes that user account from your computer. So use these options with care.*

8. On the Networking Software page of the wizard, clear the check boxes for any protocols or networking components that you don't want the connection to use.

9. Decide whether to allow callers who use the incoming connection to access only the computer providing the incoming connection or to access your network as well:

- The default setting is to allow callers to access your network. Depending on your situation, this can be a good idea or a security threat.

- To change this setting, double-click the item for the protocol on the Networking Software page to display its Properties dialog box. TCP/IP is Windows XP's preferred networking protocol, so TCP/IP is the protocol you're most likely to need to configure. The left screen in Figure 31-3 shows the Incoming TCP/IP Properties dialog box. Select or clear the Allow Callers to Access My Local Area Network check box as appropriate. Use the controls in the TCP/IP Address Assignment group box to specify how Windows XP Professional should allocate an IP address to callers. The default option, Assign TCP/IP Addresses Automatically Using DHCP, is the easiest. You can also specify a range of addresses to use; if you do this, you can limit the range to two addresses, because of Windows XP's limit of a single incoming connection. You can also allow the caller to specify their own IP address, but bear in mind that the caller might try to use an address that a computer on the network is already using.

■ If you use IPX/SPX, configure that as well by using the Incoming IPX Properties dialog box (shown on the right in Figure 31-3). Again, the key setting is the Allow Callers to Access My Local Area Network check box. Use the controls in the Network Number Assignment group box to specify how Windows XP allocates a network number to callers.

10. When you finish the wizard, it saves the incoming connection under the name "Incoming Connections" in the Network Connections folder. You can't rename the Incoming Connections item as you can other network connections.

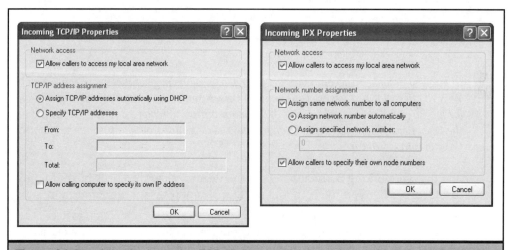

Figure 31-3. *Use the Incoming TCP/IP Properties dialog box (left) and, if necessary, the Incoming IPX Properties dialog box (right) to specify whether callers can access your LAN or just the computer providing the incoming connection.*

After you've created the Incoming Connections item, you can choose three extra settings from its Properties dialog box that the New Connection Wizard doesn't offer you:

- On the General tab, select or clear the Show Icon in Notification Area When Connected check box. This check box is selected by default, thus letting you see at a glance that an incoming connection has been established and whether data is flowing across it.

- On the Users tab, select or clear the Require All Users to Secure Their Passwords and Data check box. If you select this check box, each user must select the Require Data Encryption (Disconnect If None) check box of the connection they're using in order to connect to your computer. This check box is cleared by default.

- On the Users tab, select or clear the Always Allow Directly Connected Devices Such As Palmtop Computers to Connect Without Providing a Password check box. This check box is cleared by default.

Setting Up the Guest for a Direct Connection

To set up the guest computer for a direct connection, follow these steps:

1. Run the New Connection Wizard from the Network Connections folder.

2. On the Network Connection Type page, select the Set Up an Advanced Connection option button.

3. On the Advanced Connections page, select the option button.

4. On the Advanced Connection Options page, select the Connect Directly to Another Computer option button.

5. On the Host or Guest? page, select the Guest option button.

6. On the Connection Name page, enter the name you want to assign to the connection.

7. On the Select a Device page, select the serial, parallel, or infrared port to use.

8. If the wizard displays the Connection Availability page, choose whether to make the connection available for anyone's use or only your use.

9. On the Completing the New Connection Wizard page, choose whether to create a shortcut for this connection on your desktop. Then finish the wizard.

The wizard automatically opens the Connect dialog box for the connection after creating it. See "Connecting via a Direct Connection," later in this chapter, for a discussion of how to connect via the connection.

Considerations for Parallel Port Connections

Unless you have infrared ports on both computers you want to connect, parallel ports offer the best blend of speed and convenience. Depending on the type of parallel cable you use, you can get speeds of between 400 Kbps and 4 Mbps—plenty fast enough to be effective.

To establish a connection via parallel ports, follow these general steps:

1. Get a parallel-port data-transfer cable. Make sure that it has male DB25 (25-pin) connectors at each end. (A male connector has pins. A female connector has sockets.) Make sure that it's designed for data transfer. Not every cable with male DB25 connectors will work.

2. Attach the cable to the parallel ports on the computers.

3. Configure one computer as the host and the other computer as the guest, as described in "General Procedure for Setting Up Incoming Connections," earlier in this chapter.

4. On the guest computer, establish the connection to the host computer.

Considerations for Infrared Connections

If each of the computers between which you want to transfer data has an infrared port, you can transfer data between the computers without any cables at all. Most laptop computers include infrared ports, but very few desktop computers have them. So if you're connecting two laptops, you may well be able to use infrared, whereas if the connection involves a desktop, you're probably out of luck. It's seldom worth adding infrared to a computer that doesn't have it, because infrared costs more than other networking solutions.

The Infrared Data Association (IrDA, a trade association of computer hardware, telecommunications hardware, and software companies; www.irda.org) defines standards for infrared data transfer. Older infrared ports support IrDA 1.0, which supports speeds of 115 Kbps. Newer infrared ports support IrDA 2.0, which supports speeds of 4 Mbps. If your laptop is fast enough to run Windows XP Professional at a decent speed, it's probably recent enough to have an IrDA 2.0 port.

To establish a connection via infrared ports, follow these general steps:

1. Configure one computer as the host and the other computer as the guest, as described in "General Procedure for Setting Up Incoming Connections," earlier in this chapter.

2. Verify that the infrared ports are enabled. Many laptops that come with infrared ports include custom configuration applications that let you configure them from Windows XP. With other laptops, you may need to edit the computer's BIOS to turn on an infrared port.

3. Position the computers so that the ports are as close together as possible, facing each other, at the same height, with a clear path between them, and not in direct sunlight. Windows XP Professional automatically establishes communication between the two computers and each displays an icon in the notification area with a pop-up that alerts you the other computer is within range.

4. On the guest computer, establish the connection to the host computer. Windows XP Professional negotiates the connection and displays on the desktop a Send Files to Another Computer shortcut.

Once you've connected the guest computer to the host computer via infrared, you can transfer files by double-clicking the Send Files to Another Computer icon and working in the Wireless Link window (Figure 31-4).

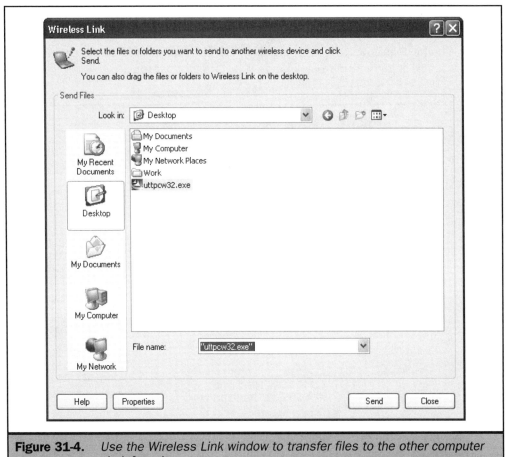

Figure 31-4.   *Use the Wireless Link window to transfer files to the other computer via infrared.*

Windows XP displays the Wireless Link icon on the desktop once it has established an infrared connection with the other computer. You can transfer files to the other computer by dragging them to the Wireless Link icon and dropping them there.

Configuring an Infrared Connection

You can configure your infrared connection by working in the Wireless Link dialog box (Figure 31-5). Display this dialog box in either of the following ways:

■ Choose Start | Control Panel | Printers and Other Hardware | Wireless Link.

■ When Windows XP Professional displays the Wireless Link icon in the notification area, right-click it and choose Properties from the shortcut menu.

The Infrared tab contains settings for the following:

■ Whether Windows XP displays icons in the notification area to indicate infrared activity.

■ Whether Windows XP plays sounds to alert you to infrared events, such as a device being within range or a device going out of range.

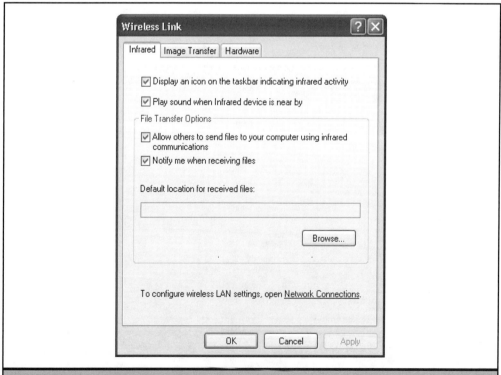

Figure 31-5.   *Configure infrared connection settings on the Infrared tab of the Wireless Link dialog box.*

- Whether others can send you files via infrared. For security, you might want to turn this option off when computing in public.
- Whether Windows XP notifies you when receiving files or just receives them automatically. In most cases, it's best to use the notification.
- Specifying the default location for placing files you've received via infrared.

Considerations for Serial Port Connections

Serial port connections are the poor cousins of parallel port connections. Serial port connections are far slower than parallel port connections, but if a serial port connection is your only option for connecting two computers, you'll probably find it tolerable.

To establish a connection via serial ports, follow these general steps:

1. Get a serial-port data-transfer cable. It may also be described as a "null-modem cable" or a "asynchronous modem eliminator cable." If your computer has regular serial ports, you'll need a cable with male DB9 connectors at each end. (Some older serial ports have 25-pin connectors.)

2. Attach the cable to the appropriate serial ports on the computers. Because many computers have two serial ports, be sure which serial port you've attached the cable to.

3. Configure one computer as the host and the other computer as the guest, as described in "General Procedure for Setting Up Incoming Connections," earlier in this chapter.

4. On the guest computer, establish the connection to the host computer.

Setting Up and Using Incoming Dial-up Connections

This section discusses considerations for setting up an incoming connection via dial-up: whether you should bother with an incoming dial-up connection at all, how and why to use callback, and the security considerations involved with incoming dial-up connections.

Balancing Convenience with Speed

Before setting up a dial-up incoming connection on your Windows XP Professional computer, perform a quick reality check on why you want to do so.

Microsoft limited Windows XP Professional's telephony capability to hosting a single incoming connection so that Windows XP Professional can't be an effective dial-in server. (Microsoft would like you to use Windows 2000 Server or Windows.NET Server for your dial-in server.) As a result of this limitation, the only reason to set up an incoming dial-up connection on Windows XP Professional is because you absolutely need to connect to your Windows XP Professional computer via modem. For any other purpose, other methods are preferable.

Dialing in to your Windows XP Professional computer via a modem will always be slow. Even if you have a 56 Kbps modem at each end of the connection, you'll get only 33.6 Kbps in each direction, so the connection is likely to feel much slower than the dial-up connection that you can establish to your ISP using the same modem and phone line. (56 Kbps modems deliver a maximum of 56 Kbps downstream and 33.6 Kbps upstream. The 56 Kbps downstream speed requires a digital connection at the upstream end—for example, at your ISP.)

Dial-up connections have the advantage of simplicity but the disadvantage of cost. If you're on the road for your own business, you probably won't want to make lengthy calls to your home-office PC at long-distance rates (even if your hotel doesn't overcharge for phone calls). A better option may be to connect to your ISP's local point of presence at local rates and from there connect to your home PC via a VPN connection, as described in "VPN Connections," later in this chapter. If you have a fast Internet connection at home, and if the location from which you're calling provides a fast connection (for example, if you're at a hotel that offers broadband connectivity), you can establish a fast connection to your home PC via a VPN connection.

Using Callback

On incoming dial-up connections, you can configure Windows XP Professional to call back callers. You may want to implement callback for any of several reasons:

- **Security** By specifying a particular phone number, you can ensure that a user can call from only one location or telephone. Unless other people have access to this location or telephone, this limitation decreases the likelihood of a malefactor being able to log in via this incoming connection.

- **Cost** By using callback, you can transfer the cost of the call to the party who owns the computer you're calling. Callback tends to be particularly appealing when it means the company is picking up the bill for you. (However, a company will usually implement callback on a remote access server rather than on individual Windows XP Professional workstations.) But it can also be good for reducing the cost of long-distance calls home from a hotel—by causing your Windows XP Professional computer to make the main call on your own phone line via callback, you can minimize your exposure to the hotel's extortionate phone rates.

You configure callback on a caller-by-caller basis from the Properties dialog box for the user. You can do so either when setting up the incoming connection (by using the user entries on the User Permissions page of the New Connection Wizard) or afterward (by displaying the Incoming Connections Properties dialog box and working on the Users tab). Either way, double-click a user's entry to display the Properties dialog box for the user, display the Callback tab (Figure 31-6), and then choose the appropriate option button:

- **Do Not Allow Callback**   This setting (the default) prevents the user from using callback.

- **Allow the Caller to Set the Callback Number**   This setting lets the user specify the number on which Windows XP Professional will call them back. This setting is good for users who will need to use callback from different locations, but it represents more of a security threat than either of the other two settings. (Windows XP Professional doesn't let you specify a list of approved callback numbers.) If you use this setting, ensure that the user uses a strong password and that they change it frequently.

- **Always Use the Following Callback Number**   This setting limits the user to the phone number specified in the Properties dialog box, even if the user tries to set a different number when they call in. This setting is more secure than allowing the user to set the callback number, but it's too inflexible for some users.

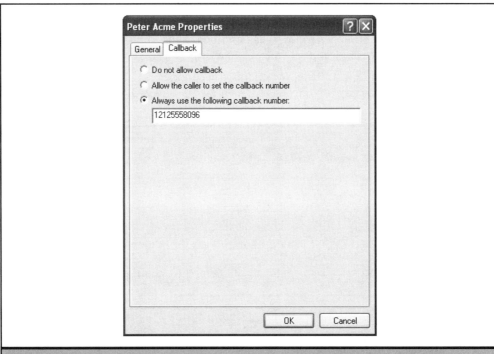

Figure 31-6.   *Configure callback options on the Callback tab of the Properties dialog box.*

If you're required to use callback with a specified number, Windows XP automatically hangs up the connection after you establish it. Your computer then waits for the callback.

If you're allowed to specify the callback number to use (this is called Set by Caller privilege), Windows XP displays the Callback dialog box (Figure 31-7) so that you can specify the callback number. If you don't need callback on this call, click the Cancel button and proceed with the call.

You'll see the Waiting for Callback notice while your computer waits to be called back. When the callback comes, your computer accepts the incoming call. The host computer registers your computer on the network. You can then begin to use resources on the computer or network, depending on how the incoming connection is configured.

Security Considerations for Dial-up Connections

Because an incoming dial-up connection makes your computer available to anyone in the world who has a phone line, you must secure your computer to prevent it from being compromised. Take the following actions:

- Use NTFS rather than FAT32 or FAT to format your disks.

- Apply NTFS permissions to your drives and network resources.

- Ensure all accounts have strong passwords. Remove any unused accounts.

- Choose suitable callback settings, as described in the previous subsection, "Using Callback." If possible, enforce callback to a single approved number for each user.

- If possible, limit incoming connections to accessing only the host computer rather than allowing them to access the network to which it's connected.

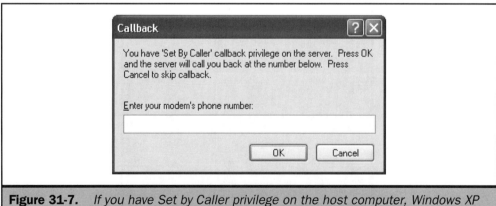

Figure 31-7. *If you have Set by Caller privilege on the host computer, Windows XP displays the Callback dialog box so that you can specify the number on which to receive the callback. You can also cancel the callback if you don't need it.*

Connecting via a Direct Connection

To connect via a direct connection that you've set up, follow these steps:

1. Display the Connect dialog box by double-clicking the connection.

2. Enter your user name and password for the computer you're connecting to.

3. Choose whether to save the user name and password. If you do, choose whether to save them for only yourself or for other users of your computer as well.

4. Click the Connect button to establish the connection. You'll see progress dialog boxes as Windows XP establishes the connection.

Once Windows XP has negotiated the connection, you can use the resources that the host computer is sharing. If the connection gives you access to the network to which the host computer is connected, you can use shared resources on the network computers as well.

To disconnect a direct connection, issue a Disconnect command from the shortcut menu for its notification area icon, from its Status dialog box, or from the Network Connections folder. You can do this from either the guest or host computer.

Troubleshooting Direct Connections

This section discusses two error messages you may run into when using direct connections.

Error 649: The Account Does Not Have Permission to Dial In

Error 649, "The account does not have permission to dial in," is more complicated than its wording suggests. It can mean any of the following on Windows XP Professional:

■ You haven't been granted remote access on the computer you're trying to connect to. If you have access to this computer, display the Incoming Connections Properties dialog box and select the check box for your entry on the Users tab.

■ You're allowed to access this computer remotely, but only during certain hours that don't include the present time.

■ Your account on the computer you're trying to connect to has been locked or disabled. Check with the administrator.

■ You may be using a protocol that the computer isn't set up to support, or the computer may require a protocol that you haven't configured.

If you're connecting to a computer running Windows 2000 Server or Windows.NET Server rather than Windows XP Professional, this error message may also have either of two further meanings:

■ For a dial-up connection, this may mean that you're calling in from a number other than one you're permitted to use.

■ Your dial-up permission may be on another domain than the one that the computer is a member of. If so, display the Properties dialog box for the connection. Select the Prompt for Name and Password, Certificate, Etc. check box and the Include Windows Logon domain check box on the Options tab. On the Security tab, if the Typical option button is selected, clear the Automatically Use My Windows Logon Name and Password (and Domain If Any) check box. Close the Properties dialog box and try again to connect. When Windows XP prompts you to provide your user name, password, and domain, do so.

Error 769: The Specified Destination Is Not Reachable

Error 769, "The specified destination is not reachable," can occur when you're trying to establish an infrared connection. In this case, the message sometimes means that the infrared feature on the computer you're trying to access has "jammed," so you can't establish the connection. Usually, you can fix this problem by restarting Windows XP on the target computer.

VPN Connections

As you're probably well aware from your own experience and from widely publicized security problems, the Internet is an insecure environment because the protocols it uses weren't designed for security. As a result, most traffic on the Internet is inherently insecure: Data packets can be intercepted in transit and, if they're not encrypted, they can be read. But because of the Internet's global reach, the Internet is a great way of getting data packets from point A to point B, wherever those two points happen to be located.

One of the ways of keeping communications secure across the Internet is virtual private networking. Virtual private networking is a networking feature for creating networks that are effectively private on media that aren't private. Virtual private network (VPN) connections use a technique called *tunneling* to create secure connections across a network that may or may not be secure (but that is assumed to be insecure).

In the real world, VPN connections are most widely implemented across the Internet, but they can be used across other networks as well. For example, companies and organizations that require ultra-tight security can use VPN connections across a company LAN or WAN to ensure the security of the communications between two computers on the network. Others use VPN connections to provide a select group of computers on a corporate network with access to a server that regular computers can't even see (let alone access). Companies and organizations that require more normal levels of security use VPNs for remote offices, offsite workers, or as extranet platforms for companies they work with.

Tunneling and Tunneling Protocols

Virtual private networking's metaphor of tunneling comes from the idea of establishing a secure channel between the two endpoints involved in the communication. Data travels from one endpoint to the other in the security of the tunnel.

The tunnel is implemented using a tunneling protocol. The two main tunneling protocols are Point-to-Point Tunneling Protocol (PPTP) and Layer 2 Tunneling Protocol (L2TP). L2TP uses IPSec and is much more secure than PPTP. Wherever possible, you should use L2TP rather than PPTP if you have the choice.

The tunneling protocol *encapsulates* the data to be transmitted by encrypting each data packet and placing it within another data packet that has a new header. At the destination, the tunneling protocol *unencapsulates* the data by removing the added header and the outer packet and decrypting the contents.

Windows XP Professional supports both PPTP and L2TP for VPN client connections it makes. For hosting incoming VPN connections, Windows XP Professional supports only PPTP.

VPN Clients and VPN Servers

Windows XP Professional provides strong features for acting as a VPN client—the computer that connects to a VPN server across a VPN connection. Typically, you'll use Windows XP Professional as the VPN client to connect to a VPN server so that you can work on the server or network to which the server provides access.

However, Windows XP Professional also includes a basic VPN server that can accept one incoming VPN connection at a time. This capability enables you to use virtual private networking to connect to your Windows XP Professional computer from a remote computer via the Internet or another network. (You can also use it to allow other people to connect to your computer if you want.) You're most likely to use this capability in a workgroup or standalone environment in which you need remote access to your computer without the costs involved in dialing direct and without the graphical overhead of an Remote Desktop Connection session.

When to Use VPN Connections

In a domain environment, you'll typically use VPN connections for the following purposes:

- To establish a secure connection from your home computer to the corporate network so that you can work remotely.

- To connect your portable computer to the corporate network across the Internet when you're out of the office.

If you work with extra-sensitive data, or if your company uses a highly secure network, you may need to use VPN connections for everyday work within the company's network.

In a standalone or workgroup environment, you may want to use VPN connections to connect remotely to your own computer or network, as discussed in the previous section.

Creating a Connection to a VPN Server

To create a connection to a VPN server, follow these steps:

1. Open the Network Connections folder and start the New Connection Wizard by clicking the Create a New Connection link.

2. On the Network Connection Type page, select the Connect to the Network at My Workplace option button.

3. On the Network Connection page, select the Virtual Private Network Connection option button.

4. On the Connection Name page, enter the name for the connection.

5. On the Public Network page, choose whether Windows XP Professional should automatically establish a dial-up Internet connection (and, if so, which connection) when you use the VPN connection.

6. On the VPN Server Selection page, enter the VPN server's host name or IP address.

7. On the Connection Availability page, choose whether to make the connection available to others or to keep it to yourself. (You can make the connection available to others only if you're an administrator.)

8. On the Completing the New Connection Wizard page, choose whether to create a desktop shortcut for this VPN connection.

Changing Your VPN Configuration

Depending on how the administrator of the VPN server has configured its incoming connections, you may need to change the VPN connection that you configured with the New Connection Wizard before you can connect to the VPN server.

To change the VPN connection, display its Properties dialog box. These are changes you may need to make:

- **General tab** You may need to change the hostname or IP address of the VPN server or change the public network to which your computer connects when trying to establish a VPN connection. The most likely scenario for needing to change the hostname or IP address is when the server has a dynamically assigned IP address rather than a static IP address. Corporate VPN servers are unlikely to have dynamic IP addresses, but personal VPN servers may well have them.

- **Options tab**   You may need to select the Include Windows Logon Domain check box to automatically pass your domain information to the server.

- **Security tab**   You may need to apply custom security settings by selecting the Advanced option button, clicking the Settings button, and then working in the Advanced Security Settings dialog box. Consult the VPN server's administrator about the authentication protocol to use for connecting to the VPN server. Windows XP Professional's default settings on the Security tab of the Properties dialog box are the Typical option button, the Require Secured Password item in the Validate My Identity As Follows drop-down list, and having the Require Data Encryption (Disconnect If None) check box selected.

- **Networking tab**   In the Type of VPN drop-down list, you can choose the PPTP VPN item or the L2TP IPSec VPN item. But in most cases, it's best to leave the Automatic item selected. This item makes Windows XP Professional try L2TP first and fall back to PPTP if L2TP doesn't work. You may need to change your Internet Protocol (TCP/IP) settings by working in its Properties dialog box and the Advanced TCP/IP Settings dialog box. (For example, you may need to specify DNS information.) Consult the server's administrator about the settings you require.

Connecting to a VPN Server

Once you've configured a VPN connection correctly, connecting to it is easy. Follow these steps:

1. If you need to establish an Internet connection manually, do so.

2. Display the Connect dialog box from the Start | Connect To menu or from the Network Connections screen.

3. Enter your user name, password, and domain (if appropriate).

4. Click the Connect button to make the connection.

5. If you need to supply more logon information (for example, domain information), Windows XP Professional displays the Connect dialog box to prompt you for it.

   To close the VPN connection, issue a Disconnect command from the connection's notification area icon, from the connection's Status dialog box, or from the Network Connections screen.

Using Windows XP's Incoming VPN Connection

As mentioned earlier in this chapter, Windows XP Professional can host a single incoming VPN connection at a time. You need to be an administrator to set up an incoming VPN connection.

   In a domain environment, you're unlikely to be able to host a VPN connection for two reasons. First, hosting VPN connections on your workstation probably won't be much use to you or anybody else. Only people with user accounts on the PC will be able to connect to it, and they're likely to be able to accomplish more by using Remote Desktop Connection or by logging on directly. Second, and more importantly, having an extra VPN server available on the network—even a single-connection VPN server—increases the network's vulnerability. So if your company needs VPN connections, your administrator will probably implement a VPN server on a corporate server, assign permissions to use it to those users who can prove they need them, and prevent users from using Windows XP Professional's VPN server.

In a small-office environment, you may want to use Windows XP Professional's VPN server to provide remote access to your computer and your network when you're on the road or working in remote locations. In this case, the ability to host a single incoming connection is plenty.

If you've already set up Windows XP Professional to accept incoming connections (for example, for a parallel port connection or an infrared connection), as described earlier in this chapter, you can add support for a VPN connection easily. Follow these steps:

1. Display the Properties dialog box for the Incoming Connections item.

2. Select the Allow Others to Make Private Connections to My Computer by Tunneling Through the Internet or Other Network check box on the General tab.

3. Click the OK button to close the Properties dialog box.

> **Tip** *To increase your computer's security, turn off incoming VPN connections temporarily when you don't need them. To do this, clear the Allow Others to Make Private Connections to My Computer by Tunneling Through the Internet or Other Network check box on the General tab of the Incoming Connections Properties dialog box.*

If you haven't yet set up Windows XP Professional to accept incoming VPN connections, follow these steps:

1. Open the Network Connections folder and start the New Connection Wizard by clicking the Create a New Connection link.

2. On the Network Connection Type page, select the Set Up an Advanced Connection option button.

3. On the Advanced Connection Options page, select the Accept Incoming Connections option button.

4. On the Devices for Incoming Connections page, you don't need to specify any devices. (If you've already configured one or more incoming connections, some of the items will be selected. Don't change these choices.)

5. On the Incoming Virtual Private Network (VPN) Connection page, select the Allow Virtual Private Connections option button.

6. On the User Permissions page, select the check boxes for the users you want to allow to connect. (See step 7 of "General Procedure for Setting Up Incoming Connections," earlier in this chapter, for a discussion of these options.)

7. On the Networking Software page, change the selection of networking components used for incoming connections if necessary.

8. From the Networking Software page, double-click the protocol that the VPN connection will use and use the Incoming Properties dialog box for that protocol to specify whether callers can access only the VPN host or the network the host is connected to. For example, for TCP/IP connections, work in the Incoming TCP/IP Properties dialog box. (See step 9 of "General Procedure for Setting Up Incoming Connections," earlier in this chapter, for a discussion of these options.)

9. Finish the wizard.

Configuring Your Firewall to Pass PPTP Traffic to the VPN Host

The incoming VPN connection you've set up will work for a computer that connects directly to the Internet. But if the computer connects through Internet Connection Sharing and Internet Connection Firewall or another firewall, you need to configure the firewall to pass to the VPN host all PPTP traffic on TCP port 1723. See "Configuring ICS to Pass Traffic to Internal Computers" in Chapter 35 for coverage of how to do this with ICS and ICF. For another type of firewall, consult its documentation.

Requiring Secure Password and Data for the Incoming VPN Connection

Like incoming dial-up connections, incoming VPN connections can seriously compromise your computer's security. To keep your incoming VPN connections as secure as possible, force users to require data encryption when connecting. To implement this, display the Incoming Connections Properties dialog box and select the Require All Users to Secure Their Passwords and Data check box on the Users tab.

Summary

This chapter has discussed how to configure incoming connections so that you (or others) can connect remotely to your computer via direct connections, dial-up connections, and VPN connections. It has also discussed how to create outgoing VPN connections.

The next chapter discusses another form of remote connection that Windows XP Professional provides: Remote Desktop Connection. This feature lets you connect remotely to your computer and run a fully graphical remote-control session.

The Complete Reference

Chapter 32

Using Remote Desktop Connections

657

This chapter discusses how to use two technologies that Windows XP Professional provides for accessing your computer remotely. The Remote Desktop feature lets you make your Windows XP Professional computer available for remote control. The Remote Desktop Connection feature lets you control your Windows XP Professional computer remotely from another computer running a version of Windows or Mac OS X. The Remote Desktop Web Connection feature lets you connect to your computer and control it from a web browser.

What Remote Desktop Connection Is and Does

Remote Desktop Connection is a remote-control technology that lets you connect to a remote computer on which you have a user account and work on that computer almost exactly as if you were sitting at it. The remote computer uses Windows XP Professional's built-in Terminal Services capabilities to provide the remote session.

The remote computer is referred to as the *remote computer* and the computer you use to access it is referred to as the *home computer*. Remote Desktop Connection uses the Remote Desktop Protocol (RDP) to communicate display information (and, optionally, sound) from the remote computer to the home computer and keystrokes and mouse clicks from the home computer to the remote computer. Applications run on the remote computer. The screen on the remote computer is locked (as if you'd locked it by issuing a Lock Computer command) so that anyone near it can't see what's happening in your user session.

Remote Desktop Connection uses two separate components:

- Remote Desktop is the component that allows the desktop to be shared. Remote Desktop is included and installed by default in Windows XP Professional and Windows.NET Server but not in Windows XP Home Edition. Remote Desktop is essentially a cut-down version of the Terminal Services included in Windows 2000 Server and Windows.NET Server.

- Remote Desktop Connection is the component that you use to connect to the remote computer. Remote Desktop Connection is included and installed by default in Windows XP Professional, Windows XP Home Edition, and Windows.NET Server, and is downloadable for other versions of Windows and for Mac OS X. (In Windows XP Professional, an administrator may have removed or disabled Remote Desktop Connection.) Remote Desktop Connection used to be called the Terminal Services Client.

Note   *You can install Remote Desktop Connection on versions of 32-bit Windows other than Windows XP by inserting the Windows XP Professional CD in the computer's CD drive and choosing Perform Additional Tasks | Set Up Remote Desktop Connection. You can install Remote Desktop Connection on Mac OS X by downloading it from Microsoft Mactopia (www.microsoft.com/mac) or the Microsoft Download Center (www.microsoft.com/downloads; then search for Remote Desktop Connection Client for Mac) and double-clicking the downloaded file.*

Because Remote Desktop isn't included in Windows XP Home Edition, you can't use Remote Desktop to remotely control a computer running Windows XP Home Edition. Most users use Remote Desktop Connection on a home computer (running just about any version of 32-bit Windows) to connect to and control a remote computer running Windows XP Professional. But because Remote Desktop Connection is a powerful tool for configuring and troubleshooting remote computers, many administrators use it to connect to remote computers running Windows.NET Server as well.

You can run multiple Remote Desktop Connection sessions at the same time to control multiple computers. This capability is useful if you have a LAN connection or a fast Internet connection.

Note

Terminal Services and Remote Desktop Connection can be configured extensively by administrators for security and performance. This section mentions the key configuration changes that may affect your Remote Desktop Connection sessions. However, if an administrator has disabled Remote Desktop Connection and Terminal Services for security reasons, you won't be able to use them at all.

Enabling and Disabling Remote Desktop

In default configurations of Windows XP Professional, Remote Desktop is disabled, so you need to enable it before you can connect to your remote computer. You'll need to be an administrator to enable Remote Desktop and specify who can use it.

To enable Remote Desktop, select the Allow Users to Connect Remotely to This Computer check box on the Remote tab (shown on the left in Figure 32-1) of the System Properties dialog box (WINDOWS KEY–BREAK). To designate users allowed to connect via Remote Desktop Connection, click the Select Remote Users button to display the Remote Desktop Users dialog box (shown on the right in Figure 32-1). To add a user, click the Add button and use the Select Users dialog box to choose the user. To remove a user, use the Remove button.

Note

Administrators automatically have the right to use Remote Desktop Connection once it has been enabled on the computer. This right is granted to members of the Remote Desktop Users group, to which administrators belong by default.

Any user who will connect via Remote Desktop must use a password to secure their user account. In a domain environment, it's almost certain that the administrator will have required each user to use a password to secure their user account in any case. But in a standalone or workgroup environment, you may need to make other users apply passwords to their user accounts—or you may need to apply one to your own account.

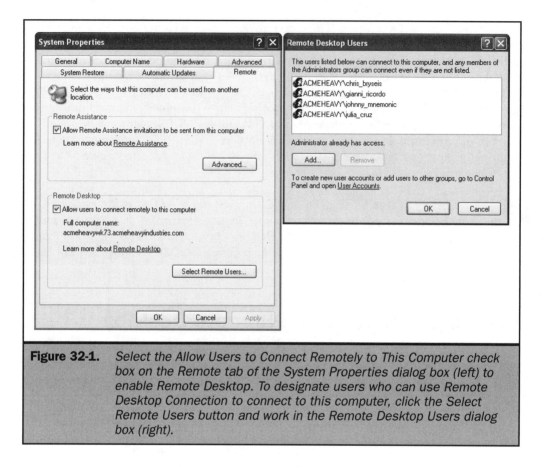

Figure 32-1.   *Select the Allow Users to Connect Remotely to This Computer check box on the Remote tab of the System Properties dialog box (left) to enable Remote Desktop. To designate users who can use Remote Desktop Connection to connect to this computer, click the Select Remote Users button and work in the Remote Desktop Users dialog box (right).*

Configuring a Remote Desktop Connection Item

Before you connect with Remote Desktop Connection, choose the configuration settings you'll use for the connection. Follow these steps:

1. Start Remote Desktop Connection by choosing Start | All Programs | Accessories | Communications | Remote Desktop Connection. Windows XP displays the smaller version of the Remote Desktop Connection window.

2. Click the Options button to expand the window to its full size (Figure 32-2).

The following subsections summarize the configuration options that Remote Desktop Connection offers.

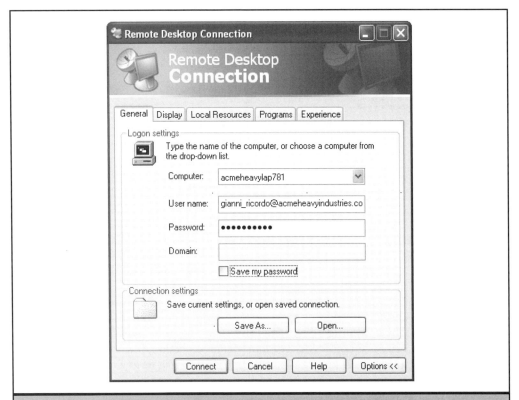

Figure 32-2.   *Choose configuration settings for a Remote Desktop Connection connection in the Remote Desktop Connection window.*

General Tab Options

Enter the name or IP address of the computer you're connecting to, the user name for your user account on that computer, your password for that account, and the domain (if any) of which that computer is part. Choose whether to save your password (if the Save My Password check box is available to you).

Note   *Instead of specifying your user name, password, and domain on the General tab of the Remote Desktop Connection window and saving them with the connection, you can specify them in the Log On to Windows dialog box when you establish the connection. Not saving this information makes your connections more secure, but it slows down the process of logging on to the remote computer. You might want to compromise by saving your user name and domain but entering your password manually at each logon. An administrator can specify that you must always enter your password when you connect.*

You can save the settings you've chosen for a Remote Desktop Connection configuration by clicking the Save As button on the General tab. Use the Open button on the General tab to open a saved configuration. By using saved configurations, you can maintain different preferences for connections to different computers.

Display Tab Options

Use the Remote Desktop Size slider to choose the screen size to use for the remote computer's desktop. Remote Desktop Connection defaults to Full Screen, which is good for when you're working continuously on the remote computer. If you're switching back and forth between the remote computer and your home computer, choose a smaller size so that the remote computer's desktop appears in a window on the home computer.

If you choose to run the remote computer's desktop full screen, select or clear the Display the Connection Bar when in Full Screen Mode check box. The connection bar lets you minimize the remote computer's desktop so that you can return to your home computer's desktop. If you don't run the remote computer's desktop full screen, you don't need to worry about this setting.

Choose the color depth to use for the remote computer's desktop in the Colors drop-down list. Typical color depths include 256 Colors, High Color (15 Bit), High Color (16 Bit), and True Color (24 Bit). Generally speaking, the fewer colors you use, the better the performance you'll get over a modest connection, but the more the look of the remote computer's desktop will suffer if it's set to use more colors. On a Fast Ethernet connection (such as many companies use), 16-bit High Color may be a reasonable setting to use. An administrator may have set a maximum color depth that you can use.

Local Resources Tab Options

Choose whether to bring sound from the remote computer to the home computer, to leave it at the remote computer, or not to play it. Bringing sound to the home computer works only for WAV files, not other sound files. Unless you have a very fast network connection or you're working on a file of which sound forms an integral part (for example, a multimedia presentation), it's rarely worth bringing sound from the remote computer to the home computer. (You may disagree, feeling that you benefit greatly from hearing Windows XP's feedback noises.) An administrator may have disabled this option in order to remove temptation from you.

Choose whether to apply Windows key combinations (such as ALT–TAB) to the local computer only, to the remote computer only, or to the remote computer in full screen mode and the local computer in windowed mode. The last of these settings tends to be the most intuitive for most people.

Choose whether to have Windows XP make your local disk drives, printers, and serial ports available to the remote computer. Doing so lets you save files from the remote computer to the local computer, print files from the remote computer to your local printers, or direct data from the remote computer to your local serial ports. An administrator may have prevented you from making your local disk drives, printers, and serial ports available—for example, for security reasons.

 Over a slow connection, saving documents from the remote computer to a local drive or printing to a local printer can take a long time.

Programs Tab Options

You can choose to make Windows XP Professional run an application automatically when you connect to the remote computer via Remote Desktop Connection. Because you can't browse to the application, you need to type in its path and filename. Likewise, if you want to specify the folder in which the application is to start, you need to type in its path and name.

Experience Tab Options

This tab contains options for specifying which Windows XP interface details Remote Desktop Connection transmits from the remote computer to the home computer and which it eliminates to improve performance. There are five check boxes: Desktop Background, Show Contents of Window while Dragging, Menu and Window Animation, Themes, and Bitmap Caching. The first four are self-explanatory: by turning off the display of less necessary interface elements, you reduce the amount of data that Remote Desktop Connection needs to transmit, and so improve performance.

Bitmap caching is a bit different from the other options. This option controls whether the home computer caches bitmaps (graphics) representing parts of the remote computer's desktop so that it can display them more quickly. Bitmap caching technically represents a security threat, because someone who breaks into your local computer might be able to retrieve bitmaps that show part of a Remote Desktop Connection session. But unless your need for security is paramount, it's a good idea to use bitmap caching to improve Remote Desktop Connection performance.

You can either choose one of the connection speeds in the drop-down list to apply a predefined set of options suitable for that speed, or you can select the Custom item in the drop-down list and choose manually which items to include. The connection speeds are Modem (28.8 Kbps), Modem (56 Kbps), Broadband (128 Kbps–1.5 Mbps), and LAN (10 Mbps or Higher).

Alternatively, specify a speed and then select or clear check boxes manually. Windows XP automatically selects the Custom item in the list.

If you've just chosen settings for connecting to a specific remote computer, now is probably a good time to save the settings by clicking the Save As button on the General tab of the Remote Desktop Connection window.

Connecting to the Remote Computer

To connect to the remote computer, click the Connect button. If Remote Desktop Connection will connect via a dial-up Internet connection, establish that connection first.

If you chose not to specify your user name, password, or domain in the Remote Desktop Connection window or your saved settings, you'll need to enter them in the Log On to Windows dialog box.

If someone is currently logged on to the remote computer, things become a little more complex.

- If you're the user who's logged on, Remote Desktop Connection picks up the session seamlessly, so you can work from the home computer in the applications that you left running on the remote computer.

- If another user is logged on, and the computer is part of a domain, what happens if you try to connect depends on whether you have administrator level privileges. The next section discusses what happens in a domain environment. The section after that discusses what happens on a standalone or workgroup computer using Fast User Switching.

What Happens in a Domain Environment

Here's what happens in a domain environment when you try to connect to a computer that another user is logged on to:

- If you have administrator privileges, Remote Desktop Connection displays a Logon Message dialog box that warns you that the other user (it names them) is logged on and points out that if you continue, their Windows session will end and their unsaved work will be lost.

- If you choose to continue, you'll see a "Remote logoff in progress" message as Remote Desktop Connection forcibly logs the user off. Remote Desktop Connection then logs you on.

- If you don't have administrator-level privileges, Remote Desktop Connection displays a message telling you that only the current user or an administrator can log on to the computer. You can't proceed past this point.

What Happens if the Computer Is Using Fast User Switching

If the remote computer is using Fast User Switching, Remote Desktop Connection handles logon conflicts in a different way than it does in a domain environment.

When you try to establish the connection, Remote Desktop Connection displays a Logon Message dialog box (shown at the top in Figure 32-3). This dialog box tells you that the other user is logged on and that they'll need to be disconnected so that you can connect. The dialog box also asks if you want to continue.

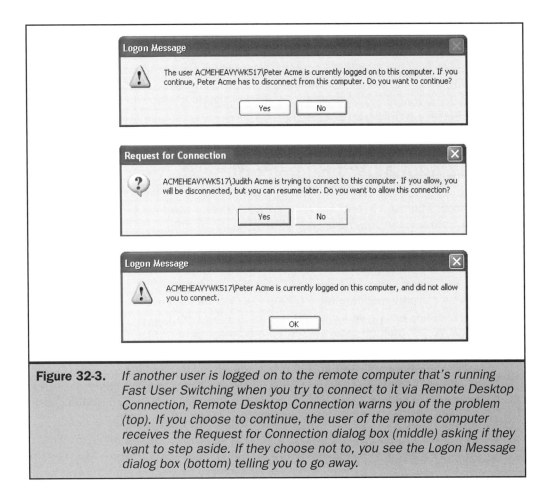

Figure 32-3. *If another user is logged on to the remote computer that's running Fast User Switching when you try to connect to it via Remote Desktop Connection, Remote Desktop Connection warns you of the problem (top). If you choose to continue, the user of the remote computer receives the Request for Connection dialog box (middle) asking if they want to step aside. If they choose not to, you see the Logon Message dialog box (bottom) telling you to go away.*

If you choose the Yes button, "continuing" involves Windows XP Professional displaying a Request for Connection dialog box (shown in the middle in Figure 32-3) to the logged-on user telling them that you're trying to log on and asking if they want to permit you to do so. If the user decides to let you do so, Remote Desktop Connection logs you on without further ado; if not, Remote Desktop Connection displays another Logon Message dialog box (shown on the bottom in Figure 32-3) telling you that the incumbent has rejected your advances.

If Remote Desktop Connection runs into a problem that prevents it from establishing the connection, it displays a Remote Desktop Disconnected dialog box to notify you of the problem. The most likely problems are as follows:

■ Remote Desktop Connection is unable to find the remote computer you specified. If you get this error, check that you've entered the correct computer name or IP address. If you're connecting via an Internet connection, make sure that the connection is working.

■ Remote Desktop Connection couldn't connect to the remote computer. This might mean that someone has configured the computer (locally or via Group Policy) so that it no longer accepts Remote Desktop Connection connections, or that an administrator has rescinded your permission to use Remote Desktop Connection. It might also mean that the computer isn't running.

Connecting from a Mac Running Mac OS X

As mentioned earlier, you can download the Remote Desktop Connection Client for Mac OS X from Microsoft Mactopia (www.microsoft.com/mactopia) or the Microsoft Download Center (www.microsoft.com/downloads). Remote Desktop Connection Client for Mac OS X (Figure 32-4) provides almost all the features that Remote Desktop Connection for Windows provides. These are the main differences:

■ On the General tab of the Remote Desktop Connection window, you can choose whether to add your Remote Desktop Connection logon settings to your Apple Keychain. (The Apple Keychain is a feature for saving passwords and other sensitive information in an encrypted but easy-to-use form.)

■ On the Display tab, you can choose whether the Remote Desktop Connection session window is resizable and whether to display the Mac OS X Dock and menu bar. If you have multiple displays, you can choose which of them to display the Remote Desktop Connection window on. Remote Desktop Connection Client for Mac defaults to 800×600 resolution rather than full screen.

■ On the Local Resources tab, you can't choose to redirect serial ports (because the Mac dispensed with them years ago) but you can specify which Mac key to use to represent the Windows ALT key and which key or keys (the choices are CONTROL, SHIFT, COMMAND, and OPTION) to use with the mouse to represent a right-click.

■ Remote Desktop Connection Client for Mac OS X is limited to connecting to one remote computer at a time. (The Windows Remote Desktop Connection client can connect to multiple remote computers at the same time.)

Working on the Remote Computer

Once you've established the connection to the remote computer, you can work on both it and the local computer. (As mentioned earlier in this chapter, you can also connect via Remote Desktop Connection to other computers as well and work on them at the same time.)

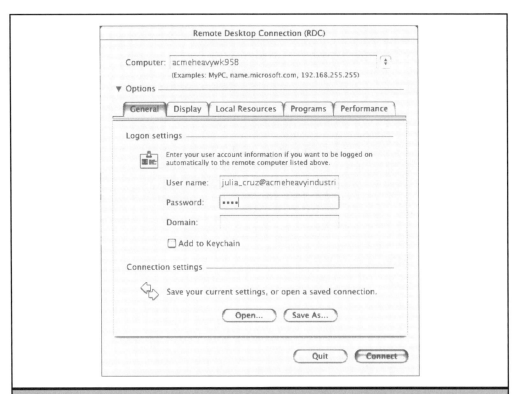

Figure 32-4.   *Remote Desktop Connection Client for Mac OS X includes most of the same options as Remote Desktop Connection for Windows, plus some Mac-specific commands.*

Mouse actions (movements and clicks) are sent to the computer with which you're currently working:

- If you have the remote computer's desktop displayed full screen, all mouse actions take effect on the remote computer.

- If you have the remote computer's desktop displayed in a window, mouse actions in that window take effect on the remote computer. Mouse actions outside that window take effect on the local computer.

Keystrokes take effect in the window you're working in, with Windows key combinations governed by the setting you chose in the Keyboard drop-down list on the Local Resources tab of the Remote Desktop Connection window. Remote Desktop Connection uses the keyboard setting on the remote computer when you're working on the remote computer. This means that if you've configured a different keyboard layout or setting on your home computer (for example, to accommodate a special keyboard), you'll need to apply those settings to the remote computer as well in order to be able to use them on it: The local computer's keyboard setting doesn't "translate" the keystrokes you send to the remote computer.

Remote Desktop Connection also provides special keyboard shortcuts for some Windows shortcuts so that you can issue them separately on your local computer and the remote computer. Table 32-1 lists these remote keyboard shortcuts with their local equivalents.

The monitor on the remote computer displays the Log On to Windows dialog box or the Welcome screen, depending on how the computer is configured. All display information is sent via RDP to the home computer. If the remote computer uses a larger desktop size than the home computer, Remote Desktop Connection reduces the size of windows so that they fit on the home computer's display. Likewise, if the remote computer has multiple monitors, Remote Desktop Connection moves all the windows from the

Remote Desktop Connection Shortcut	Local Shortcut	Effect
ALT-PAGEUP	ALT-TAB	"Coolswitches" between running applications.
ALT-PAGE DOWN	ALT-SHIFT-TAB	"Coolswitches" between running applications in reverse order.
ALT-INSERT	None	Switches among running applications in the order in which they were started.
ALT-HOME	WINDOWS KEY–ESC or CTRL-ESC	Toggles the display of the Start menu.
ALT-DELETE	ALT-–	Toggles the display of the control menu for the active window.
CTRL-ALT-– (on numeric keypad)	ALT-PRINTSCREEN	Copies the active window to the Clipboard.
CTRL-ALT-A (on numeric keypad)	PRINTSCREEN	Copies the remote desktop to the Clipboard.
CTRL-ALT-END	CTRL-ALT-DELETE	Launches or activates Windows Security or Task Manager.

Table 32-1. *Remote Desktop Connection Keyboard Shortcuts and Their Local Equivalents*

secondary monitor (or monitors) to the primary monitor so that they can be displayed on the home computer's display (which shows only the primary monitor).

If you chose (on the Local Resources tab of the Remote Desktop Connection window) to make your local drives available, they appear as *"drive on COMPUTERNAME"*—for example, "D: on ACMEHEAVYWK773." (As mentioned earlier, an administrator may have prevented redirection to local drives.)

If you chose (again, on the Local Resources tab of the Remote Desktop Connection window) to make your local printers available, they appear as *"printer on COMPUTERNAME"*—for example, "NEC870 on ACMEHEAVYWK773." (As mentioned earlier, an administrator may have prevented redirection to local printers.)

You can use the Clipboard to transfer data between the remote computer and the local computer unless an administrator has prevented you from doing so.

Switching to the Home Computer's Desktop

If you have the remote computer's desktop displayed full screen, click the Minimize button or the Restore button on the connection bar to minimize the remote computer's desktop or reduce it to a window on your home computer's desktop. (If the connection bar isn't pinned, it'll hide itself off the edge of the screen. Move the mouse pointer over the edge of the screen to make the connection bar display itself.)

Being Monitored by an Administrator

An administrator can configure Terminal Services and Remote Desktop Connection so that they're able to monitor your remote sessions. They can choose to view your sessions either with or without needing to get your consent, or they can choose to view and interact with your sessions, again either with or without needing to get your consent.

If your account is configured so that the administrator needs your permission to view or take control of your session, when they try to connect, you'll see a dialog box asking whether you want to accept the connection. Click the Yes button or the No button as appropriate. If you accept the connection, the administrator can either see what you're doing or share control of your computer with you. Both viewing and sharing control can be useful for troubleshooting Remote Desktop Connection problems.

If an administrator views a session of yours without your consent, you're unlikely to know about it. This feature is useful for administrators who need to check Remote Desktop Connection connections for security, abuse, and performance problems, but few users appreciate being monitored without warning or specific consent. (In their employment contracts, most companies reserve the right to monitor what you do on the computer to prevent abuse, avoid harassment problems, and so on.)

If an administrator starts interacting with a session of yours without consultation, you're likely to notice immediately—or assume that you've been infested by a virus.

Ending or Disconnecting Your Session

To stop working on the remote computer, you can either end your session by logging off or disconnect your session so that you can resume it later. A session may also be ended for you automatically: An administrator can configure Remote Desktop Connection sessions to time out automatically after being active for a certain time or being idle for a certain time.

To log off, choose Start | Log Off and click the Log Off button in the Log Off Windows dialog box, just as if you were logging off your local computer.

Your options for disconnecting a session depend on how an administrator has configured the remote computer:

■ The administrator may have prevented you from disconnecting a session. If not, you can disconnect by choosing Start | Disconnect.

■ The administrator may have removed the Disconnect item from the Start menu (in Windows XP) or from the Shut Down Windows dialog box to encourage you to log off rather than disconnect. However, unless the administrator has chosen not to allow disconnected sessions, you can still disconnect by clicking the Close button on the connection bar and clicking the OK button in the Disconnect Windows Session dialog box.

Caution *If anyone else shares your computer with you, it's not a good idea to disconnect Remote Desktop Connection sessions in a domain environment (or in a workgroup or standalone environment that doesn't use Fast User Switching). This is because your disconnected session will prevent other users with lower levels of privileges from using the computer until you reconnect and log off. Users with higher levels of privileges will be able to terminate your disconnected session and lose any unsaved work you had left open in it. For these reasons, your administrator may have prevented you from disconnecting your remote sessions. Disconnected sessions are more useful when you're using Terminal Services on a server or when you're using Remote Desktop Connection on a standalone or workgroup computer that uses Fast User Switching.*

If you're permitted to disconnect a session, you may be able to reconnect to it only from the computer you used to establish the session or from any other computer you're permitted to use. An administrator can also configure Windows XP Professional to close down disconnected sessions after a specified length of time, so you may find that you're not able to resume a disconnected session that you left.

Restarting and Shutting Down
the Remote Computer

If something goes wrong on the remote computer, you may need to restart it to get it working correctly again. Or if you've finished working with it, you may want to shut it down so that it's firmly locked (for example, by a boot password) until you return to the office.

Remote Desktop Connection removes the Shut Down command (or the Turn Off Computer command) from the Start menu to make restarting and shutting down the computer a little more difficult than usual, because most Remote Desktop Connection users won't need to restart or shut down the computer: Instead, they'll leave it running so that they (or other users) can log back on later. In this context, it makes sense for Remote Desktop Connection to discourage users from shutting down or restarting the computer.

 If an administrator has prevented you from shutting down the computer, as discussed in "Preventing Users from Shutting Down the Computer" in Chapter 5, you won't be able to shut down the computer remotely either.)

To shut down or restart the computer, proceed as follows:

■ In a domain environment, choose Start | Windows Security to display the Windows Security dialog box (Figure 32-5). If an administrator has removed the Windows Security item from the Start menu, press CTRL–ALT–END to display the Windows Security dialog box. Click the Shut Down button to display the Shut Down Windows dialog box. Then choose Shut Down, Restart, or Hibernate as appropriate.

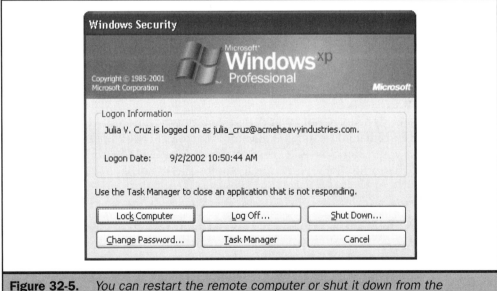

Figure 32-5. *You can restart the remote computer or shut it down from the Windows Security dialog box.*

■ In a standalone or workgroup environment, choose Start | Windows Security to launch Task Manager. (Alternatively, right-click the notification area and choose Task Manager from the shortcut menu.) If an administrator has removed the Windows Security item from the Start menu, press CTRL–ALT–END to display Task Manager. Then choose Turn Off, Restart, or Hibernate from the Shut Down menu as appropriate.

Troubleshooting Remote Desktop Connection

This section discusses several problems you may experience with Remote Desktop Connection: being unable to connect; being unable to use your local drives, local printers, local serial ports, or your Clipboard; and finding that your remote sessions end unexpectedly.

You Can't Connect via Remote Desktop Connection

This section discusses remedies for two errors you may see when trying to connect via Remote Desktop Connection.

"The Remote Computer Has Ended the Connection" Message Immediately When You Try to Establish the Connection

If you receive the message "The remote computer has ended the connection" as soon as you try to establish a connection via Remote Desktop Connection, it most likely means that the remote computer isn't configured to accept Remote Desktop Connection connections. Check the status of the Allow Users to Connect Remotely to This Computer check box on the Remote tab of the System Properties dialog box the next time you're at the computer.

"The Local Policy of This System Does Not Permit You to Logon Interactively"

The error message "The local policy of this system does not permit you to logon interactively" means that you're not a member of the Remote Desktop Users group for the computer, so you're not allowed to connect via Remote Desktop Connection. Add your account to this group (or have an administrator add it) as discussed earlier in this chapter.

You Can't Use Local Drives, Printers, Ports, or the Clipboard

If you find that you can't use your local drives, local printers, or local serial ports from Remote Desktop Connection even though you've enabled them on the Local Resources tab of the Remote Desktop Connection window, it most likely means that the administrator has prevented you from using them. The administrator may also have prevented you from using the Clipboard to share data between the remote computer and your home computer.

If you're allowed to share local printers, and you choose to do so, Remote Desktop Connection registers their presence for the remote computer when you establish the Remote Desktop Connection connection. If you add a new local printer during a Remote Desktop Connection session, you won't be able to use it from the remote computer without ending your Remote Desktop Connection session and establishing a new session.

Your Remote Session Ends Unexpectedly

This section discusses several causes of remote sessions ending unexpectedly.

"The Remote Session... Was Ended by Means of an Administration Tool..."

The error message "The remote session to the remote computer was ended by means of an administration tool. An administrator might have ended your connection," which appears in the Remote Desktop Disconnected dialog box, may mean either that an administrator has deliberately disconnected your remote session or that a policy setting has automatically terminated your session. It may also mean that someone else has logged on locally and bumped your Remote Desktop Connection session off.

"The Remote Session Was Ended Because Another User Has Connected to the Session"

The error message "The remote session was ended because another user has connected to the session" may occur when you have logged on locally using the same user account as you were using remotely. The error message could be better phrased, but the local logon shouldn't be a surprise.

Data Encryption Error Ends Remote Session

If a remote session ends with a message about a data encryption error having occurred, there's not much you can do except try to connect to the remote computer again and hope the error won't occur.

Your Remote Session Has Ended Without Notification or Error

If you return to your home computer and find that your remote session has ended without any message, chances are that you've been logged off by an administrator or timed out automatically.

Using Remote Desktop Web Connection

If for whatever reason you can't install Remote Desktop Connection or the Terminal Services Client on a computer, you may be able to use Remote Desktop Web Connection instead to connect remotely to a PC.

Remote Desktop Web Connection is an implementation of Remote Desktop Connection via a web browser. Remote Desktop Web Connection works with just about any computer that can run a version of Internet Explorer that supports ActiveX.

In order for Remote Desktop Web Connection to work, either the remote computer or a computer to which it is connected needs to be running the World Wide Web Service, a component of Internet Information Services (IIS). You need to install this on your computer separately—it's not part of the main installation of Windows XP Professional— but it's a swift and straightforward procedure.

Pros and Cons of Remote Desktop Web Connection

Remote Desktop Web Connection has several pros and cons that are worth knowing about before you set it up and start using it.

For administrators, Remote Desktop Web Connection can offer an easy solution to connectivity problems. Provided that the client has some form of Internet Explorer installed (at this writing, Internet Explorer has an estimated 96 percent of the browser market), an administrator can provide remote connectivity without installing any additional software. They can even simply embed a Remote Desktop Web Connection link in a web page to provide connectivity. These features also make Remote Desktop Web Connection good for some extranet solutions.

For end users, Remote Desktop Web Connection can provide a satisfactory remote-access solution provided that their network or Internet connection is fast enough. However, because Remote Desktop Web Connection is less configurable than Remote Desktop Connection, users can't choose performance options to suit the speed of the Internet or network connection they happen to be using. For example, while the user can choose the screen resolution at which to display the remote computer's desktop, they can't choose the number of colors to use with Remote Desktop Web Connection the way they can in Remote Desktop Connection. As a result, Remote Desktop Web Connection performance can be glacial over a slow connection.

 Remote Desktop Web Connection can also be good for roaming users who need to access their computers from computers on which they can't install any software—for example, public terminals or other people's computers.

Installing Remote Desktop Web Connection

To use Remote Desktop Web Connection, you need to install the IIS World Wide Web Service on either the remote computer or on a computer connected to it. In a domain environment, the administrator is likely to run the World Wide Web Service on a network server to which your remote computer is connected. In a standalone or workgroup environment, you'll need to install the World Wide Web service either on the remote computer itself or another of your computers to which the remote computer is connected.

To install the World Wide Web Service, follow these steps:

1. Run the Windows Components Wizard (Start | Control Panel | Add or Remove Programs | Add/Remove Windows Components).

2. Double-click the Internet Information Services (IIS) item (or select it and click the Details button) to display the Internet Information Services (IIS) dialog box.

3. Double-click the World Wide Web Service item (or select it and click the Details button) to display the World Wide Web Service dialog box.

4. Select the Remote Desktop Web Connection item. Windows XP automatically selects the World Wide Web Service item if it isn't installed.

5. Click the OK button to close the World Wide Web Service item. In the Internet Information Services (IIS) dialog box, you'll notice that Windows XP has automatically selected the Common Files item and the Internet Information Services Snap-In item (if they weren't already installed).

6. Click the OK button to close the Internet Information Services (IIS) dialog box, and then complete the Windows Components Wizard.

Allowing Remote Connections

Once you've installed the World Wide Web Service or ascertained that it's available on a server to which your computer is connected, make sure the Allow Users to Connect Remotely to This Computer check box on the Remote page of the System Properties dialog box is selected (as for a regular Remote Desktop Connection). Your computer should then be ready for Remote Desktop Web Connection connections.

Connecting via Remote Desktop Web Connection

To connect via Remote Desktop Web Connection, take these steps on the home computer:

1. Start Internet Explorer.

2. In the Address Box, enter the URL for the server. This is the computer that's running the World Wide Web Service. The URL consists of the *http://* prefix, the computer's name or IP address, and the location of the Remote Desktop Web Connection files (*Tsweb*—Terminal Services Web—by default). For example, to connect to the computer acmeheavywk801, you would enter **http:// acmeheavywk801/tsweb/** in the Address box.

3. Click the Go button or press the ENTER key as usual. Internet Explorer displays the Microsoft Windows Remote Desktop Web Connection page (shown in Figure 32-6).

4. In the Server text box, enter the name or IP address of the computer to which you want to connect. (If you're running the World Wide Web Service on the remote computer, specify the same name or IP address as in step 2.)

5. In the Size drop-down list, select the screen size you want to use: Full-Screen or one of the usual resolutions (for example, 800×600). If you're connecting via a dial-up Internet connection, use a small screen size.

6. If you need to specify logon information for the domain, select the Send Logon Information for This Connection check box. Internet Explorer reveals two previously hidden text boxes: a User Name text box and a Domain text box. Specify your user name and domain in these.

7. Click the Connect button. Internet Explorer displays the Log On to Windows bitmap. The first time you connect via Remote Desktop Web Connection,

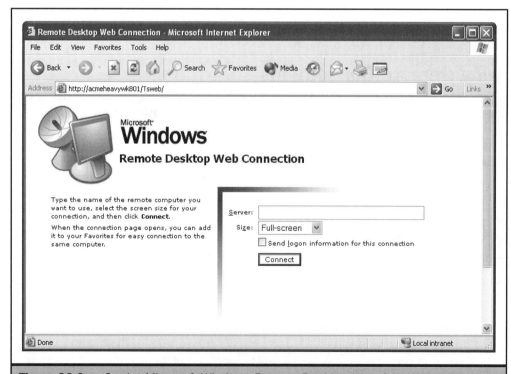

Figure 32-6. *On the Microsoft Windows Remote Desktop Web Connection page, specify the server and screen size to use.*

Internet Explorer may display a Security Warning dialog box asking if you want to install and run Microsoft Terminal Services Control. (If you've told Internet Explorer to always trust content from Microsoft, you won't see this dialog box.) Click the Yes button. Internet Explorer downloads the control and displays the Log On to Windows bitmap.

8. Enter your user name and password as usual, and then click the OK button.

If you chose to use Remote Desktop Web Connection full screen, the remote desktop occupies the entire screen.

If you chose a screen resolution less than that currently used on your home computer, the remote desktop appears within the Internet Explorer window, and you can easily switch back and forth between the home computer and the remote computer.

Work as usual, and disconnect or (preferably) log out when you've finished.

 If you'll need to access this computer frequently via Remote Desktop Web Connection, create a favorite for it in Internet Explorer.

Summary

This chapter has discussed how to use Remote Desktop Connection and Remote Desktop Web Connection to connect to and control a remote computer running Windows XP Professional.

The next chapter discusses how to use Windows XP's Remote Assistance feature to give assistance to and receive assistance from a remote user.

The

Complete
Reference

Chapter 33

Giving and Getting
Remote Assistance

This chapter discusses how to use Windows XP's Remote Assistance feature to provide help to another user across a network or Internet connection or to receive help yourself from another user, an administrator, or a Microsoft support professional. The chapter explains what Remote Assistance is, what it's for, what its limitations are, and how to use it from either end.

What Remote Assistance Is

Remote Assistance is a new help feature that uses Windows XP's terminal-services capability to enable a remote helper (for example, a corporate support technician or friend) to view what's happening on another user's computer so that they can help troubleshoot problems. For example, if you're having trouble with Windows XP, you can have a helper connect to your PC and see what's happening via Remote Assistance so that they can advise you on how to fix the problem. Similarly, someone else can ask you for help; you can connect to their computer via Remote Assistance; and you can help them by offering advice or (if they let you) taking control of their PC across the wires.

In a domain environment, you're perhaps more likely to receive Remote Assistance than to give it, so this chapter discusses receiving Remote Assistance first. But even in a domain environment, you may also need to give Remote Assistance to support less experienced users with complex procedures. So this chapter discusses how to give Remote Assistance as well.

Remote Assistance seeks to eliminate several of the problems of remote technical support at a stroke:

- The user can show their helper the problem their computer is suffering rather than having to describe it.

- The helper can walk the user through taking an action or solving a problem, watching every step of the way. Being able to see what the user is doing greatly simplifies explanations and reduces the misunderstandings endemic in phone-based remote support.

- The helper can (if the user allows them) use remote control to demonstrate how to perform an action or fix a problem. Or they can simply fix the problem (for example, if it's a configuration issue that's unlikely to recur).

These features can save both users and their helpers a great deal of time and frustration, and—in some ways, better yet—can save companies large amounts of money.

Powerful though Remote Assistance is, you still need to enable it on your computer and be able to get it to work. As you'll see in this chapter, Remote Assistance has some complications of its own.

How Remote Assistance Works

For ease of reference, the user requesting Remote Assistance is referred to as the *novice* and the user providing Remote Assistance is referred to as the *expert*. The novice's request to the expert for assistance is called an *invitation*. This chapter sticks with this terminology to keep the local and remote ends of the Remote Assistance connection clear.

Remote Assistance uses the Remote Desktop Protocol (RDP) to share the display on the novice's computer with the expert user. (In technical terms, Remote Assistance *attaches* the expert to the novice's Windows XP session.) If the novice chooses to let the expert control their desktop, RDP passes the expert's mouse movements, mouse clicks, and keystrokes to the novice's computer.

On the novice's computer, the desktop and all applications appear as usual, with a Remote Assistance window that contains controls for manipulating the Remote Assistance session and a chat panel for communicating. On the expert's computer, the novice's desktop appears in a resizable window together with the control buttons and the chat panel.

Windows XP Professional offers two types of Remote Assistance:

- **Solicited Remote Assistance**   The novice requests Remote Assistance of the expert and (if the novice is in luck) the expert responds.

- **Offer Remote Assistance**   The expert offers Remote Assistance to the novice. The novice can accept or decline the offer. The expert and novice must be members of the same domain or of domains that trust each other.

Windows.NET Server also offers both Solicited Remote Assistance and Offer Remote Assistance. Windows XP Home Edition includes only Solicited Remote Assistance.

Note   *Like Remote Desktop Connection (discussed in Chapter 32), Remote Assistance can represent a threat to the security of your computer or the network it's on (or both). But because Remote Assistance requires the novice not only to be present at the computer to accept the expert's connection but also to explicitly grant the expert control of their computer, Remote Assistance should represent less of a threat than Remote Desktop Connection. However, some administrators choose to prevent you from using Remote Assistance at all. Others allow you to receive Remote Assistance but prevent you from granting the expert control of your computer.*

Configuring Solicited Remote Assistance

Solicited Remote Assistance is enabled in default configurations of Windows XP Professional. To check that it's enabled on your computer, display the Remote tab of the System Properties dialog box (WINDOWS KEY–BREAK) and make sure the Allow Remote Assistance Invitations to Be Sent from This Computer check box is selected. Clear this check box to disable Solicited Remote Assistance.

USING REMOTE NETWORK
CONNECTIONS

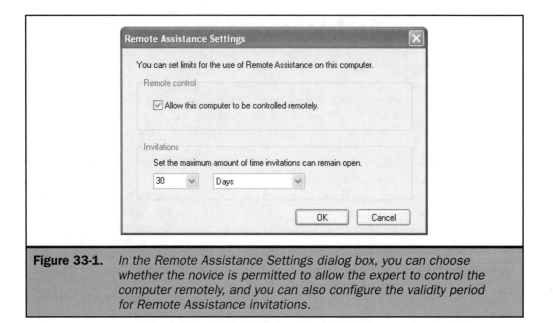

Figure 33-1.   *In the Remote Assistance Settings dialog box, you can choose whether the novice is permitted to allow the expert to control the computer remotely, and you can also configure the validity period for Remote Assistance invitations.*

Note   *In a domain environment, you may not be able to use the controls on the Remote tab of the System Properties dialog box. If so, you won't be able to display the Remote Assistance Settings dialog box. You'll need to get an administrator to configure Remote Assistance for you.*

To specify whether you (or another user of the computer) can let an expert control the computer remotely, click the Advanced button on the Remote tab of the System Properties dialog box to display the Remote Assistance Settings dialog box (Figure 33-1). Then select or clear the Allow This Computer to Be Controlled Remotely check box as appropriate.

You can use the controls in the Invitations group box in the Remote Assistance Settings dialog box to configure the validity period of Remote Assistance invitations. The default setting is 30 days, which is much longer than will be needed in most cases. If you send invitations via e-mail, you might specify a period of several hours or several days. If you send invitations via snail mail, you might need a period of several days to a week.

Enabling the Offer Remote Assistance Feature

The Offer Remote Assistance feature is "not configured" by default, which means that you can't use it. If you're a computer administrator user, you can enable it either just for computer administrator users or for all users. In a domain environment, this feature is likely to be configured via Group Policy by an administrator.

To enable Offer Remote Assistance, take the following steps:

1. Choose Start | Run to display the Run dialog box, enter **gpedit.msc** in the Open text box, and click the OK button to open Group Policy.

2. Drill down to Computer Configuration\Administrative Templates\ System\Remote Assistance.

3. Double-click the Offer Remote Assistance item to display the Offer Remote Assistance Properties dialog box (shown in Figure 33-2 with settings chosen).

4. Select the Enabled option button. Group Policy enables the controls in the group box.

5. In the Permit Remote Control of This Control drop-down list, select the degree of control you want to permit: Allow Helpers to Remotely Control the Computer, or Allow Helpers to Only View the Computer. Even if you allow helpers to remotely control the computer, the novice user has to agree to each request for control.

6. To specify which users are allowed to offer Remote Assistance, click the Show button and work in the Show Contents dialog box.

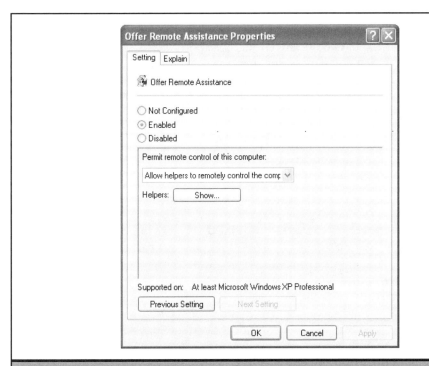

Figure 33-2. *Use the controls in the Offer Remote Assistance Properties dialog box to permit specific users to offer remote assistance to others.*

Practicing Safe Remote Assistance

Remote Assistance is a powerful and effective support tool. Given a knowledgeable and willing expert, the novice (let's assume it's you) can quickly receive solutions to configuration problems or instructions for performing awkward maneuvers. But you need to be careful when using Remote Assistance, especially when you're using it in a workgroup or standalone configuration.

First, make sure that the expert who replies to an invitation is really the person to whom you sent it:

- Before sending an invitation via Messenger, chat to your contact to make sure it's them rather than someone else using their computer. (You might even establish a video connection for a quick visual check.)

- For e-mail invitations and file invitations, use a strong password that only the expert knows. Or use a password that the expert *doesn't* know and have them phone you to get it before they make contact.

Second, consider their advice as carefully as possible before applying it. If the advice seems strange or wrong to you, you can query it in moments. If the expert has a short fuse, they might get annoyed at your querying their expertise. But you can probably restore their temper more quickly than any damage you cause to your Windows XP configuration by applying ill-considered fixes.

Third, check any files that you receive from the expert for viruses or scripts before you do anything with them. Never assume that because a file comes from someone you trust that it must be okay.

Fourth, never give the expert control of your computer unless there's a compelling reason to do so. In practice, there's almost never a compelling reason barring sudden incapacity or a breakdown of patience on your part. If the expert can't describe via text or audio chat how to fix a problem, you've probably got the wrong expert. Besides, if the expert describes to you how to fix a problem rather than fixes it for you, you'll learn from the experience.

Issuing a Remote Assistance Invitation

Windows XP lets you send a Remote Assistance invitation via Messenger, via an e-mail client that supports Messaging Application Programming Interface (MAPI), or by saving the invitation to a file and transmitting that file to the expert.

Which method of issuing a Remote Assistance invitation you find most convenient will depend on whether you use Messenger, whether you have a MAPI-compliant e-mail client, and when you need to issue the invitation. The following subsections discuss the three methods, starting with Messenger. See "Receiving Remote Assistance," later in this chapter, for a discussion of what happens when the expert responds to your invitation.

Messenger

If you use Messenger, and your expert does too, Messenger is likely to prove the simplest and quickest way to issue a Remote Assistance invitation. This is because with Messenger you can see immediately whether your contact is online. If they are, they receive your invitation almost instantly. If they're not online, you can't send them an invitation using Messenger.

> **Note**   *Messenger has a second advantage that's less apparent: It has a trick for circumventing firewall problems to establish Remote Assistance connections. After the expert has accepted a Remote Assistance invitation, Messenger on the expert's computer waits for Messenger on the novice's computer to establish the Remote Assistance connection to it. If the novice's computer fails to establish the connection, the expert's computer assumes that there's a firewall problem and attempts to establish the connection.*

To send a Remote Assistance invitation via Messenger, launch or activate Messenger and check that your contact is online. Then issue an Ask for Remote Assistance command from the Actions menu, from the shortcut menu for the contact, or from the I Want To list.

As discussed earlier in this chapter, it's a good idea to verify that the person logged on to Messenger as your contact is in fact your contact. To do so, you may prefer to start a regular Messenger conversation with them to verify their identity (or ask if they'll help you). Then issue the Ask for Remote Assistance command from the Actions menu or the I Want To list in the conversation window.

E-mail

If you have a MAPI-compliant e-mail client (such as Outlook, Outlook Express, or Qualcomm Eudora), you can use it to send a Remote Assistance invitation. Follow these steps:

1. Choose Start | All Programs | Remote Assistance to launch a Help and Support Center window showing the Remote Assistance topic. (If the All Programs menu doesn't include a Remote Assistance item, choose Start | Help and Support to open a Help and Support Center window, and then click the Remote Assistance link.)

> **Note**   *You can't use a non-MAPI e-mail client such as Hotmail, AOL, or MSN Explorer to send a Remote Assistance invitation. If your e-mail client doesn't support MAPI, save the invitation to a file as described in the next section and then attach it manually to an e-mail message to the expert.*

2. Click the Invite Someone to Help You link to display the Pick How You Want to Contact Your Assistant screen.

3. Enter the expert's e-mail address in the Type an E-mail Address text box (by clicking the Address Book button and using Address Book or by typing the address) and click the Invite This Person link.

4. On the Provide Contact Information screen, enter a message to the expert—for example, outline the problem—and click the Continue button.

5. On the Set the Invitation to Expire screen, specify the validity period for the invitation. You can specify the period in minutes, hours, or days, depending on how quickly you think the expert will get back to you.

Note *You can terminate an invitation at any time before its validity period expires.*

6. Also on the Set the Invitation to Expire screen, select the Require the Recipient to Use a Password check box and specify a strong password. It's vital to use a password for Remote Assistance invitations so that only the expert will be able to use the invitation (in case someone has hijacked the expert's e-mail account).

7. Click the Send Invitation button to send the invitation. Help and Support Center uses MAPI to create a message in your default e-mail client. To this message it attaches a file named rcBuddy.MsRcIncident containing the details of the Remote Assistance invitation. If you used a password, the invitation doesn't contain the password itself (for security) but contains the information that a password is required.

Note *If your e-mail client is configured for security, it may display a warning when Help and Support Center tries to send the Remote Assistance invitation. (This is because many viruses and other malware use MAPI to send messages automatically to spread themselves.) If your e-mail client does raise a warning, examine the message that has raised the warning to make sure it's the Remote Assistance invitation. If it is, send it.*

File

If you don't use Messenger (or if your expert doesn't or isn't online when you need them) and you don't have a MAPI-compliant e-mail client, you can save the Remote Assistance invitation to a file. You can then attach the file to an e-mail message in your non-MAPI e-mail client, burn it to a recordable CD or copy it to a floppy so that you can send it via physical mail, or place it in a tech-support folder on the network (if your company uses one).

To save a Remote Assistance invitation to a file, follow these steps:

1. Choose Start | All Programs | Remote Assistance to launch a Help and Support Center window showing the Remote Assistance topic. If the All Programs menu doesn't include a Remote Assistance item, choose Start | Help and Support to open a Help and Support Center window, and then click the Remote Assistance link.

2. Click the Invite Someone to Help You link to display the Pick How You Want to Contact Your Assistant screen.

3. Click the Save Invitation As a File link.

4. Follow through the process of creating the invitation and specifying where to save it. The default filename is RAInvitation.msrcincident.

Managing the Remote Assistance Invitations You've Sent

Windows XP tracks the Remote Assistance invitations you've sent via e-mail or saved to a file: when you sent them, to whom (those saved to a file say only Saved), their expiry data and time, and their status (Open, Expired, Resend Required). To see this information, choose Start | Remote Assistance to access the Remote Assistance page in Help and Support Center; then click the View Invitation Status link to display the View or Change Your Invitation screen.

Note *The View or Change Your Invitation screen doesn't include invitations that you've sent via Messenger.*

From this screen, you can select an invitation and take any of the following actions:

■ Click the Details button to display a Remote Assistance dialog box showing the details of the invitation.

■ Make an invitation expire immediately by clicking the Expire button.

■ Resend an invitation because your computer's IP address has changed. You'll know you need to do this because the Status column for the invitation displays Resend Required. (Typically, the reason that your network IP address will have changed is that your network uses Dynamic Host Configuration Protocol [DHCP] to allocate IP addresses to computers as needed. If you're using Remote Assistance through an ISP, the ISP may assign a dynamic IP address each time you connect rather than assign you a static IP address.)

■ Delete an invitation that you no longer need to keep. Once an invitation has served its purpose and you're sure you won't need to resend it, delete it for simplicity's sake.

Receiving Remote Assistance

If the expert accepts your invitation, Remote Assistance displays a dialog box that tells you that they've accepted your invitation and are ready to connect to your computer, and that checks that you're ready and willing to proceed. An example of this dialog box is shown next. When you click the Yes button, Remote Assistance sets up the connection. (If you click the No button, or if you don't respond to the Remote Assistance dialog box within a couple of minutes, Remote Assistance closes the connection.)

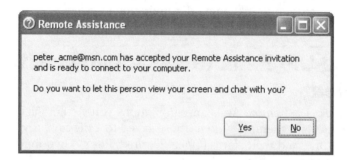

Over a LAN connection, Remote Assistance typically establishes the connection in a few seconds. Over a dial-up connection, it may take a minute or so. Remote Assistance negotiates the connection between the two computers and optimizes its settings for the speed of the connection that it detects. Once Remote Assistance has established the connection, it displays a Remote Assistance window (Figure 33-3) on your screen.

Most of the actions you can take from the Remote Assistance window on the novice's computer are straightforward. You can:

- Communicate with the expert using text-based chat by typing in the Message Entry text box and either clicking the Send button or pressing ENTER.

- Talk to the expert by clicking the Start Talking button. Click the Stop Talking button to end the audio conversation. Click the Settings button to change the audio quality you're using or to run the Audio and Video Tuning Wizard to improve the audio connection.

Note *The most awkward part of using Remote Assistance over a slow connection is the glacial speed at which the expert's window showing the novice's desktop is updated. If you're the expert, you'll spend a while twiddling your fingers waiting for the Remote Assistance window to redraw. If you're the novice, you'll need to remember that it takes a while before the expert sees the changes onscreen that you see instantly. Adding audio to the connection slows down the screen refresh speed even further, so it's best not to use audio unless you've got a fast connection. If you stick with text chat, the amount of data that Remote Assistance needs to transfer from the expert to you is minimal.*

- Give the expert control of your computer when they ask for it if you think doing so is a good idea. (As discussed earlier in this chapter, you almost never actually *need* to give the expert control, and it's much safer not to do so.) To regain control, click the Stop Control button, press ESC, or press ALT-C.

- Send a file to the expert by clicking the Send a File button and using the resulting dialog box to specify the file. Sending a large file to the expert over a slow connection will take even longer than usual because the connection is already transmitting all the data required for Remote Assistance.

- Receive a file that the expert sends to you by clicking the Save As button in the dialog box that Remote Assistance displays and specifying the folder in which to save the file. After transferring the file successfully, Remote Assistance prompts you to open it. It's a good idea to check the file for viruses before doing so.

Note   *Transferring a file from the expert to you shouldn't take as long as sending a file to the expert, provided that you're not using audio conversation. As discussed earlier in this chapter, you should check all incoming files for viruses and use common sense before applying them to your computer.*

- Disconnect the expert by clicking the Disconnect button. If the expert ends the connection, Remote Assistance displays a message box telling you that they've done so.

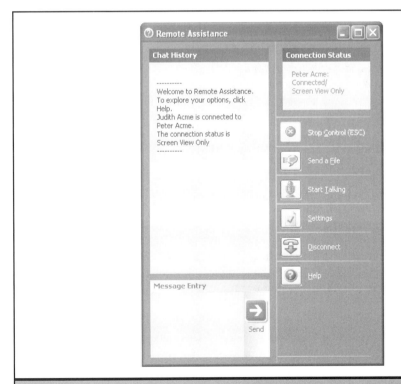

Figure 33-3.   *The Remote Assistance window on the novice's computer contains a chat pane, a Connection Status display, and control buttons.*

Responding to a Remote Assistance Invitation

This section discusses how to be the expert (in the Remote Assistance sense) and respond to an invitation from a novice.

■ In Messenger, you receive a prompt in a conversation window with the novice (or in an ongoing text conversation with other people as well) saying that the novice has invited you to start a Remote Assistance session. Click the Accept link to accept the invitation. Click the Decline link to decline it. You can also press ALT-T to accept the invitation or press ALT-D to decline it.

■ In e-mail, you receive a message with the Subject "You Have Received A Remote Assistance Invitation From" and the novice's name. The message body includes the message the novice entered and some explanatory text. The rcBuddy.MsRcIncident file comes as an attachment. Open the attachment either by using the link in the e-mail message or by double-clicking the file in the Attachments folder.

Caution	*If your e-mail Attachments folder already includes a file named rcBuddy.MsRcIncident, your e-mail application will probably rename another incoming rcBuddy.MsRcIncident file so that it doesn't overwrite the incumbent. Many e-mail applications fail to recognize MsRcIncident as an extension, so instead of renaming the file to rcBuddy1.MsRcIncident, they rename it rcBuddy.MsRcIncident1. This changes the file type from the Microsoft Remote Assistance Incident file type to an unknown file type. (See "How File Types and File Extensions Work" in Chapter 8 for a discussion of file types and file extensions.) If you try to open the renamed Remote Assistance file from the link in the e-mail message, Windows XP displays a Windows dialog box claiming "Windows cannot open this file" because it doesn't know the file type. To solve this problem, restore the file extension to MsRcIncident. (You'll need to move or rename the original rcBuddy.MsRcIncident file first.)*

■ When the novice saves the Remote Assistance invitation to a file and sends the file to you, double-click the RAInvitation.MsRcIncident file on whatever medium you receive it (for example, a recordable CD or a floppy).

For an e-mail invitation or a file invitation, Remote Assistance displays a Remote Assistance dialog box (Figure 33-4). Enter the password if one is required, and then click the Yes button to try to establish a Remote Assistance connection to the novice's computer.

Go to the section "Providing Remote Assistance," later in this chapter, for a discussion of how to provide help via Remote Assistance once you've connected.

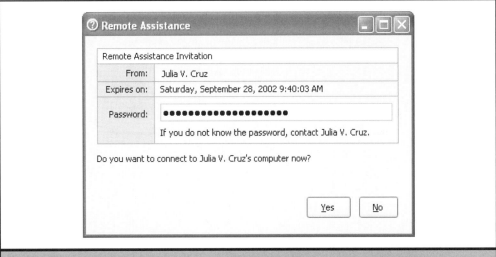

Figure 33-4.   *If the novice has applied a password to the Remote Assistance invitation, enter it in this Remote Assistance dialog box. Then click the Yes button to try to establish a Remote Assistance connection to the novice's computer.*

Offering Remote Assistance

If an administrator has enabled the Offer Remote Assistance feature (as discussed in "Enabling the Offer Remote Assistance Feature," earlier in this chapter) on your computer, you can offer Remote Assistance to other users.

To offer Remote Assistance, follow these steps:

1. Choose Start | Help and Support to open Help and Support Center.

2. In the Pick a Task list, click the Tools link to display the Tools list.

3. In the Tools list, click the Offer Remote Assistance item to display the Offer Remote Assistance page.

4. Enter the IP address or name of the target computer and click the Connect button.

The novice receives a Remote Assistance dialog box like the one shown next. If they click the Yes button, the Remote Assistance session starts. For security, there's no way to connect to the computer or take control of it via Remote Assistance without the user's consent.

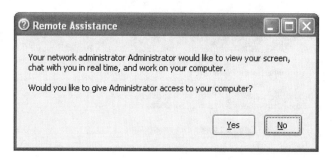

Once you've connected, you can provide assistance as described in the next section.

You can connect multiple times using the same invitation if necessary. For example, you might need to check later that the assistance you provided has actually resolved the problem. To do so, however, you need an invitation with a longer validity period than tight security recommends. It's better to have the user issue a new invitation, also with a short validity time, if they need further attention.

Providing Remote Assistance

Once you've connected to the novice's computer, the techniques for providing Remote Assistance are easy to grasp from the controls in the Remote Assistance window (Figure 33-5). Depending on the speed of your connection and the color settings Windows XP is using, the colors you see may be strange and blotchy, as in the figure. But all the controls should work as normal.

As the expert, you can take the following actions:

■ Use the chat pane to chat with the novice via text-based chat. Add audio (by using the Start Talking button) if you and the novice have enough bandwidth to make it practicable.

■ Toggle the display of the chat pane by clicking the Show Chat button (if it's hidden) or the Hide button (if it's displayed).

■ Toggle the internal Remote Assistance window between its actual size and fitting the confines of the window by clicking the Scale to Window button or the Actual Size button. If your Remote Assistance window is smaller than the novice's desktop, the Scale to Window button lets you see everything on the novice's desktop at a reduced size. If this reduced display is unreadable or mangled, use the Actual Size button to display it at its actual size. You can't make the internal Remote Assistance window bigger than its actual size. Even if you have a window much larger than the novice's desktop, the largest you can view the novice's desktop is 100% size. But in most cases this will be plenty large enough.

- Take control of the remote computer by clicking the Take Control button and convincing the novice to agree to your doing so.

- Send a file to the novice's computer by clicking the Send a File button and using the resulting dialog box to specify the file. If the novice has control of their computer, you may need to convince them to accept the file transfer. If you have control of their computer when you transfer the file, you can accept the file transfer.

- Receive a file from the novice's computer by having them click the Send a File button and specify the file to send to you. Again, if you have control of the novice's computer, you can send the file to yourself.

- Disconnect from the novice's computer by clicking the Disconnect button.

When the novice allows you to access their computer, you run applications in their security context. You can't change the security context by using the RunAs command when you're connecting via Remote Assistance.

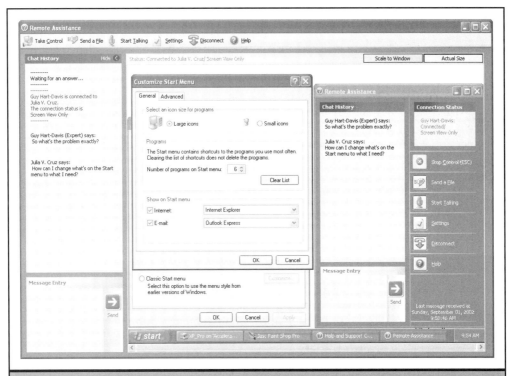

Figure 33-5.   *The expert's view of the novice's desktop in the Remote Assistance window*

Note *If administrators need to perform actions in a security context other than yours to get your computer back into shape, they're likely to connect to it via a VPN connection instead of by using Remote Assistance.*

Troubleshooting Remote Assistance

Remote Assistance is a great support tool once you've established the connection between the expert's computer and the novice's computer. This section discusses problems that arise with establishing the connection.

Remote Assistance establishes a connection by using the novice's IP address, which is included in the invitation. If the novice's IP address changes, Remote Assistance won't be able to establish the connection using the IP address from the invitation. In a domain or workgroup situation, Remote Assistance can look up the novice's computer by computer name, which is also included in the invitation. But if Remote Assistance is trying to connect across an Internet connection, it can use only the IP address.

Unable to Establish Remote Assistance Connection

If you get the error "A Remote Assistance connection could not be established" when you (as the expert) try to establish a connection to the novice, it may mean that the novice has expired the Remote Assistance invitation.

If you're trying to connect to the novice's computer across an Internet connection, it may also mean that the novice's IP address has changed. If this has happened, the novice needs to resend the invitation with the new IP address. Or they could establish a connection with you via Messenger. Failing both of these, and if you can learn the novice's new IP address (for example, by phone), you can open the rcBuddy.MsRcIncident file in a text editor (such as Notepad) and edit one of the IP addresses on the RCTICKET line. This line will look something like this:

```
RCTICKET="65538,1,192.168.0.11:3389;acmeheavywk73.acmeheavyindustries.
com:3389,*,6iToWskwgnmLcbu1g1eC3nhAKM0KftSs3eskQvNZLeg=,*,*,
s5oivPfvbTNIO/MZ/cKQW4tg/Bg="
```

Remote Assistance tries the first IP address first (in this case, 192.168.0.11, the only IP address), followed by any other IP address or computer name (here, acmeheavywk73.acmeheavyindustries.com). Change the IP address to the new IP address you've learned from the novice, and then try again to connect.

Note *The RCTICKET data is the only data in the Remote Assistance invitation (which is an XML file) that you can effectively edit. The invitation also contains a USERNAME field with the novice's name, an RCTICKETENCRYPTED field that shows whether the invitation has a password associated with it (1) or not (0), a DtStart field that specifies the start time for the invitation, and a DtLength field that specifies the duration of the invitation (in minutes). You can edit these fields, but the invitation won't work if you do.*

The "A Remote Assistance connection could not be established" error message may also mean that the novice's Internet connection is down.

Firewall: TCP Port 3389 Needs to Be Open

If the computers involved in the Remote Assistance connection are on different sides of one or more firewalls, you may find it difficult to connect. To resolve this problem, have an administrator open TCP port 3389 in the firewall. (If you're using Windows XP's Internet Connection Firewall to secure a standalone Internet connection or an Internet connection shared by a workgroup, you shouldn't need to open port 3389, because Internet Connection Firewall opens it automatically when Remote Assistance attempts to establish a connection.)

Summary

This chapter has discussed how to use Remote Assistance both to request and receive assistance from a remote helper and to provide help remotely to another user.

The next chapter discusses how to use Telnet to connect to other computers.

The Complete Reference

Chapter 34

Using Telnet

T his chapter discusses how to use the Telnet client that Windows XP Professional includes for establishing command-line remote connections with other computers and the Telnet services for hosting incoming connections. Although Telnet's capabilities are limited, knowing what Telnet can do is worth your time because you may find it useful sometimes. Being aware of the security threats Telnet can pose is also a good idea.

Understanding Telnet Client and Telnet Service

Telnet is an Internet-standard means of connecting from one computer to another. Telnet uses a server component for accepting incoming connections and a client component that connects to the server.

Both Windows XP Professional and Windows XP include a Telnet client. You can use this Telnet client to connect to another computer so that you can manage that computer or transfer data to or from it. Windows XP Professional also includes a Telnet service, which you can set up so that Windows XP Professional accepts incoming Telnet connections. (Windows XP Home Edition doesn't include the Telnet service—it has only the Telnet client.)

Note   *The Telnet client can also be useful for managing other devices remotely, such as routers.*

Making Outgoing Telnet Sessions

For outgoing Telnet sessions, you use the Telnet client software. The Telnet client is installed in default configurations of Windows XP Professional (and Windows XP Professional Home Edition).

Note   *To connect via Telnet, you need to be either a member of the TelnetClients group on the computer you're connecting to or an administrator for that computer. See "Enabling a User to Connect via Telnet," later in this chapter, for a discussion of how to create the TelnetClients group and add users to it on a computer you administer.*

To connect via Telnet client, open a command-prompt window and issue a Telnet *hostname* command, where *hostname* is the name or IP address of the computer you want to connect to. Enter your user name and password when the Telnet server prompts you for them.

Note   *If the Telnet server to which you're connecting supports the TELNET ENVIRON option, you can use a telnet –l username command to specify the user name under which to log on.*

Once you're logged in to the Telnet server, you can execute commands on it.

To end your Telnet session, enter an **exit** command. The Telnet client closes the connection and displays the message "Connection to host lost."

Tip *You can also connect to servers by using HyperTerminal as a Telnet client. In the Properties dialog box for the connection (File | Properties), select the TCP/IP (Winsock) item in the Connect Using drop-down list, and then enter the computer name or IP address in the Host Address text box and the port number in the Port Number text box.*

Running Telnet Service to Support Incoming Telnet Sessions

To support incoming Telnet sessions, you need to run the Telnet service. Windows Setup installs this service by default (unless you prevent it from doing so) and configures it for manual startup, so you have to start the Telnet service manually.

You must be an administrator to configure Telnet service.

Understanding Security Issues

Before you run the Telnet service, understand the security issues Telnet service raises. Running the Telnet service makes your computer vulnerable to unauthorized access because the Telnet protocol isn't secure (the protocol was developed in the kinder and gentler early days of the Internet) and can send passwords in clear text. This limitation doesn't mean that Telnet is useless these days, but rather that it's mostly used within already mostly secure environments. For example, Telnet is used within enterprise environments for access to resources protected by corporate security measures, but it's not used across open Internet connections.

Because of these dangers, you may choose not to use the Telnet service at all. (In a domain environment, an administrator is likely to prevent you from using the Telnet service for this reason.) If you feel you need to run the Telnet service (for example, so that you can connect to your computer from a computer running a non-Windows OS), take the following actions to limit the amount of damage a malefactor might be able to do.

- Use NTFS rather than FAT32 (or FAT) on your drives.
- Use NTFS permissions on your folders to prevent them from unauthorized access.
- Enforce strong passwords on all user accounts.
- Restrict user accounts to the folders they must access.
- Grant Telnet access only to those users who need it.
- Use NTLM authentication rather than plain-text authentication.
- Change the port used by the Telnet service from its default port (23).

"Administering and Configuring the Telnet Service," later in this chapter, shows you how to use NTLM authentication and change the Telnet port.

Starting and Stopping the Telnet Service

To start the Telnet service, follow these steps:

1. Open the Services console by choosing Start | Administrative Tools | Services, Start | All Programs | Administrative Tools | Services, or Start | Control Panel | Performance and Maintenance | Administrative Tools | Services (depending on whether you've added the Administrative Tools folder to your Start menu or your All Programs menu).

2. Select the Telnet service in the list of services.

3. Issue a Start command from the Action menu, the shortcut menu, or the toolbar. You'll briefly see a Service Control dialog box as Windows XP Professional starts the Telnet service.

To stop the Telnet service, issue a Stop command from the Action menu, the shortcut menu, or the toolbar. Again, you'll briefly see a Service Control dialog box as Windows XP Professional stops the service.

Making Sure the Telnet Service Is Working

To make sure the Telnet service is working correctly, open a command-prompt window and issue a Telnet *localhost* command. (Alternatively, issue a Telnet *hostname* command, where *hostname* is the name of your computer.)

If the Telnet service is working, you'll see a banner saying Welcome to Microsoft Telnet Server (unless someone has customized the banner) followed by a command prompt.

If Telnet service isn't working, you'll see a message saying No communication could be made because the target machine actively refused it.

Enabling a User to Connect via Telnet

To connect via the Telnet service, a user must be an administrator or a member of the TelnetClients group. You have to create the TelnetClients group manually because Windows XP Professional doesn't create it automatically.

The easiest way to create the TelnetClients group is to use the Local Users and Groups console. Follow these steps:

1. Enter **control userpasswords2** in the Run dialog box (Start | Run) to display the User Accounts dialog box.

2. Click the Advanced button on the Advanced tab to open the Local Users and Groups console.

3. Select the Groups item and issue a New Group command from the Action menu or the shortcut menu to display the New Group dialog box (Figure 34-1).

4. Enter **TelnetClients** in the Group Name text box.

5. Enter a suitable description in the Description text box. (The description is for your benefit, so you can enter whatever text suits you.)

6. Add users to the group by clicking the Add button and using the Select Users or Groups to specify the users.

7. Click the Create button to close the New Group dialog box and create the group.

Note   *You can also create the TelnetClients group by using the net localgroup command (net localgroup TelnetClients /add) from a command prompt. To add a user to the group, enter the name in this format:* **net localgroup TelnetClients "user name" /add**.

You can subsequently add other users to the TelnetClients group by issuing an Add to Group command and working on the General tab of the Properties dialog box for the group. Keep the membership of the TelnetClients group as limited as possible to maintain your computer's security.

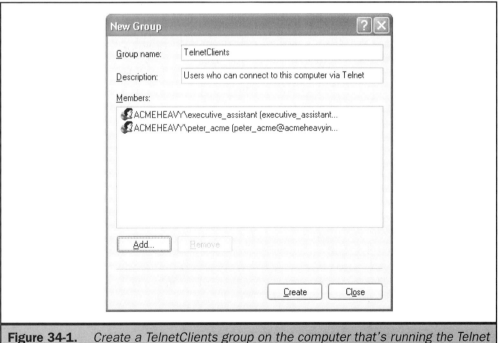

Figure 34-1.   *Create a TelnetClients group on the computer that's running the Telnet service. Add the users allowed to connect via Telnet to this group.*

Configuring Telnet Service to Run Each Time You Start Windows XP Professional

If you need the Telnet service to run every time you start Windows XP Professional, set the Telnet service to start automatically. Follow these steps:

1. In the Services console, select the Telnet service.

2. Issue a Properties command from the Action menu, the shortcut menu, or the toolbar to display the Telnet Properties dialog box.

3. On the General tab, select the Automatic item in the Startup Type drop-down list.

Be aware that Telnet can represent a security threat to your computer. See the next section for a discussion of the security issues involved in running the Telnet service.

Editing the Login Script

The banner saying Welcome to Microsoft Telnet Server comes from the login script the Telnet service automatically runs when someone makes a successful Telnet connection. You can change the message displayed by editing the file %Windir%\system32\login.cmd in a text editor such as Notepad. The lines that use the echo command are those that display text onscreen.

The default login script also includes a cd command to change directory to the %homedrive%\%homepath% folder for the user currently logged on. The %homedrive% system variable returns the drive on which your home folder is stored. The %homepath% system variable returns the path (minus the drive) to your home folder. You might want to change this command to log Telnet users into another folder.

Instead of using the default Telnet login script, you can assign a specific login script to a user. To do so, create the folder %Windir%\system32\repl\imports\scripts. (This may seem like a strange location, but it's the location Windows NT Server used. The Telnet service in Windows XP Professional uses the same folder, but you need to create it manually.) Within this folder, create another folder with the user's user name. Put the login script (named startup.bat or startup.cmd) in this folder. Then open a Computer Management window, expand \Local Users and Computers\Users so that you can see the user's account, and display the Properties dialog box for the account. On the Profile tab, enter the path to the script in the Logon Script text box as %username%\scriptname. This login script is for the Telnet service only. The user's standard logon script for Windows XP Professional won't be affected by this login script.

Administering and Configuring the Telnet Service

Windows XP Professional includes a command-line application called "tlntadmn" for administering and configuring the Telnet service. You can use tlntadmn either from the local computer or from a remote computer.

The following subsections summarize the actions you're most likely to want to take with tlntadmn. (For full details of tlntadmn's capabilities, issue a tlntadmn /? command at a command prompt.)

Viewing Your Current Settings for the Telnet Service

To view your current settings for the Telnet service, issue a tlntadmn command at a command prompt. tlntadmn returns a readout such as the following:

```
The following are the settings on localhost

Alt Key Mapped to 'CTRL+A'   :   YES
Idle session timeout         :   1 hours
Max connections              :   10
Telnet port                  :   23
Max failed login attempts    :   3
End tasks on disconnect      :   NO
Mode of Operation            :   Console
Authentication Mechanism     :   NTLM, Password
Default Domain               :   ACMEHEAVYWK517
State                        :   Running
```

Viewing, Messaging, or Terminating the Current Telnet Sessions

To view the current sessions, issue a tlntadmn –s all command. tlntadmn returns a readout that lists each Telnet session, its user ID, the user name, the client address, the logon date and time, and the idle time. Here's an example of such a readout:

```
2 telnet session(s)

ID     Domain   UserName      Client        LogonDate LogonTime IdleTime
                                                                (hh:mm:ss)
---------------------------------------------------------------------------
1084   ACME17   Judith Acme   192.168.0.19  1/14/2003 8:16:00 AM 0:51:36

1436   ACME17   Peter Acme    192.168.0.11  1/14/2003 9:53:50 AM 0:01:06
```

To send a message to a Telnet user, issue a tlntadmn –m *ID message text* command, where *ID* is the session ID and *message text* is the text of the message to send. Here's an example:

```
tlntadmn -m 1436  This server will be closing in 5 minutes. Please log off.
```

The user receives the message in their Telnet session preceded by the text "message from the administrator at *servername*", and the date and time.

To end a user session, issue a tlntadmn –k *ID* command, where *ID* is the session ID. The user receives the notice "Administrator on the server has terminated this session."

Configuring Idle Timeouts

To set the length of time a user session can remain idle before the Telnet service disconnects it, issue a tlntadmn config timeout = command with the length of time expressed in hours, minutes, and seconds. The following example sets an idle timeout of one hour:

```
tlntadmn config timeout = 1:00:00
```

To enable the Telnet service to disconnect the user after the timeout period, issue a tlntadmn config timeoutactive=yes command. To disable disconnection, issue a tlntadmn config timeoutactive=no command. (Disconnection is enabled by default.)

Configuring Connections, Authentication, Failures, and the Domain

To set the maximum number of connections the Telnet service supports, issue a tlntadmn config maxconn=*n* command, where *n* is the number of connections. Windows XP Professional's default setting is a maximum of two connections.

To set the mechanism that the Telnet service uses to authenticate users, issue a tlntadmn config sec= command with the NTLM parameter or the passwd parameter. (The Telnet service can use NTLM [encrypted] authentication or plain-text authentication. By default, it uses both. You can remove either, but not both at once.) Use a plus (+) sign to add the specified form of authentication and a minus (–) sign to remove the specified form of authentication. The following example removes plain-text authentication and adds NTLM authentication:

```
tlntadmn config sec=-passwd +ntlm
```

To change the maximum number of failed login attempts from its default setting of three, issue a tlntadmn configuration maxfail=*n* command, where *n* is the number.

To set the default domain for authenticating user names (if the names are different than those on the local computer), issue a tlntadmn config dom=*domain* command, where *domain* is the domain name.

Changing the Telnet Port

To change the port the Telnet service uses from its default port (23), issue a tlntadmn config port=*portnumber* command, where *portnumber* is the number of the port to use.

Summary

This chapter has discussed how to connect to remote computers using Windows XP Professional's Telnet client and how to configure the Telnet service to accept incoming connections. It has also covered the security issues that running the Telnet service raises.

This is the end of Part V of the book. Part VI shows you how to use the Internet effectively. Chapter 35 covers how to connect Windows XP Professional to the Internet and how to secure your Internet connection.

The
Complete
Reference

Windows XP

Part VI

Using the Internet Effectively

Chapter 35

Connecting Windows XP Professional to the Internet

This chapter discusses how to connect a computer running Windows XP Professional to the Internet.

The chapter starts by running quickly through the basics of Internet connections to make sure you're broadly familiar with the terms involved. It then covers what's perhaps the most likely scenario if you're reading this book: that your computer is a member of a corporate network that provides an Internet connection. If this is the case, you can probably skip the rest of this chapter, because an administrator will probably establish, configure, and maintain your Internet connection for you—and even secure it into the bargain.

If your computer doesn't get its Internet connection through a corporate network, you can connect it to the Internet either directly or via a connection shared by another computer or a specialized device. The rest of this chapter discusses how to set up an Internet connection, how to share it using Windows XP's Internet Connection Sharing (ICS) feature or another technology, and how to secure the connection. The chapter finishes by covering how to troubleshoot your Internet connection and ICS.

Basics of Internet Connections

You can connect to the Internet in ways that range from a private dial-up connection to a shared connection on a corporate network. This section discusses the basic components used for most Internet connections: Internet service providers, connection types and suitable devices, firewalls, and proxy servers.

Internet Service Provider

The Internet service provider (ISP) is the company or organization that provides Internet service. An ISP typically has a very fast connection to the Internet and provides slower connections to its customers.

Different ISPs provide different types of service, targeting different groups of customers. For example, some ISPs specialize in providing high-speed, dedicated connections to businesses. At the other end of the spectrum, other ISPs provide only dial-up access to individual customers. Yet other ISPs offer a full range of connection types.

Connection Type and Device

You're likely to use one of the following connection types, which are listed in approximate ascending order of speed:

- A dial-up connection via plain old telephone service (POTS) and a modem. Dial-up connections can achieve speeds of 53.3 Kbps downstream and 33.6 Kbps upstream, but are often much slower. You might be able to aggregate multiple modems by using a technology called multilink if your ISP supports it.

- An Integrated Services Digital Network (ISDN) line. An ISDN is a digital phone line. ISDN technology is capable of various speeds, but typical implementations offer two 64 Kbps channels, delivering modest but consistent speed both upstream and downstream. An ISDN connects to a terminal adapter (TA) or an ISDN router. A TA is essentially a digital "modem" for ISDN. (A TA isn't technically a modem because it doesn't modulate and demodulate the signal.) You can get internal and external TAs.

- A satellite connection, either one-way (using the satellite for downstream and a phone line for upstream data) or two-way, and a satellite dish. Satellite rates vary, but speeds of 400 Kbps to 2 Mbps are normal.

- A Digital Subscriber Line (DSL) using one of the many varieties of DSL—for example, asymmetric DSL (ADSL)—and a DSL "modem" or router. DSLs typically offer speeds of 384 Kbps to 6 Mbps downstream and 128 Kbps to 2 Mbps upstream.

- A cable connection and a cable "modem" or router. Cable connections typically offer similar speeds to DSL.

- A fiber-optic connection and an Ethernet card. Fiber-optic connections are available in few locations (some residential, some business) but offer speeds of up to 100 Mbps shared among those connected.

- A dedicated digital phone line, such as a T1 line (1.544 Mbps) or T3 line (44.736 Mbps), and a router. These lines are used almost exclusively by businesses.

Firewall

A *firewall* is a hardware or software device for protecting a network connection. A firewall acts as a security checkpoint at the border of a network, inspecting the data packets that try to cross the border and allowing only those that match the policy the administrator has set. For example, an administrator might configure a firewall to pass e-mail and web traffic but not chat.

Many different types of firewall are available, from modest software devices designed to protect home networks to complex and costly hardware devices secure enough for military usage. Windows XP includes a built-in software firewall named Internet Connection Firewall (ICF) that's suited for protecting individual computers and small networks (such as home-office networks or small-office networks).

Proxy Server

A *proxy server* is a hardware or software device positioned between the networked computers and the Internet connection. The proxy server relays Internet requests from the networked computers to the Internet, checking each request against its settings and discarding any requests for sites that aren't allowed. (For example, many companies block access to sports sites, gambling sites, and pornographic sites.) A proxy server also caches (stores) frequently requested pages so that it can deliver them quickly without needing to fetch each page afresh for each user who requests it.

Internet Connections on a Corporate Network

If your computer is part of a corporate network, and your company has decided to let you access the Internet, your computer will almost certainly be connected through a fast connection shared via the network. By centralizing Internet connections, a company can do the following:

- Keep the cost of connecting users to the Internet as low as possible

- Reduce the threat the Internet connection poses to the company's computers by using protective measures such as firewalls, proxy servers, and filtering

- Use bandwidth more efficiently by sharing it among users as necessary (as opposed to each user having a separate Internet connection)

- Restrict, manage, and track the actions that users can take on the Internet

Figure 35-1 shows an example of an Internet connection shared among a company's computers. In this example, Internet access is provided through an Internet access server that's doubling as a proxy server. Computers access the Internet via the Ethernet network.

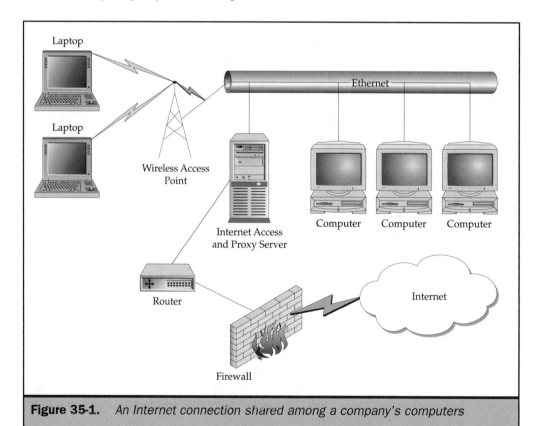

Figure 35-1.   *An Internet connection shared among a company's computers*

A wireless access point attached to the Ethernet network provides wireless connectivity for mobile computers (shown by laptops in the figure).

When your Internet connection is provided through a corporate network, you shouldn't need to worry about configuring your connection or securing it. Chances are an administrator will configure, maintain, and troubleshoot the connection centrally. All you'll need to do is use the connection. You may be restricted to using the connection only at certain times. You're likely to be prevented from accessing sites that your company deems unsuitable or a waste of time.

Note   *In a domain environment, an administrator may disable the Internet Connection Wizard to prevent you from trying to set up an Internet connection. If they've disabled it, you'll find the Setup button on the Connections tab of the Internet Options dialog box (Tools | Internet Options from Internet Explorer) is unavailable.*

Internet Connections on a Small Network

If you have a small network (for example, in your small office or home office), you probably won't be able to afford a corporate-duty Internet connection (for example, a T1 line) and the hardware that goes with it.

Figure 35-2 shows three typical configurations for connecting to the Internet:

- The top section of the figure shows a small network connected to the Internet through a connection shared by a computer running Network Address Translation. This is the type of configuration used by ICS. For the Internet connection to be available, the computer sharing the connection must be running.

- The middle section of the figure shows a small network connected to the Internet through a connection shared by a router. Because the router is connected directly to the network rather than being connected to the network via a computer, you don't need to keep any of the computers running.

- The bottom section of the figure shows a direct Internet connection from a computer that isn't shared. In the figure, the computer isn't networked, but you can also use direct Internet connections on networked computers if you need to. For example, if your office is located where no type of broadband is available, you might choose to equip each computer that needed to access the Internet with a dial-up modem connection so that each computer could connect at the best speed possible rather than trying to squeeze all the computers onto a single connection at that same dial-up speed.

If you have a small network, you're likely to use one of these configurations. Some variations are possible. For example, to connect your computers in a home office to the computer sharing the Internet connection, you might use USB or FireWire cables instead of Ethernet. You might use wireless network adapters. If the network involves only two computers, you might use a parallel cable. But the principles will remain the same.

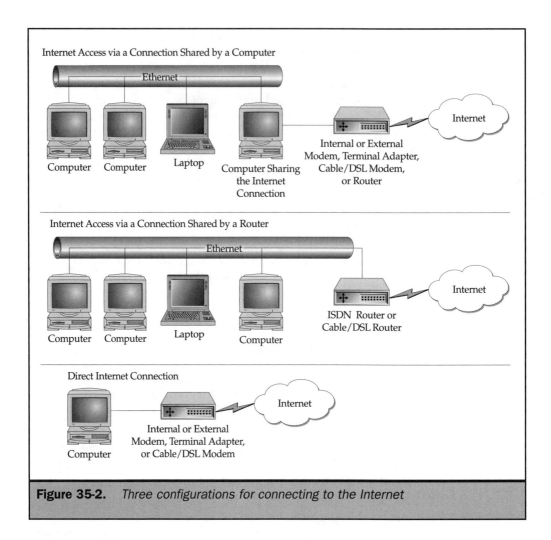

Figure 35-2. *Three configurations for connecting to the Internet*

Setting Up a Direct Connection

Once you've chosen your ISP, connected any necessary hardware to your computer and to the line that's providing your Internet connection, you're ready to configure a direct connection to the Internet. If your ISP has provided a custom setup routine, run it. If not, follow these general steps:

1. Run the New Connection Wizard by choosing Start | All Programs | Accessories | Communications | New Connection Wizard.

2. On the Network Connection Type page, select the Connect to the Internet option button.

3. On the Getting Ready page, select the Set Up My Connection Manually option button.

4. On the Internet Connection page, select the Connect Using a Dial-up Modem option button, the Connect Using a Broadband Connection That Requires a User Name and Password option button, or the Connect Using a Broadband Connection That Is Always On option button, as appropriate. If you choose the always-on option, the wizard finishes, telling you that your connection should already be connected.

Note   *For a dial-up connection, if you have multiple modems, the New Connection Wizard displays the Select a Device page so that you can specify which modem or modems to use for the connection.*

5. On the Connection page, enter a name to assign to your Internet connection. Make it descriptive so that you can easily identify the connection in the Network Connections folder.

6. The Internet Account Information page (Figure 35-3) contains three key options, each of which you can change easily later on:

Figure 35-3.   *The Internet Account Information page of the New Connection Wizard contains key options for the connection.*

- **Use This Account Name and Password when Anyone Connects to the
  Internet from This Computer**   Controls whether Windows XP uses the
  account name and password you supply for every user of this computer
  or just for you.

- **Make This the Default Internet Connection**   Self-explanatory.

- **Turn On Internet Connection Firewall for This Connection**   Controls
  whether Windows XP enables ICF for the connection. Windows XP enables
  it by default.

7. On the Completing the New Connection Wizard page, choose whether to add
   a shortcut for the connection to your desktop. Often, it's easier to access the
   connection through the Start | Connect To submenu.

Choosing Further Options for Your Internet Connection

Depending on your ISP, your computer, and your needs, you may need to change the
settings the New Connection Wizard created. To do so, select the connection's icon in
the Network Connections window and issue a Properties command from the File menu
or shortcut menu. Windows XP displays the Properties dialog box for the connection
with the General tab foremost.

The following subsections discuss the options on the five tabs of the Properties
dialog box.

Setting General Options

If your ISP has supplied you with a variety of different numbers for analog or ISDN
dial-up, you'll have entered the first number via the New Connection Wizard. This
number appears in the Phone Number group box on the General tab of the Properties
dialog box (Figure 35-4) for the connection. To add further numbers, click the Alternates
button and enter the alternate in the Alternate Phone Numbers dialog box. For each
phone number, you can add a comment (for example, *San Jose 3*) and choose whether to
use dialing rules. Windows XP selects the If Number Fails, Try Next Number check box
by default. In most cases, you'll probably want to leave this check box selected. If
appropriate, select the Move Successful Number to Top of List check box as well so that
Windows XP will use that number first next time it dials.

Apart from the alternate-number options, the key choices on the General tab of the
Properties dialog box for an Internet connection are the Use Dialing Rules check box and
the Show Icon in Notification Area when Connected check box.

Whether to use dialing rules depends on your situation. For most Internet connections,
it's helpful to display the connection icon in the notification area. The icon gives you
quick access to the connection's status, and the screens on the icon's mini-monitors give
you a quick visual readout of how much activity is happening on the connection.

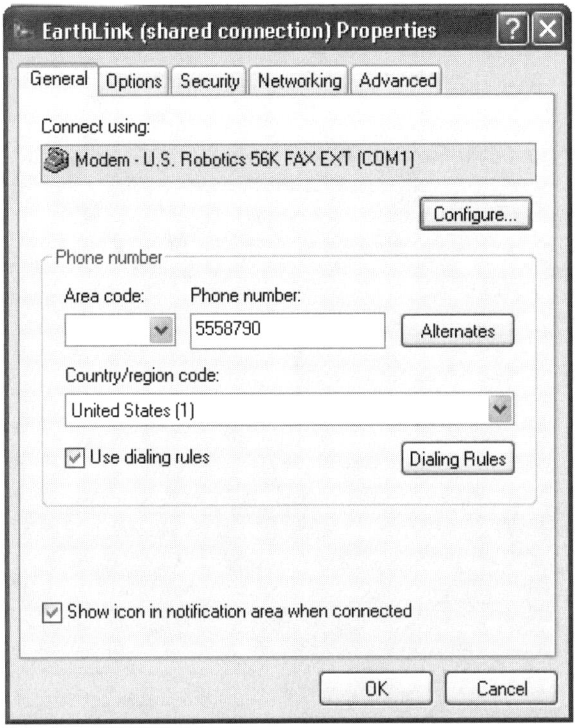

Figure 35-4. *The General tab of the Properties dialog box for an Internet connection*

Setting Dialing Options

The Options tab of the Properties dialog box (Figure 35-5) for an Internet connection contains options for controlling how Windows XP dials and redials the connection. For these options, Windows XP uses default values that you may well want to change.

The Display Progress While Connecting check box controls whether Windows XP displays the informational message boxes while connecting, authenticating your user name and password, and registering the computer on the network. This information is useful for tracking and troubleshooting connections, but it can be an annoyance if your computer needs to frequently redial to reestablish the connection.

The Prompt for Name and Password, Certificate, Etc. check box controls whether Windows XP prompts you for your user name and password in the Connect dialog box for the connection. If you've saved the user name and password for the connection, clear this check box so that you can't change them.

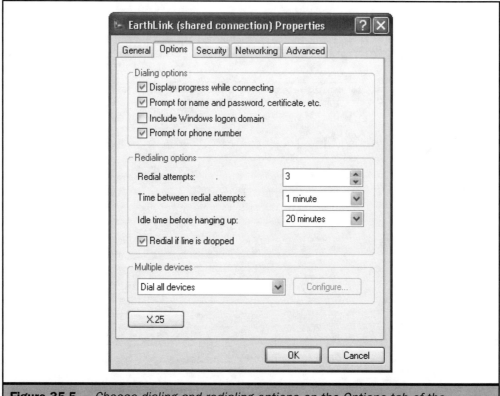

Figure 35-5. *Choose dialing and redialing options on the Options tab of the Properties dialog box for the Internet connection.*

The Include Windows Logon Domain check box controls whether the Connect dialog box for the connection includes a Domain text box. You can only use this option if you use the Prompt for Name and Password, Certificate, Etc. option. You're unlikely to need this option for connecting to an ISP. (It's normally used for connecting to a corporate network.)

The Prompt for Phone Number check box controls whether the Connect dialog box for the connection includes the Dial combo box. Unless users will need to enter or select a different phone number for the connection, clear this check box.

If you turn off the Prompt for Name and Password, Certificate, Etc. option and the Prompt for Phone Number option, Windows XP doesn't display the Connect dialog box at all—instead, it dials the connection when you double-click the connection's icon.

The options in the Redialing Options group box let you specify the number of automatic redial attempts, the time between them, whether Windows XP should redial automatically if the line is dropped, and how long to let the line languish idle before hanging it up. These settings are easy to understand. If you're paying by the minute for your Internet connection, you may well want to reduce the Idle Time before Hanging Up setting.

The Multiple Devices group box lets you specify the dialing pattern for multiple modems or ISDN channels. "Setting Up a Multilink Modem or ISDN Connection," later in this chapter, discusses these options. If you don't have multiple modems or ISDN channels, the Multiple Devices group box doesn't appear.

Setting Security Options

By default, Windows XP implements a "typical" security configuration for dial-up connections. This configuration works for most connections, but you may want to improve on it. To do so, you use the options on the Security tab of the Properties dialog box (Figure 35-6) for the connection.

Figure 35-6.   *Use the Security tab of the Properties dialog box for a connection to configure security options.*

If you choose the Typical option button in the Security Options group box, you can choose Allow Unsecured Password (the default setting), Require Secured Password, or Use Smart Card in the Validate My Identity As Follows drop-down list for an Internet connection. Some ISPs allow you to use a secured password, but others require an unsecured password. As of this writing, very few ISPs use smart cards for consumer Internet connections.

If your ISP supports using a secured password, use the Require Secured Password option. Allow an unsecured password only if you must.

If you choose Require Secured Password, Windows XP makes available the Automatically Use My Windows Logon Name and Password (and Domain If Any) check box but leaves it cleared. This option is more often used in corporate networks than by ISPs.

If you choose Require Secured Password or Use Smart Card, Windows XP makes available the Require Data Encryption (Disconnect If None) check box. You can select this check box to ensure that Windows XP uses encryption for your communications to your ISP. If you leave this check box cleared, as it is by default, Windows XP tries to use encryption but makes the connection even if it can't use encryption. If you select this check box, Windows XP drops the connection if it can't use encryption.

If you eschew the Typical option button and go for the Advanced option button, you can choose security settings in the Advanced Security Settings dialog box (see Figure 35-7). This dialog box gives you more variations and specifics on the same theme as the Typical settings we just examined.

The Data Encryption drop-down list lets you choose whether to refuse encryption, use optional encryption (connect even if your ISP doesn't support encryption), require encryption, or require maximum-strength encryption.

The options in the Logon Security group box let you choose between using the Extensible Authentication Protocol (EAP) and your selection of logon protocols. EAP is used mostly for smart cards (or other certificates) and for systems using MD5-Challenge authentication. You're unlikely to be using these outside a corporate setting, so you'll probably need to select the Allow These Protocols option button instead and use the list of check boxes to specify the protocols you want to use. Unencrypted Password (PAP) is the least secure option: The Password Authentication Protocol (PAP) uses plain-text passwords, so it should be a last resort. Consult your ISP as to which of the other protocols to use for secure logon, but note that you'll seldom want to use your Windows logon name and password (the lowermost check box in the dialog box).

Setting Networking Options

Unless you have an unorthodox ISP connection (for example, SLIP), you shouldn't need to change the options on the Networking tab of the Properties dialog box for a connection (see Figure 35-8). These are the options:

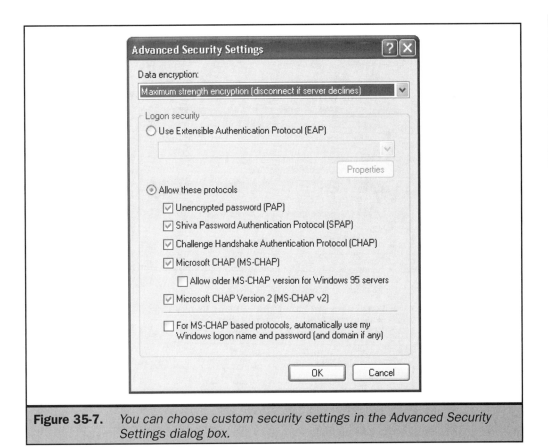

Figure 35-7. *You can choose custom security settings in the Advanced Security Settings dialog box.*

■ The Type of Dial-up Server I Am Calling drop-down list offers PPP and SLIP; almost invariably, you'll want PPP.

■ The This Connection Uses the Following Items list box lists the network protocols and services available for the connection, with check boxes indicating those in use. By default, the Internet Protocol (TCP/IP) protocol and the QoS Packet Scheduler are used. Never enable the File and Printer Sharing for Microsoft Networks service for an Internet connection, because it exposes your shared files and printers to the whole wired world. You're unlikely to need the Client for Microsoft Networks client for Internet connections. (If you have further protocols and services installed, you'll see them listed here as well.)

Figure 35-8.   *In most cases, the Network Setup Wizard chooses appropriate options on the Networking tab of the Properties dialog box for a connection.*

Setting Advanced Options

The Advanced tab of the Properties dialog box for a connection contains controls for Internet Connection Firewall and Internet Connection Sharing. "Sharing Your Internet Connection with Internet Connection Sharing," later in this chapter, and "Securing Your Internet Connection with ICF," even later in this chapter, discuss these options.

Setting Up a Multilink Modem or ISDN Connection

If DSL, cable, or optical fiber isn't available where you live, multilink modems or ISDN channels can make a worthwhile difference to your connection speed. With multilink ISDN, you get the aggregate bandwidth you'd expect; for example, two 64 Kbps channels will give you 128 Kbps. With multilink analog modems, you get a bit less than the aggregate because there's some overhead, but you get a significant increase in speed.

As mentioned earlier, you need a phone line (or ISDN channel) for each device you're using (or an ISDN terminal adapter handling two ISDN channels), and your ISP has to support multilink.

Setting Up a Multilink Modem Connection

To set up a multilink modem connection, install and configure each modem involved as usual. Use HyperTerminal or Phone Dialer to make sure each modem and phone line is working. Then open the Properties dialog box for the connection and take the following steps:

1. On the General tab, select the check box in the Connect Using list box for each modem you want to use for the connection.

2. If all the modems will call the same phone number to establish the multilinked connection, leave the All Devices Call the Same Numbers check box selected, as it is by default, and leave the existing phone number and dialing information as it is in the Phone Number group box. If the modems will dial different numbers, clear the All Devices Call the Same Numbers check box, select each modem in turn, and specify the phone number and dialing information for the modem.

3. On the Options tab of the Properties dialog box for the connection, use the Multiple Devices drop-down list to specify how to dial the modems. The default setting is Dial All Devices, which automatically dials all the modems each time you establish the connection. The Dial Devices Only As Needed setting dials the modems according to the conditions you specify (see step 4). The Dial Only First Available Device setting lets you establish a single-line connection using whichever line is available; it's primarily useful when you're sharing phone lines with other people (or with your voice calls).

4. If you selected the Dial Devices Only As Needed setting in the Multiple Devices drop-down list, configure automatic dialing and hanging up as described in the section after next.

5. Click the OK button to close the Automatic Dialing and Hanging Up dialog box, and then click the OK button to close the Properties dialog box for the connection.

Setting Up a Multilink ISDN Connection

To set up a multilink ISDN connection on a BRI, you normally need only configure the connection to use both ISDN channels (by selecting both check boxes in the Connect Using list box on the General tab of the Properties dialog box for the connection). In most ISDN configurations, both channels call the same number.

Configuring Automatic Dialing and Hanging Up

If you chose the Dial Devices Only As Needed setting for your modems or ISDN channels, click the Configure button to display the Automatic Dialing and Hanging Up dialog box (Figure 35-9). Use its controls to specify the conditions under which Windows XP should automatically dial an extra line and hang up an extra line.

Windows XP's default settings are reasonable for normal use with a modem. Depending on what kinds of operation you typically perform online (for example, frequent downloads or videoconferencing), you may want to adjust the activity thresholds

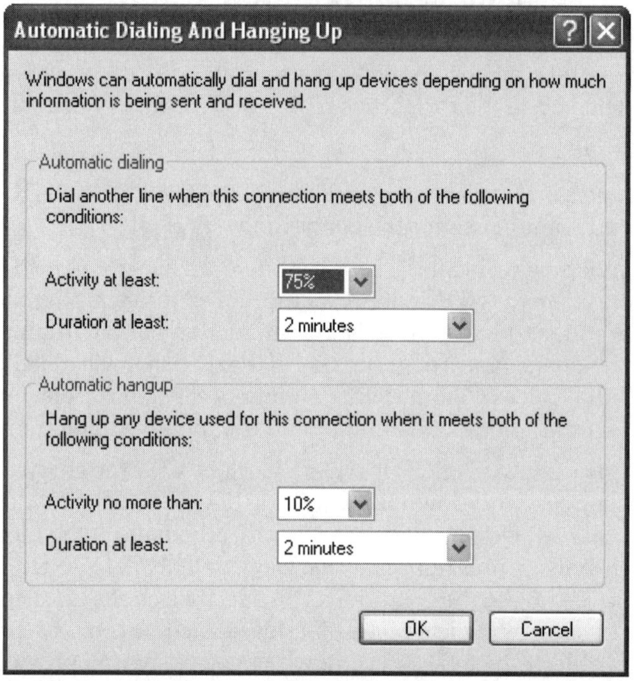

Figure 35-9. Configure settings for dialing and hanging up additional lines in the Automatic Dialing and Hanging Up dialog box.

(using the Activity at Least drop-down list and the Activity No More Than drop-down list) to ensure that Windows XP dials and hangs up the extra line or lines at the appropriate times.

Because ISDN can add a second channel almost instantaneously, you may want to sharpen Windows XP's reflexes a bit by reducing the Duration at Least setting in the Automatic Dialing drop-down list. By setting a Duration at Least value of, say, 10 seconds or 30 seconds, you can make the second channel kick in quickly when you're downloading a file of any size while avoiding having the channel added for downloading a typical web page.

For most people, the key question here is "why aren't you using the extra line or lines all the time?" For example, if you have an ISDN BRI, you might want to run only one channel most of the time because you're being charged per minute per channel. (If your ISDN is on a flat fee, you might as well run both channels the whole time.) If you're using a second (or subsequent) analog phone line, is your reason for not using it the whole time that you need to keep it open most of the time for voice calls? If so, you may prefer to dial the extra line manually when it's safe to do so.

Dial-up connections are stored in the Rasphone.pbk file in the %systemroot%\ Documents and Settings\All Users\Application Data\Microsoft\Network\ Connections\Pbk folder. You can back up this file for safety or copy it to another computer to install the dial-up connections on that computer. You'll need to restart the computer before the connections show up in Network Connections.

Choosing Between Network Address Translation and Using Multiple IP Addresses

In most cases, the easiest and least expensive method of connecting a small network to the Internet is to use a hardware or software device that performs Network Address Translation (NAT), as discussed in the following subsection. The alternative is to get multiple public IP addresses for the computers that need to connect to the Internet, as discussed in "Using Routed Internet Service and Multiple IP Addresses," later in the chapter.

Using Network Address Translation

In NAT, you share an Internet connection with a single external IP address among the computers on the network. Any TCP/IP packet sent by computers on the network to Internet destinations is forwarded to the NAT host, which replaces the local source address (that of the client computer) with the external IP address of the NAT device, replaces the source port on the client with a unique source port of its own, and routes the packet through the Internet connection. To the ISP, all packets appear to come from the single IP address they've assigned to you rather than from the various computers that originally sent them.

The NAT device associates the client information for each outgoing request with the new source port and stores these associations in a port mapping table to track what's going on. So when a reply comes back to the specified port on the external connection, NAT examines the packets, matches them to the outgoing request, and routes the packets to the client that made the request.

As mentioned earlier, you can get either software or hardware NAT devices:

- Software NAT runs on a computer. ICS is perhaps the most widely used software NAT device. Windows 98 Second Edition, Windows Me, Windows 2000, and Windows XP include ICS.

- Hardware NAT runs on a standalone hardware device. Such a device can be either a dedicated NAT device or (more likely) another network hardware device that incorporates NAT functionality. For example, many devices such as ISDN routers, DSL routers, or cable routers include NAT.

In general, NAT works well. But some applications don't work properly with NAT. Any application that expects replies to come back to a different port than the port used for sending data will have trouble via NAT, because NAT expects replies to come back to the port used for outbound traffic.

> **Caution**   *NAT devices (such as ICS) prevent IPSec from working.*

Using Routed Internet Service and Multiple IP Addresses

Instead of using NAT, you can get routed Internet service and multiple fixed IP addresses from your ISP and assign a separate external IP address to each computer that needs to connect to the Internet. To do this, you'll normally need an always-on connection with a static IP address—for example, a cable connection or DSL. You'll also need a router. Make sure the router supports UPnP so that you'll be able to use UPnP features through the hardware router.

Many ISPs charge substantially more for providing multiple IP addresses than for a single IP address, even if the connection speed is the same. So make sure that you'll benefit from using multiple IP addresses rather than NAT. The main advantage of using multiple IP addresses is that all Internet applications should work without problems, because each computer is directly accessible from the Internet. The main disadvantage is that you need to secure each computer against attack from the Internet instead of being able to secure the connection at the NAT device.

Sharing Your Internet Connection with Internet Connection Sharing

If you decide to use NAT to share your Internet connection with other computers on your small-office or home-office network, the easiest and least expensive option is to use Windows XP's built-in ICS feature. This section discusses how ICS works and how to use it.

Microsoft has made ICS and ICF as easy to use as possible. As you'll see later in this chapter, you can turn on ICS and ICF by simply selecting two check boxes. But if you administer your computer and use ICS to share an Internet connection with other computers, you'll benefit from understanding a little about how ICS and ICF work.

How ICS Works

ICS is a software NAT device integrated into Windows XP. ICS combines a Domain Name System (DNS) proxy, or *DNS forwarder*, and a Dynamic Host Configuration Protocol (DHCP) allocator (a simplified DNS server) with NAT.

The computer to which the Internet connection device is attached becomes the ICS host, and the other computers on the network become the ICS clients.

ICS uses an *internal* or *private* ICS connection and an *external* or *public* ICS connection. The internal connection is the interface between ICS and the computers on your internal network, and the external connection is the interface between your computer and the external network. The external network is typically the Internet, but it can also be another network. The internal ICS connection always has the IP address 192.168.0.1. (192.168.*n.n* is a nonroutable TCP/IP subnet.) The external ICS connection has an IP address assigned by the ISP or the other network to which the computer is connected.

ICS's DHCP server automatically supplies IP addresses to ICS clients on request, making sure there are no conflicts. The DNS forwarder resolves IP addresses for local computers and forwards nonlocal traffic out through the external ICS connection.

As described earlier in the chapter for NAT devices, packets sent by ICS clients with external IP addresses are sent to the internal ICS connection on the ICS host. The ICS host changes the source IP address and port, maps the information to an entry in its port mapping table, and routes the packets to the ISP via the external ICS connection. The host matches incoming packets to entries in the port mapping table and redirects them to the appropriate computers.

For security, each incoming packet of information needs to match a specific outgoing request. Any packets that don't match get discarded, which helps protect your network. So if you want to be able to receive incoming packets for particular services, you need to notify ICS where the packets will be coming in and what to do with them. As you'll see later in this chapter, ICS comes configured with a range of Internet services you can turn on at will, but you may also want to configure other incoming services in order to receive particular requests.

ICS uses UPnP to advertise ICS to the other computers on your network via the Simple Service Discovery Protocol (SSDP). A Windows XP client that doesn't have the advertised service then displays a screen pop-up to let the user know about it.

Note   *UPnP isn't installed by default in Windows XP or Windows Me, but you can install it manually by using the Windows Component Wizard (Start | Control Panel | Add or Remove Programs | Add/Remove Windows Components). Double-click the Networking Services item to display the Network Services dialog box, in which you'll find the check box for Universal Plug and Play. Earlier versions of Windows, such as Windows 98 and 2000, don't understand UPnP and can't benefit from the UPnP packets.*

UPnP can also implement a complex protocol stack to notify ICS that replies to outgoing packets will use different ports. By including a complex protocol stack, manufacturers can make applications work with ICS that wouldn't otherwise have worked. For example, for games created before UPnP was released and that require an IP address, manufacturers may need to produce UPnP headers (also called *UPnP extensions*) before ICS clients can participate successfully in the games.

Because the ICS host always has the IP address 192.168.0.1, ICS can be enabled on only one computer on any network. That means you can share only one connection on your home or office network via ICS. (You can have as many unshared Internet connections as you want on the ICS clients—you just can't share them via ICS. However, you may be able to share them using other sharing technologies, either hardware or software.)

If you set up a second ICS host on the same network as an existing and active ICS host, you'll get a series of error messages alerting you to the problem. The first error message appears when the second ICS host is booted or connected to the network, and it notifies you of the IP address conflict for the address 192.168.0.1. If you allow the second host to finish booting, you get a message that ICS has been disabled on it. At the same time, the existing ICS host will be displaying error messages about the address conflict.

For ICS to work consistently, the ICS Internet connection and passwords must be available in every user profile that will run the ICS host computer. Otherwise, you can end up with a user running the ICS host computer who doesn't have permission to dial the ICS connection, thus preventing ICS from functioning.

Advantages and Disadvantages of ICS

ICS offers a quick and easy way to connect a small group of networked computers to the Internet through a single connection. These are the main advantages of ICS:

- You can save money by connecting an entire office or home through a single connection device and connection. You don't need to buy multiple connection devices or pay for multiple connections.

- Using only one Internet connection reduces the number of points at which your network can be attacked. You need only one firewall to protect your whole network.

- All Internet traffic sent by ICS clients appears to originate from the ICS host. (This can also be a disadvantage, as you'll see in a moment.)

ICS also has several limitations. Some are more obvious than others:

- Unless you have a fast connection, sharing it may produce more problems than it solves. Sharing a 33.6 Kbps modem connection, for example, will seem more like torture than progress. ICS essentially divides the available bandwidth equally among active users. (The process is much more complicated than that, but roughly equal division is the most useful way of thinking of the result.)

- ICS creates a single point of failure. If the Internet connection goes down, none of the computers on the network can access the Internet. (However, you can easily switch ICS to a backup connection, either on the ICS host itself or by changing the ICS host to a computer that has another connection.)

- Some applications don't work fully through ICS. For example, NetMeeting can't send video if it's connecting to the other computer via ICS.

- ICS limits you to using the 192.168.0.*x* address range. If you use a router, you can use a different private address range.

- ICS doesn't work with one-way connections such as dial-return satellite service.

- You need to keep the ICS host running the entire time that other computers on the network may need to connect.

- ICS is intended (and designed) to handle only a relatively small number of clients—say half-a-dozen or so. If you connect more than about a dozen clients, ICS's performance deteriorates.

- As mentioned before, all Internet traffic sent by ICS clients appears to originate from the ICS host. Any embarrassing or illegal actions taken by any of the ICS clients (for example, P2P file sharing or a spot of hacking) gets blamed on the ICS host's ISP account.

For many people in home, home-office, or small-office situations, ICS's advantages greatly outweigh its disadvantages. However, your situation may mean that ICS isn't suitable for you.

NAT Alternatives to ICS

Given the centrality of the Internet to using a PC these days, and the gradual but (with any luck) inexorable spread of broadband Internet connections through urban areas, ICS is a compelling feature for most home users and many small businesses. But if ICS doesn't suit you, you should have no problem finding NAT hardware or software that will perform a similar function.

In most cases, once you've decided against ICS, you'll be better off with a hardware NAT solution than another software NAT solution. Look for an independent hardware device, such as a cable router, DSL or ISDN router, or residential gateway.

The disadvantage to using another form of NAT is that unless the device or software can handle UPnP, any program that requires UPnP won't work across it. For example, Windows XP's Remote Assistance feature requires UPnP, so you can't use it across a NAT device that isn't UPnP compliant.

Turning ICS On and Off

To turn ICS on, select the Allow Other Network Users to Connect Through This Computer's Internet Connection check box on the Advanced tab of the Properties dialog box (Figure 35-10) for the connection.

When you turn ICS on, Windows XP assigns the ICS host the static IP address 192.168.0.1. (If this address happens to be assigned to another computer on the network,

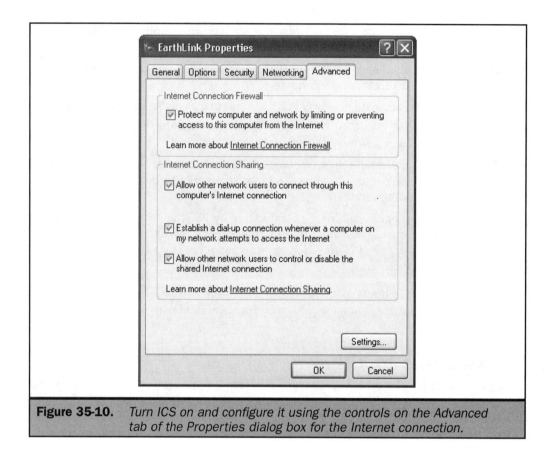

Figure 35-10. *Turn ICS on and configure it using the controls on the Advanced tab of the Properties dialog box for the Internet connection.*

Windows XP displays an error message to alert you to the problem. The following illustration shows an example of an error message.) ICS broadcasts UPnP messages about the shared Internet connection so that other computers on the network running UPnP-compliant OSs can automatically be configured to connect to the Internet via ICS.

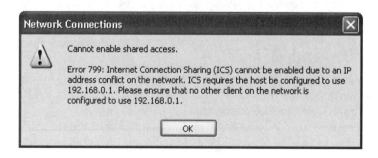

The Internet Connection Sharing group box on the Advanced tab offers two other settings. These are discussed in the next two subsections.

Configuring ICS to Start Automatically for Client Requests

If the Internet connection shared via ICS is a dial-up, you can choose whether ICS should establish the connection automatically when a client computer tries to access the Internet. In many situations, automatic connection is convenient; in others, it can have disadvantages such as racking up large phone bills or users being able to connect at times when you don't want them to connect.

Select or clear the Establish a Dial-up Connection Whenever a Computer on My Network Attempts to Access the Internet check box on the Advanced tab of the Properties dialog box for the connection as appropriate.

Allowing ICS Clients to Control the Internet Connection

The Allow Other Network Users to Control or Disable the Shared Internet Connection check box on the Advanced tab of the Properties dialog box for the connection lets you specify whether ICS clients can manually establish the connection and shut it down. Whether you want other users to be able to control the connection directly depends on your situation, but in many cases it's easier to configure ICS to start automatically when computers on the network try to reach the Internet (as discussed in the previous section) and keep this option turned off.

If you choose to let users control the connection, they use the Internet Gateway entry that appears on the Network Connections screen on their computer to manipulate the connection.

Securing Your Internet Connection with ICF

Whether you share your Internet connection or not, you need to secure it in order to keep your data safe. The best way to do so is to use a hardware or software firewall. A *firewall* is a hardware or software device that examines all incoming data packets (and in some cases outgoing traffic) and allows to pass only those packets that either match predefined rules (for example, those packets that are requests to a web server) or are replies to outgoing packets.

Note *Another tool for helping secure your Internet connection is TCP/IP filtering, which allows you to specify that only TCP/IP packets destined for specific TCP or UDP ports, or TCP/IP packets that use specific protocols, are allowed to pass across your network connections. Packets that don't match these parameters are discarded. See "Applying TCP/IP Filtering" in Chapter 30 for a discussion of how to apply TCP/IP filtering to your network connections.*

Internet Connection Firewall (ICF) is a software firewall that comes built into XP. ICF is integrated with the Network Setup Wizard, which implements ICF by default on each Internet connection you set up—so unless you chose to turn ICF off, your Internet connection probably uses it.

 ICF isn't limited to Internet connections: you can use it on other network connections if you need to.

A basic firewall is *stateless*—it retains no memory of the connections that have taken place and therefore treats each connection through it as a new connection. You essentially have to specifically permit each type of incoming traffic that you want to receive. Any other type of traffic, the firewall discards. Stateless firewalls can work well for tightly controlled environments, but they don't have enough flexibility for more dynamic environments, such as a Windows-based network connecting to the Internet through NAT.

ICF is a stateful firewall. *Stateful* means that the firewall retains a memory of connections that have passed through it. A stateful firewall stores this information in dynamic connection tables and uses it to decide which incoming packets should be allowed and which should be blocked. For example, when an ICS client is browsing the web, it sends requests for web pages. When the web server sends packets containing the page, the stateful firewall examines its connection tables, establishes from the port to which the packets have come that they match up with an outgoing request, and allows them to pass.

ICF prevents people outside your firewalled computer from scanning ports and resources, such as file shares and printer shares, while providing enough flexibility to allow most applications to work. You can configure ICF to pass specified services to designated computers inside the firewall. For example, if you want to run an FTP server on one of the ICS clients, you can do so. However, some applications can't operate fully via ICS. Other applications can't operate at all.

 ICF filters IPv4 (Internet Protocol version 4) traffic only. It doesn't filter IPv6 (Internet Protocol version 6) traffic or traffic using other protocols.

Enabling ICF

If you set up a direct Internet connection when you installed Windows XP on this computer, ICF should already be enabled. Likewise, if you let the New Connection Wizard use its default settings when you created your Internet connection, ICF should be enabled. (To check that it is, see the second bulleted paragraph.) If not, you can enable ICF either automatically or manually:

■ To enable ICF automatically, run the Network Setup Wizard by choosing Start | All Programs | Accessories | Communications | Network Setup Wizard. (Alternatively, click the Setup or Change Your Home or Small Office Network item in the Pick a Task list on the Network and Internet Connections page in Control Panel.) Choose options relevant to your network configuration. The

Network Setup Wizard enables ICF when you tell the wizard that the computer is directly connected to the Internet.

■ To enable ICF manually, select the Protect My Computer and Network by Limiting or Preventing Access to This Computer from the Internet check box on the Advanced tab of the Properties dialog box for the connection. (To turn ICF off, clear this check box and in the warning dialog box confirm that you want to proceed.)

*The Network Setup Wizard stores log information in the file %systemroot%\Nsw.log. The easiest way to view this information is to choose Start | Run, enter **nsw.log** in the Run dialog box, and click the OK button.*

What ICF Does and Doesn't Block

To protect your computer from intrusions across the Internet, ICF blocks all ports for ICS clients to unsolicited incoming traffic. To receive unsolicited incoming traffic, you need to open ports manually, as described in the section after next.

The ICS host has a lot more freedom than the ICS clients. On the ICS host, TCP port 135 and UDP port 139 are blocked in order to block server message block (SMB) requests (file and printer sharing requests) on the external ICS adapter. Were these ports not blocked, remote computers would be able to access the shares and printers on the internal network. (In exceptional circumstances, you may want to unblock these ports by using the technique described in the next section so that you can share your printers and shares on the Internet.)

Apart from ports 135 and 139, ports 1 to 1024 on the ICS host aren't blocked, so packets can be sent and received without being translated by ICS. For example, if on your ICS host you're running a web server that's listening on port 80, it can receive packets directly via port 80 without translation. Ports above 1024 on the ICS host require translation like all ports on the ICS clients.

The result of all this blocking is that the ICS host, while moderately well protected from SMB requests, can communicate directly with much regular Internet traffic, whereas the ICS clients cannot. This causes problems when you want to use an application that needs to use some of the ports in order to work. Unless you open ports in ICF, you won't be able to use these programs on one of the ICS client computers. (Provided the port is between 1 and 1024 and isn't TCP port 135 or UDP port 139, the programs should work fine on the ICS host.)

Allowing Incoming Services via ICS and ICF

ICF and ICS use the same interface for configuring the services that you're allowing Internet users to use from outside your network. That this tool is shared isn't immediately apparent from the user interface, which makes it look as though you're configuring ICS rather than ICS and ICF at the same time.

By default, incoming services are directed to the ICS host. You can redirect Internet services to particular computers on the internal network. For example, you could specify that web traffic be redirected to your web server on the internal network while Messenger file transfers be redirected to another computer.

Obviously enough, you need to be running ICS (or a similar Internet-sharing program) for computers on the internal network to be able to receive redirected services. If you're not running ICS, only the computer directly connected to the Internet can receive Internet services.

Redirecting services to a particular port without ICS running (to redirect the services to the intended computer on the internal network) can represent a security risk, because ICF passes packets through to the specified port even if the specified service isn't running.

To configure incoming services via ICS and ICF, follow these steps:

1. Display the Properties dialog box for the Internet connection. For example, choose Start | Connect To, right-click the Internet connection's item on the Connect To submenu, and choose Properties from the context menu for the item.

2. Click the Advanced tab. Windows XP displays the Advanced tab.

3. Click the Settings button. Windows XP displays the Advanced Settings dialog box, whose Services tab (Figure 35-11) provides a list of preconfigured services and lets you define further services as necessary.

4. To start a service, select its check box in the Services list box. The first time you start any given service, Windows XP displays the Service Settings dialog box (shown in Figure 35-12) for you to identify the computer running the service and check the ports used. Change the computer identified in the Name or IP Address text box if necessary.

5. To stop a service, clear its check box in the Services list box.

6. Click the OK button to close the Advanced Settings dialog box, and then click the OK button to close the Properties dialog box for the Internet connection.

If the Internet connection is currently connected, Windows XP warns you that some changes may not be applied until you disconnect it and reconnect it. Do so as soon as is practicable.

Allowing ICMP Requests

The ICMP tab of the Advanced Settings dialog box (Figure 35-13) lets you specify which— if any—Internet Control Message Protocol (ICMP) requests to respond to. ICMP is a protocol designed to handle errors at the Network layer of the OSI stack.

By default, all these check boxes are cleared so that Windows XP doesn't respond to any ICMP requests. Not responding is the safest course of action, because ICMP requests

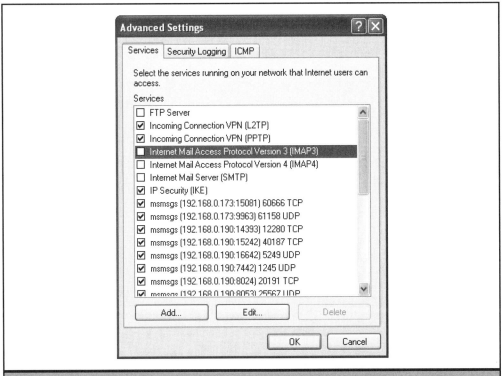

Figure 35-11.   *Use the Services tab of the Advanced Settings dialog box to specify which services can cross the firewall.*

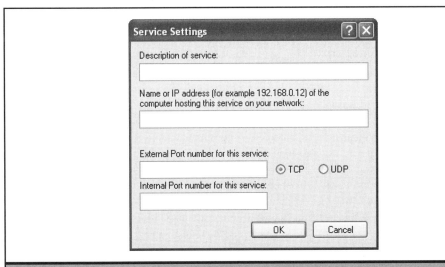

Figure 35-12.   *Use the Service Settings dialog box to edit an existing service that can cross the firewall or to add another service.*

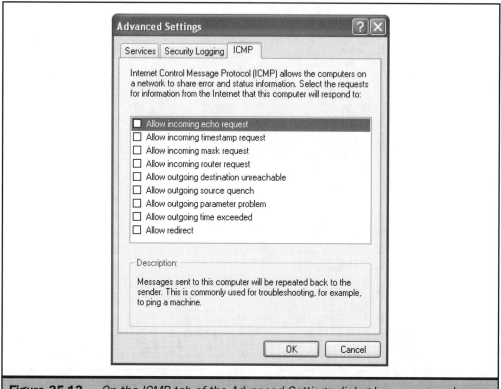

Figure 35-13. *On the ICMP tab of the Advanced Settings dialog box, you can choose whether to respond to Internet Control Message Protocol requests.*

can reveal information about your connection and your network to outsiders. For example, by selecting or clearing the Allow Incoming Echo Request check box, you can specify whether Windows XP answers ping packets. If you're outside the firewall and need to establish whether your ICS host is up, having the computer respond to the ping can show you that the computer is running. If a malefactor is looking for a computer to attack, it'd be better not to respond.

The other ICMP services can be useful too, depending on what you're trying to do. For example, a source quench message is one that ICMP sends when a computer sending data to it is supplying the data at a faster rate than the computer can handle. Given the relative speeds of computers and most Internet connections these days, this is unlikely to be a problem—but you may find a time when it's useful to allow outgoing source quench requests. Balance the benefits that answering these ICMP requests could deliver against the threats they might pose. Err on the side of caution.

To see a description of an ICMP request in the Description text box, select the request in the list box.

Using ICF's Security Logging Features

When you set up ICF, configure its security logging features on the Security Logging tab of the Advanced Settings dialog box (Figure 35-14). Select the Log Dropped Packets check box to log incoming and outgoing packets that are dropped. Select the Log Successful Connections check box to log successful inbound and outbound connections.

In the Log File Options group box, you can change the location of the firewall log file and the amount of space it can occupy. The default is 4,096KB (4MB).

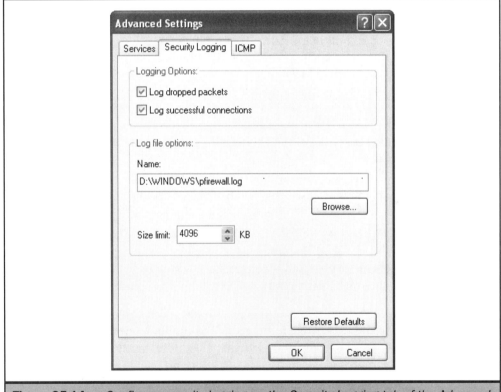

Figure 35-14. *Configure security logging on the Security Logging tab of the Advanced Settings dialog box.*

Opening Ports Manually on ICF

You may need to open ports manually on ICF in order to use some applications at all or to use certain features of other applications. To open ports manually, follow these steps:

1. Display the Advanced Settings dialog box for the Internet connection by following steps 1–3 in the section "Allowing Incoming Services via ICS and ICF," earlier in this chapter.

2. Click the Add button to display the Service Settings dialog box (refer to Figure 35-12).

3. In the Description of Service text box, enter a descriptive name for the port. This name is for your benefit, so make it understandable.

4. In the Name or IP Address of the Computer Hosting This Service on Your Network text box, enter the name or IP address of the computer hosting the service.

5. If you specify the computer's name, it's best to use a fully qualified DNS name. The default domain name for Windows XP using ICS is MSHOME.NET, so your computer's fully qualified DNS name would be *computername*.MSHOME.NET. If you want to check the fully qualified DNS name of a computer, issue an **ipconfig /displaydns** command on your ICS host and read the appropriate entry in the resulting list.

6. In the External Port Number for This Service text box, enter the external port number to use.

7. In the Internal Port Number for This Service text box, enter the internal port number to use. In many cases, this will be the same port number as the external port number.

8. Choose the TCP option button (the default) or the UDP option button, as appropriate.

9. Click the OK button. Windows XP closes the Service Settings dialog box and adds the port to the list on the Services tab of the Advanced Settings dialog box.

To edit a service you've configured in this way, double-click it in the Services list box on the Services tab of the Advanced Settings dialog box. To delete a selected service, click the Delete button.

Troubleshooting Your Internet Connection

How to troubleshoot your Internet connection depends on your connection technology and your ISP, but these are the basic steps:

1. Check your connection device:

   ■ For a dial-up connection, make sure that your modem is working, that it's powered on (if it's an external serial modem), and that it's correctly connected to your computer and to the phone line. If it's an external modem with a power supply and you suspect it of being confused, switch it off for 10 seconds or so and then switch it on again. If possible, turn on the modem's sound by selecting the Enable Modem Speaker check box in the Modem Configuration dialog box. (You can display this dialog box in various ways—for example, by selecting the modem on the General tab of the Properties dialog box for the Internet connection and clicking the Configure button.) You'll then be able to hear whether the modem's dialing.

Tip   *If you have a modem problem, run the Modem Troubleshooter in XP's Help and Support Center.*

- For an ISDN, cable, or DSL connection, make sure your terminal adapter, cable router, or DSL router is correctly plugged in and powered on. Again, if necessary, power it off and on again.

- For another type of connection, such as wireless or satellite, check the connection device for lack of power or unorthodox behavior.

2. Check your communications line (if you're using one):

   - If it's a regular phone line, place a voice call to your ISP's number and make sure a modem tone answers.

   - If it's a cable or DSL connection, check the status light on the cable modem or DSL modem.

3. Make sure the network adapters are correctly assigned. For example, Windows XP might be trying to connect to the Internet through your LAN card rather than through your external connection. Reassign the Internet connection if necessary.

4. Make sure your ISP is up. If it's temporarily down, no amount of reconfiguration will help. Phone the support number and learn what's happening. If you have a backup ISP you can use, connect using that connection and check your ISP's web site for information on problems.

5. If your ISP is alive but you can't browse the web even from the ICS host, open a command-prompt window and try pinging a host on the Internet by name. For example, you might try pinging Osborne, because Osborne is courteous enough to send a response to ping packets. (Many sites don't respond to ping packets.) Here's an example:

```
D:\>ping osborne.com
Pinging osborne.com [198.45.24.130] with 32 bytes of data:
Reply from 198.45.24.130: bytes=32 time=281ms TTL=238
```

6. As you can see in the second line, the ISP's DNS has resolved the name osborne.com to the IP address 198.45.24.130. The third line shows a reply to the ping packet, indicating that the Osborne site is online and alive. But if your ISP's DNS servers are down, as sometimes happens, the name won't be resolved to the IP address, and the command will fail. You'll still be able to access any Internet host by IP address (for example, ping 198.45.24.130 would still work)—if you know the IP address.

7. If none of the preceding helps—in other words, you're sure your communications equipment is fine, your line is fine, they're connected properly, and your ISP is up and running—try running the Network Setup Wizard again.

Understanding Common Connection Error Messages

This section discusses some of the more common error messages you may see when connecting to the Internet and how to troubleshoot them.

Error 691 or Error 734

If you get Error 691 (either "The computer you are dialing in to cannot establish a Dial-up Networking connection. Check your password, and then try again" or "Access was denied because the user name and/or password was invalid on the domain") or Error 734 ("The PPP link control protocol was terminated") when trying to connect via dial-up, check the following:

1. That your user name and password are correct for the connection.

2. That you haven't selected the Include Windows Logon Domain check box on the Options tab of the Properties dialog box for the connection.

3. That the Validate My Identity As Follows drop-down list on the Security tab of the Properties dialog box for the connection doesn't have the Require Secured Password item or the Use Smart Card item selected.

Invalid DHCP Lease

You may get an "Invalid DHCP Lease" error message when using a one- or two-way cable modem. The problem occurs because Windows XP's Autoconfiguration option automatically assigns an IP address to your cable adapter if it thinks the adapter has failed to get an address itself, whereas in fact the adapter may still be requesting an IP address from your ISP's DHCP server. The IP address that Autoconfiguration assigns is valid for your local network rather than for the ISP's network, so it prevents you from accessing the Internet.

The workaround for this problem is to open a command-prompt window and use an ipconfig command to check the IP address assigned to the network adapter for the cable modem. (For a one-way modem connection, you'll need to check the IP address for the PPP Adapter connection as well.) If the number is in the 169.254.$x.x$ range, you know that Windows XP has assigned it automatically. Issue an **ipconfig /release** command for the affected adapter to release the connection and then an **ipconfig /renew** command for the affected adapter to force Windows XP to renew the connection.

Error 633

If you get Error 633 ("The modem [or other connecting device] is already in use or is not configured properly") when you try to establish a broadband Internet connection, it usually means the connection is already open. If the connection seems not to be working, disconnect the connection and then reconnect it.

Troubleshooting ICS

This section discusses how to troubleshoot ICS. The usual problem is that ICS doesn't work, for any of a variety of reasons. ICS can also cause problems if you need to bridge two network adapters on the ICS host.

ICS works with operating systems other than Windows XP if you configure them correctly. This section shows you how to use ICS with earlier versions of 32-bit desktop Windows, with Mac OS, and with Linux.

ICS Doesn't Work

If ICS doesn't seem to be working, start by troubleshooting the ICS host, and then move to the ICS client. The first subsection discusses how to troubleshoot the ICS host. The second subsection discusses how to troubleshoot the ICS client.

Troubleshooting the ICS Host

To troubleshoot the ICS host, follow these steps:

1. Make sure the Internet connection on the host is working. Use Internet Explorer or another browser to access a web site or ping an external host.

2. Make sure you've shared the correct connection—the one connecting to the Internet.

3. If you've enabled ICF on the internal network interface, disable it before setting up ICS. Alternatively, use the Network Setup Wizard to configure ICS. (The Network Setup Wizard automatically disables ICF on internal network interfaces.)

4. Make sure the ICS host is getting an IP address from your ISP. You can do this in various ways, but one of the easiest ways is to open a command-prompt window (Start | All Programs | Accessories | Command Prompt) and issue an **ipconfig** command. Windows XP displays a list of network connections (an

example of which is shown next). In the figure, the PPP Adapter listing shows the IP address, subnet mask, and default gateway for the dial-up connection.

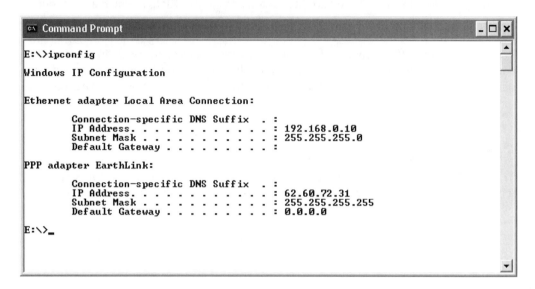

```
Command Prompt                                                        _ □ ×

E:\>ipconfig

Windows IP Configuration

Ethernet adapter Local Area Connection:

        Connection-specific DNS Suffix  . :
        IP Address. . . . . . . . . . . : 192.168.0.10
        Subnet Mask . . . . . . . . . . : 255.255.255.0
        Default Gateway . . . . . . . . :

PPP adapter EarthLink:

        Connection-specific DNS Suffix  . :
        IP Address. . . . . . . . . . . : 62.60.72.31
        Subnet Mask . . . . . . . . . . : 255.255.255.255
        Default Gateway . . . . . . . . : 0.0.0.0

E:\>_
```

5. Make sure the host's IP address on its internal connection is 192.168.0.1. Again, one of the ways to do this is by issuing an **ipconfig** command in a command-prompt window; again, the previous illustration shows an example (the Ethernet Adapter Local Area Connection entry).

6. Check the Network Setup Wizard log file (Start | Run, enter **nsw.log** in the Run dialog box, and click the OK button) and the System log for ICS configuration errors.

Troubleshooting the ICS Client

To troubleshoot an ICS client, follow these steps:

1. Use Internet Explorer or another browser to try to access a web site that you've verified you can access via Internet Explorer from the host (in other words, make sure the web site is up and functional before you use it as a test for the ICS client). If you get the web site, ICS is working.

2. Open a command-prompt window and check the IP address assigned to the ICS client by running the **ipconfig** command. The IP address needs to be in the range 192.168.0.2 to 192.168.0.254, inclusive. If it's not, take the following steps:

   ■ Choose Start | Control Panel | Network and Internet Connections | Network Connections to open the Network Connections screen.

   ■ Right-click the LAN connection and choose Properties from the context menu to open the Local Area Connection Properties dialog box.

■ In the This Connection Uses the Following Items list box, select the Internet Protocol (TCP/IP) item and click the Properties button to display the Internet Protocol (TCP/IP) Properties dialog box.

■ On the General tab, make sure the Obtain an IP Address Automatically option button and the Obtain DNS Server Address Automatically option button are selected. If they're not selected, try selecting them and closing the Internet Protocol (TCP/IP) Properties dialog box and the Local Area Connection Properties dialog box and seeing whether ICS starts working. If these option buttons are already selected, or if selecting them doesn't make any difference, try specifying an IP address and DNS server manually. Select the Use the Following IP Address option button and enter an IP address in the range **192.168.0.2** to **192.168.0.254**, the subnet mask **255.255.255.0**, and the default gateway **192.168.0.1**. Then select the Use the Following DNS Server Addresses option button and enter **192.168.0.1** in the Preferred DNS Server text box and the Alternate DNS Server text box. Close the two dialog boxes and check for connectivity.

3. Open a command-prompt window (or use the same one you used for ipconfig) and ping the ICS host by issuing a **ping 192.168.0.1** command. If you get a series of replies, you know that you have a TCP/IP connection between the ICS client and the ICS host. If you get the message "Request timed out" or "Destination host unreachable," use an ipconfig command to get the IP address of the client computer and ping it (from itself) to make sure that TCP/IP is working. If you get a response to the ping, there's most likely a problem with the physical connection between the computers (for example, your hub or switch is resting or dead, or a cable is disconnected). If you don't get a response to the ping, you have a TCP/IP problem on the ICS client.

Tip   *To find out further IP configuration information, such as the physical address of your network adapter and the address of your DNS servers, use the ipconfig command with the /all switch: **ipconfig /all**. You can also see most of the same information from the Details tab of the Status dialog box for an Internet connection or the Network Connection Details dialog box for a LAN connection. (To display the Network Connection Details dialog box, click the Details button on the Support tab of the Status dialog box for the network connection.)*

Bridging Two Internal Network Adapters on a Windows XP ICS Host

You need to turn ICS and ICF off before trying to bridge the internal ICS connection (192.168.0.1) with another internal network adapter on an ICS host. Otherwise, you'll get the error message "An unexpected error occurred when configuring the network bridge," and the bridge won't be created.

Once you've created the bridge (either manually or by using the Network Setup Wizard), turn ICS and ICF back on.

Using ICS with Earlier Versions of Windows

Windows XP's ICS works with earlier versions of 32-bit Windows. All you need to do is configure Windows to use DHCP to obtain an IP address from ICS automatically. (If the version of Windows doesn't have TCP/IP installed, you'll also need to install TCP/IP.)

Windows 98 Second Edition/Me/2000 include versions of ICS. If you already have your network set up with ICS running on one of these versions of Windows, you *can* simply patch in your Windows XP computer as an ICS client and get basic connectivity. But because versions of ICS earlier than Windows XP's version don't support UPnP, you won't be able to use any programs or features that rely on UPnP. You also won't have the firewall protection that ICF offers. So it's better to use the computer running Windows XP as the ICS host, unless you have a compelling reason for doing otherwise.

Using ICS with Macs and Linux Boxes

ICS can provide Internet connectivity for Macs and Linux boxes as well as Windows PCs. All you need to do is configure the Mac or Linux box to use DHCP so that it picks up an IP address from ICS. If a Mac won't work with DHCP, hard-code an IP address in the range 192.168.0.2 to 192.168.0.254. (You can do the same with Linux, but all current distributions of Linux grew up with DHCP in the cradle, so it's unlikely you'll need to.) On older versions of Mac OS, you may have to install TCP/IP as well.

Summary

This chapter has discussed how to connect a computer running Windows XP Professional to the Internet. Coverage has included the basics of Internet connections, the type of Internet connection you'll typically have on a corporate network, and the various options for connecting computers on a small network to the Internet. You've seen how to set up an Internet connection, share a connection with ICS, secure it with ICF, and troubleshoot both Internet connections and ICS.

The next chapter discusses how to configure and use Internet Explorer, Windows XP Professional's primary tool for accessing web content.

The Complete Reference

Windows XP

Chapter 36

Configuring and Using Internet Explorer

U nless you're coming to this chapter without having used Windows at all, or your copy of Windows XP Professional includes a browser other than Internet Explorer, you'll almost certainly have used Internet Explorer—perhaps quite extensively. So chances are you're familiar with the basic operation of Internet Explorer. You may also have a fair understanding of the more straightforward configuration options it offers. Even if not, you'll find many of the configuration options easy to understand.

This chapter discusses the more complex configuration features Internet Explorer provides and how to configure them. These features include your History settings, AutoComplete, and temporary files. Because security is a major concern for many people, the chapter also covers the security features Internet Explorer provides, including security zones, cookies, and Content Advisor. Last, the chapter provides some tips for browsing effectively, discusses how to use Internet Explorer's offline favorites feature to store web content locally so that you can access it when offline, and shows you how to access FTP sites using Internet Explorer.

In a networked environment, the Internet represents a considerable security threat. Not only can a computer on the network be exposed to attack across the Internet, but it can compromise the security of other computers on the network. To help domain administrators keep their networked computers as secure as possible, Internet Explorer ties in closely with Windows 2000 Server and Windows.NET Server to provide management features that enable tight control. An administrator can configure many separate aspects of Internet Explorer's interface and behavior for security and performance. An administrator will also typically protect the network by using firewalls and intrusion-detection systems.

What you can do with Internet Explorer—and indeed whether you can configure Internet Explorer at all—depends on how your administrator has configured it. To reflect this variety, this chapter concentrates more than other chapters on what an administrator can do and what you'll see as a result.

Configuring Internet Explorer for Security and Effectiveness

This section discusses how to configure Internet Explorer so that it provides the level of security you need while remaining as effective as possible. The section starts by giving you a general idea of the configuration options an administrator can choose for Internet Explorer in a domain. It then shows you how to choose security settings, configure temporary files, use Content Advisor and AutoComplete, configure security zones, control cookies, and choose which helper Internet applications Internet Explorer should use.

Administrative Configuration of Internet Explorer in a Domain

In its default configuration, the Internet Options dialog box contains seven tabs: General, Security, Privacy, Content, Connections, Programs, and Advanced. An administrator can prevent Internet Explorer from displaying any or all of these tabs. So if the Internet Options dialog box on your computer is missing one of these tabs, you'll know an administrator has chosen to suppress the tab so that you can't work with any of its controls. In other cases, an administrator will configure some of the settings on a tab so that you can't change them but will let you view the tab.

For example, the Content tab contains controls for the Content Advisor feature, for working with certificates, for the AutoComplete feature, and for accessing your profile in Microsoft Profile Assistant. By suppressing the Content tab through Group Policy, an administrator can prevent you from accessing any of these settings. However, the administrator might choose to allow the Content tab to appear but might prevent you from accessing some of the controls on it—for instance, they might prevent you from using the Content Adviser feature but allow you to use some AutoComplete features.

If an administrator disables all the tabs in the Internet Options dialog box, you won't be able to display this dialog box at all. When you choose Tools | Internet Options, Internet Explorer displays a Restrictions dialog box that tells you "This operation has been cancelled due to restrictions in effect on this computer" and suggests you contact your system administrator.

 An administrator can disable the Internet Options item on the Tools menu. However, you may still be able to access the Internet Options dialog box by choosing Start | Control Panel | Network and Internet Connections | Internet Options.

The following sections point out specific changes and restrictions an administrator may have made. But if one or more whole tabs are missing from the Internet Options dialog box, you'll be unable to see (let alone change) the settings that tab offers.

Here are quick examples of other settings administrators may choose in a domain environment:

- An administrator may disable the Media Explorer bar to prevent you from using this Explorer bar to play audio and video content from the Internet. (If your job doesn't require you to listen to Internet audio or watch video, your doing so would waste bandwidth.)

- An administrator may disable the option for saving a downloaded application or file to disk. (An application or file could represent a security risk or a legal risk.)

- An administrator may remove the shortcut menu for web pages to prevent you from taking actions that the shortcut menu offers.

■ An administrator may remove various commands (such as the Send Feedback command and the For Netscape Users command) from the Help menu so that you're not tempted to use them.

■ An administrator may prevent you from opening a file or web page from the File menu. Similarly, an administrator may prevent you from closing any Internet Explorer windows. These limitations may seem ludicrous the first time you learn of them—and they would be ludicrous in many corporate environments. But for specialized use such as on a demonstration computer at a booth or a tradeshow, they can be useful.

Choosing Security Settings

The Security section of the Advanced tab of the Internet Options dialog box (Figure 36-1) contains a dozen or so security-specific settings. These settings include the following:

■ **Certificates** You can make Internet Explorer warn you if a site's digital certificate is invalid. You can also make Internet Explorer check that a software publisher's certificate or a web site's certificate hasn't been revoked.

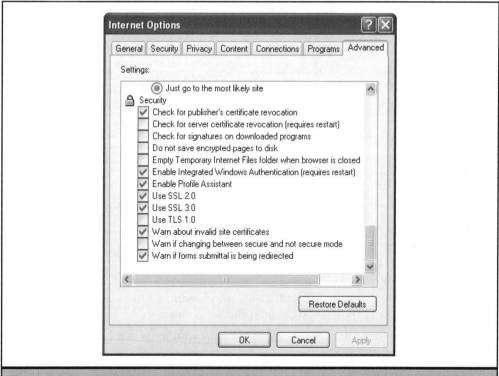

Figure 36-1. *Choose security settings in the Security section of the Advanced tab of the Internet Options dialog box.*

- **Secure Sockets Layer (SSL)**   Choose whether to use the SSL 2.0 and SSL 3.0 protocols for communicating with secure sites.
- **Moving to or from Secure Mode**   You can make Internet Explorer warn you when you move between a secure site and a nonsecure site.

 An administrator can prevent you from changing any of the controls on the Advanced tab. Alternatively, they can suppress the display of the Advanced tab so that you can't even see it.

Using and Configuring Your History

Internet Explorer keeps a list of the sites you've visited. This list, which is called your History, lets you quickly identify and access a site you've visited before. Your History can be a powerful tool for finding sites you half-remember—but it can also let anyone able to access your user account see which sites you've visited and when you've visited them.

These are the key points for using your History:

- You can access your History by clicking the History button on the toolbar, choosing View | Explorer Bar | History, or pressing CTRL-H.
- You can sort your History by the date (the default view), by the site names, by which sites you've visited the most, or by the order in which you've visited the sites today.
- You can expand and collapse the categories by which you sort your History to get at the sites you want.
- You can search through the History sites to find specific words (click the Search button).
- You can delete sites manually from the History by pressing the DEL key or right-clicking and choosing Delete from the shortcut menu.

In a domain environment, an administrator may prevent you from changing history settings. Otherwise, you can configure your History settings by using the two controls in the History group box on the General tab of the Internet Options dialog box:

- Adjust the setting in the Days to Keep Pages in History text box to keep pages for more days or fewer days. Valid settings are 0–999 days.
- Click the Clear History button and click the Yes button in the confirmation dialog box to purge your History.

Clearing your History deletes your AutoComplete entries as well.

Configuring and Deleting Temporary Files

Another group of settings an administrator can prevent you from changing is the temporary files settings. These temporary files are files Internet Explorer creates automatically when it downloads web pages to your computer. Internet Explorer caches the various components of a web page in temporary files so that it can display the page more quickly the next time you request it, either by providing the whole page from the cache or by providing elements that haven't changed in the latest version of the page (for example, graphics).

Temporary files can greatly speed up your web browsing if you have a slow Internet connection (or share a fast but busy connection). But they require disk space and make your computer retain a large amount of information from the sites you've visited. (This information is separate from your History, discussed in the previous section.)

The controls for working with temporary files are in the Temporary Internet Files group box on the General tab of the Internet Options dialog box (Tools | Internet Options). If an administrator has suppressed the display of this tab, you'll be unable to change your settings for temporary files or delete the files. You'll also be unable to change your settings for temporary files or delete the files if an administrator has specifically restricted you from doing so.

Configuring Settings for Temporary Files

To configure settings for temporary files, click the Settings button in the Temporary Internet Files group box on the General tab of the Internet Options dialog box. In the Settings dialog box (Figure 36-2), you can do the following:

- Specify how frequently to check for newer versions of the pages Internet Explorer has stored. Your options are Every Visit to the Page, Every Time You Start Internet Explorer, Automatically, or Never. The Automatically option lets Internet Explorer decide when to check for a newer version based on how frequently you access the page and how often the page changes. You can force Internet Explorer to check for a new version of the current page by pressing F5 or by issuing a Refresh command from the View menu or shortcut menu.

- Check the location of your temporary Internet files folder by looking at the Current Location display, or move the folder to another location by using the Move Folder button. (After moving the folder, restart Internet Explorer to make the change take effect.)

- Change the amount of space allocated to temporary Internet files. Saving more data may make web browsing faster, but it increases your chance of storing useless or potentially embarrassing data.

- Display the folder containing the temporary files in a Windows Explorer window by clicking the View File button. From here, you can delete specific items. But if you've been browsing actively, you'll usually find there are too many files to examine without wasting a lot of time.

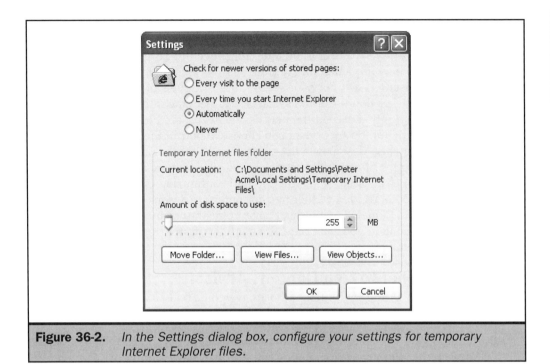

Figure 36-2. *In the Settings dialog box, configure your settings for temporary Internet Explorer files.*

■ Display the folder containing downloaded program files in a Windows Explorer window by clicking the View Objects button. This list is more useful than the list of files, because usually there are few enough downloaded program files to examine easily. You can remove an object by issuing a Remove command from the File menu or the shortcut menu.

Deleting Your Temporary Files Manually

To delete your temporary files, click the Delete Files button in the Temporary Internet Files group box on the General tab of the Internet Options dialog box, and then click the OK button in the Delete Files dialog box that Internet Explorer displays. Select the Delete All Offline Content check box in the Delete Files dialog box only if you want to delete all your offline favorites as well as the temporary files.

Deleting Your Temporary Files Whenever You Close Internet Explorer

To make Internet Explorer delete your temporary files each time you close the application, select the Empty Temporary Internet Files Folder when Browser Is Closed check box in the Security section of the Advanced tab of the Internet Options dialog box. Bear in mind that choosing this setting will slow down your browsing of sites you frequent—unless you seldom close Internet Explorer, in which case this setting won't greatly enhance your security.

Using Content Advisor

Internet Explorer's Content Advisor is a feature for preventing users from accessing inappropriate material by implementing ratings-based screening for web sites and web pages. Content Adviser lets a supervisor set permissible levels of Language, Nudity, Sex, and Violence for sites that users access. Sites that meet the rating requirements are accessible, whereas sites that exceed the permissible levels are blocked. Unrated sites are blocked by default, but the supervisor can choose to permit them.

The supervisor can also designate a list of approved sites that are always accessible no matter what rating they have and a list of banned sites that are never accessible.

This section outlines the steps for setting up and configuring Content Advisor— assuming that you get to decide whether to use Content Advisor, and (if so) that you do decide to use it. In a domain environment, an administrator can use Content Advisor to limit the range of content you can access. If an administrator does this, you won't be able to change the settings.

Deciding Whether to Use Content Advisor

When deciding whether to use Content Advisor, weigh its real and ostensible benefits against its limitations. Here are some comments:

- No ratings system yet devised and implemented is perfect and infallible. Content Advisor may allow users to access some sites that have inappropriate content; or it may block sites that you or other users may legitimately need to access.

- Whether to permit access to unrated sites is a perennial problem: Not every site will be rated, but you or other users may need to access some that aren't rated.

- The approved sites list and the disapproved sites list provide an easy way of manually blocking particular sites that don't match your overall ratings schemes.

- Many companies use Content Advisor and other content-control software to reduce their liability to harassment lawsuits. The software may not be completely effective, but it shows that the company has taken reasonable steps to prevent users from accessing inappropriate content.

Setting Up Content Advisor

To set up and configure Content Advisor, follow these steps:

1. Click the Enable button in the Content Advisor group box to display the Content Advisor dialog box.

2. On the Ratings page (Figure 36-3), select the Language, Nudity, Sex, and Violence items in turn and drag the slider to a suitable level, from 0 (none of the item) to 4 (plenty of the item).

3. Use the controls on the Approved Sites tab to build a list of sites that are always allowed and a list of sites that are never allowed.

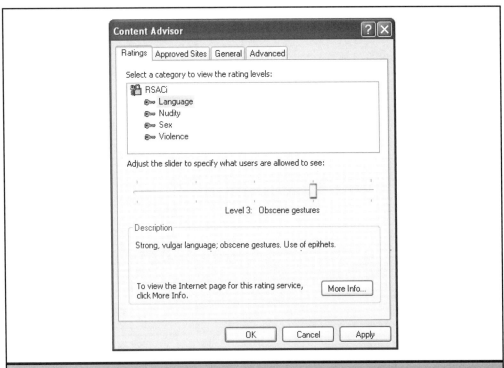

Figure 36-3.   *You can set up Content Advisor to prevent users from accessing web sites that don't meet rating requirements you specify.*

4. The General tab (Figure 36-4) offers two check boxes. By selecting one, you can permit users to access web sites that have no rating. This check box is cleared by default. The other check box is selected by default and lets the supervisor type a password to allow users to view restricted sites. This ability is normally useful, but you run the risk that a sharp-eyed user might memorize the password you type to permit them access to restricted sites.

5. To set the supervisor password, click the Create Password button in the Supervisor Password group box on the General tab. Enter the password in the Create Supervisor Password dialog box that Internet Explorer displays. You can also add a password hint to help you remember the password. Content Advisor strongly recommends you create a hint. Security experts strongly recommend you don't.

6. The General tab also provides controls for accessing Content Advisor's features for adding and removing rating systems. You're unlikely to need to change rating systems in a small- or home-office setting. You're also unlikely to need to use the controls on the Advanced page, which let you configure Content Advisor to obtain Internet ratings from a ratings bureau and to use PICSRules files.

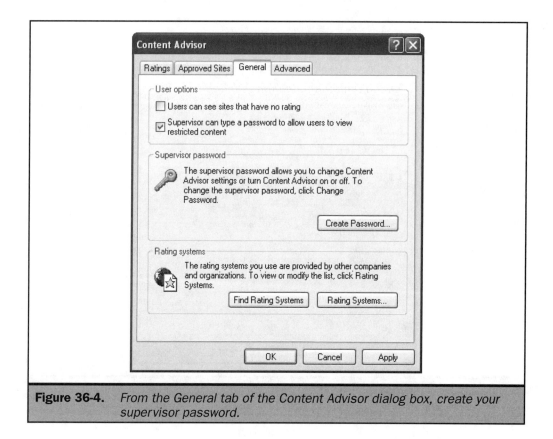

Figure 36-4.   *From the General tab of the Content Advisor dialog box, create your supervisor password.*

7. If you didn't set a supervisor password (as described in step 5), Content Advisor displays the Create Supervisor Password dialog box when you close the Content Advisor dialog box.

8. To fully apply your Content Advisor settings, exit Internet Explorer, closing all its open windows. Then restart Internet Explorer.

Disabling Content Advisor or Changing Content Advisor Settings

To disable Content Advisor, click the Disable button on the Content page of the Internet Options dialog box. To change Content Advisor's settings, click the Settings button on the Content page. In either case, you need to enter the supervisor password in the Supervisor Password Required dialog box.

Using and Configuring AutoComplete

Like AutoComplete in Windows Explorer, AutoComplete in Internet Explorer tries to save you time by automatically completing entries you start to type in the Address bar or in the Open dialog box. Because AutoComplete works by storing the URLs you access in Internet Explorer, it can present a threat to your privacy and security. For example, you might—accidentally or deliberately—visit a web site that afterward you wished you hadn't visited, or you might access an FTP site for which you had to supply a user name and password in the URL. Anyone able to access your user account would then be able to see which sites you'd visited and to log on to the FTP site under your user name. To avoid other people being able to glean this information or this access, you may prefer to turn off AutoComplete.

In a default installation of Windows XP Professional, most AutoComplete features are enabled by default. However, an administrator may prevent you from using AutoComplete for security reasons. An administrator may well prevent you from using AutoComplete for forms, because forms are especially likely to include sensitive data that could breach corporate guidelines or compromise security. If an administrator has done this, the Forms check box is unavailable.

An administrator is even more likely to prevent you from using AutoComplete for user names and passwords on forms, because this information is, by its nature, vulnerable. If an administrator has done this, the User Names and Passwords on Forms check box and the Prompt Me to Save Passwords check box are unavailable.

If you're allowed to configure AutoComplete settings, choose settings by clicking the AutoComplete button in the Personal Information group box on the Content tab of the Internet Options dialog box and working in the AutoComplete Settings dialog box (Figure 36-5). Select or clear the check boxes in the Use AutoComplete For group box to specify whether to use AutoComplete for web addresses, forms, and user names and passwords on forms. If you choose to let AutoComplete track your user names and passwords on forms, choose whether AutoComplete should prompt you before saving passwords. (Being prompted allows you to decide not to save certain passwords—for example, your most sensitive passwords—while letting you easily save other passwords.)

Click the Clear Forms button to delete all the forms data that AutoComplete has stored for you. Click the Clear Passwords button to delete all your saved passwords.

To delete all your AutoComplete entries, clear your History as discussed earlier in this chapter.

When you're working in a form or entering your password on a web site's login page, you can delete an entry that AutoComplete offers you by using the arrow keys to select the entry, and then pressing DEL. For most uses, however, this feature is too limited to be useful.

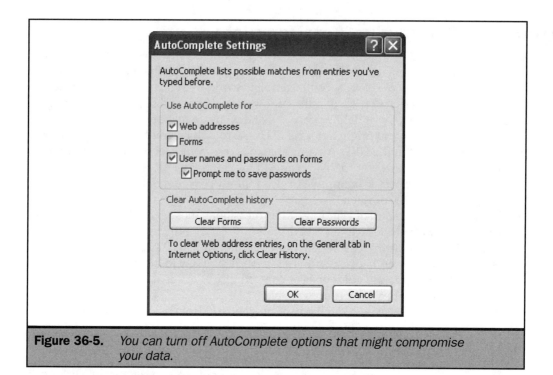

Figure 36-5.   *You can turn off AutoComplete options that might compromise your data.*

Configuring Security Zones

Internet Explorer uses the concept of *security zones*—areas of web sites that have the same security level. Table 36-1 explains the four predefined security zones Internet Explorer uses.

Note   *If there's no Security tab in the Internet Options dialog box, you'll know an administrator has prevented you from accessing these settings.*

If you administer your computer, you can define security zones, add sites to the zones, and remove sites from them. In a domain environment, an administrator will likely define security zones for you. If the administrator does so, they'll almost certainly prevent you from changing security-zone settings. If they've done so, you'll find that the Custom Level button and the Security Level for This Zone slider on the Security tab of the Options dialog box are disabled. An administrator can also prevent you from adding sites to or removing sites from security zones.

Security Zone	Explanation	Default Security Level
Local Intranet	Sites that you access on a LAN.	Medium-Low
Internet	All sites that your computer doesn't access on a LAN and that aren't explicitly trusted or restricted. You can specify how to handle cookies (information files) in this zone. (See "Configuring and Controlling Cookies," later in this chapter.)	Medium
Trusted Sites	Sites that you (or an administrator) have explicitly designated as being trusted by Internet Explorer.	Low
Restricted Sites	Sites that you (or an administrator) have explicitly restricted users from accessing.	High

Table 36-1.   *Internet Explorer's Security Zones*

Specifying Local Intranet Security Zone Sites

To specify which sites Internet Explorer treats as part of your Local Intranet security zone, display the Security tab of the Internet Options dialog box and follow these steps:

1. Select the Local Intranet item in the list box.

2. Click the Sites button. Internet Explorer displays the Local Intranet dialog box shown on the left in Figure 36-6.

3. Select or clear the three check boxes as appropriate.

4. To add specific sites, click the Advanced button. Internet Explorer displays the Local Intranet dialog box shown on the right in Figure 36-6.

5. In the Add This Web Site to the Zone text box, enter the URL of a site to add, and then click the Add button. If necessary, use the Remove button to remove a site from the Web Sites list box.

6. If your servers are secure, you can select the Require Server Verification (https:) for All Sites in This Zone check box to force Internet Explorer to check that the sites are secure before considering them part of the Local Intranet security zone.

7. Close the two Local Intranet dialog boxes.

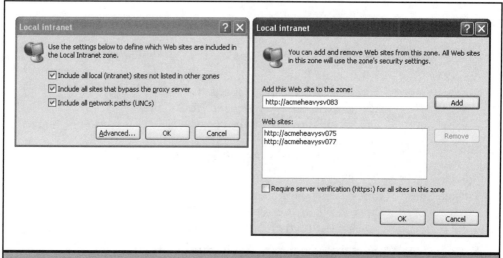

Figure 36-6. *Use these two Local Intranet dialog boxes to specify which sites Internet Explorer treats as part of your Local Intranet security zone.*

Specifying Trusted Sites and Restricted Sites

To specify which sites Internet Explorer treats as being in the Trusted Sites security zone or the Restricted Sites security zone, display the Security tab of the Internet Options dialog box and follow these steps:

1. Select the Trusted Sites item or the Restricted Sites item (as appropriate) in the list box.

2. Click the Sites button to display the Trusted Sites dialog box (shown in Figure 36-7) or the Restricted Sites dialog box. The Restricted Sites dialog box is almost identical to the Trusted Sites dialog box but doesn't offer the Require Server Verification (https:) for All Sites in This Zone check box.

3. In the Add This Web Site to the Zone text box, enter the URL of a site to add, and then click the Add button. If necessary, use the Remove button to remove a site from the Web Sites list box.

4. For trusted sites, you can select the Require Server Verification (https:) for All Sites in This Zone check box to force Internet Explorer to check the sites are secure. (This setting doesn't apply to restricted sites.)

5. Click the OK button to close the Trusted Sites dialog box or the Restricted Sites dialog box.

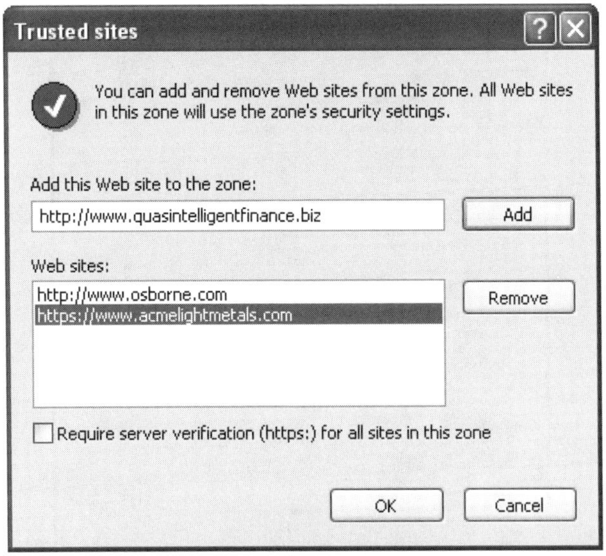

Figure 36-7. *Build a list of trusted web sites in the Trusted Sites dialog box.*

Configuring Security Settings for a Security Zone

If you administer your computer, you can configure the security settings for a security zone. Display the Security tab of the Internet Options dialog box and follow these steps:

1. Select the security zone you want to affect: Internet, Local Intranet, Trusted Sites, or Restricted Sites.

2. To apply a predefined security level, drag the Security Level for This Zone slider up or down to the appropriate position.

3. To apply a custom level of security, click the Custom Level button and work in the Security Settings dialog box (Figure 36-8). This dialog box contains a wide variety of security options including the following:

   ■ Controlling the downloading and running of ActiveX controls. For example, you might prevent users from downloading ActiveX controls that aren't digitally signed (to prove their authenticity). Or you might prevent Internet Explorer from running any ActiveX control that wasn't marked as being safe.

   ■ Allowing or preventing the downloading of files and fonts.

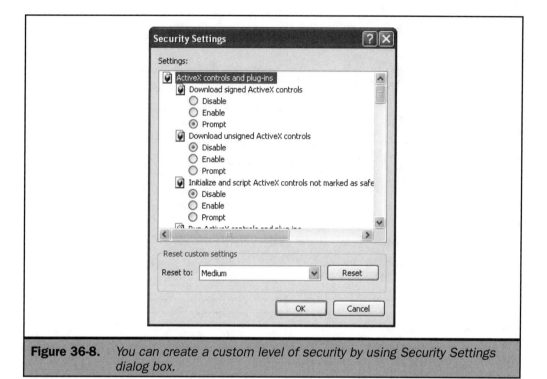

Figure 36-8. *You can create a custom level of security by using Security Settings dialog box.*

- Allowing or preventing the submission of unencrypted form data. (Ideally, form data should always be encrypted in case someone intercepts it in transit.)

- Specifying whether users can automatically log on to sites in the Local Intranet zone or whether they need to provide their user name and password for any site.

4. If necessary, you can reset your custom settings to one of the predefined security levels by using the controls in the Reset Custom Settings group box.

5. Click the OK button to close the Security Settings dialog box.

Configuring and Controlling Cookies

This section discusses the options that Internet Explorer offers for managing cookies. *A cookie*, as you'll probably know if you've been using the web for a while, is a relatively small text file that contains details of your interactions with a particular web site (or an agglomeration of affiliated web sites). For example, if you browse the amazon.com site, the amazon.com servers will cause Internet Explorer to store a cookie named *yourname*@amazon.txt, where *yourname* is your user name. The cookie stores only information you've provided to that web site, either directly (for example, by creating a user account with the site) or indirectly (for example, by browsing from page to page or by performing searches); the cookie can't (for example) grab data from files on your computer. Only the site that creates the cookie can access the cookie.

By using cookies, a web site can identify you (by your user account) each time you access that site. The site can track which pages you visit, which items you search for, which ads seem to interest you, and so on. You benefit (in theory, and often in practice) from cookies by receiving more targeted information from sites that use them, by being able to tell that you've visited a specific link before, and by not needing to identify yourself manually to the site. But cookies also mean that the companies that run web sites can build up information about your actions and preferences. The bigger the web site—or if a company owns several sites that use the same cookie—the more information companies can learn about you and your preferences.

Cookie files are stored in the %userprofile%\Cookies folder. You can access this folder and view the cookies (in a text editor such as Notepad), but usually a cookie's contents aren't intelligible unless you know the inner workings of the web site the cookie refers to.

Compared to earlier browsers (which gave you the choice of allowing all cookies, blocking all cookies, or being prompted for every cookie), Internet Explorer provides fine control over cookies. As you'll see in the next subsections, you can configure privacy preferences to tell Internet Explorer to accept some kinds of cookies but block other kinds.

In a domain environment, an administrator is likely to set cookie preferences based on corporate policy and what users are supposed to need. The administrator will probably suppress the display of the Privacy tab of the Internet Options dialog box to prevent you from accessing its options.

Choosing Privacy Settings to Control Cookies

Internet Explorer's mechanism for controlling cookies is implemented on the Privacy tab (Figure 36-9) of the Internet Options dialog box. On this tab, you can specify how to handle cookies by choosing a built-in security setting, implement a custom privacy setting of your own design, or import a set of privacy preferences that someone else has defined. You can also designate how to handle cookies from specific web sites.

To choose a built-in setting, move the Settings slider up to the appropriate setting. Table 36-2 explains the options. *First-party cookies* come from the web site itself. *Third-party cookies* come from other web sites. A *compact privacy policy* is a policy that's expressed in the web page.

To implement a custom privacy setting of your own design, click the Advanced button and work in the Advanced Privacy Settings dialog box (Figure 36-10). Select the Override Automatic Cookie Handling check box to activate the other controls; then select the appropriate option buttons to choose whether Internet Explorer should accept, block, or prompt you for first-party cookies and third-party cookies. You can select the Always Allow Session Cookies check box if you want Internet Explorer

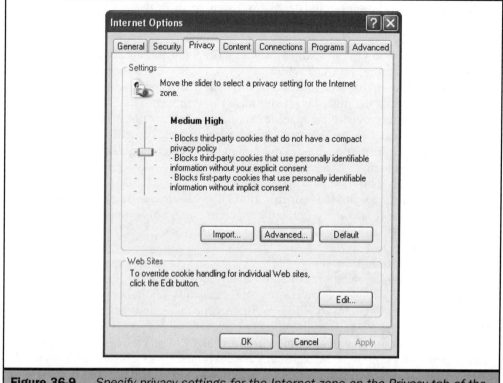

Figure 36-9. *Specify privacy settings for the Internet zone on the Privacy tab of the Internet Options dialog box.*

always to use session (temporary) cookies, whether they come from first parties or third parties. Session cookies are deleted when you close Internet Explorer.

When you close the Advanced Privacy Settings dialog box, the Privacy tab of the Internet Options dialog box shows that you've implemented a Custom level of privacy.

To import a set of privacy preferences someone else has defined, click the Import button. In the Privacy Import dialog box, navigate to the file that contains the preferences, select it, and click the Open button.

To designate how to handle cookies from specific web sites, click the Edit button on the Privacy tab and use the Per Site Privacy Actions dialog box (Figure 36-11) to specify which sites to allow and which to block.

Viewing a Privacy Report

To see whether Internet Explorer has restricted or blocked any cookies on the current page because of your privacy settings, choose View | Privacy Report and examine the information in the Privacy Report dialog box (Figure 36-12).

Type of Cookies	Block All Cookies	High	Medium High	Medium	Low	Accept All Cookies
First-Party Cookies That...						
Have a compact privacy policy	Block	Accept	Accept	Accept	Accept	Accept
Don't have a compact privacy policy	Block	Block	Accept	Accept	Accept	Accept
Use personally identifiable information without your explicit consent	Block	Block	Accept	Accept	Accept	Accept
Use personally identifiable information without your implicit consent	Block	Block	Block	Restrict	Accept	Accept
Third-Party Cookies That...						
Have a compact privacy policy	Block	Accept	Accept	Accept	Accept	Accept
Don't have a compact privacy policy	Block	Block	Block	Block	Accept	Accept
Use personally identifiable information without your explicit consent	Block	Block	Block	Block	Restrict	Accept
Use personally identifiable information without your implicit consent	Block	Block	Block	Block	Restrict	Accept

Table 36-2.   *Built-in Privacy Settings for the Internet Zone*

Select a site and click the Summary button, or double-click a site, to display the Privacy Policy dialog box (Figure 36-13). From here, you can specify how Internet Explorer should handle cookies from this site by selecting the Compare Cookies' Privacy Policy to My Settings option button, the Always Allow This Site to Use Cookies option button, or the Never Allow This Site to Use Cookies option button.

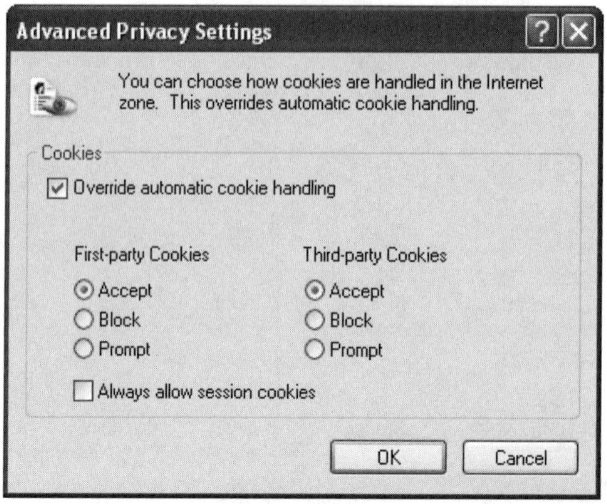

Figure 36-10.   *Create a custom privacy setting by using the Advanced Privacy Settings dialog box.*

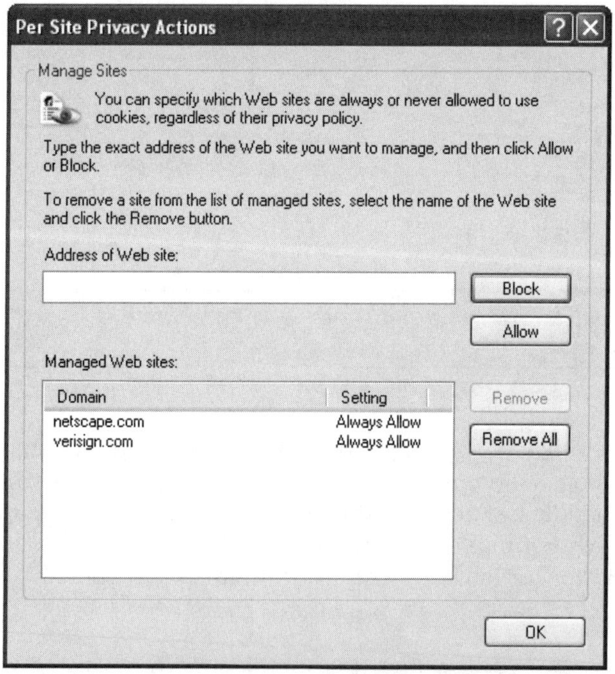

Figure 36-11.   *Use the Per Site Privacy Actions dialog box to allow or block cookies from specific web sites.*

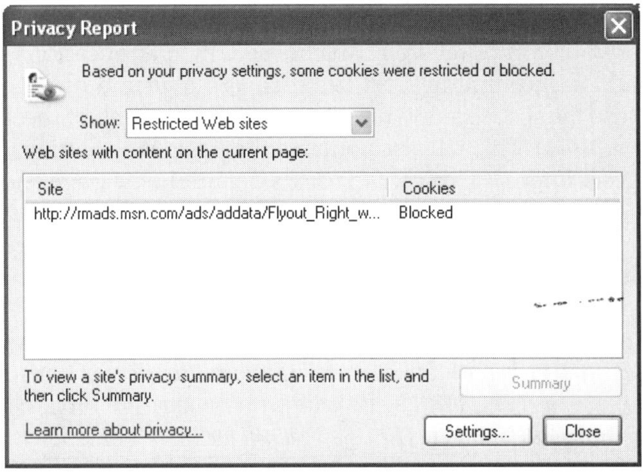

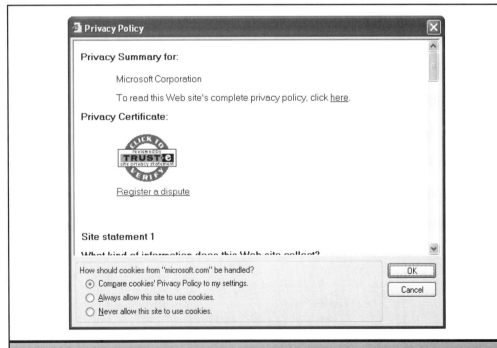

Figure 36-12. *Use the Privacy Report dialog box to see which cookies Internet Explorer has restricted or blocked for you.*

Figure 36-13. *If a site has a privacy policy, Internet Explorer automatically loads it in the Privacy Policy dialog box. From here, you can specify how to handle cookies for the site.*

Choosing Internet Applications

If you administer your computer, you can choose which applications Windows XP Professional should use for Internet services such as e-mail and newsgroups. To specify the applications, use the six drop-down lists on the Programs tab of the Internet Options dialog box (Figure 36-14). This tab also contains the Reset Web Settings button (which you can click to reset Internet Explorer to use its default home page and search page) and a check box for specifying whether Internet Explorer should check to see whether it's the default browser. When this check box is selected, Internet Explorer checks at startup to see if it's the default browser and prompts you to restore it to the default if it's not.

Your default browser is the browser associated with Internet file types and services. For example, when you click a URL in a document, Windows XP Professional activates or launches your default browser. The usual reason for Internet Explorer to stop being the default browser is that you've used another browser that's grabbed the file associations from Internet Explorer.

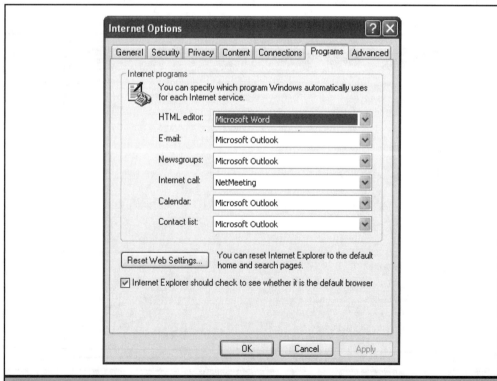

Figure 36-14.   *If you administer your computer, use the controls on the Programs tab of the Internet Options dialog box to specify the applications to use for Internet services.*

Administrators have full control over these options:

- An administrator can prevent you from configuring any of these applications (or they can suppress the Programs tab of the Internet Options dialog box altogether). Alternatively, they can prevent you from changing "messaging" settings. Doing so makes the E-mail drop-down list, the Newsgroups drop-down list, and the Internet Call drop-down list unavailable. (The other three drop-down lists remain available.) In a separate setting, an administrator can also prevent you from changing the Calendar drop-down list and the Contact drop-down list.

- An administrator can also disable the Reset Web Settings button so that you can't reset Internet Explorer to its default home page and search page.

- An administrator can also disable the Internet Explorer Should Check to See Whether It Is the Default Browser check box.

Using Internet Explorer Effectively

This section presents some tips for using Internet Explorer effectively. These tips range from setting your home page and search page, to using multiple windows and optimizing the view in each window, to accessing FTP sites.

As with much of this chapter, in a domain environment, an administrator may have prevented you from taking some of these actions.

Setting Your Home Page

Your home page is the page Internet Explorer loads when you start Internet Explorer without specifying a different location. (For example, if you launch Internet Explorer by clicking a link in an e-mail message, Internet Explorer displays the linked page rather than your home page.)

In a domain environment, an administrator will likely have set a home page for you—for example, so that all users in the domain see the same home page when they start Internet Explorer. You may be allowed to change this home page.

If you're allowed to change your home page, set it in either of the following ways:

- Browse to the page you want to use as your home page. Choose Tools | Internet Options to display the Internet Options dialog box, and then click the Use Current button in the Home Page group box. Click the Apply button.

- Choose Tools | Internet Options to display the Internet Options dialog box, and then enter the URL for the page in the Address text box. Click the Apply button.

In most cases, it's useful to have a home page that contains links to sites and pages you frequent. (If you're allowed to set your own home page, you may even want to use a custom page you create yourself that contains only the links you want.) But sometimes you may want to use a blank page as your home page. Using a blank page makes Internet Explorer load quickly and is good for when you don't have an Internet connection available—for example, when you and your laptop are on the road or in the air.

To use a blank page, click the Use Blank button in the Home Page group box on the General tab of the Internet Options dialog box.

Setting Your Search Page

An administrator may have customized Internet Explorer's search options for you, and you may not be able to change them. If you *are* allowed to change the search options, choose Change Preferences | Change Internet Search Behavior to display the Internet Search Behavior panel. Choose between Search Companion and Classic Internet Search. Then choose the default search engine to use and click the OK button.

Using Multiple Internet Explorer Windows

You can open multiple Internet Explorer windows at the same time. By opening different windows to different web sites or web pages, you can browse more quickly than by using a single window. Internet Explorer's default setting is to open each link you click in the same browser window unless the link specifies that the browser opens a new window.

The following are the easiest ways to open new Internet Explorer windows:

- To open a new window to the current page, choose File | New | Window or press CTRL-N.

- To open a new Internet Explorer window to your home page, choose Start | Internet.

- To open a link in a new window instead of the current window, right-click the link and select Open in New Window from the shortcut menu.

When you click an Internet shortcut in another application (for example, a hyperlink in an e-mail message or a Word document), Internet Explorer, by default, opens the web page in your existing Internet Explorer window. If you have several Internet Explorer windows open, Internet Explorer reuses the latest window. To prevent Internet Explorer from doing this, clear the Reuse Windows for Launching Shortcuts check box on the Advanced tab of the Internet Options dialog box.

An administrator may prevent you from opening new windows. If they do, the Window command on the File | New submenu is unavailable. The Open in New Window link on the shortcut menu is available, but it displays a Restrictions dialog box instead of opening the linked page in a new window.

Using Full-Screen View Whenever It's Helpful

Internet Explorer offers a full-screen view that maximizes the amount of information you can see in the browser. To access full-screen view, choose View | Full Screen or press F11. Press F11 again (or click the Restore button) to exit full-screen view.

Administrators can disable full-screen view, but they're unlikely to do so. Full-screen view doesn't represent a security threat. The biggest danger of full-screen view is that it might confuse a beginning user.

Hiding the Toolbars You Don't Need

If you have a small screen, you can increase the amount of information you can view at a time by hiding any toolbars you don't need. To toggle the display of a toolbar, choose its entry from the View | Toolbars submenu or the toolbars shortcut menu. (To display the toolbars shortcut menu, right-click any displayed toolbar or the menu bar.)

An administrator may prevent you from displaying and hiding toolbars.

Customizing the Toolbar

Internet Explorer's toolbar comes with a standard selection of buttons. An administrator may preconfigure the toolbar for you—for example, by adding custom buttons and removing buttons you supposedly won't need. An administrator can also prevent you from customizing the toolbar.

If you're allowed to customize the toolbar, do so as described in "Customizing the Windows Explorer Toolbars" in Chapter 8. Configure the toolbar to contain the buttons you need in the order that's most useful to you.

Customizing Your Links Bar

Your Links bar provides quick access to a selection of sites. As you saw in Chapter 7, you can also display the Links bar as one of the desktop toolbars, which lets you access key sites directly from the taskbar.

An administrator can customize the entries on the Links bar for you—for example, to provide corporate resources that you're encouraged to access. You may or may not be allowed to change these entries.

If you are allowed to customize your Links bar, do so as follows:

■ Drag the Links bar to where you want it to appear. (You may need to issue a Lock the Toolbars command from the View | Toolbars submenu or the toolbars shortcut menu to unlock the toolbars before you can move them.) For example, you might display the Links bar on a separate line under the Address bar to give yourself room for plenty of links.

- Add new links to the Links bar by displaying a page you want to add, and then dragging the page icon that appears at the left end of the Address box to the Links bar. Internet Explorer creates a new icon when you drop the link.

- Shorten any long names that buttons have so you can fit more buttons on the Links bar.

- Rearrange the buttons so that the most useful ones appear toward the left end. That way, if the window isn't wide enough to display all the buttons on the Links bar, you'll have immediate access to the most important buttons.

Using Favorites

As in Windows Explorer, you can create favorites in Internet Explorer to give yourself quick access to specific URLs. You can access your favorites either from the Favorites menu or the Favorites Explorer bar. You can even make your favorites available offline, as discussed in the next subsection.

In a domain environment, an administrator can take several actions with favorites:

- The administrator can customize favorites to provide a list of recommended sites that you can easily access. (The administrator may place some sites on both the Links bar and the Favorites menu. The Favorites menu allows for a larger number of favorites and for them to be organized into categories.)

- The administrator can delete the default favorites Internet Explorer provides.

- The administrator can delete all entries on your Favorites menu (including any favorites you've created).

- The administrator can hide the Favorites menu and Favorites Explorer bar so that you can't access the favorites at all.

- The administrator can prevent you from importing and exporting favorites. If the administrator does this, the Import/Export Wizard still runs, but when it finishes, you see a message that the feature has been disabled.

Creating Favorites

If you're allowed to create favorites, follow these steps:

1. In Internet Explorer, display the page you want to make a favorite.

2. Choose Favorites | Add to Favorites to display the Add Favorite dialog box. By default, Internet Explorer initially displays the reduced version of the Add Favorite dialog box, as shown on the left in Figure 36-15.

3. Check the name Internet Explorer has entered in the Name text box. (Internet Explorer takes this name from the title of the web page.) Change the name if necessary. In this name, you can't use any characters that you can't use in filenames. For example, you can't use a colon (:), a backslash (\) or forward slash (/), an asterisk (*), or a question mark (?).

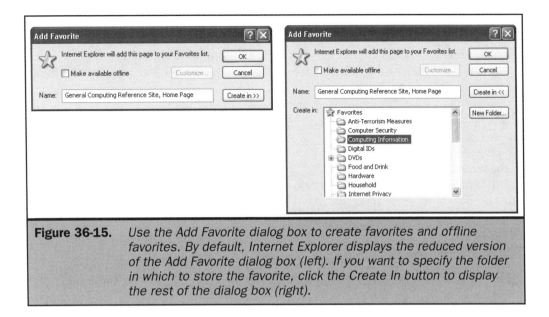

Figure 36-15.   *Use the Add Favorite dialog box to create favorites and offline
favorites. By default, Internet Explorer displays the reduced version
of the Add Favorite dialog box (left). If you want to specify the folder
in which to store the favorite, click the Create In button to display
the rest of the dialog box (right).*

4. To create the favorite directly on the Favorites menu, click the OK button.
   Internet Explorer creates the favorite and closes the Add Favorite dialog box.

5. To create the favorite in a folder on the Favorites menu, click the Create In
   button. Internet Explorer displays the rest of the Add Favorite dialog box, as
   shown on the right in Figure 36-15.

6. Select the existing folder in which to create the favorite, or click the New Folder
   button and create a new folder.

7. Click the OK button. Internet Explorer creates the favorite and closes the Add
   Favorite dialog box.

    You can create a new favorite at the top level by pressing CTRL-D.

Importing and Exporting Favorites

If you have a list of favorites from another computer, you can import it by issuing a
File | Import and Export command and following the steps of the Import/Export
Wizard. You can also use this wizard to export your favorites for importing on another
computer (or for backup).

Accessing Your Favorites

You can access your favorites either from the Favorites menu or from the Favorites
Explorer bar. Click the Favorites button on the toolbar, choose View | Explorer Bar |
Favorites, or press CTRL-I to toggle the display of the Favorites Explorer bar.

Because the Favorites Explorer bar lets you expand multiple categories of favorites at the same time, the bar provides an easier way to find favorites than does the Favorites menu, which can display only one submenu of favorites at a time. The disadvantage to the Favorites Explorer bar is that it consumes space on screen that you may need for browsing.

Organizing Your Favorites

To organize your favorites into folders, or to adjust their properties, choose Favorites | Organize Favorites or click the Organize button in the Favorites Explorer bar and work in the Organize Favorites dialog box (Figure 36-16). From here, you can rename and delete favorites and their folders, create new folders, and move favorites to folders. Most of the controls are self-explanatory. You can also change a favorite into an offline favorite by selecting in the list box, selecting the Make Available Offline check box, and then clicking the Properties button to display the Properties dialog box and choose suitable settings.

Your favorites are stored in the %userprofile%\Favorites folder. You can add shortcuts to this folder to add entries for other items on your Favorites menu.

Using Offline Favorites

If you need to be able to access certain pages when your computer is offline, use Internet Explorer's offline favorites feature to download and store copies of the pages

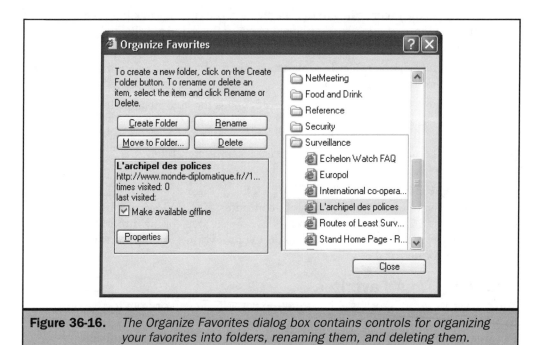

Figure 36-16.   *The Organize Favorites dialog box contains controls for organizing your favorites into folders, renaming them, and deleting them.*

you want to be able to access. For example, if you take a laptop on the road, you can use offline favorites to take with you copies of the pages you need to access.

Offline favorites can also be useful if you have a slow Internet connection (or if you're competing with many other users to share a fast Internet connection—for example, in a corporate situation). You can designate your offline favorites to be downloaded at a convenient time (for example, when your Internet connection is less busy, or when you're doing something else) so that they'll be available instantly when you want to access them.

An administrator may have prevented you from using offline favorites. If so, the Make Available Offline check box in the Add Favorite dialog box will be unavailable. (This setting is separate from, but subordinate to, the setting that prevents you from creating favorites. So if you can't create favorites, you won't be able to create offline favorites either.)

To create an offline favorite, follow the steps in the previous section for creating a regular favorite, but select the Make Available Offline check box in the Add Favorite dialog box. That sets Internet Explorer to create an offline favorite consisting of just the current web page itself.

To make Internet Explorer download pages linked to the current page, or to specify a user name or password for the site so that you won't need to enter them manually, click the Customize button. Internet Explorer starts the Offline Favorites Wizard, which walks you through the process of creating the favorite. Most of the process is straightforward, but you should be clear on the following points:

■ To download web pages linked to the current page, select the Yes option button on the Set Up the Following Page page of the wizard and enter the number of levels of links in the Download Pages *NN* Links Deep from This Page text box. You can enter 0, 1, 2, or 3. A setting of 0 downloads no linked pages. A setting of 1 downloads pages directly linked to the current page and usually nets only a moderate amount of information. A setting of 2 downloads pages directly linked to the current page and pages directly linked to those pages, which can make a lot of data. A setting of 3 downloads a third layer of linked pages, which can add up to a vast amount of data. (That said, for smaller web sites with fewer links, a setting of 3 may be appropriate: it will download most of the web site, enabling you to navigate large areas of the site when offline.)

Note *You can place some restrictions on what Internet Explorer downloads for an offline favorite by working on the Download tab of the favorite's Properties dialog box. These options are discussed next.*

■ You can set the offline favorite up to be synchronized on a schedule or manually. If you opt for a schedule, you can use an existing schedule (if you've defined one before) or create a new schedule to synchronize the page every so many days at a specified time. For example, you might create a schedule that synchronized your offline favorites very early every morning so that the updated favorites were ready for you when you started work each day.

■ If the web site the page is on requires a user name and password, you can enter them in the wizard for Internet Explorer to use automatically when synchronizing the favorite.

After finishing the wizard, select the location for the favorite and close the Add Favorite dialog box. Windows XP Professional displays the Synchronizing dialog box while Internet Explorer synchronizes the offline favorite.

After creating the favorite, you can set further properties for it. These are the other key choices you can make on the tabs of the Properties dialog box for an offline favorite:

■ On the Web Document tab, you can assign a shortcut key to the offline favorite. You can also change the favorite from being an offline favorite to being a regular favorite.

■ On the Schedule tab, you can change the schedule for the offline favorite or create a new schedule.

■ On the Download tab (shown on the left in Figure 36-17), you can specify which items to download for the favorite. Clear the Follow Links Outside of This Page's Web Site check box to prevent the offline favorite from including pages on other web sites. Use the Limit Hard-Disk Usage for This Page to *NN* Kilobytes check box and text box to prevent the offline favorite from taking up too much disk space. To specify advanced download options, click the Advanced button and work in the Advanced Download Options dialog box (shown on the right in Figure 36-17). In this dialog box, you can choose whether to download images, sound and video files, and ActiveX controls and Java applets. You can also choose whether to follow links only to HTML pages or to other types of pages as well.

■ Also on the Download tab, you can choose whether to receive notification when the main page for the favorite changes.

Saving Web Pages Locally

If you need to retain the information from a web page, consider saving the page to a local or network disk. You'll then be able to open the page at any time, whether you have an Internet connection or not. The page will remain in the state it was in when you saved it—the copy you save won't be updated as the live page may be.

To save a web page locally, display the page, choose File | Save As, and then choose suitable settings in the Save Web Page dialog box. The most important setting here is the Save As Type drop-down list, which offers the choices explained in Table 36-3.

Saving web pages locally raises several concerns, including the following:

■ Saving other people's copyrighted material may breach copyright and could expose you or your company to legal redress.

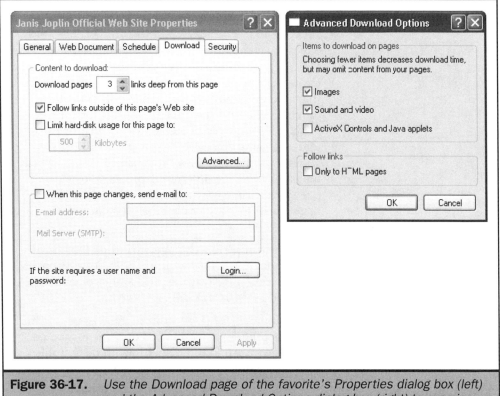

Figure 36-17. *Use the Download page of the favorite's Properties dialog box (left) and the Advanced Download Options dialog box (right) to exercise finer control over what's downloaded and what's ignored.*

- Pages that users save may contain harmful or potentially harmful scripts.
- The saved pages take up disk space.

Because of these concerns, an administrator may prevent you from saving web pages at all. Alternatively, they may prevent you from saving complete web pages but allow you to save pages as HTML files or text files.

Using View Source to See the HTML Behind a Page

You can view the HTML source code of a web page by choosing View | Source or by right-clicking a web page and choosing View Source from the shortcut menu. This feature can be useful for understanding how HTML works and getting ideas on how to code your own web pages.

Save As Type Format	Explanation
Web Page, Complete	Saves the complete web page, including the text, HTML codes, graphics, scripts, and other elements. (Note that scripts may not work because the paths they reference may not be available from the location to which you save the file.) To save the complete web page, Internet Explorer creates an HTML document with the name you assign to the page and a folder with that name and _files. (For example, if you specify the name My Page, Internet Explorer saves the web page as My Page.htm and creates the folder My Page_files.) This folder contains elements such as graphics and scripts.
Web Archive, Single File	Saves the complete web page, including the text, HTML codes, graphics, scripts, and other elements. Internet Explorer saves the page and its elements in a Modified HTML (MHTML) archive file.
Web Page, HTML Only	Saves only the HTML portions of the web page. This option is useful when you need only the formatted text of the page and can dispense with the graphics, scripts, and other elements. The resulting HTML file is relatively small but larger than a text-only file (described next).
Text File	Saves only the text portions of the web page, without the HTML codes. This option is useful when you need only the text without the formatting. For example, on an order confirmation page, you might require just the text with the order number and details rather than any graphics the page contains. The resulting text file is small.

Table 36-3.   *Formats for Saving Web Pages Locally*

An administrator can disable the Source command on the View menu. However, even if they do so, you'll still be able to use the View Source command from the shortcut menu—unless the administrator has also disabled the shortcut menu.

Accessing FTP Sites

This section discusses the key considerations for using Internet Explorer to access FTP sites—sites that provide files for download via the File Transfer Protocol.

If an FTP site permits anonymous access, Internet Explorer can access it without your supplying any information manually.

The best way to access an FTP site that requires a user name and password is by taking the following steps:

1. Browse to the site's URL.

2. Choose File | Login As to display the Log On As dialog box (Figure 36-18).

3. Enter your user name and password.

4. For security, make sure the Save Password check box is cleared.

5. Click the Log On button.

For security, it's best not to save your password for an FTP site. However, if you need to access an FTP site frequently, you may want to save your password to make the logon process quicker.

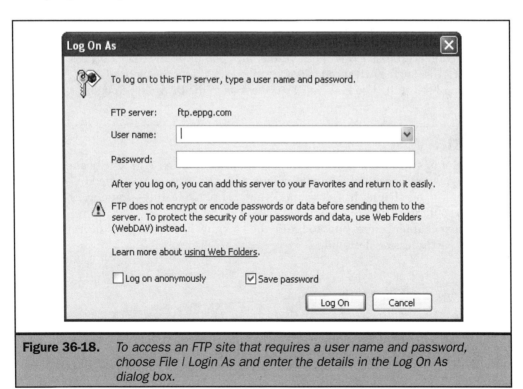

Figure 36-18.   *To access an FTP site that requires a user name and password, choose File | Login As and enter the details in the Log On As dialog box.*

You can also access an FTP site that requires a user name and password by entering this information with the URL, using the following syntax:

```
ftp://username:password@ftpserver/url
```

Here, *ftpserver* is the address of the FTP server, *url* is the URL on the server, *username* is your user name for the server, and *password* is your password for the server.

 If you're allowed to create favorites, you can create a favorite for the FTP site—including not only your user name but also your password if you want.

By default, Internet Explorer attempts to display the contents of FTP sites in Folder view. Folder view makes the FTP site look like a Windows Explorer folder so that you can use views (List view, Details view, Icon view, and so on) and manipulate the items on the site as if they were files. Folder view doesn't work for certain types of proxy connections. If you turn off Folder view, Internet Explorer displays FTP sites in an HTML list layout. To control whether Internet Explorer uses Folder view, select or clear the Enable Folder View for FTP Sites check box in the Browsing category on the Advanced tab of the Internet Options dialog box.

In regular FTP, your computer needs to supply its IP address to establish the connection with the FTP server. If your computer is located behind a firewall (as is likely if your computer connects to the Internet through a corporate connection), it may not be able to establish regular FTP connections. Instead, you may need to use passive FTP, in which the connection is established without your computer supplying its IP address. To use passive FTP, display the Advanced tab of the Internet Options dialog box (Tools | Internet Options) and select the Use Passive FTP check box in the Browsing category.

Summary

This chapter has discussed how to configure Internet Explorer for security and for ease of working. Because many of Internet Explorer's features can be configured by a domain administrator, this chapter has elaborated on many of the features you may or may not be able to configure.

The next chapter covers how to build your own web site using the tools that Windows XP Professional provides.

The
Complete
Reference

Windows
XP

Chapter 37

Creating Your Own
Web Site on IIS

This chapter briefly covers considerations for implementing your own web site using the version of Internet Information Services (IIS) included with Windows XP Professional. The chapter starts by discussing how to decide whether IIS is suitable for your needs or whether you'd be better off with another solution. It then describes how to install IIS, how to configure the options you're likely to need on Windows XP Professional, and how to put content on your web site.

Should You Host the Site on IIS or Elsewhere?

Before you spend time installing, configuring, and setting up a web site on IIS, take a quick reality check to ensure that using IIS is sensible for your situation and your needs.

In a domain environment, the administrators are unlikely to allow you to install, configure, and use IIS on your Windows XP Professional computer. In fact, the administrators will probably actively prevent you from doing anything with IIS. This is for two main reasons:

- First, most company web sites are managed centrally by administrators. This applies to both external web sites and internal web sites (for example, departmental web sites). Allowing users to host their own sites on their workstations creates unnecessary work for administrators.

- Second, users running unnecessary services decrease the performance and security of the network.

Another reason is that running IIS increases the demand on the computer and slows its performance.

If you're using Windows XP Professional in a home-office or small-office environment rather than a domain environment, and you administer your own computer, you can install and use IIS. However, before you do, be clear on the limitations on IIS in Windows XP Professional and what your alternatives are for hosting a web site.

The killer limitation is that Windows XP Professional's version of IIS is limited to ten concurrent connections. That's ten *connections*, not ten *users*; because any user who connects to your web site may use more than one connection at any given time, ten concurrent connections is typically enough for only a small handful of users at a time. This limitation on Windows XP Professional's version of IIS is intended to force anyone who wants to host a full-scale web site on Windows to use Windows 2000 Server or Windows.NET Server. These server versions of Windows include versions of IIS whose ability to accept connections is limited by the computer's power and the bandwidth available to it rather than by an artificial constraint.

This limitation makes IIS on Windows XP Professional little use for hosting a public web site—if the site gets more than a very few simultaneous users, it will have to start refusing connections, which will discourage most users from attempting to access the site. A second limitation is that Windows XP Professional doesn't provide domain name service, so you'll need to either use a third-party product or a third-party DNS service to enable users to connect to your web site by its domain name rather than by its IP address.

A third limitation is that IIS on Windows XP Professional can run only one web site at a time. However, you can create multiple sites on IIS, and then switch between them as necessary. Switching between sites won't help you maintain a web presence, but it's helpful for testing sites you're developing.

> **Caution** *In October 2002, the FBI and the SANS (SysAdmin, Audit, Network, Security) Institute issued a list of the 20 "most unwanted" security flaws for computers running Windows and Unix/Linux. IIS took the number one spot for vulnerabilities to Windows systems. Don't install and run IIS unnecessarily, because doing so may enable an attacker to take unwelcome actions on your computer or network. If you do run IIS, be diligent in applying any updates and patches Microsoft releases to reduce your security exposure.*

If you want to have a public web site, you'll do much better to pay an ISP or a web-hosting service to host the site for you. That way, you get as many connections as you're prepared to pay for; the ISP or service provides the bandwidth; and you don't have to worry about keeping the hardware or software running to make the web site continuously available to those who might want to access it.

IIS's limitations may sound severe—and they are—but they don't mean IIS on Windows XP Professional is useless. You may find IIS useful for running a small, private web site within your company or your workgroup to deploy web-based content (for example, a company knowledge base or procedure manual). You may also find IIS useful for testing web sites you're developing, making files available via the FTP service (discussed in the next chapter) for you or your colleagues to download when you're on the road, or providing remote-printing capabilities.

Installing IIS

Default installations of Windows XP Professional don't include IIS, so you'll probably need to install IIS manually. To install IIS, follow these steps:

1. Display the Add or Remove Programs window by choosing Start | Control Panel | Add or Remove Programs or running **appwiz.cpl**.

2. Click the Add/Remove Windows Components button to launch the Windows Components Wizard.

3. Select the Internet Information Services (IIS) check box in the Components list box.

   ■ Selecting the Internet Information Services (IIS) check box installs most of the IIS components: the Internet Information Services snap-in, the IIS documentation, the FrontPage 2000 Server Extensions, the SMTP Service, the World Wide Web service, and the Printers Virtual Directory. This selection omits the FTP service, the Scripts Virtual Directory, and Remote Desktop Web Connection.

Note

The World Wide Web Service is the service that enables you to make web content available, so you must install it. The Internet Information Services snap-in is necessary for configuring and managing your web site. The IIS documentation tends to be helpful if you're using IIS at all. You need the FrontPage 2000 Server Extensions only if you'll be using Microsoft FrontPage to publish your web site to the web server.

■ To include the FTP service, select the Internet Information Services (IIS) item in the Components list box and click the Details button. In the resulting Internet Information Services (IIS) dialog box (shown on the left in Figure 37-1), select the File Transfer Protocol (FTP) Service check box.

■ To include the Scripts Virtual Directory and Remote Desktop Web Connection, select the World Wide Web Service item in the Internet Information Services (IIS) dialog box and click the Details button. In the resulting World Wide Web Service dialog box (shown on the right in Figure 37-1), select the Remote Desktop Web Connection check box and the Scripts Virtual Directory check box. Close the World Wide Web Service dialog box and the Internet Information Services (IIS) dialog box.

4. Click the Next button in the Windows Components Wizard to finish installing the service. You'll need to provide your Windows XP Professional CD. If you installed Windows XP Service Pack 1 separately, you'll need to supply your Service Pack 1 CD as well.

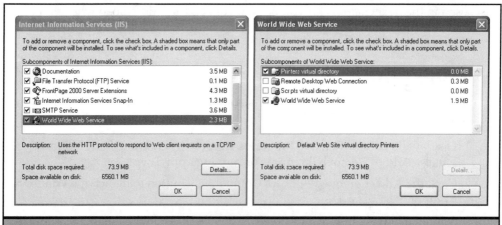

Figure 37-1. *To install all the IIS components, you need to drill down to the Internet Information Services (IIS) dialog box (left) and the World Wide Web Service dialog box (right).*

Configuring Your Web Site on IIS

When you install IIS, the Windows Components Wizard automatically creates a basic web site (named Default Web Site) that you can use as the basis for your site. While you can delete the Default Web Site and create a web site entirely from scratch, using the Default Web Site as the basis for a custom site can save you a considerable amount of time and effort.

To configure a web site via IIS, work in the web site's Properties dialog box. The following subsections describe the options you're likely to need to set for a small web site. They don't describe more advanced options you're less likely to need, such as ISAPI filters, Secure Sockets Layer (SSL) encryption, and server extensions. You might need to use some of these advanced features on web sites you're developing—but in that case, you'll benefit from getting a book that focuses on developing web sites with IIS.

Opening Your Default Web Site

To start working with your Default Web Site, open it in the Internet Information Services console. Follow these steps:

1. Choose Start | Administrative Tools | Internet Information Services or Start | All Programs | Administrative Tools | Internet Information Services (depending on how you have the Start menu configured) to open the Internet Information Services console.

2. In the left pane, double-click the item for your computer to expand it.

3. In the left pane, double-click the Web Sites item to expand it.

4. Select the Default Web Site item and issue a Properties command from the Action menu or the shortcut menu to display the site's Properties dialog box.

Choosing Options on the Web Site Tab

The Web Site tab of the Properties dialog box (Figure 37-2) contains basic configuration parameters for a web site.

Setting the Description, IP Address, and TCP Port

In the Description text box, enter the name you want to assign to the site in place of the default name, Default Web Site. This name appears in the IIS console and is primarily for your benefit, so you can make the name descriptive.

In the IP Address text box, you can assign to the web site one of the IP addresses defined in Control Panel. If your computer has only one IP address, you can safely leave the default choice—(All Unassigned)—for this setting to make this site the default web site for the computer. The default web site responds to all IP addresses assigned to this computer and not specifically to another site. If your computer has multiple IP addresses,

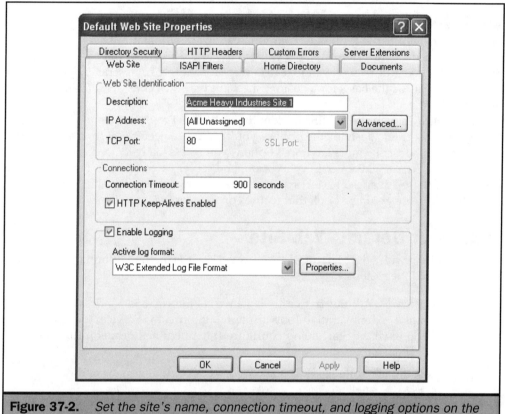

Figure 37-2. *Set the site's name, connection timeout, and logging options on the Web Site tab of the Properties dialog box.*

you should specify the appropriate IP address to prevent IIS from responding from IP traffic you don't want it to respond to.

To configure multiple identities or multiple SSL identities for the web site, click the Advanced button and choose options in the Advanced Multiple Web Site Configuration dialog box. Because of IIS's connection limitations, you're unlikely to need to use these options on Windows XP Professional.

In the TCP Port text box, you *can* change the default port (80) to a different port, but you'll seldom need to do so. Port 80 is the standard port for HTTP connections. If you change this port, anybody who needs to connect to your site will have to know the port number and will need to enter it manually. (Changing the port can be used as a security measure.)

In the SSL Port text box, enter the port to use for Secure Sockets Layer (SSL) encryption. This text box is available only after you've installed an SSL server certificate and created a server key pair and certificate request.

Configuring Connection Timeouts

In the Connection group box, you can change the timeout value in the Connection Timeout text box. The default setting is 900 seconds (15 minutes), which is longer than it needs to be for most purposes. Consider setting a shorter timeout to make sure inactive users don't hold your web site's limited number of connections open, thus denying them to other users who need to connect.

The Connection group box also contains the HTTP Keep-Alives Enabled check box, which is selected by default. *HTTP keep-alives* let a client that has connected to the server keep a connection open to the server so that it can submit further requests without needing to establish a new connection with the server for each request. Disabling HTTP keep-alives drops connections more quickly but makes your server work harder because it needs to negotiate more connections.

Configuring Logging Options

The controls in the Enable Logging group box let you control which information IIS logs about your web site.

The Enable Logging check box is selected by default. For most sites, it's a good idea to log some information so that you can see who has been accessing your site, where they're coming from, and how long they're spending at the site. However, if your site is even moderately busy, the log will gather a lot of information and fill up quickly. (Because of IIS's limit of ten concurrent connections on Windows XP Professional, log bloat tends to be less of a problem on Windows XP Professional than on Windows 2000 Server or Windows.NET Server.)

If you leave logging enabled, select the log format you want to use in the Active Log Format drop-down list. Your choices are the Microsoft IIS Log File Format, the NCSA Common Log File Format, and the W3C Extended Log File Format (the default; W3C is the abbreviation for the World Wide Web Consortium, www.w3.org). In most cases, the W3C Extended Log File Format is the best choice, because it lets you capture more information about the people who access your FTP site than do the Microsoft IIS Log File Format or the NCSA Common Log File Format. (NCSA is the National Center for Supercomputing Applications. NCSA's log file format is widely used.)

To choose logging options for the log format you chose, click the Properties button and work in the Extended Logging Properties dialog box (for the W3C Extended Log File Format), the NCSA Logging Properties dialog box (for the NCSA Common Log File Format), or the Microsoft Logging Properties dialog box (for the Microsoft IIS Log File Format). Figure 37-3 shows the two tabs of the Extended Logging Properties dialog box. The Microsoft Logging Properties dialog box and the NCSA Logging Properties dialog box offer the same options as the General Properties tab of the Extended Logging Properties dialog box except for the Use Local Time for File Naming and Rollover check box, which these two dialog boxes don't have.

The General Properties tab of the Extended Logging Properties dialog box lets you specify when IIS should create a new log file: hourly, daily, weekly, monthly, when the log file size reaches a certain size, or never (choose the Unlimited File Size button). The

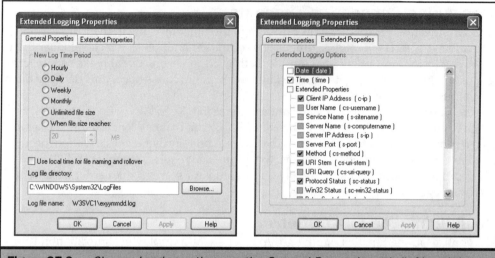

Figure 37-3.   Choose logging options on the General Properties tab (left) and the Extended Properties tab (right) of the Extended Logging Properties dialog box.

Use Local Time for File Naming and Rollover check box controls whether IIS uses local time rather than Greenwich Mean Time (GMT) for creating daily, weekly, and monthly logs, and for naming hourly, daily, weekly, and monthly logs.

 If you select the Unlimited File Size option button in the New Log Time Period group box, you need to stop the IIS service before you can access the log file.

The Log File Directory text box shows you where IIS is currently storing the folder. The default is the %systemroot%\System32\LogFiles folder. You can use the Browse button and the resulting Browse for Folder dialog box to change the location.

The Extended Properties tab of the Extended Logging Properties dialog box lets you choose which extended items of information to include in the log. For example, you might choose to include the date, time, client IP address, and user name.

Choosing Options on the Home Directory Tab

The Home Directory tab of the Properties dialog box (Figure 37-4) contains options for specifying the location of the files that make up your web site, for setting permissions on the folder, and for choosing settings for applications that will run from the site.

Specifying the Home Directory and Setting Permissions on It

Your web site's home directory can be located in a folder on your computer, in a network share on another computer, or on a web server. Specify the locations as follows:

- To use a folder on your computer, select the A Directory Located on This Computer option button. (This is the default setting.) Enter the path in the Local Path text box, either by typing the path or clicking the Browse button and using the resulting Browse for Folder dialog box to identify the folder. The default location is the %systemdrive%\inetpub\wwwroot folder. Use this folder unless you have a good reason to change it.

Tip *For security, locate your home directory on an NTFS partition and closely guard permissions for changing the directory's contents. Give the Read permission to the Everyone group and the IUSR account (IIS's automated user account) so that they can view the contents of the web site.*

- To use a folder on another computer, select the A Share Located on Another Computer option button. IIS replaces the Local Path text box with the Network

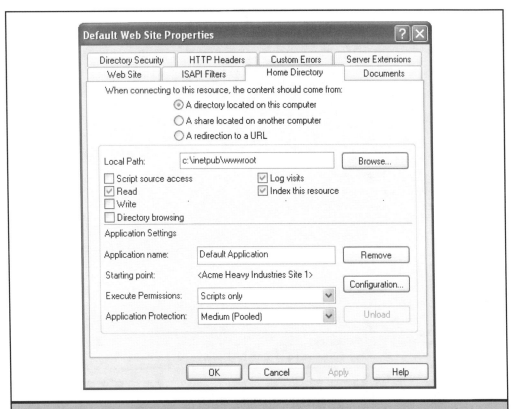

Figure 37-4. *On the Home Directory tab of the Properties dialog box, specify the folder, network share, or URL that contains the files for your web site.*

Directory text box and the Browse button with the Connect As button.
Enter a UNC path to the share in the Network Share text box (for example,
\\acmeheavy801\ourweb). Click the Connect As button and use the Network
Directory Security Credentials dialog box to specify the user name and password
to use for connecting to the network share.

■ To use a directory on a web server, select the A Redirection to a URL option button.
IIS changes the Home Directory tab of the Properties dialog box to show different
controls (Figure 37-5). Enter the URL in the Redirect To text box, and then select
the appropriate check box or boxes in the The Client Will Be Sent To list: The Exact
URL Entered Above (to redirect without adding any part of the original URL),
A Directory below This One (to redirect a parent directory to a child directory),
or A Permanent Redirection for This Resource (to attempt to force the client
browser to redirect all requests for the original URL to the redirected URL).

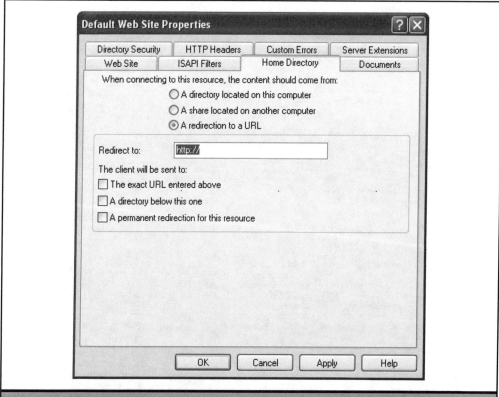

Figure 37-5.   *IIS displays a different set of controls on the Home Directory tab*
for redirecting the home directory to a web server.

If you use a local folder or a network share for your home directory, use the check boxes under the Local Path text box or the Network Directory text box to specify which permissions visitors to the site have. The default setting is Read access, which lets visitors see what's there but not change it. You'll seldom need to grant visitors Script Source Access, Write, or Directory Browsing permissions.

The Directory Browsing permission lets visitors see the folders and files that make up your web site. Some sites use this permission to let visitors access files they're offering for download. However, if you need to provide files for download, Windows XP Professional's FTP service is a better tool.

Posting Material on Your Web Site

To post material on your web site, copy files and folders to your home directory by using standard Windows techniques.

Choosing Application Settings

If you use a local folder or a network share for your home directory, the lower part of the Home Directory tab provides controls for choosing application settings. You won't usually need to configure these settings, because you're unlikely to need to run web server applications on Windows XP Professional. (However, you might need to run server applications if you're using IIS on Windows XP Professional for developing and testing web sites.)

Choosing Options on the Documents Tab

The Documents tab of the Properties dialog box (Figure 37-6) lets you specify the name of one or more default pages for the web site. The default page is the page that the site displays when the user enters the site's name but not a page name. For example, if the user enters **http://www.acmevirtualindustries.com**, the web server displays a default page such as http://www.acmevirtualindustries.com/default.htm.

IIS's default configuration is to use the default pages Default.htm, Default.asp, index.htm, and iisstart.asp, in that order. (ASP is the file extension for Active Server Pages documents.) You can rearrange this order by using the arrow buttons if necessary. For example, if your web site's home directory contains both a default.htm file and an index.htm page, IIS by default displays the default.htm file rather than the index.htm file. To make IIS display index.htm first, you would move it to the top of the list. (You could also remove Default.htm from the list.)

You can add other default page names to those on the default list. For example, if your default page is named index.html rather than index.htm, you would add **index.html** to the Enable Default Document list box and use the arrow buttons to move it to the top of the list.

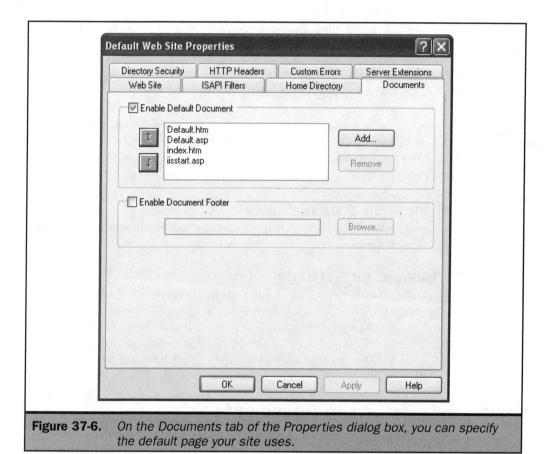

Figure 37-6.   On the Documents tab of the Properties dialog box, you can specify the default page your site uses.

You can turn off IIS's use of default documents by clearing the Enable Default Document check box. However, a default document is helpful for most sites.

Choosing Options on the Directory Security Tab

The Directory Security tab of the Properties dialog box (Figure 37-7) contains options for controlling authentication and anonymous access to your site and implementing secure communications via SSL. This section discusses authentication and anonymous access but not SSL, which is an advanced feature you're unlikely to need on a small web site.

Figure 37-7. *From the Directory Security tab of the Properties dialog box, you can control authentication and anonymous access. You can also implement SSL if you have an SSL server certificate.*

Note *The Directory Security tab also contains disabled controls for restricting access to your web site by IP addresses or domain name. These controls are disabled because IIS on Windows XP Professional doesn't offer these features—they're available only in Windows 2000 Server and Windows.NET Server.*

To control anonymous access and edit authentication methods for your web site, click the Edit button in the Anonymous Access and Authentication Control group box. IIS displays the Authentication Methods dialog box (Figure 37-8).

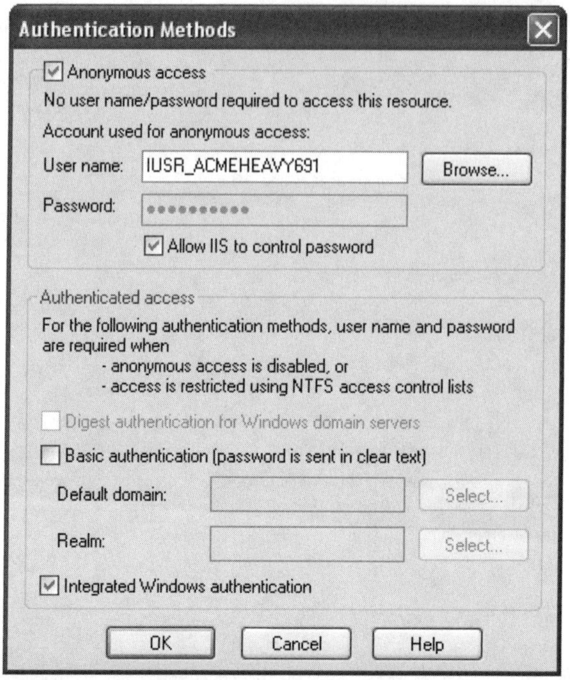

Figure 37-8.   *In the Authentication Methods dialog box, choose whether to allow anonymous access to your web site and specify which authentication methods to use for authenticated access.*

To permit anonymous access, select the Anonymous Access check box. (This check box is selected by default.) For anonymous access, IIS actually uses its built-in IUSR account (which is named *IUSR_computername*—for example, IUSR_ACMEHEAVY691). You can change this to another account if you want, but usually there's no reason to do so: it's more effective to use the IUSR account and restrict its permissions to prevent the account (and therefore any anonymous users) from taking actions they shouldn't.

For authenticated access to files and folders restricted using NTFS permissions, IIS offers the choice of Basic Authentication or Integrated Windows Authentication (select the appropriate check box). Integrated Windows Authentication uses encryption and so is more secure than Basic Authentication, which transmits passwords in clear text and so has the danger that a malefactor might intercept a password. Unfortunately, Integrated Windows Authentication doesn't work through proxy servers, but Basic Authentication does.

Integrated Windows Authentication causes the user's web browser to attempt to authenticate the user using the credentials under which they're logged on. If Integrated

Windows Authentication can't authenticate the user under those credentials, it prompts for the user name and password. By contrast, Basic Authentication immediately prompts for the user name and password.

When you permit anonymous access, IIS uses anonymous access first for every client. Only when a client is prevented by NTFS permissions from accessing a resource does IIS attempt to authenticate the user using Integrated Windows Authentication or Basic Authentication.

Choosing Options on the Custom Errors Tab

The Custom Errors tab of the Properties dialog box (shown on the left in Figure 37-9) lets you configure the error messages that IIS displays when an HTTP error occurs. IIS comes with a full set of error messages that are stored in HTML files in the %systemroot%\ help\iisHelp\common folder. You can either edit these files directly by using any HTML editor or (better) specify an alternative page to use for any given error.

To specify an alternative page, select the error in the HTTP Error list and click the Edit Properties button. In the Error Mapping Properties dialog box (shown on the right in Figure 37-9), enter in the File text box the path and name of the file to use for the error.

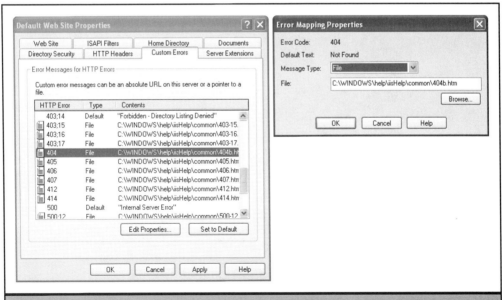

Figure 37-9.   *Use the Custom Errors tab of the Properties dialog box (left) and the Error Mapping Properties dialog box (right) to specify custom messages for HTTP errors.*

Using IIS to Share Printers on the Web

Another feature that IIS provides is sharing printers on the web. You may occasionally find it useful to be able to print to your small-office or home-office printer remotely across the web. (If you choose not to use IIS for this purpose, you can use Remote Desktop Connection to establish a remote connection to your network and print to your printer from there.)

IIS automatically shares on the Internet any printers you're sharing via Windows XP. After setting up IIS, you'll be able to connect to the printers as described in "Setting Up an Internet Printer" in Chapter 12.

Summary

This chapter has discussed how to install and configure IIS for creating your own web site on Windows XP Professional. The chapter has also covered the limitations of the version of IIS included with Windows XP Professional and why you might consider alternatives to IIS.

The next chapter covers how to use Windows XP Professional's FTP service to allow users to download or upload files.

Chapter 38

Using FTP Service

T his chapter discusses how to use the FTP service included in IIS to run an FTP site. As you know if you've used the Internet more than a little, FTP is the abbreviation for File Transfer Protocol, a standard Internet protocol for transferring files from one computer to another. While many sites now use the Hypertext Transport Protocol (HTTP) for file transfer from their web sites, FTP remains a straightforward and efficient means of making files available for download.

This chapter covers the essentials of installing, configuring, and using the FTP service.

Should You Use Windows XP Professional's FTP Service?

As with IIS (discussed in the previous chapter), you should think seriously before installing and using Windows XP Professional's FTP service.

You're unlikely to need to install the FTP service on your computer in a domain environment. In fact, an administrator will probably prevent you from installing the FTP service, because it will not only decrease the performance of your computer and increase network traffic but may also jeopardize network security. Instead, an administrator will provide you with access to the relevant areas of a centrally managed FTP site for whatever FTP needs you have.

You may wish to install and use the FTP service for home- or small-office use. Because the FTP service is part of IIS, it suffers from the limitations imposed on IIS on Windows XP Professional:

- The FTP service is limited to ten concurrent connections (as IIS is). As some users are likely to use more than one connection simultaneously, this limitation means only a small number of users can connect to the FTP service at once. So the FTP service can be useful for private usage, but it's not equipped to handle the number of connections that might result from running a public site on the Internet.

- Windows XP Professional doesn't provide domain name service, so you'll need to either use a third-party product or a third-party DNS service to enable users to connect to your FTP site by its domain name rather than by its IP address.

Given these limitations, the most likely use for the FTP service is enabling yourself or your coworkers in a small office to upload and download files remotely from whichever computer they happen to be using.

Installing the FTP Service

Windows XP Professional doesn't include the FTP service in a default installation of IIS. So unless you've performed a complete installation of IIS, you'll need to install the FTP service manually. To do so, follow these steps:

1. Display the Add or Remove Programs window by choosing Start | Control Panel | Add or Remove Programs or running **appwiz.cpl**.

2. Click the Add/Remove Windows Components button to launch the Windows Components Wizard.

3. Double-click the Internet Information Services (IIS) item to display the Internet Information Services (IIS) dialog box that lists its subcomponents.

4. Select the File Transfer Protocol (FTP) Service item.

5. Click the OK button to close the Internet Information Services (IIS) dialog box.

6. Click the Next button in the Windows Components Wizard to finish installing the service. You'll need to provide your Windows XP Professional CD. If you installed Windows XP Service Pack 1 separately, you'll need to supply your Service Pack 1 CD as well.

Configuring Your FTP Site

Installing the FTP service as described in the previous section creates a basic FTP site with default settings. Before you can use the site, you'll need to configure it as described in the following subsections.

Opening Your FTP Site

Open your FTP site in the Internet Information Services console as follows:

1. Choose Start | Administrative Tools | Internet Information Services or Start | All Programs | Administrative Tools | Internet Information Services (depending on how you have the Start menu configured) to open the Internet Information Services console.

2. In the left pane, double-click the item for your computer to expand it.

3. In the left pane, double-click the FTP Sites item to expand it.

4. Select the Default FTP Site item and issue a Properties command from the Action menu or the shortcut menu to display the site's Properties dialog box.

Choosing Options on the FTP Site Tab

The FTP Site tab of the Properties dialog box (Figure 38-1) for an FTP site contains the options discussed in the following subsections.

Setting the Description, IP Address, and TCP Port

In the Description text box, enter the name you want to assign to the site in place of the default name, Default FTP Site. This name appears in the IIS console.

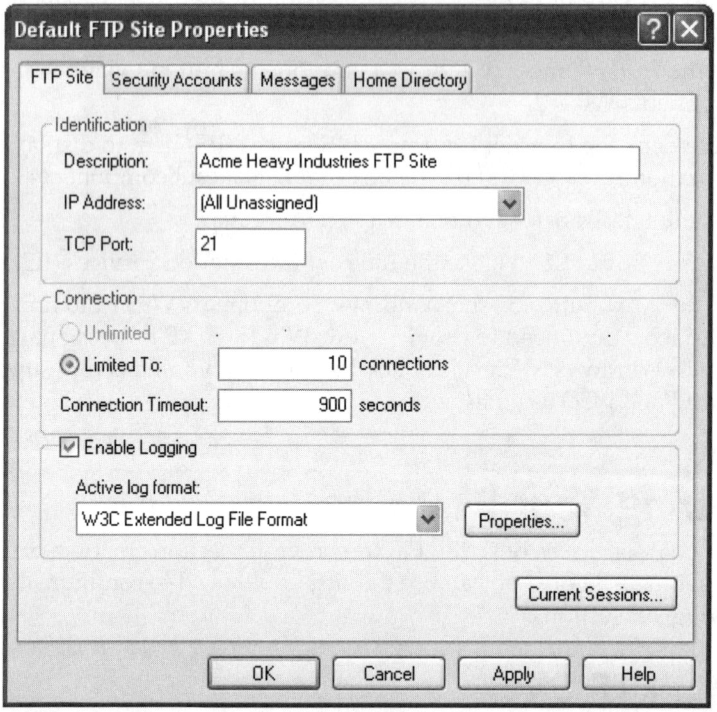

Figure 38-1.   *Set the site's name, connection timeout, and logging options on the FTP Site tab of the Properties dialog box.*

In the IP Address text box, you can assign to the FTP site one of the IP addresses defined in Control Panel. Alternatively, leave the default choice—All Unassigned—for this option.

In the TCP Port text box, you can change the default port (21) to a different port if you consider it necessary. Changing to a different port can increase your site's security, but it will also prevent legitimate users from connecting to the site if they don't know the correct port.

Limiting Connections and Configuring Timeouts

In the Connection group box, you can change the number in the Limited To *NN* Connections text box. (The Unlimited option button isn't available on Windows XP Professional.)

The default number of connections is 10—IIS's maximum number. You can set a lower number to allow even fewer connections at once. You might do this to provide better service to FTP clients over a slow Internet connection.

You can also change the timeout value in the Connection Timeout text box. The default setting is 900 seconds (15 minutes). You might set a shorter timeout to make sure inactive users don't hold your few FTP connections open, thus denying them to other users who need to connect.

Configuring Logging Options

The controls in the Enable Logging group box let you control which information IIS logs about your FTP site.

The Enable Logging check box is selected by default. You should leave this check box selected unless your site isn't connected to the Internet and is available to very few users. For example, if you run the FTP service only so that you can dial directly into your computer from remote locations and collect files, you might choose not to use logging. But usually, logging is a good idea.

If you leave logging enabled, select the log format to use in the Active Log Format drop-down list. Your choices are the Microsoft IIS Log File Format and the W3C Extended Log File Format (the default). In most cases, the W3C Extended Log File Format is a better choice, because it lets you capture more information about the people who access your FTP site.

To choose logging options for the log format you chose, click the Properties button and work in the Extended Logging Properties dialog box (for the W3C Extended Log File Format) or the Microsoft Logging Properties dialog box (for the Microsoft IIS Log File Format). Figure 38-2 shows the two tabs of the Extended Logging Properties dialog box. The Microsoft Logging Properties dialog box offers the same options as the General Properties tab of the Extended Logging Properties dialog box except for the Use Local Time for File Naming and Rollover check box, which it doesn't have.

The General Properties tab of the Extended Logging Properties dialog box lets you specify when IIS should create a new log file: hourly, daily, weekly, monthly, when the

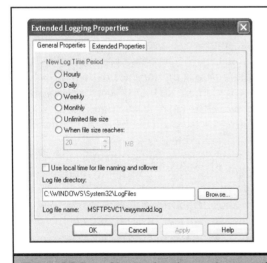
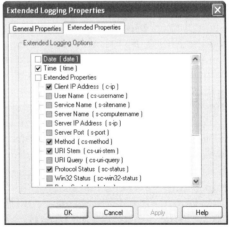

Figure 38-2.   *Choose logging options on the General Properties tab (left) and the Extended Properties tab (right) of the Extended Logging Properties dialog box.*

log file size reaches a certain size, or never (choose the Unlimited File Size button). The Use Local Time for File Naming and Rollover check box controls whether IIS uses local time rather than Greenwich Mean Time (GMT) for creating daily, weekly, and monthly logs, and for naming hourly, daily, weekly, and monthly logs.

 If you select the Unlimited File Size option button in the New Log Time Period group box, you need to stop the FTP service before you can access the log file.

The Log File Directory text box shows you where IIS is currently storing the folder. The default is the %systemroot%\System32\LogFiles folder. You can use the Browse button and the resulting Browse for Folder dialog box to change the location.

The Extended Properties tab of the Extended Logging Properties dialog box lets you choose which extended items of information to include in the log. You're likely to want to include the date, time, client IP address, and user name at least. You might also choose to log other items such as the number of bytes the user sends and receives and the length of time for which they're connected.

Choosing Options on the Security Accounts Tab

The Security Accounts tab of the Properties dialog box (Figure 38-3) for your FTP site lets you choose whether anonymous users can access the FTP site and specify who can operate the FTP site.

Allowing or Preventing Anonymous Access to Your FTP Site

Anonymous connections are widely used in public FTP sites, but for a private FTP site running on Windows XP Professional, you'll almost always want to turn off anonymous access and let only authenticated users connect to the site. To turn off anonymous access, clear the Allow Anonymous Connections check box.

If you do choose to allow anonymous access, enter in the Username text box the user account for IIS to use for authenticating anonymous users. The default setting is the IUSR account on your local computer. If you leave this account in place, leave the Allow IIS to Control Password check box selected, as it is by default, so that IIS can automatically synchronize its anonymous password settings with the corresponding Windows XP settings. Otherwise, clear the Allow IIS to Control Password check box and enter the password for the user account manually in the Password text box.

The Allow Only Anonymous Connections check box prevents authenticated users from connecting to the site. This option too applies only if you allow anonymous access. Preventing authenticated users from connecting ensures that nobody can connect with administrative privileges and change the site's configuration.

Specifying Who Can Operate Your FTP Site

The FTP Site Operators group box on the Security Accounts tab looks as though you should be able to use it to add users and groups who can operate your site. And so you

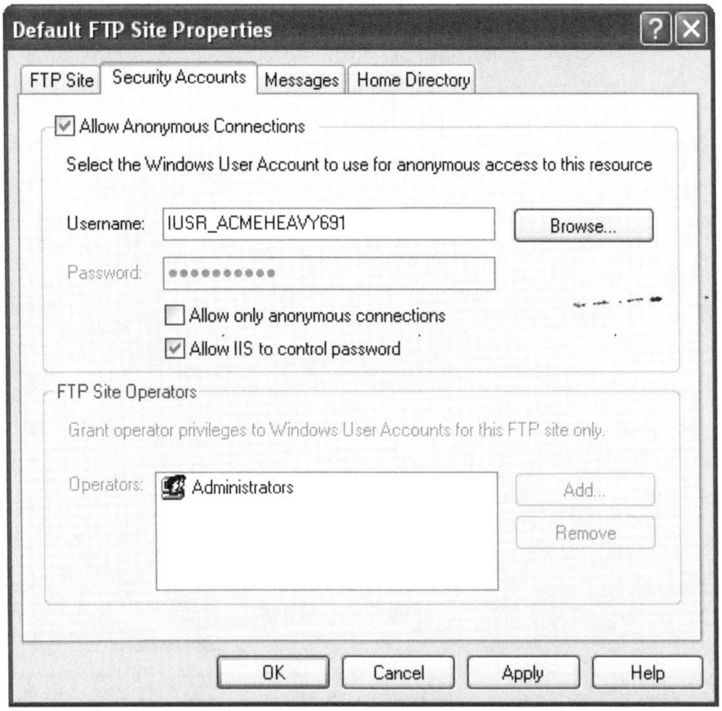

Figure 38-3.   *On the Security Accounts tab of the Properties dialog box, choose whether to allow anonymous connections to your FTP site.*

can, but only in Windows 2000 Server and Windows.NET Server, not in Windows XP Professional. Windows XP Professional assigns operator privileges to the Administrators group and prevents you from changing this assignment.

Choosing Options on the Messages Tab

The Messages tab of the Properties dialog box (Figure 38-4) lets you enter messages for the following:

- The banner that the FTP service displays to users before they log on to the site.
- The welcome message that the FTP service displays after a user has logged on successfully.
- The exit message that the FTP service displays after the user logs off.
- The message that the FTP service displays when it refuses a connection attempt because it is already at its connections limit.

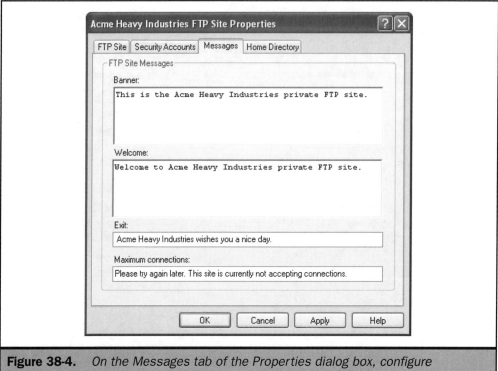

Figure 38-4. On the Messages tab of the Properties dialog box, configure messages to be displayed to users of your FTP site.

Choosing Options on the Home Directory Tab

The Home Directory tab of the Properties dialog box (Figure 38-5) contains controls for configuring the home directory of the FTP site. IIS automatically directs anonymous users to this folder. IIS directs authenticated users who have a home directory to their home directory. IIS directs authenticated users who don't have a home directory to the FTP site's home directory like the anonymous users.

Changing the Location of the Home Directory

The default location for the home directory is the %systemdrive%\inetpub\ftproot folder, which the Windows Components Wizard creates when you install the FTP service. You can change the location of the home directory as follows:

■ To specify a different folder on your local computer, make sure the A Directory Located on This Computer option button is selected. Then type the path in the Local Path text box or click the Browse button and use the resulting Browse for Folder dialog box to select the folder.

Default FTP Site Properties

FTP Site | Security Accounts | Messages | Home Directory

When connecting to this resource, the content should come from:

- ◉ a directory located on this computer
- ○ a share located on another computer

FTP Site Directory

Local Path: `c:\inetpub\ftproot`   [Browse...]

- ☑ Read
- ☐ Write
- ☑ Log visits

Directory Listing Style

- ○ UNIX ®
- ◉ MS-DOS ®

[OK] [Cancel] [Apply] [Help]

Figure 38-5. *Use the controls on the Home Directory tab to configure the location and presentation of your FTP site's home directory.*

■ To specify a folder on another computer, select the A Share Located on Another Computer option button. IIS replaces the Local Path text box with the Network Share text box and the Browse button with the Connect As button. Enter a UNC path to the share in the Network Share text box (for example, \\acmeheavy801\ ftproot). Click the Connect As button and use the Network Directory Security Credentials dialog box (an example of which is shown next) to specify the username and password to use for connecting to the network share.

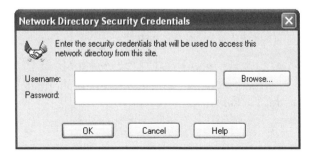

Network Directory Security Credentials

Enter the security credentials that will be used to access this network directory from this site.

Username: [   ]   [Browse...]
Password: [   ]

[OK] [Cancel] [Help]

Specifying Permissions on the Home Directory

Use the Read check box and the Write check box to specify whether the users can only read the contents of the home directory or also write to it. To provide files for download, select the Read check box. To let users post files, select the Write check box.

Choosing Whether to Log Visits to the Home Directory

Select the Log Visits check box if you want to record the FTP site's users' visits to the home directory. Doing so is usually a good idea. For this information to be recorded, the Enable Logging check box on the FTP Site tab of the Properties dialog box must also be selected.

Setting the Directory Listing Style

In the Directory Listing Style group box, select the UNIX option button or the MS-DOS option button to specify which style of directory listing to use. Using the UNIX style may convince less adept users that the FTP server is running UNIX rather than Windows.

Placing Files on Your FTP Site

To place files on your FTP site, copy or move them to the home directory, a subfolder under the home directory, or a virtual directory, by using standard Windows techniques.

Creating "Real" Folders

You can create folders under the home directory by using standard Windows techniques. For example, if your home directory is c:\inetpub\ftproot, you could create a c:\inetpub\ftproot\Incoming folder and a c:\inetpub\ftproot\Outgoing folder. These folders would appear as Incoming and Outgoing in the home directory. All users who can access the home directory will see these folders and will be able to access them.

Creating Virtual Directories

Instead of creating "real" folders in the home directory, you can create *virtual directories*. A virtual directory is an alias for a real directory located either on the local computer or on a remote computer. Users connecting to the FTP site specify an alias to connect to. When they connect to an alias, they see the contents of the real folder.

To create a virtual directory, follow these steps:

1. In the left pane of the IIS console, select the item for the FTP site.

2. Issue a New | Virtual Directory command from the shortcut menu or the Action menu to start the Virtual Directory Creation Wizard.

3. On the Virtual Directory Alias page of the wizard, enter the alias for the directory. Use standard naming conventions for directories.

4. On the FTP Site Content Directory page of the wizard, enter the path to the real folder that contains the content you want to have appear in the virtual directory. You can browse to the folder or type in the path. The folder can be on your local computer or on a remote computer.

5. On the Security Credentials page of the wizard, enter the user name and password required for accessing the virtual directory. Confirm the password in the Confirm Password dialog box. (You need do this only for a folder located on a remote computer.)

6. On the Access Permissions page of the wizard, use the Read check box and Write check box to assign the appropriate permissions for the virtual directory.

7. When you finish the wizard, it creates the virtual directory and adds it to the FTP site.

Creating User Directories

To make the FTP service direct a user to a certain folder when they connect, create a real folder or virtual directory with their user name. You can do this both for an authenticated user and for the anonymous account under which anonymous users log on.

Granting Users the Right to Log On to the FTP Site

Once you've set up your FTP site, you need to grant users the right to log on locally so that they can connect to the FTP service. If two or more users will need to access the FTP site, create a group to which you can assign the right. You can then add users to the group to assign them the right. (If only one user—for example, you—will need to log on, you can grant that user the right directly. But in most cases creating a group saves work in the long run.)

To create a group that can log on remotely, follow these steps:

1. Run **compmgmt.msc** to launch the Computer Management console.

2. Expand the System Tools\Local Users and Groups branch.

3. Select the Groups item and issue a New Group command from the shortcut menu or the Action menu to display the New Group dialog box.

4. Enter the group name in the Group Name text box and the description of the group in the Description text box.

5. Click the Add button and use the Select Users dialog box to add users to the group.

6. Click the Create button to create the group.

7. Click the Close button to close the New Group dialog box.

8. Run **secpol.msc** to launch the Local Security Settings console.

9. Expand the Local Policies\User Rights Assignment branch.

10. Display the Log On Locally policy to display its Properties dialog box (Figure 38-6).

11. Click the Add User or Group button to display the Select Users or Groups dialog box, enter the name of the group you just created, and then click the OK button.

12. Click the OK button to close the Log on Locally Properties dialog box.

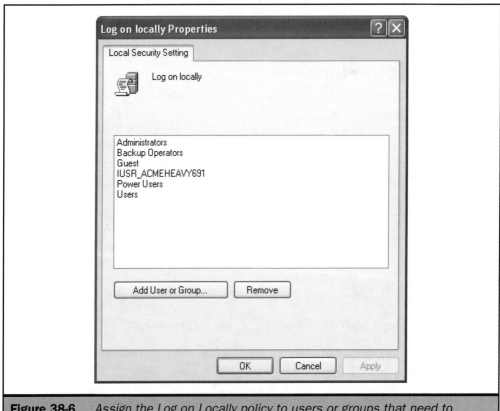

Figure 38-6.   *Assign the Log on Locally policy to users or groups that need to connect via the FTP service.*

Logging On to the FTP Site

The easiest way to check that your FTP site is working is by using Windows XP's built-in command-line FTP client as follows:

- To test the FTP site from your local computer, open a command-prompt window and enter an **ftp localhost** command. If the site is working, the FTP service prompts you for your user account and password.

- To log on from a remote computer, issue an **ftp** *hostname* command, where *hostname* is the name or IP address of the computer.

- Use a **disconnect** command to disconnect from the server. Use a **quit** command to exit the FTP utility.

Checking Current Connections

To see which users are currently connected to your FTP site, click the Current Sessions button on the FTP Site tab of the site's Properties dialog box. IIS displays the FTP User Sessions dialog box (an example of which is shown next).

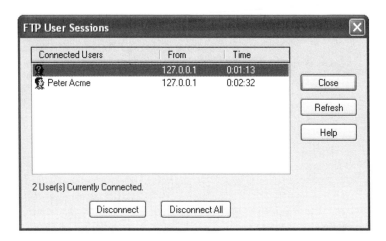

Authenticated users are identified by logon name. Anonymous users are identified by the password they entered (for example, their e-mail address). You can disconnect a user by selecting their entry in the list and clicking the Disconnect button. You can disconnect all users by clicking the Disconnect button. Any file transfers in progress for a user's connection are canceled when you disconnect the user.

Summary

This chapter has discussed how to use Windows XP Professional's FTP service. You've learned how to install and configure the service, how to place files on the FTP site, how to grant users the right to log on, and how to log on using Windows XP's FTP client. You've also seen how to check which users are currently connected to the FTP site and how to disconnect them.

This is the end of Part VI of the book. The final part covers how to manage and automate Windows XP Professional. Chapter 39, the first chapter in Part VII, discusses how to manage disks.

The Complete Reference

Part VII

Managing and Automating Windows XP Professional

The Complete Reference

Chapter 39

Managing Disks

his chapter discusses how to manage your hard disks and the volumes on them.
The chapter starts by showing you how to launch Disk Management, format
disks, and work with partitions. After that, you'll learn how to optimize disk
performance, apply quotas to restrict users to a specific amount of space, and create
and use dynamic disks.

Launching Disk Management

Windows XP's graphical tools for managing disks are Windows Explorer and Disk
Management. From Windows Explorer, you can issue a Format command (from the
File menu or the shortcut menu for the volume) or display the Properties dialog box for
a volume, from which you can run tools, such as Check Disk and Disk Defragmenter.
Windows Explorer is easy to use for these limited tasks, but Disk Management offers
a wider range of tools and should be your first resource for managing disks.

You can run Disk Management in its own console (Figure 39-1) by running
diskmgmt.msc or as part of the Computer Management console by double-clicking the
Disk Management item under the Storage item in Computer Management. Alternatively,
you can add Disk Management to a custom console. (See Chapter 43 for instructions on
creating custom consoles.)

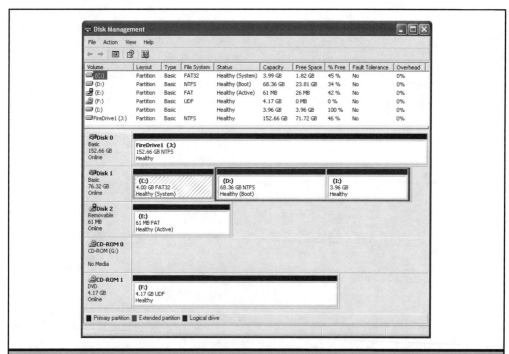

Figure 39-1.   *Disk Management is Windows XP's primary graphical tool for
managing disks and volumes.*

Item	Explanation
Volume	The volume name or letter (for example, C:, Data_Drive)
Layout	The layout of the volume: Partition, Simple, Spanned, or Striped
Type	The volume type: Basic or Dynamic
File System	The file system used: FAT, FAT32, NTFS, CDFS, UDF
Status	The status of the volume: Healthy, Healthy (System), Healthy (Boot), Healthy (Active)
Capacity	The capacity of the volume, measured in the handiest unit—usually GB or MB
Free Space	The amount of free space on the volume, measured in the handiest unit
% Free	The percentage of space free on the volume
Fault Tolerance	Whether the volume uses fault tolerance (Yes or No) to protect data
Overhead	The amount of overhead (expressed as a percentage) produced by the fault tolerance

Table 39-1. *Information Displayed in Disk Management*

Table 39-1 explains the information Disk Management's list area displays for each volume. Below the list area, Disk Management shows how each disk is laid out (for example, in the figure, Disk 0 contains one partition, whereas Disk 1 contains three partitions), the disk's capacity, the disk's type (for example, Basic, Removable, CD-ROM, DVD), and the disk's status (Online or No Media).

 Note *The View menu in Disk Management provides several commands for changing the console's configuration. For example, you can use the View | Top command to change the item displayed at the top from the Volume List (the default) to the Disk List or the Graphical View. This chapter assumes you're using Disk Management in its default configuration.*

Choosing the Best File System

As discussed in "Deciding Which File System to Use" in Chapter 2, always use the NTFS file system for your disks unless you have a compelling reason to use FAT32.

In most cases, the compelling reason will be that you need an operating system (OS) other than Windows XP, Windows 2000, or Windows NT 4 to be able to access the disk. For example, if you need to access the disk using Windows 9x or Linux, the disk must use FAT32 rather than NTFS.

You can convert a volume from FAT16 or FAT32 to NTFS without affecting the data on the disk by using the convert command. You can't convert an NTFS volume to FAT16 or FAT32 without reformatting the volume or using a third-party tool (for example, Partition Magic).

To convert a FAT volume to NTFS, make sure the disk contains some free space: 10 percent or so of the drive is enough. Then open a command-prompt window and issue the convert command in the format **convert** *drive:* **/fs:ntfs**, where *drive:* is the drive letter. When you convert the system volume, Windows XP reboots, performs the conversion, and then reboots again.

Formatting Disks

You need to format hard disks, floppy disks, and removable disks before Windows XP can use them. Formatting a disk imposes on the disk's clusters a file system Windows XP can use.

You can format fixed disks and removable disks from Disk Management, from Windows Explorer, or from the command line by using the format command. Floppy drives don't appear in Disk Management, so you can format them only from Windows Explorer and the command line.

To format a disk, follow these steps:

1. Issue a Format command from the File menu or shortcut menu (in Windows Explorer) or the Action | All Tasks submenu or the shortcut menu (in Disk Management). Windows XP displays a Format dialog box (shown on the left in Figure 39-2) customized to suit the disk type.

2. Specify the file system and the volume label. The label can be up to 32 characters for NTFS volumes, and up to 11 characters for FAT and FAT32 volumes.

3. Select the Quick Format check box and the Enable Compression check box if appropriate. It's best to perform a full format to make sure the disk doesn't contain bad sectors. Compression is available only if you use NTFS.

4. Windows XP automatically selects the best cluster size in the Allocation Size Unit drop-down list. You *can* change this setting, but you're unlikely to need to.

5. For a floppy disk, you can select the Create an MS-DOS Startup Disk check box to create a DOS startup disk, but you can't use compression. You have to use the FAT12 file system—there's no other choice. The only capacity of floppy disk that Windows XP can format is 1.44MB (the most widely used floppy disk capacity). However, you can use Windows XP to read 720K floppy disks that other operating systems have formatted.

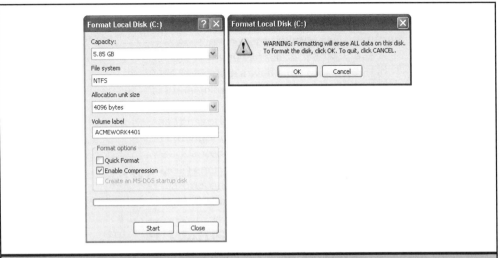

Figure 39-2. *Specify the file system and the volume label in the Format dialog box, and then acknowledge you're prepared to erase all the data on the disk.*

6. Click the OK button in the confirmation dialog box Windows XP displays (shown on the right in Figure 39-2).

In a command-prompt window, type the format command and add the appropriate switches (discussed in the following). This is the basic syntax for formatting disks using the format command:

```
format volume [/FS:file_system] [/V:label] [/Q] [/C] [/X]
```

The following list shows the most useful switches for the format command:

Switch	Meaning and Values
volume	The drive letter (for example, G:), mount point, or volume name
/FS	The file system to use: NTFS, FAT32, or FAT
/V	The label to apply to the volume
/Q	Perform a quick format instead of a full format
/C	Apply compression to the volume (only for NTFS volumes)
/X	If necessary, dismount the volume before formatting

Formatting Large Removable Storage Devices with FAT

Windows Explorer can format removable storage devices up to 2GB with FAT, FAT32, or NTFS. Windows Explorer can format removable storage devices larger than 2GB only with FAT32 or NTFS, not with FAT.

To format a removable storage device larger than 2GB, open a command-prompt window and use the format command with the /fs:fat switch:

```
format drive_letter: /fs:fat /v:drive_label
```

Formatting Large (>32GB) Drives with FAT32

Windows XP's FAT32 tools can't format FAT32 partitions larger than 32GB. The easiest way to format such a partition with FAT32 is to use the FORMAT command from a Windows 98 or Windows Me boot floppy. (If necessary, use FDISK to create the partition.)

Working with Partitions

This section discusses how to create and delete partitions, how to mount a volume in an NTFS folder, and how to assign a drive letter to a volume.

As you saw in Chapter 2 and Chapter 24, Windows XP includes a text-mode partitioning tool named diskpart that you can use to partition disks during installation or from the Recovery Console. However, Windows XP's main tool for creating partitions is Disk Management. This section concentrates on Disk Management.

Note   *Confusingly, Windows XP also includes another text-mode partition manager named DiskPart.exe. DiskPart (note the capitalization) is mostly useful for scripting, but you can use it manually instead of Disk Management if you want. If you prefer to manage your disks from the command line, you may also want to check out other command-line disk-management utilities such as chkdsk (for checking disks and repairing errors), mountvol (for mounting and unmounting volumes in NTFS folders), and fsutil (for performing tasks such as managing disk quotas and dismounting volumes).*

Creating a Partition

To create a partition using Disk Management, select the disk or free space on which to create the partition, and then issue a New Partition command or a New Logical Drive command (as appropriate) from the shortcut menu or from the Action | All Tasks submenu. The New Partition Wizard walks you through the process of creating the partition. You need to make the following choices:

- On the Select Partition Type page, specify the type of partition to create: Primary Partition, Extended Partition, or Logical Drive. Depending on your disk configuration, you may not have any choice.

■ On the Specify Partition Size page, specify the partition size. The wizard shows you the minimum and maximum sizes possible.

■ On the Assign Drive Letter or Path page (Figure 39-3), choose whether to assign the partition a drive letter (from the unused drive letters available), mount it in an empty NTFS folder, or refrain from assigning a drive letter or path. By mounting the partition in an empty NTFS folder, you can make the contents of the partition appear to be subfolders of that folder, simplifying navigation. You can also mount the partition in two or more empty NTFS folders, making it appear to be in two or more places at the same time. Further, you can give your computer access to more than the 26 drives the letters of the alphabet normally limit you to. (On many modern computers that don't have a second floppy drive, 25 drives is the limit. This is because the drive letter *B* is reserved for a second floppy drive.)

Note *You can make a partition accessible both by a drive letter and by one or more NTFS folders. Follow the procedure described in "Changing the Drive Letter or Folder Path for a Partition," later in this chapter, to add the second means of access or additional NTFS folders.*

■ On the Format Volume page (Figure 39-4), choose how to format the partition: specify the file system, change the default allocation size if you must, and enter a label for the partition (20 characters for NTFS, 11 for FAT or FAT32). You can also choose whether to perform a quick format instead of a full format (which includes a check for bad sectors on the disk) and whether to enable compression on the volume.

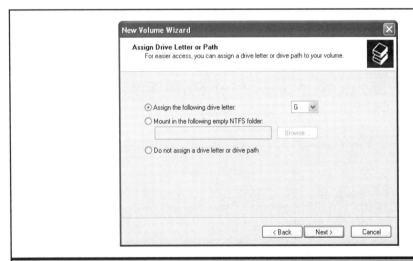

Figure 39-3. *Assign a drive letter or path to the partition you're creating by using the controls on the Assign Drive Letter or Path page of the New Volume Wizard.*

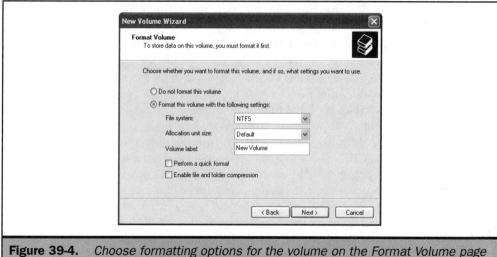

Figure 39-4. *Choose formatting options for the volume on the Format Volume page of the New Volume Wizard.*

 You can also create partitions by using a nondestructive partitioning utility such as Partition Magic or Partition Commander. These utilities can shrink existing partitions without damaging the data on them so as to make space for a new partition. The disadvantage of such utilities is that you have to pay for them.

Deleting a Partition

To delete a partition using Disk Management, select the partition, and then issue a Delete Logical Drive command from the shortcut menu or the Action | All Tasks submenu. Confirm the deletion.

Changing the Drive Letter or Folder Path for a Partition

You can change the drive letter assigned to a partition or the folder path in which the partition is mounted. You can also add the other means of access (a folder path for a partition that has a drive letter assigned, a drive letter for a partition that has a folder path assigned).

Changing the drive letter or the existing folder path will disable any application using the current mappings, so this isn't a change to make lightly. After changing a drive letter, you can use the old drive letter until you restart Windows XP, at which point the partition takes on the new drive letter.

To make one of these changes, issue the Change Drive Letter and Paths command from the shortcut menu for the partition or from the Action | All Tasks submenu and work in the Change Drive Letter and Paths dialog box.

- Click the Add button to add a drive letter to a partition that doesn't currently have one or to add an NTFS folder.
- Click the Change button to change the existing drive letter or folder.
- Click the Remove button to remove an existing drive letter or folder.

Viewing Your Mounted Volumes

If you set up mounted volumes as described in the previous sections, you can view the drive paths and their mappings by running Disk Management and choosing View | Drive Paths to display the Drive Paths dialog box. From this dialog box, you can remove drive mappings.

The Type readout on the Properties dialog box for a folder that's a mounted volume displays Mounted Volume.

Initializing a Disk

When you add a new hard disk to your computer, you may need to initialize it. If so, Windows XP automatically runs the Initialize and Convert Disk Wizard after it detects the disk. Select the disks to initialize on the Select Disks to Initialize page (Figure 39-5), and then follow through the remaining steps of the wizard to complete the procedure.

Figure 39-5. *When you add hard disks to your computer, use the Initialize and Convert Disk Wizard to initialize the disks.*

Optimizing Disk Performance

This section discusses how to use the features Windows XP Professional provides for optimizing performance on your hard disks. Steps you should take include defragmenting the disks, checking the disks for errors, scanning the disks for bad sectors, and configuring the paging file on the disks.

Defragmenting Hard Disks

Defragment (defrag) your disks regularly to keep them running as well as possible. If you work your computer hard, you might need to defragment your disks once a week or more frequently. If its workload is lighter, once a month might be enough.

Defragmentation rearranges files into contiguous or nearby clusters wherever possible, allowing the hard disk's read heads to read the file more quickly, much as you can shop more quickly at a supermarket than by running around to a dozen different stores in town.

The bigger the disk, and the more fragmented it is, the longer defragmentation takes. Allow plenty of time for defragmentation. For example, set defragmentation to go the last thing at night, when you're not using your computer (and when your backup software isn't running).

You can launch Disk Defragmenter (shown next) in any of the following ways:

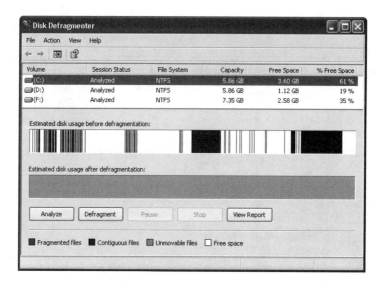

- Choose Start | All Programs | Accessories | System Tools | Disk Defragmenter.

- Click the Defragment Now button on the Tools tab of the Properties dialog box for the disk you want to defragment.

- In Computer Management, expand the Storage object and select the Disk Defragmenter object.

- Run defrag.exe.

Select a volume and click the Analyze button (or issue the Analyze command from the Action menu or the shortcut menu) to analyze it. Disk Defragmenter analyzes the volume and displays the Disk Defragmenter dialog box telling you whether you need to defragment it. Click the Defragment button to defragment the volume or the View Report button to display the Analysis Report dialog box, which presents the volume's information and details on the most fragmented files. You can print the analysis, save it to a file, or merely examine it visually.

From the Disk Defragmenter dialog box Disk Defragmenter displays when it has finished defragmenting the volume, you can access a report on the results of the defragmentation process. Again, you can print this report or save it to a file.

Checking Your Disks for Errors

To check your disks for errors, close all applications and files, and run Check Disk by clicking the Check Now button on the Tools tab of the Properties dialog box for the drive. In the Check Disk Local Disk dialog box (shown next), choose whether to automatically fix file-system errors and scan for and attempt to recover data from bad sectors, and click the Start button. Check Disk displays a readout of its progress and displays a message box to notify you when the check is complete.

When you're troubleshooting a system volume, Check Disk notifies you that "the disk check utility needs exclusive access to some Windows files on the disk" and offers to reschedule the check for the next time you restart Windows XP. Click the Yes button and restart Windows XP whenever you want to run the check.

Configuring the Paging File

As discussed in Chapter 2, your paging file is hard disk space used to supplement physical memory (RAM). This is called *virtual memory.* The paging file is a hidden system file named pagefile.sys. Its default location is the root folder of your system drive.

Using the paging file to provide virtual memory enables Windows XP to run more applications and open more files at the same time than it would be able to by just using RAM. However, because the hard disk is far slower than RAM, recalling data from virtual memory takes much longer than recalling data from RAM. So it's best to keep the applications and data you're currently working with in RAM and use virtual memory for the applications and data you're currently not working with. For example, say you have Microsoft Word and Lotus Notes running. When you're working in Word, you'll get better performance if Word and your documents are stored in RAM rather than in virtual memory. When you switch to Notes, you need Notes and your Notes data in RAM; Word can be moved from RAM to virtual memory until you activate Word again. (The reality isn't this simple, but you see the principle.)

Windows XP manages real and virtual memory automatically, moving information from RAM to the paging file and back, to always keep some RAM available (so that Windows XP doesn't run out of it), but trying to retain in RAM as much as possible of the data you're likely to need at short notice.

You can specify how much virtual memory is available to Windows XP and which drive the virtual memory is located on. Bear the following points in mind:

- Putting the paging file on a different physical drive than the system folder may improve performance. This is because Windows XP uses both the paging file and the system folder heavily, so they compete for disk reads and writes.

- You can split the paging file between different partitions or different physical drives.

- You must have a paging file on the boot partition to be able to create a memory dump. (Table 5-2 in Chapter 5 explains the different types of memory dump you can create.) That paging file must be large enough to contain the memory dump. For example, if you choose to create Complete memory dumps, the paging file on the boot partition needs to be at least as big as the amount of RAM you have.

- It's not usually worth splitting the paging file between different partitions on the same physical drive. This is because doing so won't improve performance. The only reason to do so is if you're so short of disk space that you can't spare enough space for the whole paging file on either partition.

- The paging file's default size is 1.5× the amount of RAM in your computer.

- By default, Windows XP can change the paging file's size between the minimum and maximum sizes set. You can prevent Windows XP from changing the paging file's size by setting the minimum and maximum to the same size. Doing so helps prevent the paging file from becoming fragmented, which can happen when Windows XP resizes it. Keeping the paging file in a contiguous area of the hard disk makes access to the paging file faster.

- If you fix the size of your paging file (or files), consider increasing that fixed size to 2× the amount of RAM in your computer.

- If your computer has large amounts of RAM (for example, 1GB or more), you *can* turn off the paging file and prevent Windows XP from using virtual memory at all. Doing this is something Microsoft doesn't recommend, and it prevents you from creating a memory dump.

With those points for choosing paging-file settings in mind, follow these steps:

1. Press WINDOWS KEY–BREAK to display the System Properties dialog box.

2. Click the Settings button in the Performance group box on the Advanced tab to display the Performance Options dialog box.

3. The Virtual Memory check box on the Advanced tab of the Performance Options dialog box (Figure 39-6) shows the total space allocated to paging files on all drives.

4. Click the Change button to display the Virtual Memory dialog box (shown in Figure 39-7 with some changes underway). The Total Paging File Size for All Drives group box at the bottom of this dialog box shows the minimum paging file size allowed, the recommended size, and the currently allocated size.

5. Configure the paging file for each drive as follows:

   - Select the drive in the Drive list box.

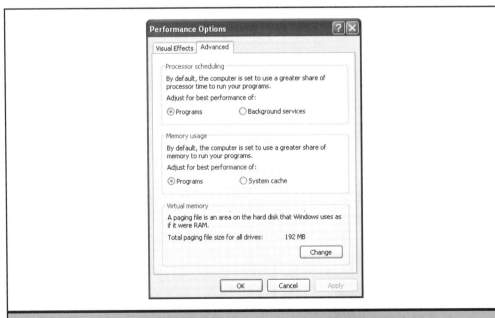

Figure 39-6.   *The Virtual Memory group box on the Advanced tab of the Performance Options dialog box shows the total space on all drives allocated to paging files.*

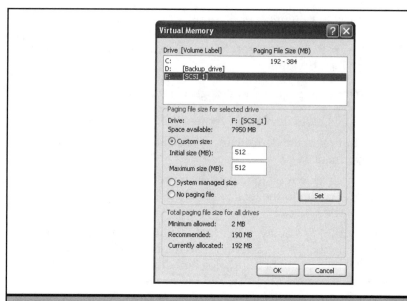

Figure 39-7.   *Use the controls in the Virtual Memory dialog box to specify the size and location of your paging file or files.*

- In the Paging File Size for Selected Drive group box, choose the Custom Size option button, the System Managed Size option button, or the No Paging File option button, as appropriate.

- If you choose the Custom Size option button, enter the minimum and maximum sizes in the Initial Size text box and the Maximum Size text box.

- Click the Set button.

6. Close the Virtual Memory dialog box. If you've made changes, Windows XP displays a System Control Panel Applet dialog box telling you you'll need to reboot your computer to make the changes take effect.

7. Close the Performance Options dialog box and the System Properties dialog box, and then either let the System Settings Change dialog box restart Windows XP or restart it manually at your convenience.

Disk Cleanup

Disk Cleanup is a tool for automatically deleting temporary files of various kinds from local hard drives. Disk Cleanup doesn't clean up network drives. You can run Disk Cleanup in any of the following ways:

- Click the Disk Cleanup button on the General tab of the Properties dialog box for the volume.

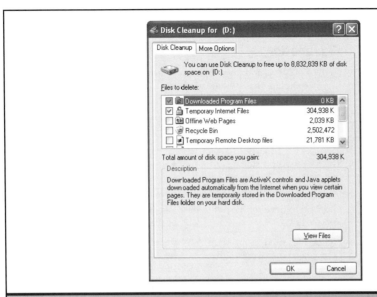

Figure 39-8. *Run Disk Cleanup periodically to automatically remove totally useless and borderline useless files from your computer.*

- Choose Start | All Programs | Accessories | System Tools | Disk Cleanup.
- Run cleanmgr.exe.

If necessary, specify the drive in the Select Drive dialog box. Disk Cleanup analyzes the drive and calculates the amount of space it can free up, and then displays the Disk Cleanup dialog box (Figure 39-8).

Table 39-2 explains the items Disk Cleanup offers to remove and any disadvantages to removing them.

Select the check boxes for the items you want to remove, and then click the OK button. Click the Yes button in the confirmation dialog box Disk Cleanup displays. Disk Cleanup then removes the items you specified. If you chose to compress old files, the Disk Cleanup operation may take a while to complete.

Using Quotas

Quotas let an administrator (let's assume *you*) restrict the amount of space users can access on an NTFS volume. (You can't use quotas on FAT volumes.) You can set either global quotas that apply to all users or assign different quotas to individual users or

Disk Cleanup Item	Explanation	Disadvantages to Removing the Item
Downloaded Program Files	ActiveX controls and Java applets Internet Explorer has downloaded	Internet Explorer may need to download these controls and applets again.
Temporary Internet Files	Cached content elements to speed up the display of web pages	May slow down web browsing.
Offline Web Pages	The files used for storing offline favorites	You won't be able to access offline favorites without resynchronizing them.
Recycle Bin	Files and folders you've put in the Recycle Bin	You won't be able to restore any of the files or folders.
Temporary Remote Desktop Files	Picture files used to speed up Remote Desktop Connection sessions	Remote Desktop Connection sessions to computers you've accessed before may be slower.
Temporary Files	Orphaned temporary files created as a workspace by applications	None—these files should have been deleted already.
WebClient/Publisher Temporary Files	Temporary storage for the WebClient/Publisher service	WebClient/Publisher performance may be slower.
Compress Old Files	Compress files you haven't used for a specified number of days (change the number if necessary)	(Compressed files aren't removed—just compressed.) Compressed files may be slower to access. Compressing the files takes Disk Cleanup a few minutes.
Catalog Files for the Content Indexer	Redundant old catalog files from indexing	None.

Table 39-2.   *Items Disk Cleanup Can Remove*

groups. A user to whom you've assigned a quota sees only that amount of disk space, not the amount there really is. For example, if you've set strict quotas, a user will see error messages saying there isn't enough disk space when they've exceeded their quota.

Quotas work on volumes rather than on individual folders, and you need to be careful which volumes you place them on. It's not a good idea to implement strict quotas on your system volume or on volumes on which you've placed paging files that can grow. Windows XP must be able to write information to disk on the system partition during the boot process, and it needs to be able to expand the paging file up to its maximum permitted size. Strict quotas can interfere with booting or running Windows XP.

You can set quotas on a standalone or workgroup computer to prevent users from taking more than their fair share of space, but quotas are more often used on file servers in domain-based networks to ensure disk space is available for all users. By using quotas, an administrator can see which users are using more disk space than they should and can take action to prevent the server from running out of space.

Enabling Quotas

To set quotas, work on the Quota tab of the Properties dialog box (shown on the left in Figure 39-9) for the disk volume you want to affect. Select the Enable Quota Management check box to enable the other controls on the tab.

Most of the controls on this tab are straightforward:

- You can choose to deny disk space to users who exceed their quota limit. Because this option may cause a user to lose work, don't use it unless you need to.

- You can set default quota limits and warning levels for new users. Set the warning level far enough below the quota limit to give users plenty of warning before they hit the limit. You can specify quota limits and warning levels in KB, MB, GB, TB (terabytes: 1,024GB), PB (petabytes: 1,024TB), and EB (exabytes: 1,024PB). At this writing, you're most likely to use MB and GB.

- You can set logging for users exceeding their quotas and exceeding their warning levels.

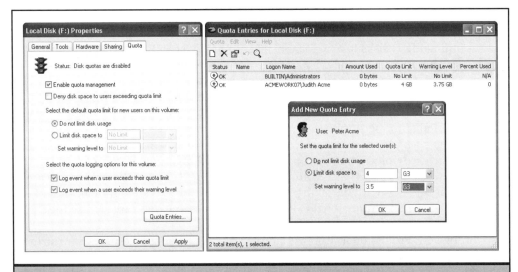

Figure 39-9. *Enable quota management on the Quota tab of the Properties dialog box for the volume, and then use the Quota Entries window and the Add New Quota Entry dialog box to add quotas for existing users.*

Creating Quota Entries

To set quota entries for existing users, click the Quota Entries button to display the Quota Entries window (shown on the right in Figure 39-9). From here, you can create a new quota entry by clicking the New Quota Entry button or choosing Quota | New Quota Entry, selecting the user or group in the Select Users dialog box, and working in the Add New Quota Entry dialog box (shown on the lower right in Figure 39-9). You can also change or delete existing quota entries from the Quota Entries window.

Close the Quota Entries window and click the Apply button or the OK button in the Properties dialog box to apply the quotas. If you've just enabled disk quotas, Windows XP displays the Disk Quota dialog box warning you Windows XP will rescan the disk to update disk usage statistics when you enable quotas. Click the OK button to proceed.

Exporting and Importing Quotas

After you create complex quotas (for example, quotas for individual user accounts) for a volume, you may want to export the quotas so that you can apply them quickly to another volume rather than having to re-create them laboriously. Use the Quota | Export and | Quota | Import command from the Quota Entries window for the volume to export and import quotas.

Using Dynamic Disks

As mentioned in Chapter 1, Windows XP Professional can use dynamic disks as well as basic disks, whereas Windows XP Home Edition can use only basic disks. *Basic* refers not to the technology used in the disk, which can be anything from the humblest of slow-spinning EIDE disks to a SCSI monster spinning at speeds that'd make Ferrari engines fail, but to the way in which the disk is formatted.

Basic disks contain basic volumes. A typical *basic* disk contains one to three primary partitions, plus an optional extended partition that can contain logical drives. The term also applies to Windows NT 3.*x* and Windows NT 4 multidisk volumes: volume sets, mirror sets, and stripe sets (with or without parity).

A *dynamic* disk contains dynamic volumes, which can be simple volumes, spanned volumes, mirrored volumes, striped volumes, or RAID-5 volumes. Like a basic disk, a dynamic disk can contain FAT16 volumes, FAT32 volumes, and NTFS volumes in any combination. Also, as with basic disks, NTFS is the best file system for computers running Windows XP Professional. All volumes on the same disk have to use the same storage type.

Windows XP Professional supports simple volumes, spanned volumes, and striped volumes (see the following list), but not mirrored volumes or RAID-5 volumes. Windows XP Professional supports these dynamic volumes only on desktop computers: You can't use dynamic disks on portable computers.

Dynamic disks can offer better performance or larger volume sizes than basic disks. You can also extend simple volumes and spanned volumes on dynamic disks to provide more space without affecting the data currently stored on the volumes.

Understanding Simple, Spanned, and Striped Volumes

Here's an explanation of the volume types:

- A *simple* volume is essentially a basic volume on a dynamic disk. Unlike a basic volume on a basic disk, you can extend a simple volume on a dynamic disk.

- A *spanned* volume is a volume that spans two or more dynamic disks to create a larger volume than either disk alone could contain.

- A *striped* volume uses two or more dynamic disks and stores data in stripes on each of them, dividing the data to give faster disk performance. However, if any disk in the striped volume fails, you can't access the data on the other disks in the striped volume either, because no disk contains complete information.

Under Windows XP Professional, striped volumes are normally used only on high-performance workstations that need to deliver the fastest possible disk performance—for example, to load colossal files quickly. Striped volumes are used more frequently on servers.

Formatting Dynamic Disks

It's best to format dynamic disks with NTFS for two reasons. First, FAT16 on Windows XP supports disk sizes only up to 2GB. Second, you can neither extend a FAT-formatted dynamic disk nor use fault-tolerance methods on it the way you can with NTFS.

Disk Management can format dynamic disks only with NTFS. To format dynamic disks with FAT or FAT32, use Windows Explorer.

Converting a Basic Disk to a Dynamic Disk

Before you convert a basic disk to a dynamic disk, make sure you're aware of the consequences:

- First, only Windows XP Professional and Windows 2000 (Professional or Server) will be able to access the dynamic disk. Other OSs need not apply.

- Second, you won't be able to boot any OS that's installed on the volumes other than the current copy of Windows XP Professional. (You'll be able to install other copies of Windows XP Professional or copies of Windows 2000 and boot them, should you need to.)

- Third, once you've converted the disk, you can't change the volumes on the disk back to partitions without deleting them and re-creating the partitions.

To convert a basic disk to a dynamic disk, log on as an administrator and follow these steps:

1. In Disk Management, right-click the gray box with the basic disk's name in the lower right-hand pane and choose Convert to Dynamic Disk from the shortcut menu to display the Convert to Dynamic Disk dialog box (shown next).

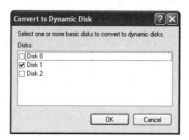

2. Make sure Windows XP has selected the check box for the disk you want to convert. If not, select this check box.

3. Click the OK button to display the Disks to Convert dialog box. From the Disks to Convert dialog box (shown on the left below), you can check the details of the basic disks you're converting to dynamic disks in the Convert Details dialog box (right). Make sure you're aware of the volumes you're about to convert. Then click the OK button.

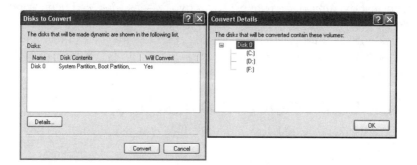

4. Click the Convert button. Disk Management may then display any of several warnings:

   ■ A Disk Management dialog box that warns you that you won't be able to start other installed OSs from any volume on those disks and asks you to confirm you want to convert them.

   ■ A Convert Disk to Dynamic dialog box that warns you the file systems on any of the disks you're converting will be dismounted and asks if you want to continue.

■ A message box that warns you the computer will restart before Disk Management converts the disk to a dynamic disk.

Creating a Volume on a Dynamic Disk

To create a volume on a dynamic disk, follow these steps:

1. In Disk Management, select free space on the disk and issue a New Volume command from the shortcut menu or the Action | All Tasks menu. Disk Management launches the New Volume Wizard.

2. On the Select Volume Type page, choose the Simple option button, the Spanned option button, or the Striped option button as appropriate.

3. Use the controls on the Select Disks page (Figure 39-10) to specify which dynamic disks to use for the volume. (For a simple volume, you can use only one disk.) Select each dynamic disk in turn in the Selected list box and use the Select the Amount of Space in MB text box to specify how much space the disk should contribute to the volume.

4. On the Assign Drive Letter or Path page (shown in Figure 39-3, earlier in the chapter), assign a drive letter to the volume or specify the NTFS folder in which to mount it.

5. On the Format Volume page (shown in Figure 39-4, earlier in the chapter), choose how to format the partition. Disk Management can use only NTFS for dynamic volumes, but you can change the default allocation size (you shouldn't need to) and enter a label (up to 20 characters) for the partition. You can also choose

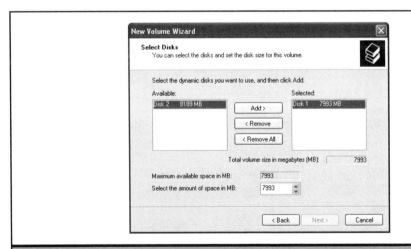

Figure 39-10. *On the Select Disks page of the New Volume Wizard, specify which disks to include in the simple, spanned, or striped volume.*

whether to perform a quick format instead of a full format and whether to enable compression on the volume.

Extending a Simple Volume or Spanned Volume

You can *extend* (increase the size of) a simple volume or spanned volume on dynamic disks. Follow these steps:

1. In Disk Management, select the volume and issue an Extend Volume command from the shortcut menu or the Action | All Tasks menu. Disk Management launches the Extend Volume Wizard.

2. On the Select Disks page, use the Available list box and the Select the Amount of Space in MB text box to specify the space to add to the volume. The Select Disks page in the Extend Volume Wizard is essentially the same as the Select Disks page in the New Volume Wizard.

Converting a Dynamic Disk Back to a Basic Disk

You can convert a dynamic disk back to a basic disk if necessary. Before you can do so, the disk must be empty, so you must either move all the volumes on the disk to another location temporarily or back them up so that you'll be able to restore them after converting the disk.

To convert the dynamic disk back to basic disk, follow these steps:

1. In Disk Management, select each volume on the dynamic disk in turn and issue a Delete Volume command from the shortcut menu or the Action | All Tasks menu. Disk Management asks you to confirm each deletion. Do so.

2. Right-click the gray box with the dynamic disk's name in the lower right-hand pane and choose Convert to Basic Disk.

Summary

This chapter has discussed how to work with disks. You have learned how to launch Disk Management, format disks, and work with partitions. The chapter also has explained how to optimize disk performance, apply quotas to restrict users to a specific amount of space, and create and use dynamic disks.

The next chapter discusses how to work with the Registry.

Chapter 40

Managing the Registry

This chapter discusses how to back up, examine, and change the Registry, Windows XP Professional's central database of configuration information. If you administer your own computer, it's always a good idea to back up your Registry in case trouble strikes your computer and you need to recover it. But under normal circumstances, you shouldn't need to access the Registry directly or change any values in it, because Windows XP Professional and the applications you run provide an interface for changing those parts of the Registry that you might reasonably need to change.

For example, the Registry setting HKEY_CURRENT_USER\Control Panel\Desktop\SCRNSAVE.EXE specifies the screensaver being used. You could change the screensaver you're using by editing this value entry, but the Display Properties dialog box provides a much friendlier and easier way of making this change than the Registry does. Only in abnormal circumstances—such as when you want to tweak Windows XP Professional in a way that Microsoft perhaps intended you not tweak it—do you need to edit the Registry directly.

If your computer is a member of a domain, you may not be able to work directly with the Registry at all, because your network administrator may have prevented you from editing the Registry. If so, be content and leave the Registry well alone. Read this chapter for light entertainment—or leave this chapter, too, well alone.

What the Registry Is and What It Does

The *Registry* is a hierarchical database of configuration information for Windows XP Professional, your hardware, and all the applications you've installed on your computer. Windows Setup creates the Registry when you install Windows XP Professional (or migrates an existing Registry when you upgrade to Windows XP Professional from an earlier version of Windows), and Windows XP Professional itself maintains the Registry. Any application can access certain parts of the Registry and write information to it. The Windows programming guidelines encourage developers to store all configuration information for their applications in the Registry, and applications routinely read settings from the Registry and write settings to it.

Caution   *Because the Registry contains a huge amount of configuration information, it's vital to running Windows XP Professional. If you damage the Registry by entering values manually or attacking (from another operating system) the files that contain the Registry, Windows XP Professional may not boot or run correctly. Similarly, a badly written application can damage data in the Registry and cause Windows XP Professional problems. So, for safety's sake, back up the Registry if you can so that you can recover it if disaster befalls you. And make sure you understand the implications of any Registry change before you implement it.*

Launching Registry Editor

For working with the Registry, Windows XP Professional provides a built-in tool named Registry Editor. (Windows NT and Windows 2000 include two Registry Editor applications: regedit32.exe and regedit.exe. Windows XP Professional has only regedit.exe but includes a stub for regedit32.exe that makes regedit.exe run if you try to run regedit32.exe.)

To launch Registry Editor, run **regedit.exe**. If you plan to run Registry Editor often, create a shortcut or Start menu item for regedit.exe.

Note *You can also get third-party applications for manipulating the Registry. These applications offer powerful features such as global search and replace, which allows you to change all instances of a value at once rather than locate and change each instance of the value manually. Examples of such Registry-editing applications include Registry Search and Replace (which you can find at assorted shareware sites on the Internet), Funduc Software's Registry Toolkit (www.funduc.com), or Norton Registry Editor (www.norton.com).*

Backing Up and Restoring the Registry

Before you make any changes to the Registry, back it up. To back it up, select the My Computer item in Registry Editor, issue an Export command from the File or shortcut menu, and then specify the name and location in the Export Registry File dialog box. The resulting file is likely to be more than 20MB, so it'll fit easily on a Zip disk or recordable CD, but not on a floppy disk.

To back up or export a root key or a subkey (a part of the Registry), select it and issue the Export command. The Export Registry File dialog box then has the Selected Branch option button selected and the root key's or subkey's name entered in the related text box. (You can enter a key name manually in this text box, but doing so is usually more effort than selecting it before issuing the Export command.) The size of the resulting file varies depending on its contents: An individual key takes up a few kilobytes, while a root key may take up several megabytes.

To restore the Registry or a key from a backup, or to import a new key, run Registry Editor, choose File | Import, select the backup file, and then click the Open button.

If you damage your Registry so extensively that Windows XP Professional won't boot, try restoring the previous version of the Registry by using Last Known Good Configuration. See "Using Last Known Good Configuration" in Chapter 24 for details.

Working with Registry Keys

The Registry contains five *root keys* (also called *subtrees* or *predefined keys*). Table 40-1 lists the root keys. Four of the five have awkwardly long names, so all five names are usually abbreviated to the three- or four-character abbreviations shown. This book follows that convention. So, whenever you see (for example) HKCC, be prepared to expand the path to HKEY_CURRENT_CONFIG.

Root Key	Abbreviation	Contains
HKEY_CLASSES_ROOT	HKCR	File types and their associations, registered classes. This root key is a mirror of HKLM\SOFTWARE\Classes (for ease of access).
HKEY_CURRENT_USER	HKCU	Settings for the current user.
HKEY_LOCAL_MACHINE	HKLM	Data about the computer's hardware and software setup.
HKEY_USERS	HKU	Data on the users configured to use the computer. Includes a DEFAULT profile for when no user is logged on.
HKEY_CURRENT_CONFIG	HKCC	Data on the hardware configuration with which the computer booted for the current session. This root key is a mirror of the current key in HKLM\SYSTEM\CurrentControlSet\Hardware Profiles\.

Table 40-1. *Root Keys of the Registry and Their Abbreviations*

Each root key contains a number of *subkeys*, each of which can contain further subkeys. (For simplicity, subkeys are usually referred to simply as *keys*.) Each root key or subkey contains one or more value entries. A *value entry* is a named item that has a name that's unique within its key, a specific data type (out of a wide range of data types that the Registry supports), and a value. Every key contains a default value entry named (Default). Each (Default) value entry either has a value or the default value (value not set).

Figure 40-1 shows a key open in Registry Editor.

Registry Editor presents the Registry in a two-pane interface reminiscent of Windows Explorer. The left pane presents a collapsible view of the Registry database. The My Computer object appears as the root object. Below My Computer are the five root keys. You can expand or collapse any of the root keys, the subkeys under a root key, and the subkeys of that subkey. The right pane shows the value entries contained in the key selected in the left pane.

Table 40-2 lists the main data types used in the Registry.

Windows XP Professional creates some of the hardware-related sections of the Registry each time it boots and examines the devices attached to your computer. But most of the Registry information is stored in binary files called *hives* in your %Windir%\system32\config\ folder (for computer-specific data) and Documents and Settings*Username*\ (for user-specific data). Table 40-3 lists the hives.

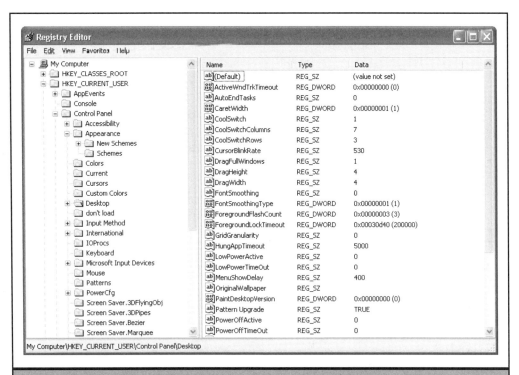

Figure 40-1. *Registry Editor is Windows XP Professional's built-in tool for working with the Registry.*

Windows XP Professional uses the hive files continuously while it's running and keeps them locked. The only way to examine the contents of the hive files while Windows XP Professional is running is through Registry Editor or another Registry-editing tool (for example, a third-party Registry editor). If you boot another operating system, you can try to open the hives directly, but doing so probably won't do you much good.

Locating Information in the Registry

Because the Registry on even a modestly configured computer contains many hundred keys and many thousand value entries, browsing for information by drilling down through root keys, keys, and subkeys isn't usually practical.

To find a specific piece of data or a specific key, you can search for it. Take the following steps:

1. Select the root key or subkey from which you want to start the search. Registry Editor's Find feature searches downward from the current selection. For example, to start your search in HKCU rather than in HKCR, select HKCU first. To start your search in a subkey of HKCU, expand HKCU and select the subkey.

2. Display the Find dialog box by choosing Edit | Find or pressing CTRL+F.

3. In the Look At group box, leave selected the Keys check box, the Values check box, or the Data check box as appropriate. (All three check boxes are selected by default.)

4. To limit matches of your search text to whole keys, values, or data entries, rather than just parts of them, select the Match Whole String Only check box.

5. Click the Find button. The Find feature finds the first match, expands the display in the left pane of Registry Editor as necessary to display the key that contains the match, selects the match in the right pane, and closes the Find dialog box.

6. To search for the next instance of the search term, press F3 or choose Edit | Find Next.

Data Type	Registry Name	Explanation
String	REG_SZ	A string value (text).
Multi-String	REG_MULTI_SZ	A string value (text) that can contain multiple values.
Expandable String	REG_EXPAND_SZ	A string value (text) that's expandable.
Binary	REG_BINARY	A binary value.
DWORD	REG_DWORD	A double-word value (a 32-bit binary value displayed in a hexadecimal format).
FileName	REG_FILE_NAME	A filename
QWORD	REG_QWORD	A quadruple-word value.
Big-Endian DWORD	REG_DWORD_BIG_ENDIAN	A DWORD value stored with its highest-order byte at the highest address and its lowest-order byte at the lowest address.
Little-Endian DWORD	REG_DWORD_LITTLE_ENDIAN	A DWORD value stored with its lowest-order byte at the highest address and its highest-order byte at the lowest address.
Resource Descriptor	REG_FULL_RESOURCE_DESCRIPTOR	A list of hardware resources used by a device.

Table 40-2.   *Main Data Types Used in the Registry*

Hive	Location on Disk	Loaded in Key	Contains Data On
DEFAULT	%Windir%\System32\Config	HKU\DEFAULT	Default user configuration
NTUSER.DAT	Documents and Settings*Username*	HKCU	The user's preferences
SAM	%Windir%\System32\Config	HKLM\SAM	User database
SECURITY	%Windir%\System32\Config	HKLM\SECURITY	Security settings
SOFTWARE	%Windir%\System32\Config	HKLM\SOFTWARE	Software
SYSTEM	%Windir%\System32\Config	HKLM\SYSTEM	Windows XP Professional and the computer's hardware

Table 40-3.   *Hive Files of the Registry*

MANAGING AND AUTOMATING WINDOWS XP PROFESSIONAL

Viewing and Editing Information in the Registry

Once you've located information in the Registry, you can view it in any of the following ways:

- View the Data column in the right pane in the Registry Editor window.
- Choose View | Display Binary Data to display the Binary Data dialog box (shown next). This view is useful primarily for binary data than for other data types. This dialog box lets you switch between Byte, Word, and DWORD formats.

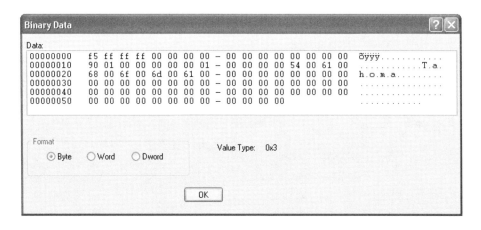

■ If the data is a string value (REG_SZ, REG_MULTI_SZ or REG_EXPAND_SZ), a binary value (REG_BINARY), or a DWORD value (REG_DWORD), you can open it for editing by double-clicking its name in the right pane and working in the resulting dialog box. You can edit string values and expandable string values in the Edit String dialog box, multistring values in the Edit Multi-String dialog box, binary values in the Edit Binary Value dialog box, and DWORD values in the Edit DWORD Value dialog box (see the following illustration).

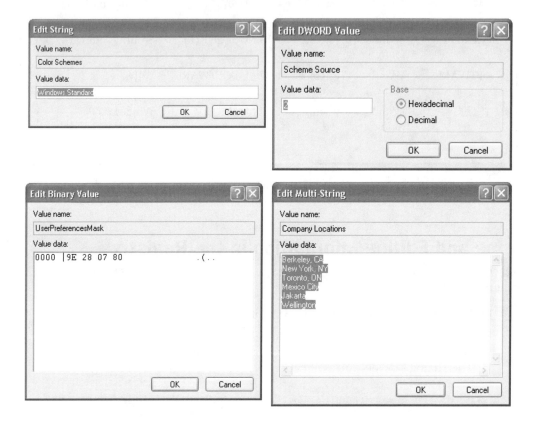

When you open a value entry for editing, you can edit it by typing in the Edit dialog box. String and DWORD values are relatively easy to edit, while binary values require great care.

Some changes you make to Registry value entries take effect immediately. Others take effect only after you restart Windows XP Professional.

Creating and Deleting Keys and Value Entries

In most cases, you won't need to create or delete keys or value entries manually, but you can do so if necessary:

- To create a new subkey in the current key, issue a New | Key command from the Edit or shortcut menu. Registry Editor applies a default name (such as New Key #1) and displays an edit box around it so that you can replace this default name immediately.

- To delete a key, issue a Delete command from the Edit or shortcut menu, or press DELETE. Confirm the deletion in the Confirm Key Delete dialog box. As with deleting a folder, deleting a key deletes all its contents—all subkeys and all value entries.

- To create a new value entry in the current key, issue a command for the appropriate data type from the New submenu on the Edit or shortcut menu: String Value, Binary Value, DWORD Value, Multi-String Value, or Expandable String Value. Registry Editor applies a default name and displays an edit box so that you can change it immediately. To set the value for the value entry, press ENTER or double-click the value entry after renaming it and work in the resulting dialog box.

- To delete a value entry, issue a Delete command from the Edit or shortcut menu, or press DELETE. Confirm the deletion in the Confirm Value Delete dialog box.

Using Registry Favorites and Copying the Current Key

You can maintain a list of favorites to quickly access keys. To add a favorite to the Favorites menu, select the key and choose Favorites | Add to Favorites. To go to a favorite, select it from the Favorites menu. To delete a favorite, choose Favorites | Remove Favorite and work in the Remove Favorites dialog box.

To copy the name of the current key to the Clipboard, issue a Copy Key Name command from the Edit or shortcut menu.

Using Permissions to Control Access to Keys

To prevent other users from accessing, modifying, or deleting keys, you can set permissions on them. Follow these steps:

1. Select the key you want to affect.

2. Issue a Permissions command from the Edit menu or the shortcut menu.

3. Use the controls on the Security tab of the Permissions dialog box to specify permissions.

4. To specify advanced permissions, click the Advanced button. From the Advanced Security Settings dialog box, use the Permission Entry dialog box (Figure 40-2) to set individual permissions.

   - Table 40-4 lists the permissions that you can set for Registry keys.

MANAGING AND
AUTOMATING WINDOWS
XP PROFESSIONAL

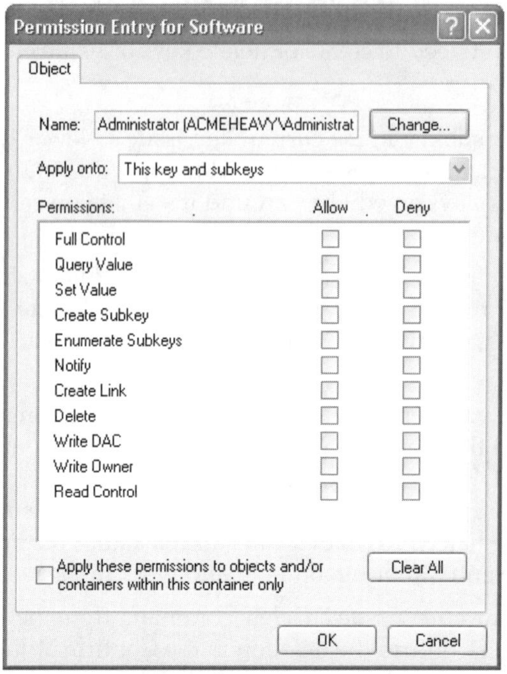

Figure 40-2. To control access to a Registry key, set permissions for it by using the Permission Entry dialog box.

■ In the Apply Onto drop-down list, choose which item to apply the permission to: This Key Only, This Key and Subkeys, or Subkeys Only.

Permission	Explanation
Full Control	The user has full control over the key and can assign permissions.
Query Value	The user can return the value of the key.
Set Value	The user can set the value of the key.
Create Subkey	The user can create a subkey within the key.

Table 40-4. Registry Permissions

Permission	Explanation
Enumerate Subkeys	The user can view the subkeys contained in the key.
Notify	Windows XP Professional notifies the user when the key is modified.
Create Link	The user can create a link from the key to another object.
Delete	The user can delete the key.
Write DAC	The user can change Discretionary Access Control (DAC) information for the key.
Write Owner	The user can change the owner record information for the key.
Read Control	This permission includes the following permissions: standard Read, Query Value, Enumerate Subkeys, and Notify.

Table 40-4.   *Registry Permissions* (continued)

MANAGING AND
AUTOMATING WINDOWS
XP PROFESSIONAL

Accessing the Registry on Another Computer

Editing the Registry on your local computer can produce dramatic effects, as you'll see in the next section. Registry Editor also lets you access the Registry on a remote computer and edit the HKLM and HKU hives.

The remote computer must be running Windows 2000, Windows NT, or Windows XP Professional. If the computer is running Windows XP Professional, it must be configured to use regular file sharing rather than Simple File Sharing. (The problem with Simple File Sharing is that it causes Windows XP Professional to authenticate network access requests under the Guest account. That prevents you from logging on as an administrator.) Windows XP Professional uses regular file sharing by default in a domain environment, but in a workgroup or standalone environment, Windows XP Professional uses Simple File Sharing by default.

The computer to which you connect also needs to be running the Remote Registry service. By default, Windows XP Professional configures the Remote Registry service to start automatically. This enables remote computers to connect to the Registry.

 Note *You can't remotely access the Registry on a computer running Windows XP Home Edition, because Windows XP Home Edition doesn't include the Remote Registry service.*

To access the Registry on another computer, follow these steps:

1. Choose File | Connect Network Registry.

2. In the Select Computer dialog box, enter the name of the computer whose Registry you want to access.

3. If Windows XP Professional displays the Enter Network Password dialog box, enter a user name and password for an account that has the appropriate access permissions on the domain.

4. Registry Editor loads the remote computer's Registry as a new branch in the left pane. Figure 40-3 shows three remote computers' Registries loaded in Registry Editor, together with the local computer's Registry. You can access the contents of the HKLM and HKU hives in the remote Registries.

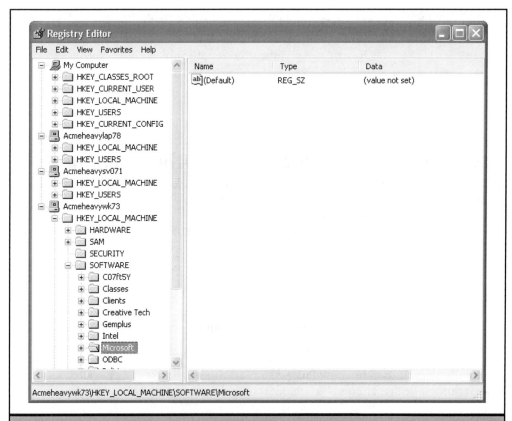

Figure 40-3.   *You can use Registry Editor to access the Registry on one or more remote computers at the same time.*

When you've finished working with the remote computer's Registry, disconnect from it in either of the following ways:

- Right-click the entry for the remote computer's Registry in the left pane in Registry Editor and choose Disconnect from the shortcut menu.

- Choose File | Disconnect Network Registry to display the Disconnect Network Registry dialog box. Select the computer to disconnect and click the OK button.

Specifying Which Users Can Access Your Registry Remotely

By default, the groups and services listed in Table 40-5 have permission to access the Registry on a computer remotely.

You can specify who can access your computer's Registry remotely by setting permissions for the HKLM\System\CurrentControlSet\Control\SecurePipeServers\ winreg key. You can also specify keys that may be accessed remotely by using the Machine entry in the HKLM\System\CurrentControlSet\Control\SecurePipeServers\ winreg\AllowedPaths key.

You'll need to restart Windows XP Professional after making this change.

Preventing Remote Access to Your Registry

You can prevent remote users and services from accessing the Registry on your computer by configuring the Remote Registry service for Manual startup and then refraining from starting it manually. Doing this can increase the security of your computer. But don't prevent the Remote Registry service from running if your computer shares folders, printers, or other resources with computers on the network. This is because the remote computers won't be able to access these resources if the Remote Registry service isn't running.

Group or Service	Types of Access	Access To
Administrators	Full Control, Read	This key and subkeys
Backup Operators	Read	This key only
LOCAL SERVICE	Read	This key and subkeys

Table 40-5. *Groups and Services That Have Permission to Access a Registry Remotely*

Examples of Customizing Windows XP Through Registry Changes

This section presents a dozen examples of changes that you can implement through the Registry. These changes are unlikely to cause problems, but make sure you have a current backup of your Registry before trying them, just in case.

Note *In the following examples, if the specified key or value entry doesn't exist in your Registry, create it.*

Editing Your Windows XP Professional Registered Owner and Registered Organization

Change the RegisteredOwner value entry or the RegisteredOrganization value entry in HKLM\SOFTWARE\Microsoft\WindowsNT\CurrentVersion. You don't need to restart Windows XP Professional.

Deleting the Contents of the Paging File at Shutdown

To delete the contents of the paging file (PAGEFILE.SYS) when you shut down Windows XP Professional, set the value to 1 for the value entry ClearPageFileAtShutdown in HKLM\SYSTEM\CurrentControlSet\Control\SessionManager\Memory Management. Restart Windows XP Professional.

Redirecting Your Program Files Folder

To redirect your Program Files folder to a different location, change the ProgramFilesDir value entry in HKLM\SOFTWARE\Microsoft\Windows\CurrentVersion. Restart Windows XP Professional.

Preventing Registry Editor from Displaying the Last Key Accessed

By default, when you open it, Registry Editor displays the last key you accessed in your previous Registry Editor session. For a clean effect, or for a clean conscience if you share your computer with others, you may want to prevent Registry Editor from doing so. Follow these steps:

1. Clear the value for the value entry LastKey in the key HKCU\Software\Microsoft\Windows\CurrentVersion\Applets\Regedit.
2. Right-click the Regedit key and choose Permissions from the shortcut menu to display the Permissions dialog box.

3. Use the Permissions dialog box and the Advanced Security Settings dialog box to remove the Full Control permission for this key from each user from whom you want to hide the last key.

Controlling SpeedStep or PowerNow Processors

As mentioned in Chapters 1 and 18, Windows XP Professional supports processor power control features such as SpeedStep and PowerNow. Windows XP Professional's support for these features is behind the scenes: Windows XP Professional handles the processor speed automatically and doesn't provide user-interface controls for manipulating it.

You can take control of the processor speed by changing the DWORD value entry named HackFlags in HKLM\SYSTEM\CurrentControlSet\Services\P3\Parameters to one of the values shown in Table 40-6. Restart Windows XP Professional to make the change take effect.

Checking Which Version of the NT Kernel You're Running

To see which version of the NT kernel your version of XP is using, check the value of the CurrentVersion value entry in the HKEY_LOCAL_MACHINE\SOFTWARE\ Microsoft\Windows NT\CurrentVersion key.

Disabling and Reenabling EFS Through the Registry

As discussed in Chapter 19, an administrator can enable and disable Encrypting File System (EFS) through Group Policy. If your computer isn't attached to a domain, you can disable EFS by creating a DWORD value entry named EfsConfiguration with the value of 1 in the HKLM\SOFTWARE\Microsoft\Windows NT\CurrentVersion key. You need to restart Windows XP Professional for this change to take effect.

Value	Effect
0	Disables Windows XP Professional's support for speed control.
1	Reestablishes the settings that SpeedStep or PowerNow was using before you upgraded from Windows 98 SE or Windows 2000 Professional to Windows XP Professional.
5	Gives Windows XP Professional full control over processor speed. You can control processor speed by making changes in the Power Options applet.

Table 40-6. *HackFlags Values and Effects*

To reenable EFS, change the EfsConfiguration value to 0 and restart Windows XP Professional.

Making Synchronization Manager Pause on Errors

As discussed in Chapter 18, by default Synchronization Manager continues with the synchronization of offline files even when it encounters an error—for example, your having requested to cache a file of a file type that you're not permitted to cache. You can make Synchronization Manager pause when errors occur by creating a DWORD value entry named KeepProgressLevel in the HKLM\Software\Microsoft\Windows\CurrentVersion\Syncmgr key. Assign the value 1 to make Synchronization Manager pause when errors occur, 2 to make it pause when warnings occur, 3 to make it pause when either an error or warning occurs, or 4 to make it pause and display information on the problem.

Turning Off HTML Scripts in Windows Media Files

As mentioned in Chapter 15, Windows Media Player has suffered several security problems. One of these involved a malefactor being able to attack computers playing Windows Media files by using scripts embedded in Windows Media files. Microsoft has issued a patch for this security vulnerability, but if you've chosen not to apply this patch, you may want to turn off HTML scripts in Windows Media files.

To turn off the processing of HTML scripts contained in Windows Media files, create a DWORD value entry named PlayerScriptCommandsEnabled with the value in the HKCU\Software\Microsoft\MediaPlayer\Preferences key. Restart Windows Media Player to make the change take effect.

Deleting Recently Played Lists for Windows Media Player

Windows Media Player stores a list of the URLs from which you've recently streamed content and a list of the files you've recently played. These lists appear from the drop-down lists in the Open dialog box for files and the Open dialog box for URLs.

To remove these lists (so that no one can see what you've been viewing or listening to), delete the HKCU\Software\Microsoft\MediaPlayer\Player\RecentURLList key and the HKCU\Software\Microsoft\MediaPlayer\Player\RecentFileList key. Windows Media Player re-creates these keys the next time you run it.

Crashing Your Computer with CrashOnCtrlScroll

To make your computer crash when you need it to (for example, for troubleshooting purposes), create a DWORD value entry named CtrashOnCtrlScroll with the value 1 in the HKLM\SYSTEM\CurrentControlSet\Services\i8042prt\Parameters key. Restart Windows XP Professional to make the change take effect. Then hold down the right-hand CTRL key and press SCROLL LOCK twice to crash your computer.

Forcing Windows XP Professional to Recognize a CD Recorder

If Windows XP Professional seems to think your CD-R or CD-RW drive is a plain CD-ROM drive, and updating the driver and reinstalling the drive does no good, try editing the DriveType value entry in the HKCU\Software\Microsoft\Windows\CurrentVersion\ Explorer\CD Burning\Drives\Volume{*GUID*}, where {*GUID*} is the GUID for the CD drive. Enter **1** for a CD-R drive, **2** for a CD-RW drive, or **3** for a plain CD-ROM drive. This should make the Recording page appear in the Properties dialog box for the drive.

Summary

This chapter has discussed how to work with the Registry, from backing it up before you do anything to it to providing some examples of configuration changes you can make to Windows XP Professional by working with the Registry.

The next chapter discusses how to use Windows XP Professional's assorted tools for scheduling tasks to run automatically.

The Complete
Reference

Chapter 41

Scheduling Tasks

851

This chapter discusses the powerful tools Windows XP Professional offers for scheduling tasks to run automatically to save time and effort. The primary tool is the Scheduled Tasks folder, which provides an easy graphical interface for scheduling mundane tasks on your local computer. For more power, you can use *schtasks*, a command-line tool with a huge number of options. Windows XP Professional also includes *at*, a command-line tool that dates back to Windows NT. at offers less power than schtasks, but you may want to use at if you're familiar with it and you don't want to invest time in learning schtasks.

Both schtasks and at can schedule tasks on remote computers as well as on the local computer. This capability tends to be more widely used by domain administrators than by end users who administer their computers, but if you run even a handful of computers, you may find this capability useful.

Using the Scheduled Tasks Folder

The Scheduled Tasks folder is Windows XP's central location for controlling tasks scheduled to run on your computer.

Note *Both administrators and users can work with the Scheduled Tasks folder. An administrator can implement various restrictions on what users can do with scheduled tasks. For example, an administrator may prevent you from altering or deleting tasks already scheduled, but may permit you to create new tasks of your own. This section points out such restrictions so that you're aware of them.*

To work with scheduled tasks, open the Scheduled Tasks folder by choosing Start | All Programs | Accessories | System Tools | Scheduled Tasks or Start | Control Panel | Performance and Maintenance | Scheduled Tasks.

From the Scheduled Tasks folder, you can create a scheduled task by using the Scheduled Task Wizard or by creating a blank task and setting its properties manually. The wizard provides an easy way to set out the basic framework of a task. After doing that, you can change the details of the task by working in the Properties dialog box. But once you've created a few tasks using the wizard, you may prefer to work directly in the Properties dialog box, which offers you more flexibility in the way you create tasks.

Note *The Scheduled Tasks folder is the %Windir%\Tasks folder. You can open this folder directly in a Windows Explorer window if you want, but there's no advantage to doing so over opening the Scheduled Tasks folder as described in this section. Windows XP saves tasks in this folder in files with the JOB file extension. This file extension is associated with the Task Object file type.*

Creating a Scheduled Task with the Scheduled Task Wizard

The Scheduled Task Wizard simplifies the process of creating a scheduled task. Because the resulting choices are relatively straightforward, this section concentrates on the nuances of scheduling a task rather than on the mechanics of the Scheduled Task Wizard.

To schedule a task using the Scheduled Task Wizard, start the Scheduled Task Wizard by double-clicking the Add Scheduled Task item. Follow the wizard's pages for creating the task. These are the main steps:

- Specify which application the task will run.

- Enter a descriptive name for the task in place of the default name the wizard suggests (the application's name).

- Choose the frequency with which to perform the task. If you choose a Daily, Weekly, or Monthly frequency, specify the schedule on which to perform the task. If you choose a One Time Only frequency, When My Computer Starts, or When I Log On, you don't need to specify the schedule.

- Specify the user account and password under which to run the task.

- On the last page of the wizard, choose whether to open the Properties dialog box for the task when you click the Finish button. (You can open the Properties dialog box at any time by double-clicking the task.) The Properties dialog box offers further options than the wizard—see "Changing the Properties for a Scheduled Task," later in this chapter.

 If you don't see the Add Scheduled Task item in the Scheduled Tasks folder, an administrator has prevented you from creating scheduled tasks.

Creating a Scheduled Task Manually

To create a new, blank scheduled task manually, follow these steps:

1. Choose New | Scheduled Task from the File menu or the shortcut menu of the Scheduled Tasks folder. Windows XP creates a new scheduled task set to run under the user account with which you're logged on (but without a password) and scheduled to run daily at 9:00 A.M. starting on the current day. The task has no application specified, so nothing will run.

2. Windows XP assigns a default name (New Task, New Task 2, and so on) to the new task and displays an edit box around the name. Type a descriptive name for the task and press ENTER.

To turn the blank task into something useful, change its properties as described in "Changing the Properties for a Scheduled Task," later in this chapter. But before you do, read the next section for an explanation of the subtleties involved in some of the task scheduling choices and the account under which you run the task.

Understanding the Subtleties of Scheduling Tasks

The Scheduled Task Wizard makes the process of scheduling a task appear a little easier than it is by glossing over several details you need to understand. The Properties dialog box for a task doesn't make matters much clearer.

Here's what you need to know:

- The account under which a task runs must have a password. (A blank password doesn't count as a password.)

- The Scheduled Task Wizard checks that the two instances of the password you enter (for the account under which to run the task) match each other. But the wizard doesn't check that you enter the correct password for the account. So if you mistype the password consistently, the wizard won't warn you.

- If you change your password, you'll need to update the password for all tasks scheduled to run under your account.

- If you change your account name in Windows XP, you'll need to change it for any tasks scheduled to run under your account.

- Scheduling a task to run When My Computer Starts runs it as a noninteractive process the next time Windows XP boots, whether someone starts or restarts the computer manually, it suffers a crash and restarts itself automatically, or it restarts when power resumes after an outage.

- When a task runs noninteractively, it's hidden from the user. The only way to see that the task is running is to open the Scheduled Tasks folder and examine the Status column for running tasks. From here, you can end a task, but doing so crashes the application.

- Scheduling a task to run When I Log On runs the task when any user logs on. This logon must be a full logon rather than the resumption of a locked session. (If the computer is using Fast User Switching, the task runs only when there are no disconnected sessions and the user is performing a full logon rather than resuming a disconnected session. If the user who logs on is the user under whose user account the task is running, the task runs interactively. If the user is anyone else, the task runs noninteractively.)

Changing the Properties for a Scheduled Task

To change the properties for a scheduled task, display its Properties dialog box by either double-clicking the task or selecting the task and issuing a Properties command from the File menu or the shortcut menu. (If you can't issue a Properties command, an administrator has prevented you from viewing and changing the properties of scheduled tasks. In this case, you can see only those task properties that Details view displays.) The following subsections discuss the controls on the three tabs of the Properties dialog box for a task.

The title bar of the Properties dialog box for a scheduled task bears only the name of the scheduled task. Unlike most other Properties dialog boxes, it doesn't contain the word "Properties."

Choosing Task Tab Settings

The Task tab (Figure 41-1) of the Properties dialog box for a task contains the following:

- A text box for specifying the application, batch file, or command to run. An administrator may have prevented you from changing the contents of this text box and may have disabled the Browse button.

- A text box for specifying the folder to start in. An administrator may have prevented you from changing the contents of this text box.

- A Comments text box in which you can enter a description of the task or notes about it.

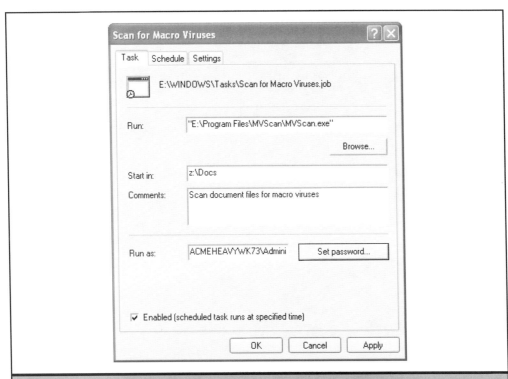

Figure 41-1. *Set the basic parameters for a task on the Task tab of the task's Properties dialog box.*

■ A text box for specifying the user account under which to run the task, and a Set Password button for displaying the Set Password dialog box in which you set and confirm the password for the user account.

■ An Enabled check box for controlling whether the task runs.

Choosing Schedule Tab Settings

The Schedule tab (shown on the left in Figure 41-2) of the Properties dialog box for a task contains controls for setting one or more schedules for the task. Most of these controls are self-explanatory, but these two points are worth mentioning:

■ To create multiple schedules for the same task, select the Show Multiple Schedules check box at the bottom of the tab. Windows XP then replaces the task summary at the top of the pane with a drop-down list for switching the display from one schedule to another, a New button for creating a new schedule, and a Delete button for deleting the currently displayed schedule.

■ To set up a schedule that includes an end date or repetition for a certain length of time (or both), click the Advanced button and work in the Advanced Schedule Options dialog box (shown on the right in Figure 41-2). To repeat the task, select the Repeat Task check box and work with the controls that Windows XP then enables.

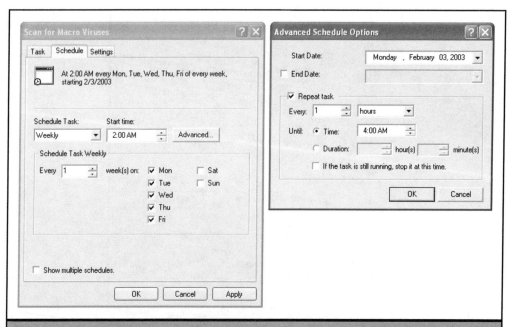

Figure 41-2. *Specify or tweak the schedule for the task on the Schedule tab of the task's Properties dialog box and in the Advanced Schedule Options dialog box.*

Choosing Settings Tab Settings

The Settings tab (Figure 41-3) of the Properties dialog box for a task contains controls for the following:

- If the task is not scheduled to run again, deleting the task after it has run successfully.

- Stopping the task if it runs for a specified length of time. (This setting lets you ensure a task doesn't run for far longer than expected in the background, degrading your computer's performance.)

- Starting the task only if the computer has been idle for a specified length of time, and stopping the task if the computer ceases to be idle. "Idle" in this context means receiving input via the keyboard or mouse.

- Refraining from starting the task if the computer is running on batteries, and stopping the task if the computer switches to battery power while the task is running.

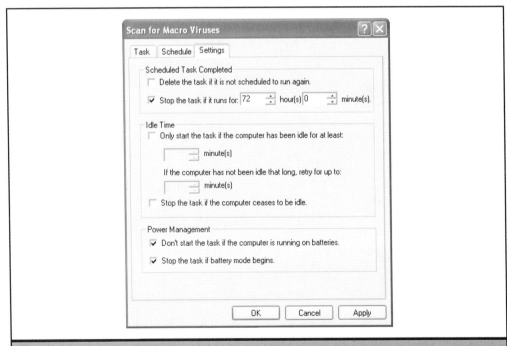

Figure 41-3. *Choose task-completion settings, idle-time settings, and power-management settings on the Settings tab of the Properties dialog box for a task.*

Examining Your Scheduled Tasks

The Scheduled Tasks folder opens by default in Details view to provide a readout of your tasks, their schedule, next run time, last run time, status, last result, and creator. Because this is Details view, you can customize it in a similar way to other folders. For example, you can rearrange the columns by dragging their column headings or by using the Choose Details dialog box. You can also toggle the display of a column by right-clicking a column heading and choosing the column's entry from the shortcut menu. And you can sort by any column by clicking its heading.

The columns are self-explanatory except for the following:

- **Status column**   Shows status descriptions such as blank (nothing is happening), Running, Missed, Did Not Start, or The Scheduled Task Did Not Run Because an Incorrect Password or User Name Was Entered. To receive notification of missed tasks when you next log on, choose Advanced | Notify Me of Missed Tasks. (An administrator can make this command, and most of the other commands on the Advanced menu, unavailable to you.)

- **Last Result column**   Displays completion codes such as 0×0 ("the task completed successfully") and 0×4001004 ("the task is running").

You can view the scheduled tasks log by choosing Advanced | View Log or by choosing Start | Run, entering **schedlgu.txt**, and clicking the OK button. The most recent entry is followed by the line

```
[ ***** Most recent entry is above this line ***** ]
```

and can be easily accessed by searching for *******. This log contains information on all tasks scheduled on the computer—those created via the Scheduled Tasks folder, those created with the schtasks command, and those created with the at command.

You can run a task immediately by selecting it and issuing the Run command from the shortcut menu. You can end a running task by issuing an End command from the shortcut menu. An administrator can prevent you from issuing either of these commands.

Stopping and Pausing the Task Scheduler

The Advanced menu in the Scheduled Tasks folder contains commands for stopping, restarting, pausing, and continuing (unpausing) the Task Scheduler. When the Task Scheduler is paused or stopped, tasks don't run.

By default, the Task Scheduler service is configured for Automatic startup. You can change this setting from the Services console.

Troubleshooting Scheduled Tasks

Take these general steps to troubleshoot scheduled tasks that don't run when they should:

- Make sure the Task Scheduler service is running. You can check this from the Services console or by using a net start command in a command-prompt window. But if you're working in the Scheduled Tasks folder, the easiest way is to check that the Advanced menu contains the Stop Using Task Scheduler command rather than the Start Using Task Scheduler command and the Pause Task Scheduler command rather than the Resume Task Scheduler command.

> **Note** *When you create a scheduled task, the Scheduled Task Wizard automatically starts or resumes the Task Scheduler service if the service is stopped or paused.*

- Verify that you've entered the correct, current password for the account. If the password has been changed, update the password in the scheduled task.
- Check that the account name hasn't changed.
- Make sure that the account has the permissions needed to run the task. If it hasn't, choose another account or acquire the permissions (for example, by working on your administrator).
- If you're getting duplication on your scheduled tasks, see if you've created an at task and a scheduled task to do the same thing. This can happen if you unintentionally change an at task to a scheduled task by editing it in the Properties dialog box, find the task missing from the at listing, and re-create it. at and the Task Scheduler don't communicate with each other, so if you create the same task in each, each will perform the task.

Using the schtasks Command

schtasks is a command-line utility for scheduling tasks on either the local computer or a remote computer. schtasks is essentially a much-improved and much-expanded replacement for the at command (discussed in "Using the at Command," later in this chapter). schtasks' improvements include being able to handle tasks with names rather than numbers, being able to run different tasks under different user accounts rather than having to run all tasks under the same account, and letting you edit an existing task.

> **Note** *Both schtasks and at can be used either from the command line or in scripts.*

schtasks is a highly complex command that can use a large number of parameters. This section covers just about everything you can do with schtasks. As a result, this section is heavy going, and there's some repetition in the tables.

Windows XP Home Edition doesn't have the schtasks command, but it does have the at command. See "Using the at Command," later in this chapter, for coverage of the at command.

Preparing to Use schtasks

To use schtasks, log on as an administrator (regular users aren't allowed to use schtasks) and open a command-prompt window (for example, Start | All Programs | Accessories | Command Prompt). Before starting work with schtasks, make sure the Task Scheduler service is running. The easiest way to check is to enter a net start command at the command prompt and verify that the resulting list includes an entry for Task Scheduler. (If the list doesn't have an entry for Task Scheduler, issue a **net start "task scheduler"** command to start the Task Scheduler service.)

To create scheduled tasks on a remote computer, you need to be an administrator on that computer.

Creating a Scheduled Task with the schtasks Command

To create a scheduled task by using the schtasks command, use the /create parameter with the following syntax:

```
schtasks /create /tn TaskName /tr TaskRun /sc Schedule [/mo modifier]
[/d day] [/m month[,month...] [/i IdleTime] [/st StartTime]
[/sd StartDate] [/ed EndDate]
[/s computer [/u [domain\]user /p password]]
[/ru {[Domain\]User | "System"} [/rp Password]]
```

Table 41-1 explains the many parameters for schtasks /create.

For example, the following command creates a scheduled task named Launch Timesheet to run an application daily at 4:45 P.M.:

```
schtasks /create /tn "Launch Timesheet" /tr
z:\public\programs\exemptts.exe /sc daily /st 16:45:00
```

To run multiple applications with the same scheduled task, create a batch file that runs the applications and configure the scheduled task to run the batch file.

Parameter	Explanation
/tn *TaskName*	The name for the task you're creating.
/tr *TaskRun*	The application, command, script, or batch file to run. Enter the full path to the file unless it's in the %systemroot%\system32 folder, in which case you can omit the path.
/sc *Schedule*	The type of schedule to use. Use the MINUTE, HOURLY, DAILY, WEEKLY, or MONTHLY argument to specify a schedule using that unit of time. Use ONCE for a task that runs once at the date and time you specify. Use ONSTART to make the task run each time Windows XP Professional starts. Use ONLOGON to run the task whenever any user logs on. Use ONIDLE to run the task when the system has been idle for the specified period of time.
/mo *modifier*	An argument required for a MONTHLY schedule and optional for MINUTE, HOURLY, DAILY, and WEEKLY schedules. For a MONTHLY schedule, use the values 1–12 to specify the monthly frequency (from every month to every 12 months). Use FIRST, SECOND, THIRD, or FOURTH with the /d *day* parameter to specify a particular day of a particular week (for example, the fourth Friday of the month). Use LAST to specify the last day (for example, the last Friday) of the month. Use LASTDAY to specify the last day of the month. For a MINUTE schedule, use the values 1–1439 to make the task run every *N* minutes. (1440 minutes is 24 hours.) For an HOURLY schedule, use the values 1–23 to make the task run every *N* hours. For a DAILY schedule, use the values 1–365 to make the task run every *N* days. For a WEEKLY schedule, use the values 1–52 to make the task run every *N* weeks.

Table 41-1.   *Parameters for the schtasks /create Command*

Parameter	Explanation
/d *day*	An argument used only for a MONTHLY schedule or a WEEKLY schedule. For a MONTHLY schedule, you must enter a three-letter day (MON, TUE, WED, THU, FRI, SAT, SUN) for a schedule that uses /mo and a FIRST, SECOND, THIRD, FOURTH, or LAST modifier. You can use a value of 1–31 for a 1–12 modifier or for no modifier. The default setting is 1 (the first day of the month). For a WEEKLY schedule, you can enter a three-letter day (MON, TUE, WED, THU, FRI, SAT, SUN) or * (every day). The default is MON.
/m *month*	This parameter is used only for a MONTHLY schedule. A value is required for a LASTDAY schedule and is optional for other schedules. Use a three-letter month (JAN, FEB, MAR, APR, MAY, JUN, JUL, AUG, SEP, OCT, NOV, DEC) or * to specify every month. The default is *.
/i *IdleTime*	This parameter is used only with, and required for, an ONIDLE schedule. Enter an integer from 1–999 to specify the idle time in minutes before the task starts.
/st *StartTime*	This parameter is required for ONCE schedules and is optional for MINUTE, HOURLY, DAILY, WEEKLY, and MONTHLY schedules. Enter the start time in 24-hour HH:MM:SS format.
/sd *StartDate*	This parameter is required for ONCE schedules and is optional for all other schedules. Enter the start date in MM/DD/YYYY format. If you omit this parameter, schtasks uses the current date.
/ed *EndDate*	This parameter isn't valid for ONCE, ONSTART, ONLOGON, and ONIDLE schedules and is optional for other schedules. Enter the end date in MM/DD/YYYY format. If you omit this parameter, the schedule is open-ended.
/s *Computer*	The name or IP address of the computer on which to create the task. If you omit this parameter, schtasks uses the local computer.

Table 41-1.   *Parameters for the schtasks /create Command* (continued)

Parameter	Explanation
/u [*domain*\]*user*	This parameter is valid only when you use the /s parameter. The user account (and domain if applicable) under which to create (not run) the scheduled task. If you omit this parameter, schtasks uses the account you're currently logged on to. Note that the /u parameter is distinct from the /ru parameter, discussed later in this table.
/p *password*	This parameter is valid only when you use the /s parameter. The password for the user account specified by /u. This parameter is required only when you use /u.
/ru {[*domain*]\ user | "System"}	The user account (and domain if applicable) under which to run the scheduled task. Use "System" or "" (paired double quotation marks with nothing between them) to specify the System account. If you omit this parameter, schtasks uses the account of the user logged on when the task runs. If that user doesn't have the required permissions to run the task, the task won't complete successfully.
/rp *password*	The password for the user account specified by /ru. The System account doesn't require a password.

Table 41-1. *Parameters for the schtasks /create Command* (continued)

The following command creates a scheduled task named Take a Break! that starts at 9:00 A.M. and runs every 30 minutes:

```
schtasks /create /sc minute /mo 30 /st 09:00:00 /tn "Take a Break!"
/tr "%programfiles%\break\qbreak.exe"
```

Tip *If you get the error message "Error 1722: The RPC server is unavailable" when trying to schedule tasks on a remote computer using schtasks or at, it means you need to enable the File and Printer Sharing for Microsoft Networks networking component on the remote computer.*

Deleting a Scheduled Task with the schtasks Command

To delete a scheduled task by using the schtasks command, use the /delete parameter with the following syntax:

```
schtasks /delete /tn {TaskName | *} [/f]
[/s Computer [/u [domain\]user /p password]]
```

Table 41-2 explains the parameters for the schtasks /delete command.

For example, the following command deletes the task named Take a Break! on the local computer. schtasks prompts you to confirm the deletion.

```
schtasks /delete /tn "take a break!"
```

The following command deletes all tasks from the computer named AcmeHeavyWk753 without confirmation:

```
schtasks /delete /tn * /f /s acmeheavywk753 /u acmeheavy\administrator
```

Parameter	Explanation
/tn *TaskName*	A required parameter specifying the name for the task you're deleting. Use * to delete all scheduled tasks on this computer.
/f	An optional parameter that suppresses confirmation of deleting the task or tasks.
/s *Computer*	The name or IP address of the computer on which to delete the task. If you omit this parameter, schtasks uses the local computer.
/u [*domain*]*user*	This parameter is valid only when you use the /s parameter. The user account (and domain if applicable) under which to delete the scheduled task. If you omit this parameter, schtasks uses the account you're currently logged on to.
/p *password*	This parameter is valid only when you use the /s parameter. The password for the user account specified by /u. This parameter is required only when you use /u.

Table 41-2.   *Parameters for the schtasks /delete Command*

Displaying All Scheduled Tasks

To display all scheduled tasks, issue a plain schtasks command or a schtasks /query command. schtasks displays a readout of the tasks (listed by name), their next run time, and their status. Here's an example:

```
TaskName                              Next Run Time             Status
==================================== ========================= =======
At2                                   00:00:00, 12/26/2002
Norton AntiVirus - Scan my computer   20:00:00, 12/20/2002      Running
Symantec NetDetect                    12:59:00, 12/19/2002
Symantec NetDetect                    At logon time
```

For more flexibility, use the /query command with the following syntax:

```
schtasks [/query] [/fo {TABLE | LIST | CSV}] [/nh] [/v]
[/s Computer [/u [domain\]user /p password]]
```

Table 41-3 explains the parameters for the schtasks /delete command.

For example, the following command returns a comma-separated, verbose list of scheduled tasks from the computer AcmeHeavyWk801 and stores it in the file z:\logs\tasklist.txt:

```
schtasks /query /fo csv /v /s acmeheavywk801 >z:\logs\tasklist.txt
```

Note   *The original version of schtasks included with Windows XP Professional has a bug that makes tasks scheduled to run between 00:00 and 00:59 be listed as "Never." This problem was fixed in Windows XP Service Pack 1.*

Changing the Properties of a Scheduled Task

To change the properties of a scheduled task, use the /change parameter with the following syntax:

```
schtasks /change /tn TaskName
[/s computer [/u [domain\]user /p password]] [/tr TaskRun]
[/ru [Domain\]User | "System"] [/rp Password]
```

Table 41-4 explains the parameters for the schtasks /change command.

For example, the following command changes the application run by the task named Employee Update:

```
schtasks /change /tn "Employee Update"
/tr \\acmeheavysv007\users\public\update3.exe
```

Parameter	Explanation
/fo {TABLE | LIST | CSV}	The output format for the query. TABLE is the default and returns a tabular format. LIST returns a list in which the HostName, TaskName, Next Run Time, and Status items each appear as a separate paragraph for each task. CSV returns a comma-separated list. Use the CSV format when redirecting /query output to a file you will subsequently load into a spreadsheet or database.
/nh	Suppresses column headings for TABLE and CSV formats.
/v	Produces a verbose report by including advanced properties of the tasks. Use /v with LIST or with CSV rather than with TABLE. (With TABLE, /v produces a display that's very hard to read.)
/s *Computer*	The name or IP address of the computer on which to display the tasks. If you omit this parameter, schtasks uses the local computer.
/u [*domain*]*user*	This parameter is valid only when you use the /s parameter. The user account (and domain if applicable) under which to display the scheduled task. If you omit this parameter, schtasks uses the account you're currently logged on to.
/p *password*	This parameter is valid only when you use the /s parameter. The password for the user account specified by /u. This parameter is required only when you use /u.

Table 41-3. *Parameters for the schtasks /query Command*

Parameter	Explanation
/tn *TaskName*	A required parameter specifying the name for the task to change.
/s *Computer*	The name or IP address of the computer on which the task is stored. If you omit this parameter, schtasks uses the local computer.
/u [*domain*\]*user*	This parameter is valid only when you use the /s parameter. The user account (and domain if applicable) under which to change the scheduled task. If you omit this parameter, schtasks uses the account you're currently logged on to.
/p *password*	This parameter is valid only when you use the /s parameter. The password for the user account specified by /u. This parameter is required only when you use /u.
/tr *TaskRun*	Use this parameter only when you need to change the application, command, script, or batch file that the task runs. This parameter specifies the replacement application, command, script, or batch file. Enter the full path to the file unless it's in the %systemroot%\system32 folder, in which case you can omit the path.
/ru {[*domain*]*user* | "System"}	The user account (and domain if applicable) under which to run the scheduled task. Use "System" or "" (paired double quotation marks with nothing between them) to specify the System account. If you omit this parameter, schtasks uses the account of the user logged on when the task runs. If that user doesn't have the required permissions to run the task, the task won't complete successfully.
/rp *password*	The password for the user account specified by /ru. The System account doesn't require a password.

Table 41-4.   *Parameters for the schtasks /change Command*

Running a Scheduled Task

To run a scheduled task, use the /run parameter with the following syntax:

```
schtasks /run /tn TaskName [/s computer [/u [domain\]user /p password]]
```

Table 41-5 explains the parameters for the schtasks /run command.

For example, the following command runs the task named Debug Input on the local computer:

```
schtasks /run /tn "Debug Input"
```

 The error message "ERROR: The data is invalid" means the task file in question has become corrupted. When this happens, the task won't run, and you won't be able to repair it. Delete the task and create a replacement.

Ending a Running Task

To end a running task, use the /end parameter with the following syntax:

```
schtasks /end /tn TaskName [/s computer [/u [domain\]user /p password]]
```

The parameters for schtasks /end are essentially the same as those for schtasks /run. See Table 41-5 for a discussion of these parameters.

Parameter	Explanation
/tn *TaskName*	A required parameter specifying the name for the task to affect.
/s *Computer*	The name or IP address of the computer on which the task is stored. If you omit this parameter, schtasks uses the local computer.
/u [*domain*]*user*	This parameter is valid only when you use the /s parameter. The user account (and domain if applicable) under which to change the scheduled task. If you omit this parameter, schtasks uses the account you're currently logged on to.
/p *password*	This parameter is valid only when you use the /s parameter. The password for the user account specified by /u. This parameter is required only when you use /u.

Table 41-5. *Parameters for the schtasks /run Command*

Using the at Command

Another command-line scheduling utility Windows XP Professional provides is the at command. at (a contraction of "at time" rather than literally "at") has been included in all Windows NT–based versions of Windows since Windows NT 4: Windows NT 4 itself (Server and Workstation), Windows 2000 (Server and Professional), Windows XP (Professional and Home Edition), and Windows.NET Server. at's wide availability and strong capabilities for scheduling tasks on both the local computer and on remote computers have made it a favorite of both administrators and those who manage a few NT-based computers of their own.

In Windows XP Professional and Windows.NET Server, at has been supplanted by schtasks to some extent. However, because many administrators have transferred to these OSs tasks they created with at for running on older versions of NT-based Windows, at is widely used even where schtasks is available.

To use the at command, log on as an administrator. (Regular users are denied access to at.) Make sure the Task Scheduler service is running. (For example, open the Advanced menu in the Scheduled Tasks folder and make sure it displays the Stop Using Task Scheduler command and the Pause Task Scheduler command.)

Creating a Scheduled Task with the at Command

To create a scheduled task with at, use the following syntax:

```
at [\\computername] time /interactive [/every:date | /next:date] command
```

Table 41-6 explains the parameters for creating tasks with the at command.

When you press ENTER, at creates the task and displays the message "Added a new job with job ID = N," where N is the next available unused number. The task then appears in the Scheduled Tasks folder under the name at$N$, where N is that number. The task is shown as having been created by NetScheduleJobAdd.

For example, the following command creates a scheduled task to run the mybackup.bat batch file on Tuesday and Thursday evenings on the local computer:

```
at 23:59 every:t,th cmd /c mybackup.bat
```

The following command creates a scheduled task to move all files from the z:\ timesheets\incoming folder on the computer AcmeHeavySv008 to the z:\timesheets\ processing folder at midnight on the first day of each month:

```
at \\acmeheavysv008 0:00 /every:1 cmd /c "move /y
z:\timesheets\incoming\*.* z:\timesheets\processing"
```

Parameter	Description
computername	The remote computer to affect. If you don't enter this parameter, at affects the local computer. You can also specify the local computer by name if you prefer.
time	The time (in 24-hour HH:MM format) to run the task.
/interactive	Run the task interactively for the current user (if any).
/every	The weekly or monthly schedule for running the command. Days of the week are expressed using the abbreviations M, T, W, Th, F, S, and Su. Days of the month are expressed using the numbers 1–31. Use commas to separate multiple dates or days. If you don't specify the date, at runs the command on a monthly schedule using the current day of the month.
/next	Runs the task on the specified day or days of the week or month. Days of the week are expressed using M, T, W, Th, F, S, and Su. Days of the month are expressed using 1–31.
command	The name of the command, application, or batch file to run. If the command isn't an executable, put cmd /c before it. Enter the full path when you need to include arguments with *command*.

Table 41-6.   *Parameters for Creating Tasks with the at Command*

A task you create for another computer is stored on that computer and run from it.

  You can renumber at tasks by changing their number to another valid ID number. For example, you could change the task at1 to at11. But if you change the "at" part of the name, or if you specify an invalid ID number (for example, at01 instead of at1), the at command no longer recognizes the task.

Deleting a Scheduled Task with the at Command

To delete a scheduled task with at, use the following syntax:

```
at [\\computername] id /delete [/yes]
```

Table 41-7 explains the parameters for deleting tasks with the at command.

Parameter	Description
computername	The remote computer to affect. If you don't enter this parameter, at affects the local computer. You can also specify the local computer by name if you prefer.
id	The ID number of the task to delete. You can delete all at tasks by using /delete without an ID number.
/delete	Delete the specified task (or all the tasks).
/yes	Skip confirmation of deleting a task or all tasks.

Table 41-7.   *Parameters for Deleting Tasks with the at Command*

For example, the following command deletes task 8 on the local computer (without confirmation):

```
at 8 /delete /yes
```

The following command deletes task 18 on the AcmeHeavyLap87 computer (with confirmation):

```
at \\acmeheavylap87 18 /delete
```

Changing a Task's Properties

You can't change an at task's properties (for example, its schedule) directly using the at command. Instead, you must delete the task and create a replacement task that has the properties you need.

Alternatively, you can edit an at task's properties by double-clicking it and working in the dialog box displayed—but the at command will no longer recognize the task afterward. See "Changing at Commands to Scheduled Tasks," later in this chapter.

Displaying the Current Tasks

To display the current tasks, enter at without any arguments. at displays a list of tasks such as the following:

```
Status ID   Day       Time      Command Line
-------------------------------------------------------------------
        8   Today     11:59 PM  every:m,t,w,th,f cmd /c mybackup.bat
```

If there are no tasks, at returns "There are no entries in the list."

Specifying the at Service Account

By default, the at command runs under the System account on the local computer. You may need to change the account. For example, you might need to run at under an administrator's account.

To set at to run under a different account, follow these steps:

1. Display the Scheduled Tasks folder.

2. Choose Tools | At Service Account to display the AT Service Account Configuration dialog box (Figure 41-4).

3. Select the This Account option button and enter the account name (once) and the password (twice).

4. Click the OK button to close the AT Service Configuration Account dialog box.

Changing at Commands to Scheduled Tasks

You can change a task scheduled by using the at command to a scheduled task by opening its Properties dialog box and editing the task in it. Once you've made any changes to the task, the at command no longer recognizes it.

As a standalone user, you'll typically have little motivation for changing at tasks to scheduled tasks, because you'll save time by creating your tasks using the Scheduled Tasks folder instead of using the at command. But in a workgroup or domain environment where an administrator uses the at command to push out tasks to other computers, you may need to change at tasks into scheduled tasks. For example, you might need to change the scheduling on a task whose running was interfering with your work.

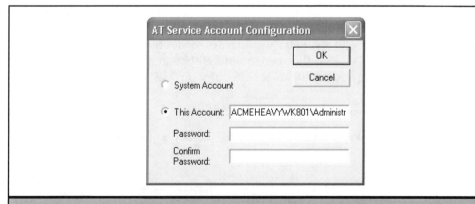

Figure 41-4. *Use the AT Service Account dialog box to configure at to run under a different account.*

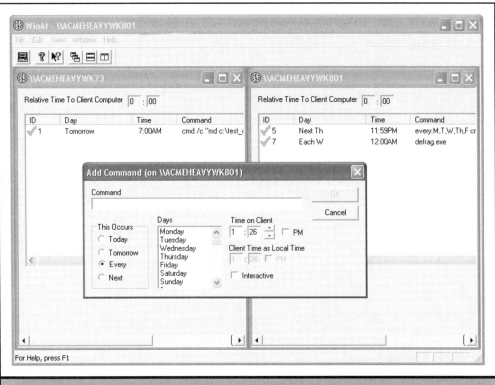

Figure 41-5.   *You can download the graphical interface WinAT to make at easier to use with a mouse.*

Giving at a GUI with WinAT

Microsoft provides a graphical application called WinAT that gives at a GUI. Perhaps the best thing about WinAT is that it can display the tasks from two or more separate computers at the same time in windows that you can position side by side. This feature lets you quickly identify a missing or surplus task on two computers that should have the same set of tasks. Figure 41-5 shows two task-list windows side by side (in the background) and the Add Command dialog box (in the foreground).

The easiest place to get WinAT is ftp://ftp.microsoft.com/reskit/nt4/x86/winat/. (If you don't find WinAT at that URL, search for it on the web.)

Summary

This chapter has discussed how to schedule tasks by using the Scheduled Tasks folder, the schtasks command, and the at command.

The next chapter discusses how to use the Management Console.

The
Complete
Reference

Chapter 42

Using the Microsoft
Management Console

875

A t various points in this book, you've seen how to use tools such as Computer Management, Disk Management, and the Services console to perform a variety of different tasks. As you've probably noticed, all these tools share a common interface that provides a framework for the functionality the tools offer. This common interface is the Microsoft Management Console (MMC). MMC is a host application into which you can load MMC *snap-ins* (modules) to create *consoles*.

As you've seen, Windows XP Professional provides several preconfigured consoles. You can work with these consoles as they are, or you can customize them so they better suit your needs. This chapter shows you how to customize the preconfigured consoles and how to build custom consoles that provide exactly the tools you need to perform day-to-day operations on your computer. Alternatively, if you administer a group of computers, you could construct custom consoles for other users, supplying the tools they need and minimizing temptation by removing all other tools.

Starting the MMC

Depending on how your computer is configured, you can run MMC in any of several ways:

- Open a preconfigured console from the Start menu. For example, if you have added the Administrative Tools menu to your Start menu or All Programs menu, choose Start | Administrative Tools | Computer Management or Start | All Programs | Administrative Tools | Computer Management to launch the Computer Management console.

- Run a console file (from the Run dialog box or a command prompt) to open it in MMC. Console files have the file type Microsoft Common Console Document and the file extension MSC.

- Double-click a console file to open the console.

- Select a Microsoft Common Console Document file and issue a Run As command from the File menu or shortcut menu; then use the Run As dialog box to run the console under a different account. For example, you might need to run a console under an administrator's privileges rather than your user account.

You can open an MMC console in any of four modes, as discussed in the next section.

Understanding Author Mode and the Three User Modes

MMC has four modes: one author mode (for configuring the console) and three user modes. The following subsections explain the different modes.

Author Mode

In Author mode, you have full access to all the controls the MMC offers. You can do the following:

- Add snap-ins to and remove snap-ins from the console
- Create taskpad views and tasks
- Access all items on the console tree
- Choose how the console will open in the future
- Choose whether users can customize the console
- Choose whether to save changes to the console
- Add entries to the Favorites menu

You can force a console to run in Author mode in any of the following ways:

- When running the console from the Run dialog box or a command prompt, use the /a switch. For example, the following command opens the Services console in Author mode:

```
services.msc /a
```

- When working in an Explorer window, select a Microsoft Common Console Document file and issue an Author command from the File menu or shortcut menu to open the console in Author mode.

- By opening an empty console with a plain **mmc** command. (When opening an empty console, you don't need to use the /a switch to open the console in Author mode.)

User Mode – Full Access

User Mode – Full Access is the least restrictive of the three user modes. You can access all items on the console tree, open new windows, and manage the existing windows. You can't add or remove snap-ins or change the configuration of the console. Nor can you change console properties or add entries to the Favorites menu.

User Mode – Limited Access, Multiple Window

User Mode – Limited Access, Multiple Window is the next stage of restriction. You can open new windows but you can't close any windows that were open when the console was last saved.

User Mode – Limited Access, Single Window

User Mode – Limited Access, Single Window is the most restrictive of the three user modes. You can access only the window that was displayed when the console was last saved. You can't open new windows. This setting essentially changes the console from being a multiple-document interface (MDI) application to a single-document interface (SDI) application.

 By default, a console runs in the same mode as it was running when it was last saved. You can change this setting, as you'll see later in this chapter.

Starting the MMC and Connecting to Another Computer

By default, MMC consoles are configured to work on the local computer, on the assumption that it's the one you'll want to manage. To connect to another computer that you have permission to access, use the /computer parameter with the computer name. For example, the following command opens the Computer Management console on the computer AcmeHeavyWk801:

```
compmgmt.msc /computer=acmeheavywk801
```

Standard Features of MMC Consoles

MMC consoles have a standard set of features that console designers can use for their consoles. Designers can hide the features they don't want to display, so not all consoles look the same. Designers can also add features to the standard MMC features by including the features in their snap-ins.

Figure 42-1 shows the standard features of an MMC console, and Table 42-1 explains them.

To choose the elements displayed in a console, choose View | Customize from either the menu bar or the shortcut menu. In the Customize View dialog box (Figure 42-2), select the check boxes for the elements you want to display and clear the check boxes for the elements you want to hide.

Working in an MMC Console

The actions you take when working in an MMC console depend largely on what snap-ins and extensions it contains. For example, you'll take different actions in the Disk Defragmenter snap-in than in the Event Viewer snap-in.

However, in most MMC consoles, you can use the following general actions:

- Use the console tree to navigate from one snap-in to another.
- If the author of the console hasn't prevented you from customizing the view, you can toggle the display of the console tree by clicking the Show/Hide Console Tree button on the toolbar.

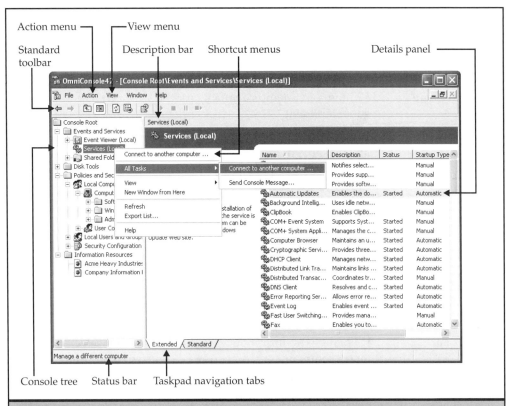

Figure 42-1. *Most MMC consoles have these standard features.*

Feature	Explanation
Console tree	The left pane in an MMC window. The console tree displays the snap-ins in the console as branches in a tree. You can navigate from object to object in the same way you navigate using the Folders Explorer bar in Windows Explorer. When the console tree is hidden, you can navigate by using the Forward button, Back button, and Up button on the toolbar.
Details pane	The right pane in an MMC window. The Details pane displays the contents of the snap-in or subcomponent selected in the console tree. Once you've drilled down to the item you want to use, work with it in the Details pane.

Table 42-1. *Standard Features of an MMC Console*

Feature	Explanation
Standard toolbar	Contains command buttons for navigating the console and taking actions with the selected object.
Action menu	Contains commands available for the selected snap-in or subcomponent.
View menu	Contains commands for switching among whichever views are available of the objects currently displayed in the Details pane. Depending on the types of objects, the choice of views might be the basic choice of Large Icons, Small Icons, List, or Details; it might offer more options, such as Full or Simple; or it may contain a selection of custom views. If you're allowed to customize the view, the View menu contains a Customize command. (See the next section for a discussion of customizing the view.)
Shortcut menus	Contains commands for taking actions, changing the view, and more. In many consoles, the shortcut menu provides the quickest way to issue a command.
Status bar	Displays extra information about the currently selected menu command or the status of the current operation.
Description bar	A bar that (when displayed) appears at the top of the Details pane and contains the name of the selected snap-in or component. When the console tree is hidden, the description bar is useful for checking which component you're using.
Taskpad navigation tabs	Tabs that appear at the bottom of a taskpad and provide navigation from one of its modes to another. For example, many consoles have a Standard tab and an Extended tab.

Table 42-1. *Standard Features of an MMC Console* (continued)

- To open a new window to the selected object, issue a New Window from Here command from the Action menu or the shortcut menu. (If you're confined to running the console in User mode – Limited Access, Single Window, you won't be able to open a new window.)
- Use the commands on the Window menu to navigate from one window to another and to arrange windows.

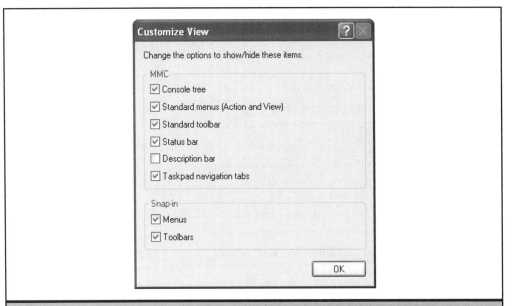

Figure 42-2.   *Use the options in the Customize View dialog box to specify which MMC and snap-in elements appear in the console.*

Note   *If you can open an MMC console in Author mode, you can add snap-ins*

Creating Custom Consoles

You can create custom MMC consoles that contain only the snap-ins that you need rather than running (for example) the entire Computer Management console or several of the smaller consoles on their own. To do so, follow these general steps:

1. Create a new blank console by issuing an **mmc** command in the Run dialog box or at a command prompt.

2. Add snap-ins and extensions to the console.

3. Specify a user mode and save the console.

4. If your console will benefit from custom taskpads, create and add them.

The following sections discuss the details of these steps toward creating a custom console.

Adding and Removing Snap-ins

You can customize your MMC consoles by adding snap-ins to them or removing snap-ins from them. To do so, follow these steps:

1. Open the console in Author mode, as discussed earlier in this chapter.

2. Choose File | Add/Remove Snap-In (or press CTRL-M) to display the Add/ Remove Snap-In dialog box (Figure 42-3).

3. In the Snap-ins Added To drop-down list, select the component to which you want to add the snap-in. The Console Root setting adds the snap-in as a new branch in the console tree. Choosing another component adds the snap-in as a new branch from that component.

4. Click the Add button to display the Add Standalone Snap-In dialog box (Figure 42-4).

5. Select the snap-in and click the Add button.

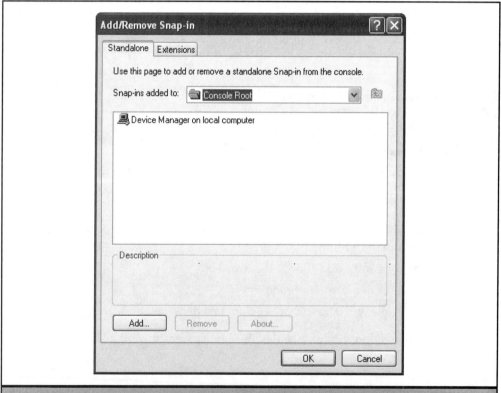

Figure 42-3. *On the Standalone tab of the Add/Remove Snap-in dialog box, choose the parent component for the snap-in you're about to add.*

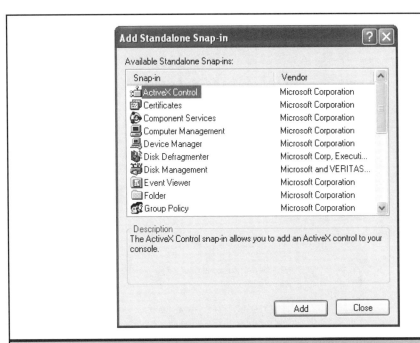

Figure 42-4.   *In the Add Standalone Snap-in dialog box, choose the snap-in to add to the console.*

Note   *You can also add ActiveX controls to your custom consoles. To do so, select the ActiveX Control item in the Add Standalone Snap-in dialog box and follow the steps in the resulting Insert ActiveX Control Wizard to specify the control to insert.*

6. If the snap-in you chose can manage remote computers as well as the local computer, MMC displays a Select Computer page or a Choose Target Machine dialog box so that you can specify which computer the snap-in will manage. Select the computer.

7. Add any further snap-ins you want in the console, and then click the Close button to close the Add Standalone Snap-in dialog box.

8. To remove any snap-in from the list on the Standalone tab of the Add/Remove Snap-in dialog box, select the snap-in and click the Remove button.

9. To enable snap-in extensions, display the Extensions tab of the Add/Remove Snap-in dialog box (Figure 42-5).

10. In the Snap-ins That Can Be Extended drop-down list, choose the snap-in you want to affect. Then select or clear the Add All Extensions check box as appropriate. If you clear this check box, use the check boxes in the Available Extensions list box to specify which extensions to use for the snap-in.

11. Click the OK button to close the Add/Remove Snap-in dialog box.

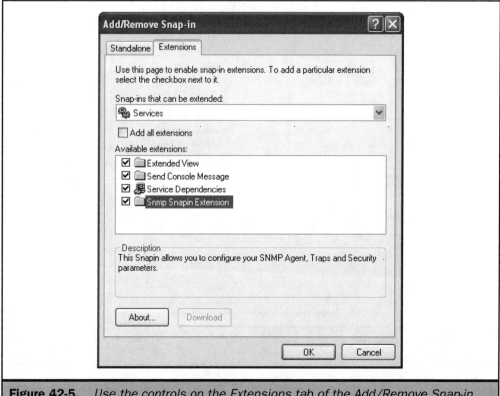

Figure 42-5. *Use the controls on the Extensions tab of the Add/Remove Snap-in dialog box to enable or disable extensions for the snap-ins you're using.*

Organizing Your Snap-ins into Folders

To organize the snap-ins in the console root into categories, you can add a folder. To do so, follow the procedure described in the previous section for adding a snap-in, but select the Folder item in the Add Standalone Snap-in dialog box.

You can then add items to the folder by specifying it in the Snap-ins Added To drop-down list in the Add/Remove Snap-ins dialog box. After closing the Add/Remove Snap-in dialog box and returning to the console, select the Folder item and issue a Rename command from the Action menu or the shortcut menu to rename the folder with a name that describes its contents.

Adding a Link to a Web Address

You can also add links to web addresses to your custom consoles. (If you refer to Figure 42-1, you'll see a couple of web links in the Information Resources branch at the bottom of the console tree.) By adding web addresses, you can provide quick access to updated content on either an intranet or extranet site or an external web site. You can also provide a link to a network folder (or local folder, but this is usually of less use) so that the user can access related files, or a mailto link for automatically starting an e-mail message to the specified address (for example, to the help desk).

To add a link to a web address, follow the procedure described in "Adding and Removing Snap-ins" (earlier in this chapter), but select the Link to Web Address Item in the Add Standalone Snap-in dialog box. Use the controls in the resulting Link to Web Address Wizard to specify the web address to link to and the text that the console should display for the entry.

Specifying a User Mode and Saving Your Console

To specify the user mode in which your console runs, and to choose other settings, follow these steps:

1. Choose File | Options to display the Console tab of the Options dialog box (Figure 42-6).

2. Enter the name for the console in the text box near the top of the tab.

3. If you like, assign a distinctive icon to the console by clicking the Change Icon button and using the Change Icon dialog box to select the icon. MMC offers a poor selection of icons, but you can browse to those contained in other DLLs or to custom icons you've created or purchased.

4. In the Console Mode drop-down list, choose the mode in which MMC should open the console next time it's run. See "Understanding Author Mode and the Three User Modes," near the beginning of this chapter, for a discussion of the four available modes.

5. If you choose one of the three user modes, you can select the Do Not Save Changes to This Console check box to prevent users from saving changes to the console. (This check box is cleared by default in a custom console.) You can also clear the Allow the User to Customize Views check box to prevent users from adding items rooted on items in the console. (This check box is selected by default in a custom console.)

Note   *By preventing users from saving changes to the console, you can ensure that they see the same console configuration each time they open it. However, preventing users from saving changes may make the console slower or more difficult to use, as the users won't be able to save any configuration improvements they make to it.*

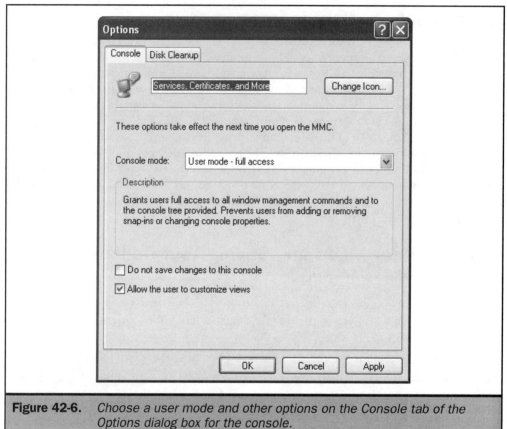

Figure 42-6. *Choose a user mode and other options on the Console tab of the Options dialog box for the console.*

6. Click the OK button to close the Options dialog box.

To save your console, issue a File | Save As command and enter the name in the Save As dialog box.

Creating Taskpads

In the custom consoles you build, you can also create *taskpads*—custom pages for use within the Details pane of an MMC snap-in. A taskpad acts as a shortcut for a number of actions you specify.

MMC provides a New Taskpad View Wizard for creating a taskpad view and a New Task Wizard for creating a task for the taskpad. By default, the New Task Wizard runs when you complete the New Taskpad View Wizard.

Note *You can't create taskpads in the preconfigured MMC consoles.*

To create a taskpad, open the console in Author mode and follow these steps:

1. In the console tree, select the snap-in you want to create the taskpad in.

2. Issue a New Taskpad View command from the Action menu or the shortcut menu to launch the New Taskpad View Wizard.

3. On the Taskpad Display page (Figure 42-7), select the layout you want for the taskpad. Use the preview to judge the effects your choices will produce. You can choose the following:

   ■ The style for the Details pane: a vertical list, a horizontal list, or no list

   ■ Whether to hide the Standard tab (so that only the Extended tab is displayed)

   ■ Whether to display the task descriptions as text or as InfoTips

   ■ Whether to make the list small, medium, or large

4. On the Taskpad Target page, choose whether to apply this taskpad view to only the selected item in the tree or all tree items that have the same type as the

MANAGING AND
AUTOMATING WINDOWS
XP PROFESSIONAL

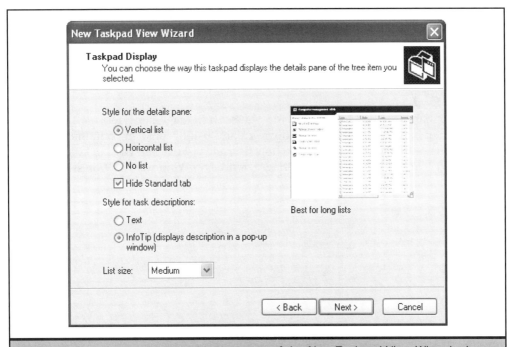

Figure 42-7.   *On the Taskpad Display page of the New Taskpad View Wizard, choose the type of display for the taskpad.*

selected item. If you choose all the items, you can specify whether MMC changes the default display for those tree items to this taskpad view.

5. On the Name and Description page, enter the name and description for the taskpad.

6. On the Completing the New Taskpad View Wizard page, choose whether to start the New Task Wizard. (This wizard starts by default.)

The New Task Wizard walks you through the process of creating a task for a taskpad. You can choose to assign a menu command, a shell command (to run a script, start an application, or display a web page), or a navigation command to a favorite. The sequence of screens that the New Task Wizard displays depends on the type of command that you choose.

Once you've created a custom taskpad view, you can take the following actions with it:

- Edit the taskpad view by selecting it, issuing an Edit Taskpad View command from the Action menu or the shortcut menu, and working on the tabs of the Properties dialog box that MMC displays. From this dialog box, you can change the configuration of the Details pane for the taskpad and the details of the tasks that it runs.

- Delete a custom taskpad view by selecting it and issuing a Delete Taskpad View command from the Action menu or the shortcut menu. MMC deletes the taskpad view without confirmation.

Summary

This chapter has discussed how to run the Microsoft Management Console and work in it. The chapter has covered why and how to create custom consoles containing only the snap-ins you need. It has also shown you how to create taskpads and assign tasks to them.

The next chapter covers how to manage services on Windows XP Professional.

The
Complete
Reference

Chapter 43

Managing Services

This chapter shows you how to manage services on your computer—if you need to. Whether you need to manage services on your computer depends on whether you administer your computer and (if not) whether you're a power user (or have ambitions to be one). However, even if you find you seldom need to manage services on your computer, you can benefit from understanding what services are, what they do, and the tools Windows XP Professional provides for examining and controlling them.

The chapter starts by discussing what services are and what they do. The chapter then shows you how to use the Services console to see what services are running and to control them. It describes how to start and stop services, how to secure services, and how to work with services on a remote computer.

In most cases, you'll need to be an administrator or a member of the Power Users group to start, stop, or configure services.

What Services Are and What They Do

Windows XP Professional uses a wide variety of services to implement many of the functions it provides. A *service* is essentially an application that provides features used by other applications. For example, the DNS Client service resolves Domain Name Service (DNS) names and caches the resulting information. Other applications and services can then use this information to find computers on the network by using their DNS names— the other applications and services don't need to resolve the DNS names themselves because the DNS Client performs that service for them.

Many services are run by the System account rather than by user accounts. This is because the System account has a high level of privileges for working with hardware. However, as you've seen earlier in this book, you can run an application to run as a service if you want to ensure it runs each time Windows XP Professional starts. You can configure an application to run under the System account, under another automated account, or under a user account that has sufficient privileges to perform the actions the application needs to take.

Table 43-1 lists the services Windows XP Professional typically runs in a domain environment. The table shows the display name (the descriptive name) of each service, the Windows XP Professional service name, the executable under which you'll find the service running (for example, in Task Manager), and a brief description of what the service does. Use this table for reference when working with services. In particular, the service name (the short name, not the display name) can be useful when you're managing services using the net commands from the command line (as described in "Managing Services with the net Commands," later in this chapter).

Note   *Each service your computer runs consumes memory and other system resources, so don't run any services you don't need to use. Conversely, because some services work in mysterious ways, make sure you understand the function of any service that's configured to run automatically before you shut it down. In particular, check for dependencies— other services that depend on this service to run. See "Checking Dependencies for a Service," later in this chapter.*

Display Name	Service Name	Executable File	Description
Alerter	Alerter	svchost.exe	Displays administrative alerts.
Application Layer Gateway Service	ALG	alg.exe	Supports third-party plug-ins for ICS and ICF.
Application Management	AppMgmt	svchost.exe	Implements software installation services via IntelliMirror.
Automatic Updates	Wuauserv	svchost.exe	Automatically checks for and downloads updated Windows files.
Background Intelligent Transfer Agent	BITS	svchost.exe	Improves network data transfer by using idle bandwidth.
ClipBook	ClipSrv	clipsrv.exe	Enables the Clipbook Viewer applet to share data with remote computers.
COM+ Event System	EventSystem	svchost.exe	Enables Component Object Model (COM) components to receive events.
COM+ System Application	COMSysApp	dllhost.exe	Configures and tracks COM+-based components.
Computer Browser	Browser	svchost.exe	Keeps a list of computers on the network. (This service has nothing to do with web browsing.)
Cryptographic Services	CryptSvc	svchost.exe	Implements cryptographic services and manages root digital certificates.
DHCP Client	Dhcp	svchost.exe	Registers and updates DNS names and IP addresses.
Distributed Link Tracking Client	TrkWks	svchost.exe	Tracks links between NTFS files on a computer or within a domain.
Distributed Tracking Coordinator	MSDTC	msdtc.exe	Coordinates transactions that take place across multiple resource managers.
DNS Client	Dnscache	svchost.exe	Resolves DNS names for the local computer and caches the results.
Error Reporting Service	ERSvc	svchost.exe	Enables error reporting for some applications.

Table 43-1.   *Windows XP Professional Services*

Display Name	Service Name	Executable File	Description
Event Log	Eventlog	services.exe	Enables Event Viewer to view messages stored in the event logs.
Fast User Switching Compatibility	FastUserSwitching-Compatibility	svchost.exe	Helps manage applications when Fast User Switching is being used.
Fax	Fax	fxssvc.exe	Enables the sending and receiving of faxes.
Help and Support	Helpsvc	svchost.exe	Enables the Help and Support Center application to run.
Human Interface Device Access	HidServ	svchost.exe	Enables input access to Human Interface Devices (for keyboards, remote controls, and so on).
IIS Admin	Iisadmin	inetinfo.exe	Enables the IIS snap-in to administer web and FTP services.
IMAPI CD-Burning COM Service	ImapiService	imapi.exe	Manages CD burning using Image Mastering Applications Programming Interface (IMAPI).
Indexing Service	cisvc	cisvc.exe	Indexes files for faster searching.
Internet Connection Firewall (ICF)/Internet Connection Sharing (ICS)	SharedAccess	svchost.exe	Runs ICS and ICF for sharing and firewalling Internet connections.
IPSec Services	PolicyAgent	lsass.exe	Manages IPSec.
Logical Disk Manager	dmserver	svchost.exe	Monitors hard disks and sends volume information to Logical Disk Manager Administrative Service.
Logical Disk Manager Administrative Service	dmadmin	dmadmin.exe	Manages hard disks and volumes.
Messenger	Messenger	svchost.exe	Transmits Alerter services messages and net send messages. (This service has nothing to do with Windows Messenger.)

Table 43-1. *Windows XP Professional Services* (continued)

Display Name	Service Name	Executable File	Description
MS Software Shadow Copy Provider	SwPrv	dllhost.exe	Manages shadow copies (a technique for copying open files).
Net Logon	Netlogon	lsass.exe	Passes through authentication for accounts in a domain.
NetMeeting Remote Desktop Sharing	mnmsrvc	mnmsrvc.exe	Enables remote control via NetMeeting.
Network Connections	Netman	svchost.exe	Manages network connections.
Network DDE	NetDDE	netdde.exe	Manages and secures Dynamic Data Exchange (DDE) transactions.
Network DDE DSDM	NetDDEdsdm	netdde.exe	Manages DDE network shares.
Network Location Awareness (NLA)	Nla	svchost.exe	Maintains a list of network configuration and location information.
NT LM Security Support Provider	NtLmSsp	lsass.exe	Secures communications for some remote procedure call programs.
Performance Logs and Alerts	SysmonLog	Smlogsvc.exe	Collects performance data for the Performance tool.
Plug and Play	PlugPlay	services.exe	Provides PnP recognition of hardware and driver loading.
Portable Media Serial Number	WmdmPmSp	svchost.exe	Returns the serial number of a portable music player.
Print Spooler	Spooler	spoolsv.exe	Spools print jobs to spool files to enable applications to finish print jobs more quickly.
Protected Storage	ProtectedStorage	lsass.exe	Provides protected storage for private keys and other sensitive data.
QoS RSVP	RSVP	rsvp.exe	Provides signaling and traffic control for quality-of-service–aware applications.
Remote Access Auto Connection Manager	RasAuto	svchost.exe	Establishes connections to remote networks when applications require them.

Table 43-1.   *Windows XP Professional Services* (continued)

Display Name	Service Name	Executable File	Description
Remote Access Connection Manager	RasMan	svchost.exe	Establishes connections to remote networks.
Remote Desktop Help Session Manager	RDSessMgr	sessmgr.exe	Provides Remote Assistance capabilities.
Remote Procedure Call (RPC)	RpcSs	svchost.exe	Provides RPC services.
Remote Procedure Call (RPC) Locator	RpcLocator	locator.exe	Maintains the RPC name service database.
Remote Registry	RemoteRegistry	svchost.exe	Lets remote users modify the Registry on this computer.
Removable Storage	NtmsSvc	svchost.exe	Provides services for removable storage.
Routing and Remote Access	RemoteAccess	svchost.exe	Provides routing and remote access services.
Secondary Logon	seclogon	lsass.exe	Allows processes to be started under alternate credentials (for example, using a Run As command).
Security Accounts Manager	SamSs	lsass.exe	Manages security information for the local user accounts.
Server	lanmanserver	svchost.exe	Provides network sharing of files, printers, and named pipes.
Shell Hardware Detection	ShellHWDetection	svchost.exe	Provides hardware detection services.
Smart Card	ScardSvr	scardsvr.exe	Enables the computer to read smart cards.
Smart Card Helper	SCardDrv	scardsvr.exe	Supports legacy smart-card readers.
SSDP Discovery Services	SSDPSRV	svchost.exe	Discovers Universal Plug and Play (UPnP) devices on the network.
System Event Notification	SENS	svchost.exe	Tracks system events and notifies COM+ Event System.
System Restore Service	Srservice	svchost.exe	Enables System Restore.
Task Scheduler	Schedule	svchost.exe	Runs scheduled tasks.
TCP/IP NetBIOS Helper	LmHosts	svchost.exe	Supports NetBIOS over TCP/IP and NetBIOS name resolution.

Table 43-1. *Windows XP Professional Services* (continued)

Display Name	Service Name	Executable File	Description
Telephony	TapiSrv	svchost.exe	Provides Telephony Application Programming Interface (TAPI) support for telephony applications.
Telnet	TlntSvr	tlntsvr.exe	Runs a Telnet server that can accept incoming Telnet connections.
Terminal Services	TermService	svchost.exe	Provides Terminal Services functionality, including Fast User Switching, Remote Desktop, and Remote Assistance.
Themes	Themes	svchost.exe	Manages desktop themes.
Uninterruptible Power Supply	UPS	ups.exe	Manages a UPS.
Universal Plug and Play Device Host	upnphost	svchost.exe	Supports the hosting of UPnP devices.
Upload Manager	uploadmgr	svchost.exe	Coordinates synchronous and asynchronous file transfers between clients and servers.
Volume Shadow Copy	VSS	vssvc.exe	Controls Volume Shadow Copy for backups and other purposes.
WebClient	WebClient	svchost.exe	Lets applications access, create, and change web-based files.
Windows Audio	AudioSrv	svchost.exe	Manages audio devices.
Windows Image Acquisition (WIA)	Stisvc	svchost.exe	Provides image capture for cameras and scanners.
Windows Installer	MSIServer	msiexec.exe	Installs, repairs, and removes applications.
Windows Management Instrumentation	winmgmt	svchost.exe	Provides an interface for accessing management information about the operating system, applications, services, and devices.
Windows Management Instrumentation Driver Extensions	wmi	svchost.exe	Transfers management information to and from drivers.

Table 43-1.   *Windows XP Professional Services* (continued)

Display Name	Service Name	Executable File	Description
Windows Time	W32Time	svchost.exe	Synchronizes the date and time with a network server.
Wireless Zero Configuration	WZCSVC	svchost.exe	Automatically configures WiFi (802.11b) network adapters.
WMI Performance Adapter	WmiApSrv	wmiapsrv.exe	Provides WMI performance library information.
Workstation	lanmanworkstation	svchost.exe	Sets up and maintains client network connections to servers.
World Wide Web Publishing	W3SVC	inetinfo.exe	Provides web publishing services through the IIS snap-in.

Table 43-1.   *Windows XP Professional Services* (continued)

Using the Services Console

Windows XP Professional's primary tool for working with services is the Services console (Figure 43-1). To run the Services console, choose Start | All Programs | Accessories | System Tools | Services or enter **services.msc** in the Run dialog box.

Note   *The Services snap-in also appears as part of the Computer Management MMC console. You can also add this snap-in to other consoles you create or modify, as described in the previous chapter.*

The Services snap-in contains a Name column, a Description column, a Status column, a Startup Type column (Automatic, Manual, or Disabled), and a Log On As column (which lists the account the service is configured to use). You can sort the display in the Services console by any column heading by clicking the heading. Click the heading again to reverse the sort order.

The Services console provides a Standard view and an Extended view. The Extended view displays the full description of the service and sometimes includes links for starting the service, stopping it, or pausing it.

Starting and Stopping Services

You don't usually need to start and stop services manually because, in most cases, Windows XP Professional is configured to start services automatically on startup and to stop them when it shuts down. To start and stop services, you need the appropriate permissions for the service.

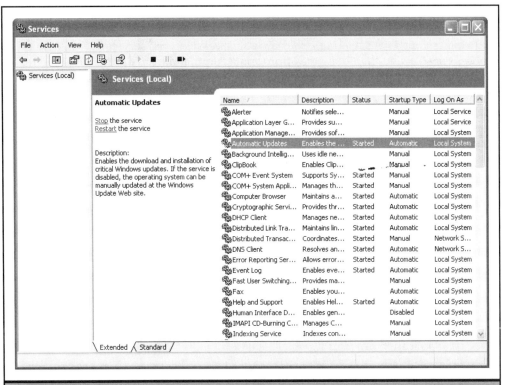

Figure 43-1. *Windows XP Professional includes the Services console for starting, stopping, pausing, and configuring services.*

However, if you find Windows XP Professional is running a service you're certain you'll never need, you can stop that service manually. After stopping the service, configure it for manual startup rather than automatic startup in the future. If you don't do this, Windows XP Professional will start the service again automatically the next time Windows XP Professional itself starts.

For some services, another option is to pause the service. Pausing a service can have two advantages over stopping a service:

■ The service neither relinquishes any connections or resources it needs nor does it cancel any tasks it's performing. For example, if you pause Fax Service, it maintains the list of the faxes queued for sending. By contrast, if you stop Fax Service, you lose the queued faxes.

■ You can resume the service more quickly than you would be able to restart it.

You may also need to restart a service you want to continue running, but that seems to be suffering from problems. For example, if you're unable to clear blockages in the print queue by deleting the jobs that appear to be affected, try stopping the Print Spooler service, and then restarting it.

To start, stop, pause, resume, or restart a service, select the service in the list in the Services console, and then issue the appropriate command from the Action menu or the shortcut menu, by using the corresponding toolbar button or by clicking a link in the Extended pane (if you're using Extended view).

Setting the Startup Type and Start Parameters

If you need to change the startup type for a service or the start parameters to use for a service, follow these steps:

1. Issue a Properties command to display the service's Properties dialog box with the General tab foremost. (For example, double-click the service's item in the list in the Services console.) Figure 43-2 shows the General tab of the Properties dialog box for the Print Spooler Service.

2. To change the startup type, select it in the Startup Type drop-down list:

   ■ Automatic startup starts the service whenever Windows XP Professional starts.

   ■ Manual startup configures the service so a user, another service, or an application can start it, as necessary.

   ■ Disabled startup prevents the service from being started.

3. To change start parameters, click the Stop button to stop the service. Enter the start parameters to use for the service in the Start Parameters group box. Then click the Start button to start the service again.

Note *From the General tab of the Properties dialog box for the service, you can also pause and resume the service (if the service supports pausing). But unless you need to change start parameters or startup type, working directly in the Services console is easier than displaying the Properties dialog box.*

Note *If you're having boot problems, you won't be able to access the Services console to disable services that might be causing problems. But you can use Recovery Console to disable the service. See "Recovering with Recovery Console" in Chapter 24 for a discussion of Recovery Console.*

Setting Service Logon Options

Like a user, each service must log on to Windows XP Professional under an account permitted to take the actions the service needs to take. For example, if a service needs to create files in a Windows XP Professional system folder, the account under which

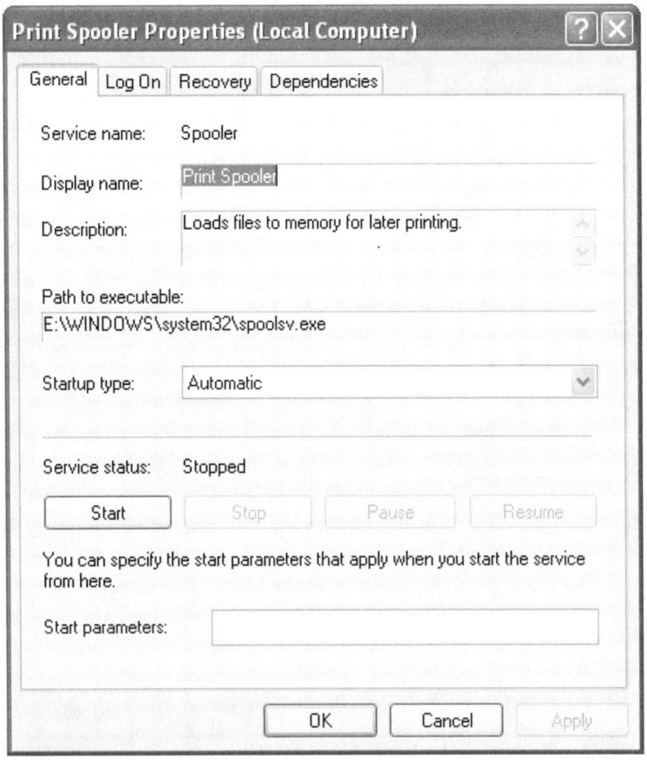

Figure 43-2. *On the General tab of the Properties dialog box for a service, you can add any necessary start parameters, choose the startup type, and start and stop the service.*

the service logs on needs the permission to create those files. Otherwise, the service won't run properly.

Most services run under the local System account, which has a full range of powers. Other services run under the NT AUTHORITY\NetworkService account. However, in rare cases, you may need to run a service under another user account. To do so, work on the Log On tab (Figure 43-3) of the Properties dialog box for the service.

On this page, choose either the Local System Account option button or the This Account option button. If you select the This Account option button, either type the name of the account or click the Browse button and use the Select User dialog box to navigate to the account. Enter the password for the account in the Password text box and the Confirm Password text box.

When a service runs under the local System account, you can select the Allow Service to Interact with Desktop check box to make the service provide a UI that allows the user

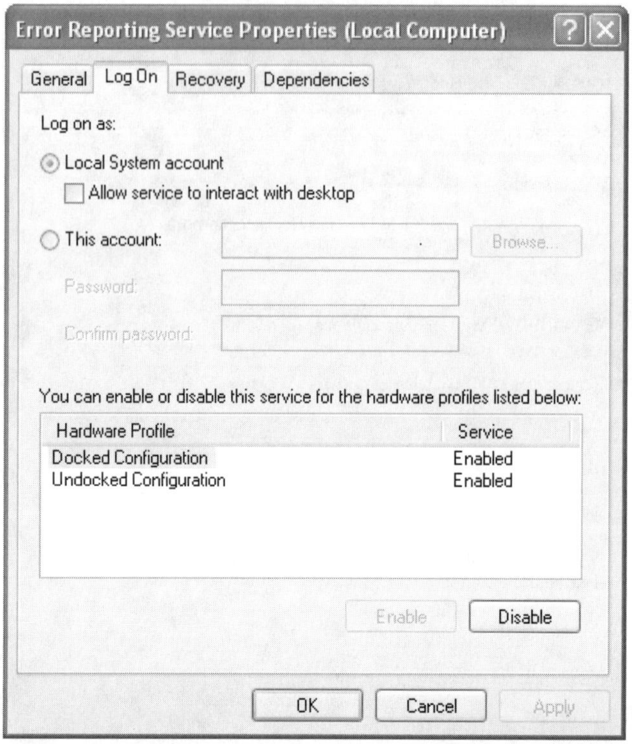

Figure 43-3. *On the Log On tab of the Properties dialog box for a service, you can change the account under which the service runs.*

who is logged on to interact with the service when it's running. In most cases, users won't need to interact with the service directly.

From the Log On tab of the Properties dialog box, you can also enable or disable the service for one or more particular hardware profiles. For example, for an undocked or mobile profile, you might turn off network services required only when connected to a network.

Setting Recovery Actions for a Service

Many services support recovery actions that you can specify on the Recovery tab (Figure 43-4) of the Properties dialog box for the service. In the First Failure drop-down list, the Second Failure drop-down list, and the Subsequent Failures drop-down list, choose from the following actions:

■ **Take No Action**   Windows XP Professional allows the service to stop—it doesn't try to restart the service or notify the user. (The service may make an entry in the event log.)

■ **Restart the Service**   Windows XP Professional tries to restart the service after the number of minutes specified in the Restart Service After *NN* Minutes text box.

■ **Run a Program**   Windows XP Professional runs the application specified in the Run Program group box. What type of application you run depends on the service involved and what you hope to do about it. For example, you might run a recovery utility or a backup utility, or you might run an application that alerted you to the failure.

■ **Restart the Computer**   Windows XP Professional restarts the computer when the service fails. By default, Windows XP Professional waits one minute before restarting the computer. You can change the length of time by clicking the Restart Computer Options button and changing the Restart Computer After *NN* Minutes

MANAGING AND
AUTOMATING WINDOWS
XP PROFESSIONAL

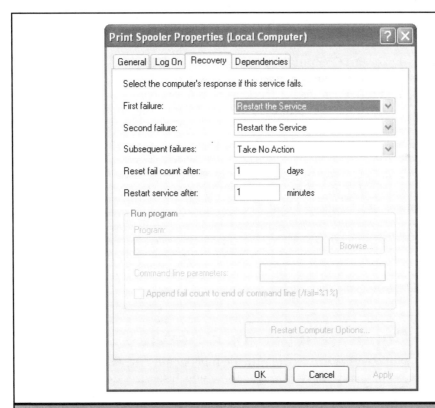

Figure 43-4.   *You can specify recovery actions for some services on the Recovery tab of the Properties dialog box.*

Figure 43-5. *If you choose to restart your computer after a service fails, configure options for the restart in the Restart Computer Options dialog box.*

text box in the Restart Computer Options dialog box (Figure 43-5). To broadcast a message to other computers on the network, select the Before Restart, Send This Message to Computers on the Network check box and enter a suitable message in the text box. Windows XP Professional provides a canned message you can adapt. Alternatively, provide a custom message of your own choosing.

Note *To receive administrative alerts, other computers on the network have to be running the Alerter service. In typical configurations of Windows XP Professional, this service is configured for manual startup. Change this service to Automatic startup to ensure the computers can receive administrative alerts.*

Note *Other services don't support recovery actions. These services are so vital to Windows XP Professional that if the service fails, Windows XP Professional restarts automatically. Examples of such services include the NetLogon service, the Event Log service, IPSec Services, and the Plug and Play Service.*

Checking Dependencies for a Service

Many services depend on other services to provide functionality they need. When you start or stop a service manually, make sure you know which services depend on it and which services it depends on. If you start a service that depends on other services, Windows XP Professional automatically starts those services. If you stop a service, Windows XP Professional automatically stops any dependent services that are running.

Use the Dependencies tab (Figure 43-6) of the Properties dialog box for a service to see which dependencies a service has and which services depend on it.

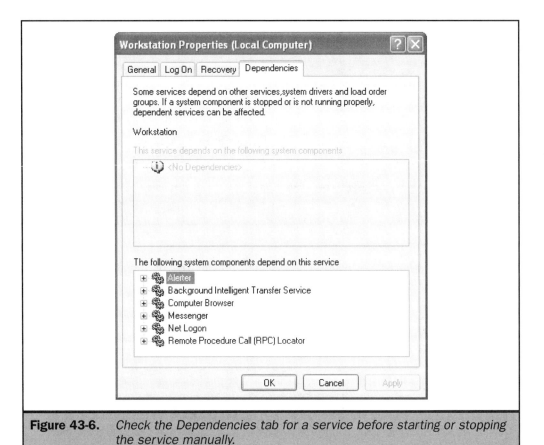

Figure 43-6. *Check the Dependencies tab for a service before starting or stopping the service manually.*

Managing Services with the net Commands

As you've seen so far in this chapter, the Services console provides an effective graphical user interface (GUI) for working with services. You can also manage services from a command prompt or from a script or batch file by using the net commands. You can start and stop most services. If a service supports being paused, you can pause it, and then resume it.

Table 43-2 lists the net commands for starting, stopping, pausing, and resuming services.

In each of these commands, you can specify the service by using either the service's name or its display name. For example, the PolicyAgent service has the display name IPSec Services and the Dhcp service has the display name DHCP Client. It's easier to use the service name if you know it, but if you don't, use the service's display name in double quotation marks. Table 43-1 (earlier in the chapter) lists the services Windows XP Professional is likely to be running, including both their display names and their short

Command	Explanation
net start	Lists all running services.
net start *service*	Starts the specified service.
net stop *service*	Stops the specified service.
net pause *service*	Pauses the specified service.
net continue *service*	Resumes the specified service.

Table 43-2. *net Commands for Managing Services*

names. If you have access to the Services console and can display the Properties dialog box for a service, you'll find the service name listed on the General tab.

For example, each of the following commands stops the Automatic Updates service (Wuauserv):

```
net stop "automatic updates"
net stop wuauserv
```

Managing Services on a Remote Computer

You can manage services on a remote computer in any of the following ways:

- By entering the command **services.msc /computer=***computername* (where *computername* is the name of the remote computer) in the Run dialog box or at a command prompt. Windows XP Professional opens a Services console for the remote computer. Alternatively, run the Services console for the local computer as usual, select the Services (Local) item, and then issue a Connect to Another Computer command from the Action menu or the shortcut menu.

- By establishing a connection to the remote computer using Remote Desktop Connection. Once you've done so, you can work directly in the Services console on that computer. For you to connect like this, the remote computer must be running Windows XP Professional or Windows.NET Server, Remote Desktop on the remote computer must be configured to accept connections, and you must have an account on the computer with sufficient permissions to configure services.

- By establishing a connection to the remote computer using Remote Assistance. For you to connect like this, the remote computer must be running Windows XP Professional Home Edition, Windows XP Professional, or Windows.NET Server, and it must be configured to accept Remote Assistance invitations. A user logged on to the computer must accept your Offer Remote Assistance session or your response to their Remote Assistance invitation and must grant you control of the computer (for you to be able to work on it directly). Even then, you'll be working in the security context of that user, so you'll have the permissions required to configure services only if that user has the permissions.

- By establishing a Telnet session to the remote computer. For you to connect, the remote computer must be running the Telnet service. (See Chapter 34 for a discussion of Telnet.)

Note *When you try to load the services on a remote computer running XP, you may get the error message "Unable to open service control manager database on \\computername. Error 1722: The RPC server is unavailable." This means the remote computer isn't running File and Printer Sharing for Microsoft Networks. To fix this problem, enable File and Printer Sharing on the appropriate connection on the remote computer.*

Summary

This chapter has discussed what services are, what they're for, and how to manage them by using both the Services console and the net start command.

The next chapter shows you how to use the command console and command history.

Index

INTERNATIONAL CONTACT INFORMATION

AUSTRALIA
McGraw-Hill Book Company Australia Pty. Ltd.
TEL +61-2-9900-1800
FAX +61-2-9878-8881
http://www.mcgraw-hill.com.au
books-it_sydney@mcgraw-hill.com

CANADA
McGraw-Hill Ryerson Ltd.
TEL +905-430-5000
FAX +905-430-5020
http://www.mcgraw-hill.ca

**GREECE, MIDDLE EAST, & AFRICA
(Excluding South Africa)**
McGraw-Hill Hellas
TEL +30-1-656-0990-3-4
FAX +30-1-654-5525

MEXICO (Also serving Latin America)
McGraw-Hill Interamericana Editores S.A. de C.V.
TEL +525-117-1583
FAX +525-117-1589
http://www.mcgraw-hill.com.mx
fernando_castellanos@mcgraw-hill.com

SINGAPORE (Serving Asia)
McGraw-Hill Book Company
TEL +65-863-1580
FAX +65-862-3354
http://www.mcgraw-hill.com.sg
mghasia@mcgraw-hill.com

SOUTH AFRICA
McGraw-Hill South Africa
TEL +27-11-622-7512
FAX +27-11-622-9045
robyn_swanepoel@mcgraw-hill.com

SPAIN
McGraw-Hill/Interamericana de España, S.A.U.
TEL +34-91-180-3000
FAX +34-91-372-8513
http://www.mcgraw-hill.es
professional@mcgraw-hill.es

**UNITED KINGDOM, NORTHERN,
EASTERN, & CENTRAL EUROPE**
McGraw-Hill Education Europe
TEL +44-1-628-502500
FAX +44-1-628-770224
http://www.mcgraw-hill.co.uk
computing_neurope@mcgraw-hill.com

ALL OTHER INQUIRIES Contact:
Osborne/McGraw-Hill
TEL +1-510-549-6600
FAX +1-510-883-7600
http://www.osborne.com
omg_international@mcgraw-hill.com